John Barten

A Complete Nautical Pocket Dictionary

English-German and German-English

John Barten

A Complete Nautical Pocket Dictionary

English-German and German-English

ISBN/EAN: 9783954270040
Erscheinungsjahr: 2012
Erscheinungsort: Bremen, Deutschland

www.maritimepress.de | office@maritimepress.de

Bei diesem Titel handelt es sich um den Nachdruck eines historischen, lange vergriffenen Buches. Da elektronische Druckvorlagen für diese Titel nicht existieren, musste auf alte Vorlagen zurückgegriffen werden. Hieraus zwangsläufig resultierende Qualitätsverluste bitten wir zu entschuldigen.

A COMPLETE

NAUTICAL
POCKET DICTIONARY
ENGLISH-GERMAN AND GERMAN-ENGLISH

BY

JOHN BARTEN

Sworn Translator and interpreter,
Author of "English and German Proverbs",
"The Echo of Colloquial English" &c., &c.

PART I
ENGLISH-GERMAN

DIETRICH REIMER (ERNST VOHSEN)
BERLIN

VOLLSTÄNDIGES

NAUTISCHES
TASCHEN-WÖRTERBUCH

DEUTSCH-ENGLISCH und ENGLISCH-DEUTSCH

VON

JOHN BARTEN

Beeidigter Übersetzer und Dolmetscher,
Verfasser von „Deutsche und englische Sprüchwörter",
„as Echo der englischen Umgangssprache" etc., etc.

TEIL II

DEUTSCH-ENGLISCH

DIETRICH REIMER (ERNST VOHSEN)
BERLIN

PREFACE.

"To make dictionaries is dull work" as Samuel Johnson aptly said. There is at first the wearisome toil of collecting the words and expressions and putting them in alphabetical order, then comparing this collection with other dictionaries and completing it accordingly, and at last there is the copying out of the collection in order to give it the desired shape. The latter part of the work alone took 12 months.

The genesis of this work may be briefly told. In his capacity as interpreter at the Hamburg Law Courts, the author felt at the beginning a great want for a handy and complete nautical dictionary, and, therefore, set at once to work to collect the words and phrases picked up from the examination of witnesses and the study of log books. If, therefore, he was not a nautical man, yet he was wide awake as to what was required of such book.

The compass of the book would not admit any explanation for technicalities which, moreover, would have necessitated the collaboration of nautical and engineering people. There are some few books of similar description edited by experts with plenty of explanations, and it might, therefore, be thought there was no occasion for this publication of an outsider. However, such books are more voluminous than complete, and more instructive than practical. A translator, whether professional or not, wants to get the translation of a word at one glance; it is in the first line quite indifferent to him what the word really signifies. Strict alphabetical order throughout the book, absence of illustrations and explanations, are, therefore, essential for facilitating his task. If a word has various applications, the difference is always made sufficiently clear without any attempt at becoming instructive.

In the German part it has been found requisite to give the gender of the substantives, or, rather, the gender that is more commonly used, for some words are used both in the masculine, feminine, and neuter gender, in

6

fact as to this subject we may safely say, "La recherche de la paternité est interdite."

The system adopted for the abridgement of repeated words will soon be grasped by the user of this book, so that its wants no special explanation, its adoption was absolutely necessary for turning out a POCKET DICTIONARY at a reasonable price, it would otherwise have become a very voluminous book, considering that it was a matter of 50,000 words and phrases.

For the same reason the description of words as to substantives, adjectives, verbs, &c., as well as the constantly recurring preposition "to" before verbs has been generally omitted, for the words of the other language were deemed to be a sufficient suggestion on this head.

If there is anything that annoyed me in all dictionaries it is the frequent cross reference to other words instead of the translation then and there. While carefully perusing other dictionaries for the purpose of completing mine, I have generally found that such cross references took up more space than the translations would have required. I have, consequently, avoided such cross references unless where whole articles were concerned.

Though not specially intended for the Navy, the book will, nevertheless, be found of good service to those who refer to the same for naval terms.

Hamburg, September, 1911.

JOHN BARTEN.

VORWORT.

„Wörterbücher zu schreiben, ist" nach dem zutreffenden Ausdrucke von Samuel Johnson, „langweilige Arbeit". — Da ist zunächst die mühsame Arbeit des Sammelns der Wörter und Ausdrücke sowie des Zusammenstellens in alphabetischer Ordnung, dann das Vergleichen der Sammlung mit anderen Wörterbüchern sowie das entsprechende Vervollständigen; und zuletzt kommt das Abschreiben der Sammlung, um ihr die gewünschte Gestalt zu verleihen. — Der letztere Teil allein nahm ein ganzes Jahr in Anspruch.

Die Genesis dieses Werkchens läßt sich mit wenigen Worten streifen. In seiner Eigenschaft als Dolmetscher bei den Hamburger Gerichten fühlte der Verfasser anfänglich das Bedürfnis nach einem handlichen und vollständigen nautischen Wörterbuche und schickte sich daher sofort an, die durch Zeugenvernehmung und Durchsicht der Schiffsjournale gelernten Wörter und Ausdrücke zu sammeln. Wenn er daher auch kein nautischer Fachmann war, so war er sich doch klar bewußt, wie ein solches Diktionär beschaffen sein müßte.

Der Umfang des Buches ließ keine Erklärung der Technikalitäten zu, was überdies die Mitarbeit von Seeleuten und Ingenieuren erfordert hätte. Zwar gibt es einige wenige ähnliche, von Experten herausgegebene Bücher, die reichlich Erklärungen enthalten, und welche die Ansicht aufkommen lassen könnten, daß für die vorliegende Veröffentlichung und außerdem von einem Nichtzünftigen, keine Veranlassung war. Jedoch diese im Auge habenden Bücher sind mehr umfangreich als vollständig und mehr belehrend als praktisch. Ein Übersetzer, gleichviel ob von Beruf oder nicht, wünscht die Übersetzung eines Wortes mit einem Blicke zu finden; was das Wort eigentlich bedeutet, ist ihm in erster Linie ganz gleichgültig. Demnach ist streng durchgeführte alphabetische Ordnung im Buche, sowie das Fehlen von Illustrationen und Erklärungen zur Erleichterung seiner Aufgabe von Wichtigkeit. — Überall, wo Wörter eine verschiedene Bedeutung haben, ist der Unterschied in diesem Werke genügend gewahrt worden, ohne daß der Versuch gemacht wurde, belehrend zu wirken.

Im deutschen Teile ist es notwendig gewesen, das Geschlecht der Hauptwörter, oder richtiger, das am meisten benutzte Geschlecht, beizufügen, weil einige Wörter sowohl als männlich wie auch weiblich und sächlich gebraucht werden, so daß man über diesen Punkt gerne sagen kann: La recherche de la paternité est interdite.

Das bei den wiederholten Wörtern angewandte Abkürzungssystem wird dem Benutzer schnell geläufig werden, so daß sich eine besondere Erläuterung erübrigt; das eingeschlagene Verfahren war zur Sicherung des Taschenformats zu einem angemessenen billigen Preise unabweisbar nötig, da das Buch sonst bei seinem Inhalt von etwa 50 000 Wörtern resp. Redensarten ein sehr umfangreiches geworden wäre.

Aus gleichem Grunde ist auch die Angabe der Gattung der Wörter, d. h. ob Substantiva, Adjektiva, Verba etc. sowie die beständig auftretende Präposition „to" vor den englischen Verben generell unterlassen worden, da die Wörter der anderen Sprache für eine genügende diesbezügliche Andeutung angesehen werden können.

Was mich bei allen Wörterbüchern stets verdroß, ist der häufige Hinweis auf andere Wörter an Stelle der sofortigen Übersetzung. Bei dem sorgfältigen Vergleichen anderer Wörterbücher zwecks Vervollständigung des meinen habe ich durchweg gefunden, daß diese Hinweise mehr Raum in Anspruch nahmen, als die Übersetzung benötigt hätte. Ich habe daher derartige Hinweise vermieden, außer wenn ganze Artikel in Frage kamen.

Obgleich dieses Buch nicht speziell für die Marine geschrieben ist, wird es dennoch denen von gutem Nutzen sein, die in ihm Marineausdrücke nachschlagen.

Hamburg, September 1911.

JOHN BARTEN.

PART I
ENGLISH-GERMAN.

A.

aak, Aak.
ab. = *abeam*.
A. B. = *able bodied sailor*,
1. Vollmatrose; 2. befahren.
action rudder, Gefechtsruder.
aback, back; *all-*, alles b., alles
gegen den Mast; *sails are
a.*, die Segel liegen b.
abaft, achter, hinter; *-the
beam*, achterlicher als dwars.
abandon, abandonnieren;
-ment, Abandonnement.
abase, streichen (die Segel).
abate, nachlassen, abflauen;
-ment, das Nachlassen.
abeam, dwars. quer ab; *-arm*,
Scherstock des Decks.
able bodied, befahren.
aboard, an Bord.
about ship! Klar zum Wenden!
Wende!
abox = *aback*.
abreast, auf der Höhe, dwars,
gegenüber, querab, neben.
absolute force, absolute Kraft;
- power, a. K.; *- pressure*. a.
Druck; *- weight*, a. Gewicht.
abstract of log, Journal-Aus-
zug.
aburton, querschiffs gebaut.
abut, zusammenstoßen.
acast, gescheitert, schiffbrüchig.
accelerated motion, beschleunigte Bewegung.
accelerating force, beschleunigende Kraft.
accommodation ladder, Fall-
reepstreppe.
accommodations,Wohnräume.
account, Besteckrechnung.
accoutrement, Ausrüstung.
accumulation of pressure,
Druckansammlung.
ace, Kettenhaken.
acoast, to lay -, nach der Küste zu anliegen.
acock bill, 1. klar zum Fallen;
2. getoppt (Rahen).
acorn, 1. Flaggenknopf; 2.
Knopf eines Flügels.
across our bow, quer vor unserm Bug; *- the sea*, dwars
See liegend; *- the stream*,
dwarsstrom; *-the tide*,dwars
zur Tide.
acting, wirkend.
action,Tätigkeit; *- of propeller*,
T. der Schraube.
acts of God, force majeure,
Höhere Gewalt, Naturereignisse.
actual power, 1. Nutzkraft; 2.
vorhandener Druck; *- pressure*, v. Druck.
acute angle, spitzer Winkel;
- angled, spitzwinkelig.
additional cargo, weitere Ladung; *- declaration*, Nacherklärung; *- freight*, Fracht-
zulage; *- keelson*, loses Kielschwein; *- longitudinal
strength*, verstärkter Längsverband; *- steering wheels*,

extra Steuerräder; -*strength*, verstärkter Verband.

adequate strength, angemessene Stärke.

adjudication of prizes, Prisenreglement.

adjust an average, die Dispache aufmachen; - *a compass*, einen Kompaß regulieren; - *the frames*, die Spanten in ein Boot setzen.

adjustable, regulierbar.

adjuster of claims, Dispacheur.

adjusting, Anpassung; -*length of shafting*, kurzes Wellenstück; - *screw*, Stellschraube; -*shaft*, kurze Schraubenwelle.

adjustment, Dispachierung; - *of loss*, die Dispache bei Partikularschaden; - *of the compass*, Kompaßregulierung.

admiralty chart, Admiralitätskarte; - *court*, Seeamt.

admission, Einströmung, Eintritt; - *port*, Eintrittskanal; - - *of slide valve*, E.-t-K.- des Schiebers.

admit air, Luft einlassen.

adornings, Verzierungen.

adrift, 1. driftig, treibend; 2. losgerissen von der Vertäuung; 3. übergegangen (Ladung).

advance, Handgeld, Vorschuß; -*note*, Vorschußanweisung; -*of freight*, Frachtvorschuß; -*on bottomry*, Bodmerei-Anleihe.

advanced passengers baggage, Gepäck der Passagiere, die in einem der nächsten Häfen an Bord kommen.

adventure, 1. Handelsunternehmen; 2. Beilast.

adze, Deichsel, deichseln, zurichten.

affreight, befrachten; -*ment*, Befrachtung, Frachtkontrakt.

afloat, flott, schwimmend.

afore, vor.

aft, achter, hinten, Achterteil.

after backstay, Hinterpardune; - *balance frame*, Achterbalancierspant; - *beam*, der hinterste Balken; -*body*, Hinterschiff; - *braces*, Achterbrassen; -*breastwork*, hinteres Geländer der Back; - *cant timber*, Hinter-Kantspant; - *capstan*, Achtergangspill; - *condenser door joint*, hintere Kondenserdeckelverbindung; - *crank shaft*, hintere Kurbelwelle; - *crosshead and guides*, hinterer Kreuzkopf und Gleitplatten; - *cuddy*, Hinterpflicht; - *deadwood*, hintere Aufklotzung; - *deck*, Achterdeck; - - *house*, Hütte; - *ebb tide*, Achterebbe; - *end*, Hinterschiff; - *flood*, Hinterflut; - *frames*, Achterspanten; - *gland*, hinterer Deckel; - *guard*, Achtergasten; - *guy of a davit*, Davits Achterholer; - - *of the sprit sail gaff*, Achterklüver - Backstag; - - *of the swing boom*, Achterkehrtau; - *hatch* od. *hatchway*, Achterluke; - - *coaming*, Achterlukensüll; - *hold*, Achterraum; - *hoods*, hinterste Planken oder Platten der Gänge der Außenoder Innenhaut; - *kant timber*, Hinterkantspant; - *ladder*, Achtertreppe; - *leech*, Hinterliek; - - *rope*, H.; -*most*, der achterlichste Teil des Schiffes; - *noon watch*, Nachmittagswache (12—4); - *part*, Achterteil; - *peak*, Hinterpiek; - - *tank*, H.-tank; - - *suction valve*, H.-tank-Saugventil; - *piece of the rudder*, Ruderhacke; - *rope*, hintere Landfeste; - *sails*, Achtersegel; - *steering gear*, Hintersteuergerät; - *stern gland*, hintere Stopfbüchse des Stevenrohrs; - *swifter*, achterste Schwichtleine der Unterwanten; -*tank*, Hintertank; - - *filling and suction box,* H.-Füll- und Saugventil-kasten; - *timbers,* Hinter-spanten; - *well suction valve,* hinteres Brunnen-Saugventil; - *yard,* Achterrahe.

aftward, achteraus.

against the tide, gegen den Strom.

agate, das Hütchen der Kompaßnadel.

agreement, Heuerkontrakt, Musterrolle; - *of ownership,* Reedereivertrag.

aground, an Grund sitzend.

ahead, voraus; - *of the reckoning,* mit dem Besteck zurück sein; - *motion,* Vorwärts-Bewegung; - *way guides,* V.-Geradführung.

ahold, dicht beim Winde.

ahoo, in Unordnung.

ahoy! ahoi! hallo! ho! all hands ahoy! Alle Mann auf Deck!

ahull, vor Topp und Takel beigedreht liegen.

air, Windhauch, auslüften; - *bag,* Luftsack; - *camel,* Kamel; - *casing of funnel,* Schornsteinmantel; - *chamber,* Windkessel; - *chambered,* mit Luftkasten versehen; - *cock,* Lufthahn; - *course,* Luftgang; - *board,* Seitenfüllung; - *ejector,* Luftauswerfer; - *funnel,* Rauchabzug; - *hole,* Luftloch; - *lid,* Lüftungspfortenklappe; - *pipe,* Luftrohr; - *port,* Luftpforte; - *pressure,* Luftdruck.

air pump, Luftpumpe; - - *air valve,* Luftpumpen-Luftauslaßventil; - - *barrel,* Luftpumpen-Zylinder; - - *bucket,* L.-kolben; - - - *ring,* L.-k.-ring; - - - *valve,* L.-K.-ventil; - - - - *guard,* L.-K.-v.-Hubbegrenzer or Klappenfänger; - - - - *seat,* L.-K.-v.-sitz; - - *chamber,* L.-körper; - - - *door,* L.-k.-deckel; - - *connecting rod,* L.-Pleuelstange; - - *cover,* L.-deckel; - - *crosshead,*

L.-Traverse; - - - *journal,* L.-T.-Halszapfen; - - *cylinder,* L.-Zylinder; - - *delivery space,* L.-Druckraum; - - - *valve,* L.-Druckventil; - - - - *guard,* L.-D.-Hubbegrenzer od. Klappenfänger; - - - - *seat,* L.-D.-sitz; - - *drain cock,* L.-Drainagehahn; - - *escape valve,* L.-Sicherheitsventil; - - *foot v.,* L.-Fußventil; - - - - *guard,* L.-Saugventil-Hubbegrenzer; - - - - *seat,* L.-S.-sitz; - - *gear,* L.-vorrichtung; - - *gland,* L.-Stopfbüchsendeckel; - - *head valve,* L.-Druckventil; - - *lever,* L.-Balancier; - - - *shaft,* L.-B.-Achse; - - - - *journal,* Halszapfen der L.-B.-A.; - - *liner,* L.-Einsatz; - - *link,* L.-Gelenk; - - - *brasses,* L.-G.-Lagerschalen; - - *man hole,* L.-Mannloch; - - *neck bush,* L.-Grundring; - - *overflow pipe,* L.-Überlaufrohr; - - - *valve,* L.-Überlaufventil; - - - - *cover,* L.-U.-deckel; - - - - *seat,* L.-U.-sitz; - - - - *spindle,* L.-U.-spindel; - - - - *spring,* L.-U.-feder; - - *pet cock,* L.-Probierhahn; - - *piston,* L.-Kolben; - - - *ring,* L.-K.-Ring; - - *plunger,* L.-Plunger; - - *relief valve,* L.-Rückflußventil; - - *rod,* L.-stange; - - - *stuffing box,* L.-Stangenstopfbüchse; - - *stuffing box,* L.-Stopfbüchse; - - - - *gland,* L.-Stopfbüchsendeckel; - - *suction pipe,* L.-Saugerohr; - - - *space,* L.-Saugeraum; - - - *valve,* L.-Saugeventil; - - - - *guard,* Klappenfänger des L.-S.; - - - - *seat,* L.-S.-Sitz; - - *top valve,* L.-Druckventil; - - - *guard,* L.-D.-Hubbegrenzer od. Klappenfänger; - - - - *seat,* L.-D.-Sitz; - - *valve,* L.-Ventil; - - - *guard,* L.-V.-Hubbegrenzer od. Klappenfänger; - - - *seat,* L.-V.-Sitz. [lüften.

air the holds, die Laderäume

air scuttle, Luftpforte; - *strake*, Luftspalt im innern Plankengang; -*valve*, Luftauslaßventil; - - *box*. Luftventilgehäuse; - - *cover*. Luftventildeckel; - *vessel* , Windkessel.

airs, light-, leichter Zug.

ake, das Aak.

alarm compass , Seekompaß mit Läutewerk; - *valve*, Alarmventil.

alee, in Lee, leewärts; - *the helm!* Ruder in Lee!

alhydic chain, Luftsackkette.

alimentary pipe, Speiserohr.

alist, mit einer Schlagseite.

all aback forward! All back vorn! - *ahoo*, alles in Unordnung; - *a-taunto*, alles in bester Ordnung; völlig getakelt; - *clear*, alles klar; - *hands ahoy!* or - *h. up!* or - *h. on deck!* Alle Mann an Deck! - *is in the wind*, alles back; - *overish*, alles in der Schwebe; - *standing*, plötzlich.

alley way, Gang; - - *of bridge*, Brückengang.

allotment note, Anweisung.

allow, zugestehen; - *ance*, Ration; - - *for drift* od. - - *for leeway*, Schätzung der Abtrift. [Kurs.

allowed course, der vergißte

alloyed steel, legierter Stahl.

almady, Baumrindenboot.

aloft, oben, nach oben; - *there!* Topp hoi!

along shore, längs der Küste; - - *boys*, Küstenschiffer; - - *navigation*, Küstenschiffahrt; - - *owner*, K—sreeder.

alongside, längsseits.

aloof, luvwärts, weitab; *keep -!* Bleib entfernt!

alter the course, den Kurs ändern; - *speed*, die Fahrgeschwindigkeit ä.

alteration, Änderung.

alternate strake, umschichtiger Gang; - *timber*, ein Imholz um das andere.

alternating light, Wechselfeuer; - Wind, abwechseln der Wind.

alternative motion, hin- und hergehende Bewegung.

altitude of a star, Höhe eines Gestirns; - *of the sun*, Sonnenhöhe.

amain, plötzlich, eiligst; *let go -, strike -*, Schnell die Segel nieder!

amidships, amidward, mittschiffs.

amora, Nordlicht.

ampère, Ampère; - *meter*, A-messer.

amplitude, Amplitude; *by -*, Mißweisung.

anchor, Anker, ankern, vor Anker gehen; - *bites*, der A. greift; - *is a-cat-head*, der A. hängt vor dem Kran; - *is a-cock-bill*, d. A. ist klar zum Fallen; - *is a-peak*, d. A. ist auf und nieder; - *is at a long peak*, das Ankertau steht stagweise; - *is a-trip*, d. A. ist triftig; - *is coming home*, d. A. geht durch; - *is dragging*, d. A. ist triftig; - *is starting*, d. A. läßt los; - *is up*, d. A. ist oben.

anchor arm, Ankerarm; - *bearings*, A-peilung; - *bed*, A-schuh; - *bill*, A-spitze; - *buoy*, A-boje; - - *rope*, A-bojereep; - *chock*, Schweinsrücken; - *clutching*, A-hals; - *crane*, A-kran; - *cross*, A-kreuz; - *crown*, A-breite; - *davit*, A-davit; - - *socket*, A-davitspur; - *deck*, A-deck; - *drag*, A-draggen; - *flue* od. - *fluke*, A-schaufel; - - *chock*, Schweinsrücken; - *forge*, A-schmiede; - *fouled by flukes* od. *stock*, stockunklarer Anker; - *hold*, 1. A-stelle; 2. das Festhalten des Ankers; - *hoy*, Leichter für Anker- und Kettentransport; - *lashing*, A-laschung; - *light*, A-licht; - *lining*, A-fütterung; - *nuts*, A-nüsse; - *palm*,

A-schar; - *ring*, A-ring;
- *rocket*, A-rakete; - *shackle*,
A-schäkel; - - *bolt*, A-s-bol-
zen; - *shaft*, A-schaft; - *shank*,
A-schaft; - - *square*, A-stock-
schaft; - *shoe*. A-schuh; - *shot*,
A-kugel mit Leine; - *slipper*,
A-schlipper; - *smith*, A-
schmied; - *smithy*, A-schmiede; - *stock*, A-stock; - - *balls*,
A-s-nüsse; - - *bolts*, A-s-
bolzen; - - *hoop*, A-s-band;
- - *planking*, Plankenbeklei-
dung in A-stockform; - -
tackle, A-talje; - - *tree nails*,
A-stocknägel; - *stopper*,
Bullentau; - *trend*, A-hals;
- *tripper*, Vorrichtung zum
Triftigmachen des Ankers;
- *tumbler*, Schlipphaken;
- *watch*, A-wache; - *yard*,
1. A-lager; 2. Secarsenal.
anchorage, 1. Ankergeld; 2. A-
platz; - *dues*, A-geld.
anchoring, das Ankern; -
ground, A-grund; - *place*,
A-platz; - *signals*, A-signale.
ancient, Nationalflagge.
anemometer, Windmesser.
anend, 1. lotrecht; 2. auf dem
Schlottholz stehend.
angelly wood, Angellyholz.
angle, 1. Winkel; 2. der Knick;
- *bar*, Winkel; - - *beam*, W-
balken; - - *carling*, W-
schlinge; - *cut*, W-schnitt;
- *iron*, W-eisen; - - *stringer*,
W-e-stringer; - *of inclination*, Neigungswinkel; - *staff*,
Winkelholz; - *steel*, W-stahl.
angular, winkelförmig; - *distance*, Winkeldistanz; - *motion*, Winkelbewegung;
- *notch*, Kluft.
annealed cast iron, schmiede-
barer Eisenguß; - *steel*,
adouzierter Stahl.
annealing, ausglühen.
anniversary wind, periodischer
Wind.
annual survey, jährliche Besichtigung.
Anordia, die Anordia.
answer the helm readily, dem

Ruder gut gehorchen; - *the
signal*, das Signal beantworten.
answering pennant, Gegen-
signalwimpel.
Antarctic circle, südliche Polarkreis; - *Ocean*, s. Eismeer.
anti corrosive composition od.
- *fouling paint*, Schutz-An-
strich; - *friction metal*,
Zapfenlagermetall; - *trades*,
Gegenpassatwinde.
anvil, Amboß; - *beak*, A-horn;
- *bed*, A-stock; - *block*, A-
klotz; - *chisel*, A-Abschroter;
- *horn*, Schweifstock.
apeak od. *apeek*, auf und nieder; *oars-!* die Riemen senkrecht! *to ride-*, mit kurzer
Kette vor Anker liegen; *to
run-*, mit dem Schiffe über
dem Anker stehen; *to set
the yards-*, die Rähen kaien.
aperture, Öffnung.
apostles, 1. Judasohren; 2. Bug-
od. Klüsholz.
apparel, Schiffsgerät.
apparels and tackles, Betake-
lung.
apparent altitude, scheinbare
Höhe; - *distance*, s. Distanz;
- *slip*, s. Slip; - *time*, Sonnen-
zeit.
*appearances of the weather
are threatening*, das Wetter
sieht drohend aus.
appendages, die überhängen-
den Teile des Schiffes.
apple pie order, alles kant.
appliance, Anwendung, Mittel.
appliances, Gerätschaften.
appointments, Schiffsgerät.
Appold's brake, Bremsvorrichtung beim Abrollen des
Kabels.
apprentice, Matrosenlehrling;
- *pilot*, Lotsenlehrling.
approachable, erreichbar, zugänglich.
apron, 1. Binnen-Vorsteven-
2. Bettung (des Trocken-
docks).
arbitrator of averages, Strand
richter.

arc, Bogen (des Himmels);
- *lamp*, Bogenlampe.
arcasse, Arcasse.
arch board, der hinterste Teil
der Gillung; - *of the cove*,
Verzierungsleiste (unter dem
Heck); - *piece of stern frame*,
Bogenstück des Schrauben-
rahmens.
arched squall, Sturmbö mit
Wolkensammlung.
archipelago, Archipel.
architecture, Bauart.
arctic circle, nördliche Polarkreis; - *ocean*, n. Eismeer.
ardency, die Eigenschaft des
schnellen Beidrehens.
ardent, schnell beidrehend.
area, Flächeninhalt; - *of
piston*, Kolbenfläche.
arm beams, Deckbalkknie;
- *cleats*, Deckklampen; - *of
a bibb* (od. *cheek) of a mast*,
der hervorstehende Mast-
backenteil; - *of a hook*, Arm
eines Bugbandes; - *of an
anchor*, Ankerarm; - *piece
of a yard*, Rahestück; - *rack*,
Gewehrgestell; - *the lead*,
das Lot speisen.
armed mast, zusammenge-
setzter Mast; - *merchantman*, bewaffnetes Kauf-
fahrteischiff.
armour bolt, Panzerbolzen;
- *plate*, Panzerplatte; - *plated*, gepanzert; - *shelf*, Pan-
zerträger.
array, Aufmarsch.
arrears, rückständige Heuer.
arris piece, Scherstück.
arterial navigation, Fluß- und
Kanalschiffahrt.
articles, Heuervertrag, Musterrolle.
artificial draught, künstlicher
Zug; - *harbour*, k. Hafen;
- *horizon*, k. Horizont.
asbestos packing, Asbestpack-
ung.
ash bag, Aschsack; - *bucket*,
Ascheimer; - *cock*, Aschhahn,
Waschhahn; - *davit*, Asch-
davit; - *damper* od. - *door*,

Aschenfalltür; - *ejector*,
Aschenauswerfer; - *hoist*,
Aschenaufzug *(see also steam
- -)*; - - *gear*, A.-Vorrichtung;
- - *piston*, Dampfaschwinden-
Kolben; - - *steam pipe*, Asch-
winden - Dampfzuleitungs -
rohr; - *hose*, Aschenschlauch;
- *pan*, Aschkasten; - *pit*,
Aschenfall; - - *damper*,
Aschenfalldämpfer; - - *door*,
Aschenfalltür; - *shoot*,
Aschenauslauf; - *wood*,
Eschenholz.   [strandet.
ashore, 1. an Land; 2. ge-
ask cable! Kette verlangen!
aslant, schräge.
asleep, oben voll stehen (Segel).
assessor, Beisitzer.
assistance signal, Notsignal.
assistant cook, Kochmaat;
- *engineer*, Maschinisten-
assistent; - *frames*, Hilfs-
spanten; - *shipwright*, Schiffs-
unterbaumeister; - *surveyor*,
Hilfsbesichtiger.
assumed position of ship,
Schiffsort.
astay, stagweise.
astern, achteraus, rückwärts,
über Steuer; - *motion*, rück-
gehende Bewegung; - *of the
reckoning*, mit dem Besteck
voraus sein; - *way guides*,
Rückwärts-Geradführung.
astronomical day, astronomische Tag; - *observation*,
a. Beobachtung; - *time*, a.
at anchor, vor Anker. [Zeit.
ataunt, *ataunto*, alles kant.
at sea, auf See.
athwart, dwars; - *hawse*, quer
vor dem Bug; - *sea*, dwars
See; - *ships*, d-schiffs; - *the
forefoot*, recht vor dem
Steven; - *the stream*, dwars-
stroms.
Atlantic chart, Karte des at-
lantischen Oceans; - *ocean*,
atlantische Ocean.
atmosphere, Atmosphäre.
atmospheric engine, atmosphärische Maschine; - *line*,
a. Linie; - *pressure*, Atmo-

sphärendruck; - *safety valve*, inneres Sicherheitsventil.

atomic weight, Atomgewicht.

atop, am Topp, oben hinauf.

atrim, gleichlastig.

atrip, 1. gesprungen; 2. frei, gelichtet (Anker); 3. aufgeheißt (Segel, Rahe); 4. klar zum Fieren (Mast).

attend the braces, klar bei den Brassen stehen. [kraft.

attractive power, Anziehungsauger, Stangenbohrer.

automatic closing valve, Selbstschlußventil; - *feeding*, Selbstspeisung; - *hammer*, selbsttätiger Hammer; - *reversing gear*, selbsttätige Umsteuerungsvorrichtung.

automatical, selbsttätig.

automatically feeding boiler, selbstspeisender Kessel.

autumnal equinox, Herbst-Äquinoctium.

auxiliary chains, Notketten; - *engines*, Hilfsmaschinen; - *exhaust tank*, Sammeltank; - *feed cock*, Hilfsspeisehahn; - *keel*, Kimmkiel; - *pipe*, Hilfsrohr; - *propeller*, H-schraube; - *pump*, H-pumpe; - *rudder*, H-ruder; - *screw steamer*, H-Schraubendampfer; - *starting valve*, H-schieber; - - - *gear*, H-s-gestänge; - - - *pipe*, H-dampfrohr; - - - *rod*, H-schieberstange; - - - *spindle*, H-schieberspindel; - *steam*, H-dampf; - - *pipe*, H-d-rohr; - - *pipes*, H-d-r-leitung; - - *power*, H-d-kraft; - - *pump*, H-d-pumpe; - - *valve*, H-d-ventil; - *steering gear*, H-steuergerät; - *stop valve*, H-schieber-Absperrventil; - - - *gear*, H-s-A.-gestänge; - *valve*, H-schieber.

available heat, nutzbare Hitze; - *power*, n. Kraft.

avast! Hört auf!

avaunt! Vorwärts! Schnell!

average, Havarie; - *adjuster*, Dispacheur; - *agreement*, Havariebond; - *bond*, H-kontrakt; - *contributions*, Beiträge zur großen H.; - *disbursement*, H-gelder; - *papers*, H-papiere; - *statement*, Dispache; - *stater*, Dispacheur; - *to be made good in case of stranding only*, H. wird nur im Strandungsfalle vergütet.

awake, wachend. [Wasser.

awash, zwischen Wind und

away aloft! enter auf! nach oben! - *off*, weit weg; - *she goes*, da geht es hin; - *there!* Zu Boot! - *with it!* drauf los! - *with the stays!* Innentakel auf! - *with the yards!* Außentakel auf!

aweather, luvwärts.

aweigh, 1. gesprungen; 2. gelichtet (Anker); -, *sir*, der A. ist gelichtet.

awning, Sonnensegel; - *boom*, S.-baum; - *curtain*, die Gardine am Sonnensegel.

awning-deck, Sturmdeck; *a. d. beam*, S-balken; *a. d. b. angle bar*, S-b-winkel; *a. d. beam stringer*, S-b-stringer; *a. d. b. s. plate*, S-b-s-platte; *a. d. b. tie plate*, S-b-Längsschiene; *a. d. hatch*, S-luke; *a. d. hatchway coaming*, S-lukensüll; *a. d. pillar*, S-stütze; *a. d. rails and stanchions*, S-geländer; *a. d. sheerstrake*, S-Schergang; *a. d. ship*, S-Schiff; *a. d. side plating*, S-Seitenbeplattung; *a. d. stanchion*, S-Geländerstütze; *a. d. stringer*, S-Stringer; *a. d. s. angle bar*, S-S-winkel; *a. d. s. plate*, S-S-platte; *a.d. vessel*, S-Schiff; *a. d. waterway*, S-Wassergang.

awning hoop, Zeltreepband; - *stanchion*, Sonnensegelstütze; - *stretcher*, Sonnensegelstrebe.

axe, Axt; - *handle*, A-stiel.

axiometer, Axiometer (am Steuerrade, um die Stellung

der Ruderpinne zu erkennen).
axis of the earth, Erdachse; - - - *rudder*, Ruderachse.

axle, Achse.
Aye, aye, sir! zu Befehl!
Azimuth, Azimuth; - *compass*, A.-Kompaß.

B.

b. = *blue sky.*
back, 1. rückwärts gehen; 2. backholen (Segel); 3. krimpen (Wind); 4. ein Borg od. einen Stopper aufsetzen (bei Ketre od. Tau).
back all! streich überall! - *and fill*, backen und füllen; - *astern*, mit den Riemen rückwärts rudern; - *her!* rückwärts! - *off*, über Steuer gehen; - *the sails*, die Segel gegen den Mast brassen; - *the anchor*, den Anker verkatten; - *the water with the oars*, mit den Riemen streichen; - *the worming*, die Trensing ausfüllen; - *one anchor by another*, einen Anker zur Unterstützung eines anderen ausbringen.
back anchor, Kattanker; - *balance*, Gegengewicht; - - *of crank shaft*, G. der Kurbelarme; - - *of eccentric*, G. des Excenters; - - *of slide valve*, G. des Schiebers; - *board*, Schlingerschlagbug; - - *of a boat*, Rückenbett eines Bootes; - *broken*, Boden durchbrochen; - *column*, Hintersäule; - *end plate*, hintere Stirnwand (des Kessels); - *freight*, Rückfracht; - *hook*, Eisenhaken; - *laid rope*, linksgeschlagenes Tau; - *landing*, Hinterstoß; - *lash*, 1. Spielraum; 2. Spielraumstöße; - *lever links*, hintere Pumpenbalanciergelenke; - *o'beyond*, wer weiß wie weit entfernt; - *of a compass timber*, Rücken

eines Krummholzes; - *of an awning*, Sonnensegel-Befestigungstau; - *of the rudder*, Fütterung des Steuerrades; - *of the ship*, 1. das Heck; 2. der Boden; - *of the stern post*, Butensteven; - *piece of the rudder*, Ruderblatt; - *plate of boiler*, Rückwand des Kessels; - - *of combustion chamber*, R. der Feuerkammer; - *platform*, hintere Platform; - *port!* streich Backbord! - *pressure*, Gegendruck; - *rabbet*, Innenkante einer Spündung; - *rope*, Backstag; - - *of a cat block*, Kattblocksteert; - *spring*, Achterspringtau; - *staff*, Sonnenhöhenmesser.
backstay, Pardune; - *a shroud with a shroud knot*, einen Wantknopf einschlagen; - *lanyards*, Taljereep der Pardune; - *plate*, Pütting d. P.; - *stool*, Rüste d. P.; - *traveller*, Leitbügel des Marsdrehreeps.
back steam, Gegendampf; - *stern post*, Außen-Achtersteven; - *stitch*, Hinterstich; - *strapped*, durch Wind und Strömung zurückgehalten; - *stroke*, Rückwärtshub; - *sweep*, die innere Bucht des Krummholzes; - - *of the waves*, Widersee; - *plate of boiler*, hintere Rohrwand des Kessels; - *view*, Rückansicht; - *wards*, hintenaus; - *wash*, Rückströmung; - - *of the propeller*, Schraubenwasser; - *water*, 1. Rücklauf (einer Welle);

2. Lagune; 3. Stauwasser (der Schleuse).

backer, Taustropp.

backing, 1. rückwärts gehen; 2. krimpen (Wind); 3. backholen (Segel); 4. die Holzlage hinter den Platten.

backing anchor, Kattanker; - *wind*, Backstagswind.

bad roadster, Schiff, das schwer vor dem Anker reibadge, falsche Tasche. [tet.

badge, falsche Tasche. [tet.

badger, verwirrt machen.

baffle plate, Schutzplatte.

baffling winds, umlaufende Winde.

bag, aufschwellen; - *fender*, Korkfender; - *of a sail*, Sack eines Segels; - *of the head rails*, tiefster Teil der Gallionsrelinge; - *pipe the mizen*, die Besahnschote an das Luvwant holen; - *racks*, Kleidersackregale; - *reef*, Unterreff; - - *of a gaff sail*, Fußreff; - - *of a top sail*, 5tes Unterreff im Marssegel; - *room*, Kleidersack-Kammer.

bagged, eingesackt.

baggy, sackartig hängend.

bail, Kaution.

bailee, Kavent.

bailer, Ösfaß.

bailes od. *bails*, die Bogen eines Bootssonnensegels.

balance, Schwichtreff; - *frame*, Balancierspant; - *piston*, Schieber - Abbalancierungskolben; - - *valve*, entlasteter Kolbenschieber; - *reef*, Balancereff; *to take in the* - -, schwichtreffen; - - *band*, Schwichtreffband; - *rudder*, Balanceruder; - *timber*, Balancierspant; - *valve*, Entlastungsventil; - *weight*, Gegengewicht; - *weights on crank shaft*, Gegengewichte der Kurbelarme.

balanced piston valve, entlasteter Kolbenschieber; - *rudder*, Balanceruder; - *slide valve*, Dampfverteilungsschieber.

balanid, Balane (Meereichel).

balcony, Achtergallerie.

bale out the water with buckets, das Wasser mit Pützen ausschöpfen; - *slings*, Seil mit doppelter Schlinge.

baler, Ösfaß.

balise, balize, ein Seezeichen, bestehend aus einer Stange mit Tonne auf einer Sandbank.

balk staff, Springstock.

ball, 1. Knäuel (Garn); 2. Ballon (einer Boje); - *and socket joint*, 1. Kugeldichtung; 2, Kugelzapfen; - *face hammer*, Kehlhammer; - *gudgeon*, Kugelzapfen; - *lamp*, Kugellampe; - *off*, Garn aufknäueln; - *pivot*, Kugelzapfen; - *valve*, Kugelventil.

ballahore, westindischer Schoner.

ballast, Ballast, ballasten; - *basket*, B-korb; - *boat*, B-schute; - *chest*, B-schlitten; - *crane*, B-kran; - *donkey*, B-pumpe.

ballast donkey bucket, Dampfballastpumpen-Kolben; - - - *valve*, D.-K-ventil; - - - - *seat*, D.-K-v-sitz; *b. d. connecting rod*, D.-Pleuelstange; - - - - *bolt*, D.-P-bolzen; - - - - *bottom end keep*, D.-Kurbelzapfenlager - Schalendeckel; - - - - - - *liner*, D. - Pleuelstangenfuß-Futter; *b. d. c. r. top end keep*, D.-Kreuzkopflagerschalendeckel; *b. d. crank pin bolt*, D.-Kurbelzapfenlager-Bolzen; - - - *brasses*, D.-K.-schalen; *b. d. c. shaft*, D.-Kurbelwelle; - - - - *bearing*, D.-K-nlager; - - - - - *bolt*, D.-K-nl-bolzen; - - - - - *brasses*, D.-K-nl-schalen; - - - - - - *keep*, D.-K-nl-deckel; - - - - - - *bolt*, D.-K-nl-Deckelbolzen; *b. d. crosshead*, D.-Kreuzkopf; - - - *bolt*, D.-K.-Lagerbolzen; - - - *brasses*, D.-K.-Lagerschalen; *b. d. cylinder*, D.-Zylinder; - - - *cover*, D.-Z-

deckel; - - - - *bolt,* D.-Z-d-bolzen; *b. d. c. drain pipe,* D.-Z.-Entwässerungsrohr; *b. d. delivery space,* D.-Druckraum; - - - *valve,* D.-Druckventil; - - - - *door,* D.-D.-deckel; - - - - *seat,* D.-D.-sitz; *b. d. discharge valve,* D.-Ausgußventil; - - *eccentric,* D.-Excenter; - - - *bolt,* D.-E.-bolzen; - - - *brasses,* D.-E.-Lagerschalen; - - - *rod,* D.-E.-stange; - - - *sheave*, D.-E.-scheibe; - - - *strap,* D.-E.-bügel; - - - - *liner,* D.-E.-b-Futter; *b. d. exhaust pipe,* D.-Ablaßrohr; - - *fly wheel,* D.-Schwungrad; - - *foot valve,* D.-Fußventil; - - - - *seat,* D.-Saugventilsitz; *b. d. gear,* D.-Geschirr; - - *head valve,* D.-Druckventil; - - *master cock,* D.-Wendehahn; - - *piston,* D.-Kolben; - - - *rod,* D.-K-stange; - - - - *crosshead,* D.-K-s-n-Kreuzkopf; - - - - *stuffing box,* D.-K-s-n-Stopfbüchse; - - - - - *gland,* D.-K-s-n-S-b-n-deckel; *b. d. slide valve,* D.-Schieber; - - *starting valve,* D.-Anlaßventil; - - *steam pipe,* D.-Dampfzuleitungsrohr; - - *stop valve,* D.-Absperrventil; - - *suction pipe,* D.-Saugerohr; - - - *space,* D.-Saugeraum; - - - *valve,* D.-Saugventil; - - - - *door,* D.-S-v-deckel; - - - - *seat,* D.-S-v-sitz; *b. d. top valve,* D.-Druckventil; - - - - *seat,* D.-D-v-sitz; *b. d. valve,* D.-Ventil; - - - *casing,* D.-Schieberkasten; - - - - *door,* D.-S-k-deckel; *b. d. valve rod,* D.-Schieberstange; - - - - *stuffing box,* D.-S-s-n-Stopfbüchse; - - - - - *gland,* D.-S-s-n-S-b-n deckel; *b. d. valve seat,* D.-Ventilsitz.
Ballast heaver, 1. Ballaststauer; 2. Baggermaschine für Ballast; - *lighter,* 1. Ballastschute; 2. Baggerschute;

- *man,* Ballaststauer; - *mark,* B-linie; - *master,* B-mann; - *pipes,* B-leitung; - *port,* B-pforte; - *pump,* B-pumpe; - - *discharge valve cover,* B - pumpen - Ausgußventildeckel; - - - - *spindle,* B-P-A-v-spindel; - *scoop* od. - *shovel,* B-schaufel; - *stowing,* B-stauung; - *tank,* Wasserballasttank; - *trenching,* das Abschotten des Ballasts; - *trim water line,* Ballasttrimm-Wasserlinie; - *trimming,* das Trimmen des Ballasts.
ballastage, Ballastabgaben.
ballasting, Beladen mit Ballast.
balloon jib, Ballonklüver; - *sail,* B-segel.
ballow, Tiefwasser hinter einer Sandbank.
balluster, Säule der Heckgallerie.
balsa od. *balse,* die Balse (Floß in S-Amerika).
Baltic Chart, Karte des Baltischen Meeres; - *trade,* 1. Ostseefahrt; 2. Ostseehandel.
band, 1. Band. Ring; 2. Bindsel (des Taus); 3. Eisenwerk (des Ruders); 4. Stoßlappen (des Segels); 5. Stringer für die Refftaljen.
bandrol, Schiffsflagge.
bangle, Ring. Band (der Spiere).
banian, gewirkte Jacke; - *day,* Fasttag.
banjo, Lager des Propellers; - *frame,* Schraubenheberahmen.
bank, 1. Bank od. Sandbank; 2. Flußufer; 3. Ruderbank; - *harbour,* Barrenhafen; - *of oars,* Ruderbank.
banker, Neufundland-Fischer od. N.-F-fahrzeug.
banking the fires, Aufbänken der Feuer.
banks, Bänke od. Stufen eines Trockendocks.
banner, Pannier.
baptise, taufen.
baptism, Taufe.

bar, 1. Spake, Stab, Stange des Spills, Kettensteg; 2. Barre, Bank, Untiefe; 3. Hafenbaum; - *harbour*, Barrenhafen; - *holes*. Spillgatte; - *iron*, Stabeisen; - *keel*, Stangenkiel; - *link*, Stangencoulisse; - *steel*, Stahl in Stangen; - *stringer*, Winkelstringer; - - *angle bar*, Stringerwinkel.

barb bolt, Bartnagel.

barbed shot, Kugel mit kleinen Enterhaken.

barca od. *barcon*, portugiesischer Zweimaster.

bare poles, vor Topp und Takel; - *wind*, schralender Wind.

barge, Ewer, Schute. Leichter; - *full*, ein Leichter voll; - *hook*, Ewerhaken; - *load*, ein Leichter voll; - *man*, Bootsknecht; - *master*, Ewerführer; - *mate*, Steuermann eines Paradeboots; - *men*, Pinnasgasten; - *of state*, Staatsboot.

bark, Bark; - *rigged*, als B. getakelt.

barkantine od. *barkentine*, Schonerbark.

barling spar, eine leichte Spiere.

barnacles, Muscheln.

barometer scale, Barometerskala.

barometrical observation, Barometer-Beobachtung.

barquantine, Barkschoner.

barque rigged, als Bark getakelt.

barquentine, Barkschoner.

barrator, Betrüger; - *ship*, Untreue, Betrug.

barratrous, betrügerisch.

barratry, Betrug, Untreue.

barrel, 1. Körper, Welle, Zylinder; 2. Trommel (bei Gangspill, Steuerapparat u. Winde); - *bulk*, Raummaß =5 Kubikfuß; - *of a capstan*, Gangspillwelle; - *of a crane*, Krantrommel; - *of a mast*, Mastenkoker; - *of a parrel*, Racktonne; - *of a pump*, Pumpenstiefel; - *of a winch*, Windentrommel; - *of the steering gear*, Trommel des Steuergeräts; - *of the wheel*, Welle des Steuerrades; - *parrel*, Tonnenrack; - *shaft*, Trommelwelle.

barricade a ship, ein Schiff verschanzen.

barrier of ice, Eisbarre; - *of reefs*, Riffenkette.

bars, all - down! Spaken aus! *to take down the -*, die S. auslegen.

base line, die Linie der Oberkante der Kielspündung; - *of a river delta*, Küstenlinie eines Flußdeltas; - *plate*, Fundamentplatte.

basin, Vordock; - *of a dock*, Außendock; - *of a port*, Binnenhafen; - *of a river*, Flußgebiet.

bast rope, Bastseil.

bastard, 1. Rücktau; 2. Großsegel einer Galeere; 3. Admiralitätsgaleere; - *file*, Vorfeile; - *pitch*, Gemisch von Harz, Pech und Teer.

batten, 1. Latte, Leiste; 2. Wegerungslatte; 3. Schalen, Schalungen (zur Verstärkung der Masten); 4. Lukenschalken, verschalken; - *and space*, Leisten mit Zwischenräumen; - - - *bulkhead*, Gitterschott; - - - *ceiling*, Lattenwegerung, offene Wegerung; - *cleat*, Lattenklampe; - *down*, verschalken.

battens of a decked top, Marsklampen; - *of the tarpaulins*, Persennigleisten.

battledores, Betingshörner.

baulks, Spieren.

bay, 1. Bucht; 2. Schafhock; - *bolt*, Hackbolzen.

be up, aufkommen.

beach, 1. Gestade, Strand 2. auf Strand setzen; *flat and sandy -*, flacher Sandstrand; *stony -*, steiniger

Strand; - *comber*, Läufor
für Händler u. Wirte; - *men*,
Bootsfahrer.

beacon, Bake, ausbaken, bebaken; *the - bears*, man peilt
die B.; - *boat*, B-boot; - *buoy*,
B-boje; - *fire*, Leuchtfeuer,
Signalfeuer; - *grate*, Feuer-
korb; - *light*, Bakenfeuer;
- - *house*, Feuerwarte; - *out*,
ausfeuern; - *tower*, Leuchtturm.   [Betonnage.

beaconage, 1. Bakengeld; 2.
beaconed rock, Bakenklippe.
beaconless, ohne Leuchtfeuer.
beading, Kehlung, Verzierung,
Verzierungsleisten.

beak, 1. Back; 2. Gallionsknie;
- *head*, Gallion, Schiffsschnabel; - - *beam*, Decksbalken; - *of the prow*, Schiffs-
schnabelspitze.

beam, 1. Balken; 2. Balancier
(der Maschine); *on the -*,
querab; - *angle bar*, Balkenwinkel; - *arm*, B-arm; - - *of
a hanging knee*, B-arm eines
Hängeknies; - *end*, Balken-
ende; *on her - ends*, zum
Kentern liegen; - *engine*,
Balancier-Maschine; - *filling*,
Ladung zwischen den Deck-
balken; - *grabs*, Balken-
klammern; - *gudgeon*, Balan-
cierzapfen; - - *brasses*, B-z-
Lagerschalen; - *hanging
knee*, Balken - Hängeknie;
- *head*, Topp; - *knee*, Balkenknie; - *lever*, Balancier;
- *line*, Linie, welche die
Durchschneidung der Deck-
balken und der Spanten
bezeichnet; - *of a forecastle
or poop*, Decksbalken einer
Back oder Poop; - *of the
anchor*, Ankerrute; - *scarph*,
Balkenlasch; - *sea*, Dwarssee; - *stringer*, Balkenstringer; - *wind*, Dwarswind.

beamy, breit.

bear, Deckbesen; *to -*, 1. sich
erstrecken (die Küste); 2.
peilen; - *a hand here!* Komm
und hilf hier! - *against the*

current, gegen den Strom
halten; - *away*, abhalten;
- - *by degrees*, allmählich
a.; - - *in the main*, die
Räumte halten; - *down*,
sinken lassen; - - *upon*, abhalten auf; - *in towards*,
zusteuern auf; - *off*, absteuern; - - *by degrees* od.
- - *gradually*, langsam immer
mehr abhalten; - - *the anchor*, den Anker vom Bug
abhalten; - *on the beams*,
quer abhalten; - *round up*,
vor dem Wind ganz ab-
halten; - *sails*, Segel tragen;
- *the land on the lee bow*,
das Land über den Leebug
peilen; - *under the lee*, nach
der Leeseite eines anderen
Schiffes steuern; - *up round*,
beim Abhalten einen Rund-
törn machen; - *up the helm!*
Luvwärts das Ruder! - *water*,
Lastigkeit haben.

bearding, Ausbugung; - *line*,
Linie der inneren Spün-
dungskante.

bearer, Fundament, Lager.

bearing, 1. Lager, L-bock, L-
stuhl; 2. L-stelle; 3. Peilung;
- *beacon*, Peilbake; - *body*,
gleichlastig; - *bolt*, Lagerbolzen; - - *nut*, L-b-mutter;
- *brasses*, Lagerschalen;
- *compass*, Peilkompaß;
- *keep*, Lagerdeckel; - *of a
shaft*, Wellenlager; - *of the
compass*, Kompaßstrich; - *of
the sails*, das Lavieren; - *oil
cup*, Schmiergefäß des Lagers.

bearings of a vessel, Wasserlinie; *to take -*, peilen; *How
are the -?* Wo befinden wir
uns?

bears S. E, der Ort peilt S. O.

beat, 1. aussegeln, schlagen,
überholen, übertreffen; 2.
lavieren, kreuzen; - *about*,
hin und her kreuzen;
- *against the wind*, gegen
den Wind ankreuzen; - *back*,
abstoßen; - *by boards*, gegen

den Wind arbeiten; - *into a river*, in einen Fluß einkreuzen; - *off*, abstoßen; - *out*, auskreuzen; - *right against the wind*, od. - - *in the wind's eye*, od. *to be on a dead* -, recht gegen den Wind ankreuzen; - *up*, aufkreuzen; - *tack for tack*, kurze Schläge machen; - *the record*, den Rekord schlagen; - *to windward*, aufkreuzen; - *with short tacks*, Schlag für S. aufkreuzen.

beaten back, durch Wind und Wetter zurück aus See; - *iron*, gehämmertes Eisen.

beating, lavieren; - *passage*, Reise in kurzen Gängen; - *sea*, Stampfsee; - *wind*, Gegenwind, der zum Kreuzen zwingt.

becalm, 1. einem Schiffe den Wind abfangen; 2. sich den Wind stehlen.

becalmed, in Windstille, Wind abgeschnitten, kein Steuer im Schiff.

becasse, großes spanisches Boot.

becket, 1. Handpferd; 2. Haken zum Aufhängen von Tauwerk etc.; 3. Behälter für altes Tauwerk; 4. Auge, Knebelstropp, Schlinge; 5. mit einem Stropp festbinden, mit Tauringen od. Klampen versehen; - *bridle*, Knebelstropp.

bed a cask, ein Faß mit Kopfhölzern festlegen; - *for a. c*, Kopfholz; - *of a bowsprit*, Bugspriet-Bettung; - *of a river*, Flußbett; - *plate*, Fundamentplatte; - - *holding down bolt*, F-plattenbolzen; - - *packing*, F-plattenpackung.

bee blocks of the bowsprit, Violinen des Bugspriets.

beech wood, Buchenholz.

bees of a bowsprit, Bugsprietviolinen.

beetle, Klameihammer.

before the beam, vorlich von dwars; - - *mast*, Dienst vor dem Mast; - - *midships*, vor dem Mittelspann; - - *wind*, vor dem Wind.

beginning of the ebb tide, die erste Ebbe; - - - *flood tide*, die Vorflut; - - - *regatta*, das Ansegeln.

behave, sich halten; - *well when scudding*, gut lenssen.

belaying, belegen; - *cleat*, Mastklampe; - *cleats for tacks and sheets*, Kreuzklampen für Halsen und Schoten; - *pin*, Belegnagel.

belee = *becalm*.

belfry, Glockengalgen.

bell, 1. Glocke; 2. das Glas = ½ Stunde; - *buoy*, Glockenboje; - *clapper*, G-klöppel; - *cover*, G-kappe; - *crank*, G-arm; - - *engine*, Maschine mit Balancier, der winkelmäßige Bewegung hat; - *rope*, Glockentau; - *shaped valve*, G-ventil; - *signal*, G-signal.

bellows, Blasebalg.

bells, Glasen = ½ Stunde.

belly, 1. Schwellung (eines Krummholzes); 2. Bauch (eines Segels); 3. gut vollstehen; - *band*, Bauchband; - *brace*, das quer über den Kessel laufende Eisenband; - *guy*, Mittelgeie; - *of the compas timber*, die hohle Seite des Krummholzes; - *stay*, Mittelstag.

bellying canvas, schwellende Segel; - *to leeward*, nach Lee zu hängend; - *to the breeze*, anfangen zu schwellen.

belting, Wallschiene, Scheuerleiste.

bench hammer, Bankhammer.

benches of a boat, Sitzbänke eines Bootes.

bend, 1. Knoten, Stich; 2. Biegung (des Flusses); - *a sail*, ein Segel anschlagen; - *mould*, Mall des Hauptspannes; - *the cable*, das

Ankertau durch den Anker-
ring stecken; - *to the oars,*
die Riemen gut vorauswer-
fen; - *two ropes together,*
zwei Taue aufeinanderstek-
ken.

bending a chain cable, eine
Ankerkette einschäkeln; - *a
plank by steaming,* eine
Planke mit Dampf sättigen
und biegen; - *a plate,* eine
Platte biegen; - *machine,*
Biegewalze; - *test,* B-probe.

bends, 1. Knoten (im Tau);
2. Bergholz.

beneaped, benept.

Bengal light, Blaufeuer.

bent knee, Winkelknie; *-timber,*
Balken mit Bucht.

bentinck boom, Baum einer
Baumfock; - *sail,* Baum-
fock; - - *sheet,* B-f-schote.

bentincks, die dreieckigen
Untersegel.

Bermuda schooner, Gaffel-
schoner.

berth, 1. Ankerplatz. Liegep;
2. Koje; 3. eine Koje an-
weisen; 4. ein Schiff hin-
legen; - *and space* od. - *and
square,* Spantenentfernung;
- *board,* Scheidewand zwischen den Kojen; - *deck,*
Zwischendeck; - *marks,* tief-
ste Ladelinie; *to give a
point a berth of 3 cables,*
Drei Kabellängen von einem
Punkte abbleiben; *t. g. a. p.
a good b.,* frei von einem P.
steuern; *t. g. a. wide b.,* weit
aus dem Wege gehen.

berthed, 1. vor Anker liegen;
2. untergebracht sein.

berther, Schlafkojen-Anweiser.

berthing, das Erhöhen des
Schiffsbords; - *master,* Ha-
fenmeister; - *of the head,*
Gallionsbretter; - *rail,* obere
Gallionsreling.

bertying, das Anlegen des
Schiffes zwecks Ausbesse-
rung.

beset, eingeengt.

best bower od. *b. b. anchor,* der

schwere Buganker; - *hawser,*
Kabeltau; - *warp,* Pferdleine.

bethel ship, Betschiff.

between decks, Zwischendeck;
- - *beam,* Z-d-balken; - - *ceiling,* Z-d-wegerung; - *the
devil and the deep sea,* zwischen zwei Übeln zu wählen
haben; - *wind and water,*
zwischen Wind und Wasser.

betwixt = between.

bevel, Schrägmaß; - *gear,* konisches Getriebe; - *pinion,*
k. G; - *wheel,* k. Zahnrad.

bevelled edge of a plank, Naht-
kante.

bevelling, das Bemallen od.
Biegen des Holzes; - *board,*
Mallbrett; - *edge of a plank,*
Notkante; - *frame,* Holz-
rahmen für ein Mallbrett.

bevil = bevel.

beyond sea, überseeisch.

bibbs, die Backen des Mastes.

bible, 1. Bibel (großer Scheuer-
stein); 2. Handaxt.

big repairs, großeReparaturen.

bight, 1. Taubucht; 2. Einbucht
(eines Flusses); - *of the peak
halliards,* das Spann des
Pikfalls; - *splice,* Buchtsplissung.

bights catch each other, die
Buchten des Kabels fangen
sich.

bilalo, Zweimaster.

bilander, kleiner holländ.
Zweimaster.

bilge, 1. Bilge, Kimm; 2. leck
werden; - *board,* Schlagwasserplatte; - *bolt,* Kimm-
bolzen; - *coads,* Tragholz;
- *cock,* Lenzhahn; - *delivery
pipes,* Lenzdruckrohrlei-
tung; - - *valve chest,* Lenz-
pumpen-Druckventilkasten;
- *discharge pipe.* Lenzdruck-
rohr; - - *valve,* Bilgeausguß-
ventil; - *ejector,* Lenzejektor;
- *free,* bauchfrei; - *heads,*
Oberende einer Boden-
wrange; - *injection,* Not-
Injektion; - - *cock,* Bilge-

Injektionshahn; - - *pipe*, B-I-rohr; - - *strainer* od. - - *strum box*, B-I-Saugesieb; - - *valve*, B-I-ventil; - - - *box*, B-I-v-gehäuse; - - - *cover*, B-I-v-deckel; - - - *mud box*, Schlammkasten des B-I-v.; - - - *pipe*, B-I-v-rohr; - - - *spindle*, B-I-v-spindel; *b. i. water*, B-I-wasser; - *inlet*, Bilge-Einlaß; - *intercostal keelson*, eingeschobenes Kimmkielschwein; - - - *angle bar*, e. K-k-s-winkel; - - - *plates*, eingeschobene K-k-s-platte; *b. i. plates*, e. K-k-s-platten; - - *stringer*, Interkostal - Kimmstringer; - - - *angle bar*, I-k-K-s-winkel; - *keel*, Kimmkiel; - - *angle bar*, K-k-winkel; - *keelson*, K-k-schwein; - - *angle bar*, K-k-s-winkel; - *log*, K-k-s.; - *piece*, K-k.; - *pipe*, Bilgenrohr; - - *flange and cap*, B-r-Flansch u. Deckel; - *pipes*, Lenzrohrleitung; - *plank*, Kimmplanke; - *planking*, Kimmbeplankung; - *planks of the ceiling*, Kimmwäger; - *plate*, Kimmplatte; - *plating*, Kimmbeplattung.

bilge pump, Lenzpumpe; - - *air vessel*, Lenzpumpen-Windkessel; - - *barrel*, L.-körper; - - *bucket*, L.-kolben; - - - *ring*, L.-k-ring; - - - *valve*, L-k-ventil; - - - - *guard*, L.-K-v-Hubbegrenzer; - - - - *seat*, L.-K-v-sitz; *b. p. chamber*, L.-Körper; - - *cover*, L.-deckel; - - *cylinder*, L.-zylinder; - - *delivery space*, L.-Druckraum; - - - *valve*, L.-Druckventil; - - - - *guard*, L.-D.-Hubbegrenzer; - - - - *seat*, L.-D.-sitz; *b. p. discharge pipe*, L.-Ausgußrohr; - - - *valve*, L.-A-g-ventil; - - - - *cover*, L.-A-g-v-deckel; - - - - *spindle*, L.-A-g-v-spindel; *b. p. foot valve*, L.-Fußventil; - - - - *guard*, L.-

Saugventil - Hubbegrenzer; - - - - *seat*, L.-S-v-sitz; *b. p. gear*, L.-vorrichtung; - - *gland*, L.-Stopfbüchsendeckel; - - *head valve*, L.-Druckventil; - - *liner*, L.-Einsatz; - - *link*, L.-gelenk; - - - *brasses*, L.-g-Lagerschalen; *b. p. neck bush*, L.-Grundring; - - *pet valve*, L.-Schnürventil; - - *plunger*, L.-Plunger; - - *ram*, L.-Kolbenstange; - - *relief valve*, L.-Rücklaufventil; - - *rod*, L.-stange; - - - *stuffing box*, L.-stangen-Stopfbüchse; *b. p. s. b.*, L.-S-b.; - - - - *gland* L.-S-b-deckel; *b. p. suction pipe*, L.-Saugerohr; - - - *space*, L.-Saugeraum; - - - *valve*, L.-Saugventil; - - - - *guard*, L.-S-v-Hubbegrenzer; - - - - *seat*, L.-S-v-sitz; *b. p. top valve*, L.-Druckventil; - - - - *guard*, L.-D-v-Hubbegrenzer; - - - *seat*, L.-D-v-sitz; *b. p. valve*, L.-ventil; - - - *cover*, L.-v-deckel; - - - *guard*, L.-v-Hubbegrenzer; - - - *seat*, L.-v-sitz.

bilge shore, Kimmstütze; - *strake*, K-gang; - *stringer*, K-stringer; - - *angle bar*, K-s-winkel; - *suction pipe*, Lenzpumpen-Saugerohr; - - *pipes*, Lenz-S-r-leitung; - - *valve*, L.-Saugventil; - - - *chest*, L.-pumpen-S-v-kasten; - *tree*, Tragholz; - *valve box*, Lenzventilkasten; - *water*, Bilgenwasser; - - *alarm*, Höhenanzeiger des B-w.; - - *discharge*, selbsttätiger Apparat zur Entleerung des B-w.; - - *gauge*, B-w-Manometer; - *ways*, Schlittenbalken.

bilged, mit eingedrückter Kimm.

bilgy, wie Schlagwasser riechend.

bill board, Ankerscheuer; - *of a compass*, Spitze eines Krummholzes; - *of admeasurement*, Meßbrief; - *of adventure*, 1. Bodmereibrief; 2. Kontrakt der Übernahme eines Risikos; - *of bottomry*, Bodmereibrief; - *of freedom*, Freibrief; - *of freight*, Frachtbrief; - *of health*, Gesundheitspaß; - *of lading*, Frachtbrief; - *of sale*, Verkaufsbrief; - *of store*, Proviantierschein; - *of sufferance*, Freihandelsbrief; - *of the anchor*, Ankerspitze; - *of tonnage*, Meßbrief; - *tricing line*, Aufholer des unteren Raatakelblocks.

billet head, 1. Pfahl; 2. Poller (eines Bootes); - *wood*, Stauholz.

billiard, Stoßeisen.

billow beaten, umbrandet.

billows, 1. Brandung; 2. Brechseen.

billy boy, Fluß- od. Küstenbarke.

binacle = *binnacle*.

binders, hölzerne Stützen zum Verlaschen.

binding, die zusammenhaltenden Schiffshölzer; - *bolt*, Bindebolzen; - *of a dead eye*, Beschlag einer Jungfer; - *strake*, Verbindungsgang.

binn, Koje.

binnacle, Kompaßhäuschen; - *compass*, Steuerkompaß; - *cover*, Kompaßbezug; - *lamp* od. - *light*, Nachthauslampe; - *list*, Krankenliste; - *stand*, Kompaßständer; - *word*, etwas, das man sich hinter's Ohr schreiben soll.

binocle od. *binocular telescope*, Doppelfernrohr.

birch wood, Birkenholz.

Birkmeyer's tarpaulin, B- geteertes Segeltuch.

bird's nest, Krähennest.

bireme, Galeere mit 2 Ruderbänken.

birlin, eine Art Ruderboot.

birth = *berth*.

biscuits, Schiffszwieback.

Bismarck lights, Zollaternen.

bit = *bitt*; *to bit the cable*, das Ankertau um die Beting legen.

bite, greifen, der Halt (des Ankers).

bits, Betinge.

bitt, 1. Beting; 2. B-schlag nehmen; 3. der Bitt (der das Wasser durchschneidende Teil des Schiffes); - *bolts*, Betingbolzen; - *head*, B-kopf; - *pins*, B-stangen; - *stopper*, B-stopper.

bitter, Betingschlag; - *end of the cable*, das Ende der Ankerkette.

bitts, Betinge.

black birch wood, Schwarzbirkenholz; - *butt w.*, Blackbuttholz; - *hitch*, einfacher Hakenschlag; - *lead*, Pottlot; - *list*, schwarze Liste; - *oakum*, Werg von getrocknetem Tauwerk; - *oil*, Zylinderöl; - *Sea*, Schwarzes Meer; - - *trade*, Schwarzemeerhandel od. S-m-fahrt; - - *trader*, S-m-fahrer; - *squall*, Gewitterbö; - *strake*, Farbegang; - *varnish*, schwarzer Teerfirnis; - *wall*, einfacher Hakenschlag; - *walnut*, Schwarzwalnußholz.

blacking, 1. schwarze Farbe; 2. schwarz streichen; - *brush*, Schwarzquast.

blade of an oar, Ruderblatt; - *of a propeller*, Flügel einer Schraube.

blare, Teer- u. Haarmischung.

blashy, Schmutzwetter.

blast, 1. Ton mit der Dampfpfeife; 2. Windstoß; - *cock*, Blashahn; - *pipe*, Blasrohr.

blather, Schlick.

bleed the buoys, Leckwasser aus den Bojen laufen lassen.

blind anchor, Hafenanker; - *buckler*, der volle Klüsendeckel; - *harbour*, eingeschlossener Hafen.

blink, der Blink (klarer Fleck zwischen Wolken); - *of ice*, Eisblink.

blirt, kurze Regenbö.

blister, Blase; - *steel*, Blasenstahl.
blizzard, eisiger Schneesturm.
block, 1. Block; 2. Lager, L-stuhl; 3. Schuh; - *and b.*, Block an B.; - *and fall*, B. mit Läufer; - *and tackle*, Zugwerk; - *heel*, Hieling; - *maker*, Blockmacher; - *maker's whip saw*, Fuchsschwanz des Blockmachers; - *seizing*, B-bindsel; - *shed*, B-macherschuppen; - *up*, unzugänglich machen; - *with several sheaves*, mehrscheibiger B.
blockade, Blockade, blockieren; - *runner*, B-brecher.
blocks, Trockendock; *to take the blocks*, 1. in's T. gehen; 2. auf die Kielblöcke gelegt werden; - *of a ship*, Blockwerk eines Schiffes.
bloody ancient, Blutflagge.
bloom iron, Frischeisen.
blow, 1. Schlag, Stoß; 2. Pfiff; 3. wehen, blasen; - *cock*, Abblashahn; - *down*, abblasen; - - *cock*, Ausblashahn; - - *pipe*, A-b-rohr; - - *valve*, A-b-ventil; - *high*, stark wehen; - *home*, dem Gestade zu wehen; - *itself out*, sich auswehen; - *off*, abblasen; - - *cock*, Abblashahn; - - *gear*, A-b-vorrichtung; - - *pipe*, A-b-rohr; - - *steam*, Dampf abblasen; - - *valve*, Abblasventil; - - - *box*, A-b-v-gehäuse; - - - *spindle*, A-b-v-spindel; - *out*, abblasen; - - *cock*, Ausblashahn; - - *pipe*, A-b-rohr; - - *pipes*, A-b-r-leitung; - - *valve*, Grundventil; - *over*, vorüberwehen; - *the gaff*, den Angeber spielen; - *through*, durchblasen; - - *cock*, Durchblashahn; - - *pipe*, D-b-rohr; - - *valve*, D-b-ventil; - *up* od. *to give a - up*, tüchtig ausschelten.
blowing weather, stürmisches Wetter.

blown from the bolt rope, vom Leik losgerissen.
blows, How - the wind? Aus welchem Loche bläßt der Wind?
blue fire, Blaufeuer; - *gum wood*, Blaugumholz; - *light*, Blaufeuer; - *Peter*, Abfahrtssignal „Blauer Peter"; - *pigeon*, Tieflot; - *water*, Blauwasser.
bluff, 1. voller, breiter Bug; 2. steiles Vorland; - *bow*, voller, breiter Bug; - *head*, Bug mit Stampfsteven.
blustering, stürmisch.
boar, Springflut.
board, 1. Bord, an B. kommen, entern; 2. Brett, beplanken, verschalen; 3. Gang, Schlag (beim Lavieren); *a-board* od. *on board*, an Bord; *b. and b.*, B. an B.; *b. of admiralty*, Marineministerium; *b. of Health*, Gesundheitsamt; *b. of trade*, Handelsamt; *b. of trade's regulations*, handelsamtliche Vorschriften; *b. plate*, Schaufelplatte; *b. up to weather*, anluven.
boardable, enterbar.
boarders, die Enterer.
boarding, das Entern; - *axe*, Enterbeil; - *grapnel*, Enterhaken; - *house*, Logierhaus, Schlafstelle; - *master*, Schlafbaas; - *nettings*, Enternetze; - *officer*, Hafen-Zollbeamter; - *pike*, Enterpike; - *plate*, Schaufelplatte.
boards, to make -, lavieren.
boat anchor, Bootsanker; - *awning*, B-sonnensegel; - *bailer* od. - *baler*, B-Ösfaß; - *bill*, B-rolle; - *boiler*, B-kessel; - *bridge*, Schiffsbrücke; - *builder*, Bootbauer; - *chock*, Bootsklampe; - - *standard*, B-klampenständer; - *cleats*, B-klampen; - *cloak*, Mantel für Offiziere im Dienst; - *cloth*, Bootsmantel; - *compass*, B-kompaß; - *cover*, B-kleid;

- *davit,* B-davit; - - *socket,* B-d-spur.

boat *deck,* Bootdeck; - - *beam,* B-d-balken; - - - *angle bar,* B-d-b-winkel; - - - *stringer,* B-d-b-stringer; - - - - *angle bar,* B-d-b-s-winkel; *b. d. guard rods,* B-d-geländerstangen; - - *pillar,* B-d-stütze; - - *rails and stanchions,* B-d-geländer; - - *stanchion,* B-d-g-stütze; - - *stringer,* B-d-balkenstringer; - - *waterway,* B-d-wassergang.

boat *detaching hook,* Haken zum Abstoßen des niedergelassenen Bootes; - *drill,* Bootdrill; - *duty,* Bootsdienst; - *engine,* Dampfbeibootmaschine; - *fast,* Fangleine; - *fender,* Bootfender; - *frames,* B-spanten; - *gear,* B-zubehör; - *grating,* B-gräting; - *gripe,* Bootskrabber; - *hoist engine,* Bootheißmaschine.

boat *hoist engine connecting rod,* BootheißmaschinenPleuelstange; - - - - - *bolt,* B.-P-stangenbolzen; - - - - *bottom end keep,* B.-Kurbelzapfen-Lagerschalendeckel; - - - - - - - *liner,* B.-Pleuelstangenfuß-Futter; *b.h.e.c.r. top end keep,* B.-Kreuzkopflagerschalendeckel; *b. h. e. crank pin bolt,* B.-Kurbelzapfenlagerbolzen; - - - - - *brasses,* B.-K-z-L-schalen; *b. h. e. c. shaft,* B.-Kurbelwelle; - - - - - *bearing,* B.-K-w-lager; - - - - - - *bolt,* B.-K-w-l-bolzen; - - - - - - *brasses,* B.-K-w-l-schalen; - - - - - - - *keep,* B.-K-w-l-deckel; - - - - - - - *bolt,* B.-K-w-l-d-bolzen; *b. h. e. crosshead bolt,* B.-Kreuzkopflagerbolzen; *b.h.e.c. brasses,* B.-K-k-l-schalen; *b. h. e. cylinder,* B.-Zylinder; - - - - *cover,* B.-Z.-deckel; - - - - *bolt,* B.-Z.-d-bolzen; *b.h. e. c. c.*

drain pipe, B.-Z.-Entwässerungsrohr; *b. h. e. eccentric,* B.-Excenter; - - - - *bolt,* B.-E-bolzen; - - - - *brasses,* B.-E.-Lagerschalen; - - - - *rod,* B.-E.-stange; - - - - *sheave,* B.-E.-scheibe; - - - - *strap,* B.-E.-bügel; - - - - - *liner* B.-E.-b-Futter; *b.h.e. exhaust pipe,* B.-Dampfablaßrohr; *b. h. e. piston,* B.-Kolben; - - - - *rod,* B.-K-stange; - - - - - *crosshead,* B.-K-s-Kreuzkopf; - - - - - *stuffing box,* B.-Kolbenstangen-Stopfbüchse; - - - - - *gland,* B.-K-s-S-b-deckel; *b. h. e. slide valve,* B.-Schieber; *b. h. e. starting valve,* B.-Anlaßventil; *b. h. e. steam pipe,* B.-Dampfzuleitungsrohr; *b. h. e. stop valve,* B.-Absperrventil; *b. h. e. valve casing,* B.-Schieberkasten; - - - - - *door,* B.-S-k-deckel; *b. h. e. v. rod,* B.-Schieberstange; - - - - - *stuffing box,* B.-S-s-Stopfbüchse; - - - - - - - *gland,* B.-S-s-S-b-deckel

boat *hook,* Bootshaken; - *house,* B-schuppen; - *lashings,* B-laschungen; - *locker,* B-kasten; - *lowering apparatus,* B - streichapparat; - *man,* Jollenführer oder Bootsgast; - *manoeuvre,* B-manöver; - *mast,* B-mast; - *oar,* Riemen; - *pads,* B-Stoßkissen; - *painter,* Fangleine eines Bootes; - *pennant,* Bootswimpel; - *planking,* B - beplankung; - *plates,* Schiffsblech; - *plating,* Bootsbeplattung; - *plug,* B-pfropfen; - - *hole,* B-p-loch; - *race,* Ruderregatta; - *rings,* Bootsringe; - *rope,* Schlepptau des Bootes; - *rudder,* Bootssteuer; - - *tiller,* B-ruderpinne; - - *yoke,* B-r-joch; - *sails,* B-segel; - *scoop,* Schöpfeimer; - *skid stanchions,* Bootsgalgenständer; - *skids,* 1. B-galgen; 2. Reibhölzer; - *sling,* Bootsstropp;

- *stem,* Vordersteven eines
Bootes; - *swifter,* Fender-
tau; - *tackle,* Bootstakel;
- *tank,* B-tank; - *tiller,* B-
ruderpinne; - *timber,* B-
spanten; - *windlass,* B-spill.
boat, to - *the anchor,* den
Anker mit dem Boote aus-
bringen; - - *the oars,* die
Riemen in das Boot legen.
boat's anchor, Bootsanker;
- *creek,* B-hafen; - *crew,*
B-mannschaft; - *gripe,* B-
krabber; - *harbour* oder
- *place* od. - *pond,* B-hafen;
- *shed,* B-haus; - *stretcher,*
Fußlatte; - *wain,* Bootsmann; - *wain's call,* B-
mannspfeife; - - *chair,* B-
m-stuhl; - - *locker,* B-manns-
Vorratskammer; - - *mate,*
B-m-maat; - - *room,* B-m-
kammer; - - *store room,* B-
m-Hellegat; - - *whistle,* B-
m-pfeife; - *wharf,* B-werfte.
boat's see also boat.
boatage, Durchschnittstrag-
fähigkeit aller Boote eines
Schiffes.
boating, 1. Versendung per
Boot; 2. Bootrudern.
bob, Wimpel.
bobbing od. *b. about,* auf und
nieder tanzen.
bobble, Kräuselwasser.
bobstay, Wasserstag; - *bar,*
W-s-stange; - *chain,* W-s-
kette; - *piece,* Gallionsschegg; - *pin,* Wasserstag-
bolzen.
boca wood, Bokaholz.
bodily, to drive - *upon the
coast,* mit der Schiffsseite
gegen die Küste treiben.
bodkin, Pfriem.
body heavier than water, ein
sanker Körper; - *hoops,*
eiserne Mastbänder; - *of
boiler,* Kesselkörper; - *of
pump,* Pumpenkörper; - *of
ship,* Schiffskörper; - *plan,*
Spantenriß; - *post,* Schrau-
bensteven.
bogie funnel, Ofenschornstein.

bogue, 1. Flußmündung; 2. den
Grund schlecht halten; 3.
dwars wegtreiben.
bogy man, Klabautermann.
boiled oil, gekochtes Leinöl.
boiler, Kessel; - *air valve,*
Luftauslaßventil des Kessels;
- *back landing,* hintere Fuge
d. K.; - *back tube plate,* hintere Rohrwand d. K.; - *barrel,*
der zylindrische Rumpf d.
K; - *bearer,* Kessellager;
- - *angle bar,* K-l-winkel;
- *blow out cock,* K-abblas-
hahn; - *braces,* Stützklam-
mern eines Kessels; - *casing,*
Schornstein-Umbau; - *composition,* Kesselbekleidung;
- *explosion,* K - explosion;
- *fittings,* K - garnituren;
- *float,* K-schwimmer; - *flue,*
innere K-rohr; - *front landing,* Vorderfuge des K.;
- *front plate,* vordere Stirnwand des Kessels; - - *tube
p.,* v. Rohrwand d. K.; - *furnace,* Verbrennungsraum;
- *grate,* Kesselrost; - *hatch,*
Kesselluke; - *inspection,*
Dampfkesselrevision; - *lagging,* Kesselbekleidung;
- *main stop valve,* K-Haupt-
absperrventil; - *maker,* K-
schmied; - *making,* K-bau;
- *mounting,* K - armatur;
- *opening,* K-luke; - *plates,*
K-platten; - *pressure,* K-
druck; - *room,* K-raum;
- *safety valve,* K-Sicherheits-
ventil; - - - *load,* K-S-h-v-
Belastung; - *seam,* Naht
eines Kessels; - *seating,*
Kesselfundament; - *shell,*
Außenhaut des Kessels;
- *shop,* Kesselwerkstatt;
- *space,* K-raum; - *stay,* K-
anker; - - *inside nut,* Innen-
mutter eines K-a; - - *nut,*
K-a-mutter; - - *outside nut,*
Außenmutter eines Kessel-
ankers; - - *washer,* Unterlagsscheibe e. K-a; - *steam
space,* Dampfraum e.Kessels;
- *stop valve,* Absperrventil

e. K.; - *survey*, Kesselbe-
sichtigung; - *test*, K-prüfung;
- *top*, K-deckel; - *tube*, K-
rohr; - - *brush*, Feuerrohr-
bürste; - - *ferrule*, F-r-ring;
- *water*, Kesselwasser; - -
space, Wasserraum des
Kessels; - *works*, Kessel-
bauanstalt.
boiling, siedend; - *point*, Siede-
punkt; - *sea*, kochende See.
boisterous, stürmisch.
bold coast, steile Küste;
- *flood*, überschwellende
Flut; - *hawse*, hoch über
dem Wasser liegende Klü-
sen; - *shore*, steiles Ufer.
bollard, 1. Pfahl; 2. Poller
(eines Bootes) ; - *timbers*,
Judasohren.
bolster, 1. Fütterung, Kissen;
2. Rüste für die Anker-
scheuer.
bolt, 1. ein Stück Zeug von
ca. 45 Yards; 2. Bolzen, verbolzen; - *boat*, seetüchtiges
Boot; - *nut*, Bolzenmutter;
- *of canvass*, Rolle Segeltuch; - *rope*, Leik; - - *line*,
L-leine; - - *yarn*, L-garn;
- *screwing machine*, Bolzen-
schneidemaschine; - *strake*,
der Gang, durch den die
Deckbalken gehen; - *with
ring and hook*, Bockshorn-
bolzen; - *yarn*, starkes
Segelgarn.
bolts of the bitts, Betingbolzen.
boltsprit, Bugspriet.
bombard od. *bomb ketch* od.
bomb vessel, Bombardier-
galiote.
bomkin = *bumkin*.
bon grace, der dicke Taufender.
bonaventure mizzen, zweiter
Besahnmast.
bond dock, Entrepotdock; - *of
bottomry*, Bodmereibrief.
bonded goods, unverzollte
Waren; - *store*, Packhofs-
lager; - *warehouse*, Zoll-
niederlage.
bonnet, Bonnet; - *of funnel*,
Schornsteinkragen; - *of the*

valve box, Ventilkasten-
deckel.
booby hatch, Kappe der Hin-
terluke.
boom, 1. Baum, Ausleger; 2.
Hafenbaum, Schlengel; 3.
Schwimmbarrikade; 4. mit
vollen Segeln fahren; - *boat*,
Deckboot; - *brace*, Leesegelspiere; - *crutch*, Baum-
krücke; - *fore sail*, Schonersegel; - - - *gaff*, Vorgaffel;
- - - *halliard*, Schonersegel-
fall; - - - *peak h.*, S-s-Piek-
fall; - - - *sheet*, S-s-schote;
- - - *tack*, S-s-hals; - - -
throat halliard, S-s-Klau-
fall; - - - *vang*, S-s-Gaffel-
gerde; - *guy*, Baumstopper;
- - *pendant*, Bullentau;
- *hoop*, Band eines Baumes;
- *iron*, Baumbügel; - *jib*,
großer Klüver; - - *downhaul*,
K-Niederholer; - - *sheet*, K-
schote; - - *stay*, K-leiter;
- - *tack*, K-hals; - *jigger*,
Leesegelspierentalje; - *main
sail*, Großsegel; - *of a harbour*, Hafenbaum; - *off*,
1. abbäumen; 2. mit der
Stange fortbewegen; - *sail*,
Baumsegel; - *sheet*, B-schote;
- *takle*, B-talje; - *to load
and unload*, Ladebaum;
- *topping lift*, Baum-Toppen-
ant; - - - *purchase*, B-Top-
penantstalje.
boomage, Hafenbaumgeld.
boomerlander, Oberländerkahn.
booming along, mit allen
Segeln gesetzt ankommen;
- *ship*, Schnellsegler.
boomkin = *bumkin*.
booms, die Barring.
boot topping, 1. Spiekerhaut;
2. Abschrapen der S.
bora, Bora.
bordage, Seitenplanken.
border pile, Außenpfahl.
bore, 1. Flutwelle; 2. anbohren,
bohren; *Cape Vincent - N.
W.*, wir peilten Kap St. Vincent N. W.; - *out*, ausbohren.

boring frame, Bohrstuhl; - *machine*, B-maschine.

borrow, sich dem Laude nähern.

borrower on bottomry, Bodmereinehmer.

bosom piece, Stoßwinkel.

boss, Hülse, Nabe, Nuß; - *of a steering wheel*, Steuerradnabe; - *of a wheel*, Schaufelradnabe; - *of a paddle wheel*, S-r-n; - *of propeller post*, Nuß des Schraubenstevens; - *of stern post*, N. d. Ruderstevens; - *plate*, Nußplatte.

botch, stümpern.

bothered, aufgehalten.

bottle paper, Zettel in einer Flasche; - *post*, Flaschenpost; - *track*, der von einer F. zurückgelegte Weg.

bottom, 1. Boden (des Schiffes u. Meeres); 2. Grund; *to carry by -*, zu Schiff transportieren; - *blow off cock*, Bodenhahn; - - - *pipe*, Ablasrohr; - - - *valve*, Ausblasventil; - *blow valve*, Bodenventil; -*board*, Bodenpflicht; - *brass*, untere Lagerschale; -*breakers*, Grundbrechseen; - *cargo*, untere Raumladung; - *chafed*, Boden abgescheuert; - *clack of a valve*, Saugklappe; -*coat*, Bodenanstrich; -*end bolt*, Kurbelzapfenlagerbolzen; - - - *nut*, K-z-l-b-mutter; - *end brasses*, K-z-l-schalen; - - *keep*, K-z-l-deckelplatte; --*liner*, Pleyelstangenfutter; - - *of a cylinder*, Endfläche eines Zylinders; - *ends*, untere Lagerschalen; - *ice*, Grundeis; - *of a dock*, Docksohle; - *of a river*, Flußbettsohle; -*of a ship*, Schiffsboden; - *of the sheave hole*, Herd des Scheibengatts; - *pile*, Raubfahl; - *plank*, Bodenplanke; - *planking*, B-beplankung; - *plate*, B-platte; - *plating*, B-beplattung; -*props*, Steekschoren;

- *sheathing*, Wurmhaut; - *shores*, Steekschoren; - *strake*, Bodengang; - *up*, kieloben; - *to the top of the main bends*, der Boden bis zur Oberkante des großen Bergholzes.

bottomrer, Bodmereigeber.

bottomry, Bodmerei; - *bond*, B-m-brief; - - *to order*, Seewechsel an Ordre; - *loan*, Bodmereischuld; - *money*, B-m-geld; - *premium*, B-m-prämie.

bouching of a block sheave, Büchse einer Scheibe.

bouge, aufschwellen.

boulders, Strandsteine.

bound home, heimwärts bestimmt.

boundary, Grenze; - *plank*, Randplanke.

bounty, Vergütung; - *boat*, subventioniertes Fischerboot.

bout ship, über Stag gehen.

bow, Bug; - *anchor*, B-anker; - *bent*, durchgebogen; *to be - bye*, die Wendung versagen; - *cable*, Bugankertau; - - *stopper*, Klüsenstopper; - *chock*, Bugaufklotzung; - - *plate*, B-a-k-platte; - *fast*, Festmachtau; - *file*, Bogenfeile; - *grace*, Wursten; - *gun*, Buggeschütz.

bowline, 1. einfacher Fahlstek; 2. Buleine; *to be on an easy* (od. *a slack*) -, mit losen Buleinen segeln; *to check the -*, die B. schricken; *to haul tight the -*, die B. anholen; *let go the -!* B. los! *to stop the -*, die B. im Mars festknebeln; *to take down the slack of the -*, die B. durchholen.

bowline bridle, Bulinspriet; - *cringle*, B-legel; - *hitch* od. - *knot*, Pfahlstich; - *of the topsail*, Marsbulin; - *on the bite*, doppelter Pfahlstich; - *tackle*, Bulintalje;

- *toggle*, B-knebel; - *upon the bight*, doppelter Pfahlstich.

bow man, Buggast; - *oar*, Bugriemen; - *of manhole door*, Bügel des Mannlochdeckels; - *of pontoon*, Vordersteven des Ponton: - *of rudder*, Rücken des Ruderrahmens; - *ornament*, Bugverzierung; - *piece*, Bugstück; - *plank*, Bugplanke; - *planking*, B-beplankung; - *plate*, B-platte; - *plating*, B-platten; - *port*, B-pforte; - *propeller*, B-propeller; - *pump*, B-pumpe; - *rope*, Vorleine; - *rudder*, Bugruder; - *sea*, Gegensee; - *swell*, G-dünung; - *waves*, Bugwellen.

bowsprit, Bugspriet; *to gammon the b.*, die Bugsprietwuhling scheren; *to run in the -*, das Bugspriet einholen; *to set up the -*, d. B. einsetzen; *the - steeves*, d. B. ist geneigt.

bowsprit bed, Bugsprietfischung; - *bees*, B-s-backen; - *bitt*, B-s-stuhl; - *cap*, B-s-Eselshaupt; - *cheek*, B-s-Violine; - *gammoning*, B-s-Wuhling; - *gear*, B-s-gut; - *heart*, das Doodshoofd des Fockstags; - *hoop*, Bugsprietband; - *horses*, Laufstagen; - *men*, Bugsprietgasten; - *netting*, B-s-netz; - *pillow*, B-s-stuhl; - *shrouds*, B-s-wanten; - *step*, B-s-spur; - *wedge*, B-s-keil.

bow the sea, in die See liegen.

bower, Buganker; - *anchor*, B.; - *cable*, B.-tau; - *chain cable*, B-a-kette.

bowing, sich begeben.

bowl, Kumme; - *of a clay pipe*, Pfeifenkopf; - *of a compass*, Kompassgehäuse; - *of wood*, Holsnapt.

bowling along, mit vollen Segeln herankommen.

bowse, auftaljen.

box, 1. Büchse, Gehäuse, Kammer, Kasten; 2. Sitz des Bootssteurers; 3. die Vorsegel backlegen; - *and needle*, Seekompaß; - *beam*, Kastenbalken; - *chronometer*, Büchsenchronometer; - *coupling*, Muffenkuppelung; - *hauling*, über Steuer halsen; - *keel*, Kastenkiel; - *keelson*, K-k-schwoin; - *angle bar*, K-k-s-winkel; - *of a cock*, Hahngehäuse; *to - off a vessel*, ein Schiff abbacken; - *plate for stop bar*, Stopper-Handspeichenbüchse; - - *training tackle bolts*, Deckbüchse für Backstaljenringe; - *spanner*, Aufsteckschlüssel; *to - the compass*, die Kompaßeinteilung ablesen können; - - - *foresails*, die Vorsegel backlegen; - *wood*, Buschbaumholz.

boxing of the stem, Laschung des Stevens; - - - - *and keel*, L. d. St. und Kiels.

boy, Schiffsjunge.

boyer, der Bujer.

brace, brassen; - *aback*, backbrassen; - *about*, herumb; - *abox*, vorn back holen; - *all flat aback*, alles back brassen; - *and haul fast!* Hol Klüverschoten an! - *at*, herumbrassen; - *a yard*, eine Rahe brassen; - *back*, beibrassen; - *by the wind*, anbrassen; - *forward*, anbrassen; - *full*, vollb.; - *in*, zurückb.; - *on*, anb.; - *round*, rundb; - *sharp up the yards*, scharf an den Wind b.; - *square*, vierkant b.; - *the sails in the wind*, in den Wind b.; - *the sprit sail and sprit top sail*, die Blinde und Oberblinde trissen; - *the yards full*, vierkant brassen; - *to*, die Vorbrassen aufschricken; - *to the mark*, die Brassen bis zur Marke anholen; - *up sharp*, scharf anbrassen.

brace, 1. Klammer, 2. Brasse;

-*block*, Braßblock; - *boom-kin*, B-baum; - *cable*, Schertau an der Schiffsbrücke; - *pendant*, Brassenschenkel.
bracer, Tragseil.
braces of a lugsail yard, Kaier; -*of the lower yards*, Brassen der Unterrahen; - *of the rudder*, Ruderösen; - *of the yard*. Brassen der Rahen.
bracket, 1. Stützplatte. 2. Träger; - *end*, Geschmiedetes Balkenknie; --*of a beam*, das heruntergebogene Knieende eines Balkens; - *frame*, Kimmstützplatte; - *of the head* od. - *of the head rail*, Gallionsknie; - *plate*, Stützplatte.
brackish, brack; -*water*, Brackwasser.
brackishness, das Salzige.
brad, Bodenspieker.
brail, aufgeien, Geitau; - *block*, G-t-block; - *in* od. - *up*, aufgeien.
brailed up, aufgegeit.
brake, 1.Pumpenhebel; 2.Bremse; - *hoop*, Bremsband; - *lever*, B-hebel; - *of the windlass*, Bremsvorrichtung des Ankerspills; - *pump*, Pumpe mit Geckstock; - *springs*, Bremsfedern.
bran new, ganz neu.
branch, Lotsenpatent; - *cable*, Zweigkabel; - *pilot*, Patentlotse; - *pipe*, Zweigrohr; - *wire*, Z-Kabel.
branches of pumps, Pumpenzüge.
brash ice, Eisbrocken.
brass bush, Metallbüchse; -*cocks of the sheaves of lignum vitae*, die metallenen Büchsen in den Scheiben von Pockholz; -*ferrule*, Metallring; - *hoop*, Messingband; - *tube*, M-rohr.
brasses, Lagerschalen.
Brazilian rose wood, Jacarandaholz.
brazing, Hartlöten.
breach, Brandung; *a clean* -,

Wellenbruch, der alles von Deck wegfegt; - *of the sea*, Abspülung durch die See; *the vessel is a - - - -*, die Wellen brechen über das Schiff wie über eine Klippe.
breachy, brack.
bread,Schiffszwieback; -*barge*, Brotback; - *binn*, B-koje; - *dust*, Zwiebackbrocken; -*locker*,Brotkammer; -*room*, B-raum.
breadth line, Hauptsente; - *ribband*, Herzsente; - *of a vessel*, Schiffsbreite; -*riders*, Mittschiffs Kattsporen.
break, 1. abbrechen, abwrakken; 2. branden, brechen (der Wellen); 3. den Hafen verlassen; - *adrift*, 1. losbrechen, losreißen (von der Vertäuung); 2. übergehen (Ladung); -*bulk*, 1.zu löschen anfangen; 2. die Ladung berauben; - *from the course*, vom Kurse abgedrängt werden; - *ground*, den Anker aufzuhieven anfangen; - *liberty*, den Urlaub überschreiten; - *off*, vom Winde oder Kurse abfallen; - *sheer*, unklar vom Anker scheren; - *the back*, den Katzenrücken setzen; - *up*, 1. aufklären; 2. abschlachten, abwracken; 3.in Stücke gehen.
break, unterbrochenes Deck; - *bulk*, Kapitän, der Ladung unterschlägt; - *bulkhead*, Frontschott; - - *of raised quarter deck*, F. des erhöhten Quarterdecks; - - *of sunk bridge*, Brückenschott; - - - - *forecastle*, Backschott; - *deck*,erhöhtes Deck; -*neck*, enge Landungsstelle; - *of the poop*, Vorderschott der Hütte.
breakage, 1. Lücken in der Stauung; 2. Bruch verstauter Güter; 3. Vergütung für Bruch.
breaker, kleines Wasserfass für ein Boot.

breakers, 1. Brechseen; 2. Brandung; - *ahead*, Brandung voraus.

breaking adrift of cargo, Übergehen der Ladung; - *in of a bank*, Abbruch des Ufers; - *of a gale*, das Auswehen eines Sturmes; - *of shaft*, Wellenbruch; - *stoppers*, Nähungen des Ankertaus; - *strain*, Bruchkraft; - *test*, B-probe; - *up and moving of ice*, Eisgang; - *up of the monsoon*, das veränderliche Wetter beim Aufhören eines Monsuns.

breakwater, 1. Wellenbrecher; 2. Brechwasser; - *glacis*, Pflasterung des Wellenbrechers.

breaming, Pech oder Teer abbrennen od. ein Schiff brennen.

breast a bar, gegen die Spaken eines Gangspills drükken; - *backstay*, Vorderpardune; - *band*, Brustleine; - *beam of the forecastle*, Frontbalken der Back; - *borer*, Brustbohrer; - *caskets*, Rahbänder; - *fast*, Dwarstau; - *gasket*, Bugzeising; - *hook*, B-band; - - *bolt*, B-b-bolzen; - *knee*, Krummholz im Vorderschiff; - *off*, breitseitig hieven; - *plate*, Brustplatte; - *rail*, Frontreling; - *rope*, Dwarsfeste; - *shore*, horizontale Dockstütze; - *the sea*, recht in der See liegen ; - *the surf*, die Brandung bewältigen; - *work*, Geländer um Back und Kajütsdeck; - - *of the forecastle*, das Vorderschott der Back; - - *of the poop*, Reling am Vorderende der Hütte; - - *of the quarter deck*, Schott der Schanze.

breath of wind, gelinde Kühlte.

breech mouldings, Zierraten des Mastes.

breeches buoy, Hosenboje; - *mat*, Stagmatte.

breeching bolt, Brokbolzen ;

- *loop*, B-loch; - *shackle*, B-schäkel. [nimmt zu.

breeze, Brise; - *up*, die B.

breezeless, windstill.

brickwork of furnace, Mauerwerk der Feuerbüchse.

bridge, Kommandobrücke; - *awning*, Brückenhaus-Sonnensegel; - *boat*, B-kahn; - *break bulkhead*, Brücken-Frontschott; - *bulkhead*, Brückenhausschott; - *cabin*, B-h-kajüte; - *deck*, B-deck; - - *beam*, B-d-balken; - - - *angle bar*, B-d-b-winkel; - - - *stringer*, B-d-b-stringer; - - - - *plate*, B-d-b-S-platte; - *deck beam tie plate*, B-d-b-Längsschiene; *b. d. guard rods*, Brückengeländerstangen; - - *pillar*, Brückendeckstütze; - - *plating*, B-d-beplättung; - - *stringer*, B-d-stringer; - - - *angle bar*, B-d-s-winkel; - - - *plate*, B-d-s-platte; - *deck waterway*, B-d-Wassergang; - *house*, Brückenhaus; - - *awning*, B-zelt; - - *coaming*, B-süll; - - - *angle bar*, B-s-winkel; - *house frame*, Brückenhausspant; - *ladder*, Brückentreppe; - *of boards*, Laufbrücke; - *of boats*, Pontonbrücke; - *rail*, Brückenhausreling; - *rails and stanchions*, Brückengeländer; - *screen*, Schutzkleid der Kommandobrücke; - *sheerstrake*, Brückenschergang; - *stanchion*, B-geländerstütze; - *the channel*, das Fahrwasser quer blockieren; - *weather boards*, Brücken-Schutzbretter; - - *cloth*, B-S-kleid.

bridle, 1. Sprute (am Segel); 2. Kettenarm (des Mooring-schäkels); - *cable*, Lenktau; - *chains*, Kettenhahnepot der Vertäuungsbojen; - *port*, Bugpforte.

bridles, Hahnepot; - *of the bowlines*, Bulienspriet.

brig, Brigg; - *cutter*, Kutter mit Briggsmast; - *rig*, B-takelage; - *rigged*, als Brigg getakelt; *brig's boom mainsail*, B.-segel; - *schooner*, Schoonerb.

brigantine, Schoonerbrigg.

bright parts, Messing- und Kupferteile; - *varnish*, heller Teerfirnis; - *work*, Messing- und Kupferteile.

brighten a plank, eine Planke weiß schrapen.

brine, 1. Salzwasser; 2. Sole; - *cock*, Abschaumhahn; - *pipe*, Salzrohr; - *pump*, Salzwasserpumpe; - *valve*, Salzventil; - - *box*, S-v-gehäuse; - - *cover*, S-v-deckel.

bring aback, back legen; - *by the lee*, anluven; - *down*, kielholen; - - *to her load*, bis zur Wassertracht laden; - *home the anchor*, den Anker mitschleppen; - *off*, abbringen; - *out an anchor* od. *a hawser*, einen Anker resp. eine Trosse ausbringen; - *the broadside to bear*, sich dwars legen und die Zähne zeigen; - *the cable to the messenger*, die Ankerkette an die Kabellaring zeisen; - *the chain to bear*, die Kette zum Tragen kommen lassen; - *the messenger to the capstan*, das Kabellaar um das Gangspill legen; - *the wind right aft*, vor dem Winde ablaufen; - *the w. r. ahead*, auf den Wind anluven; - *to an anchor*, verankern; - *to the broadside*, ein Schiff querholen; - *to the gangway*, bestrafen; - *to swing*, am Anker aufbringen; - *to the ship*, beidrehen; - *two marks* (od. *objects*) *into ore* (od. *into a line*), zwei Marken zur Deckpeilung in eine Linie bringen; - *up a ship*, 1. beim Anker aufbringen; 2. erobern; - *up a yard*, eine Rahe aufbringen;

- *up with a round turn*, suddenly, anhören lassen und plötzlich stoppen.

bringing up, Maschine hörte auf zu gehen.

brining, das Salzwasser aus dem Kessel entfernen.

briny, to cross the -, das Meer kreuzen.

brisk breeze, scharfe Brise.

British built, in England gebaut; - *owned*, in England beheimatet.

broach, 1. das Schiff mit der Breitseite gegen den Wind bringen; 2. anbrechen, anzapfen; - *to*, von selbst beidrehen.

broaching, von selbst aufluven.

broad arrow, der breite Pfeil (Zeichen als Staatseigentum); - *bottom*, flacher Boden; - *cloth*, Rahsegel; - *floor*, das breite Flach; - *pennant*, Kommodor-Stander; - *rigged*, vierkant getakelt; - *side*, Breitseite; - - *on*, dwars an; - - *through the water*, dwars ab; - - *to* --, quer ab von einander; *to bring the* - - *to bear*, sich dwars legen und die Zähne zeigen.

broken backed, mit Katzenrücken; - *down*, Maschinenbruch; - *stowage*, Staulücken; - *up*, abgewrackt; - *water*, Brandung bei einer Untiefe.

bronze metal lining, Bronzegarnitur.

broom, Besen.

brought ship to an anchor, verankerten das Schiff; - - *to the wind*, brachten das S. an den Wind.

brow, schräge Stellung.

bruise water, Butzkopf (vierkantiges Schiff).

bruising water, vorn stampfend.

bubble of the sea, Brodeln der See.

buck, ein Segel waschen.

bucket, 1. Pütze; 2. Signalball (Boote zur Rückkehr auffordernd) - *of a parrel*, Racktonne ; - *of a pump*, Pumpenkolben; - *rack*, Pützengestell; *ring*, Pumpenkolbenring; - *valve*, Kolbenventil; - - *guard*, K-v-Klappenfänger; - - *seat*, K-v-sitz.

buckle, Mastbucht.

buckled, aufgebuckelt.

buckler, Klüsendeckel.

buffalo, Schweinsrücken.

buffer, Stoßkissen; - *spring*, Pufferfeder.

buffers, Gummipuffer.

buggy boat, Räderboot für Landtransport.

build, Bauart.

build a chapel, eine Eule fangen; - *the upperworks*, vertennen.

builder's certificate, Beilbrief; - *estimate*, Bauanschlag; - *measurement*, alte Vermessungsmethode.

building block, Baublock; - *contract*, Beilbrief; - *slip*, Helgen; - *yard*, Schiffswerft.

built, gebaut; *carvel* -, karwehlartig g.; *chlincher* -, klinkerartig g.; *English* -, englische Bauart; *foreign* -, fremde B.; - *mast*, gebauter Mast; - *up crank*, zusammengesetzte Kurbel; - - - *shaft*, z-g-K-welle; - *up mast*, z-g-Mast; - *up propeller*, z-g-Schraube.

bulb angle bar, Wulstwinkel; - - *beam*, W-w-balken; - - *iron*, W-w-eisen; - *beam*, W-schienenbalken; - *iron*, W-eisen; - *plate*, W-platte; - - *carling*, W-schienenschlinge, - *steel*, W-stahl.

bulge see bilge.

bulged, ausgebaucht.

bulk, in -, Sturzladung.

bulker, Angestellter, der Stückgüter ausmißt.

bulkhead, Schott; - *angle bar*, S-winkel; - *boards*, Verschlag-

bretter; - *frame*, Schottspant; - *lamp*, Wandlampe; - *liner*, Schott-Füllplatte; - *of gratings*, Traljeschott; - *of the forecastle*, Backschott; - *of the manger*, Klüsenschott; - *of the quarter deck*, Schanzenschott; - *plate*, Schott. platte; - *plating*, S-platten; - *stringer*, S-stringer.

bull rope, Beiholer.

bullock block, Marsfallblock unter der Bramsaling.

bull's eye, 1. Blendlaterne; 2. Bullen- od. Ochsenauge; 3. hölzerne Kausche; 4. Wettergalle (Sturmzeichen); - - *squall*, Sturmbö aus heiterem Himmel.

bully beef, ganz ausgekochtes Fleisch; *to - the cask*, heißes Wasser in ein Rumfaß gießen und austrinken.

bulwark, Schanzkleid; - *angle bar*, S-k-winkel; - *netting*, S-k-netzwerk; - *planking*, S-k-beplankung; - *plate*, S-k-platte; - *plating*, S-k-platten; - *port*, S-k-pforte; - *stanchion*, S-k-stütze; - *stay*, S-k-stütze.

bumboat, Proviantboot.

bumkin, 1. Butluv; 2. Treiberbaum (eines Bootes); - *braces*, Backstagen des Butluvs; - *shroud*, Auslegerstag; - *stay*, Butluvstag.

bump, 1. Stoß, stoßen; 2. überholen; - *ashore*, mit dem Steven recht auf den Strand laufen.

bumper, 1. Eisbrecher; 2. Eishaut.

bumping on the ground, auf Grund stoßen.

bumpkin see bumkin.

bundle, sorglos verstauen.

bung, Spund; - *hole*, S-loch; - *up and bilge free*, S. oben und frei vom Boden verstaut.

bungling board, Schlagbug.

bunk, Koje.

bunker, Kohlenbunker, Kohlen

einnehmen; - *casings*, Bunkerverkleidungen; - *coal*, B-Kohlen; - *frame*, B-spant; - *lamp*, B-Lampe - *pipe*, B-Rohr; - *plate*, B-Platte; - -*stays*,B-Versteifungswinkel.
*bunkering.*Kohlen einnehmen; - *port*, Bunkerhafen.
bunt, 1. Bauch (des Segels); 2. schwellen; - *a sail*, den Bauch eines Segels aufholen und beschlagen; - *gasket*, Bauchbeschlagzeising; - *jigger*, B-talje; - *line*, B-gording; - - *block*, B-g-block; - - *cloth*, B-g-lappen; - - *cringle*, B-g-lägel; - - *lizard*, B-g-brille; - - *span*, Buggordingssprut; - *slap line*, Kerkedortje; - *whip*, Bauchtalje.
bunting, Flaggentuch; *to show all her b.*, alle Flaggen aufhissen.
buoy,Boje,aufbojen,betonnen; - *adrift*, verschlagene Boje; - *bears*, man peilt die B.; - *and beacon dues*, Tonnen- und Bakengeld; - *does not watch*, die Boje wacht nicht; - *is awake*, d. B. w.; - *is below the water*, - *is drowned*, d. B. ist blind; - *is floating in sight*, die Ankerboje wacht; - *is not f.*, d. A. w. nicht; - *up*, aufbojen.
buoy rope, Bojereep; - - *knot*, B-r-knoten; - *sling*,B-stropp; - *tun*, Tonnenboje; - *with a broom*, Besenboje.
buoyage, Betonnung.
buoyancy, Tragvermögen.
buoyant, schwimmkräftig; - *power*, Schwimmkraft.
buoys and beacons, Bojen und Baken; - - - *dues*, Tonnen- und Bakengeld.
bur pump, Bilgenpumpe.
burden, Lastigkeit.
burgee, Reedereiflagge.
burlap, grobe Leinwand.
burning hawse, sehr steif stehende Kette; - *in the hawse*, das Ankertau zerscheuert sich in den Klüsen.

burr of the moon, der kleine Hof des Mondes; - *pump*, Schlagpumpe.
burrel, alte Nägel, Metallstücke etc.
burst, bersten.
bursting, das Bersten; *strained to - point*, bis zum Platzen angestrengt.
burthen, Tragfähigkeit.
burton, 1. Stengentalje; 2. Jollentau; - *pendant*, Hanger der Marsstenge.
burying sail, ein den Bug niederdrückendes Segel.
bush, ausbüchsen, Büchse, Deckel, Ring.
bushed block, Buchsblock.
bushing, 1. Büchse, 2. Fütterung.
busk about od. to busk to and again, umherkreuzen.
bust head, Gallionsfigur.
butt against od. b. on, zusammenstoßen.
butt, Stoß; - *bolt*, S-bolzen; - *chock*, S-kalb; - *dowel*, Verbindungszapfen; - *edge*.Stoßkante; - *end bolt*, S-bolzen; - *end of a plank*, das schmale Ende einer Planke; - *joint*, Stoßverbindung; - *of a plate*, Plattenstoß; - *of a plank*, Plankenstoß; - *plate*, Stoßplatte - *riveting*, S-nietung; - *scarf*, Stufscherbe; - *seam*, Stoßfuge; - *strap*, S-blech; - - *angle bar*, S-winkel; - *strip plate*, S-platte; - *through bolt*, S-durchbolzen; - *weld*, S-Schweißung.
butted frame, durch Stoßwinkel gelaschtes Spant.
butterfly, Flußbarke; - *block*, Marsschotenblock; - *cock*, Flügelhahn; - *valve*, Schmetterlingsschieber.
buttock, 1. Billen (des Schiffes); 2. Spiegel (eines Pontons); - *line*, Schnitt des Konstruktionsrisses; - *plank*, Bugplanke; - *planking*, Billenbeplankung; - *plate*, B-platte.
buttocks, Hinterbacken.

button and loop, Tau mit Schildknopf und beiderseitiger Schleife.

butts for winding, Bughölzer.

by land, über Land; - *sea,* zu Wasser; - *the bulk,* im Ganzen; - *the day,* per Tag; - *the head,* vorlastig; - *the log,* nach Gissung; - *the piece,* per Stück; - *the stern,* achterlastig; - *the wind,* beim Winde.

C.

cabbage wood, Panakokoholz.

cabin, Kajüte; - *boy,* Kajütsjunge; - *companion,* Kajütenkappe; - *compass,* K-kompaß; - *door,* K-tür; - - *hinge,* K-t-Scharnier; - *fittings,* K-einrichtung; - *floor* od. *flooring,* K-fußboden; - *freight,* K-fracht; - *funnel,* K-schornstein; - *lecture,* Strafpredigt unter vier Augen; - *mate,* Kajütsgenosse: - *passenger,* K-passagier; - *skylight,* Kajüten-Oberlicht; - *sole,* Fußboden der K.; - *stove,* Kajütenofen; - *ventilator,* K-ventilator; - *window,* K-fenster.

cable, Ankerkette, A-tau; - *bend,* Bindsel des A-t.; - *buoy,* A-boje; - *chain,* A-kette; - *clinch,* A-stich; - *fid,* Splißhorn; - *gripper,* Ankertaukrabber; - *holder,* Kettenscheibe; - *hook,* Tauhaken; - *is at a long peak,* die Ankerkette steht stagweise; - *is chafed in the hawse,* das Ankertau zerscheuert sich in den Klüsen; - *laid rope,* kabelweise geschlagenes Tau; - *length,* Kabellänge (ca. 183 m); - *lifter,* Spillkranz; - *moulding,* tauförmige Verzierungsleiste; - *nipper,* Kabelarzeising; - *of iron wire,* Eisendrahtseil; - *reliever,* Kettenausrücker; - *serving,* Kabelkleid; - *ship,* Kabelschiff; - *splice,* K-splissung; - *stage,* K-gatt; - *test,* K-probe; - *tier,* K-gatt; - *vessel,* K-schiff; - *wise,* kabelweise.

caboose, Kombüse.

cabotage, 1. Küstenfahrt; 2. Küstenkenntnis.

caburns, die Schlarring zum Trensen.

caccle, schladden, schlarren.

cache, verborgenes Depot.

cadet, Kadett.

cage, Kohlenpfanne (für Leuchtfeuer).

caic od. *caique,* Kaik.

cairn, Mire (Steinhaufen als Marke bei Küstenaufnahmen).

caisson od. *caissoon,* 1. Senkod. Schwimmkasten; 2. Schleusenschiff desTrockendocks.

cake ice, Kucheneis.

calk see caulking.

call at a port, einen Hafen anlaufen; - *the watch,* die Wache auf Deck rufen; - - - *to relief,* d. W. purren.

calliper compasses od. *callipers,* 1. Mastenpasser; 2. Tastzirkel.

calm, windstill, Windstille; - *belt,* Windstillengürtel; - *down,* ruhig werden; - *latitude,* Calmengürtel;

calming the sea, die See besänftigen.

calms, Kalmen; - *of cancer,* K-gürtel des Krebses; - *of capricorn,* K-g des Steinbocks,

caloric, Wärmestoff.

calorifere, Heizvorrichtung.
calorimeter, Wärmemesser.
calorimetry, Wärmemessung.
calory, Wärmeeinheit.
cam, Hebedaumen; - *ball wood*, rotes Sandelholz.
camber, 1. biegen; 2. Holzhafen einer Werft; 3. Bucht eines Kiels; 4. Platz beim Dampf-kasten einer Werft.
cambered, gewölbt, gebogen; - *deck*, gekrümmtes Deck; - *keel*. durchbogener Kiel.
came in with fine weather, fing mit schönem Wetter an.
camboose, Schiffsküche.
camel, Kameel (zum Schiffs-heben).
can buoy, Birnboje; - *hook*. Schenkelhaken; - *reversed buoy*. Kegelboje.
canal dues, Kanalgeld; - *lift*, Hebemaschine; - *navigation*, Kanalschiffahrt.
candle power, Kerzenstärke.
cane buoy, Bakenboje.
canoe, Kanu, rojen.
canopy, Bootszelt.
cant block, Speckgienblock; - *body*, Vorder- od. Hinter-ende eines Schiffes, das ge-ringerenSpantenumfang hat als mittschiffs; - *fall*, Speck-gienläufer; - *floor*, Piekstück; - *frame*, Kantspant; - *hook*, K-haken; - *pieces*, die ecki-gen Schiffslatten; - *purchase*, Speckgienläufer; - *ribbands*, Latten; - *rope*, Kehrtau; - *spar*, Hakenspiere; - *timber*, Kantspant; - - *bolt*, K-s-bolzen.
cantick quoin, 1. Staukeil; 2. S.-holz.
canting, drehen;
canting coin od. *cantling*, 1. Staukeil; 2. S.-holz.
canvas od. *canvass*, Segeltuch; - *boat*, zusammenlegbares Boot; - *bucket*, Segeltuch-pütze; - *hose*, Hanfschlauch.
cap, 1. mit Kappe versehen; 2. Decke, Kappe; 3. Esels-

haupt; 4. Kerbe im Block-stropp; - *backstay*, Esels-hauptpardune; - *of a lower mast*, Mast-Eselshaupt; - *of the bowsprit*, Namen-schild; - *piece*, Lagerdeckel; - *scuttle*, Springluke; - *shore*, Eselshauptstütze.
capacity, Ladungsfähigkeit.
cape, Vorgebirge; - *fly-away*, Butterland; - *tippet of the chimney of a marine boiler*, Kaminkragen eines Schiffs-kessels.
capelage, Flechting.
capeler, Flechtung aufsetzen.
caper, Steinbock.
capes, between two -, zwischen zwei Vorgebirgen.
capping of the cutwater, Kappe des Pfeilerhauptes.
capricorn, Wendekreis des Steinbocks.
capsizal, das Kentern.
capsize, 1. kentern; 2. kanten (Faß); 3. umstürzen (Tau).
capstan, Gangspill; *to come up with the c.*, das G. zu-rückwinden; *to heave at the* -, d. G. einwinden; *to pawl the* -, pallwinden; *to rig the c.*, die Spaken einlegen; *to surge the* -, das Tau des G. lockern; *to swift the* -, das Spakenreep nehmen; *to swift the* - *bars*, die Außen-enden der Spillspaken durch ein Seil verbinden.
capstan bar, Gangspillspaken; - - *hole*, G-s-s-loch; - - *pin*, G-s-s-Sicherheitsbolzen; - *barrel*, G-s-trommel; - *cover*, G-s-Ueberzug; - *eccentric strap*, G-s-Excenterbügel; - *engine piston*, Dampfgang-spill-Kolben; - *pall*, Gang-spillpall; - - *head*, G-s-p-stopper; - - *rim*. G-s-p-ring; - *partner*, G-s-Fischung; - *pawl see* - *pall*; - *spindle*, Gangspillaxe; - - *collar*, G-s-Spindelkragen; - - *socket*, G-s-S-spur; - *steam pipe*,

G-s-Dampfzuleitungsrohr; - *swifter*, G-s-spaken-Schwichttau; - [*valve rod*, G-s-Schieberstange; - *whelp*, G-s-rippe; - - *chock*, G-s-Rippenkalb;

capstan see also steam capstan.

captain, Kapitän, Schiffer, Schiffsführer; - *of the fleet*, K. zur See; - *of the forecastle*, Quartiermeister der Back; - *of the foretop*, Q-m-des Vortops; - *of the head*, Q-m- des Bugspriets; - *of the hold*, Q-m- des Laderaums; - *of the maintop*,Q-m-des Großtopps; -*of the mess*,Backältester;-*of the port*,Hafenmeister.

captain's berth, Kapitäns Kammer; - *biscuit*, Schiffszwieback; - *certificate*, Kapitänspatent; - *clerk*, Schiffsschreiber; - *gig*, Kapitänsboot; - *protest*, Verklarung; - *room*, Kapitänskammer.

captor, Aufbringer.

capture, aufbringen, Wegnahme.

carac, die Karake.

caravel, Karavelle.

carbonic oxide, Kohlenoxyd.

carcass of a vessel, Schiffsgerippe.

card, Windrose.

cardan's rule, kardanisch.

cardinal points, Cardinalstriche; - *wind*, Hauptwind.

careenage, Kielgeld.

careening, kielholen; - *beach*, Kielholplatz; - *block*,Hollingblock; - *wharf*, Kielholwerft.

cargo, Ladung; - *adrift*, L. übergegangen; - *battens*, Wegerungslatten; - *block*, Ladungsblock;- *boat*,Frachtschiff; - *book*, Ladebuch; - *chain*, L-kette; - *compartment*,L-kompartment;-*door*, L-pforte; - *gin*, Löschrad; - *hatch* od. *hatchway*, Ladeluke; - *hold*, L-raum; - *hook*, L-haken; - *in bulk*, lose Ladung; - *in parcels*, Stückgüter; - *lamp*, Raumlampe;

- *lost or damaged by sacrifice*, durch Aufopferung verlorene oder beschädigte Ladung; - *pendant* od. *pennant*, Ladetakel; - *port*, L-pforte; - *runner*, Winschläufer; - *shifted*, Ladung übergegangen; - *steamer traffic*, Frachtdampferverkehr; - *strops*, Ladungsstropps;- *vessel*,Frachtschiff.

carline od. *carling*, 1. Schlinge; 2. Schlüssel (zum Versteifen zweier Balken; - *knee*, Scherstock des Decks; - *of the hatch*, Lukenrippe.

carpenter, Zimmermann.

carpenter's chalk line, Zimmermannsschnur; - *level*, Setzwage; - *line*, Zimmermannsschnur; - *mate*, Z-m-maat; - *room*, Z.m-kammer; - *store room*, Z-m-Hellegat; - *work*, Z-m-arbeit.

carpet man, ein stark protegierter Offizier.

carrack, die Karake.

carriage by sea, Seetransport.

carrick, die Karake; - *bend*, Kreuzknoten; - *bitt*, Spillbeting.

carried away, gebrochen, weggeschlagen, weggeflogen, über Bord geschlagen; -- *by the current*, vom Strome versetzt.

carrier, Frachtführer,F-schiff.

carries, she - a bone in her mouth od. *teeth*, das Schiff fährt so schnell, daß das Wasser vor seinem Bug aufschäumt.

carronade, Haubitze.

carry, How does she - her helm? Wie steuert das Schiff? *she carries a lee helm*, es ist luvgierig; - - - *taut* (od. *weather*) *h.*, es ist hart auf's Ruder; *to carry a vessel by boarding*, ein Schiff durch Entern nehmen; - *away*, abbrechen, wegfliegen, zerreißen, über Bord gehen; - *a-weatherly!* Luvwärts das Steuer! - *helm alee!* Ruder in Lee! *she carries her way*, das Schiff behält Fahrt; - *on one's duty*, seinen Dienst tun; - *out an anchor*, einen Anker ausbringen; - *sail*, mit ausgespannten Segeln fahren; - *the canvass*, die Hintersegel anschlagen.

carrying a press of sail, prangen; - *all sails*, alle Segel führen; - *away a vessel*, ein Schiff versegeln od. stranden lassen; - *on*, Segel pressen.

cartage, Fuhrlohn, Transportkosten.

cartel ship, 1. Kartellschiff; 2. Parlamentärschiff.

carved work, Schnitzwerk.

carvel built, karwehlartig gebaut.

casco, Kasko.

case, 1. Mantel, Umhüllung, Verkleidung; 2. Außenhaut des Schiffes; 3. Koker des Mastes; - *hardened steel*, äußerlich gehärteter Stahl; - *in*, verkleiden; - *of stranding*, Strandungsfall; - *of the boiler*, Kesselmantel.

casing, Kasten, Mantel. Schacht, Umbau; - *of engine and boiler*, Maschinen- und Kessel-Umbau; - *of the chimney*, Schornsteinmantel; - *of the cylinder*, Zylindermantel.

cask buoy, Spierentonne.

cast, 1. gießen; 2. stagen, wenden, über Stag gehen; - *adrift*, loswerfen, treiben lassen; - *anchor*, Anker werfen; - *away*, 1. gestrandet, vom Sturm verschlagen, schiffbrüchig; 2. Schiffbrüchiger; - *iron*, Gußeisen; - *loose*, loswerfen; - *of lead*, Lotwurf; - *off*, loswerfen; - *steel works*, Gußstahlwerk; - *to port*, nach Backbord abfallen.

casting, 1. abfallen; 2. Gußstück; - *the right* (od. *wrong*)

way, über den rechten resp. verkehrten Bug fallen; - *to port*, nach Backbord abfallen.

castle crew, Backgasten.

casualties at sea, Unfälle auf See.

cat, katten, aufkatten; - *the anchor*, den Anker aufkatten.

cat, 1. Ankerkatt; 2. Kattschiff; 3. neunschwänzige Katze; - *back*, Kattaufgeber; - *beam*, Decksbalken; - *block*, Kattblock; - *boat*, Schwertboot mit einem Segel; - *davit*, Kattdavit; - - *socket*, K-d-spur; - *fall*, Kattläufer; *Man the* - -! An den K-l-! *the standing part of the* - -, der stehende Part des K-l-; - *harpings*, Schwichtung; - *head*, Kranbalken; *at the* - -, unter dem Kran; *to* - - *the anchor*, den Anker am K-balken verholen; *the anchor is at the* - -, der A. ist zum Fallen klar; - - *bracket*, Kranbalkenstütze; - - *knee*, K-b-dücker; - - *of a crane*, Kranschnabel; - - *stopper*, Porteurleine; - - - *chain*, P-l-kette; - *head supporter*, Kranbalkstütze; - *hole*, 1. Hinterklüse; 2. Katzenschlupfloch; - *hook*, Katthaken; - *o'nine tails*, neunschwänzige Katze; - *purchase*, Kattakel; - *rake*, Ratschbohrer; - *rope*, Kattblocksteert; - *ship*, Kattschiff; - *tackle*, K-takel; - *tail*, Kranbalkensteert.

catamaran, 1. indisches Segelfloß; 2. widerliches Weib.

cataract, Hubregulator.

catch, hemmen; - *aback*, backlegen;

catch, 1. Knagge, Schließhaken, Schnäpper; 2. Fangreise, Fang; *there are* - *fakes in the cable*, die Buchten des Kabels fangen sich; - *of the furnace door latch*,

Feuertürriegel-Schnäpper; - *water*, Wassersammler.
caterer, Proviantmeister.
cat's paw, 1. Katzenpfote im Tau; 2. Windhauch und Kräuseln der Wasseroberfläche.
catted and fished, gekattet und gefischt.
cattle fittings, Viehverschläge; - *men*, V-wärter; - *steamer*, V-transportdampfer.
catoptric telescope, Spiegelfernrohr; - *illuminating apparatus*, Spiegel-Leuchtapparat.
caulker, Kalfater.
caulker's box, Kalfaterkiste; - *grease box*, das Fettbackje des Kalfaters; - *seat*, K-stuhl; - *tub*, K-bütte; - *work*, K-arbeit.
caulking, abdichten, kalfatern, Kalfaterung, verstemmen; - *box*, Kalfaterkiste; - *iron*, K-eisen; - *mallet*, K-hammer; - *tool*, Verstemmer.
cautionary signal, Warnungssignal.
cave of the wind, Wetterloch.
cavil, Belegklampe.
cay, Sand- od. Korallenbank.
cease oars od. *c. rowing!* Hört zu rudern auf!
cedar wood, Zedernholz.
ceiling, Wegerung; *to place the* -, das Schiff garnieren; - *hatch*, Wegerungsluke; - *of forecastle*, Wegerung der Back; - *of poop*, W. d. Hütte; - *of raised quarter deck*, W. des erhöhten Quarterdecks; - *of the between decks*, die obere W.; - *of the floor*, Bugw.; - *plank*, Garnierplanke.
cellular double bottom, Doppelboden nach dem Zellensystem; - - - *with continuous girders*, D. n. d. Längsspanten- und Stützplattensystem.
cement, Zement, mit Z. verkitten.

cemented steel, Zementstahl.
center see centre.
central force, zentrale Kraft; - *line*, Mittschiffslinie; - *stringer*, Deckbalken-Unterschlag; - - *angle bar*, D.-U.-Winkel.
centre, Mittelpunkt; - *bearer of fire bars*, Mittel-Roststabträger; - *bearing standard of a pump*, Zentrallagerständer einer Pumpe; - *bilge suction valve*, Mittellenz-Saugventil; - *bitt*, 1. Mittelbeting; 2. Zentrumbohrer; - - *bearing*, Mittelbeting-Wellenlager; - - *keep*, M.-W.-deckel; - *board*, Mittelschwert; - - *boat*, Kielschwertboot; - - *trunk*, od. - - *well*, Schwertbrunnen; - *boss*, Verstärkung in der Mitte; - *feeder*, Zenterfeeder; - *furnace*, Zentral-Feuerbüchse; - *girder*, Mittelträger; - - *angle bar*, M.-Winkel; - - *of a double bottom*, M. eines Doppelbodens; - - *plate*, M.-platte; - *gudgeon*, Pumpenbalancieraxenzapfen, - *line bulkhead*, Mittel-Längsschott; - - *keelson*, M.-Kielschwein; - *mark*, Kernpunkt; - *of a cyclone*, Zentrum eines Zyklon; - *of a fleet*, Hauptkorps einer Flotte; - *of action*, Mittelpunkt der Wirkung; - *of buoyancy* od. - *of displacement*, Schwerpunkt der Wasserverdrängung; - *of effort of the sails*, Segelpunkt; - *of giration*, Mittelpunkt der Drehung; - *of gravity* od. - *of inertia*, Schwerpunkt; - *of motion*, Bewegungsmittelpunkt; - *of oscillation*, Schwingungsmittelpunkt; - *of rotation*, Mittelpunkt der Drehung; - *pin of a compass*, Kompaßpinne; - *plate*, Mittelplatte; - *punch*, Mittelsucher; - *through plate*,

durchgehende Mittelkielplatte; - - - *keelson*, d-g-M-k-schweinplatte; - *velic*, Segelpunkt; - *vertical plate*, vertikale Mittelplatte.

centrifugal circulating pump, Zentrifugal - Zirkulationspumpe; - *power*, Z-f-Kraft; - *pump*, Z-f-pumpe.

certificate of character, 1. Klassifikationsschein; 2. Führungszeugnis; - *of competency*, Befähigungsnachweis; - - - *for distant trade*, Patent für große Fahrt; - *of mortgage*, Pfandbrief; - *of registry*, Seepaß, Flaggenzeugnis; - *of sale*, notarieller Verkaufskontrakt; - *of stowage*, Stauungsattest; - *of survey*, Besichtigungsschein; - *of tonnage*, Meßbrief; - *of valuation*, Schätzungsschein: - *of condemnation*, Kondemnationsschein.

chabee, Schloßholz.

chafed, schamfielt; - *through*, durch und durch s.

chafing batton, Schamfielungslatte; - *board*, Schalung; - *gear*, Schamfielung; - *mat*, S-f-smatte.

chafings, Schamfielung.

chain, Ankerkette; - *boat*, 1. Kettenschleppschiff; 2. Boot zum Ankerlichten; - *bolt*, Püttingsbolzen; - *cable*, Ankerkette; - - *compressor*, Kettenstopper; - - *controller*, Patentstopper; - *cargo fall*, Kettenladeläufer; - *casings*, Deckklüsen der Ankerkette; - *coupling*, Kettenkuppelung; - *drum*, K-trommel; - *hook*, K-haken; - *knot*, K-stich; - *length*, K-länge (1/10 Seem.); - *lifter*, Rolle der Ankerkette; - *locker*, Kettenkasten; - *of a crane*, Krankette; - *moorings*, Mooringsketten; - *pier*, Landungssteg; - *pipe*, Deckklüse; - - *covers*, Bekleidung des Kettenrohrs; - *plate*,

Püttingseisen; - - *bolt*, P-bolzen; - - *of a backstay*, Rüsteisen einer Pardune; - - *of lower rigging*, R. eines Unterwants; - *rack truss*, Kettenrack; - *rails*, K-reling; - *riveted butt*. K-nietungsstoß; - *riveting*, K-nietung; - *runners and gins*, K-läufer und Löschräder; - *sling*, K-schlinge; - *spans*, K-hanger; - *stopper*, K-stopper; - *strap*, K-stropp; - *swivel*, K-wirbel; - *towing*, K-schleppschifffahrt; - - *boat*, K-schleppschiff; - *wale*, Püttingsbolzenplanke; - *well*, Kettenkasten.

chains, Püttinge, Rüste.

chair, Stuhl; - *of steam winch pipe*, Dampfwindenrohrstuhl.

chalder, Ruderöse.

chaldron, unbestimmtes Kohlenmaß.

chalk down od. - *off*, ankreiden; - *line*, Zimmermannsschnur.

chalks, Kreidestriche.

chaloupe, Schaluppe.

chamber, 1. Kammer; 2. Körper einer Pumpe; 3. Fach eines Tanks; - *lock*, Kammerschleuse.

chamfered edge, Schrägkante.

change of monsoon, Monsunwechsel; - *of stroke*, Hubwechsel; - *of tack*, das Wenden durch den Wind; - *of the tide*, das Umsetzen der Tide; - *the berth*, 1. den Ankerplatz verlegen; 2. den Anker versetzen; - *the mizen*, die Besahn durchkaien.

changeable, veränderlich.

changing light, Wechselfeuer.

channel, 1. Fahrwasser; 2. Kanal; 3. Scheibengat des Blocks; 4. Rüste (oberhalb der Bortwant); - *board*, Rüste; - *bolt*, R.-bolzen; - *full of banks* od. *rocks*, unklares Fahrwasser; - *iron*, Rinneneisen; - *knee*, Rüstenknie; - *marks*, Fahrzeichen; - *pilot*,

Kanallotse; - *plate*, Pütting; - *rail*, Rüstleiste; - *support*, R-stütze; - *wale*, 1. R-bergholz; 2. Püttingsbolzenplanke.

char coal, Holzkohle.

charge the deck, das Deck versperren; *deck cargo taking full - of the deck*, die Deckladung beherrschte das Deck; *a ship of -*, ein tiefgeladenes Schiff.

Charles Wain, Großer Bär.

chart, Seekarte; - *case*, Kartenkiste; - *chest*, K-kasten; - *house*, K-haus; - - *door*, K-h-tür; - - - *hinge*, K-h-t-Scharnier; - *house window*, K-h-fenster; - *room*, Navigationszimmer.

charter, Chartepartie, chartern, befrachten; - *by the bulk* od. *for a round sum* od. *for a lump sum*, gegen eine runde Summe befrachten; - *by the voyage*, für die eine Reise b.

charterable, befrachtbar, *charterage*, Verfrachtung.

charterer, Befrachter (Mieter).

chartering, befrachten, chartern; - *broker*, Schiffsmakler; - *business*, Befrachtungsgeschäft; - *clerk*, Befrachtungsangestellter.

charterparty, Chartepartie.

chartless, auf keiner Karte aufgenommen; *the - main*, a. k. K. aufgenommene Teil des Meeres.

chase, 1. Jagd, Jagd machen auf, Verfolgung, verfolgen; 2. das verfolgte Schiff; 3. eintreiben (Bolzen etc.); - *gun*, Buggeschütz; - *in the wind's eye*, die Jagd auf ein luvwärts befindliches Schiff; - *mat*, gespickte Matte; - *port*, Jagdpforte; - *stern*, Heckgeschütz; - *to windward*, die Jagd auf ein luvwärts befindliches Schiff.

chaser, das verfolgende Schiff.

chasing hammer, Treibhammer; - *ship*, das verfolgende Schiff; - *tool*, Schraubstahl; - *wind*, umlaufender Wind.

chasse marée, Lugger.

cheat the glass, das Glas (d. h. Wacht- od. Sanduhr) schütteln und verstellen.

chebeck, Schebecke.

check, 1. abschricken; schrikken; 2. fieren, lose geben (Tau od. Kette); 3. stoppen (Kette); - *the bowlines*, die Bulienen schricken; - *the cable*, die Ankerkette abstoppen; - *the ship*, die Fahrt des Schiffes abstoppen.

check bolt, Stellbolzen; - *nut*, S-mutter; - *pin*, S-stift; - *ring*, Druckring; - *rope*, Rückhalttau; - *valve*, Regulierventil; - - *box*, Sicherheitsventilgehäuse; - - *cover*, Speiseventildeckel.

checker, Taljemann.

checkered plate, Riffelplatte.

cheek, 1. Backe (des Blocks, Bugspriets, Mastes); 2. Gaffelklaue; 3. Pumpennick; 4. Ruderklick, 5. Schließknie (des Gallions).

cheek block, Scheibenklampe; - *of carrick bitt*, Betingsklampe.

cheeks, Backenknie (des Gallions); 2. Mastspurwangen; 3. Backen (des Mastes); - *of a bowsprit*, Bugsprietbacken.

cheer, Hurrah rufen.

cheerly, mit frischer Kraft.

cheese, Fenderkissen.

chequer, Taljemann.

chequered od. - *sides*, mit Stückpforten bemalt; - *plate*, Riffelplatte.

cherry red heat, Kirschrotglühhitze.

chess tree, Halsklampe.

chest, 1. Gehäuse, Kasten; 2. Seekiste (der Matrosen); - *lock*, Kastenschloß; - *nut*, Kastanienholz; - *rope*, Bootseil.

chevron, Litze f. gute Führung.

chewed up, ausgehöhlt, vernichtet.

chief caulker, Kalfatermeister;
- *engineer*, 1. Maschinist;
- *frames*, Richtspanten;
- *mate* od. - *officer*, 1. Offizier; - *officer's log*, Schiffsjournal; - *pilot*, Oberlotse;
- *quarter master*, Steuermannsmaat.

chime and chime, Kimm an K. gestaut.

chimney, Schlot; - *shaft*, Schornsteinrohr.

China trader, Chinafahrer.

chinckle, kleine Bucht.

chine, die Rundung des Leibholzes; - *and - stowed casks*, endweise gestaute Fässer.

Chinese capstan, Differential Gangspill; - *junk*, Dschunke.

chinse, verstopfen.

chinsing iron, Stopfeisen.

chip, 1. Logbrett; 2. abklopfen;
- *fair*, abputzen, glatt meißeln; - *off*, spanähnliche Stücke abmeißeln.

chipping chisel, Abstechmeißel.

chisel, Meißel; - *scraper*, Kratzeisen.

chit, die Nota.

chock, dichten; - *a cask*, ein Faß mit Kuntjes festlegen; - *aft*, dicht achter; - *and block*, od. - *full*, vollgestopft: - *home*, dicht an; - *the cargo*, die Ladung abkeilen.

chock, 1. Aufklotzung, Kalben; 2. Klampe; 3. Staukeil; - *of the bowsprit*, Schloßholz des Bugspriets; - *of the forefoot*, Klick am Vorsteven; - *of the partners*, Unterschlag der Fischung; - *of the rudder*, Ruderkeile.

chocked, abgepallt.

choke the entrance of a harbour, den Eingang eines Hafens versperren; - *the luff*, den Läufer einer Talje unter der nächsten Part bekneifen;
- *up a port with sand*, einen

Hafen mit Sand verschütten.

chocked, 1. unklar, verstopft (bei der Pumpe); 2. bekniffen (beim Tau).

chop about, fortwährend umspringen; - *to an anchor*, hastig Anker werfen.

chopping od. *choppy sea*, hohle See.

chronometer, Chronometer;
- *chest*, C.-kasten; - *error*, C.-stand.

chuck, Scherholz; - *of a lathe*, Drehbankfutter.

chum, guter Kamerad.

chunam, Kitt.

cinder, Schlacke.

circle of altitude, Höhenkreis;
- *of amplitude*, Weitenzirkel;
great - sailing, im größten Kreise segeln.

circular sailing, Segeln in größerem Kreise; - *sector*, Kreisteil; - *stern*, Rundgat.

circulating pipe, Zirkulationsrohr; - *pump*, Z-k-l-t-pumpe.

circulating pump air valve, Zirkulationspumpen-Luftauslaßventil; *c. p. a. vessel*, Z.-Windkessel; *c.p. barrel*, Z.-körper; *c. p. bucket*, Z.-kolben; *c. p. b. and chamber*, Z.-k- und Kammer; *c. p. b. ring*, Z.-Kolbenring; *c. p. b. valve*, Z.-K.-ventil; *c. p. b. v. guard*, Z.-K-v-Hubbegrenzer; *c. p. b. v. seat*, Z.-K-v-sitz; *c. p. chamber*, Z.-körper; *c. p. c. door*, Z.-k-deckel; *c. p. cover*, Z.-deckel; *c. p. crosshead*, Traverse der Z.; *c. p. c. journal*, Halszapfen der Z.-T.; *c. p. cylinder*, Z.-zylinder; *c. p. delivery space*, Z.-Druckraum; *c. p. d. valve*, Z.-Druckventil; *c. p. d. v. guard*, Z.-D-v-Hubbegrenzer; *c. p. d. v. seat*, Z.-D-v-sitz; *c. p. discharge pipe*, Z.-Ausgußrohr; *c.p.d. valve*, Z-Ausgußventil; *c. p. d. v. cover*, Z.-A-v-deckel; *c. p. d. v. spindle*, Z.-A-v-spindel; *c. p.*

foot valve, Z.-Fußventil; *c. p. f. v. guard*, Z.-Saugventil-Hubbegrenzer; *c. p. f. v. seat*, Z.-S-v-sitz; *c. p. gear*, Z.-geschirr; *c. p. gland*, Z.-Stopfbüchsendeckel; *c. p. head valve*, Z.-Druckventil; *c. p. lever*, Z.-Balancier; *c. p. l. shaft journal*, Z.-B.-Axen-Halszapfen; *c. p. liner*, Z.-Büchse; *c. p. link*. Z.-Gelenk; *c. p. l. brasses*, Z.-G.-Lagerschalen; *c. p. neck bush*, Z.-Grundring; *c. p. pet cock*, Z.-Probierhahn; *c. p. plunger*, Z.-Plunger; *c. p. ram*, Z.-Kolbenstange; *c. p. rod*, Z.-stange; *c. p. r. stuffing box*, Z.-s-Stopfbüchse; *c. p. s. b.*, Z.-S-b; *c. p. s. b. gland*, Z.-S-b-deckel; *c. p. suction pipe*, Z.-Saugerohr; *c. p. s. space*, Z.-S-raum; *c. p. suction valve*, Z.-S-ventil; *c. p. s. v. guard*, Z.-S-v-Hubbegrenzer; *c. p. s. v. seat*, Z.-S-v-sitz; *c. p. top valve*, Z.-Druckventil; *c. p. t. v. guard*, Z-D-v-Hubbegrenzer; *c. p. t. v. seat*. Z.-D-v-sitz; *c. p. valve*, Z.-ventil; *c. p. v. guard*, Z.-v-Hubbegrenzer; *c. p. v. seat*, Z.-v-sitz; *c.p. water*, Kondensatorwasser.

circulating pump engine, Zirkulationspumpenmaschine.

circulating pump engine connecting rod, Zirkulationspumpenmaschinen - Pleuelstange; *c. p. e. c. r. bolt*, Z.-P.-s-bolzen; *c. p. e. c. r. bottom end keep*, Z.-Kurbelzapfenlagerschalendeckel; *c. p. e. c. r. b. e. liner*, Z.-Pleuelstangenfußfutter; *c. p. e. c. r. top end keep*. Z.-Kreuzkopflagerschalendeckel; *c. p. e. crank pin bolt*, Z.-Kurbelzapfenlagerbolzen; *c. p. e. c. p. brasses*, Z.-K-z-l-schalen; *c. p. e. c. shaft*, Z.-Kurbelwelle; *c. p. e. c. s. bearing*, Z.-K-w-lager; *c. p. e. c. s. b. bolt*, Z.-K-w-l-bolzen; *c. p. e. c. s. bearing brasses*, Z.-K-w-l-schalen; *c. p. e. c. s. bearing keep*, Z.-K-w-l-deckel: *c. p. e. c. s. b. k. bolt*, Z.-K-w-l-d-bolzen; *c. p. e. cross-head*, Z.-Kreuzkopf; *c. p. e. c. bolt*, Z.-K-k-lagerbolzen; *c. p. e. c. brasses*, Z.-K-k-Lagerschalen; *c.p.e. cylinder*, Z.-Zylinder; *c. p. e. c. cover*, Z.-Z.-Deckel; *c. p. e. c. c. bolt*, Z.-Z.-Deckelbolzen; *c.p.e. cylinder drain pipe*, Z.-Z.-Entwässerungsrohr; *c.p.e. eccentric*, Z.-Excenter; *c.p.e.e. bolt*, Z.-E.-bolzen; *c.p.e.e. brasses*, Z.-E.-Lagerschalen; *c. p. e. e. rod*, Z.-E.-stange; *c. p. e. e. sheave*, Z.-E.-scheibe; *c.p.e.e. strap*, Z.-E.-bügel; *c.p.e.e.s. liner*, Z.-E.-b-Futter; *c. p. e. exhaust pipe*, Z.-Dampfablaßrohr; *c. p. e. piston*, Z.-Kolben; *c. p. e. p. rod*, Z.-K-stange; *c. p. e. p. r. cross-head*, Z.-K-s-Kreuzkopf; *c. p. e. p. r. stuffing box*, Z.-K-s-Stopfbüchse; *c.p.e.p.r.s.b. gland*, Z.-K-s-S-b-deckel; *c.p.e. slide valve*, Z.-Schieber; *c. p. e. starting valve*, Z.-Anlaßventil; *c. p. e. steam pipe*, Z.-Dampfzuleitungsrohr; *c. p. e. stop valve*, Z.-Absperrventil; *c. p. e. valve casing*, Z.-Schieberkasten; *c. p. e. v. c. door*, Z.-S-k-deckel; *c. p. e. v. rod*, Z.-Schieberstange; *c. p. e. v. r. stuffing box*, Z.-S-s-Stopfbüchse; *c. p. e. v. r. s. b. gland*, Z.-S-s-S-b-deckel.

circulating water, Kondensationswasser.

circumferential joint, zirkumferentielle Dichtung; *- seam*, Umfangsnaht.

circumnavigation, Umsegelung, Weltumsegelung.

cirripede, Rankenfüßer-Muscheln.

cirrus, Federwolke.

cistern, 1. Pumpenback; 2.

Zisterne; - *block*, Hacken-block.

citadel deck, Sturmdeck.

city meters' certificate, Attest des städtischen Wiegeamts.

civil day, bürgerliche Tag; - *time*, b. Zeit.

clack box, Ventilkammer; - *valve*, Klappenventil.

claim,Forderung,Reklamation

clam, 1. Dregzange; 2. Klammer.

clamber, rasch auflaufen.

clamp, 1. Unter-Balkweger; 2. Schraubzwinge; 3. Überfall des Bootsmasts; 4. Schaalung (bei Mast od. Rahe).

clamp bolt, Unterbalkweger-bolzen; - *of a davit*, Davitshalter; - *of forecastle*, Unterbalkweger der Back; - *of mast* od. *yard*, Verschalung; - *of poop*, Unterbalkweger der Hütte; - *of raised quarter deck*, U.- des erhöhten Quarterdecks; - *of the deck beams*, Balkweger; - *of the keelson*, Backen am Kielschwein; - *canvass*, mehr Segel setzen.

clandestine trade, Schleichhandel.

clanking of chains, Kettengerassel.

clap aboard a vessel, ein Schiff entern; - *by the wind*, näher am Winde segeln: - *on*, Hand anlegen; - - *a tackle*,eine Talje anschlagen; - - *all sails*, alle Segel beisetzen od. sich beeilen; - - *the cat fall!* Hol die Katt! - - *the wind*, näher am Winde segeln; - *the messenger on the cable*, die Ankerkette an die Kabellaring zeisen; - *valve*, Klappenventil.

clapper, Klöppel; - *valve*, Klappenventil.

clarion, Rudermall.

clashy, regnerisch.

clasp, einhaken, einrücken;

- *hook*, Doppelhaken; - *hoop*, Keilband.

class, Klasse, klassifizieren.

classification, Klassifikation.

clause,Klausel,Vertragspunkt.

clave, Bohrblock.

claw, 1. Klaue; 2. Hieb mit der Katze; *to make a - to windward*, vom Ufer abhalten; - *of a grapnel*, Klaue des Dregankers; - *off from a lee shore*, sich vom Legerwall freikreuzen; - *stopper*, Klaustopper.

clawing od. - *off*, abkreuzen; - *ship*, Luvhalter; - *to windward*, luv halten.

claws of the grapnel, Klauen des Dregankers.

clay od. *clayey bottom* od. *ground*,Lehm- od. Tonboden.

clean, reinigen, schrubben; - *bill of health*, reiner Gesundheitspass; - *b. of lading*, reines Konnossement; - *bottom*, reiner Grund; - *breach*, glatt Deck; - *coast*, reine Küste; - *forward*, scharf beschnittenes Vorderschiff; - *full*, die Segel gut voll; - *run*, scharfes Hinterschiff; - *sweep*, alles von Deck fortschlagen; - *the cable*, die Ankerkette schrubben.

clear, 1. klar, sichtig; 2. klar machen, teeren, aufschießen (Tauwerk); 3. aus- od. einklarieren; - *and open channel*, klares Fahrwasser; - *away the jib!* Klüver bei! - *breach*, die Wellen rollen darüber; - *for action*, klar Deck zum Gefecht; - *for sailing*, klar zur Abfahrt; *to go -*, klar gehen; - *hawse*,klare Ketten; *to keep a - -*, klares Ankertau resp. klare Ankerketten halten; - *outward*, ausklarieren; - *the chains, the deck, the land, tackle, &c.*, die Ketten, das Deck, Land, resp. Taljen etc. klaren; - *rope*, klares Tau; - *water*, offenesFahrwasser; -*weather*, sichtiges Wetter.

clearage, Klarierung.

clearance, 1. Ausklarierung; 2. Spielraum; - *of piston*, S. des Kolbens.

clearing port, Wasserpforte; - *up*, aufklaren.

cleat, Klampe; - *of the gangway*, Fallreepsklampe.

clench, Ankerstich, Klintsch.

clew, 1. Schothorn (des Segels); 2. Knüttel (der Hängematte); 3. d. Segel aufgeien; - *cringle*, Schothornlügel; - *down*, die Segel streichen; - - *a yard*, eine Rahe mit den Geitauen herunterholen; - *garnet*, Geitau eines Untersegels; - - *block*, G-t-Block e. U.; - *iron*, ringförmiges Eisen am Schothorn großer Segel; - *jigger*, kleines Takel zum Aufholen der Topp- oder Marssegelecken; - *line*, Geitau; - - *block*, G-t-block des oberen Rahesegels; - *of a hammock*, Knüttel der Hängematte; - *piece*, Stoßlappen; - *ring*, Schothornring; - *rope*, S-h-liek; *the line from - to earing*, die Diagonallinie eines Segels von oben bis unten; - *to the wind*, den Wind abkneifen; - *up*, 1. aufgeien; 2. ein Geschäft erledigen.

cliff, Felsgestade.

climb hand over hand, sich aufpalmen; - *in through the hawse pipe*, als gemeiner Matrose beginnen.

clinch, Klinsch, Stich; - *a bolt*, einen Bolzen verklinken; - *joint*,Verband beim Klinkerwerk; - *ring*, Klinkring; - *the cable*, die Ankerkette um Mast od. Pallstützen schäkeln resp. ein Tau an den Ankerring stecken; - *work*, Klinkerwerk.

clinched and riveted, niet- und nagelfest.

clincher built boat, klinkerartig gebautes Boot; - *nail*, Schraubennagel; - *work*, Klinkerwerk.

clinching ring, Klinkring.

clinker, Schlacke; - *built boat*, klinkerartig gebautes Boot.

clip off the ropes, die Taue abputzen.

cliphook, Doppelhaken.

clipper,Klipper,Schnellsegler; - *built*, klipperartig gebaut; - *stem*, Klippersteven.

clock-calm, gänzliche Windstille.

clog, Holzschuh.

close a seam, eine Naht dicht machen; - *alongside*, Bord an Bord; - *butt*, der dichte Stoß; - *ceiling*, feste Wegerung; - *down the hatches*, die Luken schließen; - *fight*, Handgemenge; -*hauled*,dicht beim Winde laufen; - *hugged*, den Wind abkneifen; - *in on us*, über uns herfallen; - *in with the land*, dicht unter Land gehen; - *lighter*, bedeckter Leichter; - *linked chain*, Krankette; - *planked*, dicht; - - *top*, dichter Mars; - *quarters*, 1. die starken Schotten; 2. ein Gefecht Bord an Bord; - *reefed*, dicht gerefft; *a - shave*, mit blauemAuge davonkommen; - *the wind*, an den Wind gehen; - *to the land*, dicht am Lande; - *to the wind*, dicht am Winde; - *with the land*, dicht unterLand gehen; - *with a ship*, dicht neben einem Schiffe kommen.

closed in bridge, geschlossene Brücke; - *manometer*, abgeschlossenes Manometer; *we - with the island*, wir näherten uns der Insel; *under - topsails*, mit dicht gerefften Marssegeln.

closing gear, Absperr-Vorrichtung; - *of ropes*, das Zusammenschlagen vonTauen.

cloth, Bahn, Segelkleid; - *in the wind,* zu dicht mit dem Kleid am Winde.
clothed with canvass, mit gut setzenden Segeln behangen.
clothes lines, Zeugleine; - - *pendants,* Hanger der Z.; - *ropes,* Waschjollentaue.
clothing, 1. Kesselbekleidung; 2. Takelage des Bugspriets.
cloudy, bewölkt.
clout, Feul, Scheuerlappen.
clove hitch, Webeleinstich; - *hook,* Düwelshaken.
club, eine Art Bootsspiere; - *down with the current,* vor schleppendem Anker mit dem Strome treiben; - *hauling.* klubholen; - *topsail,* großes Gaffel-Toppsegel.
clubbing, vor schleppendem Anker treiben.
clue see clew.
clump block, Klampblock.
clutch, 1. Gabelstütze; 2. Schwungrad (der Maschine); 3. Kuppelungsklaue, Zahnkuppelung (der Kuppelungshülse); - *coupling,* - Klauenkuppelung; - - *box,* lösbarer Kuppelungsmuff; - *lever,* Klauenhebel; - *of winch od. windlass,* Kuppelungsklaue; - *pinion,* Schlußtriebrad.
clutching. Ankerhals.
coach, Kampanje; - *boat,* Marktschiff; - *ladder,* Kampanjetreppe; - *screw,* Holzschraube; - *whip,* langer Wimpel.
coad, Kimmkiel.
coak, 1. Büchse; 2. Zapfen, verzapfen.
coaking, Schakwerk.
coaks, 1. Zähne (eines zusammengesetzten Mastes); 2. die metallenen Büchsen (in den Scheiben).
coal, kohlen, Kohlen einnehmen; - *backer,* Kohlenträger; - *barge,* K-leichter; - *bunker,* K-bunker; - - *bulkhead,* K-b-wand; - - *door,* K-b-tür; - -

lid, K-loch-Verschluß; - - *opening.* K-bunkerloch: - - *pipe,* K-b-rohr; - - - *lid,* K-b-r-verschluß; - *b. plate.* K-b-platte; - - *stay,* K-b-stag; - *chute,* Falloch für die Kohlen; - *dust,* K-staub; - *gins,* K-schlingen; - *hammer,* K-hammer; - *hatch,* K-luke; - *heaver,* K-träger; - *hold.* K-raum; - *hulk,* K-hulk; - *jetty,* K-platz; - *lighter,* K-leichter; - *measure,* K-maß; - *poker,* Schüreisen; - *sack,* 1. Kohlensack; 2 sehr dunkle Stelle am südl. Himmel; - *screen,* Kohlenschirm; - *shoot,* K-stürze; - *shovel,* K-schaufel; - *shute,* K-stürze; - *spout,* schräge Kohlenladebühne; - *staith,* K-ladegerüst; - *station,* K-station; - *tar,* K-teer; - *tip,* K-ladeplatz; - *trimmer,* K-schaufler; - *wharf,* K-werfte; - *whipper,* K-wipper; - *whipping,* das Auskippen der K-körbe.
coalay, Kohlenträger.
coaling, Bunkerkohlen einnehmen; - *depot,* Kohlendepot; - *hatch,* K-luke; - *port,* 1. K-pforte; 2. K-station; - *station,* K-s-.
coaming, Lukensüll; - *angle bar,* Süllwinkel; - *carling,* Scherstock des Decks; - *of bridge house bulkhead,* Süll des Brückenhausschotts; - *of forecastle b.,* S. d. Backschotts; - *of poop b.,* S. d. Hüttenschotts; - *of raised quarter deck b.,* S. des Quarterdeckschotts; - *of ventilator,* feststehender Ventilatorsockel; - *plate,* Süllplatte.
coamings, Lukenränder.
coast, 1. Küste; 2. an der K. längs fahren od. Küstenhandel treiben; - *chart,* K-karte; - *guard,* K-wache, K-wächter; - *jurisdiction,* K-gebiet; - *lighting,* K-be-

leuchtung; - *pilot*, K-lotse: - *survey*, K-vermessung; - *waiter*, K-wächter.

coaster, Küstenfahrzeug.

coasting, längs der Küste fahrend, Küstenfahrt; - *craft*, K-fahrzeug; - *navigation*, K-schiffahrt; - *pilot*, K-lotse; -*steamer*, K-dampfer; - *tour*, K-reise; - *trade*, K-handel; - *vessel*, K-fahrzeug; - *voyage*, K-reise.

coastwise, Küstenfahrt, längs der Küste.

coat, 1. anstreichen, Anstrich. Lage; 2. bekleiden, verkleiden; 3. Kragen (des Mastes, der Pumpe); - *of the rudder*, Ruderbrohk; - *tack*, Pumpspiker.

coating, anstreichen, Anstrich.

coats, Teerwerg zum Umwickeln der Masten.

cobbing board, Strafbrett.

cobble, zusammenschustern.

coble, Büse.

cock, 1. Hahn; 2. Schaluppe: a-*cock bill*, klar zum Fallen; - *to cockbill a yard*, eine Rahe auftoppen; *t. c. the anchor*, den Anker unter den Kranbalken bringen; *cock boat*, hinten angehängtes kleines Boot; - *gland*, Hahnstopfbüchsendeckel; -*handle*, Hahnschlüssel; - *of a sheave*, Büchse (in Rolle od. Scheibe); - *pit*, Verbandraum.

cocked hat, Dreimaster.

cocket bread, feiner Schiffszwieback.

cockle boat od. - *shell*, Nußschale, kleines Boot.

cockling, kabbelig.

cocks and valves, die Hahnausstattung.

cockswain, Bootsmann.

cod line, Leine von 18 Garn; - *of a bay*, das Innere einer Bucht.

code od. - *book* od. - *of signals*, Signalbuch; - *signal*, S-meldung.

coefficient, Koeffizient; - *of fineness*, Völligkeitsgrad.

coelo navigation, Schiffahrtskunde durch Beobachtung der Gestirne.

cofferdam, Kofferdamm.

cog of a wheel, Kamm, Radzahn; - *wheel*, Zahnrad; - - *rim*, Z-r-kranz.

coil, Tauwerksrolle; *to - a rope*, ein Tau aufschießen; -*against the sun*, gegen die Sonne a-s-; - *away a chain*, eine Kette wegschießen; - *up a rope*, ein Tau aufschießen; - *with the sun*, mit der Sonne a-s-.

coiling, der Kink (im Tau).

coils, Schlangen (im Kessel).

coir broom, Piassavabesen; - *mat*, Bastmatte; - *rope*, B-tau.

cold chisel, Kaltmeissel; - *current*, kalter Strom; - *hammered iron*, kaltgehämmertes Eisen; - *water cistern*, Kaltwasserzisterne; *c. w. pump*, K-w-pumpe.

collapse, Eindrückung.

collapsing boat, zusammenlegbares Boot.

collapsion, Zusammenfall.

collar, 1. Ring, 2. Dichtungswinkel; 3. Auge (oberhalb eines Stags); 4. Strop, Kragen, eisernes Band (unterhalb eines Stags); 5. Schweißung (eines Knies); - *beam*, Decksbalken; - - *of a davit*, Davitshalter; - - *of the bowsprit*, Schlossholz des Bugspriets; - *of the hawse pipe*, Klüsenrohrflansch; - *of the rod*, Stopfbüchsendeckel.

collide, ansegeln, zusammenstoßen.

collier, Kohlenschiff.

colliery screened coals, zechengesiebte Kohlen.

collision, Zusammenstoß; - *Bulkhead*, Kollisionsschott; - - *angle bar*, K-s-winkel; - *mat*, Kollisionsmatte; - *pad*, K-pflaster.

colonial port, Koloniehafen.
colour chest, Flaggenkasten.
colours, Nationalflagge.
colt, Tauende. [ende.
colting, Prügel mit dem Tau-
column, Säule, Ständer.
colza oil, Rüböl.
comb, 1. Kamm (der Rahe);
2. Klampe (des Klüverhal-
ses); 3. Köpfe setzen (beim
Seegang); - *cleat,* Kamm der
Rahe. [see.
comber, 1. Leiste; 2. hohe Brech-
combined, verbunden; - *deck
erections,* verbundene Aufbauten; - *steam,* v. Dampf;
- *steering gear,* v. Steuergerät.
combing see coaming.
combustibles, Brennmaterial.
combustion, Verbrennung; -
chamber, Feuerkammer; - -
crown plate, Deckplatte der
F.; - - *side plate,* Seitenwand
der F.; - *chamber stay,* F.-
Stehbolzen; - - - *nut,* F.-S-b-
mutter.
come aboard, an Bord kommen; - *aft,* nach achtern k.;
- *alongside,* längsseits k.;
- *booming forwards,* mit allen
Segeln beigesetzt herank.;
- *home,* der Anker geht
durch; - *in sight,* in Sicht
k.; - *round on the heel,* auf
derselben Stelle wenden; -
suddenly strong (od. *heavy)
from starboard,* der Wind fiel
plötzlich stark von Steuerbord ein; - *to,* anluven; - *to a
dead halt,* aufdrehen, auftörnen; - *to an anchor,* vor Anker
gehen; - *to the wind,* an den
Wind kommen; - *up a river,*
einen Fluß heraufkommen;
- *up a rope* (od. *tackle),* ein
Tau (od. Talje) auffieren; -
up to a vessel, einem Schiffe
auflaufen; - *up the bowlines,*
die Buliens auffieren; - *up
with a vessel,* ein Schiff einholen; - *up with the capstan,*
das Gangspill zurückwinden.
coming see coaming.

command, Befehl, befehligen
not under proper -, manövrierunfähig.
commander, 1. Schiffsführer;
2. Mußkeule.
commanding breeze, günstige
Brise.
commercial code, Handelsge-
setzbuch; - - *book,* internationales Signalbuch; -
harbour, Handelshafen; -
treaty, Handelsvertrag.
commission, Offizierspatent.
commissioned officer, 1. durch
Patent angestellter Offizier;
2. beauftragter O.; *-ship,* in
Dienst gestelltes Schiff.
commissioners of customs,
Oberzolldirektion.
commodore, Kommodor.
common anchor, gewöhnlicher
Anker. - *bend,* einfacher
Schotstich; - *carrier,* Frachtschiff; - *log,* gewöhnliches
Log; - *schooner,* Gaffelschoner; - *sennit,* Plattingsleine;
- *steel,* gewöhnlicher Stahl;
- *steering gear,* gewöhnliches
Steuergerät; - *windlass,*
g. Ankerspill.
communication box, Wechsel-
ventilkasten; - *cock,* Kom-
munikationshahn; - *valve,*
K-k-ventil.
companion, Niedergangskappe;
- *hatch,* Kajütenluke; - *ladder,*
- *stairs,* K-treppe; - *way,*
Niedergang.
company, Mannschaft; - *pilot,*
Kompagnielotse; - *signal,*
K-signal; - *steamer,* K.-
dampfer.
companying steamer, mitfah-
render Dampfer.
company's pilot, Kompagnielotse.
compartment, Abschottung,
Kompartiment.
compass, Kompaß; - *adjuster,*
K-adjustierer; - *bearing,* K-
peilung; - *bowl,* od. - *box,*
K-mörser; - *card,* Windrose;
- *course made good,* gesegel-

ter Kompaßkurs; - *course steered*, K-k.; - *error*, K-fehler; - *gets* (od. *is*) *wild*, der K. fliegt; - *needle*, K-nadel; - *plane*, Schiffshobel; - *point*, Kompaßstrich; - *signal*, K-signal; - *spins*, die K-rose giert hin und her;-*stand*, K-stativ;-*timber*, Krummholz.
compasses, Zirkel.
compensation, besondere Verstärkung; - *ring*, V-ring.
complement of *men*, Vervollständigung der Mannschaft; - *of the course*, Komplement des Kurses.
complete *stroke*, Doppelhub; - *the complement of men*, die Besatzung vervollständigen.
completely *rigged*, vollständig aufgetakelt.
completion, Vollendung.
compo, monatliche Heuer.
composite *vessel*, Komposit Schiff.
composition, Kesselbekleidung.
compound, zusammengesetzt; - *air manometer*, geschlossenes Luftmanometer; - *course*, Koppelkurs; - *engine*, Hoch- und Niederdruck-maschine; - - *with surface condensation*, Kompound-maschine mit Oberflächen-kondensation; - *gauge*, kombiniertes Druck- u. Vakuum-Manometer; - - *pipe*, Kompound-Manometerrohr;
compressed *treenail*, gepreßter Holznagel.
compressive *strain*, Druck-kraft.
compressor, Armstopper.
compressors of *the windlass*, Stoppvorrichtung d. Anker-spills.
compulsory *pilotage*, Lotsen-zwang.
con, 1. den Mann am Steuer kontrollieren; 2. Steuerung.
concluding *line*, Mitteltau.

concussion, Erschütterung.
condemn, kondemnieren; - *a prize*, als gute Prise erklären.
condensation, Kondensation; - *by contact*, Oberflächen-K.; - *by injection*, K. durch Einspritzung.
condensed steam, kondensierter Dampf.
condenser, Kondensator; - *by contact*, Oberflächen - Kondensator; - *cock*, K.-hahn; - *division plate*, Trennungs-rippe des K.; - *door*, K.-deckel; - - *bolt*, K.-d-bolzen; - - - *nut*, K.-d-b-mutter; - *ferrules*, K.-röhren-Dich-tungsringe; - *gauge*, K.-Ma-nometer;-*manhole*,K.-Mann-loch;-*steam space*,K.-Dampf-raum; - *test*, K.-Druckprobe; - *tube*, K.-rohr; - - *ferrule*, K.-r-ring; - - *packing*, K-packung; - - *plate*, K.-Rohr-wand; - *water space*, K-Wasserraum.
condensing *engine*, Konden-sationsmaschine; - *jet*, Ein-spritzstrahl; - *surface*, Kon-densationsfläche.
conductibility, Leitungsver-mögen.
conductor of *heat*, Wärme-leiter.
conduit, Leitung.
cone, Konus.
coneing, die Schräge des Ruderkopfes.
confused sea, wirre See; - *swell*, w. Dünung.
conical, kegelförmig; - *pendulum*, konisches Pendel; - *valve*, Kegelventil.
conn, das Steuern beaufsich-tigen.
connect, verbinden.
connecting *bridge*, fliegende Brücke;-*gear*, Verbindungs-getriebe; - - *link*, Kulisse des V.; -*plate*, Verbindungs-platte; - *rod*, Pleuelstange; - - *bearing*, P.-lager; - - *bolt*, P.-bolzen; - - - *nut*, P.-b-

mutter; *c. r. bottom end,*
P.-fuß; *c. r. b. e. bolt.* Kurbelzapfenlagerbolzen; *c. r. b. e. b.
nut,* K.-mutter; *c. r. b. e.
brasses,* Kurbelzapfenlagerschalen; *c. r. b. e. keep,* K.-
deckel; *c. r. b. e. liner,*
Pleuelstangenfußfutter; *c. r.
fork,* Pleuelstangengabel;
c. r. gudgeon, P-s-zapfen;
*c. r. jaw.*P-s-gabel;*c. r. journal,*
Kurbelzapfen; *c. r. key,*
Pleuelstangenkeil; *c. r. liner,*
P-s-futter; *c. r. pin,* P-s-
bolzen; *c. r. top end,* P-s-kopf;
c. r. t. e. bolt, P-s-k-lager-
bolzen; *c. r. t. e. b. nut,* P-s-
k-l-b-mutter; *c. r. t. e. brasses,*
P-s-Lagerschalen; *c. r. t. e.
keep,* Deckelplatte des Kreuzkopflagers.

connection, Anschluß, Verbindung.

conning, das Steuern beaufsichtigen;-*bench,* Komman-
dobank.

consign, konsignieren.

consignee. 1. Ladungsempfänger. 2. Konsignator.

consigner, Absender.

consort od. - *ship,* Mitsegler.

constant force, dauernde Kraft;
- *pressure,* d. Druck.

construction of machinery,
Maschinenbau; - - *ships,*
Schiffsbau.

constructive total loss, konstruktiver Totalverlust.

constructor, Erbauer.

consular community, Konsular-
gemeinde;-*district,* K-bezirk;
- *fees,* K-gebühren; - *jurisdiction,* K.-gerichtsbarkeit.

consultation, Schiffsrat.

consulting engineer, beraten-
der Ingenieur.

consumption, Verbrauch.

consuming, verzehrend.

cont splice, Kuttsplissung;-*line,*
Raum zwischen den Kimmen
zweier Fässer oder den
Kardeelen eines Taues.

contend the weather gauge,

windwärts von einem andern
Schiffe zu kommen suchen.

contents, Passierschein des
Zollamts; - *unknown,* un-
bekannten Inhalts.

continuous floor, durchlaufen-
de Bodenwrange; - *jet of
water,* der kontinuierliche
Wasserstrahl.

contraband goods, Schmuggel-
ware, Konterbande;-*of war,*
Kriegskonterbande.

contract of affreightment,
Frachtvertrag;-*of recharter,*
Unterf-v-; - *ticket,* Passa-
gierbillet; - *work,* Akkord-
arbeit.

contrary wind, widriger Wind.

contrate wheel, Kronrad.

contributory values, beitragspflichtige Werte.

controlling, kontrollieren; -
valve of the steering engine,
Kontrollventil des Dampf-
steuerapparats.

convert, umwandeln.

converted steel, Halbstahl.

convex sinuosity, ausgehende
Stromkrümmung.

convexity, Ausbauchung.

convey, transportieren.

conveyance, Transport.

convict ship, Gefängnisschiff.

convoy, Eskorte, Eskortschiff.

cook, Koch; - *house,* Schiffsküche.

cooking stove, Kochofen; -
utensils, K-geschirr.

cook's mate, Kochmaat;-*shop,*
Kombüse.

cooler, Kühlapparat.

cooling, abkühlen, Abkühlung;
- *pipe,* Kühlrohr; - *surface,*
K-fläche.

co-partner in a ship, Mitreeder.

coper, Branntweinhändler.

copper, 1. Kessel; 2. Mann-
schaftskochkessel; 3. ver-
kupfern; 4. mit Kupfer beschlagen; - *bolt,* Kupferbol-
zen; - *bottomed,* K-boden,
k-bodig; - *fastened,* mit

4*

kupfernen Bolzen; - *fastening*, Kupferverbolzung; - *hammer*, K-hammer; - *punt*, Scheuerprahm; - *sheathing*, Kupferhaut; - *sheet joint*, K-blechdichtung; - *smith*, K-schmied; - *wire joint*, K-drahtdichtung.
coppers, Kochgeschirr.
coracle, ledernes Boot.
coral boat, Korallenfischerboot; - *reef*, K-riff.
cord, Leine.
cordage, Tauwerk.
cordon line, Gürtellinie.
cork buoy, Korkboje; - *fender*, K-fender; - *jacket*, K-weste.
corner of a sail, Horn eines Segels; - *piece*, Stoßlappen.
Cornish boiler, Walzenkessel mit innerer Feuerung; - *double seat valve*, Cornishventil mit Doppelsitz.
corposant, St. Elmsfeuer.
correct the course, den Kurs verbessern.
corrected course, verbesserter Kurs; - *distance*, v. Abstand; - *latitude*, v. Breite; - *longitude*, v. Länge.
corresponding sea, dementsprechender Seegang.
corrode, zerbeizen.
corrosion, Zerbeizung.
corrugated furnace, gewellte Feuerbüchse.
corvet od. *corvette*, Korvette.
cost of repairs, Reparaturkosten.
cot, Koje.
cotidal, mit gleicher Flutzeit; - *lines*, Isorachien.
cott, Pritsche, Hängematte.
cottar od. *cotter*, konischer Keil; - *for propeller*, Querkeil zur Schiffsschraube.
cotton coiling, Baumwollflechte; - *waste*, Twist.
counter, 1. Gillung (des Schiffs); 2. Hubzähler; - *act the current*, die Strömung ausgleichen; - *brace*, 1. Borgbrasse; 2. backbrassen; - *claim*, Ge-

genforderung; - *current*, G-strom; - *gear*, Hubzählvorrichtung; - *pieces*, Hukspanten; - *plate*, Gillungsplatte; - *punch*, Gegenpunze; - *rail*, unterste Heckleiste; - *sea*, Gegensee; - *signal*, G-signal; - *steam*, G-dampf; - *sink*, 1. fräsen; 2. Ausweitung; - *sunk rivet*, versenkte Niete; - - *work*, v. Nietung; - *tide*, Gegenstrom; - *timber*, Gillungsholz; - *transom*, Oberheckbalken; - *swell*, Gegendünung.
couple and uncouple, kuppeln und losmachen.
coupling, Kuppelung; - *bar*, Kuppelungsstange; - *bolt*, K-bolzen; - - *nut*, K-b-mutter; - *box*, K-hülse; - *flange*, K-flansch; - *lever*, K-hebel; - *pin*, Kulissenbolzen; - *rod*, Kuppelungsstange.
course, Kurs; - *angle*, K-winkel; - *corrected for current* (od. *drift*), wegen Stromversetzung verbesserter K.; *c. c. f. leeway*, wegen Abtrift v. K.; *c. c. f. l. and variation*, w. A. und Mißweisung v. K.; *c. c. f. l. v. and current*, der über den Grund behaltene K.; - *made good*, rechtweisender K.; - *steered*, gesteuerter K.
courses, Untersegel; - *ready for setting!* U. beisetzen! *to go under a pair of* -, mit dem Fock- und Großsegel fahren.
courset, Vorschriften für den Nachtdienst.
Court of Admiralty, Seeamt.
cove, 1. Bucht, Schlupfhafen; 2. die verzierende Kehlung unter der Heckreling.
covenant, 1. schriftlicher Vertrag; 2. sich schriftlich verpflichten.
covenantee od. *covenanter*, Kontrahent.
cover, Bezug, Kappe, Kleid,

Überzug, Deckel; - *of boiler*, das halbzylindrische Dach; - *of slide valve*, Überlappung der Dampfschieber; - *of steering apparatus*, Kappe des Steuergeräts.
covered *hatchway*, Stülpluke; - *in barge*, Kastenschute.
covering *board*, Deckbrett, Schandeckel; - *strap*, Stoßblech.
cowdie *wood*, Kaudieholz.
cowl *of the ventilator*, Kopf des Ventilators.
cowry *wood*, Kauriholz.
coxswain, Bootsführer.
C. P. = *Civil Power*.
crab, 1. Krüppelspill; 2. Segel fahren; 3. dwars wegtreiben; - *bar*, Drehbaum; - *schooner*, schonerartiges Schiff; - *winch*, Krüppelwinde; - *windlass*, das liegende K-spill.
crack, 1. Riß, Sprung; 2. mustergültig; - *boat*, Renommierschiff.
cracked, gesprungen.
cracking *in all joints*, in allen Fugen krachen.
cradle, 1. Ablaufschlitten; 2. Aufziehschlitten.
craft, Fahrzeug.
crag od. *craig*, Felsen.
cram, überfüllen.
cramp, Krampe, mit Krampen befestigen; - *iron*, Enterhaken; - *out*, aus den Krampen reißen.
crance, das eiserne Eselshoofd des Bugspriets.
crane, Kran; - *barge*, schwimmender K.: - *beam*, K-balken; - *bill*, K-fuß; - *for lower topsail yard*, Bock einer Untermarsrahe; - *handle*, Kranhandhabe; - *lines*, Schwichtleinen von den Pardunen nach dem Mars; - *post*, Kranarm; - *steam pipe*, K-Dampfzuleitungsrohr.
crane see also steam c.
crank, 1. Kurbel; 2. gekröpfte

Welle; 3. Krummzapfen; 4. *rank*, oberlastig; - *axle*, Kurbelachse; - *bearing*, K-lager; - *boss*, K-nabe; - *brace*, Bohrwinde; - *disc*, Kurbelscheibe; - *handle*, Handhabe einer Kurbel; - *hatch*, Maschinenluke eines Raddampfers; - *lever*, Kurbelarm; - *pin*, K-zapfen; c. p. *bolt*, K-z-lagerbolzen; c. p. b. *nut*, K-z-l-b-mutter; c. p. *brasses*, K-z-l-schalen: - *pit*, Kurbelgrube; -*shaft*, K-welle; c. s. *and tunnel bearing*, K-w-und Lauflager; c. s. b., K-w-lager; c. s. b. *bolt*, K-w-l-bolzen; c. s. *bearing brasses*, K-w-l-schalen; c. s. *bearing keep*, K-w-l-deckel; c. s. b. k. *bolt*, K-w-l-d-bolzen; c. s. *coupling*, K-w-kuppelung; c. s. c. *bolt*, K-w-Kuppelungsbolzen; c. s. *flange*, K-w-flansch; c. s. *journal*, K-w-lagerzapfen; c. s. *key way*, K-w-Keilnute; c. s. *water service*, K-w-Kühlrorrichtung; - *sided*, rank; - *web*, Kurbelarm.
crankiness, Rankheit.
cranky. rank.
crate, Lattenkiste.
crawl *off from a lee shore*, sich von Lee abkrabbeln.
crazy, altersschwach.
creak, stöhnen.
creaky, altersschwach.
creek, 1. Priel, 2. kleine Bucht. Schlupfhafen. 3. Hafeneinschnitt.
creep, dreggen.
creeper, Dreghaken.
creeping, das Dreggen.
crengle, od. *crenkle*, Lägel.
crest *of o wave*, Wellenkamm.
crew, Besatzung, Mannschaft; - *list*, Mannschafts-Verzeichnis; - *space*, Logis; c. s. *companion*, L-kappe; c. s. *door*, L-tür: c. s. *funnel*, L-Schornstein; c. s. *stove*, L-ofen.
crimp, 1. Heuerbaas, Matrosenmakler, Seelenverkäufer;

2. krimpen d. h. gegen die Sonne zurückgehen.

crimping house, Preß - Spelunke.

cringle, Lägel.

cripple, entmasten, stark beschädigen.

crooked chisel, Schiefbetel; - *tiller,* gebogene Ruderpinne.

croaky, stark gebogen.

cross, kreuzen; - *a lashing* od. *seizing,* eine Laschung oder Zurrung k.; - *lashed,* kreuzseitig verlascht; - *the bow of a ship,* vor dem Bug eines Schiffes passieren;-*the hawse of a vessel,* dwars vor einem Schiffe vorbeisegeln; - *the line,* den Äquator passieren; - *the path of a vessel,* den Kurs eines Schiffes kreuzen; - *the wake of a vessel,* dwars achter einem Schiffe vorübersegeln.

cross bar, Kreuzstange;-*beams,* Dwarsbalken; - *bearing,* Kreuzpeilung; - *bitt,* Querbalken; - *bulkheads,* Querschotten; - *bunker,* Querschiftsbunker, - *chock,* Stoß. kalb; - *coaming,* Querscherstock; - *cut,* 1. quer durchschnitten; 2. Trecksäge; - - *chisel,* Kreuzmeißel; - *grained,* überspänig; - *gore of a gaff sail,* die Diagonale vom Schoothorn zur Klaue eines Gaffsegels; - *hawser,* Querhalse.

crosshead, Kreuzkopf; - *block,* Gleitklotz; - *bolt,* Kreuzkopf-Lagerbolzen; - - *nut,* K-k-L-b-mutter; - *bracket,* K-k-träger; - *brasses,* K-k-Lagerschalen; - *guide,* K-k-führung; - *journal,* K-k-halszapfen.

crossjack, Kreuzsegel;-*bowline,* Kreuzbulin; - *brace,* K-brasse; *c. b. pendant,* K-b-schenkel; - *bunt line,* K-Bauchgording; - *clew garnet,*

K-geitau; *c. c. line,* Bagiengeitau; - *foot rope,* Kreuzpferd; - *leech line,* K-Nockgording, - *lift,* K-Toppenant; *c. l. purchase,* K-rahe-Toppenantstalje; - *reef tackle,* K-refttalje; - *sail,* Bagiensegel; - *sheet,* Kreuzschote; - *tack,* K-hals; - *yard,* K-rahe; - - *foot rope,* Bagienpferd.

cross in the cables, die Ankertaue haben ein Kreuz vor den Klüsen.

cross key of coupling, Querkeil der Kuppelung; - *line,* Dwarsleine; - *of an anchor,* Kreuz eines Aukers; - *pawl,* Dwarslatte; - *piece of the bitts,* Betingsbalken; - *pole,* Kreuzpfahl; - *reefs,* K-reefe der Blinden; - *sea,* kreuzender Seegang; - *section,* Querdurchschnitt; - *seizing,* Kreuzbindsel; -*spale,*Dwarslatte; - *swell,* kreuzende Dünung; - *tail,* Pleuelstangenkreuz; *c. t. butt,* Lochauflage im Kreuz; *c. t. hole,* Loch im K.; *c. t. strap,* Seitenpleuelstange des Kolbenkreuzes; - *tide,* unregelmäßiger Strom; - *timber,* Dwarsholz; - *trees,* D-salingen; - *turns,* Kreuztörns.

crossing, 1. kreuzend; 2. Kreuztörns.

crotch, Stütze.

crow bar, Brechstange: -*foot,* Hahnepoot; *c. f. dead eye,* Spinnkopfsblock; *c. f. halyard,* Spinnkopf; *c. f. lines,* Scherleinen; *c. f. of an awning,* Spinnkopf eines Sonnensegels; *c. f. of the messtable,* Ständer des Backtisches; *c. f. spanner,* einseitiger Aufsatzschlüssel; - *nest,* Krähennest.

crowd od. *to c. all possible sails* od. *t. c. every stitch of canvass,* Segel pressen.

crown, 1. Decke, Krone; 2. Hals

des Ankers; 3. größte Höhe des Sturmes; - *knot*, Kreuzknoten; - *of a combustion chamber*, Feuerkammerdecke; - *of a knot*, die Hahnepoot auf einem Knoten; - *of dome*, Domdecke; - *of donkey boiler*, Hülfskesseldecke; - *of double bottom*, Tankdecke; - *of fire box* od. - *of furnace*, Feuerbüchsendecke; - *of tank*, Tankdecke; - *of the anchor*, Ankerkreuz; - *plate of combustion chamber*, Deckplatte der hinteren Rauchkammer; - *rope*, Kreuzknoten; - *sheet*, Feuerbüchsendecke; - *wheel*, Kronrad.

crowning, einfacher Fallreepsknopf.

crow's nest, Krähennest.

crucible steel, Tiegelgußstahl.

cruise, kreuzen, Kreuzfahrt, Übungsfahrt.

cruiser, Kreuzer.

cruising ground od. - *latitude*, Station.

crumbled biscuits, Hartbrotbrocken.

crupper chain, Domperkette.

crutch, 1. Baumgabel (Stütze eines Baums); 2. Stütze des Finknetzes; 3. Hinterpiekband; 4. Rojegabel (eines Bootes); - *bolt*, Hinter-Piekbandbolzen.

cubic capacity, kubischer Inhalt.

cuckold's knot od. - *neck*, Tauschleife.

cuddy, Pflicht, Schutenkajüte.

culver tail, Schwalbenschwanz.

cumbersome, belemmernd.

cunthines, die Fauten eines Taues.

cuntline, Zwischenraum.

cuntsplice, doppelte Splissung.

cup, Kappe des Gangspills; - *chuck*, Klemmfutter; - *valve*, Tellerventil.

cure, no - no pay, ohne Erfolg keine Zahlung.

curl clouds, Federwolken.

curling iron, Brandeisen.

current, 1. Strömung; 2. Strom (elektrisch); - *chart*, Stromkarte; - *sailing*, S-segeln.

curtain of an awning, Seitenkleid eines Sonnensegels.

curtains, Feuerhemd.

curtal axe, Entermesser.

curve, 1. Krümmung; 2. Schnitt eines Schiffes; - *of weight*, Gewichtskurve; - *templet*, Kurvenlineal.

curved frame, gebogenes Spant.

cusps, Hörner der Mondsichel.

custom free, zollfrei; - *house*, Zollamt; - - *clearance* od. *c. h. entry*, Klarierung; *c. h. officer*, Zollbeamter - *regulations*, Zollverordnungen.

customable, zollpflichtig.

customs authorities, Zollbehörde; - *inwards*, Eingangszoll; - *lights*, Zollaternen; - *outwards*, Ausgangszoll; *uses and - of the sea*, Seegebräuche.

cut a feather, mit dem Bug Schaum aufwerfen; - *a sail*, ein Segel herablassen; - *a stick*, desertieren; - *and run*, den Anker schlippen und fliehen; *there is c. a. r.!* So, nun kannst du mir nachpfeifen! - *away the masts*, die Masten kappen; - *down a vessel*, ein Schiff rasieren.

cut of the jib, Schnitt des Klüvers; *to know a person by the c. o. his j.*, es jemandem an der Nase ansehen, wer er ist; - *off steam*, abgesperrter Dampf; - *off the steam*, den D. absperren; - *off valve*, Absperrventil; - *out*, Sicherung; *to - - a vessel*, ein Schiff im Hafen durch Bootsattacke aufbringen; - *splice*, Buchtsplissung; *to - the cable*, das Ankertau kappen.

cutlass, Entermesser.
cutter, 1. Kutter; 2. Schneide-
stahl; - *brig*, Kutterbrigg; -
rigging, K-zeug.
cutting away wreck, Kappen
von Trümmern.
cutting-down-line, Konstruk-
tionslinie über der Ober-
kante der Bodenwrangen
und des Todtholzes.
cutting nippers, Beißzange.
cutwater, Gallionsschegg.
cyclone, Zyklon.
cylinder, Zylinder; - *admission port*, Eintrittskanal des
Zylinders; - *boiler*, Walzenkessel; - *boring machine*,
Zylinder-Bohrmaschine; -
bottom, Z-boden; - *cock*, Z-
Abblashahn; - *column*, Z-
säule; - *cover*, Z-deckel; - -
bolt, Z-d-bolzen; *c. c. b. nut*,
Z-d-b-mutter; *c. c. stud*, Z-
d-stiftschraube; - *drain cock*,
Z-Entwässerungshahn; *c. d.*
pipe, Z-E-w-rohr; - *escape*

valve, Z-Sicherheitsventil; *c.
e. v. load*, Z-S.-Belastung; *c.
e. v. spindle*, Z-S.-spindel; *c.
e. v. spring*, Z-S.-feder; - *exhaust port*, Z-Austrittskanal;
- *face*, Z.-Schieberfläche; -
flange, Z-flansch; - *head*, Z-
deckel; - *jacket*, Z-mantel;
- - *pipe*, Z-m-rohr; - *jaw*, Z-
rand; - *lagging*, Z-beklei-
dung; - *lid*, Z-deckel; - *liner*,
Z-büchse; - *lubricator*, Z-
Schmierbüchse; - *oil*, Z-öl;
- - *cup*, Z-Schmiergefäß; -
port, Z-Dampfeintrittskanal;
- *relief valve*, Z-Sicherheitsventil; - *side rod*, Z-Pleuel-
stange; - *stuffing box*, Z-
Stopfbüchse; *c. s. b. gland*,
Z-S.-deckel; - *top*, Z.-deckel;
- *trunnions*, Z.-Trunkzapfen;
- *vacuum pipe*, Z.-Vakuum-
rohr.
cylindrical boiler, Zylinderkessel; - *valve*, Zylinderven-
til; - *wheel*, Stirnrad.
cylindriform, zylinderförmig.

D.

dab of the compass needle,
Kompaßhütchen.
dagger knee, Diagonalknie; -
piece, D-streber der Schlagbetten; - *plank*, oberster D-
s-d.S.; - *wood*, D-s-d.S.
daily rate of the chronometer,
Chronometergang; - *service*,
täglicher Verkehr.
dam, Damm, Staudamm; - *of
a harbour*, Hafendamm; - *of
stones along a river*, Ufer-
damm.
damage, Beschädigung, Havarie, Schaden; - *by jettison
and sacrifice for common
safety*, Schaden durch Seewurf und Aufopferung be-
hufs Rettung aus gemein-
samer Gefahr; - *repairs*,
Schadenreparatur; - *report*,

S-bericht; - *survey*, S-besich-
tigung; - *to engines in refloating*, Maschinenschaden
beim Abbringen des Schiffes;
- *to machinery*, Maschinenschaden; - *to or loss of sails*,
Schaden resp. Verlust an
Segeln.
damaged by grounding, &c.,
durch Angrundkommen etc.
beschädigt.
damages and costs, Schäden
mit Unkosten.
damp the fire, das Feuer
dämpfen.
damper, Dämpfer, Register; -
gear, R-vorrichtung; - *in
funnel*, Schornstein-R.
dandy, 1. Jacht mit Treiber-
mast; 2. kleines Heckboot.
danger lamps, Notlampen.

dangers of the sea, Gefahren der Seefahrt.

Daniell's stop cock, D.'s. Doppelhahn.

dark lantern, Blendlaterne; - *weather,* unsichtiges Wetter.

dash. gegenprallen; - *plate,* Schlagwasserplatte.

dasher block, Block für die Flaggenleine.

dashing and breaking of the sea, das Hin- und Herwogen des Meeres.

david od. *davit* od. *davitt,* Davit; - *chock,* Klotz; - *collar,* Davithalter; - *guy,* D-geie; - *rope,* D-tau; - *socket,* D-spur; - *topping lift,* D-ständer.

davy, Davy (d. i. seetüchtiges Beiboot); - *Jones,* Teufel; - *Jones'locker,* Meer; *to go to ---,* ertrinken.

day of entry, Tag der Einklarierung; - *service,* Tagdienst; - *shift,* Etmal; - *signal,* Tagsignal; - *watch,* T-wache; - *work,* T-schicht od. Schichtarbeit. - *worker,* S-arbeiter.

day's account, Besteck; - *of grace,* Respekttage; - *work,* 1. Etmal; 2. Mittagsbesteck; *to make up the --,* das Besteck aufmachen.

dead, to be on a - beat, recht gegen den Wind ankreuzen; - *block,* großer Stagblock; - *calm,* totenstill, Totenstille; - *door,* Blendtür; - - *of a scuttle,* Blinde eines Seitenfensters; - *eye,* Jungfernblock; - - *of the crowfoot,* Sprietblock; - *flat.* Nullspant; - *freight,* Fautfracht; - *light,* Stückpfortenklappe; - *men,* Ohrbummeln; - *neap,* Nipptide; - *on end,* recht von vorn; - *plate of furnace,* Kopfplatte der Feuerbüchse; - *point,* toter Punkt; - *reckoning.* 1. gegißtes Besteck; 2. Schiffsort; - *rising,* der Schlag des Schiffes von vorn bis hinten; - *ropes,* stehendes Tauwerk; - *sheave,* Halbscheibe; - *slow,* so langsam wie möglich; - *steam,* durch den Zylinder abgehender Dampf; - *water,* Totwasser; - *weight,* Eigengewicht; - - *carrying capacity,* Tragfähigkeit; - - *load,* Gewichtsbelastung; - - *safety valve,* Sicherheitsventil mit Gewichtsbelastung; - *wind,* Gegenwind; - *wood,* Aufklotzung; - - *bolt,* A.-bolzen; - *wood knee,* Knie auf dem Totholz; - *works,* Schiffsteile über dem Wasser; - *wreck,* abandonniertes Wrack.

deaden the ship's way, das Schiff außer Fahrt bringen; - *the blow,* den Stoß abschwächen.

deading, Kesselbekleidung.

debarkation, Ausschiffung.

decayed, verfault.

deck, Deck; - *beam,* Deckbalken; *d. b. angle bar,* D.-winkel; *d. b. clamp,* Deck-Unterbalkweger; *d. b. shelf,* Deckbalkweger; *d. b. stringer,* Deckbalkenstringer; *d. b. s. plate.* D.-platte; *d. b. tie plate,* Deckbalken - Längsschiene; - *bolt.* Deckbolzen; - *boy,* Decksjunge; - *breasthook,* Deckbugband; - *cambering,* Katzenrücken; - *cargo,* Deckladung; - - *took full charge of the deck,* D.-beherrschte das Deck; - *damage,* Deckschaden; - *dowel.* Deckpfropfen; - *ends,* Enden der Deckplanken; - *erections,* Deckaufbauten; - *fastening,* Deckbefestigung; - *fittings,* Deckeinrichtungen; - *flat,* Deckbelag; - *framing,* Deckgebälk; - *hand,* Matrose, Schiffsknecht; - *hook,* Deckl and; - - *bolt,* D.-bolzen; - *house.* Deckhaus; - - *coaming,* D.-süll; *d. h. c. angle bar,* D.-s-winkel; *d. h. window,* D.-fenster; - *light,* Deckglas;

- *line*, Decklinie; - *load*, Deckladung; - *log book*, Deckschiffsjournal; - *passenger*, Deckspassagier; - *pillar*, Deckstütze; - *pillaring*, Deckverstützung; - *pipe*, Decksklüse; - *plank*, Deckplanke; - *planking*, Deckbeplankung; - *plate*, Deckplatte; - *plating*, Deckbeplattung; - *rising*, Aufbug; - *rivet*, Deckniete; - *saloon*, Decksalon; - *scrubber*, Deckschrubber; - *seam*, Decknaht; - *sheet*, Binnenschoot; - *shelf*, oberster Balkwäger; - *stanchion*, Deckstütze; - *stores*, Deckgegenstäude; - *stopper*, Deckstopper; - *stringer*, Deckstringer; *d. s. angle bar*, D.-winkel; *d. s. plate*, eiserner Wassergang; - *structures*, Deckaufbauten; - *swept*, alles von Deck weggeschlagen; - *tackle*, Deckstalje; - *transom*, Heckbalken; - *wash hose*, Deckwaschschlauch; *d. w. pump*, D-w-pumpe; - *with a break*, gebrochenes Deck.

decked, gedeckt.

declination, Deklination; - *compass*, D.-Busole; - *map*, D.-karte.

decline, sacken (die Sonne).

decorated with bunting, Flaggengala.

decreasing motion, verzögerte Bewegung.

deduction for new, Abzug für Reparatur (ca. ¹/₃); - *from cost of repairs*, Abzüge von R.-kosten.

deep floors, Piekstücke; - *frame*, hohes Spant; - *going vessel*, tiefgehendes Schiff; - *in the hold*, tief gebaut; - *lead*, Tieflot; - - *line*, T.-leine; - *laden* od. *loaded*, tief geladen; - *neap*, höhere Nippflut; - *sea*, Tiefsee; *d. s. cable*, T.-kabel; *d. s. exploring*, T.-forschung; *d. s. fishing*, Hochseefischerei; *d. s. lead*, Tief-

wasserlot; *d. s. l. line*, Tieflotleine; *d. s. pilot*, Seelotse; *d. s. reel*, Rolle zur Tieflotleine; *d. s. sounding*, Tiefseelotung; - *tank*, Hintertank; *d. t. copper bend*, kupfernes Verbindungsrohr des H.; - *water line*, Tiefwasserlinie.

deepening, 1. auf größere Tiefen kommen; 2. ausbaggern, vertiefen.

deeps, Zwischenräume zwischen den Marken der Lotleine.

defect, Beschädigung, Fehler, Schaden.

defective, fehlerhaft, mangelhaft; - *compass*, fehlerhafter Kompaß; - *construction*, fehlerhafte Konstruktion.

deficiency, Manko.

deflection, Deviation.

deformation, Entstellung.

degree of latitude, Breitengrad; - - *longitude*, Längengrad.

degrees and minutes, Grade und Minuten.

delayed, aufgehalten.

delivering roller, Rolle, worüber das Tauwerk läuft.

delivery cock, Ausgußhahn; - *hose*, Druckrohrschlauch; - *order*, Ab- od. Auslieferungsschein; - *pipe*, Druckrohr; - *pipes*, D.-leitung; - *space*, Druckraum; - *valve*, Druckventil; *d. v. box*, D-v-gehäuse; *d. v. chest*, D-v-kasten; *d. v. guard*, D-v-Hubbegrenzer; *d. v. seat*, D-v-sitz.

demurrage, 1. Überliegetage; 2. Liegegeld.

density of steam, Dichtigkeit des Dampfes.

dented, eingebeult.

denting, Einbeulung.

dents, full of -, verbeult.

departed latitude, abgefahrene Breite; - *longitude*, a. Länge.

departure, 1. Abfahrt; 2. Abweichung; *to take a -*, den Schiffsort bei der Abfahrt bestimmen.

deployment of force, Kraftentwickelung.

depositing dock, Vorrichtung zur Hebung der Schiffe auf die Werft.

deposits, Kesselstein.

depreciation, 1. Wertverminderung; 2. Herabsetzung der Klassifikation.

depress the pole, den Pol für das Auge näher bringen.

depth, 1. Tiefe (des Raumes, Schiffes, Wassers); 2. Heiß od. Tiefe (eines Segels); 3. Zahnlänge (eines Zahnrades); 4. Höhe (des Kiels); *- for tonnage,* Vermessungstiefe.

derangement, Verwirrung.

derelict, 1. herrenlos; 2. verlassenes Wrack.

dereliction, das Abandonnieren.

derelicts, Wrackgüter.

derrick, Ladebaum; *- chain,* L.-kette; *-chocks and lashings,* Ladebaumkeile und Verlaschungen; *- crane,* Kran mit Auslieger; *- crutch stays,* Ladebaum-Krückenstützen; *- fall,* Dirkläufer; *- guy,* Ladebaumgeie; *d. g. block,* L.-block: *d. g. hoop,* Band der Ladebaumgeie; *d. pendant hoop,* Hangerband des Ladebaums; *- span,* Ladebaum-Doppelhanger.

descent of the piston, Niedergang des Kolbens.

descry land, Land erspähen.

desicated, aufgetrocknet.

despatch, 1. Depesche; 2. absenden, abfertigen, Abfertigung;3.schnelle Beförderung, Schnelligkeit; *- money,* Beförderungsgeld.

despatched vessel, abgefertigtes Schiff.

destination, Bestimmungsort.

destined for, bestimmt nach.

detachable propeller blade, abnehmbarer od. verstellbarer Schraubenflügel.

detaching hook, Auslösehaken.

detail of duty, Anordnungen für den Nachtdienst.

detained, aufgehalten.

detector, 1. Alarmapparat; 2. Meldeapparat f. verborgene Torpedos.

deterioration of thickness, Abnahme der Materialstärke.

determa, Guayanaholz.

deviate, abweichen.

deviation, Abweichung; *- book,* Kompaßjournal; *- buoy,* Deviationsboje; *- of a vessel from the voyage,* die Abweichung eines Schiffes von der übernommenen Reise.

devil's claw, Kettenstopper.

dhow, arabisches Küstenfahrzeug.

diagonal, 1. Diagonalband; 2. Diagonale; *- built,* diagonal gebaut; *- ceiling,* Diagonal-Wegerung; *- cylinder,* D.-Zylinder; *- doubling,* D.-Doppelhaut; *-engine,* schrägliegende Maschine; *- fastening,* Diagonalbefestigung; *- frame,* D-spant; *- knee,* D-knie; *- lines,* die Senten im Spannriß; *- of a gaff sail,* die Diagonale vom Schoothorn zur Klau eines Gaffsegels; *- planking,* Diagonalbeplankung; *- planks,* D-planken; *- plate,* D-schiene; *- ribbands,* Scherspannsenten; *- sheating,* Diagonalhaut; *- stay,* Kreuzanker; *- strength,* Diagonalverband; *- strengthening,* D-verstärkung; *- system,* D-verband; *- tie plate,* D-schiene; *- timbers,* D-spanten.

diagram, Riß, Diagramm; *- of the indicator,* Indikatorkurve.

dial, Zifferblatt; *- compass,* Handkompaß; *- counter,* Hubzähler mit Zifferblatt; *- of a steam gauge,* Zeigerblatt eines Manometers.

diameter, Durchmesser; *- of piston,* Kolbendurchmesser;

- *of propeller,* Schrauben-durchmesser; - *of rivet,* Nietendurchmesser.
diamond knot, Fallreepskno-ten; - *plate,* Diamantplatte; - *pointed chisel,* D-meißel.
diaphragm plate, Trennungs-platte.
die, Gewindeschneidekluppe; - *out,* ausgehen (Feuer).
difference in latitude, Breiten-unterschied; - - *longitude,* Längenunterschied.
differential block, Differenzial-Flaschenzug; - *manometer,* D.-Manometer.
dig out of the ice, loseisen.
dike, Deich; - *dam,* Stack.
dilatation, Ausdehnung.
diminishing planking, Ver-jüngungsplanken; - *strake,* V-gang.
dingey od. *dinghy* od. *dingy,* kleines Boot.
dining room, Speisesalon.
dint, Beule, einbeulen.
dip, eintauchen, am Horizont verschwinden; - *of the hori-zon,* Kimmtiefe; - *of the needle,* Inklination der Mag-netnadel; - *of the paddle wheels,* Tauchung der Schaufelräder; - *the flag,* die Flagge dippen; - *the sail,* beim Lavieren die Segel ab-wechselnd herabnehmen und aufziehen.
dipper, Plump (langer Wasser-becher an einer Schnur); 2. Schaufelbagger.
dipping compass, Inklinations-bussole; - *ladle,* Pechkelle; - *lug,* Luggersegel zum Schiften; - *needle,* Inklina-tionsnadel.
direct acting, direkteWirkung; - - *engine,* d. wirkende Ma-schine; - *course,* General-kurs; - *impact,* gerader Stoß; *to - the navigation,* die Schiffsführung leiten.
dirk, Seitengewehr.
dirt od. *dirty weather,* stür-misches Wetter.

disabled, unbrauchbar ge-worden, havariert; - *engine,* gebrauchsunfähige Maschi-ne; - *ship,* seeuntüchtiges Schiff.
disappear, auswandern, aus Sicht kommen.
disc, Scheibe; - *crank,* Kurbel-scheibe; - *valve,* Scheiben-ventil.
discharge, 1. löschen, Aus-laden; 2. abmustern, ent-lassen, Entlassung; 3. Aus-guß; - *cock,* Abflußhahn; - *orifice,* Ausguß; - *pipe,* A.-rohr; - *the pilot,* den Lotsen absetzen; - *valve,* Ausguß-ventil; *d. v. box,* A.-v-ge-häuse; *d. v. cover,* A.-v-deckel; *d. v. seat,* A.-v-sitz; *d. v. spindle,* A.-v-spindel.
discharger, Löscher.
discharging berth, Löschplatz; - *days,* L-tage; - *expenses,* L-geld; - *gear,* L-geschirr; - *permit,* L-erlaubnis; - *place* od. - *wharf,* L-platz.
disconnect, ausrücken, ent-kuppeln.
disconnected deck erections, nicht mit einander verbun-dene Aufbauten.
disconnecting gear, Entkuppe-lungsvorrichtung.
discover the land, Land in Sicht bekommen.
disembark, ausschiffen.
disembarkation, Ausschiffung.
disembogue, aus einem Kanale od. einer Bucht ausmünden resp. hinausfahren.
disemboguement, Ausmün-dung.
disengage the gear, die Ma-schinerie ausrücken.
disengaging gear, Ausrück-vorrichtung; - *of the eccen-tric rod,* Excentrikstangen-Ausrückung.
dish plate, Schaumlöffel.
disk see disc.
dislodge the anchor, den Anker vom Grunde frei hieven.

dismantled, abgetakelt, entmastet.

dismasted, entmastet.

dispatch see despatch.

displacement, Wasserverdrängung; - *scale*, W.-Skala; - *tonnage*, W.-Tonnengehalt.

display the colours od. *ensign* od. *flag*, die Flagge entfalten.

disposition plan, Dispositionsplan.

disrate, 1. ausrangieren(Schiff); 2. degradieren (Mannschaft).

disrespect, Achtungsverletzung.

distackle, abtakeln.

distance, Entfernung; - *freight*, Distanzfracht; - *made good*, Generaldistanz; - *of vision*, Sehweite; - *run*, gelaufene Distanz.

distant, entfernt; - *trade*, lange Fahrt.

distinguishing marks, Rangabzeichen; - *pendant*, Unterscheidungswimpel; - *signal*, U-s-signal; -*vane*, U-s-wimpel.

distortion, Verzerrung.

distress at sea, Seenot; - *flag*, Notflagge; - *shot*, Notschuß; - *signal*, Notsignal.

distressed seamen, notleidende Seeleute; - *ship*, Schiff in Not.

distributing box, Schieberkasten; - *cock*, Steuerungshahn; - *lever*, St-hebel; - *mechanism*, Steuerung zur Dampfverteilung; *d. m. of cocks*, Hahnsteuerung; *d. m. of slide valves*, Schiebersteuerung; *d. m. of valves*, Ventilsteuerung; - *pipe*, Dampfverteilungsrohr; - *regulator*, innere Steuerung; - *valve motion*, Steuerung.

distribution of steam, Dampfverteilung; - *of weight*, Gewichtsverteilung.

disturbed sea, unruhige See.

ditty bag, Nähbeutel; - *box*, Utensilienkasten.

diver, Taucher.

divider, Teilzirkel.

diving, mit dem Bug untertauchen; - *bell*, Taucherglocke; - *case*, T-kasten; - *dress*, T-anzug; - *rudder*, Horizontalsteuer; - *suit*, Taucheranzug.

division plate, Trennungsplatte; - - *of condenser*, T-rippe des Kondensators.

Docas men, indische Dockarbeiter.

dock, Dock, docken; - *authorities*, Dockbehörden; -*banks*, D-bänke; - *block*, D-winde; - *crane*, D-kran; - *dues* od. -*duties*, D-geld; - *entrance*, D-eingang; - *gate*, Schleusenpforte; - - *man*, S-wächter; - *master*, D-meister; - *pilot*, D-lotse od. Hafenlotse; - *rent*, Dockgebühr; - *sill*, D-drempel; - *up*, das Schothorn eines Segels aufgeien; - *walloper*, Dockbummler; - *warehouse*, Packhof; - *yard*, Arsenal, Schiffswerft; - - *matties*, Arsenalarbeiter.

dockage, Dockgebühren.

dockers, Dock- od. Hafenarbeiter; - *strike*, Streik der H.

docking, das Docken.

dodge a vessel, ein Schiff bewachen.

dodging, ganz langsam fahren.

dog, Riegel, Träger; - *cleat*, Klampe der Schlagbettung; - *of manhole door*, Mannlochdeckelriegel; - *of sludge hole door*, Schlammlochdeckelriegel; - *on crown of combustion chamber*, Feuerkammerdeckenträger; -*shore*, Schlagbettungsstrebe; -*stay*, Riegelbolzen; -*stopper*, Kettenstopper; - *strips for the brace block*, Brassenstroppe an den Rahnocken; - *strop*, zwei in einander gespließte Stroppen mit eingebundenen Kauschen; - *vane*, Verklicker; - *watch*, Abendwache.

dog's ear, Bucht eines Taues; - *tail*, Kleiner Bär.
dogger, Doggerboot.
doldrums, Äquatorialkalmen.
dolphin strikers, Stampfstage.
dolphins, 1. Pfähle; 2. Leguane (Taukränze). [Domhemd.
dome, Dampfdom; - *cover*,
domestic navigation, Küstenschiffahrt.
donkey, 1. Dampfpumpe; 2. Kleiderkasten; - *blow down cock*, Hülfskessel - Abblashahn; - *boiler*, Hülfskessel; - - *feed pipe*, H.-Speiserohr; - - *recess*, H.-nische; - *check valve*, Dampfpumpen-Speiseventil; - - - *cover*, D.-S.-deckel; - *circulating pipe*, D.-Zirkulationsrohr; - *crane*, Dampfkran; - *delivery space*, Dampfpumpen-Druckraum; - *discharge valve*, Dampfpumpen Ausgußventil; - *drain pipe*, D.-Entwässerungsrohr.
donkey engine, Dampfpumpe; - - *connecting rod*, D.-Pleuelstange; *d. e. c. r. bolt*, D.-P.-Bolzen; *d. e. c. bottom end keep*, D.-Kurbelzapfen-Lagerschalendeckel; *d. e. c. r. b. e. liner*, D.-Pleuelstangen-fußfutter; *d. e. c. r. top end keep*, D.- Kreuzkopflagerschalendeckel; *d. e. crank pin bolt*, D.-Kurbelzapfenlagerbolzen; *d. e. c. p. brasses*, D.-K-z-l-schalen; *d. e. c. shaft*, D.-Kurbelwelle; *d. e. c. s. bearing*, D.-K-w-lager; *d. e. c. s. b. bolt*, D.-K-w-l-bolzen; *d. e. c. s. bearing brasses*, D.-K-w-l-schalen; *d. e. c. s. bearing keep*, D.-K-w-l-deckel; *d. e. c. s. b. k. bolt*, D.-K-w-l-d-bolzen; *d. e. crosshead bolt*, D.-Kreuzkopflagerbolzen; *d. e. c. brasses*, D.-K-k-l-schalen; *d. e. c. cylinder*, D.-Zylinder; *d. e. c. cover*, D.-Z.-deckel; *d. e. c. c. bolt*, D.-Z.-d-bolzen; *d. e. cylinder drain pipe*, D.-Z.-Entwässe-

rungsrohr; *d. e. delivery valve*, D.-Druckventil; *d. e. eccentric*, D.-Excenter; *d. e. e. bolt*, D.-E.-bolzen; *d. e. e. brasses*, D.-E.-Lagerschalen; *d. e. e. rod*, D.-E.-stange; *d. e. e. sheave*, D.-E.-scheibe; *d. e. e. strap*, D.-E.-bügel; *d. e. e. s. liner*, D.-E.-b-futter; *d. e. exhaust pipe*, D.-Dampfablaßrohr; *d. e. piston*, D.-kolben; *d. e. p. rod*, D.-K-stange; *d. e. p. r. crosshead*, D.-K-s-Kreuzkopf; *d. e. p. r. stuffing box*, D.-K-s-Stopfbüchse; *d. e. p. r. s. b. gland*, D.-K-s-S-b-deckel; *d. e. slide valve*, D.-Schieber; *d. e. starting valve*, D.-Anlaßventil; *d. e. stop valve*, D-Absperrventil; *d. e. valve*, D.-ventil; *d. e. v. casing*, D.-Schieberkasten; *d. e. v. c. door*, D.-S.-deckel; *d. e. v. rod*, D.-Schieberstange; *d. e. v. r. stuffing box*, D.-S.-Stopfbüchse; *d. e. v. r. s. b. gland*, D.-S.-S.-deckel.
donkey feed check valve, Dampfpumpen-Speiseventil; - - *pipe*, D.-Speiserohr; - *fly wheel*, D.-Schwungrad; - *frigate*, gedeckte Korvette; - *funnel*, Schornstein d. Hülfskessels; - *injection pipe*, Dampfpumpen-Injektionsrohr; *d. i. valve*, D.-Injektionsventil; - *man*, Donkeymann; - *pump*, Dampfpumpe.
donkey pump bucket, Dampfpumpen-Kolben; *d. p. b. ring*, D.-K-ring; *d. p. b. valve*, D.-K-ventil; *d. p. b. v. seat*, D.-K-v-sitz; *d. p. delivery valve*, D.-Druckventil; *d. v. seat*, D.-D.-sitz; *d. p. foot valve*, D.-Fußventil; *d. p. f. v. seat*, D.-Saugventilsitz; *d. p. gear*, D.-geschirr; *d. p. gland*, D.-Stopfbüchsendeckel; *d. p. head valve*, D.-Druckventil; *d. p. rod*, D.-stange; *d. p. stuffing box gland*, D.-Stopfbüchsendeckel; *d. p. suction*

valve, D.-Saugventil: *d. p. s. v. seat*, D.-S.-sitz; *d. p. top valve*, D.-Druckventil; *d. p. t. v. seat*, D.-D.-sitz; *d. p. valve*, D.-ventil; *d.p.v.seat*,D.-v-sitz.

donkey sea suction cock key, Dampfpumpen-Saugehahnschlüssel; *d. s. s. rose plate*, D.-saugesieb; - *steam pipe*, D.-Zuleitungsrohr; - *suction pipe*, D.-Saugerohr; *d. s. space*, D.-S-raum.

door, 1. Deckel; 2. Tür; - *mat*, Fußmatte; - *of fire box*, Feuerkammertür; - *sill*, Türschwelle.

dot a line, punktieren.

double a cape, ein Kap umsegeln; - *a vessel*, ein Schiff mit einer Spiekerhaut versehen; *d. acting*, doppelwirkend; *d. a. air pump*, doppelwirkende Luftpumpe; *d. a. circulating pump*, d-w-Zirkulationspumpe; *d. a. engine*, d-w-Maschine; *d. a. pump*,d-w-Pumpe;-*and single fastening*, doppelte und einfache Befestigung; - *angle bar*, doppelter Winkel; *d. a. b. bilge keelson*, Doppelwinkel-Kimmkielschwein; *d. a. b. keelson*, D.-Kielschwein; *d. a. b. side keelson*, D.-Seitenkielschwein; *d. a. iron*, doppeltes Winkeleisen; - *banked boat*, doppelrudriges Boot; *d. b. oar*, kurzer Riemen; - *bar link*, Spurkulisse; - *benched boat*, doppelruderiges Boot; - *bend*, doppelter Flaggenstich; - *bitted*, mit zwei Rundtörns belegt; - *black wall hitch*, doppelter Hakenschlag; - *block*, d. Block; - *boat*, Doppelboot; - *bodied capstan*, doppeltes Gangspill; - *bollard*, Doppelpoller; - *bottom*, D-boden; *d. b. aft*, hinterer D-b-; *d. b. forward*, vorderer D-b-; *d. b. on ordinary floors*, D-b- mit Längsträgern auf gewöhnlichen Bodenwran-

gen; *d. b. test*, Prüfung des D-b-; - *butt strap*, doppelte Stoßplatte; - *capstan*, d. Gangspill; - *clinker fashion*, doppelklinkerartiger Bau; - *combustion chamber boiler*, Kessel mit doppelter Feuerkammer; - *crank*, doppelte Kurbel; - *crown knot*, türkischer Knoten; - *cylinder steam engine*, zweicylindrige Dampfmaschine; - *decker*, Zweidecker; - *diamond knot*, englischer Fallreepsknoten; - *dredger*, doppelte Baggermaschine; - *ended boiler*, Doppelkessel; *d. e. spanner*, Schlüssel mit D-enden; - *ender*, vorn und hinten egales Boot; - *expansion engine*, zweifache Expansionsmaschine; - *fastening*, doppelte Befestigung; - *floor*, Bauchstück; - *flue boiler*, Kessel mit zwei Feuerröhren; - *frame*, Doppelspant; - *futtock*, doppelter Auflanger; - *gear*, Doppelgeschirr; - *headed capstan*, doppeltes Gangspill; - *light*, Doppelleuchtfeuer; - *ported slide valve*, Zweiwegschieber; *d. p. v.*, Doppelpfortenventil; - *purchase winch*, doppelte Winde; - *reefed*, doppelt gerefft; - *reversed angle bar*, d. gekehrter Winkel ;- *riveting*, doppelte Nietung; - *scored block*, Block mit Doppelreep; - *scull*, mit zwei Riemen wricken; - *seat valve*, Doppelsitzventil; - *sheaved block*, zweischeibiger Block; - *shroud knot*, doppelter Wantknoten; - *Spanish burton*, Wientakel; - *steering wheel*, Doppelsteuerrad; - *strap* od. *strop*, 1. Doppelstropp; 2. mit D. versehen; - *thimble*, Doppelkausche; - *tides*, doppelte Schicht; - *timber*, Bauchstück; - *T-iron*, doppeltes T-eisen; - *topsails*, doppelte Marssegel; - *wall*,

d. Schauermannsknoten; *d. w. and crown knot,* d. Fallreepsknoten; *d. w. k.,* d. Schauermannsknoten; - *whip,* d. Jollentau.

doubler, Umschiffer.

doubling, Doppelhaut; - *nail,* Hauptnagel; - *plate,* Verdoppelungsplatte; - *strake,* V-d-gang.

dough boy, Teichkloß.

douse, plötzlich loswerfen; - *a sail,* ein Segel streichen.

dousing chock, Kalb des Binnenvorstevens.

Dover fees, Abgabe beim Passieren der Straße von Calais.

dovetail, 1. einschwalben; 2. Schwalbenschwanz; - *cutter,* Bohrenschneide; - *plate,* Schwalbenschwanzplatte.

dovetailing, Schwalbenschwanzverbindung.

dow, arabischss Küstenfahrzeug.

dowal od. *dowel,* 1. Zylinderzapfen; 2. Dübel; 3. verdübeln; - *borer,* Dobelbohrer.

dowling pin, Zylinderzapfen.

down along, längs der Küste; - *by the head,* sich nach vorn senkend; - *east,* weit weg nach Ost; - *fall,* Stromschnelle; - *fore sail!* Runter mit der Fock! - *haul,* 1. Niederholer; 2. Segel niederholen! - - *block,* Niederholerblock; - *hauler,* N-h-; - *killock!* Laß den Bootsanker fallen! - *oars,* die Riemen fallen lassen; - *stroke,* Kolbenniedergang; - *the helm!* Ruder in Lee! - *the main tack!* Großhals daal! - *the river,* flußabwärts; - *the sound,* den Sund hinunter; - *the wind,* mit dem Winde; - *the yard!* streicht die Rahe! - *with the helm!* Ruder in Lee!

downs, Dünen.

dowsing chock, Klüsenband.

drabler od. *drablet,* das untere Bonnet.

draft see draught.

drag, 1. Schleppnetz; 2. Dreghaken, dreggen; 3. mitgehen, triftig sein; - *anchor,* Treibanker; - *bar,* Kuppelstange; - *boat,* Baggerboot; - *for,* fischen nach; - *link,* Zugstange; - *net,* Schleppnetz; - *rope,* Dreggtau; - *sail,* Treibsegel.

dragging anchor, schleppender Anker; - *her moorings,* mit der Vertäuung triftig.

drags, das Mitgeschleppte.

drain, Abzugskanal; - *board,* Tellerbord; - *cock,* Entwässerungshahn; - - *gear,* E.-vorrichtung; - *pipe,* E-w-rohr.

draught, 1. Schiffsplan; 2. Tiefgang; 3. Zug (im Schornstein etc.); - *marks,* Ahming.

draw, 1. tief gehen; 2. ziehen (Segel); - *aft,* achterlich gehen (Wind); - *ahead,* vorlich gehen (Wind); - *ashes,* Asche ziehen; - *asunder,* auspflükken (alte Taue); - *close,* anziehen (Schraube); - *in on top,* oben einholen (Schiffbau); - *in the tail shaft,* die Schraubenwelle einziehen; - *the fires,* die Feuer auslöschen; - *the sheets aft,* die Schoten abholen; - *up into a line,* sich in Linie arrangieren; - *up water,* Wasser schöpfen; - *water,* Lastigkeit haben.

drawback, Ausfuhrprämie.

draw bucket, Schlagpütze; - *gate,* Schleusentor; - *screw,* große Ziehschraube.

drawing bucket, Schlagpütze; - *points,* Zeichen; - *sails,* Wind auffangende Segel.

dredge, baggern; - *boat,* Austernfischerboot; - *down the river,* über Steuer mit dem Strome und schleppendem Anker flußabwärts fahren.

dredger, Bagger; - *bucket,* B-eimer; - *ladder,* B-leiter; - *ladle,* B-löffel.

dredging boat, Baggerboot; - *bucket,* B-eimer; - *engine,* Bagger; - *ladder,* B-leiter; - *machine.* Bagger; - *plant,* B-Maschinerie.

dredgings, das Ausgebaggerte.

dredgy. Gespenst eines Ertrunkenen.

dress a ship with bunting, mit Flaggen und Wimpeln schmücken; - - - *with overall flags,* über die Toppen beflaggen; - *up,* abrauhen.

dressing, Flaggengala; - *with masthead flags,* kleine F.; - *with overall f.,* über die Toppen beflaggt; - *with up and down f.,* über die Nokken b.

dribble. Staubregen.

dried up, aufgetrocknet.

drift. 1. Stromversetzung; 2. Lochdorn; - *anchor,* Treibanker; - *angle,* Driftwinkel; - *bolt,* Jagdbolzen; - *current,* Triftstrom; - *fishery,* Treibnetzfischerei; - *hoop,* Treibband des Mastes; - *ice,* Treibeis; - *keel,* Schlingerkiel; - *of a current,* Geschwindigkeit und Richtung des Stromes; - *of a vessel,* die treibend zurückgelegte Strecke; - *pieces,* die festen Stützen des Fallreeps; - *rail,* der zerbrochene Gang; - *sail,* Treibsegel; - *way,* Abtrift; - *wood,* Treibholz.

drifter, Treibnetzfischer.

drifting of ice, Eisgang.

drifts. Schanzkleid der Wandering.

drill, Drehbohrer, bohren; - *mast,* Exerziermast; - *ship,* E-schiff; - *stand,* Bohrstock.

drilling machine, Bohrmaschine.

drip pan, Oeltropfschale; - *pipe,* Entwässerungsrohr.

dripping pan, Bratpfanne.

drive, 1. treiben, Abtrift haben; 2. eintreiben (Pfahl etc.); -

a-hull, vor Topp und Takel treiben; - *ashore,* auf Strand t.; - *at anchor,* den Anker schleppen; - *bodily to leeward,* dwars nach Lee zu abtreiben; - - *upon the coast,* d. nach Land zu treiben; - *far from the course,* verwehen; - *in the oakum with a horsing iron,* den Werg mit dem Klameieisen in die Nähte eintreiben; - *to leeward,* in Lee sacken; - *under bare poles,* vor Topp und Takel treiben; - *up a river,* flußaufwärts t.; - *upon the anchor,* auf dem Anker t.; - *winches,* an den Winschen arbeiten; - *with the anchor,* mit dem Anker treiben; - *with the tide,* mit der Tide treiben.

driven ashore, auf Strand getrieben; - *by the current* od. *tide,* durch Strom od. Flut abgetrieben; - *far from the right course,* weit vom richtigen Kurse abgetrieben.

driver, Treiber; - *boom,* Besahnbaum; - *halliard,* Treiberfall; - *yard,* Brotwinner; - *of the spring catch,* der erste Sektor der Hebelsteuerung.

driving anchor, Treibanker; - *axle,* T-achse; - *collar,* Druckring; - *rain,* peitschender Regen; - *rod,* Schubstange; - *shaft,* Antriebswelle; - *wheel,* Treibrad.

drizzle od. *drizzling rain,* Sprühregen.

droger od. *drogher,* Küstenbarke.

droghing, Küstenfahrt.

drogue, Schleppholz.

dromoscope, Kursmesser.

drop. 1. Tiefe (des Segels); 2. Lauf (des Decks); 3. die nach unten gerichtete Bucht eines Holzes; - *astern,* 1. achteraussacken; 2. zurückbleiben; - *bolt,* Schloßbolzen; - *down the river*, flußabwärts treiben; - *keel*, Schwert; - *strake*, Splißgang; - *pawl*, Sperrkegel; - *the anchor*, den Anker fallen lassen; - - - *under foot*, d. A. an den Grund fieren; - *the ensign*, die Flagge senken, salutieren.

drops, kleine Verzierungen.

drowned, 1. ertrunken; 2. am Horizont verschwunden; - *land*, versunkenes Land.

drum head of capstan, Gangspillkopf; - *of a crane*, Krahntrommel; - *of steering gear*, Trommel des Steuergeräts.

dry bottomed boiler, Kessel ohne Wasserraum unter der Feuerung; - *cask*, Schiff mit trockenen Waren; - *condensation*, trockene Kondensation; - *dock*, Trockendock; - *felt*, ungeteerter Filz; - *harbour*, Fluthafen; - *nurse*, Lehrmeister eines Vorgesetzten; - *provisions*, trockener Proviant; - *rot*, Trockenfäule; - *squall*, Bö ohne Regen; - *steam*, trockener Dampf; - *the sails*, die Segel trocknen.

dryer, Trockenmittel. [nung.

drying of steam, Dampftrock-D-slide valve*, D-schieber.

dub, abdechseln.

dubbing, das Abschlichten.

duck, 1. einen Mann von der Rahe fallen lassen; 2. taufen (beim Passieren der Linie); 3. leichtes Segeltuch; - *up a sail*, 1. ein Segel auftuchen; 2. ein Untersegel etwas aufducking*, Linientaufe. [holen.

ductility, Dehnbarkeit.

due east, & c., genau östlich etc.

dues, Abgaben.

dull, 1. windstill; 2. schwerfällig (Schiff).

dumb chalder, Ruderträger; - *cleat*, Hornklampe; - *compass*, Windrose ohne Magnetnadel; - *craft*, Boot ohne Segel; - *pintle*, Ruderhaken; - *sheave*, tote Scheibe; - *snatch*, Verholklampe.

dumby, die an einem Pfeiler befestigte Barke.

dump a load, eine Ladung stürzen; - *bolt*, Stuufbolzen; - *fastening*, S.-befestigung.

dumping ground, Abladeplatz für Ausgebaggertes.

dunnage, Garnierung; - *battens*, G.-latten; - *mats*, G.-matten; - *planks*, G.-planken; - *wood*, Stauholz.

dunnaged, garniert.

dusk, to - the horizon, den Horizont verdunkeln.

dust haze, Höhenrauch.

dusty, stürmisch.

Dutch built, kuffähnlich; - *galliot*, holländische Kuff; - *screw*, Wasserschraube.

Dutchman's breeches, zwei blaue Streifen am bewölkten Himmel.

duty, 1. Dienst; 2. Zollabgaben; - *free*, zollfrei; - *on board ship*, Borddienst.

D-valve, D-schieber.

dygogram, Dygogramm.

dying away, abnehmen (des Windes).

dynamo, Dynamo; - *circuit*, Stromkreis.

dynamometer, Kraftmesser; - *trial*, Kraftmessung mit dem Bremszaum.

dynamometrical brake, Bremsdynamometer.

E.

ear, Öse (eines Taus).

earing, Nockbindsel, N-ohr; -

cringle, Nockohrenlägel; - *thimble*, Nockhornkausche.

ease, 1. erleichtern, vermindern; 2. ein Schiff in See luven; 3. ein wenig mit dem Ruder aufkommen; 4. Tau od. Kette etwas loser machen; - *away*, T. o. K. e. l. m.; - *down*, Fahrt verlangsamen; - *her!* Langsam! - *in*, einfieren; - *off*, etwas loser machen; - - *the jibs!* Klüverschoten los! - - *the tacks!* die Halsen aufstechen! - *sail*, die Segel vermindern; - *the engines*, langsam fahren; - *the headway*, die Fahrt vermindern; - *the helm*, mit dem Ruder aufkommen; - *up*, langsam; - - *the tack* od. *sheet*, die Schote auffieren.

easing gear, Sicherheitsventil-Entlastungsvorrichtung.

East India Trader od. *E. Indiaman*, Ostindienfahrer; - *latitude*, östliche Breite; - *longitude*, ö. Länge; - *variation*, ö. Mißweisung.

easterly variation, östliche Mißweisung.

eastern amplitude, Morgenamplitude.

easting, 1. zurückgelegter östlicher Kurs; 2. ö. Entfernung von einem bestimmten Meridian; 3. Annäherung an eine östliche Richtung od. Umschlagen nach Ost; *wind with - in it*, Wind mit Ost.

easy, langsam, gemächlich; *of an - access*, leicht zugänglich; - *ahead*, langsam vorwärts; - *astern*, langsam rückwärts; *on an - bowline*, mit losen Buliens segeln; *under - sails*, unter handlichen Segeln.

eat, *to-the wind out of a vessel*, einem Schiffe die Luv abkneifen; - *to windward*, Luv halten; - *up into the wind*, Luv gewinnen.

ebb, Ebbe; - *anchor*, Ebbanker; - *and flood*, Ebbe und Flut; *beginning ebb*, erste E; *end-*,

Dreiviertel E.; *first quarter -*, Viertel E.; *half -*, halbe E.; *last quarter -*, Dreiviertel E ; *lowest of the -*, Stillwasser bei E.; *the - makes* od. *runs*, das Wasser läuft ab; - - *sets to south*, die Ebbe setzt nach Süden; - *tide*, Ebbe.

ebony, Ebenholz.

ebullition, das Sieden.

eccentric, Excenter; - *bolt*, E-bolzen; - - *nut*, E.-b-mutter; - *brasses*, E.-Lagerschalen; - *catch*, E.-knagge; - *disk*, E.-scheiben; - *gab*, E.-auge; - *gear*, E.-vorrichtung; - *governor*, E.-regulator; - *key*, E.-keil; - - *way*, E.-k-nute; - *motion*, E.-Bewegung; - *pulley*, E.-scheibe; - *radius*, E.-radius; - *rod*, E.-stange; - - *fork*, E.-stangengabel; - - *gab*, E.-s-auge; - - *gear*, E.-Transmission; - *pin*, E.-stangenwarze; - *shaft*, E.-welle; - - *bearing*, E.-Wellenlager; - *sheave*, E.-scheibe; - - *feather*, E.-scheibenfeder; - *key way*, E.-s-Keilnute; - - *set screw*, E.-s-Druckschraube; - *snug*, od. - *stop*, E.-knagge; - *strap*, E.-bügel; - - *bolt*, E.-b-bolzen; - - - *nut*, E.-b-b-mutter; *e. s. liner*, E.-bügelfutter; - *tappet*, E.-scheibe; - *throw*, E.-weg.

eclipse, Finsternis.

economiser, Speisewasser-Vorwärmer.

ectropometer, Instrument zur Bestimmung der Kompaßrichtung von Gegenständen

eddy, Neerstrom; - *water*, Rückströmung; - *wind*, Fallwind.

edge along, langsam nähern; - *away*, etwas abhalten; - *down*, langsam auf etwas zusteuern; - *in with*, sich allmählich nähern; - *near*, sich heranschlängeln; - *off*, sich allmählich entfernen.

edge of a plank, Schmalseite einer Planke; - - - *plate*,

Kante einer Platte; - *riveting*, Längsnahtnietung.

eduction, Ableitung; - *gear*, Ausströmungsvorrichtung; - *pipe*, A-s-m-rohr; - *port*, A-s-m-öffnung; - *valve*, A-s-m-ventil.

effect, Leistung od. Wirkung.

effective horse power, od. *e. p.*, effektive Pferdekraft; - *pressure*, Überdruckspannung.

efficiency, Leistungsfähigkeit; -*of steam*, Dampfkraft.

egg ended boiler, Kessel mit ovalen Enden.

ejector, Auswerfer; - *pipe*, Ejektorrohr.

eke, den Proviant strecken.

ekeing od. *eking* od. *e. piece*, Bug Füllstück,

elastic chuck. Klemmfutter.

elasticity, Spannkraft.

elbow cock, Elbogenhahn; - *in the hawse*, Kabelschlag; - *in the channel* od. *river*, starke Biegung im Fahrwasser od. Flusse; - *of a pipe*, Krümmer eines Rohrs; - *of the cable*, Schlag im Ankertau; - *pipe*, Krümmerrohr.

electric cable, elektrischer Kabel; - *current*, e. Strom; - *installation*, elektrische Einrichtung.

electric light engine, elektrische Lichtmaschine; *e.l.e. connecting rod*, Pleuelstange der elektrischen L.; *e.l e.c r. bolt*, P.-bolzen d. e. L.; *e.l.e. c. r. bottom end keep*, Kurbelzapfenlagerschalendeckel d. e. L.; *e. l. e. c. r. b. e. liner*, Pleuelstangenfußfutter d. e. L.; *e. l. e. c. r. top end keep*, Kreuzkopflagerschalendeckel d. e. L.; *e. l. e. crank pin bolt*, Kurbelzapfenlagerbolzen d. e. L.; *e. l. e. c. p. brasses*, K-z-l-schalen d. e L.; *e. l. e. c. shaft*, Kurbelwelle d. e. L.; *e. l. e. c. s. bearing*, K-wellenlager d. e. L.; *e. l.*

e. c. s. bearing bolt, K-w-l-bolzen d. e. L.; *e. l. e. c. s. bearing brasses*, K-w-l-schalen d. e. L.; *e. l. e. c. s. bearing keep*, K-w-l-deckel d. e. L.; *e. l. e. c. s. b. k. bolt*, K-w-l-d-bolzen d. e. L.; *e. l. e. crosshead bolt*, Kreuzkopflagerbolzen d. e. L.; *e. l. e. c. brasses*, K-k-l-schalen d. e. L.; *e. l. e. cylinder*, Zylinder d. e. L.; *e. l. e. c. cover*, Z.-deckel d. e. L.; *e. l. e. c. bolt*, Z.-d-bolzen d. e. L.; *e. l. e. cylinder drain pipe*, Z.-Entwässserungsrohr d. e. L.; *e. l. e. eccentric*, Excenter d. e. L.; *e. l. e. e. bolt*, E.-bolzen d. e. L.; *e. l. e. e. brasses*, E.-Lagerschalen d. e. L.; *e. l. e. e. rod*, E.-stange d. e. L.; *e. l. e. e. sheave*, E-scheibe d. e. L.; *e. l. e. e. strap*, E.-bügel d. e. L.; *e. l. e. e. s. liner*, E.-b-futter d. e. L.; *e. l. e. exhaust pipe*, Dampfablaßrohr d. e.L.; *e.l.e.e. piston*, Kolben d. e. L.; *e. l. e. p. rod*, K.-stange d. e. L.; *e. l. e. p. r. crosshead*, K-s-Kreuzkopf d. e. L.; *e. l. e. p. r. stuffing box*, K-s-Stopfbüchse d. e. L ; *e. l. e. p. r. s. b. gland*, K-s-S-b-deckel d. e. L.; *e. l. e. slide valve*, Schieber d. e. L.; *e. l. e. stop valve*, Absperrventil d. e. L.; *e. l. e. starting valve*, Anlaßventil d. e. L.; *e. l. e. valve casing*, Schieberkasten d. e. L.; *e. l. e. v. c. door*, S-k-deckel d. e. L.; *e. l. e. v. rod*, Schieberstange d. e. L.; *e. l. e. v. r. stuffing box*, Schieberstangen-Stopfbüchse d. e. L.; *e. l. e. v. r. s. b. gland*, S.-S.-deckel d. e. L.

electric lighting, elektrische Beleuchtung; - *propulsion*, e. Fortbewegung.

electrical engineer, Elektro-Techniker; - *ventilating motor*, Ventilationsmaschine.

electrically driven, mit Elektricität betrieben.

electromotor, Elektromotor.
elevation, Seitenriß.
elevator, Elevator.
eleven o' clock wind, steife Brise.
Elliot's eye, Elliotsauge.
elliptical boiler, elliptischer Kessel: - *stern*, elliptisch geformtes Heck.
elm wood, Ulmenholz.
St. Elmo's fire od. *light*, St. Elmsfeuer.
embankment, Kai.
embargo, Beschlagnahme; *to lay an - on*, *to put under an -*, mit Beschlag belegen: *to raise* od. *to take off the -*, den B. aufheben: - *law*, Embargogesetz.
embark, sich einschiffen; - *ation* od. *-ment*, Einschiffung
embay, in eine Bai einlaufen.
embayed, besetzt (zwischen Vorgebirgen eingeschlossen).
embayment, Bucht von Klippen umgeben.
embedded, eingegraben.
embezzlement of the cargo, Veruntreuung der Ladung.
embrail, aufgeien.
emery cloth, Schmirgelleinen; *-paper*, S-papier; - *stick*, S-feile.
emigrant, Auswanderer; - *commissioner*, A.-Kommissar.
emigrate, auswandern.
emigration commissioner, Auswanderungskommissar: - *officer*, A-w-Beamter.
empty a boiler, einen Kessel leeren.
enclosed space, eingeschlossener Raum.
encumbered, belemmert.
encumbrance, Belemmerung.
end for end, der Länge nach; - *journal*, Endzapfen; - *of a sail*, die Pünte; - *of the ebb*, Hinterebbe; - *on*, recht von vorn od. in der Längenlinie; - *plate of a double bottom*, Querschott eines Doppelbodens.

endless chain propeller, die archimedische Schraube mit geschlossener Kette; - *rope*, Seil ohne Ende; - *shake*, die unregelmäßige Bewegung der Enden einer Welle.
ends of a boiler, die Böden eines Kessels.
engine, Maschine; - *bearers*, Maschinenlager; - *bed*, M-fundament; - - *plate*, M-f-platte; - *casing*, M-raumschacht; - *casting*, M-formguß; *-commands*, M-kommandos; - *floor* od. *flooring*, M-kammer-Flurplatten; - *forging*, M-schmiedestück; - *guard rail*, M-raumgeländer; - *hatch* od. *hatchway*, M-luke; - *indicator*, M-indikator; - *oil*, M-öl; - *opening*, M-luke; - *power*, M-kraft; - *pumps*, Pumpen des M-raums; - *repairs*, M-reparaturen.
engine room, Maschinenraum; - - *after bulkhead*, M.-schott; - - *b.*, M.-schott; - - *b. angle bar*, M.-s-winkel; - *coamings*, M.-süll; - - *door*, M.-tür; - *d. hinge*, M.-t-scharnier; - - *flooring*, M.-Flurplatten; - - *forward bulkhead*, Kesselraumschott; - - *ladder*, Maschinenraum-Leiter; - - *lamp*, M.-Lampe; - - *platform*, M.-Plattform; - - *skylight*, M.-Oberlicht; - - *stores*, M.-Vorräte; - - *telegraph*, Maschinentelegraph; - - *tools*, Maschinenraum-Werkzeug; - - *ventilator*, M.-Ventilator; - - *well*, M.-brunnen.
engine seating, Maschinen-Fundament; - - *angle bar*, M-F.-winkel; - *shaft of steam winch*, Dampfwindenwelle; - *shop*, Maschinenwerkstatt; - *sleepers*, M-fundament; - *survey*, M-besichtigung; - *turned treenail*, gedrehter Holznagel; - *works*, Maschinenbauanstalt.
engineer, Ingenieur od. Ma-

schinist; - *surveyor*, Maschinenbesichtiger.
engineering office, 1. Bureau für Ingenieurwesen; 2. Maschinenbauanstalt.
engineer's berth, Maschinistenkammer; - *certificate*, M-i-patent; - *log* od. *logbook*, M-i-Journal; - *mess room*, M-i-messe; *for* - *purposes*, um Maschinenreparaturen vorzunehmen; - *room*, Maschinistenkammer; - *store room*, Maschinendepot.
engulf, 1. verschlingen (Schiff); 2. sich stürzen (Fluß); 3. unterirdisch verschwinden (Fluß); 4. einschneiden (Küste).
enlarge, räumen, achterlich gehen.
enlist, anwerben, sich a. lassen; - *ment*, Anwerbung.
ensign, 1. Nationalflagge; 2. Fähnrich; -*halliard*, Flaggenleine; - *staff*, Flaggenstock.
enter, 1. klarieren; 2. einkommen, einlaufen, einsegeln; - *short*, zu wenig klarieren; - *the service*, den Dienst antreten.
entering ladder, Bootsleiter, Sturmleiter; -*port*, Fallreeppforte; - *rope*, Fallreepstau; - - *stanchion*, F-r-ständer.
entire deck, durchgehendes Deck.
entrance, Einfahrt; - *of a vessel*. Splißgang des Bugs.
entry, Einklarierung.
ephemeris, die Ephemeriden.
equation, Gleichung.
equator, Äquator.
equatorial current, Äquatorialstrom; - *doldrums*, Äquatorstillen.
equiangular, gleichwinkelig.
equibalance, Gleichgewicht.
equicural, gleichschenkelig.
equidistant from, in gleicher Entfernung von.
equiformity, Gleichförmigkeit.
equilateral, gleichseitig.

equilibrium, Gleichgewicht; - *valve*, G.-Ventil.
equinoctial compass, Äquinoktial Kompaß; - *storms*, Ä.-Stürme.
equinox, Äquinoktium.
equip, ausrüsten; - *ment*, Ausrüstung.
equipoise, Gleichgewicht; - *rudder*, Balanceruder.
erect, 1. montieren (Maschine etc.); 2. aufsetzen (Spanten).
erecting shop, Montierungswerkstätten.
erection, Aufbau.
erections, Aufbauten.
error by amplitude, Mißweisung; - *in dead reckoning*, Mißgissung; - *in observation*, Beobachtungsfehler; - *of a planet*, Differenz zwischen dem beobachteten und berechneten Platze eines Planeten; - *of the compass*, Kompaßfehler; - *of the dead reckoning*, Mißgissung.
escape, entweichen, Entweichung; - *pipe*, Ausströmungsrohr; - *valve*, Sicherheitsventil; - - *gear*, S.-Gestänge; - - *load*, S.-Belastung; - - *seat*, S.-sitz; - - *spindle*, S.-Spindel; - - *spring*, S-Feder.
escutcheon, Wappenschild am Heck.
essaying glass, Wasserstandsglas.
establishment of a vessel, das vorschriftsmäßige Inventar; - *of the tides*, Hafenzeit.
estimate, Kostenanschlag.
estimated horse power, ungefähre Pferdekraft.
estivage, Stauung der Fracht.
estuary, Mündung.
euphroe, Spinnkopf.
European trade, europäische Fahrt.
evacuation pipe, Ausleerungsrohr.
evaporate, verdampfen.
evaporating apparatus, Abdampfapparat.

evaporation, Verdampfung.
evaporative heat, Verdampfungswärme; - *power*, V-d-fähigkeit.
evaporator,Evaporator; - *brine cock*,E.-Schaumhahn; - *coils*, E.-schlangen; - *door*, E.-Deckel; - *equilibrium valve*, E.-Gleichgewichtsventil; - *escape valve*, E.-Sicherheitsventil; - - - *load*, E.-S.-Belastung; - *float*, E.-schwimmer; - *gauge cock*, E.-Probierhahn; - *g. glass*, E.-Wasserstandsglas; - *pressure gauge*, E.-Manometer; - *vacuum gauge*, E.-Vacuumeter.
even keel, gleichlastig.
evening gun, Abendschuß; - *watch*, A-wache.
every rope an end, alles klar legen; - *stitch set*, alles beigesetzt.
evolutionary squadron, Übungsgeschwader.
examine the depth and quality of the ground, den Grund ausloten; - *the seams*, die Nähte untersuchen.
excentric see eccentric.
excess of hatchway, Übermaß an Luken.
excessive pressure, übermäßiger Druck.
excused from duty, dienstfrei; - *idlers*, Freiwächter.
executive officer, der beauftragte Offizier.
exercise at quarter, Klarschiff-Exerzieren.
exhaust cock, Auslaßhahn; - *column*, Ableitungssäule; - *lap*, innere Deckung eines Schiebers; - *pipe*, Dampfablaßrohr; -*pipes*,D.-Leitung; - *port*, Dampfaustrittskanal; - - *of slide valve*, D.- des Schiebers; - *regulator*, Retourdampfregulator; - *steam*, Abdampf; - *tank*, Sammeltank; - *trunnion*, Exhaustzapfen; - *valve*, Ausströmungsventil.

exhausting chamber, Dampfraum.
exhaustion, Abführung; - *of steam*, Dampfabführung.
expand the steam, Dampf absperren.
expansion, 1. Ausdehnung; 2. Expansionsvorrichtung; - *eccentric*, E-p-excenter; - *engine*, E-p-maschine; - *gear*, E-p-vorrichtung; - *gland*, E-p-verdichtung-Stopfbüchsendeckel; - *hatch* od. *h-way*, E-p-luke; - *joint*, E-p-dichtung; - *ring*, E-p-ring; - *slide valve*, E-p-schieber; - *steam*, expandierter Dampf; - *tank*, E-p-tank; - *valve*, E-p-ventil; - - *gear*, E-p-v-gestänge; - - *piston*, E-p-v-kolben; - - *rod*, E-p-v-stange; - - *spindle*, E-p-v-spindel; - - - *guide*, E-p-v-s-führung; - *force*, Ausdehnungskraft; - *power*, A-d-vermögen; - *steam*, Expansivdampf.
expell the oakum out of the seams, den Werg auskauen.
explode, explodieren.
explosion, Zersprengung; - *of a boiler*, Dampfkesselexplosion.
export dock, Ausfuhrdock; - *dues* od. - *duty*, A-f-zoll.
exposed anchorage, ungeschützter Ankerplatz.
extend protest, Verklarung belegen.
extended protest od. *extension of p.*, Verklarung; *extension pipe*, Verlängerungsrohr.
external condenser, Röhrenkondensator; - *pressure*, äußerlicher Druck; - *safety valve*, äußeres Sicherheitsventil.
extractor, Extraktor.
extreme breadth, größte Breite; - *length*, äußerste Länge.
eye, Auge; - *of a block strap*, A. eines Blockstropps; - *of a crank*, Kurbelauge; - *of a pair of backstays*,Auge einer

Spannpardune: - *of a rope*, A. eines Taues: - *of a stay*, Stagauge: - *of a vessel*, Bugklüse: - *of the anchor*, Ankerauge; - *of the storm*, windstilles Zentrum eines Zyklons.

eye bolt, Augenbolzen: - *gasket*, A-bindsel: - *reach*, Sehweite; - *screw*,Schraubenring: - *shot*, Sehweite: - *splice*, Augsplissung.

eyelet holes, Gatchen im Segel.

eyes in a rope, Augen in einem Tau; - *of her*, Bugklüsen.

eyot, kleine Insel.

F.

F. stands for "Fog".

F. A. A. stands for "Free of all average".

face of a tooth of a wheel, Stirnfläche eines Radzahns; - *piece*, Füllstück zwischen den Knien des Gallionsscheggs; - *plate*, vertikale Gurtplatte; - - *of a lathe*, Planscheibe einer Drehbank; - *the piston rings*, die Kolbenringe schlichten; - *wheel*, Kronrad.

facing, ebnen. schlichten.

fag end, Kuhschwanz (aufgedrehtes Tauende); - *out*, aufpflücken.

fagged, aufgedreht.

faggot od. *fagot*, 1. Knepeling (blinderMatrose):2.Stauholz.

fair, 1. schön (Wetter): 2. günstig (Wind):3.abschlichten; 4. eben, glatt: - *lead truck*, Wegweiserklotje.

fairing the body, das Übertragen und Vergleichen der Schiffsrisse.

fairleader, 1. Wegweiser, gefüttertes Gatt (in der Bordwand);2. Scherbrett: - *batten*, Scherlatten.

fairleaders for steering rods, Steuerstangenstühle.

fairway, Fahrwasser: - *buoy*, F.-boje.

fairways, Seegatten.

fake, Bucht (einer Rolle Tauwerk).

faker, der Mann, der die Taue in Buchten legt.

fakes catch each other, die Buchten des Kabels fangen sich.

faking box, Kasten für die Rettungsleinen.

fall, 1. Läufer (des Takels); 2. Bruch (des Decks);3. Herbst; 4. Gefälle (des Flusses); - *of the vangs*, Geerdläufer; - *proof*, Schlag- od. Wurfprobe.

fall aboard of another vessel, gegen ein anderes Schiff stoßen od. treiben; - *astern*, 1. über Steuer gehen; 2. achteraus sacken od. zurückbleiben; - *calm*, 1. windstill werden; 2. sich glätten (die See); - *down a river*, einen Fluß hinunter treiben od. geschleppt werden; - *dry at low water*, bei Niedrigwasser trocken fallen; - *foul of another vessel*, mit einem andern Schiffe unklar werden; - *in with*, begegnen; - *light*, flau werden; - *off*, abfallen; - - *round*, rund um wenden; - *over board*, über Bord fallen; - *to leeward*, leewärts treiben.

falling, fallen, sich legen (See und Wind): - *tide*, fallende Tide.

falls of a deck, Erhöhungen eines Decks.

false face, aufgesetzte Schie-

bertläche (des Zylinders): -
fire, falsches Feuer; - *keel*,
loser Kiel; - *keelson*, zweites
Kielschwein; - *muster*, Knepeling (blinder Matrose); -
rail, Verstärkungsleiste; -
stem, Brustholz des Gallions:
- *sternpost*, loser Achtersteven.
family head, große Gallionsfigur.
fan along, stoßweise vorwärts-
kommen; - od. - *blast*, Zentrifugalventilator; - *engine*,
Maschine zur Erzeugung
künstlichen Zugs.
fanal, kleines Leuchtfeuer.
fancy line, Niederholer einer
fane, Windfahne. [Rahe.
fang the pump, die Pumpe anschlagen.
fanning breeze, flaue Brise.
fare, Passagegeld.
fash, zackige Naht.
fashion piece, Heckspant; -
timber, Randsomholz.
fast, 1. fest; 2. Festmachtau;
- *aground*, festgeraakt; - *ice*,
festes Eis; - *sailing ship*,
Schnellsegler: - *there*! Festmachen!
fasten, anbolzen, befestigen,
verbolzen; - *the ends of a
seizing*, einen Bindsel besetzen; - *with bolts*, anbolzen, verbolzen; - *with spikes*,
spiekern. [bolzung.
fastening, Befestigung. Ver-
fat quartered, von hinten voll
gebaut.
fathom, Faden, abfadmen, fadmen: - *line*, Lotleine; - *wood*,
Stauholz.
fathomable, ergründlich.
fathomless, unergründlich.
faucet joint, Randdichtung.
favour, 1. vorsichtig verfahren;
2. günstiger sein (Wind).
fay, genau aneinander passen.
faying, anliegend, an-
schließend.
fearn, kleines Bratspill.
fease, ein Tau aufdrehen.

feat of power, Kraftleistung.
feather an oar, einen Boots-
riemen platt werfen: - *cloud*,
Federwolke; - *grass mat*,
Binsenmatte; - *of a shaft*,
Rippe einer Welle etc.;
feathering float, verstellbare
Radschaufel; - *paddle*, bewegliche Schaufel; - *wheel*,
Schaufelrad mit verstell-
baren Schaufeln; - *propeller*,
Schraube mit v. Flügeln.
*feathers of the rudder braces
and pintles*, Schmiegen der
Haken und Fingerlinge des
Ruders.
feazings, Kuhschwanz.
feed, speisen; - *the fishes*, ertrinken.
feed apparatus, Speiseapparat:
- *check valve*, Speiseregulier-
ventil; - *cock*, Speisehahn;
- *delivery pipe*, Speisepum-
pendruckrohr; - - *valve chest*.
S-p-Druckventilkasten.
feed donkey, Dampfspeisepumpe: *f. d. bucket*, Dampf-
speisepumpen-Kolben; *f. d.
b. valve*, D.-K-Ventil: *f. d. b.
v. guard*, D.-K.-V.-Klappen-
fänger: *f. d. b. v. seat*, D.-K.-
V.-sitz; *f. d. connecting rod*,
D.-Pleuelstange; *f. d. c. r.
bolt*, D.-P-stangenbolzen; *f.
d. c. r. bottom end keep*, D.-
Kurbelzapfen-Lagerscha-
len-Deckel; *f. d. c. r. b. e.
liner*, D.-Pleuelstangenfuß-
futter; *f. d. c. r. top end
keep*, D.-Kreuzkopflager-
schalendeckel; *f. d. crank
shaft*, D.-Kurbelwelle; *f. d.
c. pin bolt*, D.-Kurbelzapfen-
lagerbolzen; *f. d. c. p. brasses*, D.-K-z-l-schalen: *f. d. c.
shaft bearing*, D.-Kurbel-
wellenlager; *f. d. c. s. b. bolt*,
D.-K.-bolzen; *f. d. c. s. bearing keep*, D.-K.-Deckel: *f. d.
c. s. b. k. bolt*, D.-K.-D.-bol-
zen; *f. d. c. s. bearing brasses*, D.-K.-schalen; *f. d.
crosshead bolt*, D.-Kreuzkopf-
lagerbolzen; *f. d. c. brasses*,

D.-K-k-l-schalen; *f. d. cylinder*. D.-Zylinder; *f. d. c. cover*, D.-Z.-Deckel; *f. d. c. c. bolt*, D.-Z.-D.-Bolzen; *f. d. cylinder drain pipe*, D.-Z.-Entwässerungsrohr; *f. d. delivery pipe*, D.-Druckrohr; *f. d. d. space*, D.-Druckraum; *f. d. d. valve*, D.-Druckventil; *f. d. d. v. chest*, D.-D.-Kasten; *f. d. d. v. door*, D.-D.-Deckel; *f. d. d. v. seat*, D.-D.-Sitz; *f. d. discharge valve*, D.-Ausgußventil; *f. d. eccentric*, D.-Excenter; *f. d. e. bolt*, D.-E.-Bolzen; *f. d. e. brasses*, D.-E.-Lagerschalen; *f. d. e. rod*, D.-E.-Stange; *f. d. e. sheave*, D.-E.-Scheibe; *f. d. e. strap*, D.-E.-Bügel; *f. d. e. s. liner*, D.-E.-B.-Futter; *f. d. exhaust pipe*, D.-Dampfablaßrohr; *f. d. fly wheel*, D.-Schwungrad; *f. d. foot valve*, D.-Fußventil; *f. d. f. v. seat*, D.-Saugventilsitz; *f. d. gear*, D.-Geschirr; *f. d. head valve*, D.-Druckventil; *f. d. master cock*, D.-Wendehahn; *f. d. piston*, D.-Kolben; *f. d. p. rod*, D.-K.-Stange; *f. d. p. r. crosshead*, D.-K.-S.-Kreuzkopf; *f. d. p. r. stuffing box*, D.-K.-S.-Stopfbüchse; *f. d. p. r. s. b. gland*, D.-K.-S.-S.-Deckel; *f. d. pump*, D.; *f. d. slide valve*, D.-Schieber; *f. d. starting valve*, D.-Anlaßventil; *f. d. steam pipe*, D.-Dampfzuleitungsrohr; *f. d. stop valve*, D.-Absperrventil; *f. d. suction pipe*, D.-Saugerohr; *f. d. s. space*, D.-S-raum; *f. d. s. valve*, D.-S-ventil; *f. d. s. v. door*, D.-S-v-deckel; *f. d. s. v. seat*, D.-S-v-sitz; *f. d. top valve*, D.-Druckventil; *f. d. t. v. seat*, D.-D.-Sitz; *f. d. v., D.-Ventil; *f. d. v. casing*, D.-Schieberkasten; *f. d. v. c. door*, D.-S.-Deckel; *f. d. v. rod*, D.-Schieberstange; *f. d. v. r. stuffing box*, D.-S.-Stopfbüchse; *f. d. v. r. s. b. gland*,

D.-S.-S.-Deckel; *f. d. v. seat*, D.-Ventilsitz.
feed engine, see *feed donkey.*
feed head, selbstwirkende Speiseröhre; *- heater*, Speisewasser-Vorwärmer; *- - coils*, S.-V.-Schlangen; *- - door*, S.-V.-Deckel; *- - steam pipe*, S.-V.-Dampfzuleitungsrohr; *- pipe*, Speiserohr; *- pipes*, S.-Leitung; *- pump*, Speisepumpe.
feed pump air vessel, Speisepumpen-Windkessel; *f. p. barrel*, S.-Körper; *f. p. bucket*, S.-Kolben; *f. p. b. valve*, S.-K.-Ventil; *f. p. b. ring*, S.-K.-Ring; *f. p. b. valve*, S.-K.-Ventil; *f. p. b. v. guard*, S.-K.-V.-Hubbegrenzer; *f. p. b. v. seat*, S.-K.-V.-Sitz; *f. p. chamber*, S.-Körper; *f. p. cover*, S.-Deckel; *f. p. cylinder*, S.-Zylinder; *f. p. delivery pipe*, S.-Druckrohr; *f. p. d. space*, S.-D-raum; *f. p. d. valve*, S.-D-ventil; *f. p. d. v. guard*, S.-D-v-Hubbegrenzer; *f. p. d. v. seat*, S.-D-v-sitz; *f. p. escape valve*, S.-Sicherheitsventil; *f. p. e. v. load*, S.-S.-Belastung; *f. p. foot valve*, S.-Fußventil; *f. p. f. v. guard*, S.-Saugventil-Hubbegrenzer; *f. p. f. v. seat*, S.-S.-Sitz; *f. p. gear*, S.-Geschirr; *f. p. gland*, S.-Stopfbüchsendeckel; *f. p. head valve*, S.-Druckventil; *f. p. liner*, S.-Einsatz; *f. p. link*, S.-Gelenk; *f. p. l. brasses*, S.-G.-Lagerschalen; *f. p. neck bush*, S.-Grundring; *f. p. overflow valve*, S.-Ueberlaufventil; *f. p. pet cock*, S.-Probierhahn; *f. p. p. valve*, S.-Schnürventil; *f. p. plunger*, S.-Plunger; *f. p. ram*, S.-P.; *f. p. relief valve*, S.-Rücklaufventil; *f. p. rod*, S.-Stange; *f. p. r. stuffing box*, S.-S.-Stopfbüchse; *f. p. s. b. S.-Stopfbüchse; *f. p. s. b. gland*, S.-S.-Deckel; *f. p.

suction pipe, S.-Saugerohr;
f. p. s. space, S.-S-raum; *f. p.
suction valve*, S.-S-ventil; *f.
p. s. v. chest*, S.-S-v-kasten;
f. p. s. v. guard, S.-S-v-Hubbe-
grenzer; *f. p. s. v. seat*, S.-S-
v-sitz; *f. p. top valve*, S.-
Druckventil; *f. p. t. v. guard*,
S.-D.-Hubbegrenzer; *f. p. t.
v. seat*, S.-D.-Sitz; *f. p. valve*,
S.-Ventil; *f. p. v. cover*, S.-
V.-Deckel; *f. p. v. guard*, S.-
V.-Hubbegrenzer; *f. p. v. seat*,
S.-V.-Sitz.
feed suction valve chest, Speise-
pumpen-Saugventilkasten; -
valve, Speiseventil; - - *box*,
S.-Gehäuse; - - *cover*, S.-
Deckel; - *water*, Speise-
wasser; - -*filter escape valve
load*, S.-Filter-Sicherheits-
ventilbelastung; - - *heater*,
Speisewasser-Vorwärmer; - -
tank, S.-Behälter.
feeder, Feeder.
feeding, Speisung; -*apparatus*,
Speisevorrichtung; -*gale*, zu-
nehmender Sturm; - *means*,
Speisevorrichtung.
feeding see also feed.
feel the helm, dem Ruder gehorchen.
fell across our bows, das Schiff
trieb direkt vor unsern Bug;
- *calm*, es wurde windstill.
felt, Filz.
felucca, Feluke.
fend off, abwehren.
fender, Fender; - *beam*, Reibholz; - *bolt*, Kopfbolzen.
fenders, Reibhölzer; - *of old
cable* od. *junk*, Taukränze.
ferrule, 1. Endring, Zwinge;
2. Nockband (an den Rahen);
- *press*, Zwingpresse.
ferry od. - *boat*, Fähre.
fetch, von oben holen; - *a
harbour*, einen Hafen er-
reichen; - *a pump*, eine
Pumpe anschlagen; - *headway*, anfangen vorauszu-
gehen; - *sternway*, a. über
Steuer zu gehen; - *to wind-*

ward, Luv gewinnen; - *up*,
plötzlich anhalten; - *way*,
hin- und herschütteln.
fid, 1. das Fid (des Segel-
machers); 2. Schloßholz der
Stengen); 3. auftreiben (auf
einer Fid); - *hole*, Schloß-
holzgatt.
fidded, auf dem Schloßholz
stehend.
fiddle, Schlingerborden; -*block*,
Violinblock; - *figure head*,
nach innen gekehrte Gal-
lionsfigur.
fiddler's green, Seemanns-Ver-
gnügungslokal.
fidley, Oberheizraum; -*bunker*,
Querschiffsbunker.
field of view, Gesichtsfeld.
fife rail, Nagelbank.
figure head, Gallionsfigur; -
of eight knot, Achterstich.
file brush, Feilenbürste.
filings, Feilspäne.
fill and stand on, vollbrassen
und Kurs anliegen; - *away*,
die Segel vollbrassen; - *in
an opened vessel*, ein offenes
Schiff voll planken; - *the
boilers*, die Kessel füllen; -
the sails, die Segel vollbrassen; - *up between the
beams*, den Raum zwischen
den Deckbalken vollstauen;
- *up the seams with oakum*
(od. *old rope yarn*), die Nähte
mit Werg abstopfen.
fillet, Nase; - *of a crank shaft*,
N. einer Kurbelwelle.
filling chocks of the cutwater,
Füllstücke des Gallions;
-*floor*, Füllstück; - *futtock*,
Füllholz; - *of a ship*, das
Vollaufen eines Schiffs; -
piece, Füllstreifen; - *pipe*,
Füllrohr; -*timber*, Füllspant;
- *transom*, Füllungsworp.
*fillings between the head
cheeks*, der Kamm zwischen
den Schlußknien d. Gallions.
fined steel, gefrischter Stahl.
finished with engines, wir
stellten die Maschine ab.

finishing tools, Schlichtwerkzeug.

finishings, Verzierungen.

fir lining, Fütterung der Betinge; - *wood*, Kiefernholz.

fire a boiler, einen Kessel heizen; - *a rocket*, eine Rakete abfeuern; - *flare rockets*, lodernde Raketen a.

fire arrow, Feuerpfeil zur Entzündung der Segel und Takelage; - *bar*, Roststab; -- *bearer*, R.-träger; - *bare*, Feuerbake; - *bill*, F-rolle; - *boat*, Dampfspritzenboot; - *boom*, Brandbalken; - *box*, Feuerkammer; - - *door*, F.-tür; - - *shell*, Feuerbüchsenmantel; - - *sides*, Seitenwandungen d. Feuerbüchse; - - *stay*, Feuerkammer-Stehbolzen; - - - *nut*, F.-S.-mutter; *f. b. top*, Feuerbüchsendecke; - *bricks*, feuerfeste Steine; - *bridge*, Feuerbrücke; - *bucket*, Feuerpütze; - *clay*, feuerfester Ton; - *door*, Feuertür; - - *latch*, F.-klinke; - *drill*, Feuerdrill; - *engine*, Dampffeuerspritze.

fire engine connecting rod, Dampffeuerspritzen - Pleuelstange; *f. e. c. r. bolt*, D.-P.-bolzen; *f. e. c. r. bottom end keep*, D.-Kurbelzapfen-lagerschalendeckel; *f. e. c. r. b. e. liner*, D.-Pleuelstangenfußfutter; *f. e. c. r. top end keep*, D.-Kreuzkopflagerschalen - deckel; *f. e. crank pin bolt*, D.-Kurbelzapfenlagerbolzen; *f. e. c. p. brasses*, D.-K-z-l-schalen; *f. e. c. shaft*, D.-Kurbelwelle; *f. e. c. s. bearing*, D.-K.-lager; *f. e. c. s. b. bolt*, D.-K.-l-bolzen; *f. e. c. s. bearing brasses*, D.-K.-l-schalen; *f. e. c. s. bearing keep*, D.-K.-l-deckel; *f. e. c. s. b. k. bolt*, D.-K.-l-d-bolzen; *f. e. crosshead brasses*, D.-Kreuzkopflagerschalen; *f. e. cylinder*, D.-Zylinder; *f. e. c. cover*, D.-Z.-deckel; *f. e. c. c. bolt*,

D.-Z.-d-bolzen; *f. e. cylinder drain pipe*, D.-Z.-Entwässerungsrohr; *f. e. eccentric*, D.-Excenter; *f. e. e. bolt*, D.-E.-bolzen; *f. e. e. brasses*, D.-E.-Lagerschalen; *f. e. e. rod*, D.-E.-stange; *f. e. e. sheave*, D.-E.-scheibe; *f. e. e. strap*, D.-E.-bügel; *f. e. e. s. liner*, D.-E.-b-futter; *f. e. exhaust pipe*, D.-Dampfablaßrohr; *f. e. hose*, D.-schlauch; *f. e. piston*, D.-Kolben; *f. e. p. rod*, D.-K-stange; *f. e. p. r. crosshead*, D.-K-s-Kreuzkopf; *f. e. p. r. stuffing box*, D.-K-s-Stopfbüchse; *f. e. p. r. s. b. gland*, D.-K-s-S-b-deckel; *f. e. slide valve*, D.-Schieber; *f. e. starting valve*, D.-Anlaßventil; *f. e. steam pipe*, D.-Dampfzuleitungsrohr; *f. e. stop valve*, D.-Absperrventil; *f. e. valve casing*, D.-Schieberkasten; *f. e. v. c. door*, D.-S.-deckel; *f. e. valve rod*, D.-Schieberstange; *f. e. v. r. stuffing box*, D.-S.-Stopfbüchse; *f. e. v. r. s. b. gland*, D.-S.-S.-deckel.

fire extinguisher, Feuerlöschapparat; - *grate*, Rost; - *hearth*, Unterlage der Kombüse; - - *carline*, Stütze der K.; - *hook*, Feuerhaken; - *hose*, Feuerspritzenschlauch; - *man*, Heizer; - *man's cock*, Aschhahn; - *picker*, Schürhaken; - *place top*, Feuerbüchsendecke; - *proof*, teuerfest; - *rake*, Feuerharke; - *roll*, F-rolle; *to beat the* - -, F-lärm schlagen; - *screen*, F-schirm; - *ship*, Brander; - *slice*, Schüreisen; - *shovel*, Feuerschaufel; - *station*, der beim Feuer einzunehmende Platz; - *tube*, F.-rohr; - *boiler*, F-r-kessel; - *up*, auffeuern; - *wood*, Brennholz.

firing, sich erhitzen; 2. Beheizung; - *shovel*, Feuerschaufel; - *with back flame*, Pultfeuerung.

first bower, der große Bug-anker; - *class pilot*, Vollotse; - *coat*, der erste Anstrich; - *flood*, Vorflut; - *lining of the bow*, Eisgang; - *of the ebb*, Vorebbe; - *quarter ebb*, Viertel Ebbe; - *reef*, erstes Reff; - - *band*, e. R-band; - *watch*, e. Wache (8—12 p. m.).

firth, Meerenge.

fish a mast od. *yard*, einen Mast od. eine Rahe fischen; - *the anchor*, den Anker fischen; - *with a running hitch*, mit einer Schlinge nach etwas t.

fish, 1. Ankerkippung; 2. Blatt (des Bugspriets); 3. Schalung (des Mastes); - *back*, Fisch-reep; - *boom*, Ankerauf-windebaum; - *davit*, Fisch-davit; - - *socket*, F.-spur; - *front of a mast*, Schwalpe vorn am Maste; - *gig*, Elger; - *hook*, Penterhaken; - *mart-ingale*, Domper der Fisch-davits; - *oil trade*, Tranfahrt; - *pendant*, Fischreep; - *pro-peller*, Fischschwanzschrau-be; - *shackle*, Fischschäkel; - - *bolt*, F.-bolzen; - *tackle*, Fischtakel; - - *block*, F.-block; - - *fall*, F.-läufer; - - *pendant*, F.-hanger; - *tail propeller*, Fischschwanz-schraube.

fisherman, Fischerfahrzeug - 's *bend* od. *knot*, Fischer-knoten.

fishery, Fischereigrund; - *harbour*, Fischerhafen; - *police*, Fischereipolizei.

fishing boots, Wasserstiefel; - *boundary*, Fischereigrenze; - *craft*, Fischerfahrzeug; - *fleet*, F-flotte; - *gear*, Fische-reigerät; - *ground*, F-grund; - *harbour*, Fischerhafen; - *smack*, F-schaluppe; - *tackle*, F-gerät; - *vessel*, F-fahrzeug.

fit, bestroppen, beschlagen, zutakeln, anschließen, an-einanderlegen, fugen; - *close*, dicht anschließen; - *out*, aus-rüsten; - *the planks on a vessel*, ein Schiff beplanken; - *the rigging on a mast head*, das stehende Gut auflegen; - *the stanchions underneath the beams*, die Deckbalken-stützen anbringen.

fit rod, Fitt.

fitter, Maschinenschlosser, Monteur.

fitting out and manning, Aus-rüstung und Bemannung.

fittings, Armaturen, Garnitu-ren, Einrichtungen, Zubehör.

five boater, Walfischschiff mit 5 Booten; - *crank engine*, Maschine mit 5 Kurbeln; - *mast barque*, Fünfmast-Bark; - *fore and aft schooner*, F.-Gaffelschoner; - - *full rigged ship*, F.-Vollschiff; - - *schooner*, F.-Schoner.

fix a vessel, ein Schiff befrach-ten od. verfrachten; - *the course*, den Kurs festsetzen; - *removed ceiling in its place again*, abgenommene Wege-rung wieder an ihrem Platz befestigen; - *the rigging on a mast head*, das stehende Gut auflegen.

fixed blade propeller, Schraube mit festen Flügeln; - *block*, 1. Scheibe im Schanzkleide; 2. Steertblock; - *engine*, fest-stehende Maschine; - *expan-sion*, feste Expansion; - *light*, festes Feuer; - *parrel*, fixes Rack; - *propeller blade*, fester Schraubenflügel; - *pump*, feststehende Pumpe; - *sector*, fester Sektor.

fizgig, Elger.

flag, Flagge; - *bag*, Flaggen-sack; - *chart*, F-karte; - *chest*, F-kasten; - *flag covers the cargo*, die Flagge deckt die Ladung; - *line*, F-leine; - *maker*, F-fabrikant; - *of distress*, Notflagge; - *of truce*, Parlamentärflagge; - *pole*, F-stock; - *share*, Prisenanteil des Admirals: - *ship*, Flaggenschiff; - *signal*, F-signal: - *staff*, F-stock; - - *stay*, Krückstag; - *with a waft*, Flagge im Schau.

flame tube, Feuerrohr.

flanche od. *flange*, Flansche: - *joint*, Flanschendichtung; - *of a pipe*, Rohrflansch.

flanged plate, geflanschte Platte.

flank of a tooth of a wheel, Zahnflanke.

flap, 1. Klappe; 2. klappern, schlagen: *to - backstays*, &c., Pardunen etc. durch gegenseitiges Schnüren stützen.

flapping, the sails are -, die Segel schlagen gegen den Mast.

flare up, aufflackern, Flackerfeuer; - - *light*, Flackerlicht.

flaring bow, überhängender Bug.

flash, 1. Blink (eines Leuchtturmes): 2. Goldstreifen (an der Mütze); 3. Blitz, Aufblitzen; - *light*, Blinkfeuer; - *pan*, Pfanne zum Abbrennen von Pulver als Signal; - *sector*, Blitzsektor; - *signal*, Lichtblitzsignal.

flashing see flash.

flat, 1. Watt, Untiefe; 2. Prahm; 3. mittschiffs Bodenwrange: - *aback*, ganz back; *to - aft*, dicht anholen; - *bank*, Watt: - *bastard file*, schlichte Bastardfeile; - *bottomed*, flachbodig: - - *boat*, Landungsboot; - - *punt*, flachbodige Schauke; - *built*, f.; - *calm*, Totenstille; - *chisel*, Flachmeißel; - *coast*, flache Küste; - *file*, Schlichtfeile; - *floor timbers*, die flachen Bodenwrangen; - *floored*, flachbodig; *to - in*, dicht anholen; - - - *the jibs*, die Luvklüverschoten anholen; - *iron*, Flacheisen; - *keelson plate*, Flachkielschweinplatte; - *of*

the bottom, das Flach des Bodens; - *of the deck*, Decksplanken; - *plate keel*, der flache Kiel; - - *keelson*, Flachkielschweinplatte; - *quarter*, flaches Hinterschiff; - *scarf*, Plattscherbe; - *seam*, platte Naht; - *seizing*, Plattbindselung.

flats, mittschiffs Bodenwrangen.

flatten a sail, ein Segel in der Längsrichtung des Schiffes stellen.

flaw, 1. Riß; 2. Flage (jäher Windstoß).

flawed, rissig.

fleet, 1. Flotte; 2. verfahren (Kette, Tau, Talje): *to - aft*, achtern gehen; - *dyke*, Flutdeich; *to - off*, losmachen; *to - the dead eyes of the standing rigging*, das stehende Gut verbinden.

flemish, Taue in Scheiben aufschießen; - *eye*, flämisches Auge; - *fakes*, die klar liegenden Buchten eines aufgeschossenen Taues; - *horse*, Nockpferd.

flexible, biegsam; - *coupling*, biegsame Kuppelung.

flight, Flucht (des Holzes).

float, 1. Floß; 2. Schwimmer (im Kessel); 3. flott sein, schwimmen; - *away*, wegtreiben; - *gauge*, 1. Schwimmer; 2. Stand des S.; - *of the paddle wheel*, Radschaufel; - *stick*, Zeiger am Manometer.

floatage, Treibgut.

floated by her own resources, durch eigene Hilfsmittel flott geworden.

floating anchor, Treibanker; - *beacon*, T-bake; - *body*, Schwimmkörper; - *booms*, Schlängel; - *breakwater*, der schwimmende Wellenbrecher; - *bridge*, Floßbrücke; - *buoy*, wachende Boje; - *coffin*, seeuntüchtiges Schiff;

- *crane*, - *derrick*, Schwimm-kran; - *dock*, S-dock; - *elevator*, schwimmende Getreideheber; - *harbour*, s. Hafendamm; - *hospital*, Krankenschiff; - *ice*, Treibeis; - *light*, treibendes Feuer, Feuerschiff; - *line*, Wasserlinie; - *object*, treibender Gegenstand; - *pier*, schwimmende Landungsbrücke; - *safe*, über Bord geworfener Behälter für Wertpapiere; - *stage*, Kalfaterfloß; - *wharf of a flying bridge*, Landungsbrücke einer Fähre; - *wreckage*, treibende Schiffstrümmer.

floe, Eisscholle.

flog, auspeitschen; - *the glass*, das Glas od. die Sanduhr od. Wachtuhr schütteln und vorstellen.

flogging hammer, Vorschlaghammer.

flood, Flut, überfluten; - *anchor*, Flutanker; - *cock*, F-hahn; - *gate*, F-tor; *the - makes*, die Flut beginnt; - *mark*, Hochwassermarke; - *tide*, Flut, F-tide.

floor, 1. Bodenwrange, Flach des Schiffes; 2. Lanen des Bootes; 3. Sohle des Docks; - *ceiling*, Flachwegerung; - *guide*, Sente zwischen Kimm und Kiel; - *head*, Bodenwrangenende; - - *ceiling*, Stauchwegerung; - - *chock*, Bodenwrangenkalb; - *hollow*, Rundung des Bodens; - *plan*, der wasserpasse Riß; - *plate*, Bodenwrangenplatte; - *riband*, Kimmkolschwein; - *ribbon*, Flursente; - *rider*, Katspor; - *sweep*, die Normale auf der Flursente; - *tier*, Bodenwrangenreihe; - *timber*, Bauchstück.

flooring adrift, Fußboden ist versetzt; - *of water wheel*, Radboden.

floors, Bodenwrangen; *long and short armed* -, doppelte oder lang- und kurzarmige Bodenwrangen.

flory boat, Passagierboot.

flotage, Treibgut.

flotilla od. *flotille*, Flotille.

flotsam, Treibgut; - *and jetsam*, Wrackgut.

flotson, Treibgut.

flour binn, Mehlkoje.

flow, 1. Abfluß; 2. Zufluß; 3. fieren (Schote etc.); - *of tide*, Steigen der Flut.

flowage, Überströmung.

flower of the winds, Windrose.

flowing sheets, raumschots segeln; - *water*, das auflaufende Wasser.

flue, 1. Feuerrohr; 2. F-zug; - *boiler*, Röhrenkessel; - *cleaner*, Feuerrohrreiniger.

fluid, flüssige Substanz.

fluke, Flügel des Ankers.

fluking, all -, in rascher Fahrt.

flunkey, Schiffskoch.

flurry, leichte umspringende Brise.

flush, glatt; - *bolt*, eingelassener Schubriegel; - *deck*, Glattdeck; - - *ship*, G.-Schiff; - *head rivet*, plattköpfige Niete; - *keel*, Flachkiel; - *pipe*, Spülrohr; - *rivet*, versenkte Niete; - *riveting*, Nietenversenkung; - *with*, auf gleicher Höhe mit.

flute, Fleutschiff.

flutter, flattern, im Winde spielen.

fluttering sail, killendes Segel.

fluvial insurance, Flußversicherung.

flux and reflux, Ebbe und Flut.

fly about, rasch und häufig umspringen (Wind); - *and hoist of the flag*, Länge und Tiefe der Flagge; - *block*, Schlingerblock; - - *of the topsail tye*, Marsdrehreepsblock; - *boat*, Flieboot; - *by night*, halbe Breitfock und Leesegel; - *of the compass*, Kompaßrose; - *of the flag*, Länge der Flagge; - *out*, auswehen, im Winde flattern;

to let - the sheets, die Schoten fliegen lassen; - *to the
wind* od. - *up in the w.*, in
den Wind auffliegen; - *wheel*,
Schwungrad.
fly see also flying.
flying boom, Außenklüverbaum; - - *iron*, A-k-Brille; -
bridge, Verbindungsbrücke;
- - *rails and stanchions*, V.-
Geländer; - - *stanchions*, V.-
G.-stütze; - *jib*, Außenklüver;
- - *boom*, A-baum; - - - *foot
rope*, A.-pferd; - - - *guy*, A.-
geie; - - - *iron*, A-bügel; - - -
stay, A.-Stampfstag; *f. j.
downhaul*, A.-Niederholer; *f.
j. guy*, A.-Backstag; *f. j. halliard*, A.-fall; *f.j. martingale*,
A.-Stampfstag; *f. j. sheet*,
A.-schote; *f. j. stay*, A.-leiter;
f j. tack, A.-hals; *f. j. topsail*,
Jager; - *light*, zu leicht beladen; - *martingale stay*,
Außenklüverdomper; *in a -
mess*, schlecht verproviantiert sein; - *royals*, lose Royal;
- *sails*, die obersten Segel; -
sheets, fliegende Schoten.
foam, Schaum, - *cock*, S-hahn;
- *collector*, S-sammler.
foddering, der lose Leikstopfen.
fog alarm, Nebelalarmsignal;
- *bank*, N-bank; - *bell*, N-
glocke; - *bow* od. - *dog* od.
- *eater*, N-streifen mit sehr
hellem Glanz; - *gun*, N-ka-
none, N-signal; - *horn*, N-
horn; - *patches* od. *showers*,
N-schwaden; - *signal*, N-
signal.
fold of the block, Blockscheibe;
to - the sails, die Segel auftuchen.
folding boat, Klappboot; -
chair, Bordsessel.
follow in the wake, im Kielwasser folgen.
following sea, *swell*. *wind*.
fortlaufende See, Dünung,
Wind.
foot, 1. Fuß (des Masts, Segels,
Stenge); 2. mit Füßen schie-

ben; - *band*, Fußband; -
board, Laufplanke; - *brail*,
Fußgeitau; - *clew*, F-hahn-
pot; - *gore*, F-gillung; - *grating*, F-gräting; - *hook*, Auflanger; - - *shrouds*, Püttingswanten; - - *staff*, Schwichtungslatte; - *lining*, Fuß-
band; - *mat*, F-matte; - *of
a mast*, F. eines Mastes; -
of a topmast, F. einer Marsstenge; - *rails*, abgerundete
Heckleisten; - *rope*, 1. Pferd
(unter den Rahen); 2. Fuß-
leik (des Segels), Fußsaum,
Fußsaum; - *valve*, Fußventil;
- - *box*, Saugventilgehäuse;
- - *guard*, S-v-Hubbegrenzer;
- - *seat*, S-v-sitz; - *waling*,
Bauchdielen.
footing, 1. Fußhalt; 2. Hänsel-
geld; *to miss one's-*, fehl-
treten.
force a vessel on shore, ein
Schiff auf den Strand setzen;
- *and lifting pump*, Saug-
und Druckpumpe; - *of wind*,
Windstärke; - *pump*, Druckpumpe; - *the fires*, auffeuern.
forced draught, künstlicher
Zug; - - *engine*, Maschine
zur Erzeugung von künst-
lichem Z.
*forced draught engine connect-
ing rod*, Künstlichen Zug-
erzeugungsmaschinen -Pleu-
elstange; *f. d. e. c. r. bolt*,
K. Z.-P.-bolzen; *f. d. e. c. r.
bottom end keep*, K.Z.-Kurbel-
zapfenlagerschalendeckel; *f.
d. e. c. r. b. e. liner*, K. Z.-
Pleuelstangenfußfutter; *f. d.
e. c. r. top end keep*, K. Z.-
Kreuzkopflagerschalendek-
kel; *f. d. e. crank pin bolt*,
K. Z. - Kurbelzapfenlagerbolzen; *f. d. e. c. p. brasses*,
K. Z.-K-z-l-schalen; *f. d. e.
c. shaft*, K. Z.-Kurbelwelle;
f. d. e. c. s. bearing, K. Z.-
K.-Lager; *f. d. e. c. s. b.
brasses*, K. Z.-K.-L-schalen;
f. d. e. c. s. bearing bolt, K.
Z.-K.-L-bolzen; *f. d. e. c. s.*

bearing keep, K. Z.-K.-L-deckel; *f. d. e. c. s. b. k. bolt*, K. Z.-K.-L.-d-bolzen; *f. d. e. crosshead bolt*, K. Z.-Kreuzkopflagerbolzen; *f. d. e. c. brasses*, K. Z.-K-k-l-schalen; *f. d. e. cylinder*, K. Z.-Zylinder; *f. d. e. c. cover*, K. Z.-Z.-deckel; *f. d. e. c. c. bolt*, K. Z.-Z.-d-bolzen; *f. d. e. cylinder drain pipe*, K. Z.-Z.-Entwässerungsrohr; *f. d. e. eccentric*, K. Z.-Excenter; *f. d. e. e. bolt*, K. Z.-E.-bolzen; *f. d. e. e. brasses*, K. Z.-E.-Lagerschalen; *f. d. e. e. rod*, K. Z.-E.-stange; *f. d. e. e. sheave*, K. Z.-E.-scheibe; *f. d. e. e. strap*, K. Z.-E.-bügel; *f. d. e. e. s. liner*, K. Z.-E.-b-futter; *f. d. e. exhaust pipe*, K. Z.-Dampfablaßrohr; *f. d. e. piston*, K. Z.-Kolben; *f. d. e. p. rod*, K. Z.-K-stange; *f. d. e. p. r. crosshead*, K. Z.-K-s-Kreuzkopf; *f. d. e. p. r. stuffing box*, K. Z.-Kolben-stangen-Stopfbüchse; *f. d. e. p. r. s. b. gland*, K. Z.-K.-S.-deckel; *f. d. e. slide valve*, K. Z.-Schieber; *f. d. e. starting valve*, K. Z-Anlaßventil; *f. d. e. stop valve*, K. Z.-Absperrventil; *f. d. e. valve casing*, K. Z.-Schieberkasten; *f. d. e. v. c. door*, K. Z.-S.-deckel; *f. d. e. valve rod*, K. Z.-Schieberstange; *f. d. e. v. r. stuffing box*, K. Z.-S.-Stopfbüchse; *f. d. e. v. r. s. b. gland*, K. Z.-S.-S.-deckel.

forcer, Kolben.

forcing pump, Druckpumpe; - *valve*, Austrittsventil.

fore, vorn; - *and aft*, 1. längsschiffs; 2. vorn und hinten; *f. a. bridge*, Verbindungsbrücke; *f. a. a. fender*, Scheuerleiste; *f. a. a. line*, Längenlinie; *f. a. a. rigged*, nur mit Schraatsegeln getakelt; *f. a. a. r. mast*, Schonermast; *f.a.a. sails*, Schraatsegel; *f. a. a. schooner*, Gaffel-schoner; - *and after*, 1. Längsträger (in einer Luke); 2. Gaffelschoner; 3. Zeltbaum; - *bay*, Lazarett; - *beak*, Schiffsschnabel; - *body*, 1. Vorderschiff; 2. V-spanten; - *boom*, Vorbaum; *f. b. topping lift*, V.-Toppenant; *f. b. t. l. purchase*, V.-Dirktalje; - *bowline*, Fockbulin; - *brace*, F-brasse; - - *pendant*, F-b-schenkel; - *bunt line*, F-Bauch-gording; - *cabin*, Vorderkabine; - *cant timber*, Vorkantspant.

forecastle, 1. Back; 2. Volkslogis; - *awning*, Sonnensegel der Back; - *bulkhead*, B-schott; - *coaming*, B-süll; - - *angle bar*, B-s-winkel; - *deck*, B-deck; *f. d. beam*, B-d-balken; *f. d. b. angle bar*, B-d-b-winkel; *f. d. b. hanging knee*, B-d-b-Hängeknie; *f. d. b. lodging knee*, horizontales Knie des B-d-b; *f. d. b. shelf*, Backbalkweger; *f. d. b. stringer*, Backdeckbalken-stringer; *f. d. b. s. plate*, B.-platte; *f. d. b. tie plate*, Backdeckbalken - Längsschiene; *f. d. fastening*, Back-deck-Befestigung; *f. d. pillar*, B-d-Stütze; *f. d. plating*, B-d-beplattung; *f. d. stringer*, B-d-stringer; *f. d. s. angle bar*, B-d-s-winkel; *f. d. s. plate*, B-d-s-platte; *f. d. waterway*, B-d-Wasserweg; - *frame*, Backspant; - *guard rods*, Backgeländerstangen; - *head*, Backdeck; - *ladder*, Backleiter; - *man*, B-gast; - *rail*, B-reling; - *rails and stanchions*, B-geländer; - *sheerstrake*, Schergang der B.; - *skylight*, Oberlicht der B.; - *sole*, Fußboden des Logis; - *stanchion*, Geländerstütze der Back; - *stove*, Logisofen; - *ventilator*, Backventilator; - *waterway*, Wassergang der Back.

fore cat harpings, Fockschwichtingen; -*chain plates*, F-rüsteisen; - *chains* od. *channels*, F-rüsten; - *clew garnet*, F-geitau; - *cockpit*, Bootsmannsgat; - *concern*, Vordergeschirr; - *courses*, Focksegel; - *cuddy*, Vorderpflicht; - *deadwood*, Vorsteven-Auf klotzung; - *deck*, Vordeck; - *foot*, Stevenlauf; - - *rope*, Fockpferd; - *frames*, Vorderspanten; - *futtock shrouds*, Vor-Marspüttingswanten; - *futtocks*, Vor-Marspüttingen; - *gaff*, Schonersegelgaffel; *f. g. topsail*, Vorgaffel-Toppsegel; *f. g. t. downhaul*, V.-T.-Niederholer; *f. g. t. halliard*, V.-T.-fall; *f. g. t. sheet*, V.-T.-schote; *f. g. t. tack*, V.-T.-hals; - *gear*, Vordergeschirr; - *guy*, V-geie; - *hatch*, V-luke; - *hatchway coaming*, V-l-süll; - *hold*, Vorderraum; - *hoods*, vorderste Planken od. Platten der Innen- od. Außenhautgänge; - *hook*, Bugband; - *jeer*, Fockfall; - *land*, Vorland; - *leech*, Stagkante; - - *line*, Fock-Nockgording; - - *rope*, Vorleik; - *lift*, Focktoppenant; - - *purchase*, Fockrahe - Toppenantstalje; - *lock of the anchor stock*, Ankerstocksplint; - *lower cross trees*,Fockmast-Dwarssahlinge; *f. l. rigging*, Fockwanten; *f. l. shroud*, Fockwant; *f. l. studding sail*, Vor-Unterleesegel; *f. l. s. s. halliard*, V.-U.-fall; *f. l. s. s. inner h.*, V.-U.-Binnenfall; *f. l. s. s. outer h.*, V.-U.-Außenfall; *f. l. s. s. sheet*, V.-U.-schote; *f. l. s. s. tack*, V.-U.-hals; *f. l. s. s. yard*, V.-U.-rahe; *f. l. trestle trees*, Fockmast-Längssahling; - *man*, Bootsbugmann; - *mast*, Fockmast; *f. m. braces*, Vorbrassen; *f. m. cap*, Fockmast-Eselshaupt; *f. m. coat*, F.-kragen; *f. m. cross trees*, F.-

Dwarssahlingen; *f. m. head*, Topp des Fockmastes; *f. m. h. pendant*, F-masthanger; *f. m. men*, Matrosen; *f. m. shrouds*, Fockwanten; *f. m. step*, F-mastspur; *f. m. tackle*, F-hangertakel; *f. m. trestle trees*, F-mast-Längssahling; *f. m. wedges*, F-m-keile; - *most backstay*, Vorderpardune; - - *frame*, Ohrspant; - - *shrouds*, Fockwant; - *part*, Vorschiff; - *peak*, V-piek; - - *deck*, V-p-deck; - - *halliard*, V-p-fall; - - *tank*, V-p-tank; - - - *suction valve*, V-p-t-Saugventil; - *pendant tackle*, Fockseitentakel; - *preventer stay*, loser F-stag; - *propeller*, Vorpropeller; - *rake*, das Überhängende des Bugs; *to - reach in stays*, beim Wenden an Fahrt gewinnen; *to - reach on a ship*, ein Schiff totsegeln; - *reef tackle*, Fock-Refftalje; - *rigging*, 1. Fockwanten; 2. F-takelage.
fore royal, Vor-Royal; *f. r. backstay*, V-R-Pardune; *f. r. bowline*,V-R-Bulin; *f.r. brace*, V-R-Brasse; *f. r. bunt line*, V-R-Bauchgording; *f. r. clew line*, V-R-Geitau; *f. r. cross trees*, V-R-Sahlingen; *f. r. foot rope*, V-R-pferd; *f. r. halliard*, V-R-fall; *f. r. h. purchase*, V-R-fall; *f. r. lift*, V-R-Toppenant; *f. r. mast*, V-R-stenge; *f. r. m. head*, Flaggentopp der V-R-s-; *f. r. rigging*, V-R-want; *f. r. sheet*, V-R-schote; *f. r. stay*, V-R-stag; *f.r. studding sail*, V-R-Leesegel; *f. r. s. s. boom*, V-R-L-s-spiere; *f. r. s. s. downhaul*, V-R-L-s-Niederholer; *f. r. s. s. halliard*, V-R-L-s-fall; *f. r. s. s. sheet*, V-R-L-s-schote; *f.r. s.s. tack*, V-R-L-s-hals; *f. r. s. s. yard*, V-R-L-s-rahe; *f. r. yard*, V-R-r-.
fore runnings, Vorlaß; - *sail*, 1. Fock; 2. Schonersegel;

- - *boom*, S.-baum; - - *halliard*,
S.-fall; - - *sheet*, S.-schote; -
sheet, 1. Fockschote; 2. Scho-
nersegelschote;-*ship*,Vorder-
schiff: - *shore*, Seeufer; -
shrouds, Fockwanten; - *skysail*,Vor-Scheisegel;*f.s. backstay*, V-S.-Pardune;*f.s.brace*,
V-S.-Brasse; *f. s. clew line*,
V-S.-Geitau; *f. s. foot rope*,
V-S.-pferd; *f. s. halliard*, V-
S.-fall; *f. s. lift*, V-S.-Top-
penant;*f.s. mast*,V-S.-stenge;
f. s. sheet, V-S.-schote; *f. s.
stay*, V-S.-stag; *f. s. yard*,
V-S.-rahe; *f. stay*, Fockstag;
f. staysail, Stagfock; *f. s.
downhaul*, S.-Niederholer;
f. s. halliard, S.-tall; *f. s.
sheet*, S.-schote; *f. s. stay*,
S.-leiter; *f. s. tack*, S.-hals;
- *stem*,Vordersteven;-*stroke
of the piston*, der Kolbenhub vorwärts; - *studding
sails*, Fockleesegel; - *tack*,
Fockhals; - - *block*, F.-block;
- *tackle*, Vortakel;- - *pendant*,
Fockmasthänger; - *tank*,
Vortank; - - *filling and
suction valve box*, V.-Füll-
und Saugventilkasten; -
throat halliard, Vorklaufall;
- *thwart*, vordere Sitzbank;
- *top*, Vormars; - - *braces*,
V.-brassen.
fore topgallant,Vorbramsegel;
f. t. backstay, V-b-pardune;
f. t. bowline, V-b-bulin; *f. t.
brace*. V-b-brasse; *f. t. buntline*, V-b-Bauchgording; *f. t.
cap*, V-Bramstenge - Eselshaupt; *f. t. clew line*, V-b-
Geitau; *f. t. cross trees*,
Dwarssahlingen der V-b-
stenge; *f. t. foot rope*, V-b-
pferd; *f. t. futtock shrouds*,
V-b-Püttingswanten; *f. t.
futtocks*, V-b-Püttingen; *f. t.
halliard*, V-b-fall; *f. t. leech
line*. V-b-Nockgording; *f. t.
lift*,V-b-Toppenant;*f.t.mast*,
V-b-stenge; *f. t. m. cap*, V-
b-s-Eselshaupt; *f. t. rigging*,
V-b-s-wanten; *f. t. sail*, V-b-

segel; *f. t. sheet*, V-b-schote:
f. t. shroud, V-b-want; *f. t.
stay*, V-b-stag: *f. t. s. sail*.
V-b-s-segel: *f. t. studding
sail*, V-b-Leesegel; *f. t. s. s.
boom*, V-b-L-s-spiere:*f.t.s.s.
downhaul*, V-b-L-s-Nieder-
holer; *f. t. s. s. halliard*, V-b-
L-s-fall; *f. t. s. s. sheet*, V-b-
L-s-schote; *f.t.s.s. tack*, V-b-
L-s-hals; *f.t.s.s.yard*, V-b-L-
s-rahe; *f. t. trestle trees*, V-b-
stengen-Längssahling; *f. t.
tye*, V-b-Drehreep:*f. t. yard*,
V-b-rahe.
fore topmast, Vor-Marsstenge:
f. t. backstay, V-M-pardune;
f. t. cap, V-M-stenge-Esels-
haupt:*f.t.cross trees*, Dwarssahlingen derV-M-stenge;*f.t.
head*,V-M-s-topp; *f.t.rigging*,
f. t. shrouds, V-stengewanten;
f. t. stay, V-Stengestag; *f. t.
staysail*,V-S.-segel;*f.t.s.down-
haul*,V-S.-s-Niederholer;*f.t.s.
halliard*, V-S.-s-fall; *f. t. s.
sheet*, V-S.-s-schote; *f. t. s. s.
pendant*,V-S.-s-s-schenkel;*f.t.
s.stay*,V-S.-s-leiter;*f.t.s.tack*,
V-S.-s-hals;*f.t. studding sail*,
V-Oberleesegel;*f.t.s. s.boom*,
V-O.-spiere: *f. t. s. s. downhaul*, V-O.-Niederholer; *f. t.
s. s. halliard*, V-O.-fall; *f. t.
s. s. sheet*, V-O.-schote; *f. t.
s. s. tack*, V-O.-Hals; *f. t. s.
s. yard*, V-O.-rahe; *f. t. trestle trees*, V-Marsstengen-
Längssahling.
fore topping lift, Vordirk.
fore topsail, Vor-Marssegel;
f. t. bowline, V-M-bulin; *f. t.
brace*, V-M-brasse; *f. t. b.
pendant*, V-M-b-schenkel: *f.
t. buntline*, V-M-Bauchgord-
ing; *f. t. clew line*, V-M-
Geitau; *f. t. foot rope*, V-M-
pferd; *f. t. halliard* od. *f. t.
h. purchase*, V-M-fall; *f. t.
lift*, V-M-Toppenant; *f. t.
reef tackle*, V-M-rettalje; *f.
t. sheet*, V-M-schote; *f. t.
tye*, V-M-drehreep; *f. t. yard*,
V-M-rahe.

6*

foretop staysail, Vorstagsegel.
fore trysail, Vor-Treisegel; *f. t. boom,* V-T.-baum; *f. t. brails,* V-T.-geitane; *f. t. gaff,* V-T.-gaffel; *f. t. halliard,* V-T.-fall; *f. t. inhaul,* V-T.-Einholer; *f. t. outhaul,* V-T.-Ausholer; *f. t. peak halliard,* V-T.-Piekfall; *f. t. sheet,* V-T.-schote; *f. t. tack,* V-T.-hals; *f. t. throat halliard,* V-T.-Klaufall; *f. t. vang,* V-T.-gerde; *f. t. v. pendant,* V-T.-Gaffelgerdenschenkel.

fore tye, Drehreep des Vormarsfalls; - *vang,* Vor-Gaffelgerde; - - *pendant,* V-G-gerdenschenkel; - *wind*, Wind nach vorn; - *yard,* Fockrahe; - - *boom,* F-spiere; - - *foot rope,* F-pferd;

foreign bottom od. *foreigner,* ausländisches Schiff; *foreign flag,* fremde Flagge; - *going vessel,* Schiff für großeFahrt; - *service,* Dienst auf ausländischen Stationen; - *trade* od. *voyages,* die große Fahrt; - *yard,* fremde Werft.

foremost backstay, Vorderpardune; - *beam,* vorderste Balken; - *frame,* Ohrspant; - *shroud,* Fockwant.

forge, schmieden, Schmiede; - *ahead,* vorausschießen; - - *of a vessel,* ein Schiff überholen; - *a vessel off,* ein Schiff mit aller Kraft abbringen; - *a v. over a bank* od. *shoal,* e. S. über eine Bank hinüberzwingen; - *tongs,* Schmiedezange.

forged iron, geschmiedetes Eisen.

forging, Schmiedestück; - *hammer,* S-hammer; - *machine,* S-maschine.

fork, Gabel; - *and lashing eye,* Hahnepot und Sorrauge; - *beam,* Scherstock des Decks; - *link,* Gabelglied; - *wrench,* G-schraubenschlüssel.

forked connecting rod, gegabelte Pleuelstange.

formation, Gestaltung.
formed abreast, in Frontlinie.
former, Kardusstock.
forward, vorn; - *crank shaft,* vordere Kurbelwelle; - *eccentric,* Vorwärts-Exzentrik; - *stroke,* V-Hub; - *well suction*, vorderes Brunnen-Saugventil.
forward see also fore.
fother a leak, ein Leck futtern; - *mat,* Futtermatte.

foul, 1. faul, bewachsen, schmutzig (Schiffsboden); 2. unklar; 3. seicht (Küste); 4. stürmisch (Wetter); 5. ungünstig (Wind); - *air,* unreine Luft; *to - another vessel,* mit einem andern Schiffe unklar werden; - *berth,* unklarer Ankerplatz; - *bill of health,* unreiner Gesundheitspaß; - *bottom,* 1. bewachsener Boden; 2. unklarer Grund; - *coast,* u. Küste; - *hawse,* unklare Ketten; - *running rope,* unklar laufendes Tau; - *shore,* seichte Küste; *the ship makes - water,* das Schiff rührt den Grund auf; *the ship is - of a rock,* das Schiff ist gegen Felsen gefahren; - *weather,* unsichtiges, schlechtes Wetter; - - *Jack,* ein Unheilbringer.

fouled, anchor - by the flukes armunklarer Anker; *a. - by the stock,* stockunklarer A.

foundation bolt, Fundamentbolzen; - *plate,* F-d-m-platte; - - *bolt,* F-d-m-Plattenbolzen; - - - *nut,* F-d-m-P-b-mutter.

founder at anchor, vor Anker untergehen; - *head down,* Kopf über u.; - *under sails,* unter Segel u.

four bladed propeller, vierflügelige Schraube; - *cant,* vierschäftiges Tauwerk; - *crank engine,* Maschine mit vier Kurbeln; - *cylinder compound engine,* vierzylindrige

Verbundmaschine; - *cylinder engine*, v. Maschine; - *deck ship*, Vierdeckschiff; - *fold block*, vierscheibiger Block; - - *purchase*, Gien; - *mast barque*, Viermast-Bark; - - *ship*, V.-Schiff; - *oared*, vierruderig; - *point bearing*, vier Strich-Peilung; - *sheave block*, vierscheibiger Block; - *sided sail*, viereckiges Segel; - *stranded rope*, vierschäftiges Tau; - *thread spun yarn*, vierdrähtiges Schiemannsgarn; - *way cock* od. *valve*, Vierwegehahn.

fourth bower, der vierte Buganker.

fother, futtern.

fox wedge, Gegenkeil.

foxes, Fuchsjes.

foxy, fuchsig.

F. P. A. stands for "free of particular average".

fracture, brechen, Bruch.

frame, 1. Spant; 2. Schiffsgerippe; - *a hatchway*, eine Luke mit Rahmen versehen; - *a masthole*, ein Mastloch mit R. v.; - *angle bar*, Spantwinkel; - *bolt*, S-bolzen; - *bolting*, das Aneinanderbolzen der Spanten; - *floor*, Bodenwrange; - *liners*, Spant-Füllstreifen; - *of a crane*, Krangestell; - *of bridge house*, Brückenhausspant; - *of raised quarter deck*, Spant des erhöhten Quarterdecks; - *of the poop*, Hüttenspant; - *of the slip* od. *stocks*, Bettung der Helling; - *of the vessel is put up* od. *is standing* od. *the v. is in* -, das Schiff steht in Spanten; - *riders*, Diagonalschienen; - *rivet*, Spantniete; - *saw*, Spannsäge; - *timber*, Inholz; - *work*, Spanten.

framing, Gestell. *See also frame.*

frap, mit Tauen zusammenzeisen.

frapping in lashings, die Verlaschungen zusammenzeisen.

fray, abnutzen, fressen, mahlen.

free, 1. lenzpumpen, ausschöpfen; 2. klaren (Pumpe); - *from leakage*, frei von Leckage; *to go* -, raumschots segeln; - *of breakage*, frei von Bruch; - *of damage except in case of stranding*, f. v. Beschädigung, außer im Strandungsfalle; - *of particular average*, f. v. besonderer Havarie.

freeboard, Freibord;

freebooter, Freibeuter.

free port, Freihafen; - *pratique*, Verkehrserlaubnis; - *trade*, Freihandel.

freeing, lenzpumpen; - *port*, Wasserpforte.

freezing point, Gefrierpunkt.

freight, befrachten, verfrachten, Fracht; - *in a lump sum*, Pauschalfracht; - *out and home*, Aus- und Rückfracht.

freightage, Fracht.

freighter, Befrachter.

freighting business, Befrachtungsgeschäft.

French fake, französische Bucht eines Taues; - *sennit*, französische Platting; - *shroud knot*, f. Wandknoten; - *the ballast*, Ballast umkörten.

fresh breeze, frische Brise; - *gale*, f. Sturm; - *shot*, Überschwemmungswasser; - *water*, Trinkwasser; - - *condenser*, Meerwasser-Destillierapparat; - - *Jack*, unbefahrener Seemann; - - *pipe*, Trinkwasserrohr; - - *pump*, T-w-pumpe; - - *tank*, T-w-behälter.

freshen, 1. auffrischen (Wind); 2. auffieren (Tau); 3. umkörten (Ballast); - *way*, wieder in Fahrt kommen.

freshes, Brackwasser.

freshet, Hochwasser.
Fresnel lamp, Lampe mit Fresnelscher Linse.
friction, Reibung; - *coupling*, Friktionskuppelung; - - *box*, F.-muff; - *gear*, Friktionsgetriebe; - *of piston*, Kolbenreibung; - *of slide valve*, Schieberreibung; - *plate*, Friktionsscheibe; - *rollers*, F-rollen; - *socket*, F-kegel; - - *coupling*, lösbare F-kegelkuppelung; - *wheel*, F-rad.
frictional resistance, Reibungswiderstand.
friezing, Verzierungsleiste auf der Reling.
frigate, Fregatte.
frigid zone, kalte Zone.
fringing reef, das ausliegende Riff.
frith, Meerenge.
frog od. *frock*, Troier (Seemannsjacke).
front bulkhead, Frontschott; - - *of bridge*, Brückenhausschott; - - *of forecastle*, Backschott; - - *of poop*, Hüttenschott; - *column*, Vordersäule; - *landing*, V-stoß; - *lever links*, vordere Pumpenbalanciergelenke; - *plate*, v. Stirnwand; - - *of boiler*, Frontwand des Kessels; - *rail*, F-reling; - *tube plate of boiler*, vordere Rohrwand des Kessels.
fudge a day's work, das Mittagsbesteck berechnen.
fuel, Heizmaterialien.
fulcrum, Stütze; - *of pumps*, Pumpenbockständer.
full and by, voll und bei; *very* - *aft*, hinten voll gebaut; - *bottomed*, voll gebaut; - *bow*, volle Bug; - *built*, voll gebaut; - *cargo*, volle Ladung; - *for stays*, voll halten zum wenden; - *form*, voll gebaut; - *man*, Vollmatrose; - *manned*, vollbemannt; - *pay*, ganze Heuer; - *poop*, überwölbte Hütte; - *power*, volle Kraft;

- *pressure*, Hochdruck; *in* - *range*, im vollen Bereiche; - *rigged*, voll getakelt; - - *ship*, Vollschiff; - *sheered*, mit viel Spring gebaut; - *speed ahead*, Volldampf voraus; - - *astern*, V. rückwärts; - *spread sails*, alles bei; - *twisted*, voll hart geschlagen.
fully manned, voll bemannt.
fumigate, ausräuchern.
fumigation, Ausräucherung,
functionment, Gang.
fungle, stümpern.
funnel, 1. Schornstein; 2. Trichter; - *blast pipe*, Schornstein-Blasrohr; - *bonnet*, S.-kragen; - *cape*, S.-kragen; - *casing*, S.-mantel; - *cover*, S.-kappe; - *damper*, S.-dämpfer; - *draught*, S.-Zug; - *guys*, S.-stagen; - *hood*, S.-kappe; - *light*, S.-licht; - *mark*, S.-zeichen; - *ring*, S.-band; - *shrouds*, S.-stagen; - *stage*, S.-stellage; - *stays*, S.-stagen.
fur, Kesselstein ansetzen.
furr out, die Schiffsseiten mit doppelten Planken versehen.
furl, beschlagen, festmachen; - *a sail in a body*, ein Rahsegel am Topp f.; - *the sails with rope yarns*, die Segel auf Stoßgarn setzen.
furling gasket, Beschlagzeising; - *line*, B-s-leine.
furnace, 1. Feuerbüchse; 2. Verbrennungsraum; - *bar*, Roststab; - - *bearer*, R.-träger; - *bridge*, Feuerbrücke; - *crown*, Feuerbüchsendecke; - *door*, Feuertür; - *flue*, Feuerbüchse; - *front*, Feuertürzarge; - *gases*, Feuerbüchsen-
furniture, Ausrüstung. [gase.
furr, 1. das Spunt in einem Holz; 2. mit einer Spiekerversehen. [setzt.
furred up, mit Kesselstein besetzt.
furren, das Spunt im Holze.
furring, 1. Spikerhaut; 2. das Spunt im Holze.
furrow between two waves, Wellenfurche.

furse, Reisig zum Abbrennen des Schiffsbodens.

fusible plug, leicht schmelzbarer Propfen; - - *of boiler*, Sicherheitspfropfen des Kessels.

fusibility, Schmelzbarkeit.

futtock, 1. Auflanger (Teil der Spanten); 2. Pütting (der Wanten); - *band*, P.-Band; - *chain*, P.-kette; - *head*, die fünfte, siebte und neunte Diagonale im Schiffsriß; - *hoop*, Püttingsband; - *line*, Querschnitt; - *plank*, Kielwegerungsplanke; - *plate*,

Beschlag der unterenStengewantjungfer; - *rider*, Auflanger der Kattsporen; - *ring*, Püttingsring; - *shrouds*, Püttingswanten; - *staff* od. *stave*, Schwichtungslatte; - *timbers*, Sitter u. Auflanger.

futtocks, 1. Püttingen (der Wanten); 2. Sitter und Auflanger (Teil der Spanten); *first* -, der erste Sitter; *second* -, d. e. Auflanger; *third* -, d. zweite Sitter; *fourth* -, d. z. Auflanger; *fifth* -, d. dritte A.

fuzzy, morsch.

G.

gab, Auge; - *hook*, od. - *of the eccentric*, Gabel des Excenters; - *lever* od. *lifter*, Gabelhebel.

gabbard od. *gabert*, Leichter.

gaff, 1. Gaffel; 2. Staken, Bootshaken; *to blow the* -, den Angeber spielen; - *end*, Gaffelende; - *fall*, G-läufer; - *sail*, G-segel; - - *boom*, G-sbaum; - *setter*, Bootshaken; - *topsail*, Gaffeltoppsegel; - - *downhaul*, G.-Niederholer; - - *halliard*, G.-fall; - - *sheet*, G.-schote; - - *tack*, G.-hals; - *traveller*, Gaffel-Ausholring.

gaffers, Spieren.

gain fast to windward, schnell Luv gewinnen; - *on a bearing*, ein Merkzeichen nach Änderung einer Peilung gewinnen; - *on the tide*, die Gezeit aussegeln; - *the weather gage* od. *side*, Luv gewinnen; - *to windward by backing*, auflavieren; - *upon a vessel*, gegen ein Schiff gewinnen.

galaxy, Milchstraße.

gale, Sturm; - *away*, vor dem S. weglaufen.

galeas od. *galeasse*, Galeasse.

galeongee, türk. Matrose.

galiot, Kuffgaleasse.

galleass, Galeasse.

galled, schamfielt.

gallery ladder, Sturmleiter.

galley, 1. Kombüse; 2. Galeere; - *arch*, Bootshaus; - *door*, Kombüsentür; - - *hinge*, K.-Scharnier; - *foist*, Staatsbarke; - *funnel*, Kombüsen-Schornstein; - *hitch*, Galeerenknoten; - *house*, Bootshaus; - *news*, Klatsch; - *punt*, offenes Küstenboot; - *stoker*, pflichtloser Matrose; - *stove*, Kombüsenofen; - *yarn*, Räubergeschichte.

gallion, Gallion; - *cheek*, Schließknie des G.

galliot, Kuff.

gallon measure, Gallonenmaß.

gallows od. - *bitts*, Galgen; - *stanchion*, Gerüst für Rundhölzer, Galgenstreber.

galvanized bolt, verzinkter Bolzen; - *iron*, verzinktes Eisen; - - *bucket*, verzinkte eiserne Pütze; - *steel*. v. Stahl·

gammon the bowsprit, das Bugspriet zurren; - *knee*, Stevenknie; - *plate*, Schäkelplatte der Bugsprietzurring; - *ring*, Herzring d. B.; - *shackle*, Schäkel d. B.

gammoning, Bugsprietzurring; - *chain*, Zurringskette; - *hole*, Bugsprietzurringsgatt; - *hoop*, B-s-bügel; - *of a bowsprit*, B-s-zurring; - *piece*, Lieger.

gang, Trupp; - *of riveters*, Nieterkolonne.

gangboard, Laufplanke.

gang cask, kleines Wasserfaß; - *plank*, Steg.

gangway, 1. Laufplanke; 2. Fallreep; 3. Fallreepspforte; *to bring to the* -, mit Schlägen bestrafen; - *door*, Ladepforte; - *ladder*, Fallreepsleiter; - *in scaffolding*, Laufbrücke; - *port*, Fallreeppforte; - *rail*, F-r-reling.

gangways in the hold, Wallgänge.

gantlet see *gauntlet*.

gant line, Jolltau; - *lope*, Hangmattsjolle.

gape, aufgesprungen, offen stehen.

garbage scow, Flachboot zur Müllabfuhr.

garbel, Kielgang.

garboard, Kielgang; - *bolt*, K.-bolzen; - *plank*, K.-planke; - *plate*, K.-platte; - *seam*, K.-naht; - *strake*, Kielplanke.

garland, 1. Taukragen; 2. Rationsnetz.

garnet, Ladetakel.

garnish, besetzen, verzieren.

garniture of a boiler, Kesselgarnitur.

gas buoy, Gasboje.

gases, Gase.

gasket, 1. Beschlagzeising; 2 geflochtene flache Hanfliederung.

gat, Seegatt (Fahrwasser zwischen Banken).

gate, 1. Schleusentor; 2. Mün-

dung od. Seegrenze; *in a* -, durch eine Welle gegen einander geworfen.

gather fresh way, wieder gut in Fahrt kommen; - *headway*, in Fahrt kommen; - *steerage way*, dem Ruder zu gehorchen anfangen; - *in* od. *up the sails*, die Segel auftuchen; - *up the skin*, Brook nehmen beim Segel festmachen; - *way*, in Fahrt kommen.

gatt od. *gatway*, Seegatt,

gaub line, Achterholer des Stampfstocks.

gauge, 1. Manometer; 2. Meßinstrument; 3. Pegel; 4. Zeiger; 5. Tiefgang; 6. aichen, messen; - *cock*, Probierhahn; - *glass*, Wasserstandsglas; - - *ring*, W-s-Dichtungsring; - *pipe*, W-s-rohr; - *rod*, Peilstock der Pumpen; - *steam pipe*, Dampfdruckmesserrohr; - *tap*, Probierhahn.

gauging rod, Peilstock.

gauntlet, Hangmattsjolle; *to run the* -, Spießruten laufen.

gaunt lope, Hangmattsjolle.

gauntree, Kopfhölzer.

gauze wire and red lead joint, Metalldrahtgaze- und Mennigkitt-Dichtung.

gauger, Aichmeister.

gear, Geschirr, Gestänge, Getriebe, Triebwerk, Vorrichtung, Zubehör; *to be in* -, 1. brauchbar, in Ordnung; 2. eingreifen (Zahnräder); *to* - *together*, see 2; *out of* -, unbrauchbar, nicht in Ordnung; - *capstan*, kleines Gangspill.

geared engine, Maschine mit Übersetzungswirkung.

gearing, Vorgelege; - *shaft*, Steuerungswelle.

general average, große Havarie; - - *statement*, H. g. Dispache; - *cargo*, Stückgüter; - *course*, Generalkurs.

generator, Dampferzeuger.

gentle breeze, leichte Brise; - *gale*, frische Kühlte.

gentlemen of the jacket, Matrosen.

gently, sacht, vorsichtig.

geo - navigation, Besteck durch Gissung.

German Ocean, Nordsee.

get aground, festgeraten, stranden; - *ashore*, 1. an Land kommen; 2. stranden; - *clear*, klar bekommen od. kommen; - *ground*, Grund bekommen; - *her afloat*, das Schiff flott bekommen; - *her off*, d. S. abbringen; - *pooped*, hinten eine Sturzsee über- bekommen; - *sight of*, in Sicht bekommen; - *the an- chor ready*, den Anker klar machen; - *the offing*, offene See gewinnen; - *under sail* od. *way* od. *weigh*, den An- ker lichten od. segelfertig machen; - *up steam*, Dampf aufmachen.

getting up, the --, Dampfent- wickelung.

gib, 1. Gegenkeil, Hakenkeil; 2. Kranbalken (der Ma- schine); - *and cotter*, Keil und Lösekeil.

gibe see gybe.

Giffard's injector, der Giffard Injektor.

gift rope, Schlepptau.

gig, Gig.

gil - guy, Ladebaumholer.

giller, Steuerreep.

gimbal of a compass, Kompaß- bügel.

gimbals od. *gimbels* od. *gimbles*, Balancierbügel.

gimblet, 1. Frittbohrer; 2. einen Anker am Grunde um seinen Stock drehen.

gimbols see gimbals.

gimlet see gimblet.

gin, Löschrad; - *block*, Fla- schenzug; - *cheeks*, Schenkel des Hebebocks; - *sling*, Tau- kranz.

gipsies, Kettenscheiben.

giration, Drehung,

girder, Bindebalken, Trag- balken, Träger, Kielschwein, Längswinkeleisen; - *angle bar*, Trägerwinkel; - *plate*, Trägerplatte,

girdle, Doppelung.

girt, zu steif vertäut; - *line*, Jollentau; - - *block*, J.-block; - - *of the sheers*, Jolltau; - - *of the mizzen brails*, Auf- holer der Besahnbrok; - *strain of a staysail*. Span- nung in der Schotstrak.

girth band, Bauchband; - *of a vessel*, Spantumfang eines Schiffes.

give a coat of paint, an- streichen; *g. a. c. of tar*, lab- salben; - *a full twisting to a rope*, ein Tau zur vollen Härte drehen; - *a wide berth*, weit aus dem Wege gehen; - *bail*, Kaution stellen; - *chain*, Kette ausstecken; - *chase*, verfolgen; - *her a sheer*, das Schiff gieren lassen; - *her an overhaul*, das S. überholen; - *out*, nachgeben, versagen; - *the course*, den Kurs angeben; - *the ship her sheer*, das Schiff schlichten; - *to the wind*, dem Winde nachgeben; - *topping*, kränzen; - *up tacks and sheets*, Halsen und Schoten aufstechen; - *way*, sich begeben, springen; - - *with a will*, gut ausholen (beim Rudern).

gland, 1. Deckel; 2. Stopf- büchsendeckel; - *bush*, S.; - *cock*, der Hahn, dessen Lilie durch eine Stopfbüchse geht; - *of a plumber block*, Pfannendeckel; - *of a stuff- ing box* od. *of the rod*, Stopfbüchsendeckel; - *pack- ing*, S-b-packung; - *safety stud*, Stopfbüchsen-Siche- rungsstift; - *stud*, Stopf- büchsenstift.

glass, 1. Barometer; 2. Fern-

glas; 3. Logglas; - *gauge*, Wasserstandsglas.
glazed frost, Glatteis.
glin, Nebelerscheinung vor schlechtem Wetter.
globe lamp od. *lantern* od. *light*, Kugellampe.
globular chart, Planiglob; - *light*, Kugellampe; - *sailing*, im größten Kreise segeln.
gloomy, trübe.
glut, 1. Wuhling (um Gangspill); 2. Unterlage unter einer Handspake; 3. das Gugsplit (im Segel); - *a rope*, ein Tau mit Sand bestreuen.
go about, über Stag gehen: - *ahead*, vorwärts g.; - - *eccentric*, Vorwärts-Excenter; - - - *strap*, V.-E.-bügel; - *aloft*, nach oben gehen; - - *hand over hand*, sich aufpalmen; - *and haul*, vorangehen; - *astern*, rückwärts gehen; - - *eccentric*, Rückwärts-Excenter! - - - *strap*, R.-E.-bügel; - *by the board*, dicht über Deck abbrechen (Mast); - *clear*, klar kommen; - *down*, 1. abnehmen (Wind; See); 2. fallen (Barometer); 3. in's Meer sinken; - *free*, raumschotts segeln; - *in ballast*, mit Ballast beladen; - *to sea*, in See gehen; - *to the bottom*, in's Meer sinken; - *to the weather side* od. - *to windward*, luvwärts kommen.
go-ashores, die Kleider zum Landbesuch.
goblet, Becher, Eimer.
gobline, Achterholer des Stampfstocks.
godsend, Strandgut.
gondola, Gondel.
gondolier, Gondolier.
gone, vernichtet, verloren.
good board, Schlagbug.
goods plundered from a wreck, Strandraub.
goose neck, Schwanenhals; - *wing*, Schothorn; - - *of the foresail*, S. der Fock.

gore, Gillung (des Segels).
gores, Schrägen.
gorge, Rinne (der Rolle).
goring, Ausschnitt (des Segels); - *cloth*, schräg geschnittenes Segelkleid.
gorze, Reisig (zum Abbrennen des Schiffsbodens).
gouge, Bossiereisen.
government steamer, Regierungsdampfer; - *tug*, R-schlepper; - *yard*, Marinewerft.
governor, Regulator; - *balls*, R.-kugeln; - *cut off*, regulierte Expansion; - *of Watt*, Schwungkugelregulator; - *rod*, Regulatorstange; - *spindle*, R-spindel; - *spring*, R-feder; - *valve*, Drosselventil; - - *gear*, Regulatorsteuerung,
gowk storm, Frühjahrssturm.
grab, Klammer; - *line*, auf Deck herabhängendes leicht zu ergreifendes Tau.
grabble, mit Haken fischen.
graft, bestricken.
grain ceiling, Getreidewegerung; - *cut*, überspänig; - *elevator*, Getreideheber; - *feeder*, G-t-d-feeder; - *upset*, geknickte Faser (im Maste); *in the - of the vessel*, in gleicher Richtung und dicht vor dem Schiffe.
granny's bend od. *knot*, Altweiberknoten.
graphite Graphit.
grapline od. *grapling* od. *grappnel*, Dreganker; - *rope*, Dregtau.
grapple, 1. verankern; 2. Schiffshaken; 3. Enterhaken werfen; 4. anhaken; - *shot*, Geschoß mit Tau und Greifhaken.
grappling, 1. Enterhaken; 2. nach dem Anker fischen.
graps, Greifer.
grasshopper beam, Balancier; - *engine*, B.-maschine mit schwingendem Hebel.

grate, Rost; - *surface*, R-fläche.

grated top, Röstermars.

grating, Gräting; - *beam*, Rostschwelle; - *deck*, Deck aus Gitterwerk; - *hatch*, Lukengräting; - *of cabin skylight*, Kajüten-Oberlichtgräting; - *of crew space skylight*, Logis O.; - *of engine room s.*, Maschinen-O.; - *of messroom s.*, Messen-O.; - *of the head*, Gallionsgräting; - *top*, Röstermars.

grave, den Schiffsboden reinigen.

gravel ground od. *gravelly bottom*, Kieselgrund.

graving, das Reinigen und Labsalben desSchiffsbodens; - *beach*, Kielbank; - *dock*, Trockendock; - *piece*, 1. Spunt; 2. hölzernes Ersatzstück.

gravity, Schwere.

grazing blow, ein streifender Schlag; - *the ship*, das Schiff streifen.

grease, schmieren, Schmiermittel; - *cock*, S-hahn; - *cup*, S-büchse; - *tap*, S-hahn.

greaser, Maschinenschmierer.

great cabin, große Kajüte; - *circle sailing*, Segeln in größerem Kreise; - *coasting trade*, große Küstenfahrt.

greave, den Schiffsboden abbrennen.

green hand, unbefahrener Seemann; - *heart*, Grünholz; - *light*, grünes Seitenlicht.

greve, flacher Sandstrand.

grey elm wood, Grauulmenholz; - *hound*, Schnelldampfer.

gridiron, 1. Kielbank; 2. Balkenrost; - *evolution*, beim Einfahren einen Kreis von außen nach innen beschreiben und dann parallel neben einem andern Schiffe fahren; - *expansion valve*, Gitterschieber; - *valve*, Rostschieber.

grind, 1. abnutzen, abreiben, fressen, mahlen; 2. abziehen, einschleifen, schleifen.

grindstone, Schleifstein.

grip, fassen.

gripe, 1. Anlauf, Stevenanlauf; 2 Bootskrabber; 3. greifen (Kette).

griping, luvgierig.

groin, Stack.

gromet, Schiffslehrling.

grommet, Taukranz; - *of a royal mast*, Kragen der Royalstenge; - *of a stay*, Stagring.

groove, Rille (der Rolle); - *and tongue joint*, Verspundung.

grooving machine, Nutmaschine.

groper, englisches Kriegsschiff in der Nordsee.

gross adventure, Bodmerei; - *average*, große Havarie; - *effect*,Totalleistung;-*freight*, Bruttofracht;-*measurement*, Bruttotonnengehalt; - *sea*, grobe See; - *tonnage*, Bruttotonnengehalt; - *weight*, B-gewicht.

ground, 1. Grund; 2. an G. geraten od. sitzen; - *a vessel*, ein Schiff aufwinden; - *chain*, Grundkette; -*futtock*, der erste Sitter; - *hold*, 1. Ankergrund; 2. Ankerwerk; - *ice*, Grundeis; - *log*, G-log; - *sea*, G-see; - *strake*, Kielgang; - *swell*, Grunddünung; - *tackle*, Ankergeschirr, Grundgeschirr; -*tier*,unterste Lage;-*timber*,Bauchstück; - *way*, Stapelklotz-Unterbau.

ground, *headway over the -*, Fahrt voraus über den Grund.

groundage, Ankerzoll.

grounder, leicht strandendes Schiff.

grounding, an Grund geraten; - *lights*, Notlampen; - *signal*, Signal für das Festsitzen.

grow, stehen, weisen (Kette); - *a short stay*, wie ein Steng-

stag stehen; - *exceedingly,* zum Springen steif stehen; - *underneath the bottom of the vessel,* die Kette steht unter dem Schiffsboden.
growing pay, Heuer (nach Abarbeiten des Handgeldes).
growler od. *grumbler,* Unzufriedener.
grummet, Grummetstropp.
guage see gauge.
guarantee engineer, Garantiemaschinist.
guard, Schutzvorrichtung; - *board,* kleines Bergholz; - *boat,* Rondeboot; - *iron,* eiserner Schutzbügel; - *of a skylight,* Gitter eines Oberlichts; - *of a valve,* Ventilanschlag; - *plates of steam pipes,* Schutzbleche der Dampfrohre; - *rail,* Maschinenraumgeländer; - *ring,* Sicherungsring; - *rod,* Geländerstange; - *rods of raised quarter deck,* Geländerstangen des erhöhten Quarterdecks; - *ship,* Wachtschiff.
gudgeon, Lagerzapfen; - *of a bitt,* Einschnitt für das Spillwellenlager; - *of the rudder,* Fingerling des Ruders.
Guese stands for Portuguese.
guess rope od. - *warp,* Schlepptrosse; - *warp boom,* Schwingbaum.
guest rope, Bootstau.
guide, Geradeführung, Gleitbahn, Leitung; - *bar,* Führungsstange; - *block,* Gleitschuh; - *pulley,* Leitblock; - *rod,* Führungsstange; - *of high pressure piston,* Hochdruckkolben-F.; - - *of intermediate p. p.,* Mitteldruckkolben-F.; - - *of low p. p.,* Niederdruckkolben - F.; - *shoe,* Gleitschuh.
guiding light, Richtfeuer.
gulf, Golf; - *stream,* G-strom.
gulleting of the rudder, Gillung des Ruders.

gum wood, Gummibaumholz.
gun boat, Kanonenboot; - *deck,* Batteriedeek; - *fire,* Morgen- und Abendschußzeit; - *port,* Stückpforte; - *room,* Offiziersmesse; - *shot,* Kanonenschuß; - *tackle purchase,* doppelt einscheibige Talje.
gunnel see gunwale.
gunner, Feuerwerker; - '*s mate,* Unter-F.
gunny bag, Jutesack.
Gunter's rig, Schiebe-Toppmast; - *scale,* Rechentafel.
gunwale, 1. Schandeckel; 2. Dollbord (im Boot); **3.** Mit dem Schandeck zu Wasser liegen; - *angle bar,* Schandeckelwinkel; - *of bridge house,* Schandeckel der Brücke; - *of forecastle,* S. d. Back; - *of poop,* S. d. Poop; - *of raised quarter deck,* S. d. erhöhten Quarterdecks; - *plate,* Wetterdeck-Stringerplatte; - *stringer,* Stringer des Oberdecks.
gusset, Fächerplatte; - *in a boiler,* Blechzwickel; - *plate,* horizontale Knieplatte; - *stay,* Eckanker.
gust of wind, Windstoß.
gusty, stürmisch.
gutted, ausgebrannt, leer gewaschen.
gutter, Rinne; - *angle bar,* innerer Rinnsteinwinkel; - *board,* Rinnleiste; - *deck angle bar,* Innenwinkel des Oberdeckstringers; - *plank,* Rinnleiste; - *waterway,* Rinnstein.
guy, mit Ketten verlaschen; - *clear,* freihalten, freibolen.
guy, Gei; - *of sheers,* G. eines Bocks; - *of the boom,* Bullentau; - *of the cargo pendant,* Vorausholer des Toppreeps; - *of the jib boom,* Klüverbackstag; - *of the main boom,* Bullentau; - *of the swinging boom,* Kehrtau des Backsbaums; - *tackle,* Stoppertalje.

gybe a sail, 1.ein Segel beim Segeln vor d. Winde übergehen lassen; 2. ein S. durchkaien.

gybing, giepen.
gyn tackle, Hebezeug.

H.

h. stands for *hail*.
haaf boat, Fischerboot.
haar, 1. Haarrauch (bei östl. Winde); 2. heulender Oststurm.
haberdden od. *haberdine*, getrockneter Stockfisch.
hackmatack, amerik. Lärchenholz.
hack watch, Beobachtungsuhr.
Hadley's quadrant, engl. Quadrant.
hag's teeth, Unregelmäßigkeiten in einer Matte.
hail, 1. ein Schiff anrufen; 2. Hagel; - *fellow*, guter Kamerad; - *from*, beheimatet in; - *squall*, Hagelbö; - *stones*, Schlossen; *within -*, innerhalb Rufweite.
half a crown, rundes Auge; - *beam*, Bastardbalken; - *angle bar*, B-winkel; - *engine*, Halb-Balanciermaschine; - *breadth plan*, der wasserpasse Riß; - *deck*, Halbdeck; - *drowned land*, Watt; - *ebb*, halbe Ebbe; - *flood*, h. Flut; - *floor*, Sitter; - *hitch*, Halbstich; - *and seizing*, Trossenstich; - *and timber hitch*, halber Stich und Zimmermannsstich; *at - mast* od. - *mast high*, halbstocks; - *minute glass*, Halbminutenglas; - *moon in the mast thwart*, Mastloch in der Segelducht; - *pay*, halbe Heuer; - *pike*, Enterpieke; - *poop*, halbüberwölbte Hütte; - *port*, halbe Stückpfortenklappe; - *round bar iron*, Halbrundeisen; - - *bastard file*, halbrunde Bastardfeile;

- *round iron*, halbrundes Eisen; - - *smooth file*, halbrunde Schlichtfeile; - *seas over*, halb betrunken; - *sheave*, Halbscheibe; - - *hole*, totes Scheibengatt; - *speed ahead*, halbe Kraft vorwärts; - - *astern*, h. K. rückwärts; - *staff high*, halbstocks; - *tide*, zwischen Ebbe und Flut; - - *rock*, bei halber Ebbe sichtbare Klippe; - *timbers in the cant body*, die unteren Auflanger der Kantspanten; - *time survey*, Halb-Zeit-Besichtigung; - *tub*, Balje; - *turn ahead* oder *astern*, halber Schlag vorwärts resp. rückwärts.
haliard od.*halliard* od.*halyard*, Fall: - *block*, F-block; - *of a yard*, F- einer Rahe; - *purchase*, F.; - - *fall*, F.-Taljeläufer; - *tub*, Marsfallbalje.
hamber od. *hambro line*, Bindselleine.
hammer test, Prüfung mit dem Hammer.
hammock, Hängematte; - *batten*, H.-latte; - *clew*, H.-Hahnepot; - *cloth*, H-mdecke; - *clue*, H-m-Hahnepot; - *gantline* od. *girtline*, Hangmattsjolle; - *lashing*, H-m-steert; - *nettings*, Finknetz; - *rack*, H-m-latte.
hamper, Kramstücken.
hance, Fall des Decks.
hand along, weiter langen od. w. mannen; - *a sail*, ein Segel beschlagen; - *beckets*, Handpferde; - *bellows*, H-blasebalg; - *crane*, H-kran; - *cuffs*, H-schellen; - *distri-*

buting lever, H-steuerungs-hebel; - *drag*, 1. H-bagger; 2. Baggerhaken; - *drill*, Handbohrer; - - *machine*, Handbohrmaschine; - *feed pump*, Handpumpe; - *gear*, H-steuer; - - *lever*, Anlaß-hebel; - *glass*, Halbminuten-glas; - *grapling*, Handhaken; - *grommets*, H-pferde; - *guide*, H-führer; - *hole*, H-loch; - *hook*, 1. H-haken; 2. Granat-haken; - *lead*, Handlot; - - *line*, H.-leine ; - *lever*, Hand-hebel; - *mast piece* od. *spar*, Mastholz; - *over hand*, Hand über H.; - *power lever*, H-hebel; - *pump*, H-pumpe; - - *bucket*, H-p-kolben; - - - *ring*, H-p-k-ring; - *pump rod*, Handpumpenstange; - - *valve*, H-p-ventil; - *punching machine*, Handlochmaschi-ne; - *rail*, Handgeländer; - *reversing gear*, Handum-steuerungsvorrichtung; - *riveting*, Handnietung; - *sail*, Handsegel; - *saw*, H-säge; - *seizing*, Obenbindsel; - *shears*, Handschere; - *spike*, H-spake; - - *of the windlass*, Spill-spake; - *starting lever*, Hand-steuerungshebel; - *steering gear*, H-steuergerät; - - *wheel*, H-s-rad; - *swab*, Boots-schwabber; - *taught* od. *tight*, mit Händen steif ge-holt; - *tiller*, Ruderpinne; - *to the helm* od. *wheel!* Mann an's Ruder! - *turning gear*, Handdrehvorrichtung; - *vice*, Handschraubstock; - *wheel*, Handrad.

handle, hantieren, Griff, Hand-habe, Schwengel.

hands, all - to quarters! Klar Schiff!

handsomely, sacht, vorsichtig.

handy billy, die dritte Hand; - *vessel*, gut steuerndes Schiff; - *weather*, handiges Wetter.

hang, 1. sacken; 2. fallen, hangen (Mast etc.); - *aback*,

sich treiben lassen; - *aft*, achter überhangen; - *for-ward*, zu viel gestagt sein; - *on to the booms!* An die Bockspiere! - *up with a becket*, aufknebeln.

hanging block, Drehreeps-block unter dem Stengen-topp; - *clamp*, Boiklampe; - *compass*, Hängekompaß; - *keel*, H-kiel; - *knee*, H-knie; - - *bolt*, H-k-bolzen; - *lamp*, Schlingerlampe; - *mat*, Schamfielungsmatte; - *pawls*, Hängpallen; - *stage*, leichte Stellage; - *valve*, Gelenk-ventil.

hangman's knot, Schifter-knoten.

hank, 1. Strähne, Strang; 2. Säuger (des Segels); - *for -*, Schlag für S.

harbour authorities, Hafen-behörde; - *bar*, H-barre; - *boom*, H-schlängel; - *deck* H-deck; - - *stanchions*, H-d-Geländerstütze; - *dues*, H-geld; - *duty*, H-dienst; - *leech line*, Schmiergording; - *light*, Hafenfeuer; - *log*, H-journal; - *master*, H-meister; - *pilot*, H-lotse; - *reach*, der zum Hafen führende Teil eines Flusses; - *of distress*, Not-hafen; - *of refreshment*, Er-frischungshafen; - *of refuge*, Schutzhafen; - *police*, Hafen-polizei.

harbourage, Hafengebühren.

hard a board, hart an Bord; - - *lee*, h. in Lee; - - *port*, h. Rechtsruder; - - *starboard*, h. Linksruder; - - *weather*, h. luvwärts das Ruder; - *down*, h. daal; - *and fast*, 1. hoch und trocken; 2. rückt und rührt sich nicht; - *laid rope*, hartgeschlagenes Tau; - *of steerage*, hart auf's Ruder sein; - *solder*, Hart-lot; - *up* od. - - *the helm* od. - - *weather*, hart auf das Ruder; - *wood*, hartes Holz.

harden up, 1. ganz voll laufen lassen (Tank); 2. steifholen, steifsetzen.
hardened steel, gehärteter Stahl.
harl, Haąrrauch.
harmattan, Harmattan.
harness cask, Rationsfaß; *men's - for towing boats,* Halskoppel; *- hitch,* Notstich.
harpen od. *harpin* od. *harping,* Sente mit Schmiege.
harpoon, Harpune, harpunieren; *- line,* Harpunleine.
harpooner, Harpunierer.
harr, Haarrauch.
harsh steel, unschweißbarer Stahl.
hasp, 1. Klappe; 2. Bügel; 3. das Halbrund für das Bugspriet eines Bootes.
hat money, Extragratifikation.
hatch, 1.Luke; 2. Lukenöffnung; 3. L-deckel; *- bar,* L-stange; *- batten cleats,* Schalkleistenklampen; *- battens,* S-l-; *- beam,* Lukenbalken; *- - angle bar,* L.-winkel; *- boat,* Fischerboot mit Behälter; *- carling,* Lukenschlüssel; *- coaming* od. *combing* od. *coming,* L-süll; *- - angle bar,* L-s-winkel; *- companion.* Lukenkappe; *- cover,* Stülpluke; *- frame,* Lukenrahmen; *- grating,* L-gräting; *- house,* L-haus; *- - protectors,* Lukenkappen - Schutzvorrichtung; *- ladder,* L-leiter; *- lid,* Stülpluke; *- ring,* Lukenring; *- scuttle,* 1. Fenster; 2. Lichtpforte; *- stanchions,* Lukenstützen; *- survey,* L-besichtigung.
hatchel, kleine Axt.
hatches, under -, wohlverwahrt im Raum.
hatchet, Beil.
hatchway bulkhead, Lukenkoker; *- netting,* L-netz; *- stopper,* L-stopper; *- tarpaulin,* 1. Schalkpersenning; 2. Matrosenhut; *- trunk,* Lukenkoker.

hatchway see also hatch.
haul, holen, ziehen, schleppen; *- aboard the tack,* den Hals dicht anholen: *- aft,* anholen: *- - jibs starboard sheets!* Klüverschoten Steuerbord! *- - the sheets!* Untersegelschoten an Bord holen! *- ahead,* vorausholen; *- alongside,* längsseits holen; *- ashore,* ans Land ziehen; *- astern,* achterausholen: *- close aft the sheet,* die Schote dicht anholen; *- down,* niederholen; *- home,* beiholen: *- in,* einholen; *- - and fasten the braces,* die Brassen anholen und festmachen; *- - for Algiers,* das Schiff nach Algier bringen: *- - the log,* das Log einholen; *- - the slack,* das Lose einholen; *- off,* anluven; *- - all,* achter und vorn zugleich rundbrassen; *- out,* ausholen; *- over the boom,* die Baumschote anholen; *- round,* rund brassen; *- - a point,* eine Landspitze vorsichtig umsegeln; *- taught* od. *taut* od. *tight,* steifholen; *- the sheets aft,* die Schoten anholen; *- the ship up,* das Schiff aufholen; *- the tacks aboard,* die Halsen anholen; *- the topsail sheets home,* die Marsschoten vorholen: *- the wind,* beim Winde brassen: *- - again,* wieder an den Wind gehen; *- the wind on the port tack,* scharf an den Wind mit Backbordhalsen über Steuerbordbug gehen; *- two blocks,* Block an B. holen; *- under the chains,* sich unter die Rüsten begeben; *- up the courses,* die Untersegel aufholen; *- the helm,* das Ruder luvwärts legen: *- - the tack,* den Hals aufholen; *- the ship on the stocks,* das Schiff auf die Helgen holen; *- the wind,* beim Winde brassen.

haulage, Transportkosten von od. nach dem Schiffe.

hauling *line*, Verholleine; - *part of a tackle*, Anholpart eines Takels.

haunch, der Fall des Decks.

haven, Hafen; - *master*, H-meister. *(See also harbour & port.)*

havenage, Hafenabgabe.

hawse, 1. Klüse; 2. vor zwei Ankern liegend; - *bags*, Klüsensäcke; - *block*, K-deckel; - *bolster*, K-backe; - *box*, K-fütterung; - *buckler*, K-deckel; - *chock*, K-band; - *fallen*, die See bricht durch die Klüsen; - *flap*, K-deckel; - *full*, durch die Klüsen Wasser übernehmen; - *hole*, K-loch; - *hook*, K-band; - *pieces*, K-hölzer; - *pipe*, K-rohr; - - *collar*, K-r-flansch; - - *cover*, K-r-Deckel; - - *flange*, K-r-flansch; - *plug*, K-pfropfen; - *timber*, Klüsholz; - *plug*, Klüsenpfropf; - *wood*, Klüsholz.

hawser, Trosse; - *bend*, Kabelstich; - *laid cordage*, trossweise geschlagenes Tauwerk; - - *rope*, t. g. Tau; - *port*, Schleppforte; - *wise laid cordage*, trossweise geschlagenes Tauwerk.

hawsing *mallet*, Kalfater-hammer.

haze, Dies.   [hammer.

hazy, diesig.

head, 1. Kopf od. Vorderende eines Schiffes; 2. Fallhorn; *by the-*, vorderlastig; *How is the-?* Wie liegt es an? - *another vessel*, rascher als ein anderes Schiff laufen.

head and heel of a timber, das obere und untere Ende eines Auflangers; - *board*, Galliousbrett; - *boom*, Jägerstock; - *braces*, Vorbrassen; - *cloth*, Gallionskleid; - *clew* oder *clue of a hammock*, Kopfende oder Knüttel einer Hängematte; - *cringle*, Kopflägel; - *earing*, Nockbindsel; - *fast*, vordere Landfeste; - *gallery*, Gallionsgalerie; - *gear*, Vordergeschirr; - *gore*, Kopfgillung; - *grating*, Gallionsgräting; - *hole*, Gaatche am Rahliek; - *knee*, Gallionsknie; - *land*, Vorgebirge; - *ledge*, Querstück eines Luksülls; - *plate*, querschiffs liegende Süllplatte; - *leech*, Oberleik; - *light*, Topplaterne; - *line*, Rahtau; - *lining*, Verdoppelung am Rahliek; - *most*, vorderst; - *netting*, Seitengräting des Gallions; - *of a beam*, Topp; - - *galley*, Schnabel; - - - *mast*, Topp; - - - *sail*, Kopf eines Segels; - - - *stockless anchor*, K. e. stocklosen Ankers; - - - *timber*, das obere Ende eines Auflangers; - *of the bow*, Bugspitze; - - - *capstan*, Kopf des Gangspills; - - - *careen*, Unterlauf zum Vordersteven; - *of water*, Wasserhöhe; - *piece*, Fallappen; - *pilot*, Lotsenkommandeur; - *pump*, Bugpumpe; - *rails*, Gallionsreling; - *ring*, Leitring; - *rope*, 1. Rahleik; 2. Anschlagleik (eines dreieckigen oder Gaffelsegels); 3. vordere Verholleine; - *sails*, Vorsegel; - *sea*, Gegensee; - *serang*, Meister; - *sheets*, Vorschoten; - *stick*, Fallknüppel; - *swell*, Gegendünung; - *tabling*, Kopfsaum; - *timber*, Stütze der Gallionsreling; *to-the sea*, in See liegen; *with-to sea*, mit dem Kopfe gegen die See liegen; - - *to wind*, mit der Nase im Winde liegen; - *valve*, Druckventil; - - *box*, D-v-gehäuse; - *way*, Fahrt voraus; - - *eccentric*, Vorwärtsexzenter; - - - *rod*, V.-stange; - - - *sheave*, V.-scheibe; - - - *strap* V.-bügel; - *way over the ground*, Fahrt voraus über den Grund; - *wind*, Gegenwind; - *yard*, Fockrahe.

health officer, Quarantäne-Arzt.

heaping sea, Kabbelsee.

heart, 1. Zunge (eines hölz. Mastes); 2. Stagblock (B. mit einem Loch); 3. Herz (Ducht im Tau); 4. Herzrad (Maschine); - *block*, großer Jungfernblock; - *wheel*, Herzrad; - *with scores for the lanyard*, Dodshoft mit Einkerbungen für das Taljereep; - *without s. f. t. l.*, D. mit glattem Gatt.

hearth, Herd.

hearty, mit aller Kraft.

heat by friction, Erhitzung durch Wärme; - *wave*, Hitzwelle.

heated, erhitzt; - *steam*, heißer Dampf.

heater, Vorwärmer.

heating, Heizung; - *apparatus*, Heizvorrichtung; - *by steam*, Dampfheizung; - *power*, Heizkraft; - *surface*, H-fläche; - *the feed water*, Vorwärmen des Speisewassers; - *tube*, Siederöhre.

heave, einhieven, hieven, werfen; - *about*, rasch über Stag gehen; - *ahead*, voraus hieven; - *anchor h.*; - *and a-weigh!* Reiß den Anker aus! - *and paul!* Hiev pall! - *and rally!* Hiev mit Kraft! - *and set*, auf und nieder stampfen; - *astern*, achteraus hieven; - *astrain*, mit Kraft h.; - *at the windlass*, mit dem Ankerspill einhieven; - *down*, niederhieven, kielholen, auf die Seite legen; - *in*, einhieven; - *by means of a heaver*, zusammenzwingen; - - *sight*, in Sicht kommen; - - *stays*, über Stag gehen; - - *the slack*, das Lose einhieven; - *off*, abhieven; - *out*, losmachen; - *pawl*, pallhieven; - *short*, kurz hieven; - *taught*, steif h.; - *together!* Hiev zugleich! - *the lead*, das Lot werfen; - *the log*, das

Log w.; - *to*, beidrehen, backbrassen; - *up*, aufhieven; - *upon a rope*, an einem Tau hieven.

heaver, Drehknüppel, Hebebaum.

heaving, hieven, einhieven, werfen; - *line*, Wurfleine; - *mallet*, Klopfkeule; - *motion*, aufsteigende Bewegung.

heavy gale, schwerer Sturm; - *repairs*, große Reparaturen; - *sea*, hochgehende See; - *swell*, schwere Dünung; - *warp*, Pferdleine; - *weather*, schweres od. vollhandiges Wetter.

heck boat, Heckboot.

heel, krängen, überlegen; - *gunwale to*, mit dem Schandeckel im Wasser liegen; - *to port*, nach Backbord krängen.

heel, der Hiel, die Hieling, die Hacke, das Vierkant; - *of a mast*, Fuß eines Mastes; - - - *pillar*, Stützenfuß; - - - *spar*, Spierenfuß; - - - *timber*, Unterende eines Inholzes; - - - *topmast*, Fuß einer Marsstenge; - *of the keel*, Hieling des Kiels; - *of the rudder*, Sohle des Ruders; *to come round on the -*, auf gleicher Stelle wenden; - *brace*. Hacköse; - *chain of the jib boom*, Fußkette des Klüverbaums; - *hoop*, Hackenband; - *jigger*, Fußtalje; - *knee*, Fußknie; - - *bolt*, F-k-bolzen; - *lashing*, 1. Fußlaschung; 2. Spiersteert der Leesegelspiere; - *pintle*, Fußzapfen; - *post*, hinterer Propellersteven; - *rope*, Fußlaschung der Bockspieren; - - *of the jib boom*, Jollentau des Klüverbaums; - *tackle*, Fußtalje; - - *of the props* (od. *spars*) *of a pair of sheers*, Fußlaschung der Bockspieren; - *tenon*, Fußzapfen (eines Mastes); - - *of the bowsprit*, Bugspriet-F.;

to give a heel to port, nach Backbord krängen.
heeling angle, Krängungswinkel; *- error,* K-fehler; *the lower part of the -,* Hacke der Bramstenge.
height of the tide, Fluthöhe; *- - - tween decks,* Höhe des Zwischendecks; *- of water in boiler,* Wasserstand im Kessel. [graph.
heliograph, Sonnenlicht-Tele-
heliographic communication, Mitteilung durch den Heliographen.
helm, Ruder; *- alee!* od. *put the - -!* Ruder in Lee! *- amidships!* Mittschiffs das R.! *- close to!* R. luvwärts an Bord! *- lashed,* festgebundenes R.; *- less,* steuerlos; *- manoeuvre,* Rudermanöver; *- on board* od. *- over,* das Ruder an Bord gelegt; *- port,* Hennegat; *- - transom,* unterster Heckbalken; *- tackle,* Nottalje; *- put up,* Ruder nach Luv gelegt.
helmsman, Rudersmann.
helve of an axe, Axtstiel.
hemisphere, Halbkugel. [holz.
hemlock, Schierlingstannen-
hemp cable, Hanf-Ankertau *- packing,* H-packu ng; *- rope* H-tau.
hemped piston, Kolben mit Hanfliderung.
hen coop, Hühnerstall.
hermaphrodite brig, Briggschoner.
herring buss, Heringsbüse, H-boot; *- smack,* H-fischer.
hickory, Hickoryholz.
hide drogher, Häuteschiff; *- rope,* Ledertau.
high and dry, hoch und trocken sitzen; *- between decks,* tief verbunden im Zwischendeck; *- land,* hohes Land; *- latitudes,* hohe Breiten.
high pressure, Hochdruck; *- - boiler,* H.-Kessel; *- - connect-*

ing rod, H.-Pleuelstange; *h. p. c. r. bolt,* H.-P.-bolzen; *h. p. c. r. bottom end,* H.-Kurbelzapfenlagerschalen; *h. p. c. r. b. e. keep,* H.-K.-deckel; *h. p. c. r. b. e. liner,* H.-Pleuelstangenfußfutter; *h. p. c. r. top end keep,* H.-Kreuzkopflagerschalendeckel; *h. p. crank pin,* H.-Kurbelzapfen; *h. p. c. p. bolt,* H.-K.-Lagerbolzen; *h. p. c. p. brasses,* H.-K.-Lagerschalen; *h. p. c. shaft,* H.-Kurbelwelle; *h. p. c.s. bearing,* H.-Kurbelwellenlager; *h. p. c. s. b. bolt,* H.-K.-bolzen; *h. p. c. s. bearing brasses,* H.-K.-schalen; *h. p. c. s. bearing keep,* H.-K.-deckel; *h. p. c. s. b. k. bolt,* H.-K.-d-bolzen; *h. p. c. s. journal,* H.-K.-zapfen; *h. p. c. web,* H.-Kurbelbacke; *h. p. crosshead bolt,* H.-Kreuzkopflagerbolzen; *h. p. cylinder,* H.-Zylinder; *h. p. c. admission port,* H.-Z.-Eintrittskanal; *h. p. c. cover,* H.-Z.-deckel; *h. p. c. c. bolt,* H.-Z.-d-bolzen; *h. p. cylinder drain cock,* H.-Z.-Drainagehahn; *h. p. cylinder drain pipe,* H.-Z.-Entwässerungsrohr; *h. p. c. escape valve,* H.-Z.-Sicherheitsventil; *h. p. c.e.v.load,* H.-Z.-S.-belastung; *h. p. c. e. v. spindle,* H.-Z.-S.-spindel; *h. p. c. e. v. spring,* H.-Z.-S -feder; *h. p. c. exhaust port,* H.-Z.-Austrittskanal; *h. p. c. jacket,* H.-Z.-mantel; *h. p. c. liner,* H.-Z.-Einsatz; *h. p. c. stuffing box gland,* H.-Z.-Stopfbüchsendeckel; *h. p. eccentric,* H.-Excenter; *h. p. e. brasses,* H.-E.-Lagerschalen; *h. p.e. bolt,* H.-E.-bolzen; *h. p.e.gear,* H.-E.-Vorrichtung; *h. p. e. rod,* H.-E.-stange; *h. p. e. sheave,* H.-E.-scheibe; *h. p. e. strap,* H.-E.-bügel; *h. p. e. s. liner,* H.-E.-b-futter; *h. p. engine,* H.-maschine; *h. p.*

gear, H.-gestänge; *h. p. gland*, H.-Stopfbüchse; *h. p. guide*, H.-Geradführung; *h. p. g. shoe*, H.-Gleitschuh; *h. p. piston*, H.-kolben; *h. p. p. gland*, H.-k-deckel; *h. p. p. guide rod*, H.-k-Führungsstange; *h. p. p. packing ring*, H.-k-Liderungsring; *h. p. piston rod*,H.- Kolbenstange; *h. p. p. r. crosshead*, H.-K.-Kreuzkopf; *h. p. p. r. c. brasses*, H.-K.-K.-Lagerschalen; *h. p. p. r. c. guide*, H.-K.-K.-führung; *h. p. p. r. stuffing box*, H.-Kolbenstangen-Stopfbüchse; *h. p. p. r. s. b. gland*, H.-K.-S.-deckel; *h. p. plunger piston*, H.-Plunger-Kolben; *h. p. receiver pipe*, H.-Dampfreservoir-Rohr; *h. p. slide valve*, H.-schieber; *h. p. steam*, H.-dampf; *h. p. sternway guides*, H. - Rückwärtsbewegungs-Gleitplatten; *h. p. tube*, H.-rohr; *h. p. turbine*, H.-Turbine; *h. p. t. engine*, H.-Turbinenmaschine; *h. p. valve balance piston*, H.-schieber-Abbalanzierungskolben; *h. p. v. b. p. cylinder*, H.-s-A.-Schutzkappe; *h. p. v. casing*, H.-Schieberkasten; *h. p. v. c. door*,H.-S-k-deckel;*h. p.v.c. escape valve load*, H.-S-k-Sicherheitsventilbelastung ; *h. p. v. chest*, H.-S-k-; *h. p. v. c. door*, H.-S-k-deckel; *h. p. v. c. escape valve load*, H.-S-k-Sicherheitsventilbelastung ; *h.p.v.gear*,äußere Steuerung des H.-Zylinders; *h. p. v. rod*, H.-Schieberstange; *h. p. v. r. stuffing box*, H.-S.-Stopfbüchse; *h. p. v. r. s. b. gland*, H.-S.-S.-deckel; *h. p. v. spindle*,H.-Schieberstange; *h. p.v.s. guide*, H.-S.-führung. *high rigged*, hoch getakelt; *on the - seas*, auf hoher See; *- tide*, Hochwasser; *- top*, Mastspitze; *- water*, Hochwasser; *- - by force of*

wind, Windstau; *- - level*, Hochwasserniveau; *- - mark*, H-w-marke; *- - spring*, Springflut; *- wind*, starker Wind.

hind part, Hinterschiff.

hinge, Scharnier; *- bolt*, S.-bolzen; *- hook*, Stützhaken; *- pin*, Scharnierstift.

hire, heuern, mieten, Heuer.

hitch, Schlag, Stich, Knoten, festmachen, mit dem Bootshaken erfassen; *- a rope to*, ein Tau feststecken an; *- the buoy*, die Ankerboje fangen; *- the tug*, den Schlepper festmachen.

hitcher, Bootshaken.

H. M. S. = S. M. S.

hoar frost, Reif.

hobbler,Strandläufer,Treidler.

hog, 1. Schrubber, spanischer Besen; *- brace*, *- chain*, *- frame*, eine Art Längsverband über Deck, um eine Biegung zu verhüten.

hogged, durchgebogen.

hogging frame, Längsverband; *- moment*, Bruchmoment.

hoist, 1. Tiefe od. Breite (der Flagge); 2. T. od. Heiß (des Segels); 3. H. (des Mastes); *to - a boat or flag*, ein Boot od. eine Flagge heißen; *- ashes*, Asche h.; *- away!* Heiß weg! *- in a boat or flag*, ein Boot od. eine Flagge einheißen; *- out a b.*, ein Boot aussetzen; *- the flag with a waft*, die Flagge im Schau wehen lassen; *- up*, aufbringen, aufheißen.

hoisting, heißen; *- engine*, Heißmaschine; *- gear*, H-vorrichtung; *- machine*, H-maschine.

hold, greifen, fassen (Anker); *- her own*, sich gut halten; *- her way*, Fahrt behalten; *- her wind*, sich gut am Winde halten; *- off*, frei halten; *- on*, beibleiben; *- -*

7*

a rope, ein Tau festhalten od. stoppen; - *tack with*, Kurs und Geschwindigkeit einhalten mit; - *water*, mit den Riemen streichen.

hold, Laderaum, Raum; - *beam*, R-balken; - - *angle bar*, R-b-winkel; - - *clamp*, R-b-Unterbalkweger; - - *hanging knee*, R-b-Hängeknie; - - *knee rider*, R-b-Kattspor; - - *lodging k.*, horizontales Knie des R-b-; - - *shelf*, R-b-weger; - - *spirketting*, R-b-Setzweger; - - *stringer*, R-b-stringer; - - - *angle bar*, R-b-s-winkel; - - - *inner a. b.*, Innenwinkel des R-b-s-; *h. b. stringer plate*, R-b-s-platte; *h. b. s. shell lugs*, kurze R-b-s-winkel; *h. b. waterway*, R-b-Wassergang; - *bunker*, Unterbunker; - *ceiling*, Raumwegerung; - *coal bunker*, Unterbunker; -*fast*, 1. Tau zum Festhalten; 2. Federbolzen; - *gang*, Raum-Arbeitertruppe; - *ladder*, Raumleiter; *to keep a good - of the land*, sich nahe am Lande halten; - *pillar* od. *stanchion*, Raumstütze; - *stringer*, R-stringer; - - *angle bar*, R-s-winkel; - *ventilator*, R-ventilator.

holder, Raumarbeiter.

holding bolt, Riegelbolzen; - *down bolt*, Fundamentbolzen; - - - *nut*, F.-mutter; - *ground*, Ankergrund; - *up bolt*, Kielbolzen; -*up hammer*, Gegenhalter.

hole for a thole pin, Dollengatt; - *in the sky*, sehr dunkle Stelle am südlichen Sternenhimmel; - *of the hawse*, Klüsenloch; - - - *privy*, Brillgat.

holes in the head of the windlass od. *capstan*, Spakenlöcher im Spillkopf.

holiday tour, Feiertagsausflug.

holidays, Freiaugen.

hollow, 1. Toppauflanger; 2. Ausschnitt (des Holzes); - *chisel*, Hohlmeißel; - *cleat*, Sorrklampe; - *keel*, Hohlkiel; - - *plate*, gewölbte Kielplatte; - *pillar*, hohle Stütze; - *sea*, h. See; - *shaft*, Hohlwelle.

holy, durchlöchert; - *stone*, Scheuerstein, mitS.scheuern.

home, anchor is coming -, der Anker geht durch; *a sheet is -*, eine Schote ist vor; - *freight*, Rückfracht; - *port*, 1. inländischer Hafen; 2. Heimats-H., beheimatet; - *trade*, Binnenhandel; - *ward bound*, auf der Heimreise; - - *bounder*, Heimatswimpel; - - *cargo*, Rückladung; - - *freight*, Retourfracht.

homogeneous iron, Homogeneisen.

honour with a sulate, mit Kanonenschüssen begrüßen.

hood, 1. Kappe (der Luke od. Pumpe); 2. Kragen (über den Augen des stehenden Gutes); 3. Luke (eines Fischerbootes); - *end fastening*, Bolzen der vorderen und hinteren Außenbeplankung; - *ends*, Plankenenden (der Spündung des Vor- und Hinterstevens).

hoodings od. *hoods*, Hoods.

hook, 1. Bugband; 2. Haken, einhaken; 3. Huk od. Landspitze; - *a tackle*, eine Talje einhaken; - *and butt scarph*, Hakenlaschung; - *block*, Hakblock; - *bolt*, 1. Hakenbolzen; 2. Schaufelbolzen (des Schaufelrades); - *scarph*, Hakenlaschung.

hooker, Hukergaleass.

hooking, das Verzapfen.

hoop, Bügel; - *iron*, Bandeisen; - *of a yard*, Band einer Rahe; - *of the anchor stock*, Ankerstockband; - *steel*, Bandstahl.

hoops for bobstay, Band für Wasserstage; - *of a tilt*, Bogen eines Bootssonnensegels; - *of the bowsprit*, Bänder des Bugspriets; - *on the topmasts*, Marsstengenbänder.

hope, kleine Bucht.

hopper od. - *barge*, Baggerprahm; - *dredger*, Dampf-od. Seebagger.

horary angle, Stundenwinkel; - *circle*, S-kreis.

horizon, Kimm; - *glass*, K-spiegel.

horizontal air pump, horizontale Luftpumpe; - *bilge p.*, h. Lenzpumpe; - *circulating pump*, h. Zirkulationspumpe; - *cylinder*, h. Zylinder; - *drilling machine*, liegende Bohrmaschine; - *engine*, horizontale Maschine; - *feed pump*, h. Speisepumpe; - *knee*, h. Knie; - *rudder*, h. Steuer; - *steering engine*, h. Dampfsteuermaschine; - *through bolt*, h. Durchbolzen; - *trunk engine*, h. Trunkmaschine; - *tubular boiler*, h. Röhrenkessel.

horn beam, Hagebuchenholz; - *bowsprit*, Bugspriet und Klüverbaum aus einem Stück; - *card*, Hornscheibe; - *cleats*, H-klampen; - *the frames*, die Spanten genau einsetzen; - *timber*, Mittelheckspant.

horns, 1. Enden, Pünten; 2. die Ösen am abgeplatteten Ende der Ruderpinne.

horse, 1. Pferd (Fußtau unter der Rahe); 2. Leuwagen (einer Schote); 3. Lotbrook (am Handlot); 4. Leiter (auf und nieder am Mast); 5. Sprut, Spann (für Buggordings); 6. Reling (der Back); 7. Jückstag (der Gaffel, des Baumes); 8. Nockpferd (unter der Marsrahe); - *barge*, vom Pferde gezogene Barke; - *box*, Pferderaum; - *ferry*, Zugfähre; - *iron*, Klameieisen; - *latitudes*, Roßbreiten;

- *path*, Leinpfad; - *power*, Pferdekraft; - *shoe clamp*, Klammer zur Verbindung des Kiels und Vorderstevens; - - *plate*, Kokerplatte; - - *rack*, Hufeisenreling um den Mast; - - *splice*, H-e-splissung; - *shoes*, Drucklagerschuhe; - *track*, Leinpfad; - *transom*, Heckbalken; - *up*, klameien.

horses, Pferde.

horsing, klameien; - *iron*, Klameieisen.

hose, Schlauch; - *wrench*, S-Verschraubungsschlüssel.

hospital ship, Krankenschiff.

hot air engine, Heißluftmaschine; - - *heating*, Luftheizung; - *chisel*, Setzeisen; - *water heating*, Heißwasserheizung; - - *pipe*, Warmwasserrohr; - - *pump*, W-w-pumpe; - - *well*, Luftpumpendruckraum.

hotwell, Luftpumpendruckraum; - *connections*, L.-Verbindungen; - *discharge orifice*, L.-Ausgußöffnung.

hound, Hummer; - *piece of a mast*, Mastbacke.

hounding of the bowsprit, Bugsprietsteil außerhalb des Stevens.

hounds of a mast, Backen eines Mastes; - *of a topmast*, Hummer einer Stenge.

house, 1. Deckhaus; 2. eine Stenge in das Hol fieren; 3. binnenbords holen und festmachen; - *boat*, Hausboot; - *flag*, Redereiflagge; - *line*, Hüsing.

housing, 1. Hüsing (dünne Leine); 2. Hausung (des Bugspriets oder des unteren Mastes); - *of the bowsprit*, Bugspriethausung.

hove down, bettlägerig; - *to*, beigedreht, wir drehten bei.

how is the head? Wie liegt es an?

howker, Hukergaleaß.

hoy, 1. Hallo! Ho! 2. Küstenfahrer.

hub, Nabe.
hug, anschmiegen; - *the coast*, sich dicht am Lande halten; - *the wind*, sich dicht am Winde halten; - - - *close!* . Nichts vergeben!
hulk, Hulk, Speicherschiff.
hull, 1. Rumpf des Schiffes; 2. in den R. schießen; 3. vor Topp und Takel treiben; - *and appurtenances* od. *equipment*, Kasko und Aurüstung; - *down*, Rumpf unter der Kimm (nur die Segel sichtbar); - *to*, vor Topp und Takel treiben.
hullock, Lappen eines Segels.
hummock of ice, Eishöcker.
hump, Höcker; - *backed*, durchgebrochen.
hunting skiff, Jagdboot.
huon pine, Gummitanne.
hurd, Ducht eines Taues.
hurricane, Orkan; - *deck*, Promenadendeck; - - *lamp*, Sturmlaterne; - *force*, von orkanartiger Stärke; - *house*, Haus auf dem Promenaden-

deck; *to be - swept*, vom Orkan schwer mitgenommen.
husband, Bestätter; - *age*, Provision des B.
hydraulic crane, hydraulischer Kran; - *dock*, Schwimmdock; - *dredger*, hydraulischer Bagger; - *engine*, hydraulische Maschine; - *engineer*, Wasserbau-Ingenieur; - *jack*, hydraulischer Hebeapparat; - *pressure*, Wasserdruck; - *riveting*, hydraulische Nietung; - *slip*, h. Helgen; - *test*, Wasserdruckprobe.
hydraulics, Wasserbau.
hydrographer, Hydrograph.
hydrographical map, Seekarte; - *office*, Hydrographisches Amt.
hydrography, Hydrographie.
hydrokineter, Dampfstrahlvorwärmer.
hydrometer, Salzgehaltmesser.
hydrostatic pressure, hydrostatischer Druck.
hydrostatics, Hydrostatik.

I.

iati-wood, javanisches Thekabaumholz.
ibex, Steinbock.
ice anchor, Eisanker; - *beam*, Verstärkungsbalken gegen Eisgang; - *berg*, E-berg; - *blink*, E-blink; - *bound*, eingeeist; - - *harbour*, vom Eise besetzter Hafen; - *breaker*, Eisbrecher; - *canoe*, E-boot; - *chart*, E-karte; - *clause*, E-klausel; - *claws*, E-haken, E-klaue; - *cock*, E-hahn; - *doubling*, E-haut; - *drift*, Treibeis; - *engineer*, E-maschinist; - *fender*, E-fender; - *field*, E-feld; - *floe* od. *float*, Treibeis-Scholle; - *island*, E-flarde; - *lane*, Durchfahrt im Eise; - *lining*, Eis-

haut; - *locker*, E-kammer; - *master*, E-lotse; - *patch*, E-flarde; - *region*, E-region; - *room*, E-kammer; - *sea*, E-meer; - *shelf*, E-zunge; - *sludge*, E-schlamm; - *tongue*, E-zunge.
identity, Gleichheit.
idler, Freiwächter.
ignite, anzünden.
ignition lamp, Glühlampe.
ill footing, gefährlicher Ankerplatz; - *used*, ausgenutzt.
illuminating power, Leuchtkraft.
immersed midship section, der eingetauchte Querriß des Mittelspanten.
immersion, 1. Eintauchung; 2. Tiefgang.

impact, Stoß (der Kollision).

impassible, unpassierbar.

impelling power, Treibkraft.

impermeator, Dampföler.

import dock, Einfuhrdock; - *duty*, E-f-zoll.

imports, Einfuhrwaren.

impress men for sea od. - *seamen*, Matrosen pressen; - *money*, Preßgeld.

in and out, von innen nach außen durchgehend; - - - *bolts*, Bolzen, die abwechselnd von innen nach außen und umgekehrt geschlagen werden.

inboard, binnenbords.

inbow, Bug.

incandescent lamp,Glühlampe.

inclination compass, Inklinations-Bousole.

increase of pressure, Drucksteigerung.

increased draught, vermehrter Tiefgang; - *temperature*, erhöhte Temperatur.

increasing motion, beschleunigte Bewegung.

incrustation, Kesselsteinbildung.

indemnity club, Entschädigungsverband.

indent, Einschnitt, Schießscharte; *to - with a pin*, verpinnen.

indentation, Einbeulung.

indented, eingebeult; - *mortise*, versetztes Zapfenloch; - *port*, Eckpforte.

indenting of stores, das Quittieren über Ausrüstungsgegenstände.

indenture, Einbeulung, Einbuchtung.

indentures, Frachtkontrakt.

independent piece of the head, Rückenstück des Gallions; - *rudder pintle*, abnehmbarer Ruderfingerling.

Indiaman, Ostindienfahrer.

india rubber hose, Kautschukschlauch; - - *joint*, Gummidichtung; - - *packing*, G-

packung; - - *ring*,Kautschukring. *(See also rubber)*.

Indian Ocean,IndischerOzean.

indicated horse power, indizierte Pferdestärke; - *power*, i. Kraft; - *thrust*, i. Druck.

indicator, Indikator; - *barrel*, I.-trommel; - *card*, I.-papier; - *cock*, I.-hahn; - *cord*, I.-schnur; - *cylinder*,I.-zylinder; - *diagram*, I.-diagramm; - *gear*, I.-zubehör; - *pencil*, I.-stift; - *pipe*, I.-rohr; - *piston*, I.-kolben; - - *rod*, I.-k-stange; - *spring*, I-k-feder.

indirect acting engine,indirekt wirkende Maschine.

indraught, einsetzende Strömung.

induction gear,Einströmungsvorrichtung.

inexplosive boiler, unexplodierbarer Kessel.

inextinguishable, unauslöschbar.

inflammable cargo, entzündbare Ladung.

infusible, unschmelzbar.

ingulf see engulf.

inhaul, Einholer; - *block*, E.-block.

inhauler, Einholer.

inhibition,1.Arrest; 2. Handelssperre.

initial pitch,Eintrittssteigung; - *pressure*, Anfangsdruck.

injection, Einspritzung, Injektion; - *cock*, Injektionshahn; - *gear*, I-j-vorrichtung; - *handle* od. *lever*, I-j-handhabe; - *pipe*, I-j-rohr; - *pump*, Dampfstrahlpumpe; - *slide* od. *s. valve*, Einspritzventil; - *valve box*, E.-gehäuse; - - *cover*, E.-deckel; - - *pipe*, E.-rohr; - - *spindle*, E.-spindel; - *water*, Injektionswasser.

injector, Dampfstrahlpumpe; - *of Giffard*, Giffardscher Injektor; - *receiving pipe*, I.-Dampfdüse.

injure, havarieren, beschädigen.

inland navigation, Binnenschiffahrt; - *sea*, Binnenmeer; - *vessel*, B-fahrzeug; - *water communication*, Verkehr durch B-gewässer.
inlet, 1. kleine Bucht; 2. Eintritt, Einlaß, Einlaßöffnung; - *pipe*, E-rohr; - *sluice*, Einflußschleuse; - *valve*, Einlaßventil.
inner bar, Innenbarre; - *binding strake of the decks*, Schlüssel der Decksbalken; - *bottom*, Innerboden; - *plate*, Tankdeckenplatte; - *plating*, Innerbodenbeplattung; - *end of the cat head*, innerer Teil des Kranbalkens; - *halliard*, Binnenfall; - *harbour*, B-hafen; - *jib*, B-klüver; - - *downhaul*, B-k-Niederholer; - - *halliard*, B-k-fall; - - *sheet*, B-k-schote; - - *stay*, B-k-leiter; - - *tack*, B-k-hals; - *peak brail*, Gaffel-Innengeitau; - *port*, Binnenhafen; - *post*, B-Achtersteven; - *roads*, Innenreede; - *screw shaft*, innnere Schraubenwelle; - *sheet of a studding sail*, Binnenschote eines Leesegels; - *sheets*, Binnenschoten; - *skin*, Innenbekleidung; - *stern post*, Binnenhintersteven; - *strake*, innerer Plattengang; - *stringer angle bar*, Stringer-Innenwinkel; - *waterway*, Innen-Wassergang.
inrush of water, Einströmen des Wassers.
insertion cloth joint, Dichtung mit Einlagetuch.
insertions of india rubber, Gummieinlage.
inset, Einsetzen der Flut.
inshore, nach Land zu.
inside butt strap, Innen-Stoßplatte; - *callipers*, Hohlzirkel; - *clinch*, Binnenstich; - *plank*, Innenplanke; - *planking*, Innenbeplankung; - *screw tool*, inwendiger

Schraubstahl; - *strake*, Innengang.
inspection of quarters, Besichtigung des Volkslogis.
inspirator, Dampfstrahlpumpe.
Instance Court, Admiralitätsgericht, Abteilung für Seemannskontrakte.
instantaneous generator, sofort wirkender Dampferzeuger.
insubmersible, unsinkbar.
intake as per bill of lading, Einnahme laut Konnossement.
intense heat, intensive Hitze.
intensity of draught, Stärke des Zuges.
intercostal, Einschiebsel, eingeschoben; - *floors*, Bodenwrangenstücke; - *girder*, Zwischenträger; - *keelson*, eingeschobenes Kielschwein; - *plates*, eingeschobene Platten; - *stringer*, Interkostalstringer.
interest in a vessel, Schiffsanteil.
interior planking, Innenbeplankung; - *screw*, Schraubenmutter.
interlocutary decree, Zwischenurteil.
interloper, Schmuggler, Kaper.
intermediate beam, Bastardbalken; - - *angle bar*, B.-winkel; - *connecting rod*, Mitteldruck-Pleuelstange; *i. c. r. bottom end keep*, M.-Kurbelzapfenlagerschalendeckel; *i. c. r. b. e. liner*, M.-Pleuelstangenfußfutter; *i. c. r. top end keep*, M.-Kreuzkopflagerschalendeckel; - *crank pin bolt*, M.-Kurbelzapfenlagerbolzen; *i. c. p. brasses*, M.-K-z-l-schalen; - *crank shaft*, M.-Kurbelwelle; *i. c. s. bearing*, M.-K.-lager; *i. c. s. b. brasses*, M.-K.-l-schalen; *i. c. s. bearing keep*, M.-K.-l-deckel; *i. c. s. b. k. bolt*, M.-

K.-l-d-bolzen; *i. c. s. journal,* M.-K.-Lagerzapfen; *- cylinder,* M.-Zylinder; *i. c. admission port,* Eintrittskanal des M.-Z.; *i. c. cover,* M.-Z.-deckel; *i. c. escape valve.* M.-Z.-Sicherheitsventil; *i. c. e. v. load,* M.-Z.-S.-belastung; *i. c. e. v. spindle,* M.-Z.-S.-spindel; *i. c. e. v. spring,* M.-Z.-S.-feder; *i. c. exhaust port,* Austrittskanal des M.-Z.; *i. c. liner,* M.-Z.-büchse; *i. c. stuffing box gland,* M.-Z.-Stopfbüchsendeckel; *- eccentric,* M.-Excenter; *i. e. brasses,* M.-E.-Lagerschalen; *i. e gear,* M.-E.-vorrichtung; *i. e. rod,* M.-E.-stange; *i. e. sheave,* M.-E.-scheibe; *i. e. strap,* M.-E.-bügel; *i. e. s. liner,* M.-E.-Bügelfutter; *- frame,* Zwischenspant; *- gear,* Mitteldruck-Gestänge; *- gland,* M.-Stopfbüchse; *- piston,* M.-kolben; *- - guide,* M.-K-Geradführung; *- - rod,* M.-k-stange; *i. p. r. crosshead,* M.-k-s-Kreuzkopf; *i. p. r. c. brasses,* M.-k-s-K-k-Lagerschalen; *i. p. r. c. guide,* M.-k-s-K-k-Gleitplatte; *i. p. r. stuffing box,* M.-k-s-Stopfbüchse; *i. p. r. s. b. gland,* M.-Zylinder-S-b-deckel; *- port,* Zwischenhafen; *- pressure connecting rod,* M.-Pleuelstange; *i. p. c. r. bolt,* M.-P-s-bolzen; *i. p. crank pin,* M.-Kurbelzapfen; *i. p. c. shaft bearing bolt,* M.-Kurbelwellenlagerbolzen; *i. p. c. web,* M.-Kurbelbacke; *i. p. c. bolt,* M.-Kreuzkopflagerbolzen; *i. p. cylinder,* M.-Zylinder; *i. p. c. cover,* M.-Z.-deckel; *i. p. c. c. bolt,* M.-Z.-d-bolzen; *i. p. cylinder drain cock,* M.-Z.-Drainagehahn; *i. p. c. d. pipe,* M.-Z.-Entwässerungsrohr; *i. p. c. escape valve spindle,* M.-Z.-Sicherheitsventilspindel; *i.*

p. c. jacket, M.-Z.-Mantel; *i. p. eccentric,* M.-Exzenter; *i. p. e. bolt,* M.-E.-bolzen; *i. p. e. gear,* M.-E.-vorrichtung; *i. p. e. rod,* M.-E.-stange; *i. p. gear.* M.-Gestänge; *i. p. guide,* M.-Geradführung; *i. p. guide shoe,* M.-Gleitschuh; *i. p. piston,* M.-Kolben; *i. p. p. guide rod,* M.-K-Führungsstange; *i. p. p. packing ring,* M.-Kolbenliderungsring; *i. p. piston rod crosshead,* M.-Kolbenstangen - Kreuzkopf; *i. p. p. r. c. guide,* M.-K-s-K.-Führung; *i. p. p. r. stuffing box,* M.-K-s-Stopfbüchse; *i. p. receiver pipe,* M.-Dampfreceivorrohr; *i. p. slide valve,* M.-Schieber; *i. p. steam chest,* M.-S-kasten; *i. p. turbine,* M.-Turbine; *i. p. t. engine,* M.-Turbinenmaschine; *i. p. valve balance piston,* M.-Schieber-Abbalanzierungskolben; *i. p. valve casing* od. *i. p. v. chest,* M.-S-kasten; *i. p. v. gear,* äußere Steuerung des M.-Zylinders; *i. p. v. rod stuffing box,* M.-Schieberstangen-Stopfbüchse; *i. p. v. spindle guide,* M.-S-s-führung; *i. reversed frame,* Zwischen-Gegenspant; *- ribband,* Z-sente; *- shaft,* Schraubenwelle; *- slide valve,* Mitteldruckschieber; *- starting valve,* M-d-Anlaßventil; *- steam chest,* M-d-Schieberkasten; *- stop valve,* Hülfsabsperrventil; *i. s. v. gear.* Mitteldruck - Absperrventilgestänge; *i. s. v. spindle,* Hülfs-Absperrventilspindel; *- valve balance piston cylinder,* Schutzkappe des Mitteldruck-Schieber-Abbalanzierungskolbens; *- valve casing,* M.-S-kasten; *i. v. c. door,* M.-S-k-deckel; *i. v. c. escape valve load,* M.-S-k-Sicherheitsventilbelastung; *i. v. chest,* M.-S-k; *i. v. gear,* äußere Steuerung des M.-Zylinders; *i. v. rod*, M.-Schieberstange; *i. v. r. stuffing box gland*, M.-S-s-Stopfbüchsendeckel; *i. v. spindle guide*, M.-S-s-führung.

intermittent od. *intermitting light*, Blinkfeuer.

internal block, Block mit Stropp im Gehäuse; - *blow down pipe*, inneres Ausblasrohr; - *bound block*, Block mit Stropp im Gehäuse; - *distributing mechanism*, innere Steuerung; - *donkey feed pipe*, i. Hülfsspeiserohr; *i. f. p.* i. Speiserohr; - *flue*, i. Feuerzug; - *pipe*, i. Rohr; - *pressure*, inwendiger Druck; - *safety valve*, inneres Sicherheitsventil; - *scum pipe*, i. Schaumrohr; - *steam pipe*, i. Dampfrohr; - *water gauge pipe*, i. Wasserstandsrohr.

international code of signals, internat. Signalbuch.

interscalm, Raum zwischen 2 [Rudern.

inventory, Inventar.

inverted cylinder, umgekehrt liegender Zylinder; - - *engine*, Maschine mit u. l. Z.; - *vertical c. e.*, vertikale Maschine.

inward bound, nach Hause bestimmt; - *cargo*, einkommende Ladung; - *freight*, e. Fracht.

Irish pennants, Reffzeisinge; - *reef*, Kopf eines gerefften Segels.

iron ballast, Eisenballast; - *bark wood*, Eisenholz; - *binding of a dead eye*, eiserner

Beschlag einer Jungfer; - *block*, Eisenblock; - *boat*, eisernes Boot; - *boiler*, eiserner Kessel; - *bolt*, e. Bolzen; - *bound*, 1. eisenbeschlagen; 2. felsig und steil (Küste); - - *block*, eisengestroppter Block; - - *snatch block*, Kinnbackenblock; - *cased*, gepanzert; - *casting*, Eisenfassonguß; - *clad* od. *coated*, gepanzert; - *deck*, eisernes Deck; - *dog*, eiserne Klammer; - *fastened*, mit Eisen verbolzt; - *fastening*, Eisenverbolzung; - *frame*, eisernes Spant; - *hook*, e. Bugband; - *hoop*, e. Band; - *horse of a ship's head*, Papageistock; - *knee*, eisernes Knie; - *mast*, eiserner Mast; - *maul*, Maker; - *of a block*, der eiserne Beschlag eines Blocks; - *of a studding sail boom*, Bügel einer Leesegelspiere; - *piston*, eiserner Kolben; - *plated*, gepanzert; - *rail*, eiserne Reling; - *sick*, eisenkrank; - *stanchion*, eiserne Stütze; - *strap*, Eisenstropp; - *strapped block*, Block mit eisern. Beschlag; - *waterway*, Deckstringer; - *wedge*, eiserner Keil; - *wire rigging*, Eisendrahttakelung; - *work*, Schmiedearbeit; - *works*, Eisenhütte; - *yard*, eiserne Rahe.

island harbour, durch Inseln geschützter Hafen.

isle, Eiland.

islet, kleine Insel. [raum.

issue room, Proviantausgabe-

J.

jabble sea, unruhige See.

Jabez, by -, zum Henker!

jack, 1. Bugflagge (Union J.); 2. Teerjacke (Matrose); 3. Dwarssahling (des Topps); 4. Daumkraft (Schrauben-

winde); - *block*, Oberblock des Bramfalls; - *boots*, Wasserstiefeln; - *braces*, Bagienbrassen; - *carpenter*, Modellschnitzer; - *cross trees*, Royalsahling; - *flag*,

Gösch; - *in the basket*, Korbbake; - *in the bread room*, Proviantmeisters-Maat; - *knife*, Klappmesser; - *nasty face*, Küchenjunge; - *plane*, Schrubhobel; - *pin*, Belegnagel; - *screw*, Schraubenwinde; - *staff*, Göschstock; - *stay of a gaff*, Jackstag einer Gaffel; - - *of a yard*, J. einer Rahe; - *tar*, Jan Maat; - *with a lantern*, St. Elmsfeuer.

jackass bark, Schonerbark; - *brig*, Brigg mit 4 eckig. Topp- und Bramsegel.

jacket, Dampfmantel; - *drain cock*, D.-Drainagehahn; - *gauge*, Mantelmanometer; - *pipe*, Mantelrohr; - *safety valve*, Dampfmantel-Sicherheitsventil; - *steam pipe*, D.-rohr.

Jack's quarter deck, Back.

jackyard topsail, Schotrahe-Toppsegel.

jackyarder, Toppsegel mit Schotrahe.

Jacob's staff, Jakobsstab.

jagged bolt, Hackbolzen.

jam nut, Stellmutter.

jammed, bekniffen, festgeklemmt, eingepreßt.

janty, aufgeputzt, beflaggt.

jar, klappern, rasseln.

jarrah timber, Mahagoni-Gummibaumholz.

jarring, klappern, rasseln.

jaunty, aufgeputzt.

jaw, 1. das große Wort führen; 2. Klaue (bei Gaffel und Baum); 3. Scheibengatt (des Blocks); 4. Gabel (der Pleuelstange); - *rope*, Racktau.

jear od. *jeer*, Rahhanger; - *bitts*, Betinge der Masten; - *block*, Rahtakelblock; - *capstan*, kleines Gangspill.

jerk, Ruck, Stoß; *to give a -*, einen Pull holen.

jerker, Küchenmeister.

jerquer, der untersuchende Zollbeamte.

jerquing, Zolluntersuchung.

Jersey frock, der blaue Troier.

jet, Strahl; - *condenser*, Einspritz-Kondensator; - *injection cock*, Notinjektionshahn; - - *pipe*, Injektionsrohr; - - *valve*, Notinjektionsventil; - *of steam*, Dampfstrahl; - *pipe of a hose*, Schlauchmundstück; - - - - *pump*, Pumpenmundstück; - *propelled steamer*, Reaktionsdampfer; - *propeller engine*, R-a-maschine; - *pump*, Strahlpumpe.

jetsam od. *jetson*, Seewurf.

jettage, Abgabe der einkommenden Schiffe.

jettison, Seewurf, über Bord werfen.

jetty, Hafendamm, Landungsbrücke.

jewel block, Leesegel-Fallblock.

Jew's harp, Ankerschäkel.

jib, 1. Klüver; 2. übergehen lassen; 3. *the cut of one's -*, der Gesichtsausdruck; - *boom*, 1. Klüverbaum (beim Segler); 2. Kranschnabel (beim Kran); - - *foot rope*, Klüverpferd; - - *guy*, K-geie; - - *hoop*, Klüverbaumband; - *netting*, K-b-netz; - - *stay*, K-stampfstag; - - *traveller*, Ausholring des Klüvers; - *cover*, Klüverkleid; - *downhaul*, K-Niederholer; - *frame*, Gestellwand; - *guy*, Klüverbackstag; - *halliard*, K-fall; - *hank*, K-lägel; - *head*, K-kopf; - *iron*, K-bügel; - *man*, K-gast; - *martingale*, K-stampfstag; - *netting*, K-baumnetz; - *of a crane*, Kranausleger; - *of jibs*, Vorroyalstagsegel; - *sheet*, Klüverschote; - - *pendant*, K.-schenkel; - *stay*, 1. Klüverleiter; 2. Gestellwand (bei der Maschine); - *tack*, Klüverhals; - *topsail*, Klüver-Toppsegel; - - *downhaul*, K.-T.-Niederholer; - - *sheet*, Jager-

schote; - - *tack*, K.-T.-hals;
- *traveller*, Ausholring des
Klüvers; - *tye*, Klüverfall.
*jibe*od.*jibing see gybe* u. *gybing.*
jibs downhaul! Klüver bergen!
jig, stoßweise holen.
jigger, 1. Besahn; 2. Jigger
(4 Mast-Dampfer); 3. Treiber
(Boot); 4. Handtalje (bei Tau
und Kette); - *boom*, Besahnbaum; - - *hoop*, Klüverbaumband; - - *topping lift*, Be-
sahnbaum-Toppenant; - - - -
purchase, B.-T.-talje; - *bowline*, Besahnbulin; - *brace,*
B-brasse; - - *pendant*, B-b-
schenkel; - *brails*, B-geitaue;
- *bunt line*, B-Bauchgording;
- *chain plates*, B-Rüsteisen; -
- *channel*, B-Rüste; - *clew
garnet*, B-geitau ; - *foot rope,*
Jiggerpferd; - *futtock
shrouds*, - *futtocks*, Besahn-
Püttingswanten; - *gaff*, B.-
Gaffel; - - *topsail*, Jigger-
gaffel-Toppsegel; - - - *downhaul*, J.-T.-Niederholer; - - -
halliard, J.-T.-fall; *j. g. topsail sheet*, J.-T.-schote; *j. g.
t. tack*, J.-T.-hals; - *halliard,*
Besahnfall; - *leech line*, B-
Nockgording; - *lift*, B-
Toppenant; - - *purchase*, B-
rahe-T.-talje; - *lower cross
trees*, B-mast-Dwarssahlinge;
- - *rigging*, B-wanten; - -
trestle trees, B-mast-Längs-
sahling; - *mast*, B-mast; - -
cap, B-m-Eselshaupt; - - *coat*,
Jiggermastkragen; - - *cross
trees,* Besahnmast-Dwars-
sahlinge; - - *head*, Topp des
Jiggermastes; - - *trestle trees,*
Besahnmast-Längssahlinge;
- - *wedge*, B.-keil; - *middle
staysail*, Besahn-Mittelstagsegel; - - - *downhaul.* B.-M.-
Niederholer; - - - *halliard*, B.-
M.-fall; - - - *sheet*, B.-M.-schote;
- - - *stay*, B.-M.-leiter; - - - *tack*,
B.-M.-hals; - *outhaul*, B.-Aus-
holer; - *peak halliard*, B.-Piek-
fall; - *reef tackle*, B.-Refftalje;
- *rigging*, B.-Wanten; - *royal,*

B.-Royal; - - *backstay*, B.-
R.-Pardune; - - *brace*, B.-
R.-brasse; - - *bunt line*, B.-
R.-Bauchgording; - - *clew
line*, B.-R.-Geitau; - - *foot
rope*, Jigger-R.-pferd; - -
halliard od. - - - *purchase,*
B.-R.-fall; *j. r. lift*, B.-
R.-Toppenant; - - *mast*, B.-
R.-stenge; - - *sheet*, B.-R.-
schote; - - *stay*, Jigger
R.-stag; - - *staysail*, J.-R.-
Stagsegel; - - - *downhaul,*
Besahn-R.-S.-Niederholer;
- - - *halliard*, B.-R.-S.-fall;
- - - *sheet*, B.-R.-S.-schote;
- - - *stay*, B.-R.-S.-leiter; - - -
tack, B.-R.-S.-hals; - *royal
yard*, B.-R.-rahe; - *sheet*, B.-
schote; - *shroud*, B.-want;
- *skysail*, B.-Scheisegel; - -
backstay, B.-S.-pardune; - -
brace B.-S.-brasse; - - *clew
line*, B.-S.-geitau; - - *foot
rope*, B.-S.-pferd; - - *halliard*,
B.-S.-fall; - - *lift*, B.-S.-
Toppenant; - - *mast*, B.-S.-
stenge; - - *sheet*, B.-S.-schote;
- - *stay*, B.-S.-stag; - - *yard*,
B.-S.-rahe; - *stay*, B.-stag;
- *staysail*, B.-Stagsegel; - -
downhaul, B.-S.-Niederholer;
- - *halliard*, B.-S.-fall; - -
sheet, B.-S.-schote; - - - *pendant*, B.-S.-Schotenschenkel;
- *staysail stay*, B.-Stagsegel-
leiter; - - *tack*, B.-S-s-hals;
- *tack*, B.-hals; - *tackle*, die
dritte Hand; - *throat halliard*, Besahn-Klaufall; - *top*,
B.-mars; - *topgallant backstay*, B.-Brampardune; - -
brace, B.-B-brasse; - - *bunt
line*, B.-B-bauchgording; - -
cap, B.-B-stenge-Eselshaupt;
- - *clew line*, B.-B-geitau; -
- - *cross trees*, Dwarssahlinge der B.-B-stenge; - -
futtocks, B.-Brampüttings-
wanten; - - *halliard* od. - - -
purchase. B.-Bramfall; - *topgallant leech line*, B.-B-Nock-
gording; - - *lift*, B.-B-Toppe-
nant; - - *mast*, B.-B-stenge;

- - - *cap*, B.-B-s-Eselshaupt;
- *topgallant rigging*, B.-B-wanten; - - *sail*, B.-B-segel;
- - *sheet*, B.-B-schote; - - *shroud*, B.-B-want; - - *stay*, B.-B-stag; - - *staysail*, B.-B-Stagsegel; - - - *downhaul*, B.-B-S.-Niederholer; - - - *halliard*, B.-B-S.-fall; - - - *sheet*, B.-B-S.-schote; - - - *stay*, B.-B-S.-leiter; - - - *tack*, B.-B-S.-hals; - *topgallant trestle trees*,B.-Royal-Längs-sahling; - - *tye*, B.-Bram-drehreep; - - *yard*, B.-B-rahe; - *topmast*, B'-Marsstenge; - - *backstay*, B.-stengepardune; - - *cap*, B.-Marsstenge-Eselshaupt; - - *cross trees*, B.-M.-Dwarssahlinge; - - *rigging*, - - *shroud*, B.-Stengewanten; - - *stay*, B.-S-stag; - - *staysail*, Be-sahnstenge-Stagsegel; - - - *downhaul*, B.-S.-Niederholer: - - - *halliard*, B.-S.-fall; - - *sheet*, B.-S.-schote; - - - *stay*, B.-S.-leiter; - - - *tack*, B.-S.-hals; - *topmast trestle trees*, Besahn-Bram-Längsahling; - *topping lift*, Besahnbaum-dirk; - *topsail*,Besahn-Mars-segel; - - *brace*,B.-Marsbrasse; - - - *pendant*, B.-M.-schenkel; - *topsail bunt line*, B.-Mars-Bauchgording; - - *clew line*, B.-M.-geitau; - - *foot rope*, B.-M.-pferd; - - *halliard* od. - - - *purchase*, B.-M.-fall; - *topsail lift*,B.-M.-Toppenant; - - *reef tackle*, B.-M.-Refftalje; - - *sheet*, B.-M.-schote; - - *tack*, B.-M.-hals; - - *tye*, B.-M.-Drehreep; - - *yard*, B.-M.-rahe; - *vang*, B -gerde; - - *pendant*, B.-Gaffelgerde-schenkel; - *yard*, B.-rahe; - - *foot rope*, B.-pferd.

jimble od. *jimmal*, Bügel des Kompasses.

job, das Stück Arbeit; - *Captain*, Setzschiffer; - *watch*, Beobachtungsuhr.

jobble, kurze schwere See.

jocy, Seesoldat.

jog, Sohle des Ruders.

joggle of the paddle box, Rad-kastenknie.

join, 1. zusammenfügen; 2. an-mustern; 3. sich treffen, zu-sammenbleiben.

joining shackle, Ankerketten-schäkel.

joint, verbinden, Dichtung, Verbindung; - *bolts*, Schließ-bolzen; -*dowel*,Verbindungs-zapfen; - *owner*, Mitreeder; - *pipe*, Verbindungsrohr.

jollies, Seesoldaten.

jolly boat, Jolle.

jolt, stoßen, rütteln.

jonah, Unglücksbringer; - *trip*, unglückliche Reise.

journal, 1. Hals- oder Lager-zapfen; 2. Schiffsjournal; - *bearing*, Achsenlager; - *box*, A-büchse; - - *lubricator*, A-b-Schmiervorrichtung; - *of observations*, Observations-journal.

jugle, Radkastenknie.

jump pointed, karwehlartig gebaut; - *weld*, Stoßschweiß-ung.

jumper of the sprit sail gaff, Blinderahe-Domper; - *stay*, Grosstag vom Eselshoofd aus.

junction dock, Verbindungs-dock; - *plate*, Deckplatte.

juniper wood, Wachholder-holz.

junk, 1. Dschunke (Schiff); 2. kondemniertes Tauwerk; 3. zähes Pökelfleisch; - *ring*, 1.Liderungsring; 2. Kolben-deckel; - - *bolt*, K-d-bolzen; - - *eye bolt*, Schraubenbolzen mit Splint.

jury mast,Notmast; - *propeller*, N-schraube; - *rig* od. *rigged* od. *rigging*, N-takelung; - *rudder*, N- ruder; - *topmast*, N-stenge.

jute linen rope, Seil aus Jutehanf.

K.

kajak, Kanu.
kalassy, indischer Seemann.
kayak, Kanu.
keckle, schladden, schlarren.
keckling, Schladding.
kedge, 1. warpen, verholen;
2. Warpanker; - *anchor*, W.;
- - *rope*, W.-tau.
kedging, warpen, verholen.
keel, Kiel; *from - to sticks*, von
vorn bis hinten; *to give the -*,
kielholen; *to heave the - out*,
den Kiel flößen; *to set the -*,
den K. legen; *upon an even -*,
gleichlastig.
keel blocks, Kielblöcke; - *boat*,
K-boot; - *chain*, Füllungs-
kette; - *piece*, Kielstück; - -
of stern frame, Schrauben-
stevenknie; - - - - *post*, Hinterstevenknie; - *plates*, Kiel-
platten; - *rabbet*, K-spün-
dung; - *rivet*, K-niete; - *rope*,
Füllungstau; - *scarph*, Kiel-
laschung; - - *bolt*, Kielver-
scherbungsbolzen.
keelage, Kielgeld, K-recht.
keelhale od. *keelhaul*, 1. kielholen, Kielholung; 2. einen
Matrosen bestrafen.
keeler, 1. Kalfaterfaß; 2. Führer eines Kohlenbootes.
keelman, Führer eines Kohlenbootes.
keelson, Kielschwein; - *angle
bar*, K.-winkel; - *bolt*, K.-bol-
zen; - *casing*, K.-kasten; - *plate*,
K.-platte; - *rider*, zweites
K.; - *scarph*, K.-laschung.
keep, halten, stehen, steuern;
- *afloat*, flott halten, an Bord
od. in See bleiben; - *a good
look out*, gut Ausguck halten;
- *ahead*, sich voraus halten;
- *aloof*, sich in guter Entfernung luvwärts halten; -
astern, sich achteraus halten;
- *away*, abhalten; - - *again*
od. - - *on her course again*,
wieder auf Kurs setzen; -

anchor watch, Ankerwache
gehen; - *a weather eye*, auf
Böen achten; - *clear*, ausweichen; - *close in with the
land*, dicht unter Land
bleiben; - *close to the wind*,
dicht anhalten; - *course*,
Kurs halten; - *fast*, festhalten, gut stoppen (Tau, Kette);
- *full*, voll halten (Segel,
Schiff); - *good hold of the
coast*, sich dicht unter der
Küste halten; - *harbour
watch*, Hafenwache halten;
- *her off*, das Schiff abfallen
lassen; - *her own*, sich gut
am Winde halten; - *hold of
the land*, sich dicht unter
Land halten; - *off*, abhalten;
- *out of the way*, ausweichen;
- *sea watch*, Seewache gehen;
- *stroke*, Schlag halten; - *the
broadside to the wind*, sich
dwars zum Winde halten;
- *the land*, dicht unter Land
halten; - - - *aboard*, d. u. L.
h.; - *the log*, das Journal
führen; - *the luff*, luv halten;
- *the offing*, frei vom Lande
halten; - *the port side of the
river*, sich an der Backbordseite des Flusses halten; -
the sails shivering, killbras-
sen; - *the sea*, sich in See
halten; - *the ship in position*,
das Schiff gerade halten; -
the watch, Wache halten; -
the weather gage od. - *t. w.
side* od. - *the wind* od. - *to
windward*, sich luvwärts
halten; - *under easy sail*, sich
unter kleinen gerefften Segeln halten; - *up steam*,
Dampf aufhalten; - *watch*,
Wache gehen; - *way*, Fahrt
beibehalten; - *within hail*,
sich in Rufweite halten; -
within signal distance, sich
in Signalweite halten; - *your
luff!* Nichts ab! - *your*

weather eye lifting! Guck gut aus!
keep, Deckel, Deckelplatte; - *bolt*, Lagerdeckelbolzen; - - *nut*, L.-mutter; - *for crank pin brasses*, Kurbelzapfenlagerschalendeckel; - *for crosshead brasses*, Deckelplatte des Kreuzkopflagers; - *for link brasses*, Gelenklagerdeckel; - *for main bearing brasses*, Hauptlagerdeckel; - *for pump lever shaft brasses*, Pumpenbalanzieraxen - Lagerdeckel; - *for rocking shaft brasses*, Balanzieraxen-Lagerdeckel.
keg, 1/4 Ankerfäßchen.
kelson see keelson.
kelter, in prime -, aufgezeugt, fein-fein, in bester Ordnung.
ken speckled, deutlich gemarkt.
kenk, Kinke.
kennet, Belegklampe.
kenning, ca. 20 Seemeilen; - *glass*, Taschenfernrohr.
kennings, Kennungen, Landmarken.
kent, mit Stangen stoßen.
kentledge, Ballasteisen; - *goods*, Ballastgüter.
kersey, Pfortlaken.
ketch, die Kits od. Schnigge (2 master); - *barge*, Besahnewer.
kettle bottom, Boden mit runder Kimm; - *of the compass*, Kompaßdose.
kevel od. *kevil*, 1. Kreuzholz; 2. Belegklampe; - *head*, Poller.
key, 1. Keil, Schlüssel, Splint; 2. Sand- od. Korallenbank; 3. das Cay (blinde Klippen); - *bit*, Schlüsselbart; - *bolt*, Splintbolzen; - *hole*, 1. Keilloch; 2. Schlüsselloch; - *model*, Schiffsmodell; - *of a cock*, Hahnschlüssel; - *of the anchor stock*, Ankerstocksplint; - *of the cock wheel*, Schlüssel des Zahnrades; - *of the rudder*, Schloß des Ruders; - *porter*,

Hafendammarbeiter; - *rack*, Schlüsselbrett; - *shank*, Schlüsselschaft; - *way*, Keilnute.
keyage, Kaigeld.
kid, Back od. Schüssel.
kiddy, geputzt.
kidnapper, Seelenverkäufer.
killock, 1. Wurfanker; 2. Ankerflügel.
kiln, Dampfkasten.
kingston valve, Kingstonventil; - - *spindle*, K.-spindel; - - *strainer*, K.-saugesieb.
kink in a cable, 1. eine Kinke in einer Trosse; 2. Kinken bilden.
kinky, voll von Kinken.
kiss the mud, den Schlamm berühren.
kit. 1. Schaufel; 2. Seesack, Matrosengepäck.
kite, eines der höchsten und leichtesten Segel.
knag, Felsspitze.
knave line, Racktalje.
kneck, Zusammendrehung eines Taues.
knee, Knie; - *bolt*, K.-bolzen; - *of the head*, Gallion; - *of the steering gear*, K. des Steuerapparats; - *plate*, K.-platte; - *rider*, K.-Kattspor; - - *bolt*, K.-K.-bolzen; - *timber*, Krummholz.
knees up and down, auf- und niederstehende Knie.
knigt head, Judasohr.
knights, Belegpoller hinter den Masten.
knittle, 1. Knüttel einer Leine; 2. Hängematten-Nitzel.
knock, klopfen, stoßen, Stoß, Schlag; - *off*, 1. abschlagen; 2. Schicht machen; - *out boiler scales*, Kesselstein ausklopfen.
knot, 1. Knopf, 2. Knoten = 1 Seemeile; - *a shroud with a shroud knot*, einen Wantknopf einschlagen.
knotted stopper, Knopfstopper.
knuckle, Bucht, Knick; -

moulding od. - *rail*, unterste Heckleiste; - *timber*, Inholz mit Knick.

koff, die Kuff.

krennel, kleine Lägel, k. Mutte.

kub house, Kochhaus.

kuff rigged as bark, Barkentine; - - - *brigg*, Brigantine.

L.

the three l's, viz. lead, latitude, and look-out.

labouring, arbeiten.

lace, anreihen; - *piece*, Gallionsschegg.

laces, Reester (Stahlstreifen zur Verstärkung der Segelnähte).

lacing, 1. Anschlagleine; 2. das Anreihen, die Litzung; 3. Rückenknie der Gallionsfigur; - *holes of an awning*, Schnürlöcher eines Sonnensegels; - *of a. a.*, Schnürleine e. S.

ladder, Leiter, Treppe; - *rope*, Fallreepstau; - *to fire room*, Niedergang zum Heizraum.

laden, beladen; - *by the head*, vorlastig beladen; - - - *stern*, achterlastig b.; - *in bulk*, mit Sturzgütern b.; - *in parcels*, mit Stückgütern b.; - *on even keel*, gleichlastig; - *to sink*, tief beladen.

ladies room, Damenzimmer.

lading port, Ladungshafen.

ladle, 1. Gießlöffel, Schöpflöffel; 2. ausschöpfen.

ladroneship, chinesisches Seeräuberschiff.

lagan, mit Schwimmer geworfenes Gut.

lagging, Bekleidung.

lagoon, Lagune.

laid aback, gegengebraßt; - *on the shelf*, ausrangiert, pensioniert; - *out with dunnage wood and mats*, mit Stauholz garniert und mit Matten unterschlagen; - *to the wind*, bei dem Winde gebraßt; - *up*, aufgelegt; *the land is -*,

das Land ist gelegt (d. h. hinter uns verschwunden).

lake, Binnensee; - *craft*, Landseefahrzeug.

lamp cotton, Lampendocht; - *glass*, L-zylinder; - *halyard*, L-fall; - *locker*, Lampisterie; - - *door*, Tür d. L.; - *oil*, Lampenöl; - *room*, L-raum; - *scissors*, L-schere; - *trimmer*, L-trimmer; - *wick*, L-docht; - - *box*, Dochtbüchse.

land, 1. Land; 2. landen, ausschiffen; - *blink*, Landblink; - *breeze*, L-brise; - *fall*, Land in Sicht bekommen; - *fang*, Ankergrund; - *feather*, Meeresbucht; - *ice*, Landeis; - *in sight*, Land in Sicht; - *laid*, außer Gesicht des Landes; - *locked*, vom Lande eingeschlossen; - *lubber*, Strandläufer, Binnenschiffer; - *marks*, Landmarken; - *of a plate*, die Stelle, wo die Platte an ein Spant stößt; - *pirate* od. *shark*, Straßenräuber; - *sick*, nach Land sich sehnend; - *the pilot*, den Lotsen absetzen; - *turn* od. *wind*, Landwind; - *waiter*, Strandwächter.

land, the - is laid, das Land ist gelegt; - *looms high*, das L. erscheint hoch.

landing, 1. Ladung; 2. Stoß; - *certificate*, Landungsbescheinigung; - *charges*, L-kosten; - *edge*, Nahtstreifen; - - *of a plate*, Längsnaht einer Platte; - *of a plate started*, die Nahtstreifen lockerten sich; - *place*,

Landungsplatz; - *stage*, L-brücke; - *strake*, die 2. obere Planke eines Bootes; - *surveyor*, Oberzollbeamter; - *waiter*, Zollbeamter.

landsman, Landratte.

lane route, bestimmter Kurs der atlant. Dampfer.

laniard see lanyard.

lantern, Laterne; - *braces*, L-eisen: - *girdles*, Gitterwerk der L.; - *keg*, Proviantfäßchen mit L.; - *signal*, L-signal; - *stuffing box*, Stopfbüchse in Gestalt einer L.

lanyard, Taljereep; - *mat*, T.-matte; - *seizing*, T.-bindsel.

lap, Nahtstreifen; - *butts*, überlappte Stöße; - *joint*, Dichtung mittelst Ueberlappung; - *jointed*, klinkerweise gebaut; - *of slide valve*, Schieberüberdeckung; to - *over*, überschießen; - *seam*, Überblattung; - *side*, die schwerere Seite, - *weld*, Schweißung durch Überlappung.

lapped frames, Spanten, die durch Überlappung der Enden gelascht sind.

lapping, durch Raddampfer verursachte Wellen.

lapside, Schlagseite.

lapsided, schief.

lapsider, Schlagseiter.

lapstreak, klinkergebautes Boot.

larboard, Backbord; - *bow*, B. Bug: - *brace*, B. Brasse; - *watch*, B. Wache.

larbowlines, Leute der Backbord-Bugwache.

larch wood, Lärchenholz.

large, raum; - *wind*, raumer Wind.

largest floor timber, das größte Bauchstück im Nullspant.

lark, Nußschale.

Lascar, ind. Matrose.

lash, laschen, verlaschen, zurren; - *of the wind*, Windstoß; - *up*, auffangen; - - *the*

hammocks, die Hängematten zurren.

lasher, Tromptau.

lashing, Laschung, Zeising; - *around a fished spar*, L. einer gefischten Spiere; - *by flat seizing*, L. mit gewöhnlichen Bindseln; - *chain*, Sorrkette: - *eye*, Bändselauge; - *of a studding sail boom*, Steerttau einer Leesegelspiere; - *of a tail block*, Befestigung eines Steertblockes; - *of the heel of a topmast with the masthead*, Fußlaschung; - *of the head of sheers*, Kopflaschung; - *of two eyes*, Laschung zweier Augen aufeinander; - *rope*, Sorrtau.

lask, mitBackstagswind segeln.

lask od. *lasket of a bonnet*, Lißleine eines Bonnets.

last, 1. Last = 2 Tonnen; 2. Ladung; - *quarter ebb*, Dreiviertel Ebbe.

lastage, 1. Trächtigkeit; 2. Lastgeld.

latch, 1. Klinke; 2. Lißleine eines Bonnets.

latching od. *l. key*, Schloß eines Bonnets.

Lateen rigged, mitLateinsegeln getakelt; - *sail*, Lateinsegel; - *yard*, lateinische Rahe.

Lateener, Lateinsegelboot.

latent heat, gebundene Wärme.

lateral fastening, Querverbindung; - *impact*, Seitenstoß.

lathe, Drehbank; - *frame*, D.-gestell; - *mandrel*, D.-spindel; - *screw*, Leitspindel.

laths of the chain wales, Latten der Rüsten.

latitude, Breite: - *by dead reckoning*, gegißte B.; - *by observation*, beobachtete B.; - *in*, angekommene B.; - *south*, südliche B.

launch, 1. Barkasse; 2. Stapellauf, vom Stapel laufen lassen.

launching, vom Stapel lassen;

- *block*, Werftblock; - *cradle*, Ablaufschlitten; - *fast*, Törntau; - *planks*, Ablaufplanken; - *slip*, A-l-helgen; - *ways*, Gleitplanken; - *wedges*, Stoßkeile.

laundry boat, Waschboot.

laveer, lavieren.

law of gravitation, Gravitationsgesetz; - *of merchant shipping*, Seerecht; - *of salvage*,Strandungsordnung.

lawful merchandise, gesetzlich zulässige Waren; - *prize*, gute Prise.

lay, to - a bend od. *hitch around the hook of a block*, einen Hakenschlag machen; - *a deck*, ein Deck legen; - *a rope*, ein Tau schlagen; - *a vessel close to the wind*, an den Wind gehen; - - - *in the roads*, ein Schiff auf die Reede legen; - - - *on a careen*, ein S. kielholen; - - - *on the stocks*, e. S. zum Bau aufsetzen; - *aback*, back brassen; - *aboard of a vessel*, einem S. längsseits laufen; - *acoast*, nach der Küste zu anliegen; - *aft*, nach hinten kommen; - *aloft*, aufentern; - *alongside*, längsseits; - *all flat aback!* Brass back überall! - *down a vessel*, ein Schiff abschnüren; - *down buoys*, ausbojen; - *hold of*, anfassen, sich bemächtigen; - *on a metal sheating*, eine Metallhaut anlegen; - *the keel*, den Kiel legen; - *the land*, das Land aus Sicht verlieren; - *the sails aback*, die Segel gegen den Mast brassen; - *the vessel alongside of another*, sich bei einem andern Schiffe längsseits legen; - *to*, beidrehen, unter den Wind legen; - *up*, auflegen.

lay, Schlag eines Taues; - *days*, Liegetage; - *Lords of the Admiralty*, die höheren Zivilbeamten d. Admiralität.

layer, Lage; - *of planking*, Plankenschicht.

laying down, Übertragung des Schiffbauplans in natürlicher Größe auf den Mallboden; - *on a careen*, Kielholung.

lazaret, Lazarett.

lazy guy of the mizzen boom, Stoppertalje d. Besanbaums.

leach see leech.

lead a rope, ein Tau leiten: - *a seafaring life*, die See befahren.

lead, 1. Lot, Blei; 2. Schiebervoreilung; - *arming*, Ausfüllung des Senkbleies mit Talg; - *block*, Leitblock; - *joint*, Bleidichtung; - *line*, Lotleine; - - *tub*, L.-balje; - *nail*, Bleinagel; - *of slide valve*, Schiebervoreilung; - *of the steering gear*, Führungsstange des Steuergeräts; - *off*, ableiten; - *wire joint*, Bleidrahtdichtung.

leading block, Leitblock; - *buoy*, Fahrwassertonne; - *fair*, 1. sich klar in der Scheibe bewegen; 2. gut fahren (Tauwerk); - *lights*, Leitfeuer; *to get the - - in a line*, die L. durcheinander bringen; - *marks*,Leitmarken; - *part of a tackle*, der laufende Teil eines Takels; - *screw*, Leitspindel; - *strings of a boat's yoke*, Jochleinen; - *wind*, Raumwind.

leads of steering rods, Führungsstangen der Steuerung.

leadsman, der Mann am Lote.

league, Lige = 3 Seemeilen.

leaguer, Wasserlieger.

leak, Leck, lecken; - *alarm*, Läutewerk zum Anzeigen eines Lecks; - *has been stopped accidentally*, das Leck hat sich zugezogen.

leakage, Leckage, das Lecken; - *finder*, Lecksucher.

leaky, leck, leckend; - *from dryness*, aufgetrocknet und undicht geworden.

lean bow, scharfe Bug.
leather hose, Lederschlauch.
leave of absence, Urlaub.
ledge between the beams, Rippe zwischen den Deckbalken; *- of a hatch,* Lukenrippe; - *of rocks,* Felsenriff.
lee, das Lee, die Leeseite; *by the -,* mit dem Wind von Lee ein; *to go - - -,* den Wind verlieren; *on the - beam,* dwars nach Lee; - - - *bow,* in L. voraus; *under the lee,* in L.; *on the - quarter,* achtern auf der L-seite.
lee anchor, Leeanker; *- arm,* L-nock; *- board,* Schwert; *- boat,* Leeboot; *- bow,* L-bug; *- bowline,* L-bulin; *- brace,* L-brasse; *- brail,* L-geitau; *to - clew,* die L-seite eines Segels aufgeien; *- fall,* das Überholen nach L.; *- fang,* Strecktau; *- fange,* Leuwagen (eines Schratsegels); *- gauge,* die Lage unter dem Winde; *to have the - -,* sich in Lee eines anderen Schiffes befinden; *- going tide,* Flut von Luv nach Lee setzend; *- helm,* Leeruder; *the ship carried lee helm,* das Schiff ist luvgierig; *don't give so much - helm!* Nicht soviel Leeruder geben! *- hitch* od. *latch,* vom Kurse abfallen; *- lurch,* Überholen nach Lee zu; *- sheet,* L-schote; *- shore,* L-küste; *- side,* L-seite; *- tide,* L-tide; *- wheel,* 2ter Mann am Ruder.
leech, 1. Kante; 2. stehendes Liek; *- line,* Nockgording; - *- block,* N.-block; *- lining,* Verstärkungsband; *- rope,* Stehleik; *- tabling,* Kantensaum.
leeward, 1. in Lee, leewärts; 2. viel Abtrift haben; *to drive to -,* abtreiben; *to fall to -,* vom Winde abkommen; *- coast,* Leeküste; *- islands,* Antillen; *- tide,* Leetide; *-*

vessel, Schiff mit viel Abtrift.
leewardness, starke Neigung zum Abtreiben.
leeway, Abtrift; *to make -,* stark abtreiben; *to make up for -,* das Versäumte nachholen.
left handed propeller od. *screw,* linksdrehende Schraube; *- - rope.* linksgeschlagenes Tau.
leg, 1. Stütze, Strebe; 2. Schenkel (des Zirkels etc.); *- of a reef point* od. *of a sheet,* *leech line, &c.,* die Part eines Reffzeisings od. einer Schote, Nockgording etc.; *- of the fork of a stay,* Schenkel eines Stagauges.
legger, Wasserlieger.
legs, all - and wings, schnell fahrendes Schiff.
lender on bottomry, Bodmereigeber.
length between perpendiculars, Länge zwischen den Perpendikeln; *- of a chain cable,* Kettenlänge; *- of stroke,* Hublänge; *- of a wave,* Wellenlänge; *- on load line,* Länge in der Höhe der Ladelinie; *- over all,* äußerste Länge.
lengthen a vessel, ein Schiff länger machen.
lengthening, Verlängerung; *- piece,* Toppauflanger.
lengthway, der Länge nach.
lengthwise, der Länge nach; *- built bulkheads,* Langschotten.
let, verfrachten od. vermieten; *- all sails come aback,* durchdrehen lassen; *- a. s. out,* alle Segel ausspannen; *- come down,* fallen lassen; *- down an iron plate,* eine Platte einlassen; *- everything run,* alle Segel mit einem Mal laufen lassen; *- fly the sheets,* die Schoten fliegen lassen; *- go!* Werft los! *- - amain!* Los! *- - and haul!*

Rund vor! - - *everywhere!*
Los überall! - - *the anchor,*
den Anker fallen lassen;
- - - - *before the sails are
taken off, with all sails set*
od. *standing,* mit den Segeln
im Topp zu Anker gehen;
- *go the main sheet,* die Groß-
schote loswerfen; - *out a
reef or two,* es sich bequem
machen; - *out the reefs,* die
Reffe ausstecken.
letter board, Namenbrett; - *of
marque* od. *of reprisal,* 1.
Kaperbrief; 2. K-schiff.
Levant trader, ein Levante-
fahrer.
Levanter, heftiger Ostwind.
levee, Damm, Deich.
level, Stand; - *line,* Wasserlinie; - *of the sea,* Meeres-
spiegel.
lever, Balanzier, Hebel; - *engine,* B.-Maschine; - *handle,*
Hebelgriff; - *link,* Pumpen-
gelenk; - - *brasses,* P.-Lager-
schalen; - *of a winch,* Kurbel einer Winsch; - *of a windlass,* Handspeiche eines Ankerspills; - *of the chain cable
compressor,* Hebel des Kettenstoppers; - *safety valve,*
Sicherheitsventil mit Hebel;
- *shaft,* Balanzieraxe; - - *journal,* Halszapfen der Balanzieraxe.
liberty day, Urlaubstag; - *men,*
beurlaubte Mannschaft; -
ticket, Urlaubspaß.
licensed pilot, Patentlotse.
lick, Prügel, prügeln; - *into
shape,* durch Strenge er-
ziehen.
lid, Deckel; - *of a hatchway,*
Lukendeckel; - *of an air
port,* Klappe der Lüftungs-
pforte.
lie, How does she lie? Wie
liegen wir an? - *across,*
dwars liegen; - *aground,* festsitzen; - *ahull,* zum Treiben
liegen; - *along the land,* am
Lande entlang steuern; -

alongside, längsseits liegen;
- *athwart,* dwars liegen; -
balanced, auf der Dump
liegen; - *by,* unter kleinen
Segeln beiliegen; - *the course,*
Kurs anliegen; - *gunwale to,*
mit dem Schandeckel zu
Wasser liegen; - *head to
wind,* auf dem Winde liegen;
- *hove to,* beigedreht liegen;
- *in!* Leg ein! - *off!* Freiblei-
ben! - *in stays,* in der Wendung liegen; - *on even keel,*
gleichlastig liegen; - - -
weight, auf der Dump liegen;
- *on the beam ends* od. *on
the broadside,* zum Kentern
liegen; - *on the oars,* auf den
Riemen liegen; - *out!* Leg
aus! - *over,* überliegen; - *to,*
beigedreht liegen; - - *the
course,* Kurs halten; - - *the
north,* Nord anliegen; - *well
to in a gale* od. - *steady and
dry when hove to in a gale,*
im Sturm gut und trocken
beiliegen; - *with yards apeak,*
mit gestoppten Rahen liegen.
lien, Retentionsrecht.
life arrow, Pfeil mit Rettungs-
leine; - *belt,* Schwimmgürtel;
- - *box,* S.-kiste; - *boat,* Rettungsboot; - - *drill,* Übung
mit den Rettungsbooten; - -
station, Rettungsstation; -
buoy, R-boje; - - *line,* Strecktau; *to let go the* - -, die Rettungsboje werfen; - *car,*
Rettungswagen; - *cutter,* R-
kutter; - *preserver* od. *pro-
tector,* 1. R-apparat; 2. Tot-
schläger (in der Tasche); -
line, 1. Strecktau; 2. Ret-
tungsleine; - *mortar,* Mörser
zum Abfeuern von Raketen
mit Rettungsleinen; - *raft,*
R-floß; - *rocket,* R-rakete; -
saving apparatus, R-gerät;
- *s. service,* R-dienst; - *shot,*
R-leine mit Kugel; - *signal,*
R-signal; - *station,* R-station;
- *whale gig,* R-gig.
*lift the anchor by means of a
boat,* den Anker mit einem

Boote lichten; - *the chain into the sprocket wheel*, die Kette in die Kettentrommel des Gangspills einlegen; - *the propeller*, die Schraube heben; - *the shaft*, die Welle herausheben.

lift, 1. Toppenant; 2. das Spielen des Segels im Winde; 3. Ladung, Last; 4. Hebebaum; 5. Aufzug, Fahrstuhl; - *block*, Toppenantsblock; - *purchase*, Toppenantstalje; - - *block*, T.-block; - - *fall*, T.-läufer.

lifter up of a topsail, Hahnepot für die Bauchtalje der Marssegel.

lifting apparatus, - *gear*, Hebevorrichtung; - *sail*, ein das Vorderschiff hebendes Segel.

ligan, mit Schwimmer geworfenes Gut.

light, 1. Feuer (Leuchtf.); 2. Licht (Laternenl.); - *airs*, leichter Wind; - *beacon*, Leuchtbake; - *breeze*, flaue Brise; - *dues*, Feuergeld; - *goods*, leichte Güter; - *handed*, leicht bemannt; - *horseman*, Gigsgast; - *house*, Leuchtturm; - - *book*, L-feuerbuch; - - *keeper*, L-turmwächter; - *laden* od. *loaden*, leicht geladen; - *oared*, leicht bemannt; - *port*, Lichtpforte; - *room*, Laternenkammer; - *sails*, Beisegel; - *ship*, Feuerschiff; - *squall*, leichte Bö; - *the fires*, die Feuer anzünden; - *timbered*, mit schwachen Inhölzern gebaut; - *vessel*, Feuerschiff; - *warp*, Jagleine; - *water draught*, Tiefgang bei leichter Beladung; - *w. line* od. *mark*, leichte Wasserlinie.

lighten, ableichtern.

lightened frame, durchbrochenes Spant.

lightening, ableichtern, leichtern; - *conductor*, Blitzableiter.

lighter, Leichter; - *man*, L-führer.

lighterage, 1. Leichtern; 2. Leichtergeld.

lighting, Befeuerung.

lights visible in full range, Feuer in voller Sehweite.

lignite, Braunkohle.

lignum vitae, Pockholz; - - *bearing*, P.-lager; - - *sheave*, P.-scheibe; - - *strips*, P.-streifen.

limber boards, Füllungen des Wasserlaufs; - *chain* oder *clearer*, Reinigungskette; - *gate*, Speigat; - *hole*, Wasserlaufloch; - *passage*, die Reihe der Füllungen; - *plate*, Füllungsplanke; - *rope*, Nüstergattau; - *strake*, Kielwegerungsgang; - - *bolt*, K-w-bolzen.

limbers choked, Wasserläufe verstopft.

limit of trade winds, Passatgrenze.

limmer, Seitentau einer Sturmtreppe.

line, 1. ausfüllen, garnieren; 2. beplanken; 3. die Leisten der Farbestreifen anmerken; 4. Leine; 5. Linie, Sonnenlinie; *to cross the* -, den Äquator passieren; *to get the leading lights in a* -, die Leitfeuer durcheinander bringen; - *ahead*, Kielwasserlinie; - *breadth*, Hauptsente; - *of battle ship*, Linienschiff; - *of bearing*, Peilungslinie; - *of direction*, Richtungslinie; - *of flotation*, Wasserlinie; - *of shafting*, Wellenstrang; - *up*, ausgießen.

liner, 1. Schiff einer Dampferlinie; 2. Futter, Füllblech, Füllstreifen; 3. Büchse; 4. Einsatz; - *for ballast donkey crank shaft brasses*, Dampfballastpumpen - Kurbelwellenlagerschalenfutter; - *for boat hoist engine c. s. b.*, Bootheißmaschinen-K.; - *for circulating pump e. c. s. b.*,

Zirkulationspumpen-K.; - *for c. s. b.*, K.; - *for donkey engine c. s. b.*, Dampfpumpen-K.; - *for electric light e. c. s. b.*, Elektrischlichtmaschinen-K.; - *for feed donkey c. s. b.*, Dampfspeisepumpen-K.; - *for fire engine c. s. b.*, Dampffeuerspritzen-K.; - *for forced draught e. c. s. b.*, Künstlichen Zugerzeugungsmaschine-K.; - *for high pressure c. s. b.*, Hochdruck-K.; - *for intermediate p. c. s. b.*, Mitteldruck-K.; - *for low p. c. s. b.*, Niederdruck-K.; - *for oil pump c. s. b.*, Ölpumpen-K.; - *for refrigerating engine c. s. b.*, Eismaschinen-K.; - *for reversing e. c. s. b.*, Umsteuerungsmaschinen-K.; - *for steam ash hoist c. s. b.*, Dampfaschwinden-K.; - *for steam capstan c. s. b.*, Dampfgangspill-K.; - *for steam crane c. s. b.*, Dampfkran-K.; - *for steam winch c. s. b.*, Dampfwinden-K.; - *for steering engine c. s. b.*, Dampfsteuerapparat K.; - *for turning engine c. s. b.*, Drehvorrichtungsmaschinen-K.; - *for warping e. c. s. b.*, Verholmaschinen-K.; - *for windlass c. s. b.*, Dampfankerspill-K.; - *of sheet iron*, Futterblech.

lining, 1. Bekleidung (des Schiffes); 2. Garnitur (innere B. der Lagerschalen); 3. Verstärkungsbänder (für Segel); - *of the bitts*, Kissen der Betinge; - *of the bow*, Ankerfütterung; - *piece*, Füllstreifen.

link, Coulisse, Gelenk; - *block*, Coulissenstein; - *brasses*, Gelenklagerschalen; - *motion*, Coulissensteuerung; - *of a chain cable*, Ankerkettenglied; - *worming*, Ausfüllen der spiralförmigen Vertiefungen des Tauwerks mit Ketten.

linseed oil, Leinöl.

lip of a scarph, Lippe einer Laschung.
lipper, Spritzung.
lipping the whole of the hawse pipe, das Loch des Klüsenrohrs wurde von der See bespült.
liquefaction, das Flüssigwerden.
liquid fuel, flüssiges Heizmaterial.
list, Schlagseite, S. annehmen.
little cabin, kleine Kajüte.
littoral, Küstenland.
live, sich oben halten; - *lumber*, lebendige Ballast; - *oak wood*, Steineichenholz.
lively, flott schwimmend.
livid, schwärzlich rot und blau.
living quarters, Volkslogis.
lizard, Sprut (am Drehreep).
load, 1. beladen, einladen; 2. Belastung; *shipper's* - *and count*, nach Abladers Einladung und Zählung; - *of the safety valve*, Belastung des Sicherheitsventils; - *water line*, Tiefladelinie; - *w. section*, Ebene der T.
loading and discharging crane, Ladekran; - *berth*, L-platz; - *days*, L-tage; - *expenses*, L-kosten; - *gear*, L-geschirr; - *port*, L-hafen.
lobby, Vorkajüte.
lobe plate, Grundplatte.
loblolly, Hafergrützbrei; - *boy*, Heilgehülfe.
lobscourse, Labskaus.
local attraction, Kompaßdeviation.
lock, 1. Schleuse; 2. Schloß; - *bars*, Lukenstangen; - *bolt*, Sicherheitsbolzen; - *chamber*, Schleusenkammer; - *gate*, S-tor; - *nut*, Gegenmutter.
lockage, Schleusengeld.
locked up chamber, der verschlossene Kasten eines Sicherheitsventils; - - *safety valve*, Sicherheitsventil mit verschlossenem Kasten.

locker, 1. Kettenkasten; 2. Kammer, Kasten, Spind; *not a shot in the -*, kein Geld im Beutel.

locust wood, Akazienholz.

lode star, Polarstern.

lodging knee, horizontales Knie; - - *bolt*, horizontale K-bolzen.

loft, Werkstatt.

log, 1. Log, loggen; 2. Schiffsjournal; - *board*, Logbrett; - *book*, Schiffsjournal; - *canoe*, Kanu; - *chip*, Logbrett; - *glass*, L-glas; - *line*, L-leine; - *reel*, L-rolle; - *rotator*, L-schraube; - *ship*, L-scheit; - *slate*, L-tafel.

log, by the -, nach dem gegißten Besteck.

logged, auf der Seite liegend.

logger head, Poller eines Bootes.

logging head, Balancier.

logs, the ship - 10 knots, das Schiff läuft 10 Knoten in der Stunde.

long and short armed floors, doppelte Bodenwrangen; - - - *boards*, lange Gänge od. Schläge; - *b.*, l. G. o. S.; - *boat*, Großboot; - *bolt*, Betingbolzen; - *D-slide valve*, langer D-Schieber; - *floor*, das lange Flach; - *jawed*, ausgereckt; - *logger*, ein sehr langes und schnelles Schiff; - *poop*, lange Hütte; - *scarph*, Langscherbe; - *sea*, lange See; - *skeined*, langsträhnig; - *splice*, Langsplissung; - *swell*, lange Dünung; - *tackle*, Segeltakel; - - *block*, Violinblock; - *timbers*, Bugstücke der Kaatspanten; - *togs*, Zivilanzug; - *ton*, lange Tonne = 21×112 lbs.; - *top timbers*, Bugstücke der Kaatspanten; - *topgallant mast*, lange Bramstenge.

longitude, Länge; - *by dead reckoning*, gegißte L.; - *by observation*, beobachtete L;

- *E.*, östliche L.; *in*, bekommene L.; - *left*, abgefahrene L.; - *W.*, westliche L.; - *watch*, Chronometer.

longitudinal, Längsspant; - *bulkhead*, L-schott; - - *stringer*, L-s-stringer; - *frame*, Längsspant; - *girder*, L-träger; - *key of propeller*, Schrauben-L-keil; - *seam*, L.-naht; - *section*, Längendurchschnitt; - *strain*, Längsspannung; - *strength*, Längsverband; - *strengthening*, Längsverstärkung.

longshore, längs der Küste; - *butcher*, Küstenwächter; - *fishery*, K-fischerei; - *lubber*, Landratte; - *lawyer*, Stranddieb; - *man*, Schauermann; - *owner*, geiziger Reeder; - *thief*, Stranddieb.

loof, Backe (Rundung des Bugs); - *frame*, Luvspant; - *tackle*, Zwei- und Einscheiber-Talje; - *timbers*, Balanzierspannen.

loof, to bring the - round od. *to spring the -*, Luv gewinnen.

look-out, Ausguck, Ausgucksmann; - - *bridge*, A-g-brücke; - - - *rails and stanchions*, A-g-brückengeländer; - - - *stanchions*, A-g-b-zepter; *l. o. for squalls!* steh klar für die Bö! - - *man*, Ausgucksmann.

loom, 1. Seegesicht; 2. sichtbar werden; - *gale*, leichte Brise; - *of an oar*, Riemenschaft; - *up*, sich undeutlich zeigen.

looming, 1. Seegesicht; 2. sichtbar werden; - *high*, hoch aussehen.

loop hole, Schießgatt; - *of a river*, Krümmung eines Flusses.

loose, 1. loswerfen, losmachen; 2. locker, lose; *to work -*, locker werden; - *bulwark*, das lose Schanzkleid; -

ceiling, lose Wegerung; - *coupling*, lösbareKuppelung; - *deck*, Stellung; - *eccentric*, loses Exzenter; - *flying jib boom*, der lose Außenklüverbaum; - *on the shaft*, lose auf der Welle; - *paddle wheels*, lose Schaufelräder; - *part*, das Lose; - *propeller*, lose Schraube; - *pulley*, lose Scheibe; - *royal*, das loseOberbramsegel; *to - sails to dry*, Segel trocknen; - *wheel*, loses Rad.

loosen, abbinden, Spielraum geben; - *a key*, einen Keil lösen; - *amain*, schnell die Segel streichen; - *a sail*, ein Segel losmachen.

lopsided, mit einer Schlagseite gebaut.

lose, vergeben, verlieren; *nothing to -!* Nichts vergeben! - *her steerage way*, aus dem Steuer laufen; - *sight of*, aus Sicht verlieren; - *the number of one's mess*, sterben; - *way*, aus der Fahrt kommen; - *the weather gauge*, Luv verlieren.

loss book, Verlustbuch; - *of heat*, Wärmeverlust; - *of power*, Kraftverlust.

lost effect, nutzlose Leistung.

low and aloft, von oben bis unten mit Segeln bedeckt; - *between decks*, mit niedrigem Zwischendeck gebaut; - *cherry red heat*, anfangende Kirschrotglühhitze; - *latitudes*, die niedrigen Breiten.

low pressure, Niederdruck; - - *ahead and astern way guides*, N.-Vor- und Rückwärts-Geradführungen; - - *boiler*, N.-kessel; - - *connecting rod*, N.-Pleuelstange; *l.p.c.r.bolt*, N.-P.-bolzen; *l. p. c.r. bottom end keep*, N.-Kurbelzapfen-Lagerschalendeckel; *l. p. c. r.b.e. liner*,N.-Pleuelstangenfußfutter; *l. p. c. r. top end*

keep, N.-Kreuzkopf-Lagerschalendeckel; - - *crank pin*, N.-Kurbelzapfen; *l. p. c. p. bolt*, N.-K.-Lagerbolzen; *l. p. c. p. brasses*, N.-K.-Lagerschalen; *l. p. c. shaft*, N.-Kurbelwelle; *l.p.c.s.bearing*, N.-K.-lager; *l. p. c. s. b. bolt*, N.-K.-l-bolzen; *l. p. c. s. bearing brasses*, N.-K.-l-schalen; *l. p. c. s. bearing keep*, N.-K.-l-deckel; *l.p.c.s. b. k. bolt*, N.-K.-l-d-bolzen; *l. p. c. s. journal*, N.-K.-Lagerzapfen; *l. p. c. web*, N.-Kurbelbacke; - - *crosshead bolt*, N.-Kreuzkopflagerbolzen; - - *cylinder*, N.-Zylinder; *l.p.c. admission port*, Eintrittskanal des N.-Z.; *l. p. c. cover*, N.-Z.-deckel; *l. p. c. c. bolt*, N.-Z.-d-bolzen; *l.p.cylinder drain cock*, N.-Z.-Drainagehahn; *l. p. c. d. pipe*, N.-Z.-D-n-rohr; *l. p. c. escape valve*, N.-Z.-Sicherheitsventil; *l. p. c. e. v. load*, N.-Z.-S.-belastung; *l. p. c. e. v. spindle*, N.-Z.-S.-spindel; *l. p. c. e. v. spring*, N.-Z.-S.-feder; *l. p. c. exhaust port*, N.-Z.-Austrittskanal; *l. p. c. jacket*, N.-Z.-mantel; *l. p. c. liner*, N.-Z.-Büchse; *l. p. c. stuffing box*, N.-Z.-Stopfbüchsendeckel; - - *eccentric*, N.-Exzenter; *l. p. e. bolt*, N.-E.-bolzen; *l. p. e. brasses*, N.-E.-Lagerschalen; *l.p.e.gear*, N.-E.-vorrichtung; *l. p. e. rod*, N.-E.-stange; *l. p. e. sheave*, N.-E.-scheibe; *l. p. e. strap*, N.-E.-bügel; *l.p.e.s. liner*, N.-E.-b-futter; - - *engine*, N.-Maschine; - - *gear*, N.-gestänge; - - *gland*, N.-Stopfbüchse; - - *guide*, N.-Geradführung; - - - *shoe*, N.-Gleitschuh; *l. p. piston*, N.-Kolben; *l. p. p. packing ring*, N.-K-liderungsring; *l. p. piston rod*, N.-K.-stange; *l. p. p. r. crosshead*, N.-K-s-Kreuzkopf; *l.p.p.r. c. brasses*,

N.-K-s-K-k-Lagerschalen: *l.
p. p. r. c. guide*, N.-K-s-K-k-
führung: *l. p. p. r. stuffing
box*, N.-K-s-Stopfbüchse;
l. p. p. r. s. b. gland, N.-
Zylinder-K-s-S-b-deckel; *l. p.
plunger piston*, N.-kolben:
- - *receiver pipe*, N.-Dampf-
reservoirrohr; - - *slide valve*,
N.-schieber; - - *starting
valve*, N.-Anlaßventil; - -
steam, N.-dampf; - - *turbine*,
N.-Turbine: *l. p. t. engine*,
N.-T.-Maschine; - - *valve
balance piston*, N.-schieber-
Abbalanzierungskolben; *l. p.
v. b. p. cylinder*, N.-s-A.-
Schutzkappe; *l. p. v. casing*,
N.-Schieberkasten; *l. p. v. c.
door*, N.-S.-deckel; *l. p. v. c.
escape valve load*, N.-S.-
Sicherheitsventilbelastung ;
l. p. v. gear, äußere Steuerung des N.-Zylinders; *l. p.
v. rod*, N.-Schieberstange; *l.
p. v. r. stuffing box*, N.-S.-
Stopfbüchse; *l. p. v. r. s. b.
gland*, N.-S.-S-b-deckel: *l. p.
v. spindle guide*, N.-Schieber-
stangenführung.
low rigged, niedrig getakelt;
- *sails*, kleine Segel; - *shore*,
niedriges Ufer; - *tide*, Niedrigwasser; - *water*, N.; - -
alarm od. *detector*, Alarm-
apparat bei zu niedrigem
Wasserstande; - - *mark*, Nie-
drigwasserlinie.
lower a boat, ein Boot niederlassen; - *a yard*, eine Rahe
fieren; - *a sail for a squall*,
ein Segel wegen einer Bö
laufen lassen; - *amain*,
schnell die Segel streichen;
- *away!* Fier weg! - *cheer-
fully*, willig streichen; -
handsomely, langsam fieren:
- *with a turn round a cleat*
od. *kevel*, um eine Klampe
od. einen Poller fieren; - *the
flag*, die Flagge streichen;
- *the sails*, die Segel streichen.
lower anchor, Windanker; -
boom, Bockspiere; - *brace*,

Brasse der Unterrahe; -
breadth sweep, Radius der
größten Breite; - *braces and
lifts!* An die Fock- u. Großbrassen! - *bunt line*, Bauchgording des Untersegels; -
channel, Unterrüste; - *collar
of a stay*, Kragen am Unterende eines Stags; - *counter*,
der untere Teil der Gillung;
- *cross trees*, Marssahlinge.
lower deck, Unterdeck; - -
beam, U.-balken; - - - *angle
bar*, U.-b-winkel; - - - *clamp*,
U.-Balkweger; - - - *hanging
knee*, U.-balken-Hängeknie;
- - - *knee rider*, U.-b-Kattspor;
- - - *lodging knee*, horizontales
Knie des U.-b-; - - - *shelf*, U.-
Balkweger; - - - *stringer*, U.-
Balkenstringer; - - - - *plate*,
U.-B.-platte; *l. d. b. tie plate*,
U.-balken-Längsschiene; - -
bolt, U.-bolzen; - - *fastening*,
U.-befestigung; - - *hatch*, U.-
luke; - - *hatchway coaming*,
U.-Lukensüll; - - *hook*, U.-
band; - - *mast wedges*, U.-
Mastkeile; - - *pillar*, U.-
stütze; - - *planking*, U.-be-
plankung; - - *spirketting*, U.-
Setzweger; - - *stanchion*, U.-
stütze; - - *stringer*, U.-strin-
ger; - - - *angle bar*, U.-s-win-
kel; - - - *inner angle bar*, Innenwinkel des U.-s-; - - - *plate*,
U.-s-platte; - - - *shell lugs*,
kurze Stringerwinkel des U.:
- - *waterway*, U.-Wassergang.
lower fore topgallant brace,
Vor-Unterbrambrasse; - - -
foot rope, V-U-brampferd;
- - - *sail*, V-U-b-segel; - - -
yard, V-U-b-rahe.
lower fore topsail, Vor-Unter-
marssegel; - - - *brace*, V-U-m-
brasse; - - - - *pendant*, V-U-m-
Brassenschenkel; *l. f. t. foot
rope*, V-U-m-pferd; *l. f. t.
yard*, V-U-m-rahe.
lower futtocks od. *lower futtock shrouds*, Marspüttings-
wanten; - *hold*, Unterraum;
- - U.-balken.

lower jigger topgallant brace,
Besahn - Unterbrambrasse;
- - - *sail,* B.-U-bramsegel; - - -
yard, B.-U-b-rahe: *l. j. topsail,* B.-Untermarssegel; *l. j.
t. brace,* B.-U-m-brasse; *l. j.
t. b. pendant,* B.-U-m-b-
schenkel; *l. j. t. foot rope,*
B.-U-m-pferd; *l. j. t. yard,*
B.-U-m-rahe.
lower keel, Unterkiel; - *lift,*
Unterrahe-Toppenant; - -
purchase, Untertoppenants-
talje; - - - *fall,* U.-läufer;
lower main topgallant brace,
Groß-Unterbrambrasse; *l. m.
t. foot rope,* G.-U-brampferd;
l. m. t. sail, G.-U-b-segel; *l.
m. t. yard,* G.-U-b-rahe; *l. m.
topsail,* G.-U-marssegel; *l. m.
t. brace,* G.-U-m-brasse; *l. m.
t. b. pendant,* G.-U-m-b-
schenkel; *l. m. t. foot rope,*
G.-U-m-pferd; *l. m. t. yard,*
G.-U-m-rahe; - *mast,* Untermast; - - *cap,* U.-Eselshaupt;
- - *cross trees,* U.-Dwarssah-
linge; - - *hound,* U.-hummer;
- - *trestle trees,* Untermars-
Längssahling; - *middle topgallant brace,* Mittel-Unter-
brambrasse; *l. m. t. foot
rope,* M.-U-brampferd; *l. m.
t. sail,* M.-U-b-segel; *l. m. t.
yard,* M.-U-b-rahe; *l. m. topsail,* M.-Untermarssegel; *l. m.
t. brace,* M.-U-m-brasse; *l. m.
t. b. pendant,* M.-U-m-b-
schenkel; *l. m. t. foot rope,*
M.-U-m-pferd; *l. m. t. yard,*
M.-U-m-rahe; - *mizen topgallant brace,* Kreuz-Unter-
brambrasse; *l. m. t. foot rope,*
K-U-b-pferd; *l. m. t. sail,* K-
U-b-segel; *l. m. t. yard,* K-
U-b-rahe; *l. m. topsail,* K-
Untermarssegel; *l. m. t. brace,*
K-U-m-brasse; *l. m. t. b.
pendant,* K-U-m-b-schenkel;
l. m. t. foot rope, K-U-m-
pferd; *l. m. t. yard,* K-U-m-
rahe; - *orlop deck,* Raumdeck;
- - - *beam,* R.-balken; - - -
stringer angle bar, R.-Strin-

gerwinkel; -*pendants,* Seiten-
hanger der Untermasten; -
platform, Maschinisten-
stand; - *pump box,* Pumpen-
eimer; - *reef tackle,* Unter-
Refftalje; - *rigging,* Unterwanten; - *ropes,* das untere
Tauwerk; - *sheets of a studding sail,* Unterleesegelscho-
ten; - *shroud,* Unterwant; -
stay, Untermaststag; - *stern,*
Gillung; - - *timber,* G.-holz;
- *studding sail,* Unterleesegel;
l. s. s. boom, U.-spiere; *l. s.
s. b. guy,* Backspierengeie;
l. s. s. halliard, Unterleesegel-
fall; *l. s. s. inner h.,* U-l-s-
Innenfall; *l. s. s. sheet,* U-l-s-
schote; *l. s. s. tack,* U-l-s-
hals; *l. s. s. tripping line,*
U-l-s-Aufholer; *l. s. s. yard,*
U-l-s-rahe; -*topgallant brace,*
Unterbrambrasse; *l. t. sail,*
U-bramsegel; - *topsail,* U-
marssegel; - - *brace,* U-m-
brasse; - - *jackstay,* U-m-
segel-Jackstag; - - *yard,* U-m-
rahe; - *trestle trees,* U-m-
Längssahling; - *turn of bilge
keelson,* Kielschwein in der
unteren Rundung der Kimm;
- *t. of the bilge,* die untere
Rundung der Kimm; - *yard,*
Unterrahe.
lowest of the ebb, Stillwasser
bei Ebbe.
loxodromic course, der loxodromische Kurs; - *tables,*
Tafeln zur Bestimmung des
Schiffsortes nach Kurs und
durchlaufenem Wege.
lubber, unbefahrener Matrose.
lubber's hole, Soldatengatt; -
point, Steuerstrich (der im
Kompaßgehäuse den Kurs
andeutet).
lubricate, schmieren.
lubricating bearing, selbst-
schmierendes Lager.
lubrication, Schmieren.
lubricator, Schmiervorrichtung.
luff, anluven; - *all you can!*

Luv all was geht! - *alee!* od. - *and lie!* L. dicht an den Wind! - *and touch her!* Laß den Wind ein wenig an das Liek kommen! - *round!* Laß in den Wind schießen! *Keep your -!* Halt dicht an den Wind!

luff, 1. Luv, Luvseite; der luvwärts vom Schiffe liegende Teil des Horizonts; 2. Luvleik eines Segels; 3. Stagkante (3eckiges Stagsegel); 4. Rundung des Bugs; - *frame*, Vorderbalanzierspant; - *hook*, Haken einer Handtalje; - *tackle*, Talje aus einem ein- und zweischeibigen Block; - *timbers*, Luvbäume; - *upon*, Talje auf T.

lug boat, Lugger; - *foresail*, L.-fock; - *fore topsail*, Vor-Toppsegel; - *mainsail*, Großsegel; - *main topsail*, Groß-Toppsegel; - *mizen*, Treiber; - - *topsail*, T.-Toppsegel; - *piece*, kurzer Gegenwinkel; - *sail*, Luggersegel; - *yard*, L.-rahe.

lugger, Lugger.

lull, abflauen; - *of a gale*, kurz anhaltendes Abnehmen des Sturmes; - *of the surf*, k. a. A. der Brandung.

lumber, 1. unnützer Ballast; 2. gesägtes Nutzholz; - *iron*, Mastengabel; - *port*, Ladepforte für Bauholz.

lumbered, belemmert.

lumbering sea, kabbelige See.

lumper, Schauermann.

lumpy sea, kabbelige See.

lunar corona, Mondring; - *halo*, M-hof; - *distance*, M-distanz; - *eclipse*, M-finsternis; - *method*, Bestimmung der geographischen Länge durch M-distanz; - *observation*, Beobachtung der M-d- von einem Stern zur Berechnung der geogr. Länge; - *tables*, M-tafeln.

lurching, überholen, schwer schlingern.

lurking reef, wachendes Rift; - *rock*, blinde Klippe.

lying at anchor, vor Anker liegen; - *to*, beigedreht.

lymphad, einmastige Galeere.

M.

machine riveting, Maschinennietung.

mackerel breeze, frische Brise; - *gale*, f. Sturm.

mad, rund umlaufend.

made block, zusammengesetzter Block; - *eye*, flämisches Auge; - *mast*, gebauter Mast.

Magellan jacket, Wachtmantel.

magged, aufgebraucht.

magnet, Magnetnadel.

magnetic, magnetisch; - *course*, mitweisender Kurs; - *declination*, Mißweisung; - *pole*, magnetischer Pol.

magnus hitch, Stopperstek.

mahogany, 1. Mahagoniholz; 2. altes zähes Fleisch.

maiden trip, Jungferreise.

mail flag, Postflagge; - *of a chain*, Kettenviereck zum Abreiben neuer Taue; - *steamer*, Postdampfer.

main, 1. der offene Ozean; 2. Festland; - *beam*, Hauptspantbalken; - *bearing*, Kurbelwellenlager; - - *bolt*, K.-bolzen; - - - *nut*. K.-bmutter; - *bearing brasses*, K.-schalen; - - *keep*, Hauptlagerdeckel; - - - *bolt*, K.-Deckelbolzen; - - - - *nut*, K.-D.-mutter; - *bearing liner*, K.-schalenfutter; - *bends*, die großen Berghölzer; - *body*, Hauptrumpf; - - *frames*,

H.-spanten; - *boom*, Groß-baum; - - *topping lift*, G.-Toppenant; - - - - *purchase*, G.-Dirktalje; - *boiler*, Haupt-kessel ; - *bowline*, Großbulin; - *brace*, G-brasse; - - *pendant*, G-b-schenkel ; - *breadth*, die größte Breite; - *bulwark*, Schanzkleid; - *bumkin*, Großbutluv; - *bunt line*, Groß-Bauchgording; - *cable*, Hauptkabel; - *capstan*, großes Gangspill; - *chain plate*, Großrüsteisen; - *channel*, große Rüste; - *check valve*, Hauptspeise-ventil ; - *clew garnet*, Groß-geitau; - *cone driving wheel*, Haupttriebrad; - *course*, das große Segel.

main deck, Hauptdeck; - - *awning*, H.-Sonnensegel; - - *beam*, H.-balken; - - - *angle bar*, H.-b-winkel; - - - *clamp*, H.-Unterbalkweger; - - *hanging knee*, H.-Balken-hängeknie; - - - *lodging knee*, horizontales Knie desHaupt-deckbalkens; - - - *shelf*, Hauptdeck-Balkweger; - - - *stringer*, H.-Balkenstringer; - - - - *plate*, H -B.-platte; *m. d. b. tie plate*, H.-balken-Lukenstringer; *m. d. bolt*, H.-bolzen; *m. d. fastening*, H.-befestigung; *m. d. hatches*, H.-luken ; *m. d. hatchway coaming*, H.-l-süll; *m. d. hook*, H.-band; *m. d. mast wedges*, H.-Mastkeile; *m. d. pillar*, H.-stütze; *m. d. planking*, H.-beplankung; *m. d. plating*, H.-beplattung; *m.d. sheerstrake*, H.-Schergang; *m. d. spirketting*, H.-Setz-weger; *m. d. stanchion*, H.-stütze; *m. d. stringer*, H.-stringer; *m. d. s. angle bar*, H.-s-winkel; *m. d. s. inner a. b.*, Innenwinkel des H.-stringers; *m. d. s. plate*, H.-Stringerplatte; *m. d. s. shell lugs*, kurze Stringerwinkel des Hauptdecks; *m. d. water-way*, H.-Wassergang.

main discharge pipe, Haupt-ausgußrohr; *m. d. valve*, H-a-g-ventil; *m. d. v. cover*, H-a-g-v-deckel; *m. d. v. seat*, H-a-g-v-sitz; *m. d. v. spindle*, H-a-g-v-spindel; - *engine*, Schiffsmaschine; - *feed check valve*, Maschinenpumpen-Speiseventil; *m.f. pipe*,Haupt-speiserohr; - *floor*, Boden-wrange des Hauptspants; - *foot rope*, Großpferd; - *frame*, Hauptspant; - *funnel*, H-schornstein; - *futtock shrouds*, Groß-Marspüttings-wanten; - *futtocks*, G-M-Püttinge; - *gaff*, große Gaffel; - - *topsail*, Großgaffel-Topp-segel; - - - *downhaul*, G.-T.-Niederholer; - - - *halliard*, G-T.-fall; - - - *sheet*, G.-T-schote; - - - *tack*, G-T.-hals; - *hatch*, Großluke; - *hatch-way coaming*, G.-süll; - *hold*, Hauptraum; - *injection pipe*, Hauptinjektionsrohr; - - *valve*, H-i-j-ventil; - - - *cover*, H-i-j-v-deckel; *m. i. v. rose plate*, Haupteinlaßventilsieb; *m. i. v. spindle*, Haupt-Ein-spritzventilspindel; - *jeer*, Großfall; - *jib*, großer Klüver; - *keel*, Hauptkiel; - *keelson*, H.-schwein; - *land*, Festland; - *leech line*, Groß-Nockgording; - *lift*, Groß-toppenant; - - *purchase*, Großrahe - Toppenantstalje; - *lower cross trees*, Groß-mast-Dwarssahlingen; - *l. rigging*, Großwanten; - - *trestle trees*, Großmast-Längssahlingen; - *mast*, Großmast; - - *cap*, G.-Esels-haupt; - - *coat*, G.-kragen; - - *cross trees*, G.-Dwars-sahlingen; - - *head*, Topp des G.; - - *step*, G.-spur; - - *tackle*, Großhangertakel; - - *trestle trees*, Großmast-Längssahlingen; - - *wedge*, G.-keil; - *middle staysail*,

Großmittelstagsegel; - - - *downhaul*, G.-Niederholer*;* - - - *halliard*, G.-fall; - - - *sheet*, G.-schote; - - - *tack*, G.-hals; *to go a - pace*, mit vollen Segeln fahren; - *peak halliard*, Großpiekfall; - *pendant tackle*, G-seitentakel; - *piece*, Spillstamm; - - *of rudder*, Ruderherz; - - *of the stern post*, Hauptholz des Achterstevens; - - *of the windlass*, Spillwelle; - *post*, Achtersteven; - *purchase*, Mastgien; - *rail*, Reling; - - *angle bar*, R.-winkel; - *reef tackle*, Groß-Refftalje; - *rigging*, Großwanten; - *rope*, Hauptseil.

main royal. Groß-Royal; - - *backstay*, G-R-pardune; - - *brace*, G-R-brasse; - - *bunt line*, G-R-Bauchgording; - - *clew line*, G-R-Geitau; - - *foot rope*, G-R-pferd; - - *halliard* od. - - *h. purchase*, G-R-fall; - - *lift*, G-R-Toppenant; - - *mast*, G-R-stenge; - - *sheet*, G-R-schote; - - *stay*, G-R-stag; - - *staysail*, G-R-Stagsegel; - - - *downhaul*, G-R-S.-Niederholer; - - - *halliard*, G-R-S.-fall; - - - *sheet*, G-R-S.-schote; - - - *stay*, G-R-S.-leiter; - - - *tack*, G-R-S.-hals; - *royal studding sail*, G-R-Leesegel; - - - - *boom*, G-R-L.-spiere; - - - - *downhaul*, G-R-L.-Niederholer; - - - - *halliard*, G-R-L.-fall; - - - - *sheet*, G-R-L.-schote; - - - - *tack*, G-R-L.-hals; - - - - *yard*, G-R-L.-rahe; - *royal yard*, G-R-rahe.

main sail, Großsegel; - - *halliard*, G.-fall; - - *haul!* Rund achter! - *shaft*, Hauptwelle; - - *of steering engine*, H.-desDampfsteuerapparats; - *sheerstrake*, Hauptschergang; - *sheet*, Großschote; - - *horse*, Großsegel-Leitwagen; - *shroud* Großwant.

main skysail, Groß-Scheisegel;

- - *backstay*, G-S.-pardune; - - *brace*, G.-S.-brasse; - - *clew line*, G-S.-geitau; - - *foot rope*, G-S.-pferd; - - *halliard*, G-S.-fall; - - *lift*, G-S.-Toppenant; - - *mast*, G-S.-stenge; - - *sheet*, G-S.-schote; - - *stay*, G-S.-stag; - - *yard*, G-S.-rahe.

main spur wheel, großes Stirnrad; - *stay*, Großstag.

main staysail, Groß-Stagsegel; - ,- *downhaul*, G-S.-Niederholer; - - *halliard*, G-S.-fall; - - *sheet*, G-S.-schote; - - - *pendant*, G-S.-Schotenschenkel; *main staysail stay*, G-Stagsegel-Leiter; *m. s. tack* G-S.-hals.

main steam, Hauptdampf; - - *pipe*, H.-rohr; - - *pipes*, H.-r-leitung; - - *valve*, H.-ventil; - *stock of the rudder*, Ruderpfosten; - *stop valve*, Hauptabsperrventil; - - - *spindle*, H.-spindel; - *stream*, Stromrichtung; - *studding sail*, Großleesegel; - *tack*, Großhals; - - *block*, Haupthalsblock; - *tackle*, Großstagtakel; - - *pendant*, G.-hanger; - *throat halliard*, Groß-Klaufall; - *thwart*, Mastducht; -*top*,Großmars; - -*bowline*,G.-bulin; - - *braces*, G.-brassen.

main topgallant backstay, Großbram-Pardune: - - *bowline*, G.-bulin: - - *brace*, G.-brasse; - - *bunt line*, G.-Bauchgording; - - *cap*, G.-stenge-Eselshaupt; - - *clew line*, G.-geitau; - - *cross trees*, Dwarssahlinge derG.-stenge; - - *foot rope*, G.-pferd; - - *futtock shrouds*, G.-Püttingswanten; - - *futtocks*, G.-püttingen; - - *halliard* od. - - *h. purchase*, G.-fall; - - *leech line*, G.-Nockgording; - - *lift*,G.-Toppenant; - - *mast*, G.-stenge; - - - *cap*, G.-s-Eselshaupt; *m. t. rigging*, G.-s-wanten; - - *royal mast*, große Oberbramstenge; - -

royal sail, g. O-b-segel; - - *sail,* Großbram-Segel; - - *sheet,* G.-schote; - - *shroud,* G.-want; - - *stay,* G.-stag; - - *staysail,* G.-Stagsegel; - - - *downhaul,* G.-S.-Niederholer; - - - *halliard,* G.-S.-fall; - - - *sheet,* G.-S.-schote; - - - *stay,* G.-S.-leiter; - - - *tack,* G.-S.-hals; *m.t. studding sail,* G.-Leesegel; - - - - *boom,* G.-L.-spiere; - - - - *downhaul,* G.-L.-Niederholer; - - - - *halliard,* G.-L.-fall; - - - - *sheet,* G.-L.-schote; - - - - *tack,* G.-L.-hals; - - - - *yard,* G.-L.-rahe; *m. t. trestle trees,* G.-stengen-Längssahling; *m. topgallant tye,* G.-Drehreep; *m. topgallant yard,* G.-rahe.
main topman, Großtoppgast.
main topmast, Großmarssten-ge; - - *backstay,* G.-pardune; - - *cap,* G.-Eselshaupt; - - *cross trees,* Dwarssahlingen der G.-; - - *rigging,* Groß-mars - Wanten; - - *shroud,* Großstenge-Want; - - *stay,* G.-stag; - - *staysail,* G.-Stag-segel; - - - *downhaul,* G.-S.-Niederholer; - - - *halliard,* G.-S.-fall; - - - *sheet,* G.-S.-schote; - - - *stay,* G.-S.-leiter; - - - *tack,* G.-S.-hals; *m. t. studding sail,* Großoberlee-segel; - - - - *boom,* G.-spiere; - - - - *downhaul,* G.-Nieder-holer; - - - - *halliard,* G.-fall; - - - - *sheet,* G.-schote; - - - - *tack,* G.-hals; - - - - *yard,* G.-rahe; *m. t. trestle trees,* Groß-marsstengen-Längssahling.
main topping lift, Großbaum-dirk.
main topsail, Großmarssegel; - - *brace,* G-m-brasse; - - *b. pendant,* Großmars-Brassen-schenkel; - - *bunt line,* G.-Bauchgording; - - *clew line,* G.-geitau; - - *foot rope,* G.-pferd; - - *halliard* od. - - *h. purchase,* G.-fall; - - *lift,* G.-Toppenant; - - *reef tackle,* G.-Refttalje; - - *sheet,* G.-schote;

- - *tye,* G.-Drehreep; - - *yard,* G.-rahe.
main transom, Heckbalken.
main trysail, Großtreisegel; - - *boom,* G.-baum; - - *b. topping lift,* G.-b-toppenant; - - *p. t. l. purchase,* G.-b-Dirktalje; - - *brails,* G.-Geitaue; - - *gaff,* Großtreisegel-Gaffel; - - *halliard,* G.-fall; - - *inhaul,* G.-Einholer; - - *outhaul,* G.-Ausholer; - - *peak halliard,* G.-Piekfall; - - *sheet,* G.-schote; - - *tack,* G.-hals; - - *throat halliard,* G.-Klaufall; - - *topping lift,* G.-Baumdirk; - - *vang,* G.-gerde.
main valve, Hauptventil; - *vang,* Großgaffelgerde; - - *pendant,* G.-schenkel; - *wales,* die großen Berghölzer; *-yard,* Großrahe; - - *boom,* Groß-spiere; - - *foot rope,* Groß-pferd; - - *men,* Mannschaft der Krankenliste. [aufhalten.
maintaining steam, Dampf *maintenance of crew,* Unterhalt der Mannschaft.
make a good board, einen guten Schlagbug (od. Streckbug) machen; *- a sternboard,* über den Achtersteven wenden; *- a tack,* einen Schlag tun; *- bad weather,* den Sturm schlecht aushalten; *- errors in the dead reckoning,* sich vergissen; *- fast,* festmachen; *- foul water,* muddern; *- free with the land,* ganz dicht an das Land heransegeln; *- good the damage,* Schaden ausbessern; *- good the course,* den Kurs verbessern; *- good weather,* den Sturm gut aushalten; *- headway,* Fahrt machen; *- leeway,* Abtrift haben; *- long boards* od. *tacks,* lange Gänge machen; *- more water than the pumps can throw up,* mehr Wasser machen als man auspumpen kann; *- out,* erkennen; *- sail,* Segel setzen od. unter Segel gehen; *-short boards* od. *tacks,*

kurze Gänge machen; - *signals,* Signale machen; - *sternway,* über Steuer gehen; - *up a sail,* auftuchen; - *up the average,* Havarie aufmachen; - *the land,* Land machen; - *water,* Wasser machen; - *way,* Fahrt haben.
make, rigging, and apparel, Schiff mit sämtlichem Zubehör und Ausrüstung.
making, sea -, See nimmt zu.
making iron, Rabatteisen.
malleability, Schmiedbarkeit.
mallet, Klopfkeule.
man, bemannen; - *before the mast,* Matrose; - *bound,* durch ungenügende Bemannung zurückgehalten; - *broder,* Heuerbaas; - *handle,* durch Menschenkraft bewegen; - *hole,* Mannloch; - - *cover* od. *door,* M.-deckel; - *of war,* Kriegsschiff; - *rope,* Manntau; - *ropes,* Fallreepstaue; *ship!* Mann die Rahen! - *the boat!* Zu Boot! od. Bootsgasten! - *the capstan!* An's Spill! - *the rope along!* Mann weiter! - *the side!* Mann das Fallreep!
manageable, manövrierfähig; - *ness,* Steuerfähigkeit.
management, Führung, Leitung.
managing owner, Korrespondenzreeder.
mandrel od. *mandrell* od. *mandril* od. *mandrill,* 1. Drehbankspindel; 2. Spitzhammer.
manger, Schaafhock; - *board,* Waschbord.
manifest of the cargo, Ladungsmanifest.
manilla rope, Manilatau.
manless, unbemannt.
manned, bemannt.
manning, bemannend, Bemannung.
manoeuvre, manövrieren, Manöver.
manometer, Manometer.

maple, Ahornholz.
mapping out, die graphische Darstellung.
mare's tales, Streifenwolken.
margin plank, Randplanke; - *plate,* Tankseitenplatte.
marine. 1. Marine; 2. Seesoldat; - *barometer,* Schiffsbarometer; - *boiler,* Schiffskessel; - *engine,* S-maschine; - *engineer,* S-ingenieur; - *engineering,* Marine-Ingenieurwesen; - *flue boiler,* Schiffszugkessel; - *glue,* S-leim; - *governor,* S-maschinen-Regulator; - *insurance clauses,* Seeversicherungsbedingungen; - *jurisdiction,* Seegerichtsbarkeit; - *stores,* Schiffsutensilien.
mariner, Seefahrer; - *'s compass,* Schiffskompaß.
maritime affairs, Seewesen; - *code,* Schiffahrtsgesetzbuch; - *commerce,* Seehandel; - *country,* Seeufer-Staat; - *Court,* Seeamt; - *jurisdiction,* Seegerichtsbarkeit; - *law,* Seerecht; - *lien,* Seepfandrecht; - *powers,* Seemächte; - *prize,* Prise auf hoher See; - *tort,* Verbrechen auf See.
mark boat, festliegendes Zielboot; - *the draught of a vessel,* den Tiefgang eines Schiffes aichen.
marking yarn, Kabelgarn mit farbigem Herzgarn.
marks and deeps of the lead line, Marken und Zwischenräume der Lotleine.
marl, marlen.
marline od. *marling,* Marleine; - *hitch,* Marlienstich; - *knot,* Marlschlag; - *spike,* Marlpfriem; - - *hitch,* M.-stich.
marry, anbändeln, Taue doppelt einholen.
martinet, 1. strenger Offizier; 2. Sklaventreiber; 3. Nockgording.
martingale, Stampfstock; - *backrope,* S.-Achterholer; -

boom, S.; - *boom hoop*, S.-band; - *down*, dompen; - *guy*, Stampfstock-Geie; - *stay*, Klüverdomper.

martnet see *martinet*.

mast, bemasten, Mast, Stenge; - *beam*, Mastbalken; - - *angle bar*, M.-winkel; - *cap*, Mast-Eselshaupt; - *carline* od. *carling*, M.-schlüssel; - *cheek*, M.-backe; - *cleat*, M.-klampe; - *cloth*, Stoßlappen; - *coat*, M.-kragen; - *collar*, Spiel-kragen; - *gore*, M.-gillung; - *head*, M.-topp; - - *angle*, M.-t-winkel; - - *cover*, M.-t-deckel; - - *flag halliard*, Flaggleine eines Mastes; - - *hoop*, Toppband; - - *lantern* od. *light*, Topplicht; - - *light traveller*, Leiter des T.; - - *man*, der Ausguck im Topp; - - *pendant*, Masttakelhanger; - - *tenon*, Masttoppzapfen; - - *truck*, Flaggenknopf; - *heel*, Fuß des Mastes; - - *tenon*, Mastfußzapfen; - *hole*, Mastloch; - - *collar*, Wandel-kragen; - *hoop*, Mastband; - - *for derrick*, M. für Lade-baum; - - *for lower rigging*, M. für Unterwanten; - *hound*, Masthummer; - *hounding*, Mastteil zwischen Oberdeck und Längssahling; - *house*, Mastschuppen; - *housing*, Masthausing; - *less*, mastlos; - *lining*, Verdoppelung im Mastliek; - *maker*, Masten-bauer; - *man*, Mastgast; - *partner*, Mastfischung; - - *chock*, M.-kalben; - - *plate*, M.-platte; - *pond*, Masten-hafen; - *prop for careening*, Mastbaumstütze; - *room*, Mastloch; - *rope*, Windreep; - *shed*, Mastbaumwerkstatt; - *sheers*, Block zum Masten-einsetzen; - *step*, Mastspur; - *tabling*, Mastkantensaum; - *tackle*, Haugertakel; - - *fall*, Masttakelläufer; - *tenon*, Mastzapfen; - *timber*, Masten-holz; - *trunk*, Mastkoker;

- *wedge*, Mastkeil; - *with top and topgallant cross trees*, Vollmast.

master, 1. Schiffer, Kapitän; 2. Obersteuermann (Kriegs-schiff); - *at arms*, Schiffs-profoß; - *attendant*, Hafen-meister; - *cock*, Wendehahn; - *mariner*, Seeschiffer; - *ship-wright*, Marine-Schiffsbau-meister.

master's certificate, Schiffer-patent; - *mate*, Obersteuer-manns-Maat; - *store room*, Schiffersgatt.

masting sheers, Mastenkran.

mat, 1. Matte; 2. Garnierungs-matte.

match chest, Luntenkiste; - *hook*, Doppel-Takelhaken; - *staff*, Zündleinenstock; - *tub*, Kühlbalje.

mate, Offizier, Steuermann; -'s *certificate*, Steuermannspa-tent; - *receipt*, S-m-quittung; - *room*, S-m-kammer.

material, Material; - *fastenings*, die wichtigen Verbandteile.

Matthew Walker knot, Talje-reepsknoten.

maul, Maker (schwerer Ham-mer).

maximum pressure, Maximal-druck.

meaking iron, Kratzeisen.

meal pendant od. *pennant*, ro-ter Wimpel während der Essenszeit.

mean draught, mittlerer Tief-gang; - *height*, mittlere Segel-höhe; - *pressure*, Durch-schnittsdruck; - *proportion*, D-s-verhältnis; - *time*, mitt-lere Zeit.

measure brief, Meßbrief; - *goods*, Maßgüter.

measurement, Schiffsvermes-sung; - *capacity*, Raumig-keit; - *goods*, Maßgüter; - *of the tonnage*, Tonnengehalt; - *ton*, Raumtonne.

meat safe, Fleischschrank; - *tub*, Frischbalje.

mechanical engineer, Maschinenbau-Ingenieur; - *power*, mechanische Leistung; - *stoker*, selbstwirkende Feuerung.

medicine chest, Arzneikiste.

medium midshipman, älterer Seekadett; - *pressure*, Mitteldruck; - - *boiler*, M.-kessel; - - *cylinder*, M.-Zylinder; - - *engine*, M.-Maschine.

meet her! Stütz! - *the helm*, das Ruder stützen.

meeter, Gegendampfer, G-segler.

meeting steamer, Gegendampfer.

megaphone, Sprachrohr.

melt, schmelzen.

melting point, Schmelzpunkt; - *pot*, S-topf.

mend, ausbessern; - *a furled sail*, ein beschlagenes Segel besser festmachen.

mercantile affairs, Handelssachen; - *law*, Handelsgesetz; - *marine*, H-marine; - - *office*, Seemannsamt.

mercator's chart, die wachsende Karte; - *sailing*, nach vergrößerter Breite segeln.

merchant flag, Handelsflagge; - *fleet*, H-flotte; - *man*, Kauffahrteischiff; - *navy*, Handelsmarine; - *seaman*, Matrose eines Handelsschiffes; - *service*, Handelsmarine; - *shipping act*, Handelsschiffahrtsgesetz; - *trading*, Großhandel; - *vessel*, Kauffahrteischiff.

mercurial barometer, Quecksilber-Barometer; - *gauge*, Luftleeremesser.

mercy, at the - of, ein Spielball von etc.

meridian, Meridian; - *altitude*, Mittagshöhe; - *circle*, Mittagskreis; - *mark*, Meridianzeichen; - *of a place*, Ortsmeridian.

meridional distance, Meridiandistanz; - *part*, Meridianteil.

mess, Messe; - *beef*, gepökeltes Rindfleisch; - *bill*, Backsrolle; - *bowl*, Brotback; - *boy*, Backschafter; - *chest*, Messegeschirrkasten; - *cloth*, Tischtuch; - *kid*, Brotback, Fleischback; - *kit*, Kochgerätschaften; - *locker*, Backschrank; - *mate*, Backgenosse; - *pork*, Pökelschweinefleisch; - *room*, Messe; *m. r. companion*, Messenkappe; *m. r. door*, M-tür; *m. r. d. hinge*, M-t-Scharnier; *m. r. funnel*, M-Schornstein; *m. r. skylight*, M-Oberlicht; *m. r. stove*, M-ofen; *m. r. ventilator*, M-ventilator; - *stool*, Backsbank; - *table*, B-tisch; - *traps*, Messegeschirr; - *tub*, Fleischfaß.

mess, to lose the number of one's mess od. *to be scratched out o. o. m.*, sterben.

messenger, Kabelaring; - *chain*, Kabelarkette; - *shackle*, Kabelarschäkel; - *wheel*, Kabelarrad.

metacentre, Metazentrum.

metacentric height, metazentrische Höhe.

metal bolt, Metallbolzen; - *canopy*, Bogenkreuz über der Niedergangsluke; - *fastening*, Metallbefestigung; - *lining*, M-garnitur; - *sheathing*, M-haut; - *sheave*, M-scheibe.

metallic joint, Metalldichtung; - *packing*, M-dichtung; - *piston*, Kolben mit M-liderung.

metalling, mit Metall beschlagen.

meteorological observation, meteorologische Beobachtung; - *observatory*, Wetterwarte; - *tide*, Ebbe und Flut infolge von Witterungseinflüssen.

meteorology, Meteorologie.

metestick, Meßstab.

mid channel, mitten im Fahrwasser.

middle band, Mittelband; - *bowline*, M-bulin; - *brace*, M-brasse; - - *pendant*, M-Brassenschenkel; - *brail*, M-geitau; - *bunt line*, M-Bauchgording; - *clew garnet*, M-geitau; - *deck*, Mitteldeck; - - *beam*, M.-balken; - - - *angle bar*, M.-b-winkel; - - - *clamp*, M.-Unterbalkweger; - - - *hanging knee*, M.-balken-Hängeknie; - - - *lodging knee*, horizontales Knie des M.-balkens; - - - *shelf*, M.-Balkweger; - - - *tie plate*, M.-balken-Lukenstringer; - *deck hatch*, M.-luke; - - *hatchway coaming*, M.-Lukensüll; - - *hook*, M.-band; - - *pillar*, M.-stütze; - - *spirketting*, M.-Setzweger; - - *stanchion*, M.-stütze; - - *tie plate*, M.-Lukenstringer; - - *waterway*, M.-Wassergang; - *foot rope*, Mittelpferd; - *futtock shrouds*, Mittel-Marspüttingswanten;-*futtocks*,M.-M-püttinge; - *ground*, seichte Stelle mit tieferem Wasser an beiden Seiten; - *jib*, Mittelklüver; - - *halliard*, M.-fall; - *latitude sailing*, Mittelbreite-Rechnung; - *leech line*, Mittel-Nockgording; - *lift*, M.-Toppenant; - - *purchase*, M.-rahe-T.-talje; - *line*, Kiellinie; - - *bolt*, Kielschweinbolzen; - - *box keelson*, Mittel-Kastenkielschwein; - - *bulkhead*, M.-Längsschott; - - *centre through plate keel and keelson*, Mittelplatten - Kiel und Kielschwein; *m. l. c. t. p. keelson*, M.-K-s-; - - *continuous plate keelson*, Mittel-K-s-; - - *intercostal keelson*, eingeschobenes M-K-s-; *m. l. i. k. angle bar*, e. M-K-s-winkel; *m. l. i. k. plate*, e. M-K-s-platte; - - *keelson*, M-K-s-; *m. l. k. angle bar*, M-K-s-winkel; - - *pillar*, Mittschiffsstütze; - - *single plate keelson*, Träger-Kielschwein; - - *vertical centre plate keelson*, Mittelplatten-K.; *m. l. v. p. k.*, vertikales Mittelkiel-

schwein; - *lower cross trees*, Mittelmast-Dwarssahling; - - *rigging*, Mittelwanten; - - *trestle trees*, Mittelmast-Längssahling; - *mast*, Mittelmast; - - *cap*, M.-Eselshaupt; - - *cross trees*, M.-Dwarssahlingen; - - *shroud*, Wanttau des M.; - - *stay*, Mittelstag; - - *staysail*, Mittelstagsegel; - - *tackle*, Mittelhangertakel; - - *trestle trees*, Mittelmast-Längssahling; - - *wedge*, M.-keil; - *middle staysail*, M-Mittelstagsegel; - - - *downhaul*, Kreuz-Mittelstagsegel-Niederholer; - - - *halliard*, Mittel-M.-fall; - - - *sheet*, M-M.-schote; - - - *tack*, M-M.-hals; - *pendant tackle*, Mittelseitentakel; - *platform*, Mittel-Plattform;-*reef tackle*, M-Refftalje; - *rigging*, Mittelwanten; - *rope of an awning*, Mittelliek eines Sonnensegels; - *royal*, Mittel-Royal; - - *backstay*, M-R.-Pardune; - - *brace*, M-R.-brasse; - - *bunt line*, M-R.-Bauchgording; - - *clew line*, M-R.-Geitau; - - *foot rope*, M-R.-pferd; - - *halliard* od. - - - *purchase*, M-R.-fall; *m. r. lift*, M-R.-toppenant; - - *mast*, M-R.-stenge; - - *sheet*, M-R.-schote; - - *stay*, M-R.-stag; - - *staysail*, M-R.-Stagsegel; - - - *downhaul*, M-R.-S.-Niederholer; - - - *sheet*, M-R.-S.-schote; - - - *stay*, M-R.-S.-leiter; - - *tack*, M-R.-S.-hals; - *royal yard*, M-R.-rahe;-*sail*, Mittelsegel; -*sheet*, Mittel-Schote; - *shroud*, M-want; - *skysail*, M-Scheisegel; - - *backstay*, M-S.-pardune; - - *brace*, M-S.-brasse; - - *clew line*, M-S.-geitau; - - *foot rope*, M-S.-pferd; - - *halliard*, M-S.-fall; - - *lift*, M-S.-toppenant; - - *mast*, M-S.-stenge; - - *sheet*, M-S.-schote; - - *stay*, M-S.-stag; - - *yard*, M-S.-rahe; - *stay*, Mittelstag; - *staysail*, M.-segel; - - *downhaul*, Mittelstagsegel-Niederholer; - - *halliard*, M.-fall; - - *sheet*, M.-Schote; - - - *pendant*, M.-Schotenschenkel; - *staysail stay*,M.-leiter; - - *tack*,M.-hals; - *stitched seam*, Mittelnaht; - *stitching*, durchgenähte Naht eines Segels; - *tack*, Mittelhals; - *thwart*, Mastducht; - *timber*, mittlere Heckstütze; - *top*, Mittelmars. *middle topgallant backstay*, Mittelbram-Pardune; - - *brace*, M.-brasse; - - *bunt line*, M.-Bauchgording; - - *cap*, M.-stenge-Eselshaupt; - - *clew line*, M.-geitau; - - *cross trees*, Dwarssahlingen der M.-stenge; - - *foot rope*, M.-pferd; - - *futtock shrouds*, M.-Püttingswanten; - - *futtocks*, M.-Püttingen; - - *halliard* od. - - - *purchase*, M.-fall; *m. t. leech line*, M.-Nockgording; - - *lift*, M.-toppenant; - - *mast*, M.-stenge; - - - *cap*, M.-stenge-Eselshaupt; - - *rigging*, M.-stengewanten; - - *sail*, M.-segel; - - *sheet*, M.-schote; - - *shroud*, M.-want; - - *stay*, M.-stag; - - *staysail*, M.-s-segel; - - *downhaul*, M.-s-s-Niederholer; - - - *sheet*, M.-s-s-schote; - - - *stay*, M.-Stagsegelleiter; - - - *tack*, M.-S-s-hals; *m. t. trestle trees*, M.-stengen-Längssahlingen; - - *tie*, M.-Drehreep; - - *yard*, M.-rahe. *middle topmast*, Mittelmars-Stenge; - - *backstay*, M.-pardune; - - *cap*, M.-stenge-Eselshaupt; - - *cross trees*, Dwarssahlingen der M.-stenge; - - *rigging*,M.-wanten; - - *shroud*, M.-want; - - *stay*, M.-stag; - - *staysail*, Mittelstenge-Stagsegel; - - - *downhaul*, M.-S.-Niederholer; - - - *halliard*, M.-S.-fall; - - - *sheet*, M.-S.-schote; - - - *stay*, M.-S.-leiter; - - - *tack*, M.-S.-hals; *m. t. trestle trees*, M.-stengen-Längssahling.

middle topsail, Mittelmars-Segel; - - *brace*, M.-brasse; - - *b. pendant*, M.-Brassenschenkel; - - *bunt line*, M.-Bauchgording; - - *clew line*, M.-geitau; - - *foot rope*, M.-pferd; - - *halliard* od. - - *h. purchase*, M.-fall; - - *lift*, M.-toppenant; - - *reef tackle*, M.-Refftalje; - - *sheet*, M.-schote; - - *tie*, M.-Drehreep; - - *yard*, M.-rahe.

middle transom, mittlerer Heckbalken; - *watch*, Mittelwache (12—4 a. m.); - *yard*, M.-rahe; - - *foot rope*, M.-pferd.

midnight sun, Nordersonne.

midship, mittschiffs; - *beam*, M.-balken; - *bend*, Nullspant; - *deep tank*, mittschiffs hoher Tank; - *floor*,Bodenwrange d. Mittelspants; - - *timber*, die Bodenwrange im Nullspant; - *frame*, Mittelspant; - - *section*, Flächeninhalt des M.; - *section*, Hauptspant-Querschnitt.

midshipman, Seekadett; - 's *hitch*, Maulstich.

midships, mittschiffs; - *the helm!* M. das Ruder!

mild steel, weicher Stahl.

miles, to make short -, schnell segeln.

milky way, Milchstraße.

mill board joint, Pappedichtung.

mind the helm! Auf das Ruder achten! - *your port helm!* Nicht mehr Steuerbordruder! - - *starboard* -*!* N. m. Backbordruder!

miner's light, Kohlendepotlampe.

minimum pressure, Minimaldruck.

mirage, Luftspiegelung.

missing stays, die Wendung versagen; - *the anchorage*, den Ankerplatz verfehlen; - *vessels*, verschollene Schiffe.

misstay, die Wendung versagen.

mist, Dunst.

mistral, kalter N. W.-Wind.
misty, dunstig; - *rain*, unsichtiges Regenwetter.
mitre plane, Gehrungshobel; - *wheel*, Kegelzahnrad.
mixed cargo, gemischte Ladung; - *steam*, g. Dampf; - *timber*, g. Holz.
mizen, Besahn; - *boom*, B-baum; - - *topping lift*, B.-b-Toppenant; - - - - *purchase*, B.-b-Dirktalje; - *braces*, B.-brassen; - *brails*, B.-Geitaue; - *chain plates*, B.-Rüsteisen; - *channel*, B.-rüste; - *courses*, Sturmsegel; - *fife rail*, Besahn-Nagelbank; - *futtock shrouds*, B.-Püttingswanten; - *futtocks*, B.-Püttingen; - *gaff*, B.-gaffel; - - *topsail*, B.-Gaffeltoppsegel; - - - *downhaul*, B.-G.-Niederholer; - - - *halliard*, B.-G.-fall; - - - *sheet*, B.-G.-schote; - - - *tack*, B.-G.-hals; - *halliard*, B.-fall; - *lower cross trees*, B.-mast-Dwarssahlingen; - *lower rigging*, B.-wanten; - *lower trestle trees*, B.-mast-Längssahlingen.
mizen mast, Besahnmast; - - *cap*, B.-Eselshaupt; - - *coat*, B.-kragen; - - *cross trees*, B.-Dwarssahlingen; - - *head*, B.-topp; - - *step*, B.-spur; - - *trestle trees*, B.-Längssahlingen; - - *wedges*, B.-keile.
mizen middle staysail, Besahn-Mittelstagsegel; - - - *downhaul*, B.-M.-Niederholer; - - - *halliard*, B.-M.-fall; - - - *sheet*, B.-M.-schote; - - - *tack*, B.-M.-hals.
mizen outhaul, Besahn-Ausholer; - *peak halliard*, B.-Piekfall; - *rigging*, B.-wanten.
mizen royal, Kreuz-Royal; - *backstay*, K-R-pardune; - - *brace*, K-R-brasse; - - *bunt line*, K-R-Bauchgording; - - *clew line*, K-R-geitau; - - *foot rope*, K-R-pferd; - - *halliard*, od. - - *h. purchase*,

K-R-fall; - - *lift*, K-R-top-penant; - - *mast*, K-R-stenge; - - *m. head*, K-R-topp; - - *sheet*, K-R-schote; - - *stay*, K-R-stag; - - *staysail*, K-R-Stagsegel; - - - *downhaul*, K-R-S.-Niederholer; - - - *halliard*, K-R-S.-fall; - - - *sheet*, K.-R-S.-schote; - - - *stay*, K-R-S.-leiter; - - - *tack*, K-R-S.-hals; *m. r. yard*, K-R-rahe.
mizen sail, Besahnsegel; - *sheet*, Besahnschote; - *shroud*, Besahnwant.
mizen skysail, Kreuz-Scheisegel; - - *backstay*, K-S.-pardune; - - *brace*, K-S.-brasse; - - *clew line*, K-S.-geitau; - - *foot rope*, K-S.-pferd; - - *halliard*, K-S.-fall; - - *lift*, K-S.-toppenant; - - *mast*, K-S.-stenge; - - *sheet*, K-S.-schote; - - *stay*, K-S.-stag; - - *yard*, K-S.-rahe
mizen stay, Kreuzstag.
mizen staysail, Besahn-Stagsegel; - - *downhaul*, B.-S.-Niederholer; - - *halliard*, B.-S.-fall; - - *sheet*, B.-S.-schote; - - *s. pendant*, B.-S.-Schotenschenkel; - - *stay*, B.-S.-leiter; - - *tack*, B.-S.-hals.
mizen tack, Besahnhals; - *tackle*, Achterseitentakel; - *throat halliard*, Besahn-Klaufall; - *top*, B.-mars; - - *bowline*, B.-Segelbulin; - - *braces*, Kreuzbrassen.
mizen topgallant backstay, Besahnbram-Pardune; - - *brace*, B.-brasse; - - *bunt line*, B.-Bauchgording; - - *cap*, Besahn-bramstenge-Eselshaupt; - - *clew line*, B.-Geitau; - - *cross trees*, Dwarssahlingen der B.-stenge; - - *foot rope*, B.-pferd; - - *futtock shrouds*, B.-Püttingswanten; - - *futtocks*, B.-Püttings; - - *halliard* od. - - *h. purchase*, B.-fall; - - *leech line*, B.-Nockgording; - - *lift*, B.-Toppenant;

- - *mast*, B.-stenge; - - - *cap*,
B.-s-Eselshaupt; *m.t.rigging*,
B.-Stengewanter; - - *sail*,
B.-segel; - - *sheet*, B.-schote;
- - *shroud*, B.-want; - - *stay*,
B.-stag; - - *staysail*, B.-Stag-
segel; - - - *downhaul*, B.-S.-
Niederholer; - - - *halliard*,
B.-S.-fall; - - - *sheet*, B.-S.-
schote; - - - *stay*, B.-S.-leiter;
- - - *tack*, B.-S.-hals; *m. t.*
trestle trees, B.-stengen-
Längssahling; - - *tye*, B.-
Drehreep; - - *yard*, B.-rahe.
mizen topmast, Besahnstenge;
- - *backstay*, B.-Pardune; - -
cap, B.-Eselshaupt; - - *cross*
trees, B.-Dwarssahling; - -
rigging,B.-wanten; - - *shroud*,
B.-want; - - *stay*, B.-stag; - -
staysail, B.-Stagsegel; - - -
downhaul, B.-S.-Niederholer;
- - - *halliard*, B.-S.-fall; - - -
sheet.B.-S.-schote; - - - *stay*,B.-
S.-leiter; - - - *tack*, B.-S.-hals;
m. t. trestle trees, B.-Längs-
sahling.
mizen top men Kreuztopp-
gasten; - - *sail*, Kreuzsegel;
- *topping lift*, Besahnbaum-
dirk.
mizen topsail, Kreuzmars-
Segel; - - *brace*, K.-brasse;
- - *b. pendant*, K.-Brassen-
schenkel; - - *bunt line*, K.-
Bauchgording; - - *clew line*,
K.-Geitau; - - *foot rope*, K.-
pferd; - - *halliard* od. - - *h.*
purchase, K.-fall; - - *lift*, K.-
Toppenant; - - *reef tackle*,
K.-Refftalje; - - *sheet*, K.-
schote; - - *tye*, K.-Drehreep;
- - *yard*, K.-rahe.
mizen trysail, Besahn; - *vang*,
B.-gerde; - - *pendant*, B.-
Gaffelgerdenschenkel; -*yard*,
B.-rahe.
mizzen see mizen.
modelling loft, Mallboden.
moderate breeze, mäßige
Brise; - *gale*, m. Sturm.
moist steam, feuchter Dampf.
mole, Mole, Wellenbrecher; -

cular weight, Molekulargewicht.
momentum of flexion, Biegungsmoment; - - *force*,
Kraftm-; - - *inertia*, Träg-
heitsm-.
monk seam, durchgenähte
Naht.
monkey, to sling the -,Matrosen-
spiel; - *to suck the* -, mit
einem Strohhalm einem
Fasse Wein entziehen.
monkey, 1. Trinkkanne; 2.
Steuerindikator; - *block*,
Buggordingsblock am Stag;
- *boat*, kleines Dockboot;
- *bulwark*, Bastardrelings-
brett; - *forecastle*, halbe
Back; - *gaff*, Flaggengaffel;
- *jacket*, Überzieher; -*pump*,
feines Saugrohr resp. Strohhalm; - *rail*, Monkeyreling;
- *spanner*, Universalschrau-
benschlüssel; -*spar*, Übungs-
mast; - *wheel*, Rolle des
Hebebocks.
monkey's allowance, mehr
Schläge als Brot; - *tail*,
Hebebaum.
monoxyle, Einbaum.
monsoon, Monsun; - *drift*, M.-
drift.
monthly charter, Monats-
charter; - *service*, monat-
licher Verkehr.
moonlight night, mondhelle
Nacht.
moon raker, Wolkenschraper;
- *rise*, Mondaufgang; - *sail*,
M.-segel; - - *brace*, M-gucker-
brasse; - - *sheet*, M-g-schote;
- *sheered*, mit sehr viel
Spring gebaut.
moor, vertäuen; - *a cable each*
way, mit je einem Anker
vorn und hinten vertäuen;
- *across*, einen A. dwars ab-
legen; - *against ebb and*
flood, für Ebbe und Flut
vertäuen; - *along*, längs dem
Lande vertäuen; - *along the*
quay, längs dem Kai vertäuen; - *head and stern*, vorn

und hinten vertäuen; - *with
a span*, in einer Hahnepoot
vertäuen; - *with a spring on
the cable*, mit einem Spring
auf der Kette v.; - *with two
anchors ahead*, mit zwei
Ankern voraus v.

moorage, Ankerplatz.

mooring anchor, Vertäuanker;
- *bend*, V-t-knoten; - *berth*,
Ankerplatz; - *bitts*, V-t-
poller; - *block*, Anbindeblock;
- *bridle*, Kettenarme des
Mooringschäkels; - *buoy*,
Vertäuboje; - *chain*, V-t-
kette; - *chocks*, Reitpallen;
- *lead*, Vertäuführung; - *pall*,
Poller am Lande; - *pipe*,
Vertäuklüse; - *post*, V-t-pfahl;
- *ring*, V-t-ring; - *rope*, V-t-
tau; - *shackle*, V-t-schäkel;
- *stone*, Anbindeblock; -
stump, A. für Boote; - *swivel*,
Vertäuwirbel; - *works*, V-t-
arbeiten.

moorings, Vertäuung: - *of the
flying bridge*, Giertau der
fliegenden Brücke; *to let go
the* -, die Vertäuung loswerfen.

mooter, Nagelschneider.

mop, Dweil; - *board*, Scheuerleiste.

morning gun, Morgenschuß;
- *watch*, M-wache (4–8 a. m.).

mortgaged vessel, verpfändetes
Schiff.

morticed block, ausgestemmter
Block.

mortise, Zapfenloch; - *chisel*,
Lochbetel; - *to be bolted*,
das verbohrte Zapfenloch
zum Vernageln.

mortising, Verzapfung.

moses, Zuckerfaß-Prahm; -
boat, kleines Kielboot.

mosquito fleet, Flotte kleiner
Schiffe.

motion, 1. Bewegung; 2. Transmission; - *bars*, Führungen;
- *of piston*, Kolbenbewegung.

motive power, Betriebskraft.

motor, Motor.

mould, 1. Schablone; 2. Form,
Gießform; 3. bemallen; - *loft
floor*, Mallboden.

moulded breadth, Konstruk-
tionsbreite; - *depth*, Modell-
tiefe.

moulding, Mallung, Verzierungsleisten; - *edge*, Mall-
kante; - *of a beam*, Mall-
breite eines Balkens; - *of a
floor*, M. einer Bodenwrange;
- *of a frame*, M. eines Spants;
- *of a keel*, M. eines Kiels;
- *of a keelson*, M. eines
Kielschweins; - *of the stem*,
M. des Vorderstevens; - *of
the sternpost*, M. des Hinterstevens.

mountainous sea, berghohe
See; - *waves*, Wellenberg.

mounting Garnitur.

mouse a hook, einen Haken
einmausen; - *of the stay*,
Stagmaus.

mousing, mausen, Mausing.

mouth, Mündung.

movable beams in hatchways,
abnehmbare Lukenbalken;
- *coupling*, lösbare Kuppelung; - *pillar*, abnehmbare
Stütze; - *propeller blade*, a.
Schraubenflügel; - *stanchion*,
versetzbare Stütze.

move, verholen.

moving, verholen, das V.; -
apparatus, Triebwerk; -
force, T-kraft; - *of ice*, Eisgang; - *power*, Triebkraft;
- *water*, Aufschlagwasser.

mud, Schlamm, Schlick; -
anchor, Schildanker; - *bank*,
Morastbank; - *boat*, Moderprahmboot; - *box*, Schlammkasten; - - *door*, S.-deckel;
- - *joint*, S.-dichtung; - *cock*,
Schlammausblaseventil; -
hole, Schlammloch; - *hopper*,
S-boot; - *land*, Watt; -
lighter, Mudderprahm; - *rake*,
Schlammharke; - *shovel*, S-
schaufel.

mudderer, Mudderprahm.

muddy, schlickig; - *bottom*,

Schlickgrund; - *water,* schlammiges Wasser.
muffle, umwickeln.
mug, Becher, Mucke, Krug.
muggy, schwül und feucht.
mulberry, Maulbeerbaumholz.
mulet, Geldstrafe.
multiple expansion, mehrfache Expansion; - - *engine,* m. E.-maschine. [scheibe.
multiplying sheave, Patent-*multitubular boiler,* vielröhriger Kessel].

mushroom, Muschel; - *anchor,* Pilzanker: - *valve,* pilzförmiges Ventil; - *ventilator,* Muschelventilator.
muster, mustern; - *roll,* Musterrolle.
mutineer, Meuterer.
mutiny, meutern, Meuterei.
mutinying, meutern.
mutton legger, 1. Art Segel; 2. Boot mit demselben.
muzzle lashing, Kopfzurring.

N.

nadir, Fußpunkt.
nail, Nagel, Spiker; *to - the trip,* die Seereise verderben resp. vereiteln.
naked, ohne Kupfer- und Zinkbeschlag.
name a ship, ein Schiff taufen; - *board,* Namenbrett.
narrow boat, Kanalschiff von 30 Tonnen; - *channel,* 1. enges Fahrwasser: 2. Priel; - *floor,* der scharfe Boden: - *passage,* enges Fahrwasser; - *pennant,* Toppwimpel; - *seas,* englischer Kanal.
narrows, Meerenge.
nasty weather, schlechtes Wetter.
national pennant, Reichsflagge.
natural defect, Beschaffenheitsschaden; - *harbour,* natürlicher Hafen; - *steel,* Schmelzstahl.
nauropometer, Krängungsmesser.
nauscopy, die Kunst, Schiffe in großer Entfernung sehen zu können.
nautical almanack, nautischer Kalender; - *assessor,* n. Beisitzer; - *day,* n. Tag; - *indicator,* Instrument zur Feststellung der richtigen Breite und Länge sowie Magnetnadelabweichungen;

- *instrument,* naut. Instrument; - *mile,* Seemeile; - *signal,* Schiffssignal; - *stationer,* naut. Buchhandlung; - *stationery,* n. Papierwaren; - *surveyor,* n. Sachverständiger; - *tables,* n. Tabellen; - *term,* Schiffsausdruck; - *time,* S-zeit.
nautilus propeller, hydraulischer Propeller.
naval agency, Agentur für die Angelegenheiten von Marine-Offiziere; - *architect,* Schiffsbauingenieur; - *architecture,* S-b-kunst: - *Court,* Seeamt; - *demonstration,* Flottendemonstration; - *hood,* Klüsenback; - *officer,* Marineoffizier; - *reserve,* Marinereserve; - - *flag,* Flagge der M.; - *review,* Flottenschau: - *school,* Seemannschule; - *science,* Seewissenschaft; - *service,* Marinedienst; - *station,* M-station; - *stores,* Schiffsmaterialien; - *tactics,* Seetaktik; - *war,* Seekrieg; - *yard,* Marinewerft.
navel hood, Klüsenback; - *timbers,* der erste Sitter des Flachs.
navigable, schiffbar.
navigate a vessel, ein Schiff führen.

navigating officer, Navigationsoffizier.

navigation, Schiffahrt. Schifffahrtskunde; - *act*, Schifffahrtsgesetz; - *bounty*, S-f-prämie;-*school*, Navigationsschule; - *subsidy*,Schiffahrtsprämie; - *treaty*, S-f-vertrag.

navigation, to direct the - of the ship, die Schiffsführung haben.

navigator, Seefahrer.

navy, Marine; - *board*, Admiralitätsbehörde; - *court*, Seeamt; - *yard*, Marine-Werft.

nealed to, mit tiefem Ankergrunde dicht an der Küste.

neap, abnehmend; - *tide*, Nippflut.

neaped, benept.

near! no -! Nicht höher! - *the coast*, 1. nahe der Küste; 2. sich der K. nähern; *to go - the wind*, hart am Winde liegen.

N. E. by E, N. O. zu O.

neck bush, Grundring; - *lace*, Püttingsringkette; - *of a crane*, Kranbalken; - *of a hoop*, Bügelarm; - *of a sail*, Klauhorn; - *of land*, Landspitze;- *of the anchor*, Ankerhals; - *ring*, Führungsauge der Abzugsleine; - - *of a stuffing box*, Stopfbüchsenring.

needle yaws, die Nadel schwankt hin und her.

needles, Felsenspitzen.

negative slip, negativer Slip.

negociate the bar, die Barre kreuzen.

Neptune's sheep, Kammwellen.

net tonnage, Netto-Tonnengehalt.

netting, Netzwerk; - *of the top*, Marsnetz.

nettle, das Knüttel.

neutral bottom, neutrale Schiff; - *flag*, n. Flagge.

new measurement, Moorsomsche Vermessungsmethode.

night awning, Nachtdecke, N-zelt; - *glass*, N-teleskop; -

mark, N-marke; - *orders*, Befehle für den N-dienst; - *pendant*, N-wimpel; - *quarters*, N-Klarschiff; - *service*, N-dienst; - *signal*, N-signal; - *watch*, N-wache; - *work*, N-schicht.

nine pin block, Leitblock.

nip, 1. kurze Kinke; 2. einen Stopper aufsetzen; - *cheese*, Proviantmeister-Maat; - *the cable*, die Kette an das Kabelar aufzeisen.

nipped by the ice, vom Eise eingeschlossen.

nipper, 1. Stopperende; 2. Hängematten mit sehr wenig Bettzeug; 3. zwei Teile eines Taues aneinander befestigen; - *men*, die Aufzeiser der Kette an das Kabelar; - *of the cable*, Kabelarzeising.

nippers, Kneifzange.

nipping the cable, Befestigung des Zeisings an das Kabel.

nipple, Nippel.

no higher! nicht höher!

nock of a fore and aft sail, Binnennock.

nog, Fußbolzen eines Strebers.

nohowish, unwohl.

no-man's land, Deckteil, für den niemand zu sorgen hat.

nominal horse power, nominelle Pferdestärke; - *power*, Nominalkraft.

non-condensing engine, Auspuffmaschine; - *conductor*, 1. Nichtleiter; 2. Wärmeschutzmasse; - *expansive engine*, Volldruckmaschine; - *return valve*, Rückschlagventil.

nook, kleine Bucht.

normal pressure, Normaldruck; - *speed*, N-Geschwindigkeit; - *thrust*, N-druck.

Norman, Normann od. Katzenkopf (am Bratspill).

north-east monsoon, Nordost-Monsun; - - *trades*, N.-passatwinde; - *sea chart*, Nordseekarte; - *sun*, Nordersonne; - *west monsoon*, Nordwest-Monsun.

norther, Norder.
northern amplitude, Mitternachtsweite; - *hemisphere*, nördliche Halbkugel.
northing, 1. nördliche Richtung; 2. n. Abweichung; *to gain* od. *make* -, Nord gewinnen.
nose of a ship, Schiffsschnabel.
notch, Kerbe; - *block*, Lotblock.
notching up, Verminderung des Schieberhubes.
nothing off! od. - *to lose!* Nicht abfallen!
notice of abandonment, Abandon-Erklärung.
nozzle, Düse, Dampfkasten; - *of a hose*, Schlauchmund-

stück; - *of a pump*, Pumpenmundstück; - *plate*, Dampfventilsitz.
number, to lose the - of one's mess, sterben; - *of strokes*, Zahl der Kolbenhube.
nun buoy, Spitz- od. Flaschenboje.
nut, 1. Mutter; 2. Ankernuß; 3. Spindelmutter (des Steuergeräts); - *bolt*, Mutterbolzen; - *of the anchor stock*, Ankerstocknuß; - *shaping machine*, Mutterfräßmaschine; - *wood*, Nußbaumholz; - *wrench*, Mutterschraubenschlüssel.
nuts, Nußkohlen.
N. W. by W., N. W. zu W.

O.

O, 1. overcast; 2. Lloyds Klassifikation für 4. Klasse.
oakum, Werg; *black* -, geteertes W.; *white* -, ung. W.
oar, Ruder, Riemen; - *blade*, R.-blatt; - *handle*, R.-heft; - *lock*, - *swivel*, R.-Gabel; - *web*, äußeres R.-blatt.
oars! Riemen hoch!
oarsman, Ruderer.
obey the helm, dem Ruder folgen.
oblique impact, schiefer Stoß; - *sailing*, Segeln in der loxodromischen Linie.
observation, Beobachtung; *by* -, nach B.; *to work an* -, eine B. ausrechnen.
observatory, Sternwarte, Warte.
observe the sun's amplitude, die Sonnenhöhe peilen.
obtuse angle, stumpfer Winkel.
o'cast = overcast.
occidental variation, westliche Mißweisung.
occurrences of the voyage, Begebenheiten während der Reise.

Ocean steamer, Seedampfer.
off, 1. auf der Höhe von; 2. Haltet ab! - *and on*, vom Lande ab und nach dem Lande zu kreuzen; - *duty*, Freiwacht haben; - *she goes!* Da geht es hin! - *the land*, vom Lande ab; - *the reel*, plötzlich.
offal, Abfall.
officer of the watch, wachthabender Offizier; - *on duty*, diensttuender O.; -*'s berth*, Offiziers-Kammer; - *mess room*, O.-messe; - *room*, O.-kämmer.
official log book, offizielles Schiffsjournal.
offing, draußen, offene See; *to have a good* -, gut frei vom Lande sein; *to stand for the* -, seewärts anliegen; - *anchor*, Seeanker.
offset, Absatz.
off-shore, von der Küste her.
offward, buten, seewärts.
oil, Oel; - *bag*, O-sack; - *box*, O-büchse; - *can*, O-kanne; - *carrying vessel*, Petroleum-

transportschiff; - *cloth*, Wachstuch; - *cock*, Oelhahn; - *cup*, Schmierbüchse; - *distributer*, Vorrichtung zur Oelverbreitung; - *feeder*, Schmierkanne; - *funnel*, Oeltrichter; - *groove*, O-nute; - *hole*, O-loch; - *lubricating pipe*, Schmierrohr; - *measure*, Oelmaß; - *pipe*, O-rohr.

oil-pump, Oelpumpe; - - *bucket valve*, Oelpumpen - Kolbenventil; - - - - *seat*, O.-K.-sitz; *o.p. connecting rod*, O.-Pleuelstange; *o. p. c. r. bottom end keep*, O.-Kurbelzapfen-Lagerschalendeckel; *o. p. c. r. top e. k.*, O.-Kreuzkopf-L.; *o. p. c. r. bottom end liner*, O.-Pleuelstangenfußfutter; *o. p. crank pin bolt*, O.-Kurbelzapfenlager-bolzen; *o. p. c. p. brasses*, O.-K.-schalen; *o. p. c. shaft bearing*, O.-Kurbelwellenlager; *o. p. c. s. b. brasses*, O.-K.-schalen; *o. p. c. s. bearing keep*, O.-K.-dekkel; *o. p. c. s. b. k. bolt*, O.-K.-d-bolzen; *o. p. crosshead bolt*, O.-Kreuzkopflager-Bolzen; *o. p. c. brasses*, O.-K.-schalen; *o. p. cylinder cover*, O.-Zylinder-Deckel; *o. p. c. c. bolt*, O.-Z.-D-bolzen; *o. p. cylinder drain pipe*, O.-Z.-Entwässerungsrohr; *o. p. delivery space*, O.-Druckraum; *o. p. d. valve*, O.-Druckventil; *o. p. d. v. seat*, O.-D.-sitz; *o. p. discharge valve*, O.-Ausgußventil; *o. p. eccentric*, O.-Excenter; *o. p. e. bolt*, O.-E.-bolzen; *o. p. e. brasses*, O.-E.-Lagerschalen; *o. p. e. rod*, O.-E.-stange; *o. p. e. sheave*, O.-E.-scheibe; *o. p. e. strap*, O.-E.-bügel; *o. p. e. s. liner*, O.-E.-b-futter; *o. p. engine connecting rod bolt*, O.-Pleuelstangenbolzen; *o. p. e. crank shaft*, O.-Kurbelwelle; *o. p. e. c. s. bearing*, O.-K.-Lager; *o. p. e. c. s. b. bolt*, O.-K.-L-bolzen; *o. p. e. cylinder*, O.-

Zylinder; *o. p. e. piston*, O.-Kolben; *o. p. e. slide valve*, O.-Schieber; *o. p. exhaust pipe*, O.-Dampfablaßrohr; *o. p. foot valve*, O.-Fußventil; *o. p. f. v. seat*, O.-Saugventilsitz; *o. p. head valve*, O.-Druckventil; *o. p. piston rod*, O.-Kolbenstange; *o. p. p. r. crosshead*, O.-K.-Kreuzkopf; *o. p. p. r. stuffing box*, O.-Kolbenstangen-Stopfbüchse; *o. p. p. r. s. b. gland*, O.-K.-S.-deckel; *o. p. starting valve*, O.-Anlaßventil; *o. p. stop valve*, O.-Absperrventil; *o. p. suction pipe*, O.-Saugerohr; *o. p. s. space*, O-Saugeraum; *o. p. suction valve*, O.-Saugventil; *o. p. s. v. seat*, O.-S.-sitz; *o. p. top valve*, O.-Druckventil; *o. p. t. v. seat*, O.-D.-sitz; *o. p. valve*, O-ventil; *o. p. v. casing*, O.-Schieberkasten; *o. p. v. c. door*, O.-S.-deckel; *o. p. v. rod*, O.-Schieberstange; *o. p. v. r. stuffing box*, O.-S.-Stopfbüchse; *o. p. v.r.s.b. gland*, O.-S.-S.-deckel; *o. p. v. seat*, O.-Ventilsitz.

oil receiver, Oelsammler; - *sieve*, O-sieb; - *skin*, O-zeug; - *tank*, O-tank; - *tight*, öldicht; - *tracks* od. *ways*, Schmiernuten.

oiler, Dampfschiff mit Oelfeuerung.

old salt, Seebär; - *stager*, ein gut Beschlagener; - *whale*, Seebär.

oldster, Seekadett mit 4 jähr. Dienstzeit.

olive wood, Oelbaumholz.

ombrometer, Regenmesser.

one-and-a-half master, Anderthalbmaster; *one and all*, alle zugleich; *one armed anchor*, einarmiger Anker; *one crank engine*, Maschine mit einfacher Kurbel; *one deck vessel*, Eindeckschiff.

oozy bottom, Schlickgrund.

open, in Sicht bekommen; - *a bearing*, eine Marke von

einer anderen offen bekommen od. aussegeln; - *a port*, einen Hafen dem Handel öffnen; - *out*, auseinander nehmen; - *the entrance of a port*, eine Einsegelung offen bekommen.

open bridge house, offene Brücke; - *handed*, zwei Ruder benutzend; - *linked chain*, Kette mit offenen Gliedern; - *manometer*, offenes Manometer; - *policy*, offene Polize; - *road*, o. Reede; - *seam*, o. Naht; - *water*, eisfreies Wasser.

opened, 1. sich begeben; 2. aufgetrocknet, offen; 3. geöffnet, offen gelegt; *engines - out*, auseinandergenommene Maschine; *we - the lights of . .*, wir bekamen die Feuer von . . offen.

opposite angle, Scheitelwinkel; - *cranks*, Gegenkurbeln; - *tacks*, über den andern Bug.

optic signal, Lichtsignal.

optional, nach Belieben.

order in line abreast, Aufstellung in gerader Frontlinie; *o. i. l. ahead*, Kielwasserformation; *o. i. quarter line*, Staffelformation; - *of sailing*, Segelordnung.

orders, for -, für Order.

ordinary, in -, außer Dienst gestellt; - *cargo steamer*, gewöhnlicher Frachtdampfer; - *seaman*, Leichtmatrose.

Oregon pine wood, Oregonfichtenholz.

Oriental variation, östliche Mißweisung.

orifice, Öffnung, Mündung.

orlop beam, Raumbalken; - - *angle bar*, R.-winkel; - - *stringer*, R-stringer; - - - *angle bar*, R.-s-winkel; - - - *inner a. b.*, Innenwinkel des R.-s-; - - - *plate*, R.-s-platte; - - - *shell lugs*, kurze R.-s-winkel.

orlop deck, Orlopdeck; - - *beam*, O.-balken; - - - *angle bar*,

O.-b-winkel; - - - *stringer*, O.-b-stringer - - - *s-plate*, O.-b-s-platte; - - *tie plate*, O.-b-Längsschiene; *o. d. hatches*, O.-luken; *o. d. hatchway coaming*, O.-l-süll; - - *mast wedge*, O.-Mastkeil; - - *pillar*, O.-stütze; - - *stringer*, O.-stringer, O.-stringer; - - - *angle bar*, O.-s-winkel; - - - *inner a. b.*, Innenwinkel des O.-s-; - - - *plate*, O.-Stringerplatte; - - - *shell lugs*, kurze Stringerwinkel des O.

orlop stringer, Orlopstringer; - - *angle bar*, O.-winkel; - - *inner a. b.*, Innenwinkel des O.

ornament, Verzierung.

orthodromic course, geradläufiger Kurs.

oscillating cylinder, oscillierender Zylinder; - - *trunnion*, Trunkzapfen des o. Z.; - *engine*, o. Maschine.

oscillation, Schwingung.

out. to be -, auslaufen; *to let all sails -*, alle Segel beistehen lassen.

out and home freight, Hinund Rückfracht; - *board*, außenbords; - *boats!* Boote aus! - *oars!* Riemen aus! - *of gear*, ausgerückt; - *of joint*, aus den Fugen gewichen; - *of order*, beschädigt; - *of soundings*, außerhalb lotbaren Grundes; - *of trim*, außer Trimm.

outer bar, Außenbarre; - *bearing*, Außenlager; - *fore topsail sheet*, Vor-Obermarssegelschote; - *garboard strake*, Nebenkielgang; - *halliard*, Außenfall; - *harbour*, Außenhafen; - *jib*, 2ter Klüver; - *downhaul*, Niederholer des großen Klüvers; - - *halliard*, Großklüverfall; - - *sheet*, G-k-schote; - - *stay*, G-k-leiter; - - *tack*, G-k-hals; - *leech line*, Nockgording; - *peak brail*, Gaffel-Außengeitau; - *screw shaft*, äußere Schraubenwelle; - *sheet*, Außenschote; - *skin*, Außenbekleidung; - *strake*, äußerer Plattengang; - *turn of an earing*, die Ausholschlagen eines Nockbindsels; - *turns of a seizing*, die inneren Parten eines Bindsels; - *waterway*, äußerer Wassergang.

outfit, Ausrüstung, ausrüsten.

outhaul, outhauler, Ausholer.

outlet, Auslaß, Auslauf; -*valve*, Auslaßventil.

outlier, die vom Lande entfernt liegende Klippe.

outmanoeuvre, ausmanövrieren.

outmost, äußerste.

outpoint, dichter am Winde segeln.

outports, Außenhäfen.

outrange, überholen.

outrigger, 1. Auslegerboot; 2. Maststütze od. Luvbaum; 3. Schnabel (eines Krans).

outsail a vessel, ein Schiff totsegeln.

outside bilge planks, Kimmplanke; - *butt strapp*, äußere Stoßplatte; - *clinch*, Außenstich - *plank*, A-planke; - *planking*, A-beplankung; - *plating*, A-haut; - *strake*, A-gang.

outstand, die See halten.

outward, ausgehend; - *bend*, Ausbuchtung; - *bound*, ausgehend; - *cargo*, a. Ladung; - *freight*, Ausfracht; - *passage*, Ausreise; - *trade*, Ausfuhrhandel.

oval boiler, ovaler Kessel; - *linked chain*, Schakenkette.

overall hook, ganz herumgehender Haken.

overbear, mehr Segel als ein anderes Schiff führen.

overblow, starker Wind, der kein Marssegel zuläßt.

overboard, über Bord; *masts rolled -*, die Masten schlingerten über Bord.

overbound, dwars.

over-carriage, zuweitgeführter Transport.

overcast, bedeckt.

overdue, überfällig.

overfall, Brechsee.

overflow pipe, Überlaufrohr - *valve*. Ü-l-ventil; - - *seat*, Ü-l-v-sitz; - - *spindle*, Ü-l-v-spindel; - - *spring*, Ü-l-v-feder.

overfreight a vessel, ein Schiff überlasten.

overhand knot, gewöhnlicher Knoten.

overhaul, 1. überholen; 2. totsegeln; - *the papers*, die Papiere ü.; - *the rigging*, die Takellage nachsehen; - *the seams*, die Nähte nachschlagen.

overhead beam engine, Maschine mit nach oben liegendem Balancier; - *compass*, Hängekompaß; - *cylinder engine*, Maschine mit umgekehrten Zylindern; - *travelling crane*, Laufkran.

overheat the steam, überhitzen.

overheating of steam, Überhitzung; - *pipe*, Ü-rohr.

overhung crank, überhängende Kurbel; - *paddle wheel*, ü. Schaufelrad.

overladen, überladen.

overlap, 1. überlappen, Überlappung; 2. sich decken (2 Landmarken); *the sails - each other*, die Segel stehlen einander den Wind.

overlapping strake, abliegender Gang.

overlay days, Überliegetage.

overload, überladen.

overlooker, Inspektor.

overmasted, übermastet.

overpressed with sails, mit Segeln überladen.

overpressure, übermäßiger Druck.

overrake, Seen über den Bug nehmen.

overreach, beim Lavieren zu weit segeln.

overrigged, übertakelt.
overrun the log, die Distanz überlaufen.
oversetting, das Umschlagen.
overshoot, zu weit laufen.
oversparred, übertakelt.
over supply, überreiches Angebot.
overtaken, 1. überholen, einholen; 2. überfallen; *the sun has - the wind*, die Sonne ist durch den Windstrich gegangen.
overtime, Überzeit.
overturned boat, umgekipptes Boot.

own a share in a vessel, einen Schiffsanteil haben; - *a vessel*, Reeder eines Schiffes sein; *the ship hlods her -*, das Schiff geht mit dem Winde.
owner, Reeder; - *ship*, Eigentumsrecht.
oxide, Oxyd.
oxidise, oxydieren.
oxter plate, Gillungsplatte.
oxyde, Oxyd.
oxydise, oxydieren.
oxygen, Sauerstoff; - *gas*, S.-gas.
oxyhydrogen gas, Knallgas.
oylet hole, Reefgatt.

P.

p. = passing.
pace, Schritt; *to go a main -*, mit vollen Segeln fahren; *the wind keeps - against the sun*, der Wind dreht gegen die Sonne auf.
pack, packen, verpacken; - *ice*, Packeis.
packet boat, Packetschiff.
packing, Packung, Liderung; - *bolt*, Packungsbolzen; - *box*, Stopfbüchse; - *drawer*, Pakkungszieher; - *gasket*, flach geflochtene Hanfliderung; - *gave out*, die Liderung drang heraus; - *knife*, Pakkungsmesser; - *of the piston*, Dampfkolbenliderung; - *of the stuffing box*, Verpackung der Stopfbüchse; - *port*, Schieberkastenöffnung zur Liderung; - *ring*, Liderungsring; - *screw*, Packungszieher; - *stick*, P-stock; - *tow*, P-werg; - *washer*, Liderungsscheibe; - *worm*, Stopfbüchsenreiniger.
packs, Wolkenmassen.
pad, 1. Füllstück; 2. Taukranz.
paddle, Schaufel; - *arm*, Radarm; - *beam*, Radkastenbalken; - *bearer*, Langsahling der Radwelle; - *board*, Schaufel; - *boat*, Raddampfer; - *bolt*, Schaufelnagel; - *box*, Radkasten; - - *annex*, R-anbau; - - *boat*, R.-boot; - - *cabin*, R.-kajüte; - - *framing*, Rahmenwerk des Radgehäuses; - - *stay*, Radkastenstütze; - *bracket*, Lagerträger des Schaufelrades; - *cargo steamer*, Radfrachtdampfer; - *case*, Radkasten; - *deck*, R.-deck; - *float*, Schaufel; - - *connecting rod*, S-lenker; - *plate*, S-platte; - *propulsion*, Fortbewegung durch S-räder; - *ring*, Radring; - *saloon steamer*, Rad-Salondampfer; - *shaft*, Ruderradwelle; - - *bearing*, Radwellenlager; - - *inside b.*, Innenlager der Radwelle; - - *outside b.*, Außenlager der R.; - *steamer*, Raddampfer; - *tug*, Radschleppdampfer; - *wheel*, Schaufelrad; - *arm*, S-arm; - - *boss*, S.-nabe; - - *bracket*, S.-stuhl; - - *engine*, Raddampfmaschine; - - *float*, Radschaufel; - - *propeller*, Radpropeller; - - *radius*, Radius des Schaufelrades;

- - *rim*, Radkranz des S.; - - *ring*, Radring des S.

paddy's hurricane, der ganz leicht umlaufende Wind; - *land*, Irland.

padlock, Vorhängeschloß.

paint brush, Farbenpinsel; - *bucket*, F-topf; - *locker*, F-spind; - - *door*, F-s-tür; - *oil*, F-öl; - *scrubber*, F-schrubber; - *silk*, einen neuen Anstrich benötigen; - *strake* od. *streak*, Malgang.

painter, 1. Maler; 2. Fangleine.

pair of backstays, Spann-Pardunen; - - *shrouds*, S-want.

pales, innere Stütze der Spanten.

palinurus, Palinurus.

pall see *pawl*.

pallet, Ballastkasten.

palm, Segelhandschuh; *to - a person*, schmieren; - *of the anchor*, Ankerhand; - *oil*, Schmiergeld; - *stay*, Winkelanker.

pampero, heftiger, kalter Südwind in den Pampas.

pan, Pfanne.

panch, Stoßmatte.

panel, Füllung.

pannekin od. *pannikin*, kleine Pfanne.

panscale, Kesselstein.

panting, keuchen (Spanten und Beplattung biegen sich nach innen und außen); - *beam*, Piekverstärkungsbalken; - - *angle bar*, P.-winkel; - - *stringer a. b.*, P.-Stringerwinkel; - - *inner a. b.*, Innenwinkel des P.-stringers; - - - *shell lugs*, kurze Stringerwinkel der Piekbalkenstringer.

panting deck, Piekdeck; - - *beam*, Piekdeckbalken-Winkel; - - - *stringer*, P.-stringer; - - - - *plate*, P.-Stringerplatte; *p. d. stringer*, Piekdeckstringer; - - - *angle bar*, P.-winkel; - - - *inner a. b.*,

Innenwinkel des P.; - - - *plate*, P.-platte; - - - *shell lugs*, kurze Stringerwinkel des Piekdecks.

panting stringer, Piekstringer.

pantry, Bottlerei; - *door*, B.-tür; - - *hinge*, B.-t-Scharnier.

paper cylinder of the indicator, Indikator-Papierzylinder.

parade in review order, Flottenparade.

parallel bar, Parallelstange; - *motion*,1.Parallelbewegung. 2. Parallelogramm; - *motion links*, die Glieder am Parallelgestänge; - *m. radius bar*, Leitstange des Parallelogramms; - *m. shaft*, Parallelogramm-Welle; - - - *bearing*, P.-Wellenlager; - *sailing*, im Breitenparallel segeln.

parbuckle, 1. aufschroten; 2. Schrottau.

parcelling, 1. Schmarting; 2. mit S. belegen; - *canvass*, S.-tuch; - *upon a seam*, der Streifen S.

paring hammer,Beulenklopfer.

parliament, to make a - heel, eine halbe Kielholung geben.

parrel, Rack; - *cleat*, R-klampe; - *halliard*, R-taljenaufholer; - *lashing*, Sorrung zweier Augen eines Taues ineinander; - *of royal yard*, Rack der Royalrahe; - *of skysail y.*, R. d. Scheisegelrahe; - *of topgallant y.*, R. d. Bramrahe; - *of topsail y.*, R. d. Marsrahe; - *rib*, R-schlitten; - *rope*, R-tau; - *truck*. R-klotje; - *with short and long leg*, Stopprack.

part, brechen, zerreißen; *to - from the anchor*, durch Brechen der Ankerkette in's Treiben geraten.

part, 1. Part eines Takels; 2. Schiffsanteil; - *double bottom*, teilweiser Doppelboden; - *in a vessel*, Schiffsanteil; - *of sea*, Seestrich; - *owner*, Mit-

reeder; - - *of the cargo,* Ladungsinteressent.
partial awning deck vessel, Schiff mit teilweisem Sturmdeck; - *bulkhead,*Halbschott; - *iron deck,* teilweise eisernes Deck; - *steel d.,* t. stählernes D.
particular average, einfache Havarie; - - *statement,* e. H. Dispache.
parting, 1. brechen, zerreißen; 2. Triftiggehen (infolge gebrochener Ankerkette).
partition of average, Havarieverteilung; *to - off,* abschotten; - *plate,* Scheideplatte.
partners, 1. Teilhaber; 2. Fischungen; - *plates,* Fischungsplatten.
parts and fittings, Teile und Zubehör; - *of a tackle,* Parten eines Takels.
pass, durchlassen, passieren, vorbeisegeln; 2. scheren (ein Tau); - *along,* weiter mannen; - *an earing,* ein Nockbändsel um die Rahe nehmen; - *as close as is safe,* so dicht wie möglich vorbeisegeln; - *astern,* am Heck passieren; - *from hand to hand* od. *from man to man,* einmannen; - *in sight of Dover,* in Sicht von D. passieren; - *port to port,* Backbord an B. passieren; - *right over,* übersegeln; - *starboard to s.,* Steuerbord an S. passieren; - *survey,* besichtigen; - *the hatches,* die Luken in gutemZustande finden;-*the nippers,*die Kabelarzeisinge aufsetzen; - *the quarantine,* Quarantaine durchmachen; - *to leeward,* in Lee passieren; - *through a lock,* durchschleusen; - *within hail* od. *hailing distance,* in Rufweite passieren.
pass boat, Prahm, Marktkahn.
passage, 1. Fahrt, Reise, Überfahrt; 2. Durchfahrt; 3. Fahrwasser; 4. Dampfweg (der

Maschine); - *boat,* Fährboot; - *broker,* Passagier-Vermittler; - *days,* Reisetage, Seetage; - *home,* Heimreise; - *money,* Fahrgeld; - *out,* Ausreise.
passaree, 1. Bullentau des Fockhalses; 2. den Fockhals mit einem B. ausholen.
passe, 1. Balje; 2. Flutrinne auf den Watten.
passenger, Reisender; - *accommodation,* Einrichtungen für Passagiere; - *act,* Passagiergesetz; - *broker,* Passagier-Vermittler; - *certificate,* Zertifikat für ein P.-schiff; - *lift,* P.-aufzug; - *rates,* P.-preise; - *steamer,* P.-dampfer.
paste, Kitt.
*patches of fog,*Nebelschwaden.
patent anchor, Patentanker; - *dryer,* Feul, Scheuerlappen; - *fuel,* Preßkohlen; - *jackstay of a gaff,* Patent-Jackstag einer Gaffel; - *lights,* konvexe Gläser im Deck; - *log,* Patentlog; - *packing,* P-liderung; - *shackle,* P-schäkel; - *slip,* Aufschlepphelling; - *steering gear,* Patent-Steuergerät;-*topsail,* P.-Marssegel; - *windlass,* P.-spill.
patron, Schiffsherr.
pattern, Modell.
paul see pawl.
paulin, Persennig.
paunch mat, Stoßmatte.
pawl, pallsetzen, Pall; - *and half -,* zwei Pallen verschiedener Länge; - *bitt,* Pallbeting; - *box,* Pallkasten; - *cleats,* P-klampen; - *of the cradle,* P-pfosten des Schlittens; - *post,* P-beting; - *rack* od. *rim,* P-kranz; - *ring,* P-ring;-*the capstan,*pallwinden.
pawls, to lower the -, die Pallen niederlassen.
pay a vessel, 1. ein Schiff resp. die Mannschaft bezahlen; 2. ein S. außer Dienst stellen; 3. ein S. teeren; - *away,* nach-

stecken; - *down a rope*, ein Tauende nach unten geben; - *off*, 1. abmustern; 2. abfallen; 3. abrüsten; - *out*, nachstecken; - *round*, ganz abfallen; - *the bottom*, den Schiffsboden labsalben; - *the mast*, den Mast anstreichen; - *the seams*, die Nähte auspichen; - *with the topsail*, fortgehen ohne zu bezahlen.

pay, Heuer; - *clerk*, Schreiber des Zahlmeisters; - *day*, Lohntag; - *master*, Zahlmeister.

paying ladle, Pechlöffel.

pea jacket, Piejacke; - *of the anchor*, Ankerspitze.

peak, 1. Piek (des Schiffes und der Gaffel); 2. Nockhorn (des Segels); 3. Spitze der Ankerhand; - *brail*, Gaffelgeitau; - *bulkhead*, Piekschott; - - *angle bar*, P.-winkel; - *cringle*, Pieklägel; - *downhaul*, Niederholer der Piek; - *frame*, P.-spant; - *halliard*, P.-fall; - *line*, P.-leine; - *of a gaff*, P. einer Gaffel; - *pendant*, Gaffelstander; - *piece*, Nocklappen derGaffelsegel; - *tank*, Piektank.

peak, the cable is at a long -, die Ankerkette steht stagweise.

pearl lashing, Zurring der Gaffelklauen.

peat drag, Torfbagger.

pedestal, Lagerbock.

peel of an oar, Ruderblatt.

peg ladder, Bootsleiter; - - *of a crane*, Kranleiter.

pelorus, Instrument zur Entdeckung eines Kompaßfehlers.

pen, Stall.

pendant, 1. Wimpel; 2. Schenkel (des Tauwerks); - *of a vang*, Gerdenschenkel; - *of the lower booms*, Hanger der Backspieren; - *tackle*, Seitentakel.

peninsula, Halbinsel.

pennant, Wimpel; - *halliard*, Flaggenleine des Großtopp; - *ship*, Kommodoreschiff.

penny boat, Themsedampfer.

perch, Strauchbake.

percussive force, Stoßkraft.

perils of the sea, Seegefahren.

periodical survey, periodische Besichtigung; - *winds*, p. Winde.

perishable cargo, leicht verderbliche Ladung; - *goods*, l. v. Güter.

permanent bottom ceiling,feste Bodenplattform; - *repairs*, gründliche Reparaturen; - *ventilators*, feststehendeVentilatoren.

permit, 1. Erlaubnis, E.-schein; 2. Zollabfertigungsschein.

perturbating power, störende Kraft.

pesterable goods, lästige resp. viel Raum einnehmende Güter.

pet cock, Probierhahn; - *valve*, Schnüffelventil.

peter-man, *peterer*, Fischermann.

petroleum wharf, Petroleumwerfte.

petties, kleine Kosten.

petty average, gewöhnliche Havarie; - *expenses*, kleine Kosten; - *officer*, Maat.

pewter, Weißmetall.

phantom ship, Geisterschiff.

pharology, Lehre von den Leuchtsignalen.

pharos, Feuerwarte.

picaroon, Strandräuber.

pick, to - *a soft plank*, es sich bequem machen; - *up the mail*, die Post aufnehmen.

picked up anchor, gingen Anker auf.

pickle the timbers, die Inhölzer salzen.

piece goods, Stückgüter; - *work*, S-arbeit.

pier, Hafendamm; - *dues*, H.-Abgaben; - *head*, Spitze des H.; - - *light*, Molenfeuer.

pierage, Hafendammzoll.

piercer, die Handfit des Segel-
machers.

pig iron, Roheisen; - *of ballast*,
Ballasteisen; - *pen*, Schwei-
nestall; - *yoke*, Seequadrant.

pigeon holes, Spillspakengatt.

pile driver, Ramme; - *for
armour plates*, Schlußpaket;
- *withdrawer*, Pfahlausheber.

pillage, Plünderung.

pillar, abstützen, Deckstütze;
- *beacon*, Pfahlbake; - *between
decks*, Deckstütze; - *head*,
Stützenkopf; - *ladder*, S-
leiter.

pillaring, Verstützung.

pillow, Lager; - *block*, Tunnelwellenlager; - - *bearer*, Lagerbock; - - *bolt*, Tunnelwellen-
lagerbolzen; - - *keep*, T-w-l-
deckel; - *of a stay*, Beklei-
dungskissen eines Stags; - *of
the bowsprit*, Kissen des Bugspriets.

pilot, 1. lotsen. Lotse; 2. Segel-
handbuch; 3. Instrument zum
Auffinden von Kompaßfeh-
lern; - *boat*, Lotsenboot; -
bridge, Kommandobrücke;
- - *rails and stanchions*, K.-
geländer; - - *stanchion*, K.-
g-stütze; - *chart*, Kurskarte;
- *cutter*, Lotsenkutter; *to -
down*, niederlotsen; - *flag*,
Lotsenflagge; - *house*, Ruder-
haus; *to - in*, einlotsen; *to -
in and out*, ein- und auslotsen; - *jack*, Lotsenflagge;
- *master*, Lotsenkomman-
deur; - *office*, Bureau für
das Lotsenwesen; *to - out*,
auslotsen; -'s *fairway*, Lot-
senfahrwasser; - *signal*, L-
signal; -'s *orders*, L-anwei-
sung; - *station*, L-station;
- *steamer*, L-versetzdampfer;
to - up, auflotsen; - *waters*,
Lotsengewässer.

pilotage, 1. Lotsenkunde; 2.
L-geld; - *inwards*, L-g- beim
Eingang; - *outwards*, L-g-
beim Ausgang.

pin, 1. Bolzen, Stift, Zapfen;
2. Scheibennagel (eines

Blocks); 3. Pinne (des Kompaß); - *hole*, Nagelgatt; - *maul*,
Treibhammer; - *of a block*,
Blockpinne; - *of a crane
post*, Kransäulenpinne; - *of
steering rod*, Bolzen der
Steuerstange; - *rack*, Loch-
leiste für die Belegpinnen;
- *rails*, Nagelbänke; - 's *head*,
N-kopf.

pinch bar, Brechstange.

pine wood, Fichtenholz.

pinion, Drehling; - *wheel*,
Triebrad.

pink ship, Pinkschiff; - *stern*,
hohes, schmales Heck.

pinky, Pinkschiff.

pinnace, Pinasse.

pintle, Fingerling; - *score*,
Fingerlings-Ausschnitt.

pipe, 1. Rohr; 2. Bootsmannspfeife; - *bracket*, Rohrstütze;
- *connections*, Röhrenver-
bindung; *to - down*, hin-
unterschicken; - *flange*,
Rohrflansch; - *of the boatswain*, das Flöten des Boots-
mannes; - *of the W. C.*,
Klosettrohr; *to - up*, auf
Deck rufen.

pipes, Rohrleitung.

piracy, Seeraub.

pirate, Seeräuber, S.-schiff.

pirogue, Piroge.

pirry, plötzlicher Seesturm.

piston, Kolben; - *body*, K.-
körper; - *boss*, K.-nabe; -
cover, K.-deckel; - - *eye bolt*,
K.-d-Handhabe; - *expansion
valve*, K.-Expansionsventil;
- *eye*, K.-öse; - *gland*, K.-
deckel; - *gland* od. - *junk ring*,
K.-deckel; - *nut*, Kolben-
mutter; - *packing*, K-pak-
kung; - - *ring*, K-p-ring; -
paste, K.-kitt; - *pump*, K-
pumpe; - *ring*, K-ring; - *rod*,
K-stange; - - *bolt*, Kreuzkopflagerbolzen; - - *collar*,
K-k-l-Stopfbüchse; - - *crosshead*, Kolbenstangen-Kreuz-
kopf; - - - *bolt nut*, Kreuz-
kopflager-Bolzenmutter; - - -

brasses, K.-schalen; - - - *guide*, Kolbenstangen - Kreuzkopfführung; - *rod guide*, Kolbenstangenführung; - *rod keep*, Deckelplatte des Kreuzkopflagers; - *rod nut*, Kolbenstangenmutter; - *rod packing*, K-s-packung; - *rod stuffing box*, K-s-Stopfbüchse; - - - - *gland*, K-s-S.-deckel; - *speed*, Kolbengeschwindigkeit; - *spring*, Feder des Kolbenrings; - *stroke*, Kolbenhub; - *travel*, K-spiel; - *valve*, K-schieber; - - *cover*, K-s-deckel; - - *exhaust port*, K-s-Austrittskanal; - - *junk ring*, K-s-deckel; - - *packing ring*, K-s-Metalliderung; - -*spindle*, K-s-stange; - - - *gland*, K-s-s-Stopfbüchsendeckel; - *valve steam port*, K-s-Eintrittskanal; - *valve stuffing box*, K-s-Stopfbüchse; - *valve tongue piece*, K-s-Füllstück.
pitch, 1. Abstand, Steigung; 2. Pech, verpechen; 3. stampfen; - *and scend*, beim Stampfen mit dem Vorschiff aus dem Wasser kommen; - *astern*, hinten stampfen; - *boat*, Kalfaterprahm; - *chain*, kalibrierte Kette; - *kettle*, Pechtopf; - *ladle*, P-löffel; - *mop*, P-quast; - *of propeller*, Steigung der Schraube; - *pine*, Pechtannenholz; - *pot*, Pechtopf; - *tow*, P-werg.
pitcher, stampfendes Schiff.
pitching, stampfend.
pitted, pitting, angefressen.
pivot, stehender Zapfen; - *of a compass*, Kompaßpinne; - *of a crane post*, Kranbaumzapfen; - *of a windlass*, stehender Zapfen eines Spills.
pivoted scuttle, auf Zapfen drehendes Seitenfenster.
place of call, Ordrehafen; - *of stranding*, Strandungsstelle; *to - the ceiling*, das Schiff

garnieren; *to - the shrouds on the masthead*, die Wanten anlegen; *to - the standing rigging*, das stehende Gut auflegen.
plain chart, Plankarte; - *furnace*, glatte Feuerbüchse.
plait, Kabelgarn.
plaited rope, geflochtenes Tau.
plan drawing, Planzeichnung. - *of a sail*, Segelplan; - *of the pipes*, Rohrplan; - *of projection*, Spantenriß; - *of the ship*, Riß des Schiffes.
plane, Hobel; - *chart*, gleichgradige Karte; - *iron*, Hobeleisen; - *of flotation*, Wassertracht; - *sailing*, Plansegeln; - *tree*, Platanenholz.
planesheer see *planksheer*.
planing machine, Hobelmaschine.
planisphere, Planiglob.
plank, Planke, beplanken; - *clamp*, Balkwäger aus Planken; - *timbers*, Bretter.
planking, 1. Beplankung; 2. Dampfkessel-Bekleidung; - *of a cylinder*, Zylindermantel; - *of the topsides*, die oberen Seitenteile eines Schiffes; - *screw*, Plankenschraube.
planks between the wales, Füllungsbalken; - *for the ceiling*, Garnierungsbalken; - *of the bottom*, Flachgänge; - *of the floor heads*, Kimmplanken; - *starting*, Planken gaapen.
planks, to work the - on a vessel, die Beplankung bei einem Schiffe anbringen.
planksheer, Schandeckel; - *of forecastle*, S. der Back; - *of poop*, S. der Hütte; - *of raised quarter deck*, S. des erhöhten Quarterdecks.
plant, 1. Werkzeug; 2. Anlage.
plastic metal, plastisches Metall.
plat, die Serving.

plate, Platte,Schiene; - *armour*, Plattenpanzerung; - *compressor*, Lamellenbremse; - *iron*, Platteneisen; - *keel*, P-kiel; - *knee*, Knieplatte; - *riders*, Diagonalschienen; - *shelf*, Tellerbort; - *steel*, Plattenstahl; - *stringer*, P-stringer; - - *angle bar*, P-s-winkel.

platform, Plattform; - *grating*, P.-Gräting.;

plating, Beplattung.

platter, eine Back (große Schüssel).

play, Spielraum: - *of piston*, Kolbenspiel.

pleasant gale, angenehme Kühlte.

pleasure boat, Lustfahrzeug; - *trip*, L-fahrt.

pledget, ein Wergzopf.

plier, Luvhalter.

pliers, Drahtzange.

Plimsoll's mark, gesetzlich vorgeschriebene Lade-Wasserlinie.

ploc, Mischung von Haar und Teer.

plough the sea, gut durch das Wasser gehen.

ploughing, das Reiben.

plug, Pfropfen; - *hole*, Pfropfen-loch; - *of a boat*, Boots-pfropfen; - *of a cock*, Kücken eines Hahnes; - *up a hole*, ein Loch verstopfen.

plumbago, Pottlot.

plumber od. *plummer block*, Tunnelwellenlager; - - *bolt*, T.-bolzen; - - - *nut*, T.-B-mutter; - *block bottom*, Unterlagsplatte; - *block cover*, Zapfenlagerdeckel; - *block keep*, Tunnelwellenlager-Deckel; - - - *bolt*, T.-D-bolzen; - - - - *nut*, T.-D-b-mutter.

plummet, Handlot.

plunder, berauben, Raub; - *of a wreck*, Strandraub.

plunderage, Unterschlagung von Gütern.

plunger, Plunger; - *piston*, P.-Kolben; - *pump*, P.-pumpe.

plunging, untertauchen.

plush, Rest der Branntwein-ration einer Backschaft.

ply an oar, den Riemen gebrauchen; - *between two places*, zwischen zwei Orten regelmäßig fahren; - *by small* od. *short boards*, kurze Gänge machen: - *to windward*, gegen den Wind aufkreuzen; - - - *by boards*, lavieren.

plyer, Aufkreuzer.

plyers, Biegezange.

p. m. = post meridiem (nach 12 mittags).

pneumatic tools, pneumatisches Werkzeug; - *transmission*, p. Übertragung.

pneumatometer, Luftmesser.

pocket bunker, Taschenbunker.

point a rope, eine Hundepünte an ein Tau legen; - *a sail*, die Reffzeisige in ein Segel nähen; - *a topmast*, den Topp der Stänge richtig zwischen die Sahlings einführen; - *out rope yarns*, Kabelgarne ausschrapen: - *the yards*, die Rahen scharf anbrassen.

point, 1. Kompaßstrich; 2. Hundepünt (eines Taues); 3. Reffzeising (eines Segels); *four - bearing*, Vier-Strich-Peilung; - *hole*, das Gaatje für einen Reffzeising; - *line*, Bändselgut; - *of departure*, Abfahrtspunkt; - *of impact*, Treffpunkt; - *of intersection*, Schnittpunkt; - *of sailing*, Segelstellung; *What is your best - - -?* Mit welcher S. läuft Ihr Schiff am besten? - *of the ram*, Spornspitze; - *quarter*, Viertel-Kompaß-strich; - *run to*, erreichte Position: - *sailed from*, verlassene Position.

pointed laid rope, Tau mit Katsteert; - *stopper*, Steert-stopper.

pointer, Schlagholz; - *bolt*, Schlangenbolzen.

pointing, Hundepünt; - *line*, Trensgarn.
poker, Schüreisen.
polar axis, Polarachse; - *circle*, P-kreis; - *distance*, P-distanz; - *light*, Nordlicht. - *line*, P-linie; - *star*, Nordstern.
pole, 1. Flaggentopp; 2. Bootshaken; 3. äußerste Spitze einer Stänge; 4. Pol; *to - a boat*, ein Boot mit Stangen fortbewegen; - *axe*, Enterbeil; - *compass*, Pfahlkompaß; - *hook*, Bootshaken; - - *mast*, Pfahlmast; - *of a royal* od. *topgallant mast*, Flaggentopp.
poles, under bare -, vor Topp und Takel.
police watch vessel, Hafenpolizeiboot.
polishing hammer, Polierhammer.
ponche, Abschottung der Sturzgüter.
pontoon, Ponton; - *crane*, Schwimmkran; - *for careening ships*, Verschlußponton.
poop, Hütte; - *awning*, Hüttensonnensegel; - *bulkhead*, H-schott; - *cabin*, Kajüte unter dem Hinterdeck; - *coaming angle bar*, Hüttensüllwinkel; - *deck*, H-deck; - - *beam*, H-d-balken; - - - *angle bar*, H-d-b-winkel; - - - *hanging knee*, H-d-b-Hängeknie; - - - *lodging knee*, horizontales Knie des H-d-b-; - - - *shelf*, Hüttenbalkweger; - - - *stringer*, H-deck-Balkenstringer; - - - - *plate*, H-d-B.-platte; *p. d. b. tie plate*, H-d-balken-Lukenstringer; *p. d. fastening*, H-d-Befestigung; *p. d. pillar*, H-d-stütze; *p. d. plating*, H-d-Beplattung; *p. d. stringer*, H-d-Stringer; - - - *angle bar*, H-d-S.-winkel; - - - *plate*, H-d-S.-platte; *p. d. waterway*, H-d-Wassergang; - *frame*, Hüttenspant; - *guard rods*, H-geländerstangen; - *ladder*, H-treppe;

- *lantern*, Hecklaterne; - *port*, H-fenster; - *rail*, Hüttenreling; - *rails and stanchions*, H-geländer; - *royal*, Obenhütte; - *sheerstrake*, Hüttenschergang; - *stanchion*, H-geländerstütze; - *waterway*, Hütten-Wassergang; - *weather boards*, H.-Schutzbretter.
pooped, eine See brach über das Heck.
pooping sea, eine hinten überkommende Sturzsee.
popped head of a lathe, Drehbankreitstock.
poppets, Schlittenstützen.
port, 1. Backbord; 2. Rechtsruder geben; 3. Pforte, Stückpforte; 4. Hafen; 5. Kanal im Zylinder; 6. Dampfeintritt des Schiebers; - *Admiral*, Hafenadmiral; - *anchor*, Backbordanker; - *bar*, 1. Pfortenhebel; 2. Hafenbaum; 3. Untiefe im Hafen; *on the - beam*, querab an Backbord; - *bilge suction valve*, B.-Lenzsaugventil; - *boiler*, B.-kessel; - *bow*, B.-bug; *on the - -*, querab an B.-b-; - *charges*, Hafenabgaben; - *clearing*, Auslaufen; - *dues* od. *duties*, Hafengebühren; - *engine*, Backbordmaschine; - *flange*, Lukenlatte; - *flap*, Pfortenklappe; - - *hinge*, P.-Scharnier; - *frame*, Pfortenrahmen; - *hinges*, P-angeln; - *hole*, 1. P-öffnung; 2. Dampföffnung eines Zylinders; - *hook*, Hängenhaken; - *lanyard*, Pfortensteert - *lid*, P-deckel; - *light*, Backbord-Licht.
port of call, Anlegehafen; - - *destination*, Bestimmungshafen; - - *discharge*, Löschungshafen; - - *distress*, Nothafen; - - *entry*, Eingangshafen; - - *exit*, Ausflußöffnung; - - *loading*, Ladehafen; - - *refuge*, Nothafen; - - *registry*, Heimats-

hafen; - - *sailing*, Abgangs-hafen ; - - *transhipment*, Um-ladehafen.

port pendant, Pfortenhanger; - *quarter*, Backbord-Achter; *on* - -, querab an B.-A.; - *regulations*, Hafenordnung; - *rope*, Pfortentau; - *sail*, Ballastkleid; - *sash*, Klappen-fenster; - *shackle*, Pforten-ring; - *side*, Backbordseite; - *sill*, Pfortendrempel; - *tack*, mit Backbordhalsen über Steuerbordbug; - *tackle*, Pfortentalje; - *toll*, Hafen-gebühr; - *the helm*, Rechts-ruder geben; - *warden*, Hafenmeister; - *watch*, Back-bordwache; - *way*, Dampf-leitung.

portable crane, Fahrkran; - *pump*, versetzbare Pumpe.

portage, 1. Lastigkeit; 2. Heuer beim Hafenaufenthalt; - *bill*, Musterrolle.

ported helm, legten das Ruder nach Steuerbord.

Portland race, Stromkabbe-lung bei P.

position, Schiffsort; - *assumed*, S.; - *lights*, Positionslichter; *to have the lights in* -, die Lichter an Ort und Stelle haben.

post captain, Kapitän zur See; - *service*, Postdienst; - *windlass*, Winde.

potato pen, Kartoffelbehälter.

pouch, kleine Abschottung.

pounding, 1. stampfen (der Maschine); 2. das Anstürmen (der See).

powder chest, Feuerkiste; - *flag*, Pulverflagge; - *room*, P-kammer.

power, Kraft.

pram, Prahm.

pratique, Verkehrserlaubnis; - *boat*, das mit V. versehene Landungsboot; *to admit to* -, V. erteilen; *to take* -, V. ein-einholen; *to get* -, V. er-halten.

prayer book, kleiner Scheuer-stein.

preservation of boilers, Kessel-unterhaltung.

press a ship on shore, ein Schiff auf den Strand jagen; - *gang*, Preßgang; - *man*, Matrosenpresser; - *of sails*, unter vollen Segeln; - *of steam*, Dampfdruck; *to* - *sailors*, Matrosen pressen.

pressure, Druck, Spannung; - *cylinder junk ring*, Druck-zylinder-Liderungsring; - *gauge*, Dampfdruckmesser; - *governor*, D-d-regulator; - *reducing valve*, Druck-reduzierventil; - *required*, erforderlicher Druck; - *test*, D-probe.

presumptive loss, mutmaß-licher Verlust.

prevailing winds, vorherr-schende Winde.

preventer, Borgtau; - *backstay*, B-pardune; - *bobstay*, B-was-serstag; - *bolt*, Klappbolzen; - *brace*, Borgbrasse; - *brail*, B-brohk; - *chain bolt*, unte-rer Püttingsbolzen; - *c. plate*, P-klappe; - *deck*, Stilling; - *guys*, Borggeie; - *leech line*, Schmiergording; - *lift*, Borg-toppenant; - *of the bonnet*, Borgbindsel des Bonnets; - *plate*, Püttingsklappe; - *rope*, Borgtau; - *rudder*, Notruder; - *sheet*, Borgschote; - *shroud*, B-want; - *slings*, B-hanger; - *stay*, B-stag; - *stopper*, B-stopper; - *tiller*, Ruderhorn; - *tow rope*, Borg-tau; - *vang*, B-gerde.

preventers, Borgbindsel.

prick the chart, das Besteck in der Karte absetzen; - *the seams*, eine Segelnaht in der Mitte durchnähen.

pricker, Pricker; - *bar*, Schür-eisen.

pricking, absetzen (auf der Karte); - *note*, Zollhaus-erlaubnis zur Verschiffung von Gütern.

primage, Frachtzuschlag.
priming, 1. Grundfarbe; 2. Preimen (Überkochen und Eindringen des Wassers in die Zylinder); - *paint*, Grundfarbe; - *valve of the cylinder*, Sicherheitsventil.
principal frames, Richtspanten; - *light*, Kursfeuer; - *owner*, Hauptreeder.
prisage, Prisenanteil der Krone.
private yard, Privatwerft.
privateer, Kaper, K-schiff; - *ing*, Kaperei.
privilege of fishing, Fischereirecht.
prize, 1. Prise; 2. auflichten mit einer Handspake; - *cause*, Prisenprozeß; - *court*, Prisengericht; - *goods*, P-güter; - *money*, P-geld; *to condemn as lawful -*, als gute Prise erklären.
prizes, adjudication of -, Prisenreglement.
proceed, abfahren, fahren, weiterfahren; - *on*, w.
proceedings during the voyage, die Begebenheiten während der Reise.
production of steam, Dampferzeugung.
professional stevedore, berufsmäßiger Stauer.
profile draught, Riß eines Querschnitts.
projected plan, Entwurf.
projector, Scheinwerfer.
promenade deck, Promenadendeck; - - *beam*, P.-balken; - - - *angle bar*, P.-b-winkel; - - - *stringer*, P.-b-stringer; - - *guard rods*, P.-Geländerstangen; - - *pillar*, P.-stütze: - - *rails and stanchions*, P.-geländer; - - *s.*, P.-G-l-stützen: - - *stringer*, P.-stringer; - - *waterway*, P.-Wasserweg.
promontory, Vorgebirge.
prong, der schräge Scherstock des Decks.
proof mark, Versuchstempel; - *strain*, Prüfungskraft.

prop, abstützen, Stütze; - *of the sheers*, Bockspier; - *of the stem*, Stevenstütze.
propeller, Schraube; - *blade*, S.-flügel; - - *area*, Flächeninhalt der S.-f-; - - *flange*, S.-f-flansch; - *boss*, S.-nabe; - *engine*, S.-Dampfmaschine; - *frame*, S.-rahmen; - *key*, S.-keil; - - *way*, S.-k-nute; - *nut*, S.-mutter; - *post*, S.-steven; - - *rivet*, S.-s-niete; - *shaft*, S.-welle; - - *flange*, S.-w-flansch; - - *key way*, S.-w-Keilnute; - - *liner*, S.-w-hülse; - - *nut*, S.-w-mutter; - - *sleeve*, S.-w-hülse; - - *stay*, S.-w-bock: - - *stuffing box*, S.-w-Stopfbüchse; - *stud*, Stiftschraube der Schraubennabe; - - *bolt*, S-s-bolzen d. S.; - - - *nut*, S-s-b-mutter d. S.; - *wheel*, Schiffsschraube; - *with feathering blades*, Schraube mit verstellbaren Flügeln.
propelling power, 1. Vorwärtsbewegungskraft; 2. Treibapparat.
proper navigation, Hochsee-Schiffahrt.
proppet, senkrecht stehende Stütze.
propulsion, Fortbewegung.
protactor, Winkelfasser.
protecting club, Schutzverband; - *sheath of a cable*, Bekleidung eines Taues.
protection club of shipowners, Reederei-Schutzverband.
protest, 1. Protest; 2. Verklarung.
provide ballast, Ballast liefern.
proving house, Kettenprobieramt.
provision boat, Proviantboot; - *list*, P-verzeichnis; - *room*, P-kammer.
provisions, Proviant.
prow, Bug; - *post*, Vordersteven.
public water, schiffbares Wasser.
puddening, 1. Schamfielungsmatte; 2. Taukränze; 3. das

Leguan (alte Rahen und Masten); - *of an anchor ring*, Ankerrührung.
pudding see puddening.
puddled steel, Puddelstahl.
puff of wind, Fallwind.
puffy, böig.
pull, rojen, rudern; - *ahead*, vorwärts r.; - *all at once*, alle zugleich r.; - *cheerily*, hart r.; - *even stroke*, Schlag r.; - *hard*, ausholen; - *long stroke*, langen Schlag r.; - *on*, vorwärts r.; - - *a rope*, an einem Tau ziehen; - *short stroke*, kurzen Schlag r.; - *stroke*, denTakt beim Rudern angeben; - *strong*, stark r.; - *together*, alle zugleich r.; - *towards*, r. nach; - *up*, aufhissen.
pulley, Rolle (Windezeug); - *block*, Gehäuse einer R.
pulsometer, Pulsometer (eine Art Pumpe).
pump, pumpen, Pumpe; *to - dry*, lenz pumpen; *the - blows*, die Pumpe lorcht; *t. p. does not fetch*, d. P. faßt nicht; *t. p. is dry*, d. P. schlägt lenz; *t. p. is fetched*, d. P. faßt; *t. p. is free*, d. P. ist lenz; *t. p. sucks*, d. P. schlägt lenz; *to fetch t. p.*, die P. ansaugen lassen.
pump back, Pumpen-back; - *barrel*, P-Körper; - *beam gudgeon brasses*,P-balanzier-zapfen-Lagerschalen; - *bit*, P-bohrer; - *bolt*, P-bolzen; - *borer*, P-bohrer; - *box*, P-eimer; - *brake*, P-hebel; - *bucket*, P-kolben; - - *rod*, P-k-stange; - *carlines*, Fisch für die Pumpen; - *casing*, P-sood; - *chamber*, P-körper; - - *liner*, P-einsatz; - *cheeks*, P-mick; - *cistern*, P-kasten; - *coat*, P-kragen; - *cover*, P-deckel; - - *bolt nut*, P-d-Bolzenmutter; - *crank*, P-Kurbelwelle; - *crosshead guide rod*, P-Kreuzkopf-Führungsstange; *p. c. g. r.*

bracket, P-K.-F.-träger; *p. c. journal*, Halszapfen der P-traverse; - *cylinder*, P-zylinder; - *dale*, P-rinne; - *dredger*, P-bagger; - *escape valve spindle*, P-Sicherheitsventil-spindel; - *foot*, P-fuß; - *gauge*, P-sonde; - *gear*, P-vorrichtung; - *gland*, P-Stopfbüchsendeckel; - *hammer*, P-hammer; - *handle*, P-schwengel; - *head*, P-aufsatz; - *hook*, P-haken; - *kettle*, P-kessel; - *leather*, P-leder; - *lever*, P-balanzier; - - *brasses*, P-b-Lagerschalen; - - *gudgeon*, P-b-Lagerzapfen; - - - *bearing*, P-b-zapfenlager; - - - - *keep*, P-b-z-l-deckel; *p. l. g. brasses*, P-b-z-l-schalen; *p. l. link*, P-b-gelenk; - - - *keep*, P-b-g-deckel; *p. lever shaft journal*, Halszapfen der P-b-axe; - *lift*, P-hub; - *liner*, P-einsatz; - *link*, P-gelenk; - - *brasses*, P-g-Lagerschalen; - *links*, P-gelenke; - *partner*, P-fischung; - *pipe*, P-rohr; - *piston*, P-kolben; - *plunger*, P-plunger; - *rocking shaft*, P-Balanzieraxe; - - - *gudgeon brasses*, P-B.-zapfen-Lagerschalen; - *rod*, P-stange; - *room*, P-kammer; - *scraper*, P-schraper; - *spear*, P-stange; - *staff*, P-stock; - *stock*, P-kasten; - *stuffing box*, P-Stopfbüchse; - - - *gland*, P-S.-deckel; - *suck*, P-schuh; - *tack*, P-spieker; - *tube*, P-rohr; - *valve*, P-ventil; - - *seat*, P-v-sitz; - *well*, P-sood.
pumps choked, Pumpen unklar; - *thrashing heavily*, P. arbeiten schwer.
punch, durchlochen, Lochmaschine.
punched rivet hole, mit der Lochmaschine gemachtes Nietenloch. [schine.
punching machine, Lochma-
punt, 1. Schauke (viereckiger Prahm); 2. mit Ruderstangen fortbewegen.

punter, Prahmführer.
puppet clack, Schnarchventil.
puppets of a cradle, Schlittenständer; - *of the wash board*, Dollbaum.
purchase, Talje; - *block*, T.-block; - *fall*, Takelläufer; - *rim*, Spillkranz; - *rod*, Zugstange; - *the anchor*, den Anker aufwinden.
purser, 1. Zahlmeister; 2. Proviantmeister; -*'s steward*, Stuart des P.
put a seal on the mast, das Schiff an die Kette legen; - *a vessel on the beach*, ein S. auf den Strand holen; - - - - - *blocks*, ein S. auf Stapelklötze legen; - *aback*, zurückbacken; - *aboard*, an Bord bringen; - *about*, über Stag gehen; - *back*, aus See zurückkehren;-*in for shelter*, zum Schutze einlaufen; - *in in a damaged condition*, mit Havarie einlaufen; - *into a becket*, aufknebeln; - *into port*, in einen Hafen einlaufen; - *off*, unter Segel gehen; - *on a seizing*, einen Bindsel aufsetzen;-*on board*, an Bord bringen; - *out to sea*, auslaufen; - *tabling on a sail*, Verdoppelungen auf ein Segel setzen.
put the helm alee, das Ruder in Lee legen; - - - *amidship*, d. R. mittschiffs legen; - - - *aport*, d. R. nach rechts legen; - - - *astarboard*, d. R. nach links legen; - - - *close on board*, d. R. hart an Bord legen; - - - *down*, d. R. in Lee legen; - - - *up*, d. R. auflegen.
put the planks on a vessel, ein Schiff beplanken; - *the rigging on the masthead*, das stehende Gut auflegen; - *the strands of a rope into the lays of another*, die Duchten eines Taues in die Schlagen eines anderen stechen; - *up*, aufrichten; - - *for X.*, in Ladung liegen nach X.
puttock see futtock.
putty, Kitt; - *up*, verkitten.
pyrometer, Hitzegradmesser.
pyx, Kompaßhäuschen.

Q.

quade, unbeständig.
quadrant, Quadrant; - *arc*, Q.-bogen; - *tiller*, Ruderquadrant.
quadrantal deviation, die viertelkreisartige Deviation.
quadruple expansion engine, vierfache Expansionsmaschine; - *riveting*, v. Nietung.
quarantine, Quarantäne; - *flag*, Q.-flagge; - *ground* od. *harbour* od. *station*, Q.-Station; - *officer*, Q.-beamte; *to pass q.*, Q. halten; *to discharge* od. *release from* -, aus der Q. entlassen.
quarter, 1. Achterteil (des Schiffes); 2. das Achtkant (einer Rahe); 3. Quartier (der Besatzung); *the ship has a fat* -, das Schiff geht tief im Wasser; *on the* -, backstagsweise.
quarter badges, blinde Hecktasche; - *block*, Geitau- und Schotblock; - *board*, Oberschanzkleid; - *boat*, Seitenboot; - *bumkin*, Brassenbaum; - *cloth*. 1. Schanzkleid von Segeltuch; 2. Bezug der Finknetzkasten; - *deck*, Achterdeck; - - *cabin*, obere Kajüte; - - *hatch*, Achterluke;-*fast*, hintere Seitenfeste; - *fishes*, Schalstücke des Mastes; - *gallery*, Heck-

gallerie; - *hatch*, Achterluke; - *iron of a yard*, Innen-Spierenbügel; - *lanterns*, Seitenlaternen am Hinterdeck; - *line*, Backstagslinie; - *master*, 1. Steuermannsmaat; 2. Quartiermeister; - *nettings*, Finknetze der Hütte; - *of a yard*, Rahearm; - *pieces*, Seitenstütze des Hecks; - *pillar*, S.; - *point*, ein Viertel - Kompaßstrich; - *points*, Seitenstücke des Hecks; - *port*, S-pforte am Heck; - *rail* od. *railing*, Reling am Quarterdeck; - *seizing*, Mittelbändsel; - *slings*, Rahestroppen; - *stanchion*, Sonnensegelstütze am Heck; - *strop*, Stoßtaljenstropp; - *tackle*, Klappläuter; - *timber*, hinterer Seitenauflanger; - *tracing* od. *tricing line*, Aufholer des oberen Rahetakelblocks; - *watch*, Hälfte der Wache; - *wind*, achterlicher Wind.

quartering, das backstagsweise Segeln; - *wind*, der b. Wind.

quarterly breeze, Backstagsbrise; - *wind*, B-s-wind.

quarters, from both - alternately, abwechselnd von beiden Achterseiten; *Keep good -!* Seid wachsam! *Pipe the men to -!* Alle Mann auf!

quay, Kai; - *berth*, K-platz; - *wall*, K-mauer.

quayage, 1. Kaimauer; 2. Kaigeld.

quick sand, beweglicher Sand; - *wales*, Berghölzer des Oberschiffs; - *water*, Setzweger; - *work*, unter Wasser befindliches Werk; - *of the topsides*, die inneren Schanzkleidbretter.

quicken, stärker krümmen; - *the sheer*, viel Spring geben.

quilting, Netz über dem Wasserbehälter.

quoin for stowing, Staukeil.

quoins, to drive in -, verkeilen.

R.

ra, Rahe.

R.A. = RearAdmiral, Contre-A.

rabbet, 1. Falz, Nut, Spündung; 2. Rinne (im Lukensüll); 3. einfalzen.

race, 1. Regatta; 2. Stromkabbelung; - *boat*, Rennboot; - *championship*, Meisterschaftsrennen; - *knife*, Kratzeisen; *to - timber*, abkrabben; *a - on t.*, ein Schrapp.

racing, Wettrennen; - *boat*, Rennboot; *engines -*, die Schraube lief blind; - *knife*, Kratzeisen; - *yacht*, Rennjacht.

rack, 1. Gestell, Recken; 2. Reling um das Kajütendeck; 3. Wegweiserlatte mit Scheiben; 4. mit einem Stopper versehen; 5. zusammenzeisen; - *bar*, Spannholz für Taue; - *block*, Puppenblock; - *wheel*, Sperrad.

racking, Kreuzbändsel; - *seizing*, K.

radial drilling machine, Radial-Bohrmaschine; - *float*, feststehende Radschaufel; - *paddle wheel*, Strahlschaufelrad.

radiating heat, strahlende Wärme.

radiation, Strahlung.

radius, Halbmesser; - *bar*, Gegenlenker; - *shaft*, G.-welle.

raft, 1. Floß, flößen; 2. Törnholz (für Stappellauf); - *for life saving*, Rettungsfloß; - *of casks*, Tonnenfloß.

raft bridge, Floßbrücke, - dog,
F-krampe; - port, Piekpforte.
raftsman, Flößer. [bolzen.
rag bolt od. ragged b., Hack-
rail od. railing, Reling; - of
the hammock nettings, Finknetzreling; - of the head,
R. des Gallions; - of the top,
Marsreling.
rails and stanchions, Geländer.
railway berth, Eisenbahn-
Liegeplatz; - ferry, Eisen-
bahnfähre.
rain region, Regenregion; -
squall, R-bö.; - taking off,
der R. ließ nach.
raise a blockade, eine Blockade
aufheben; - a mouse, eine
Maus aufsetzen; - a purchase,
ein Hebezeug zurichten; -
a screw, eine Schraube
lichten; - a sunken vessel,
ein gesunkenes Fahrzeug
heben; - steam, Dampf aufmachen; - the coast, sich
der Küste nähern; - the
frames, die Spanten auf-
richten; - the land, sich dem
Lande nähern; - the stem,
den Vordersteven aufsetzen.
raised deck, erhöhtes Deck;
- fore d., e. Vorderdeck; - - -
plating, Beplattung des e. V.;
- quarter deck, e. Quarterdeck; - - - awning, Sonnensegel des e. Q.; - - - beam,
Balken d. e. Q.; - - - - clamp,
Unterbalkweger d. e. Q.;
- - - - hanging knee, Hängeknie d. e. Q-balkens; - - - -
lodging knee, horizontales
Knie d. e. Q.-b-; - - - - shelf,
Balkweger d. e. Q.; - - - -
stringer, Balkenstringer d.
e. Q.; - - - - - plate, B.-platte
d. e. Q.: r. q. d. b. tie plate,
Lukenstringer d. e. Q.; r. q.
d. coaming angle bar, Winkel
d. e. Q.-sülls; r. q. d. fastening, Befestigung d. e. Q.; r. q.
d. frame, Spant d. e. Q.; r.
q. d. ladder, Treppe zum e.
Q.; r. q. d. plating, Beplattung d. e. Q.; r. q. d. rail,

Reling d. e. Q.; r. q. d. rails
and stanchions, Geländer d.
e. Q.; r. q. d. sheerstrake,
Schergang d. e. Q.; r. q. d.
stanchion, Geländerstütze d.
e. Q.; r. q. d. stringer, Stringer
d. e. Q.; - - - - angle bar, S.-
winkel d. e. Q.; - - - - plate,
S.-platte d. e. Q.; r. q. d.
waterway, Wassergang d. e.
Q.; - vessel, ein hoch auf-
gebautes Schiff.
rake, 1. Harke; 2. Fall (des
Mastes); 3. Ausschießen (des
Stevens); 4. Kielwasser; -
of the rudder, Hinterteil des
Ruders; - of the stem, das
Ausschießen des Vorder-
stevens; - of the stern, d. A.
d. Hinterstevens; - up the
ground, den Boden auf-
wühlen.
raking stem, ausschießender
Vordersteven; - stern post,
a. Achtersteven.
rakish appearance, wie ein
Schnellsegler aussehend.
ram, 1. rammen, Ramme; 2.
Sporn (eines Panzerschiffes);
3. Kolbenstange (einer Pumpe); 4. Kardeelblock; - head,
oberer Marsfallblock; - line,
Strohkleine.
ramed, in Spanten stehend.
ramp, Rampe.
range, 1. Kochhausherd; 2.
Sog; 3. Belegknecht; 4. Nagelbank; 5. überholte Anker-
kette; to have a light in
full -, im vollen Bereiche
eines Feuers sein; he caused
such a heavy - that our vessel
took the ground, er verursachte einen derartig schwe-
ren Sog, daß unser Schiff
an Grund geriet.
range beacon, Richtungsbake;
- heads, Bratspillbetings; -
lights, Richtungsfeuer; - of
the cable, Bucht der aufge-
holten Ankerkette.
range, to - by, vorübersegeln;
- the coast, längs der Küste
fahren.

ranges, the - catch each other, die Buchten des Kabels fangen sich.

ranging, 1. ausscheren an der Kette; 2. ausbreiten (Ketten parallel nebeneinander a.).

rank keel, tiefer Kiel.

ransom, loskaufen, Lösegeld; - *bill,* Ranzionskontrakt.

rap full, geschwellt (Segel).

rapids, Stromschnellen.

rarefaction, Verdünnung.

*rasing iron,*Nahthaken; - *knife,* Kratzeisen.

rasp, Raspel.

ratchet, Sperrklinke; - *drill,* Ratschbohrer; - *wheel,* Sperrad.

rate, 1. Rate; 2. Gang (des Chronometers); 3. Geschwindigkeit (der Strömung und des Schiffes).

rate, to - a chronometer, den Gang eines C. bestimmen; 2. *to - a man as officer,* einem Manne einen Offiziersposten geben.

rater, a first -, ein Schiff ersten Ranges.

rating, Posten.

ratle down, ausweben.

ratline, Webeleine; - *seizing,* W.-bindsel; - *stuff,* W.

ratlings, Webeleinen.

rat's tail, Katsteert.

rattle, mit Webeleinen versehen; - *down,* ausweben; - *of chains,* Kettengerassel.

rave hook, Nahthaken.

raven duck, Raventuch.

*raw cast steel,*roher Gußstahl; - *oil,* rohes Öl; - *sailor,* unbefahrener Matrose; - *steel,* Rohstahl.

raze a ship, ein Schiff rasieren.

razee, das rasierte Schiff.

reach, 1. Stromstrecke. 2. *to -,* mit raumem Winde fahren; *to - across the fairway,* querab in das Fahrwasser kommen.

reaction, Gegen- od. Rückwirkung.

read the log, das Log ablesen.

ready about, klar zum Wenden; - *all!* Ruder in Lee! - *for sail* od. *sea,* seeklar; - *to discharge,* zum Löschen bereit; - *to load,* zum Laden bereit.

real slip, wirklicher Slip.

ream, to -, Nähte zum Dichten öffnen.

reamer od. *reaming iron,* Räumahle.

rearing, einfallend.

rebate see rabbet.

rebatten, wieder verschalken.

rebend, wieder anschlagen.

*re-boilering,*mit neuen Kesseln versehen.

re-bolted, neu verbolzt.

re-building, Umbau.

re-built, umgebaut.

re-bush, neu ausbüchsen.

rebut a charge, eine Anschuldigung wiederlegen.

recall, Signalflagge zum Umkehren.

recapture, wiedergenommene Prise.

receipt for goods, Ladungsempfangsschein.

*receiver,*1. Ladungsempfänger; 2. Dampfreservoir, Receiver; - *gauge,* R.-Manometer; - *of wrecks,* Strandvogt; - *pipe,* Überströmrohr.

receiving note, Anlieferungsschein; - *ship,* Matrosenquartierschiff.

recess, Nische; - *bulkhead,* Ausbau einer N.; - - *of donkey boiler,* Hülfskessel-A.; - - *of shaft tunnel,* Schaft-tunnel-A.; - *of tunnel,* Tunnelkammer.

rechange, Reserve-Segel od. Rundhölzer.

recharter, wieder- od. weiterverfrachten, Wieder- oder Weiterverfrachtung.

reciprocal bond, Revers.

reciprocating, umwechselnd; - *motion,* wechselweise Bewegung.

reckoning, Besteck, Gissung; *ahead of the* -, mit seinem B. zurück sein; *astern of the* -, m. s. B. voraus s.; *out of one's* -, außer s. B. s.; *to work the ship's* -, B.machen.

reclassification, Reklassifikation.

recoil, wieder aufschießen.

recopper, neu mit Kupfer belegen.

record, Rekord.

recover, bergen; - *damages*, Schadenersatz erhalten.

recovery of damages, Schadenersatz.

rectangular boiler, Kofferkessel.

rectifier, Instrument zur Berichtigung des Kompasses.

red flag, Pulverflagge; - *gum wood*, Rotgummibaum; - *heat*, Rotglut: - *lead*, Mennige; - - *joint*, Mennigkittdichtung; - *light*, rotes Seitenlicht; - *pine wood*, Rottannenholz.

redemptioner, ein Mann, der sein Passagegeld abarbeitet.

reduce sails, Segel mindern; - *speed*, Fahrt vermindern.

reduced distance, die gegißte Weite; - *temperature*, verminderte Temperatur.

reduction of pressure, Druckverminderung.

reef, 1. blinde Klippen; 2. reffen, Reff; *to take in a* -, einreffen; *to let out the reefs*, die Reffe losmachen.

reef band, Reffband: - *cringle*, R-lägel; - *earing*, R-bindsel; - *knittle*, R-zeising; - *knot*, R-knoten; - *line*, R-leine; - *pendant*, Schmierreep; - - *cleat of a boom*, S.-klampe eines Baumes; - *points*, Reffbändsel; - *span*, R-taljenlägel mit Steert; - *tackle*, R-talje; - - *block*, R-t-block; - - *cringle*, R-t-lägel; - - *patch*, R-t-lappen; - - *piece*, R-t-l-; - - *span*, R-t-lägel mit Steert; - *topsails!* Marssegel reffen!

reefed, gerefft; - *topmast*, verkürzter Toppmast.

reefer, Seekadett.

reefing, reffen; - *becket*, Reffknebelsteert; - *cleat of a boom*, Reffhangerklampe; - *gear*, Mechanismus zum Segelreffen; - *jacket*, enganliegende Jacke; - *jigger*, kleines Takel zum Strecken des Reffbändsels; - *point*, Reffzeising.

reel, Rolle; - *of the log*, Logrolle.

reeling, schlingern.

re-embark, wieder einschiffen.

re-embarcation, Wieder-Einschiffung.

reeming, aufweiten; - *beetle*, Klameihammer; - *iron*, Scharfeisen.

re-engined, mit neuen Maschinen versehen.

re-entering bend, Einbucht; - *e. sinuosity*, eingehende Krümmung.

reeve, durchscheren, einscheren.

reeving, durchscheren, einscheren; - *line*, Scherleine.

re-ferrule, die Zwingen erneuern.

refined charcoal steel, raffinierter Stahl; - *iron*, Feineisen.

refit, 1. ausbessern (Takelage); 2. wieder ausrüsten (Schiff); - *ment*, 1. Ausbesserung; 2. Wieder-Ausrüstung.

reflecting quadrant, Spiegel-Oktant.

refloated, wurde wieder flott.

reflux, Rückfluß, Abfluß, Ebbe.

refreight, wieder befrachten.

refrigerating chamber, Kühlraum; - *engineer*, Gefrier-Maschinist; - *machine*, Eismaschine; - - *connecting rod*, E.-Pleuelstange; - - - - *bolt*, E.-P.-bolzen; - - - - *bottom end keep*, E.-Kurbelzapfen-Lagerschalendeckel; - - - - - *liner*, E.-Pleuelstangenfußfutter; *r. m. c. r. top e. k.*, E.-Kreuzkopf-Lagerschalendeckel; *r. m. crank pin bolt*, E. - Kurbelzapfen - Lagerbolzen; *r. m. c. p. brasses*, E.-K.-L-schalen; *r. m. c. shaft*, E.-Kurbelwelle; *r. m. c. s. bearing*, E.-K.-Lager; *r. m. c. s. b. bolt*, E.-K.-L-bolzen; *r. m. c. s. bearing brasses*, E.-K.-L-schalen; *r. m. c. s. bearing keep*, E.-K.-L-deckel; *r. m. c. s. b. k. bolt*, E.-K.-L-d-bolzen; *r. m. crosshead bolt*, E. - Kreuzkopf-Lagerbolzen; *r. m. c, brasses*, E.-K.-L-schalen; *r. m. cylinder*, E.-Zylinder; *r. m. c. cover*, E.-Z.-deckel; *r. m. c. c. bolt*, E.-Z.-d-bolzen; *r. m. cylinder drain pipe*, E.-Z.-Entwässerungsrohr; *r. m. eccentric*, E.-Excenter; *r. m. e. bolt*, E.-E.-bolzen; *r. m. e. brasses*, E.-E.-Lagerschalen; *r. m. e. rod*, E.-E.-stange; *r. m. e. sheave*, E.-E.-scheibe; *r. m. e. strap*, E.-E.-bügel; *r. m. e. s. liner*, E.-E.-b-futter; *r. m. exhaust pipe*, E.-Dampfablaßrohr; *r. m. piston*, E.-Kolben; *r. m. p. rod*, E.-K.-stange; *r. m. p. rod crosshead*, E.-K.-s-Kreuzkopf; *r. m. p. r. stuffing box*, E.-K.-s-Stopfbüchse; *r. m. p. r. s. b. gland*, E.-K.-s-S.-deckel; *r. m. slide valve*, E.-Schieber; *r. m. starting valve*, E.-Anlaß-ventil; *r. m. stop v.*, E.-Absperrventil; *r. m. valve casing*, E.-Schieberkasten; *r. m. v. c. door*, E.-S.-deckel; *r. m. valve rod*, E.-Schieberstange; *r. m. v. r. stuffing box*, E.-S.-Stopfbüchse; *r. m. v. r. s. b. gland*, E.-S.-S.-deckel; *r. m. steamer*, Dampfer mit Kühlvorrichtung.

refrigerator, Kühlapparat.

refuge beacon, Rettungsbake; - *harbour*, Zufluchtshafen.

refuse, Abfall, Versatz (bei Kohlen); - *staying*, die Wen-

dung versagen; - *to answer the helm*, dem Ruder nicht gehorchen; - *to do duty*, 1. die Arbeit verweigern (Mannschaft); 2. nicht funktionieren wollen (Maschinerie).

regatta, Wettrudern, Wettsegeln.

region of calms, Region der Windstillen; - *of trade winds*, Passatregion.

register, 1. Seebrief; 2. Schiffsregister; 3. Hubzähler; - *book*, Registerbuch; - *measurement*, die vom Zollamt festgesetzte Lastigkeit; *to - sailors*, Matrosen anwerben; - *tonnage*, Register-Tonnengehalt.

registered port, Heimatshafen.

regular line, regelmäßige Linie; - *liner*, r. Fahrer; - *service*, r. Verkehr; - *trade*, r. V.; - *trader*, r. Fahrer.

regulate, in Ordnung bringen.

regulating, regulieren, die Regulierung; - *screw*, Regulierschraube; - - *of a steering chain*, Spannschraube einer Steuerkette; - *valve*, Regulierventil; - - *gear*, Druckreduzierventilgestänge; - - *rod*, D-r-v-stange; - - *spindle*, D-r-v-spindel; - *wheel*, Regulierrad.

regulation lights, vorschriftsmäßige Lichter.

regulator, Moderator, Regulator; - *rod*, R.-stange.

reigning wind, der vorherrschende Wind.

rejoint, verschließen, wieder zusammenfügen.

relaunch, wieder vom Stapel lassen.

relief cock, Entlastungshahn; - *frame*, E-l-rahmen; - *gangs*, ablösende Arbeitergänge; - *valve*, Rücklaufventil; - - *spindle*, Überlaufventilspindel.

relieve, ablösen, verfangen; -

the watch, die Wache ablösen.

relieving rope, Grundtau, Aufhalter der Ankerkette; - *tackle*, Nottalje.

re-line, wieder ausfüllen.

remast, neu bemasten.

remetalling, eine neue Metallhaut anlegen.

render, kommen, mitkommen, lose geben, durchscheren.

rendering, klar laufend.

rends, Fugen, Nähte.

renewing the stays in boiler, einen Kessel neu verankern.

repair, reparieren, Reparatur; *in -*, in Ausbesserung; *to - on board*, sich an Bord begeben.

repairer, Ausbesserer.

repairing, reparieren; - *dock*, Reparatur-Dock; - *shop*, R.-Werkstatt.

repairs to a wooden hull, Zimmerungsreparatur; - *to the hull*, Schiffsrumpfreparaturen.

repeat a signal, ein Signal wiederholen.

replenish stores, die Vorräte ergänzen.

report, melden, Meldung, Bericht; *to - oneself to . .*, sich bei . . melden.

reprise, eine dem Feinde wieder abgenommene Prise.

required pressure, erforderlicher Druck.

re-reeve, wieder durchscheren.

re-rove, wieder durchgeschoren.

reserve buoyancy, Deplacements-Überschuß; - *spar*, &c., Reservespiere etc.; - *valve*, inneres Sicherheitsventil.

re-set log, das Log wieder stellen.

reship, 1. wiedereinnehmen (Ladung); 2. w-einhängen (Ruder); 3. w-einsetzen (Mast).

resistance by friction, Widerstand durch Reibung.

resisting power, Widerstandskraft.

resources, Hülfsmittel.

respondentia, uneigentliche Bodmerei; - *bond*, B.-brief; *borrower at -*, B.-nehmer; *lender at -*, B.-geber.

rest, Zapfenlager.

restaying, neu verankern.

resting part, Zapfenlager.

restoration, Wiederaufnahme.

restow, umstauen.

resultant, Diagonalkraft.

retaining valve, Kugelventil.

retard of the tide, Verzögerung der Flut.

retarder, Retarder.

retire from service, sich vom Dienst zurückziehen.

re-treenailed, neu vernagelt.

retrogade motion, Rückwärtsbewegung.

return cargo, Rückladung; - *freight*, R-fracht; - *ticket*, Retourbillet; - *connecting rod*, rückwirkende Pleuelstange; - - - *engine*, Maschine mit r. P.; - *flame boiler*, Kessel mit rückkehrender Flamme; - *flue b.*, K. m. r. Flamme; - *in ballast*, in Ballast zurückkommen; - *of a voyage*, Reisebericht; - *sea*, zurückgeworfene Welle; - *stroke*, zurückgehende Hub; - *valve*, Rückflußventil; - *voyage*, Rückreise.

revenue cutter, Zollkutter; - *officer*, Z-beamter.

reversal, Umsteuerung.

reverse, 1. umsteuern; 2. umdrehen, umkehren; - *valve*, Luftventil.

reversed angle bar, Gegenwinkel; - *angle iron*, das gekehrte Winkeleisen; - *frame*, Gegenspant.

reversible, umsteuerbar.

reversing, 1. umsteuern; 2. umkehren; - *engine*, Umsteuerungsmaschine; - *connecting rod*, Pleuelstange der U.; - - - - *bolt*, P.-bolzen d. U.; - - - - *bottom end keep*, Kurbelzapfen-Lagerschalen-

deckel d. U.; - - - - *b. e.
liner*, Pleuelstangenfußfutter d. U.; - - - - *top end
keep*, Kreuzkopf - Lagerschalendeckel d. U.; *r. e.
crank pin bolt*,Kurbelzapfen-Lagerbolzen d. U.; *r. e. c. p.
brasses*, K.-L-schalen d. U.;
r. e. c. shaft, Kurbelwelle d.
U.; *r. e. c. s. bearing*, Kurbelwellenlager d. U.; *r. e. c. s.
b. bolt*, K.-bolzen d. U.; *r. e.
c. s. bearing brasses*, K.-schalen d. U.; *r. e. c. s.
bearing keep*, K.-deckel d.
U.; *r. e. c. s. b. k. bolt*, K.-d-bolzen d. U.; *r. e. crosshead bolt*, Kreuzkopflagerbolzen d. U.; *r. e. c. brasses*,
K-k-l-schalen d. U.; *r. e.
cylinder*, Zylinder d. U.; *r.
e. c. cover*, Z.-deckel d. U.;
r. e. c. c. bolt, Z.-d-bolzen d.
U.; *r. e. cylinder drain pipe*,
Z.-Entwässerungsrohr d. U.;
r. e. eccentric, Exzenter d.
U.; *r. e. e. bolt*, E.-bolzen d.
U.; *r. e. e. brasses*, E.-Lagerschalen d. U.; *r. e. e. rod*, E.-stange d. U.; *r. e. e. sheave*,
E.-scheibe d. U.; *r. e. e. strap*,
E.-bügel d. U.; *r. e. e. s. liner*,
E.-b-futter d.U.; *r. e. exhaust
pipe*, Dampfablaßrohr d. U.;
r. e. piston, Kolben d. U.;
r. e. p. rod, K.-stange d. U.;
r. e. p. r. crosshead, K.-s-Kreuzkopf d. U.; *r. e. p. r.
stuffing box*, K.-s-Stopfbüchsendeckel d. U.; *r. e. slide
valve*, Schieber d. U.; *r. e.
starting v.*, Anlaßventil d.
U.; *r. e. starting valve handle*,
A.-habe d. U.; *r. e. stop
valve*, Absperrventil d. U.;
r. e. valve casing, Schieberkasten d. U.; *r. e. v. c. door*,
S.-deckel d. U.; *r. e. valve
rod*, Schieberstange d. U.;
r. e. v. r. stuffing box, S.-Stopfbüchse d. U.; *r. e. v.
r. s. b. gland*, S.-S.-deckel d.
U.; - *gear*, Umsteuerungsvorrichtung; - *hand wheel*,

Handumsteuerungsrad; - - - *brake*, H.-bremse; - *handle*,
Umsteuerungshebel; - *lever*,
U.; - *link*, Umsteuerungs-Koulisse; - *motion*, Umsteuerung; - *rod*, Umkehrstange;
- *shaft*, Umsteuerungs-Spindel; - *turbine*, U.-turbine;
- *valve*, Luftventil; - *wheel*,
Umsteuerungsrad; - *worm*,
U-s-schnecke; - - *wheel*, U-s-rad.
reverting, rücklaufender Zug
im Kessel.
revolution, Umdrehung.
revolve, umdrehen.
revolving light, Drehfeuer; - - *house*,Leuchtturm mit Blinkfeuer.
rhumb, Kompaßstrich; - *card
of a compass*, Windrose; - *card socket*, Hütchen der
Kompaßrose; - *line*, die loxodromische Linie; - *lines*,
Kompaßlinien; - *point*, K-p-strich; - *sailing*, Segeln in
der Loxodrome.
rib, 1. Rippe (flache Verstärkung eines Maschinenteils);
2. Rackschlitten; 3. Inholz,
Spant.
ribband, Sente; - *batten*, S.;
- *line*,Vorderende eines Bergholzganges; - *of the bulkheads*, Leiste zur Bekleidung
der Schottenfugen.
ribbing nail, Sentennagel.
ribbon, die gemalte Schiffsleiste; - *line*, Linie der Senten auf dem wasserpassen
Riß.
ribbons of a sail, Segelfetzen.
rickers, unbearbeitete Bootmasten.
ride across, quer ankern; - *aperture*,mit gekaiten Rahen
vor Anker liegen; - *at anchor*,
vor A. l.; - *athwart*, zwischen
Wind und Strom vor A. gieren; - *between wind and tide*,
z. W. u. S. liegen; - *down*,
1. hinunter gleiten; 2. gewaltsam niederholen; - *easy*,
bequem vor Anker liegen;

- *hard*, schwer v. A. **reiten**;
- *out a gale*, einen Sturm
abreiten; - *to the tide*, auf
dem Strome liegen; - - - *wind*,
a. d.Wind liegen; - *upon the
main*, die See halten; - *windward tide*, auf einem luvwärts setzenden Strom ge-
schwoit liegen.

rider, Kattspor; - *bolt*, K.-bol-
zen; - *keelson*, Kielschwein-
sohle; - *plate*, Gurtplatte.

riders, die oberen Lagen der
im Raum verstauten Fässer.

ridge chain of an awning,
Streckkette eines Sonnen-
segels; - *lining o. a. a.*, Verstärkungsband des Rückens
eines Sonnensegels; - *of a
wave*, Wellenkamm; - *of an
awning*, Rücken eines Sonnensegels; - *of banks*, Rük-
ken einer Bank; - *of rocks*,
Klippenreihe; - *of waves*,
Wellenkamm; - *rope of an
awning*, Sonnensegelreep; -
ropes, 1. Laufstagen (am
Bugspriet); 2. Strecktaue
über Deck (bei schlechtem
Wetter).

riding bitts, Ankerbetings;
- *buckler*, Klüsendeckel mit
Kerbe; - *fakes*, obere Buch-
tenlage; - *light*, Ankerlicht;
- *sail*, 3eckiges Segel; - *scope*,
ausgesteckte Kettenlänge.

riff, Riff, Sandbank; -*of rocks*,
Felsenriff.

rig, 1. Takelage; 2. auftakeln
(Fahrzeug); 3. zustellen
(Pumpe, Gangspill); 4. aufzeugen (Baum, Mast); -*anew*,
umtakeln; - *down*, abtakeln;
- *in*, einholen, einziehen;
- *out*, ausbringen, ausrüsten;
- *out the booms!* Spieren aus!

rigger, Takeler.

rigging, Takelage; - *chain*,
Takelkette; - *cutter*, Vor-
richtung zum Abhauen des
Takelwerks; - *loft*, T-boden;
- *master*, T-bootsmann; -*mat*,
Stoßmatte; - *screw*, Want-

schraube; - *span*, W-kreuz;
- *stopper*, Borg für stehendes
Gut; - *works*, Takelarbeiten.

right a vessel, ein Schiff aufrichten.

right abeam, recht dwars; -
aft, r. achteraus; - *ahead*, r.
voraus; - *angle*, rechter
Winkel; - *astern*, recht
achteraus; -*handed propeller*,
rechts drehende Propeller;
- *h. rope*, r. geschlagenes
Tau; - *h. screw*, r. drehende
Schraube; - *in the wind's
eye*, recht in den Wind; -
in your teeth, r. auf die
Nase; - *on end*, senkrecht;
- *the helm!* mittschiffs das
Ruder! - *up channel*, gerade
mit dem Kopfe in den Kanal
hinein; - *of salvage*, Strandrecht; - *of search*, Durchsuchungsrecht; - *of visit*,
Recht der Flaggenprüfung;
- *of way*, Wegerecht; - - -
lamp od. *light*, W.-lampe; -
sailing, Segeln in der recht-
weisenden Linie.

righten a vessel, ein Schiff
aufrichten.

rigid, steif; -*ity*, S-heit.

rim, Kranz, Pallkranz; - *of a
steering wheel*, Steuerrad-
kranz; - *of the top*, Mars-
band.

rime, 1. ausräumen; 2. Reif
(als Niederschlag).

rimer, Räumahle.

ring, Ring; - *bolt*, R-bolzen;
- - *for painter*, Fangleine-
bolzen; - *bush*, Büchse einer
Blockscheibe; - *dog*, Kant-
haken; -*eye bolt*, Ringbolzen;
- *of a cant hook*, Kantring;
- *of a chain*, Kettenring;
- *of the piston*, Kolbenring;
- *rope*, Taustopper; - *stopper*, Kattstopper; - *tail*, 1.
Baumleesegel; 2.Brotwinner;
- - *boom*, Spiere des Brotwinners; - - *mast*, Treiber-
mast; - *up the anchor*, den
Ankerring bis an den Kranbalken ziehen.

rip, Kabbelung; - *off planks*, die Haut von den Planken abtrennen; - *open*, auftrennen; - *up an old vessel*, ein altes Schiff abwracken.

ripping adze, Brechdeißel; - *chisel*, Schroteisen; - *iron*, Nahthaken.

ripple, kochen, kabbeln, kräuseln.

ripples, Kräuselung.

rippling, Kabbelung.

ripps, Stromrippling.

rise and fall, Steigen und Fallen; - *of a floor*, Aufkimmung einer Bodenwrange; - *rise! Reise! Reise!* (Weckruf).

rising floor timbers, eingezogene Bauchstücke; - *line*, Flursente; - *main*, Druckrohr; - *of a boat*, Duchtenwäger eines Bootes; - *of a star*, Aufgang eines Gestirns; - *of the floor* od. - *of the floor timbers amidships*, die Aufkimmung der Bodenwrangen; - *of the tide*, das Steigen der Flut; - *of the timbers*, das Aufsteigen der Inhölzer; - *of the water*, das Anschwellen des Wassers; - *scaffold bridge*, Bumbam; - *tide*, steigende Tide; - *timber*, eingezogenes Bauchstück; - *wood of a keel*, Gegenkiel.

river barge, Flußbarke; - *bed*, F-bett; - *boat*, F-boot; - *channel*, Fahrwasser; - *craft*, Flußfahrzeug; - *harbour*, F-hafen; - *navigation*, F-schifffahrt; - *pilot*, F-lotse; - *police*, F-polizei; - *regulating*, Stromregulierung; - *risk*, Versicherung für Flußtransport; - *ship*, F-schiff; - *steamer*, F-dampfer; - *wall*, Ufermauer.

rivered, mit Flüssen versehen.

riveret, Flüßchen.

rivet, nieten, Niete; - *bolt*, Klinkbolzen; - *hole*, Nietenloch; - *iron*, Nieteisen; -

plate, N-blech; - *stamp*, N-kopfmacher; - *steel*, Nietenstahl; - *work*, Vernietung.

riveter, Nieter.

riveting, Nietung, Vernietung; - *hammer*, Niethammer; - *machine*, N-presse; - *punch*, N-eisen.

roach, Fußgillung.

road, Reede; - *of refuge*, Zufluchtsreede.

roader see roadster.

roadstead, Reede.

roadster, 1. ein auf der Reede liegendes Schiff; 2. Küstenfahrer.

roam the sea, auf der See umherschweifen.

roar, brausen, brüllen.

roaring forties, Strich des Atlant. Ozeans zwischen 40 und 50⁰ nördl. Breite.

roband stitch, Rahbändselstek.

robands, *robbens*, *robbins*, Anschlagbindsel.

rock, 1. Klippe; 2. wiegen; - *elm wood*, Steinulmenholz; - *island*, Klippeninsel; - *maple wood*, Zuckerahornholz; - *steep to*, die steil aufsteigende Klippe.

rocker keel, vorn und hinten nach oben gekrümmter Kiel.

rockered, vorn und hinten nach oben gekrümmt.

rocket, Rakete; - *signal*, Raketensignal.

rocking lever, oszillierender Hebel; - *shaft*, oszillierende Welle; - - *bearing*, Pumpenbalanzieraxenlager; - - *brasses*, Balanzieraxen - Lagerschalen; - - *gudgeon brasses*, B.-Zapfen-L.; - - *journal*, Lagerzapfen der B.

rocky bottom, felsiger Grund.

rod, Stange; - *collar*, Stopfbüchsendeckel; - *iron*, Bundeisen.

Rodger's anchor, R.-Anker.

rogue's yarn, der rote Faden im Tau.

roll up, aufrollen.

rolled iron, Walzeisen; - *plates,* gewalzte Platten; - *steel,* Walzstahl.

roller, 1. Laufrolle; 2. Roller (hohe rollende Dünung); - *flag,* Warnungsflagge; - *of the cable,* Rollbank.

rolling, rollen, schlingern; - *and tossing of the sea,* das Hin- und Herwogen der See; - *chock,* 1. Kimmkiel, Schlingerkiel; 2. Rackklampe; - *circle,* der von Schaufelrädern beschriebene Kreis; - *cleat,* Rackklampe; - *friction,* rollende Reibung; - *hitch,* Rollstich; - *rope,* Stoßtaljentau; - *swell,* die lange, rollende Dünung; - *tackle,* Rolltakel.

rollocks, Rojeklampen.

rombowline, unbrauchbares Segeltuch und Tauwerk.

roof, Bedachung.

room, Raum, Kammer, Saal.

roomer, Schiff mit viel Gelaß.

rope, 1. anlieken; 2. Liek (eines Segels); 3. Tau; - *bands,* Anschlagsbändsel; - *fender,* Taufender; - *is stranded,* eine Ducht im Tau ist gebrochen; - *ladder,* Sturmleiter; - *maker,* Reepschläger; - *mat,* Taumatte; - *messenger,* T-kabelar; - *packing,* T-pakkung; - *rides,* das T. läuft unklar; -'s *end,* T-ende; - *sling,* T-stropp; - *stopper,* T-stopper; - *strop,* T-stropp; - *stropped block,* taugestroppter Block; - *yarn,* Kabelgarn; - - *knot,* K.-knoten.

ropery, Reepschlägerei.

roping needle, Lieknadel; - *palm,* Segelhandschuh; - *twine,* Liekgarn.

rose, 1. Saugesieb; 2. Windrose; - *boxes,* Brausen; - *knot,* Rosenlaschung; - *lashing,* R-zurring; - *plate,* Saugesieb; - *seizing,* Rosenbindselung; - *sponge,* Seiher für Pumpenrohre; - *wood,* Rosenholz.

rotary, drehend; - *engine,* rotierende Maschine; - *motion,* r. Bewegung; - *pump,* Rotationspumpe; - *speed,* Umdrehungsgeschwindigkeit.

rotation, Drehung, Umdrehung.

rotator, Logschraube.

rotten stone, Tripelstein; - *row,* die Reihe abgetakelter alter Schiffe.

rough, 1. stürmisch; 2. unbehauen; - *mast,* unbehauener Mast; - *sea,* grobe See; - *spar,* unbehauene Spiere; - *timber,* u. Holz; - *tree,* 1. Schanzkleidreling; 2. unbearbeitete Spiere; - - *rail,* Schanzkleidreling; - - *spar,* unbehauene Spiere; - - *stanchion* od. *timber,* Schanzkleidstütze; - *weather,* stürmisches Wetter.

round, runden; - *a cape,* ein Kap umsegeln; - *and hollow cleats,* Sorrklampen; - *charter,* Rundreise-Befrachtung; - *chisel,* Stielmeißel; - *down of a beam,* die Niederbucht eines Deckbalkens; *to - down,* nach unten überholen; - *file,* runde Feile; - *house,* Deckhaus; - *in,* einholen, aufholen; - *linked chain,* weite Ringkette; - *nose chisel,* Hohlkehlmeißel; - *of a beam,* Bucht eines Balkens; - *policy,* Rundreisepolice; - *ribbed,* mit rundem Boden; - *seizing,* Kreuzbindsel; - - *with a crossing* od. *with cross turns,* K.; - *sennit,* Rundplatting; - *sheered,* mit gutem Sprung gebaut; - *splice,* glatte Splissung; - *stern,* rundes Heck; - *the world,* die Welt umsegeln; - *timber,* Rundholz; *to - to,* beidrehen; - *top,* Mastkorb; - *turn in the hawse,* Rundtörn in den Ketten; *to - up,* vom Winde abhalten; - - - *the slack of a tackle,* das Lose einer

hängenden Talje aufholen; *a - voyage*, Rundreise; - *wood*, Rundholz. *rounded gunwale*, gerundeter Schergang; - - *plate*, Platte eines gerundeten Scherganges; - - *plating*, Platten e. g. S.; - - - *of bridge*, P. e. g. S. des Brückenhauses; - - - *of forecastle*, P. e. g. S. der Back; - - - *of poop*, P. e. g. S. der Hütte; - *hammer*, Kehlhammer. *rounding*, 1. Rundung, Bucht (im Schiffsholze); 2. Schladding, Wuhling (Tau zum Umwickeln); - *down*, Niederbucht; - *in*, Einbucht; - *of the beam*, Balkenkrümmung; - *out*, Ausbucht; - *seizing*, Plattbindsel; - *to*, anluven; - *up*, 1. Aufbucht od. Krümmung der Balken nach oben; 2. die Blöcke näher zusammen bringen.
roundly, willig (beim Fieren).
rounds, Stufen einer Bootsleiter.
rouse, anholen, steifholen; - *block*, großer Fußblock; *to - in* od. *up*, rasch holen.
rousing, holen.
routine, Routine (Diensteinteilung); - *book*, D.-sbuch.
rove, durchgeschoren, eingeschoren.
roven, 1. Rahband; 2. durchgeschoren; - *about*, umherschweifend.
row, to -, rudern, rojen; - *all at once*, alle zugleich r.; - *dry*, nicht Wasser werfen; - *long stroke*, lang rudern; - *short stroke*, kurzen Schlag r.; - *standing*, stehend r.
row barge, Ruderbarke; - *board*, Rojeplatte; - *boat*, Ruderboot; - *galley*, Ruderschiff; - *lock*, R-gabel; - *of rivets*, Nietenreihe; - *peg*, R-pflock; - *plate*, Rojeplatte; - *port*, R-pforte; - *stringer*, R-leiste.

rowel, Rolle des Kolderstocks.
rowing barge, Ruderbarke; - *championship*, Meisterschaftsrudern; - *club*, Ruderklub; - *galley*, R-schiff; - *gear*, R-apparat; - *guard*, Hafenwachtboot; - *match*, Wettrudern.
rowl, Löschrad.
royal, Royal; - *backstay*, R-Pardune; - *brace*, R-brasse; - *bunt line*, R-Bauchgording; - *clew line*, R-Geitau; - *cross tree*, R-Sahling; - *foot rope*, R-pferd; - *gear*, R-geschirr; - *halliard* od. *r. h. purchase*, R-fall; - *lift*, R-toppenant; - *mast*, R-stenge; - - *fid*, R-s-Schloßholz; - - *hole*, R-s-S.-gatt; - *mast head*, R-topp; - *m. pole*, Flaggentopp der R-stenge; - *rigging*, R-wanten; - *sheet*, R-schote; - *stay*, R-stag; - *staysail*, R-Stagsegel; - - *downhaul*, R-S.-Niederholer; - - *halliard*, R-S.-fall; - - *sheet*, R-S.-schote; - - *tack*, R-S.-hals; - *studding sail*, R-Leesegel; - - - *boom*, R-L.-spiere; - - - *downhaul*, R-L.-Niederholer; - - - *halliard*, R-L.-fall; - - - *sheet*, R-L.-schote; - - - *tack*, R-L.-hals; - - - *yard*, R-L.-rahe; - *top*, R-topp; - *topgallant mast*, Oberbramstenge; - *yard*, Royalrahe; - - *man*, Oberbramgast; - - *parrel*, Rack der Royalrahe; - - *rope*, Royaljolle; - - *tripping line*, Royal-Niederholer.
rubber, 1. Armfeile; 2. Gummi, Kautschuk; - *for packing*, Dichtungsgummi; - *hose*, Gummischlauch; - *joint*, G-dichtung; - *mop*, Wischer mit breiter G-platte; - *packing*, G-packung; - *ring*, G-ring.
rubbing, Reibung; - *batten*, Stoßschale; - *paunch* od. *punch*, Schalung des Mastes; - *strake*, Wallschiene, Scheu-

erleiste, Reibholz; - *surface,* Reibungsfläche.

rubble ice, loses Packeis.

rudder, Ruder, Steuer; - *arms,* Ruderarme; - *back,* R-hacke; - *bands.* R-scheren; - *bearings,* R-Fingerlinge und Fußzapfen; - *brace,* R-öse od. R-schere; - - *bolt,* R-scherenbolzen; - *brake,* Armstopper; - *breeching,* der Ruderlichter; - *bushes,* R-büchsen; - *carriage,* R-lager; - *case* od. *casing,* R-koker; - *chains,* Sorgketten; - *chalder,* Ruderschere; - *chocks,* R-klicks; - *coat,* R-kragen; - *commands,* R-kommandos; - *frame,* R-rahmen; - *gear,* R-geschirr; - *gudgeon,* R-öse; - *hanger,* Vorrichtung zum Einhaken des Steuerruders; - *head,* Ruderkopf; - - *gland,* R-deckel; - - *hoop,* R.-band; - - *plate,* Fischungsplatte des Ruders; - *heel,* Ruderhacke; - *hole,* Ruderkopfloch; - *horn,* R-horn; - *house,* R-haus; - *irons,* R-beschlag; - *less,* ohne Steuerruder; - *lines,* Ruderseile; - *lock,* R-schloß; - *mould,* R-mall; - *nails,* R-nägel; - *partner,* R-fischung; - *pendant,* Sorgleine; - *chain,* S.-kette; - *pintle,* Ruderfingerling; - - *bolt,* R.-bolzen; - - *scores.* Ausschnitte für die R.-e; - - *straps,* Fingerlingfeder; - *plating,* Ruderbeplattung; - *port,* R-kopfloch; - *post,* Hintersteven; - *pressure,* Ruderdruck; - *rake,* Schegg des Ruders; - *rivet,* Ruderniete; - *shaft,* R-herz; - *stay,* Quersteg des Ruderrahmens; - *stock,* R-pfosten; - *stopper,* R-lichter; - *stops,* R-knaggen; - *strap,* R-stropp; - *surface,* R-fläche; - *tackle,* R-talje; - *tiller,* R-pinne; - *trunk,* R-koker.

ruffled sea, kräuselnder Seegang.

rules of the road, Seestraßenrecht.

rumbowline, Lodding.

rumbowling, geringwertig.

rummage, 1. Umstauung; 2. durchstöbern.

rummager, 1. Umstauer; Durchstöberer.

run. 1. Scharf des Hinterschiffes; 2. zurückgelegte Distanz; *by the -,* für die Überfahrt angemustert.

run, to - a little changed, ein wenig unklar laufen; - *aground,* auf Grund laufen; - *ahead of one's reckoning,* mit seinem Besteck zurück sein; - *ashore,* auf Strand laufen; - *by the lead,* beim Fahren fortwährend loten; - *clear,* klar fahren; - *close upon the wind,* dicht beim Winde segeln; - *down and sunk,* gerammt und in den Grund gebohrt; - *down another ship,* ein anderes Schiff ansegeln; - *down latitude,* Breite machen; - *end for end,* ganz aus dem Block laufen; - *fair,* ruhig werden; - *foul,* 1. unklar laufen; 2. ansegeln, zusammenstoßen; - *full,* raumsegeln; - *high,* hohl gehen; - *hot,* warmlaufen; - *in a rope,* ein Tau einlaufen; - *in lead, &c.,* mit Blei etc. vergießen; - *in the slack of a rope,* das Lose einer Trosse einholen; - *into a vessel,* ein Schiff ansegeln; - *out a warp,* eine Trosse ausbringen; - *out a kedge,* einen Warpanker ausbringen; - *over the seams,* die Nähte untersuchen; - *short of provisions,* Proviant wird knapp; - *up a tank,* einen Tank vollaufen lassen; - *up a yard,* eine Rahe auflaufen; - *up in the rigging,* in den Wanten aufentern.

rundle head, Kopf od. Trommel der unteren Spillwelle.

rung, 1. Leitersprosse; 2. Bauchstück der Bodenwrange; 3. Dreher eines Steuerrades; - *head*, Oberende einer Bodenwrange.

runner, 1. Läufer (eines Schlafbaases); 2. Mantel (Tau); 3. Vorläufer der Logleine; - *and tackle* od. - *purchase* od. - *tackle*, Manteltakel.

running agreement, die offene d. h. halbjährige Musterrolle; - *block*, laufender Block; - *bowline*, laufender Ptahlstich; - - *knot*, laufender P.; - *bowsprit*, einlaufendes Bugspriet; - *days for loading*, laufende Ladezeit inclus. Sonntags; - *end of a rope*, Widerhalttau; - *eye*, laufendes Auge; - *gear*, laufendes Gut; - *hitch*, laufender Knoten; - *in bowsprit*, Bugspriet zum Einlaufen; - *knot*, laufender Knoten; - *lights*, Warnungsfeuer; - *part of a tackle*, laufender Part eines Takels; - *rigging*, laufendes Gut; *the* - - *leads fair*, das laufende G. fährt gut.

rupture, Bruch; - *of shaft*, Wellenbruch.

Russian duck, russisches Segeltuch; - *sheeting*, Schiertuch.

rust, Rost, rosten; - *preventive*, R-schutzanstrich; - *proof*, rostsicher; - *putty*, Eisenkitt; - - *joint*, E.-dichtung.

rut of the sea, Wellenschlag; - *of the shore*, Brandung an der Küste.

S.

saccade, das Klappen der Segel gegen die Masten.

sacrifice, opfern, Opfer: *at a -*, aufs Spiel setzen.

sad weather, schlechtes Wetter.

saddle, Klampe; - *back bunker hatchway*, Mittelbunkerluke; - *crutch*, Hohlklampe; - *of a boom*, Baumkragen; - *of the bowsprit*, Backen des Bugspriets; - *of a jib boom*, Sattel eines Klüverbaums.

safe anchorage, sicherer Ankerplatz; - *arrival*, wohlbehaltene Ankunft; - *conduct*, Sicherheitspaß; - *port*, sicherer Hafen; - *road*, sichere Reede.

safety buoy, Rettungsboje; - *collars*, Sicherungsring; - *device*, Sicherung; - *keel*, Sicherheitskiel; - *lamp*, S-h-lampe; - *lock*, S-h-schloß; - *pin*, S-h-pinne; - *ring*, Sicherungsring; - *space*, Kofferdamm; - *stud*, Sicherungsstift; - *valve*, Sicherheitsventil; - - *box*, S.-gehäuse; - - *cover*, S.-deckel; - - *drain pipe*, S.-Entwässerungsrohr; - - *gear*, S.-gestänge; - - *lever*, S.-hebel; - - *load*, S.-belastung; - - *pipe*, S.-rohr; - - *seat*, S.-sitz; - - *spindle*, S.-spindel; - - *spring*, S.-feder; - - *weight*, S.-belastung.

sagged, durchgebogen.

sagging moment, Durchsackmoment; - *to leeward*, Abtrift nach Lee, nach L. abtreibend.

sail, to - before the wind, vor dem Winde segeln; - *by the wind*, beim Winde segeln; - *close hauled*, dicht b. W. s.; - *down*, hinuntersegeln; - *free*, raumschots s.; - *in ballast*, in Ballast s.; - *large*, raumschots s.; - *on a bowline*, mit angeholten Buliens s.; - *on a taught b.*, dicht beim Winde s.; - *on an easy b.*, mit losen Buliens segeln; - *on the wind*, beim Winde s.; - *up*, heraufsegeln; - *upon the anchor*, über den Anker segeln; - *well by the wind* od. *well on a bowline*, gut beim Winde segeln; - *with a flowing sheet* od. *with a fore topsail*, raumschots segeln; - *with both sheets aft* od. *with a stern wind*, platt vor dem Winde s.; - *with a quartering wind*, mit Backstagswind s.; - *with the wind abeam*, mit halbem Winde s.

sail binn, Segelkoje; - *burton*, S-takel; - *cloth*, S-tuch; - *cover*, S-bezug; - *drill*, S-exerzieren; - *duck*, S-tuch; - *exercise*, S-exerzieren; - *hook*,S-macherhaken; - *hoop*, Mastband; - *locker*, Segelkoje; - *loft*, Segelmacher-Werkstatt; - *maker*, S.; - -'s *mate*, S.-maat; - -'s *splice*, S.-Splissung; - *needle*, Segelnadel; - *netting*, Finknetz des Stagsegels; - *room*, Segelkammer; - - *door*, S.-tür; -*tackle*,Segeltakel; -*trimmer*, S-trimmer; - *twine*, S-garn; - *yard*, S-stange.

sailer, Segelschiff.

sailing, segeln, navigieren; - *boat*, Segelboot; - *craft*, S-fahrzeug; - *dates*, Abfahrtstage; - *directions*, Segelanweisungen; - *evolutions*, Evolutionen unter Segel; - *ice*, mürbes Eis; - *instructions*, Segelanweisungen; - *list*, Fahrplan; - *master*, Navigationsoffizier; - *match*, Wettsegeln; - *navigation*, Segelschiffahrt; - *on a parallel of latitude*, im Breitenparallel segeln; - *orders*, Abfahrtsbefehl; - *qualities*,Segeleigenschaften; - *tactics*, Segeltaktik; - *trawler*, Fischsegler; - *trim*,

Segelfähigkeit; - *vessel*, Segelschiff; - *yacht*, S-jacht.

sailings, Abfahrten.

sailless, ohne Segel.

sailor, Matrose, Seemann; - *boy*, Schiffsjunge; - *fashion* od. - *like*, seemäßige Art; *a bad* -, leicht seekrank werden.

sailor's bag, Matrosensack; - *book*, Seefahrtsbuch; - *chest*, Matrosenkiste; - *custom*, Seemannsbrauch; - *home*, S-m-heim; - *parlance*, S-m-sprache.

sails, Segelage ; - *were flapping the mast*, die Segel schlugen gegen den Mast.

saline deposit, Salzniederschlag.

salinometer,Salzgehaltmesser; - *cock*, S.-hahn.

sally port, 1. Ausfalltor; 2. Bootshafen.

saloon, Salon; - *accommodations*, S.-Einrichtung; - *steamer*, S.-dampfer.

salt, tüchtiger alter Seemann; - *beef*,gesalzenes Rindfleisch; - *box* od. - *case*, Salzdose; - *eel*, Tauende; - *junk*, zähes Salzfleisch; - *provisions*, gesalzener Proviant; - *stops*, Salzpfropfen; - *water*, S-wasser.

salvage, Bergung; - *agreement*, Bergungskontrakt; - *association*, B-g-gesellschaft; - *bond*, B-g-kontrakt; - *claim*, Anspruch auf Bergelohn; - *law*, Strandungsordnung; - *money*, Bergelohn; - *remuneration*, B.; - *right*, Strandrecht; - *steamer*, Bergungsdampfer.

salvagee, Eigner einer geborgenen Ladung.

salvager, Strandwächter.

salver od. *salvor*, Berger.

sampan, Sampankahn.

sampling order, Ermächtigung zum Probenziehen; - *stick*, P-stecher; - *tube*, P-stechheber.

samsons post, Simsonspfosten.
sand, Sand, Watt; - *bagger*,
Segler mit Sandballast; -
ballast, S-b-; - *bank*, Sandbank; - *glass*, S-glas; - *passing through after gland*,
durch den hintern Deckel
kam Sand; - *pump dredger*,
S-pumpenbagger; - *ridge*, S-
rücken; - *spit*, S-zunge; -
strake, S-strak; - *warpt*, durch
die Gezeit auf eine S-bank
gesetzt.
sanding up, versanden.
sands, Sandbank.
sandy bottom, Sandgrund.
sanitary pipe, Rohr für hygienische Zwecke; - *pump*,
Pumpe f. h. Z.
sap wood, Sapanholz.
Sargasso Sea, Sargassomeer.
satin wood, Atlasholz.
sattie, großes Frachtschiff im
Mittelmeer.
saturate, sättigen.
saturated steam, gesättigter
Dampf.
saturation, Sättigung.
saucer, Spur des Gangspills.
save, abbergen, bergen, retten;
- *all*, Ölfänger; - *alls*, Schutz-
tücher.
saved cargo, geborgene Ladung.
saving of weight, Gewichts-
ersparnis; - *raft*, Rettungsfloß.
saw, Säge; - *file*, S.-feile.
scale, 1. Maßstab; 2. Kesselstein; 3. abpicken; - *of pressure*, Druckskala.
scaling hammer, Pickhammer;
- *tools*, P-werkzeug.
scant wind, knapper Wind.
scanting, schralen.
scantling, 1. Materialstärke,
Profil; 2. die Vorzeichnung
auf dem Werkstück; - *of
frames*, Breite und Dicke
der Spanten.
scaphander, Taucherrüstung.
scarcity of provisions, Pro-
viantmangel.
scarf od. *scarph*, laschen, an-

laschen, verscherben; La-
schung, Verlaschung, Scher-
be; - *bolt*, Verscherbungsbolzen; *to - up upon a
stump*, einkluften; - *weld*,
Schweißung durch Über-
lappung.
scaze, to -, Kreuzung legen.
scend, das Stampfen und Aufsteigen des Vorderschiffs.
scheme of scantling, Bauvor-
schrift.
schooner, Schoner; - *rig*, S.-
Takelung; - *smack*, als S.
getakelte Schmack.
scintillating light, Funkelfeuer.
scoop, 1. Schaufel, Ösfaß,
schaufeln; 2. Gießer.
scope, die ausgesteckte Kette.
score, 1. Rille, Rinne, Kerbe;
2. Spur; 3. Einschnitt (der
Rolle); 4. schrammen.
Scotch coffee, gekochtes Wasser mit geröstetem Zwie-
back; - *man*, Schamfielungslatte; - *mist*, feuchter Nebel.
scour, schrubben, scheuern;
- *the coast*, längs der Küste
fahren.
scourge, neunschwänzige
Katze.
scout, Schute.
scow house, Arche.
scrap iron, Alteisen; - *log*,
Decknotizen; - *steel*, Bruch-
stahl.
scrape, schrapen; - *along*, entlang schrammen; - *over the
ground*, über den Grund
schurren.
scraper, Schabeisen, Schraper.
scraping iron, Kratzeisen.
screen, Schirm, Vorhang; -
bulkhead, Schutzschott; -
casing, S-umhüllung.
screens, Schutzwände.
screw, 1. Schraube, schrauben; 2. Spindel des Steuergeräts; - *alley*, Schraubentunnel; - *aperture*, S-brunnen; - *blade*, S-flügel; - *bolt*,
S-bolzen; - - *nut*, S-b-mutter;
- - *stay*, S-b-steg; - *brake*, S-

bremse; - - *nut*, Bremsmutter; - *cargo steamer*, Schrauben-Frachtdampfer; - *cutting machine*, S. - Schneidemaschine; - *dies*, Schraubenbakken: - - *and stocks*, doppelte Schraubenschneidekluppen; - *dock*, hydraulisches Dock; - *down*, anziehen, festschrauben, zuschrauben; - *driver*, Schraubenzieher; - *fan*, Zentrifugalventilator; - *gammoning*, Bugsprietbügel; - *hoop*, Schraubband; - *key*, Schraubenschlüssel; - *life boat*, S.-rettungsboot; - *lifting gear*, S-hebevorrichtung; - *off*, losschrauben; - *passage*, Schraubentunnel; - *pin shackle*, S-bolzenschäkel; - *plate*, Gewindeschneideeisen; - *post*, Propellersteven; - *propeller*, Schiffsschraube; - *propulsion*, Fortbewegung durch Schrauben; - *race*, Schraubenbrunnen; - *rudder*, S-ruder; - *saloon and cargo steamer*, Schrauben-Salon- und Frachtdampfer; - *shackle*, Schraubenbügel; - *shaft*, S-welle; - - *pipe*. Stevenrohr; - - - *bulkhead*, Stopfbüchsenschott; - *shaft tunnel*, Schraubenwellentunnel; - *steam engine*, S-schiffsmaschine; - *steamer*, S-dampfer; - *stock*, Nietkolben; - *tap*. Schraubenbohrer; - *tool*, Schraubstahl; - *tug*, Schraubenschleppdampfer; - *up*, die Schraube anziehen; - - *the wind. lass*, das Ankerspill zusammenschrauben; - *vice*, Schraubstock; - - *pinchers*, Schraubenkloben; - *well*, S-brunnen; - *with variable pitch*, Schraube mit verstellbaren Flügeln; - *wrench*, Schraubenschlüssel.
screwed stay. Stehbolzen.
screwing machine, Schraubenschneidemaschine; - *tool*, Schraubstahl.

scrimshanker, Drückeberger.
scrimshaw, Schnitzwerk.
scrive board, Bretter zum Aufreißen der Umrisse eines Schiffes.
scroll head, die Krull; - *wheel*, Schneckenrad.
scrub, schrubben; - *broom*, Schrubbesen; - *gang*, Deck-schrubber-Abteilung.
scrubber, Schrubber.
scruff, Bart eines Schiffes.
scud, leichtes Dunstgewölk; *to* -, lenzen; - *away*, ausreißen; - *under bare poles*, vor Topp und Takel lenzen.
scull, wriggen, Wrickriemen.
sculler boat, Nachenfähre.
scullerage, Ewerführerlohn.
sculling, wricken; - *oar*, Wrickriemen.
scum, abschäumen; - *cock*, Schaumhahn; - *dish*, S-löffel; - *of the sea*, Triftholz u Schaum; - *pipe*, Schlammrohr; - *valve*, Salzablaßventil.
scupper od. - *hole*, Speigat; - *hose*, S.-schlauch; - *leather*, S.-leder; - *nail*, Presennignagel; - *pipe*, Speigatrohr; - *plug*, S-g-pflock; - *shoot*, S-g-röhre; - *valve*, S-g-klappe.
scuttle a ship, ein Schiff wegsetzen.
scuttle, 1. Fenster, F-loch; 2. kleine Luke; - *butt*, Trinkwassertonne; - *cap*, Springluke; - *cask*, Trinkwassertonne; - *frame*, Fensterrahmen; - *hatch*, Deckel einer kleinen Luke.
scuttling, anbohren.
sea, See, Seegang, Sturzsee; - *anchor*, Seeanker; - *biscuit*, Schiffszwieback; - *boat*, Seeschiff; - *borne*, von See kommend; - *bow*, Regenbogen von Flugwasser; - *breach*, Klopfsee; - *bread*, Schiffszwieback; - *breakers*, Brandung; - *breaking*, Dwarssee; - *breeze*, Seebrise; - *brief*, Seepaß; - *cable*, S-kabel;

- *cap*, 1. Schaum; 2. Südwester; - *card*, Windrose;
- *carriage*, Seetransport; -
chart, S-karte; - *chest*, See-
mannskiste; - *clam*, Klammer der Lotleine; - *coast*,
Küste; - - *cable*, Küsten-
kabel; - *cock*, Bodenhahn;
- *compass*, Seekompaß; -
connections, Unterwasser-
teile; - *cook*, Schiffskoch;
- *craft*, oberster Plankengang; - *cunny*, indischer
Steuermann; - *current*, See-
strömung; - *damage*, See-
schaden; - *day*, S-tag; - *drag*,
Anhängsel eines Schiffes;
- *drift*, Seetrift; - *faring
man*, Seefahrer; - *f. nation*,
seefahrende Nation; - *foam*,
Seeschaum; - *folk*, S-leute;
- *gait*, langes Wellental; -
gasket, Beschlagzeising: -
gate, 1. Seeschleuse; 2. lange
rollende Dünung; *in a - -*,
von einer Welle gegen einander geworfen; - *gauge*,
Wassertracht; - *going*, see-
gehend; - - *vessel*, Seeschiff;
- *injection*, See-Injektion;
- - *strainer*, S-I.-Saugesieb;
- - *valve*, S-I.-Ventil; - -
water, S-I.-Wasser; - *lawyer*,
rechthaberischer Seemann;
- *lead*, Tieflot; *to have -
legs*, Seefüße haben; - *letter*,
Seebrief; - *level*, Meeres-
spiegel; - *light*, Seeleuchte;
- *line*, Meereshorizont; - *log*,
Seejournal; - *making*, der
Seegang nimmt zu; - *man*,
Matrose, Seemann; - *man-
like style*, seemännische Art;
- *manship*, Seefahrerkunst;
- *marks*, S-zeichen; - *navigation*, S-schiffahrt; - *pass*,
S-paß; - *pay*, Sold; - *pie*,
gesalzenes Fleisch und Ge-
müse; - *pilot*, Seelotse; -
policy, Schiffspolize; - *port*,
Seehafen; - *protest*, Verklarung; - *provisions*, Dauer-
proviant; - *quake*, Seebeben;
- *rate*, Gang (des Chrono-

meters); - *reach*, der sich in
das Meer ergießende Teil
eines Flusses; - *risk*, Seegefahr; - *roke*, S-rauch; -
room, S-raum; *to get - -*, die
hohe See gewinnen; *to have
- -*, auf der hohen S. sein;
- *shore*, Seegestade; - *sick*,
seekrank; - *sickness*, See-
krankheit; - *side*, S-ufer;
- *stock* od. *stores*, S-vorräte;
- *suction cock*, S-hahn; -
timber, Schiffsbauholz; -
tossed, von der See umhergeworfen; - *trade*, S-handel;
- *traffic*, S-verkehr; - *trip*,
S-fahrt; - *turn*, 1. ein Gang
nach S. zu; 2. S-wind; -
valve, Bodenventil; - *view*,
1. Seeansicht; 2. S-aussicht;
- *voyage*, S-reise; - *wall*, S-
deich, S-mauer; - *ward*, seewärts; - *watch*, S-wache;
- *water tank*, S-wasserkasten;
- *way*, S-gang; - *weeds*, S-
tang; - *wolf*, Kaperschiff;
- *worm*, Seewurm; - *worthiness*, S-tüchtigkeit; -
worthy, seetüchtig.
seal the hatches, die Luken
dicht kalfatern; *to put a -
on the mast*, an die Kette
legen.
sealer, Robbenfänger.
sealing vessel, Robbenfänger.
seam, Naht; - *with butt straps*,
Fuge mit Überdeckungs-
platten.
seaming needle, Nähnadel.
seamless tube, nahtloses Rohr.
search light, Scheinwerfer.
seasoned wood, lufttrockenes
Holz.
seat of a cock, Sitz eines
Hahns; - - - *valve*, Ventilsitz;
- *of ease*, Abort; - *of the
fire*, Herd des Feuers; - *of
water*, Lage des Schiffes im
Wasser; - *locker*, Kasten-
bank; - *valve*, Doppelsitzventil.
seating, 1. Fundament; 2. Lager
(d. h. der auf dem Kiele

ruhende Teil des Schiffs-
bodens).
second awning, oberes Sonnensegel; - *bower*, der tägliche
Buganker; - *dog watch*,
Abendwache; - *hawser*,
Pferdeleine; - *hand*, 1. alt;
2. zweiter Maat; - *mate*, z.
M.; - *preventer stay*, Schlin-
gerstag; - *reef*, zweites Reff;
- - *band*, z. R-band.
section, Durchschnitt.
sectional boiler, Gliederkessel;
- *dock*, Sektionsdock.
sector, 1. Sektor; 2. Spurkulisse (der Exzenterstange).
secunny, indischer Steuermannsmaat.
secure, befestigen, festmachen;
- *a mast*, einen Mast versichern; - *a rope*, ein Tau
feststecken; - *the anchor*,
den Anker zurren; - *the dead
eyes*, die Jungfern einbinden;
- *the end of a zeising*, einen
Bindsel besetzen; - *the hatches*, die Luken versichern;
- *the yards with chains*, die
Rahen mit Ketten fangen;
- *with a bolt*, verbolzen; -
with woodwork, verschalen.
sediment, Kesselstein, Niederschlag; - *cock*, Schlamm-
hahn; - *collector*, S-sammler.
seeling, schlingern.
segment of a sphere, Kugel-
abschnitt.
seine boat, Fischerboot mit
Schleppnetz.
seining ground, die mit dem
Schleppnetz bedeckte Stelle.
seize, 1. zurren; 2. aufbringen,
kapern; - *a block on a stay*,
einen Block an ein Stag
nähen; - *two bights* (od.
eyes) *of ropes together* od.
- *two ropes end on end*, die
Buchten zweier Taue an-
einander nähen; - *up*, fest-
schnallen.
seizing, Bindsel, Sorrtau,
Zeising; - *stuff*, Bindselgnt;
- *wire*, Drahtbindsel.

seizure, Beschlagnahme.
self acting feeding apparatus,
selbsttätiger Speiseapparat;
s. a. f. means, selbsttätige
Speisevorrichtung; *s. a. lubricator*, Selbstöler; *s. a.
stoker*, selbstwirkende Feuerung; - *closing valve*, Selbstschlußventil; - *feeding apparatus*, selbsttätige Speisevorrichtung; - *feeding
furnace*, s. Feuerbüchse; -
lubricating bearing, selbst-
schmierendes Lager; - *oiling
blocks*, selbstölende Blöcke;
- *stowing bower*, stockloser
Buganker.
selvage, der blaue Einstrich
im Segeltuch.
selvaged, mit Sahlleiste versehen.
selvagee od. - *strop*, Garnstropp; - *tail*, Steert mit zu-
sammengemarlten Garnen.
selvedge see selvage.
semaphore, Küstentelegraph.
semi box beam, Kastenbalken;
- - - *angle bar*, K.-winkel.
semicircular deviation, die
halbkreisartige Deviation.
send down, herunterbringen;
- *in a door, &c.*, eine Tür etc.
einschlagen; - *up*, aufbringen.
sending, das Vorderschiff
tauchte tief unter.
sennit, Platting; - *eye*, P.-auge.
sensible heat, empfundene
Hitze.
sentinel valve, Alarmventil.
separation cloths, Separations-
tücher.
serang, indischer Bootsmann.
serious damage, schwere Beschädigung.
serro motor, Umsteuerungsmaschine.
serve a rope, ein Tau bekleiden.
serves, the tide -, die Flut tritt
ein.
service, 1. Dienst; 2. Verkehr;
3. Kleidung eines Taues;
- *boat*, Arbeitsboot; - *cock*,
Zweighahn; - *pipe*, Z-rohr;

to take off the - of a rope, ein Tau abkleiden.
serviceable, brauchbar; - *stores,* b-b-e Seevorräte.

serving, Bekleidung; - *board,* Kleidspan; - *hammer* od. - *mallet,* Kleidkeule.

set, setzen; - *course,* Kurs s.; - *down the rigging,* das stehende Gut niedersetzen; *s. d. t. sheets,* die Schoten n.; *s. d. t. ship's position on the chart,* den Schiffsort nach der Seekarte feststellen; *s. d. t. tack,* den Hals niedersetzen; - *in,* einsetzen, eintreten; - *out,* aufbrechen, aussetzen; - *over board,* außenbords setzen; - *sail,* Segel setzen; unter S. gehen; - *the land,* das Land peilen; - *the log,* das Log stellen; - *the stays of a mast,* einen Mast stagen; - *the watch,* die Wache aufsetzen; - *up the rigging,* das stehende Gut aufsetzen; *the current - us to the north,* der Strom versetzte uns nach Norden.

set, How will the ebb -? Wohin setzt die Ebbe? *The tide sets to the south,* die Flut läuft nach Süden; *the current sets westward,* der Strom setzt nach West.

set of a current, Richtung der Strömung; - *of flags,* Stellflaggen; - *of riveters,* Nieterkolonne; - *of sails,* ein Gestell Segel; - *of timbers,* ein Satz Inhölzer; - *off,* Absatz; - *screw,* Hemmschraube.

settee, 1. Kanapee; 2. Settie (2mast. türk. Barke).

settie sail, Schebeckensegel.

setting, regulieren; - *boom,* Ausleger; - *fid,* Kegel zum Weiten der Reffsegel; - *of the current,* Stromrichtung; - *of the safety valves,* Sicherheitsventil-Regulierung; - *of the slide v.,* Schieber-R.; - *pole,* 1. Bootshaken; 2. Setz-

stange; - *tide,* Anfang der Flut.

settle down, sacken; - *the average,* die Havariekosten decken; - *the halliards,* die Fallen abfieren; - *the land,* das Land aus Sicht verlieren.

settled, vor Anker liegend; - *deck,* ausgetrocknetes Deck; - *down,* 1. gesackt (Schiff); 2. niedergeknickt (Mast); - *weather,* beständiges Wetter; - *wind,* stehender Wind.

sew, auf dem Grunde sitzen; - *the bolt ropes to a sail,* ein Segel anlieken.

sewed, she - four feet while aground, das Schiff war beim Festsitzen 4 Fuß aus der Last gehoben.

sextant, Sextant.

shack lock, Schäkel.

shackle, einschäkeln, Schäkel; - *bolt,* S.-bolzen; - - *pin,* S.-b-stift; - *crow,* Kuhfuß mit Schäkel; - *jack,* Klobenschraube; - *of a chain cable,* Ankerkettenschäkel.

shackled two wires on the cable, wir schäkelten 2 Drahttrossen an die Schlepptrosse.

shade deck, Schattendeck; - - *beam,* S.-balken; - - - *angle bar,* S.-b-winkel; - - - *stringer,* S.-b-stringer; - - - - *plate,* S.-b-s-platte; *s. d. b. tie plate,* S.-b-Lukenstringer; *s. d. hatch,* S.-luke; *s. d. hatchway coaming,* S.-Lukensüll; *s. d. pillar,* S.-stütze; *s. d. rails and stanchions,* S.-geländer; *s. d. stanchions,* S.-G-l-stützen; *s. d. ship,* S.-schiff; *s. d. stringer,* S.-stringer; - - - *angle bar,* S.-s-winkel; - - - *inner a. b.,* Innenwinkel des S.-s-; - - - *plate,* S.-Stringerplatte; *s. d. vessel,* S.-schiff; *s. d. waterway,* S.-Wassergang.

shaft, Welle; - *alley,* Schrauben-Wellengang; - *bearing,*

Wellenlager; - *coupling*, W-kuppelung; - *hole of propeller*, Schraubengat; - - - - *post*, Auge des Schraubenstevens; - *journal*, Halszapfen der Welle; - *key way*, Wellenkeilnute; - *of steering gear*, Welle des Steuergeräts; - *of the anchor*, Ankerschaft; - *trunk*, - *tunnel*, Wellentunnel.

shafting. Wellenleitung.

shake a ship, ein Schiff beim Stapellauf in Gang bringen; - *in the wind*, den Bug so hart an den Wind bringen, daß die Segel killen; - *of a sail*, das Schlagen eines Segels; - *out a reef*, ein Reff ausstecken.

shakes, Risse.

shakings, Abfall von altem Tauwerk.

shallop, Schalupe.

shallow, 1. seicht; 2. Untiefe; - *waisted*, mit glattem Deck gebaut.

sham Abraham, Drückeberger; - *port*, blinde Luke.

shan, schadhafte Stelle an den Spieren.

shank, Gießpfanne; - *of the anchor*, Ankerschaft; - *painter*, Rüstleine; - - *chain*, R.-kette.

shanty, Gesang beim Gangspillwinden.

shape the course for, den Kurs setzen auf . .

shapes hoisted, wir hißten 3 schwarze Bälle, um unser Aufgrundsitzen zu signalisieren.

shaping, das Schneiden und Biegen der Planken; - *machine*, 1. Fräsmaschine; 2. Maschine zum Abdrehen von Blöcken.

share in a vessel, Schiffspart.

sharesman, anteilsberechtigtes Mitglied der Bemannung eines Fischerboots.

shark hook, Haifischhaken;

-'*s mouth*, Mastöffnung im Sonnensegel.

sharp bottom, scharfer Boden; - *bow*, s. Bug; - *floor*, s. Boden; - *keel*, s. Kiel; - *look out before!* Da vorne gut ausgucken! - *on!* Hart anbrassen! - *trimmed*, scharf beim Winde gebraßt; - *up!* Hart anbrassen!

shave, vollbrassen; *a close* -, mit blauem Auge davonkommen.

sheaf, die Schove.

shear see sheer.

shearing force, Scherkraft; - *machine*, S-maschine.

shears, 1. Bock zum Einsetzen der Masten; 2. große Schere; - *of the mast*, Mastenkran.

sheathe a ship, ein Schiff verhäuten; - - - *with boards*, einem S. eine Spiekerhaut geben; - - - *with copper*, e. S. e. Kupferhaut g.

sheathing, Beschlag, Haut; - *copper*, Kupferblech; - *hammer*, Beschlaghammer; - *nail*, Hautspiker; - *of copper*, Kupferhaut; - *of fir boards*, Spiekerhaut; - *paper*, Futterpappe; - *sheet*, Beschlagblech.

sheave, Scheibe; - *hole*, Scheibenloch; - - *for topgallant tye in a topgallant mast*, Bramstengen - Drehreepgat; - - *for top rope in a t. m.*, B.-Windreepgat; - - *f. t. r. in a topmast*, Scheibengat für den Windreep in einer Marsstenge; - - *for topsail tye in a t.*, S. f. d. Drehreep in e. M.; - - *in the bulwarks*, S. im Schanzkleide; - - *of a yard*, S. einer Rahe.

sheep pen, Schafstall; - *shank*, Trompetenstich.

sheer about, umher scheren od. gieren; - *across the current* od. *tide*, quer über den Strom s.; - *alongside*, längsseits s.; - *and nail the rib-*

bands, die Senten s.; - *away* od. - *off*, abgieren; - *home*, vorschoten; - *the decks*, die Decks schlichten; - *up alongside*, längsseits scheren; - *up to the anchor*, auf den Anker scheren.

sheer, Spring od. Sprung eines Schiffes; - *batten*, Spreizlatte; - *draught*, Schiffsplan; - *hook*, Enterhaken; - *hulk*, Bollen; - *lashing*, Kopflaschung der Spieren eines Bocks; - *legs*, Mastenkran; - *line*, Schertau; - *mould*, Mall für den Strak; - *plan*, Seitenriß; - *pole*, 1. Bockstange; 2. Spreizlatte; - *rail*, Leiste des Schandeckels; - *ribband*, Sente; - *sail*, Treibsegel; - *strake*, oberster Plankengang; - *wales*, Berghölzer.

sheer, to give a -, scheren lassen; *ship taking a - against the helm*, das Schiff scherte dem Steuer entgegen aus.

sheered, mit Spring gebaut.

sheers, 1. Mastenkran; 2. Bock zum Einsetzen der Masten; 3. Bockspieren.

sheerstrake, Schergang; - *of bridge*, S. der Brücke; - *of forecastle*, S. d. Back; - *of poop*, S. d. Hütte; - *of raised quarter deck*, S. des erhöhten Quarterdecks; - *plate*, S.-platte.

sheet, 1. Schote; 2. Sitzbank im Boote; 3. Platte; - *anchor*, Pflichtanker; - *bend*, einfacher Schotenstich; - *bitts*, Schotenpoller; - *block*, S-block; - *cable*, Pflichtankertau od. -kette; - *chain*, P-akette; - *cleat*, Schotenklampe; *to - close home*, die Segel dicht anholen; - *clouds*, Schichtenwolke; -*hole*, Schotengat; *to - home a sail*, ein Segel verschoten; - *knot*, Schotenstich; - *lightning*,

Wetterleuchten; - *of ice*, Eisscholle; - *stopper*, Schotenstopper.

sheets of the courses, Untersegelschoten; - *of a studding sail*, Wasserschoten.

shelf, 1. oberer Balkwäger; 2. Sandbank, Riff; *laid on the -*, ausrangiert, pensioniert; - *bolt*, Balkwegerbolzen; - *of rocks*, eine unter Wasser befindliche Felsenreihe; - *piece*, Balkweger.

shell, 1. Außenbekleidung; 2. Rumpf (eines Schiffes); 3. Büchse od. Sitz des Hahns; 4. Gehäuse; - *back*, Seebär; - *boat*, leichtes Ruderboot; - *lugs*, kurze Stringerwinkel; - *plating*, Außenhaut; - - *of boiler*, Kesselwandung; - *rivets*, Außenhautnieten; - *riveting*, A-h-nietung.

shells, Muscheln.

shelly ground, Muschelgrund.

shelter, Schutz; - *deck*, Schutzdeck; - - *beam*, S.-balken; - - - *angle bar*, S.-b-winkel; - - - *stringer*, S.-b-stringer; - - - - *plate*, S.-b-s-platte; *s. d. b. tie plate*, S.-b-Längsschiene; *s. d. hatch*, S.-luke; *s. d. hatchway coaming*, S.-Lukensüll; *s. d. pillar*, S.-stütze; *s. d. rails and stanchions*, S.-geländer; *s. d. sheerstrake*, S.-Schergang; *s. d. ship*, S.-schiff; *s. d. stanchions*, S.-Geländerstütze; *s. d. stringer*, S.-Stringer; - - - *angle bar*, S.-S.-winkel; - - - *inner a. b.*, Innenwinkel des S.-stringers; - - - *plate*, S.-Stringerplatte; *s. d. vessel*, S.-schiff; *s. d. waterway*, S.-Wassergang.

sheltered road, geschützte Reede.

shelves, Untiefen.

shelving, flach ansteigend.

shelvy, voller Klippen und Sandbänke.

shift a tackle, 1. ein Takel

verschlagen; 2. ein Tau abschricken; - *anchorage*, den
Ankerplatz wechseln; - *an
anchor*, einen Anker ver-
setzen; - *ballast*, den Ballast
umstauen; - *the berth*, den
Ankerplatz verändern; - *the
helm*, das Ruder überlegen;
- *the jibs*, die Klüver umlegen; - *the mizen*, die Besahn
übergehen lassen; - *the sails*,
die Segel wechseln; - *the
scarfs*, die Scherben verschießen; - *the spars*, die
Rundhölzer wechseln; - *the
stowage*, die Ladung um-
stauen; - *the vessel*, das
Schiff verholen.
shift, 1. Schicht (Arbeit); 2.
Stoß (Planken); - *of butts*,
Stoßverteilung; - *of two
butts*, das Überschießen
zweier Plankenenden; *to
begin the -*, die Schicht antreten.
shifted cargo, übergegangene
Ladung; - *wind*, umgesprun-
gener Wind.
shifter, Kochsmaat.
shifting backstay, Schlinger-
pardune; - *ballast*, fliegender Ballast; - *beam*, Schiebbalken; - - *angle bar*, S.-
winkel; - *board*, Getreide-
schott; - - *stanchion*, G.-
stütze; - *cargo*, übergehende
Ladung; - *ground*, Well-
grund; - *of cargo*, das Übergehen der Ladung; - *of
planking*, Verschuß der Planken; - *sand*, Triebsand; -
spanner, verstellbarer
Schraubenschlüssel; - *wind*,
umspringender Wind.
shin up, zwischen zwei Tauen
emporklettern.
shine, to take the - off, eine
Sache zum ersten Male in
Gebrauch nehmen; *t. t. t. s.
out of a person*, jemand
übertreffen.
shingle, Grant.
ship, 1. einnehmen, übernehmen; 2. sich einschiffen; 3.

anmustern; - *and unship*,
ein- und ausrücken; - *the
hand steering gear*, den
Handsteuerapparat ein-
schalten; - *the oars*, die Riemen klar machen; - *the propeller*, die Schraube aufsetzen; - *the rudder*, das
Ruder einhängen; - *the
ventilators*, die Ventilatoren
aufsetzen.
ship, 1. Schiff; 2. Vollschiff; -
ahead, ein S. voraus; - *astern*,
e. S. achteraus; - *biscuit*,
Schiffszwieback; - *board*, S-
planke; - *borne goods*, durch
Schiff bezogene Waren; -
boy, Schiffsjunge; - *bread*,
S-zwieback; - *breaker*, Schiff-
abbrecher; - *broker*, Schiffsmakler; - *builder*, Schiffbauer; - *building*, S-bau; - -
timber, S-b-holz; - - *yard*,
S-b-werft; - *canal*, Schiff-
fahrtskanal; - *carpenter*,
Schiffszimmermann; - *carriage*, Schiffsfracht; - *carver*,
S-bildhauer; - *casting*, Schiff-
formguß; - *chandler*, Schiffs-
lieferant; - *forging*, Schiffs-
schmiedestück; - *jack*, Schiffs-
winde; - *in company*, Mitsegler; - *keeper*, Schiffs-
lieger; - *load*, S-ladung; -
master, S-führer; - *mate*, S-
kamerad; - *ment*, Ladung;
- *owner*, Reeder; - -'s *association* od. *society*, Reederei-
verein; · *owning business*,
Reedereigeschäft; - *piercer*,
Bohrwurm; - *plates*, Schiffs-
bleche; - *repairer*, Schiffs-
ausbesserer; *the - rides between wind and tide*, das
Schiff giert vor seinem
Anker zwischen Wind und
Strom; - *rig*, Schiffstakelage;
- *rigged*, als Vollschiff getakelt; - *scraper*, Schiffs-
kratze; - *shape fashion*, seemännische Art; - *sheathing*,
Schiffblech; - *surveyor*,
Schiffsbesichtiger; - *way*,
Stapel; - *worm*, Bohrwurm;

- *wreck*, Schiffbruch, S. leiden; - *wright*, Schiffbauer, Zimmerbaas; - -'s *yard*, - *yard*, Schiffswerft.
shipped by the run, für die Ueberfahrt angemustert.
shipper, Ablader: -'s *load and count*, nach Abladers Einladung und Zählung.
shipping, 1. Schiffe; 2. Schifffahrt; - *affairs*, Schiffahrtsangelegenheiten; - *agent*, Schiffsagent; - *bill*, S-zettel; - *business*, Reedereigeschäft; - *by the run*, für die Überfahrt anmustern; - *charges*, Verladungskosten; - *clerk*, Waterklark; - *expenses*, Verladungskosten; - *gazette*, Schiffsnachrichten; - *house*, Exportgeschäft; - *intelligence*, Schiffsnachrichten; - *legislation*, Schiffahrtsgesetzgebung; - *list*, Schiffsverzeichnis; - *manifest*, Manifest; - *master*, Heuerbaas; - *news*, Schiffsnachrichten; - *note*, Schiffszettel; - *office*, Heuerbureau; - *opportunity*, Schiffsgelegenheit; - *season*, Verschiffungszeit; - *trade*, 1. Seehandel; 2. Schiffahrtsbetrieb; - *weight*, Verschiffungsgewicht.
ship's apparatus, Schiffsausrüstung; - *articles*, Musterrolle; - *bell*, Schiffsglocke; - *biscuits*, S-zwieback; - *boy*, S-junge; - *carpenter*, S-zimmermann; - *classification*, S-klassifikation; - *clock*, Borduhr; - *company*, Schiffsvolk; - *cook*, S-koch; - *crane*, S-kran; - *crew*, S-besatzung; - *duty*, S-dienst; - *engine*, S-maschine; - *husband*, S-inspektor; - *hygiene*, Gesundheitspflege auf Schiffen; - *length*, Schiffslänge; - *log book*, S-journal; - *mate*, S-maat; - *model*, S-modell; - - *trying station*, S-m-Versuchsstation; - *outfit*, S-ausrüstung; - *papers*, S-doku-

mente; - *part*, S-part; - *place by bearings*, gepeiltes Besteck; - *p. b. observation*, astronomisches B.; - *position*, Schiffsort; - *protest*, Verklarung; - *register*, Schiffsregister; - *service*, S-dienst; - *side*, S-wand; - *smith*, S-schmied; - *surgeon*, S-arzt; - *time*, Bordzeit; - - *piece*, B-uhr; - *tonnage*, Tonnengehalt des Schiffes.
shiver, 1. killen; 2. Scheibengat; - *hole*, S.; - *my timbers!* Gott verdamm mich!
shivering sail, killendes Segel.
shoal, 1. flache Stelle; 2. flacher werden; - *indicator* od. - *mark*, Bake; *to - to 5 fathoms*, sich bis auf 5 Faden Wassertiefe dem Lande nähern; - *water*, seichtes Wasser.
shoaler, Küstenfahrer; - *draught*, leichter Tiefgang.
shoaling, good - ground, langsam ansteigender Grund.
shoaly, voll Üntiefen.
shock, Stoß; - *of the waves*, Wellenschlag.
shoe, Ankerschuh; - *block*, Schuhblock; - *of a keel*, loser Kiel; - *of a pipe*, Ausmündung; - *of an anchor*, Ankerschuh; *to - an anchor*, od. *to put the - under the fluke*, den Ankerschuh unterschieben; - *piece*, Schuhplanke.
shole, Stützen-Unterlage.
shoot, Stürze, Ladungsschacht, Schütte; *to - ahead*, vorausschießen; - *anchor*, Pflichtanker; *to - ballast*, Ballast schießen.
shop, Werkstätte.
shorage, Strandrecht.
shore, 1. Küste, Land, Ufer; 2. Stütze, Strebe; - *anchor*, Landanker; - *battery*, Strandbatterie; - *boat*, Landungsboot; - *dues*, Ufergeld; - *fast*, Landfeste; - *going togs*, Kleider zum Landbesuch; - *horizon*, Strandkimm; -

light, Küstenfeuer; - *man*, Schauermann; - *off by bulkheads*, abschotten; - *purser*, Oberzahlmeister; - *service*, Küstendienst; - *up*, abstützen.

shoring, abstützen.

short allowance, gekürzte Ration; - *boards*, kurze Gänge; - *bolt*, Stuufbolzen; - *D-slide valve*, kurzer D-shieber; - *handed*, schwach bemannt; - *jeer*, kurzes Rahtakel; - *laid rope*, das zu fest gedrehte Tau; - *link chain cable*, Ankerkette ohne Stege; - *of*, Mangel haben an ..; - *poop*, kurze Hütte; - *sails*, kleine, gereffte Segel; - *screw bolt*, Holzschraube; - *sea*, kurze See; - *shipped*, nicht mit verladen; - *splice*, Kurzsplissung; - *stay*, kurz Stag; - *stick*, kurze Bramstenge; - *tonnage*, Ladungsmanko; - *topgallant mast*, kurze Bramstenge.

shorten, einhieven, einnehmen; - *a rope*, ein Tau kürzen; - *canvass*, Segel mindern; - *in the cable*, Ankerkette einkürzen; - *sail*, Segel bergen od. mindern.

shortening, Verkürzung.

shot, 1. aneinander gesplißt; 2. eingeschossen; - *ballast*, ungestauter Ballast; - *garland*, Kugelrecken; - *line*, Raketenleine; - *locker*, Kugelraum; - *of a cable*, Ankertausplissung; - *of distress*, Notschuß; - *plug*, Schmierpfropfen; - *rack*, Kugelrecken.

shoulder block, Schulterblock; - *of mutton sail*, Schafschinken; - *strap*, Achselband; *to - the anchor*, den Anker aus dem Grund reißen.

shout, Leichter; - *man*, L-schiffer.

shove off, abstoßen.

shovel, Schaufel; - *board*, Scheibenspiel auf Deck.

shovelling flat, Schaufelraum für Kohlen im Heizraum.

show lights, Signale mit Lichtern geben; - *one's colours* od. *flag*, seine Flagge zeigen.

showery, regenböig; - *scuds*, Regenwolken.

shredding, Tasche (Verdoppelung von Plankengängen).

shreds, Fetzen.

shrinkage, Schwund.

shroud, Wanttau; - *bridle*, Knebelstropp; - *cleat*, Wantklampe; - *knot*, W-knoten; - *laid cordage*, kabelweise geschlagenes Tauwerk; - *laid rope*, wantweise g. Tau; - *lanyard*, Taljereep der Wanten; - *plate*, Püttingseisen; - *rope*, Wanttau; - *stopper*, W-stopper; - *tackle*, W-takel; - *truck*, W-klotje.

shrouds, Wanten; *a pair of -*, das Spannwant.

shut, zumachen; - *in one mark by another*, zwei Marken zur Deckpeilung bringen; - *off steam*, Dampf abstellen; - *off the tank*, wir schlossen den Tank ab (so daß kein Wasser mehr zulaufen konnte).

shute, Stürze, Ladungsschacht.

shy, schralen; - *a biscuit on board of another vessel*, so dicht an ein anderes Schiff kommen, daß man einen Zwieback an Bord werfen kann.

sick, 1. krank; 2. schadhaft; - *bay*, Schiffslazarett; - *berth*, Krankenkoje; - - *attendant*, Krankenwärter; - *flag*, Quarantäneflagge; - *mess*, Krankenmesse; - *ship*, rankes Schiff; - *ticket*, Krankenschein.

side, Seite, Wand; - *arm of a hanging knee*, Seitenarm eines Hängeknies; - *bar keel*, Seitenplattenkiel; - *bar of a keel*, Seitenplatte eines Kiels; - *bitt*, Seitenbeting; - - *bearing*, S.-Wellenlager; - - *keep*, W.-deckel des S.; - *boat*, Seitenboot; - *boy*, Fallreepsgast; - *bunker*, Seitenbunker; - *by* -, Bord an B.; - *coal bunker*, Seitenkohlenbunker; - *connecting rod*, Seiten-Pleuelstange; - *counter timber*, Heckstütze; - *fish*, Vorder- und Hinterstück eines zusammengesetzten Mastes; - *gallery*, Seitengallerie; - *girder*, Seitenträger; - - *angle bar*, S.-winkel; - - *of a double bottom*, S. eines Doppelbodens; - - *plate*, S.-platte; - *hole of a pump*, Pumpengat; - *house*, Seitenhaus.

side intercostal keelson, eingeschobenes Seitenkielschwein; - - - *angle bar*, e. S.-winkel; - - - *plate*, e. S.-platte; *s. i. plate*, e. S.-p-; *s. i. stringer*, e. Seitenstringer; - - - *angle bar*, e. S.-winkel; - - - *plate*, e.-S.-platte.

side keelson, Seitenkielschwein; - - *angle bar*, S.-winkel; - *ladder*, Seitenleiter; - *lantern*, S-laterne; - *lever*, S-balanzier; - - *engine*, S-b.-maschine; - *light*, Seitenfenster; - - *screen*, Laternenkasten; - - - *stanchions*, L.-stützen; - *lights*, Seitenlichter; - *line*, Sente der Vertäuung; - *of a ship*, Schiffsseite; - *piece of a wooden built mast*, Schalstück eines hölz. Mastes; - *planks*, Seitenplanken; - *plate of combustion chamber*, Seitenwand der Feuerkammer; - *plating*, Seitenbeplattung; - - *of bridge*, Brückenhaus-S.; - - *of forecastle*, Back-Seitenbeplattung; - - *of poop*, Hütten-S.; - - *of raised quarterdeck*, S. des erhöhten Quarterdecks; - *rod*, Pleuelstange; - *rope*, 1. Fallreepstau; 2.

Strecktau eines Sonnensegels; - - *stanchions*, Fallreepsständer; - *stringer*, Seitenstringer; - - *angle bar*, S.-winkel; - - *inner a. b.*, Innenwinkel des S.; - - *shell lugs*, kurze S.-winkel; - *tackle*, Seitentalje; - *trees*, die unteren Seitenstücke eines zusammengesetzten Mastes; - *view*, Seitenansicht; - *wheel*, Schaufelrad.

sideral day, Sterntag; - *time*, S-zeit.

siding, das Zurichten der Planken in der Breite; - *of a beam*, seitenrechte Dicke eines Balkens; - - - *floor*, s. D. einer Bodenwrange; - - - *frame*, s. D. eines Spants; - - - *keel*, s. D. e. Kiels; - - - *keelson*, s. D. e. Kielschweins; - - - *stem*, s. D. e. Vorderstevens; - - - *stern post*, s. D. e. Hinterstevens.

sight, sichten, in Sicht bekommen; - *for deviation*, Deviationsbeobachtung ; - *for variation*, Mißweisungsbeobachtung; *to - the anchor*, den Anker in Sicht hieven; *to take a* -, die Höhe eines Gestirns messen; *in* -, in Sicht.

sighting distance, Sichtweite.

sign of distress, Notsignal; *to sign on* od. *to sign the agreement* od. *the articles*, anmustern.

signal, Signal; - *ball*, S.-ball; - *beacon*, S.-bake; - *bell*, S.-glocke; - *book*, S.-buch; - *chest*, S.-kasten; - *code*, S.-ordnung; - *flag*, S.-flagge; - *for sailing*, Abfahrtssignal; - *halliard*, Flaggenleine; - *lantern*, Signallaterne; - *letters*, S-buchstaben; - *light*, S-feuer; - *locker*, Flaggenspind; - *log*, Signaljournal; - *number*, S-nummer; - *of distress*, Notsignal; - *rocket*, Signalrakete; - *ship*, Wachtschiff; - *station*, Signalstation; - *torch*, S-fackel; - *whistle*, S-pfeife.

sill, Schwelle; - *ometer*, Fahrt-Geschwindigkeitsmesser.

silt, Schlick.

silted, silty, verschlickt.

silver thaw, Rauhfrost.

simple average, einfache Havarie.

sing out, aufsingen, aussingen.

single acting air pump, einfachwirkende Luftpumpe; *s. a. circulating p.*, e. Zirkulationspumpe; *s. a. engine*, e. Maschine; *s. a. pump*, e. Pumpe.

single anchor, einziger Anker; - *angle bar beam*, Winkelbalken; - *banked oar*, der lange Riemen; - *bar link*, Stangenkoulisse; - *beam engine*, Maschine mit einfachem Balanzier; - *bend*, einfacher Flaggenstich; - *block*, einscheibiger Block; - - *with a hook*, Hakenblock; - *boater*, ganz allein fischender Schleppnetzkutter; - *bodied capstan*, einfaches Gangspill; - *canvas*, Bramtuch; - *crank*, einzelne Kurbel; - *diamond knot*, einfacher Diamantknoten; - *dredger*, e. Bagger; - *ended boiler*, nur von einem Ende zu heizender Kessel; - *expansion engine*, einfache Expansionsmaschine; - *fastening*,e.Befestigung; - *frame*, das e. Spant; - *flue boiler*, Kessel mit einer Feuerröhre; - *plate keelson*, einplattiges Kielschwein; - - *rudder*, e. Ruder; - *ported slide valve*, Drehschieber; - *purchase winch*, Krüppelwinde; - *reefed*, einmal gerefft; - *riveting*, einfache Nietung; - *screw steamer*, Einzelschraubendampfer; - *shroud knot*, einfacherWantknoten; - *thread screw*, ein-

fache Schraube; - *tree mast*, Mast aus einem Stück; - *wall and crown knot*, einfacher Fallreepsknoten; - *w. k.*, e. Schauermannsknoten; - *whip*, Jollentau.

singled ship up, zogen die Vertäuung bis auf eine Trosse ein.

sinical quadrant, Reduktionsquadrant.

sink, sinken, versenken, in den Grund bohren.

sinker, Senkblei an der Lotleine.

sinuosity, Flußkrümmung.

siren, sirene, Sirene.

sirocco, Sirokko.

sister od. - *block*, zweischeibiger Puppblock; - *hook*, Federhaken; - *keelson*, Seitenkielschwein; - - *bolt*, S.-bolzen; - *ships*, Schwesterschiffe.

six cylinder engine, sechszylindrige Maschine; - *penny nail*, $1\frac{1}{2}$ zöll. Spiker; - *water grog*, sehr schwacher Grog.

size, Dicke.

skeet, Gießer.

skeg of the keel, Kielbacke.

skegg shores, die Stützen gegen den Achtersteven.

skeleton of a vessel, Schiffsgerippe; - *pier*, Landungsgerüst; - *ship*, Schiffsgerippe.

sketch blocks, Schattenrisse.

skid beams, Bootsgalgen.

skids, 1. Bootsgalgen; 2. Ladeschlitten; 3. Reibhölzer (außenbords).

skiff, Skiff.

skilligolee, Matrosensuppe.

skim up, ebnen, glätten.

skin. 1. Brook eines Segels; 2. Innenbeplankung; *to - up a sail in the bunt*, das Tuch zur Stauung des Bauches eines Segels glatt legen; *to gather up the -*, beim Segelfestmachen Brook nehmen.

skipper, Führer, Schiffer; - *boy,* Schiffsjunge; -'s *daughter,*Welle mit weißem Kamm.

skirt, Saum des Segels.

skulker, Drückeberger.

skylight, Oberlicht; - *coaming,* O.-süll; - *cover,* O.-persennig; - *grating,* O.-Gräting; - *of crew space,* Logis-O.

sky line, Horizontlinie; - *rocket,* Signalrakete.

skysail, Scheisegel; - *backstay,* S.-pardune; - *brace,* S.-brasse; - *clew line,* S.-Geitau; - *foot rope,* S.-pferd; - *halliard,* S.-fall; - *lift,* S.-Toppenant; - *mast,* S.-stenge; - - *pole* od. - *p.,* Flaggentopp der S.-s-; - *sheet,* S.-schote; - *stay,* S.-stag; - *yard,* S.-rahe; - - *parrel,* Rack der S.-r-.

skyscraper, dreieckiger Wolkenraper.

slab line, Schlappleine; - *reef line,* Reffleine an der Achterkante der Segel.

slabs, 1. loses Segeltuch; 2. Schillen (Schiffbau).

slack, to - a rope, ein Tau fieren; - *away,* wegfieren; - *back,* lose schrauben; - *handsomely,* langsam fieren; - *over the wheel,* mit dem Ruder nachgeben; - *speed,* die Fahrt vermindern.

slack, lose, schlaff; *to be on a - bowline,* mit losen Buliens segeln; - *breeze,* schwache Brise; *to bear a - helm,* gern abfallen; - *in stays,* beim Wenden langsam sein; - *water,* Stauwasser; - - *navigation,* Schiffahrt auf Gewässern mit wenig Gefäll; - *wind,* schwacher Wind.

slack, the - of a rope, das Lose eines Taues.

slacken, auslaufen (Ebbe und Flut); - *speed,* die Fahrt verlangsamen.

slackening of the tide, Kentering der Flut.

slag, Schlacke.

slant of wind, kurz anhaltender, besserer Wind, - *tack,* Schlagbug.

slatch, von kurzer Dauer.

slate of a boiler deposit, Kesselstein.

slave trade, Sklavenhandel.

slaver, Sklavenschiff.

sledge, die Schleep der Helling; - *hammer,* großer Schmiedehammer; - *without head,* Schlitten ohne Hoofd.

slee, Ablaufschlitten.

sleep, to -, eben voll stehen (Segel).

sleeper, 1. Holzstrebe; 2. Lager, Fundament des Kessels; 3. Schlefer (Knie des Heckbalkens).

sleeping berth, Schlafkoje.

sleeve, 1. Hülse; 2. der englische Kanal.

slew see slue.

slice, 1. Schlagkeil (Stapellauf); 2. Bohlenstück zwischen den Inhölzern; 3. Brecheisen.

slide bar, Gleitschiene; - *block of a gaff,* G-block einer Gaffel; - *board for steering chain,* G-planke einer Steuerkette; - *box f. s. c.,* G-rohr einer S.; - *bridge,* Schieberbahn; - *chest,* S-kasten; - - *cover,* S-k-dekkel; - *of the steering wheel,* Welle des Steuerrades; - *rod,* Schieberstange; - *spindle,* S.; - *sweep,* Gleitschuh; - *valve,* Schieber; - - *balance,* Ventilgegengewicht; - - *box,* Schieberkasten; - - *case* od. *casing,* S.; - - - *door,* S.-deckel; - - - - *bolt,* S.-d-bolzen; - - - - - *nut,* S.-d-b-mutter; *s. v. exhaust port,* Austrittskanal des Schiebers; *s. v. face,* Schieberfläche; *s. v. gear,* äußere Steuerung; *s. v. guide,* Führung des Schieberventils; *s. v. lap,* Deckfläche des

Schiebers; *s. v. link,* Koulisse; *s. v. packing ring,* Schieber-Packungsring; *s. v. reversing gear,* S.-Umsteuerungsvorrichtung; *s. v. rod,* Schieberstange; - - - *bolt,* S.-bolzen; - - - *guide,* Führung der S.; - - - - *bracket,* S.-Führungsstützplatte; *s. v. r. packing,* S.-packung; *s. v. r. stuffing box,* S.-Stopfbüchse; *s. v. spindle,* Schieberstange; - - - *check nut,* S.-Gegenmutter; - - - *guide bracket brasses,* S.-Führungsträger-Lagerschalen; - - - *nut,* S.-mutter; *s. v. spring,* Schieberfeder; *s. v. travel,* Schieberweg; *s. v. weight,* Ventilgegengewicht.

slider, Gleitblock.

slides for steering gear, Gleitplanken des Steuergeräts; - *of the crosshead,* Geradführungsbacken des Kreuzkopfes.

sliding balk od. *baulk,* Tragholz; - *bilge block,* Ständer der Schlagbetten; - *door,* Schiebetür; - *flying jib boom,* der lose Außenklüverbaum; - *friction,* Gleitreibung; - *gunter* od. - - *mast,* Schiebstenge; - *sail,* portugiesisches Segel; - *head of a lathe,* Spitzdocke; - *joint,* Gleitdichtung; - *keel,* Schieberkeil; - *plank,* Tragholz; - *stop cock* od. - - *valve,* Absperrschieber; - *ways,* Ablaufplanken; - *weight,* Laufgewicht.

slight damage, leichte Beschädigung; - *repairs,* kleine Reparaturen.

slimy ground, Schlickgrund.

sling, 1. Schlinge; 2. fangen (eine Rahe); 3. anschlagen (ein Faß); - *band,* Eisenband des Hangers; - *cleats,* Rackklampen; - *dogs,* Teufelsklaue; - *hoop,* 1. Dreehreeps-

ring (für das Fall); 2. Hangerband (einer Rahe); - *of a gaff,* Hanger einer Gaffel; - *of a lower yard,* H. e. Unterrahe; - *of a yard,* Stropp e. Rahe; - *strop,* Hangerstropp.

slip, 1. Helgen; 2. Aufschlepphelgen; 3. Slip (Unterschied in der Fortbewegung einer Schraube im Wasser od. in der Luft); 4. slippen, schießen lassen (Kette od. Tau); 5. schlieren (von selbst auslaufen); - *dock,* Dock mit geneigtem Boden; - *down,* niedergleiten; - *hook,* Sliphaken; - *knot,* Weiberknoten; - *off,* abschlieren; - *rope,* Schlipptau; - *shackle,* S-schäkel; - *stopper,* S-stopper; - *way,* Helling, Aufschlepphelgen.

slipping knot, Bauernknoten.

sloop, Schaluppe; - *hire,* Bootsheuer; - *of war,* Korvette; - *rigged,* mit Schaluppentakelung; - *smack,* Fischerfahrzeug; - *yacht,* Jacht mit Schaluppentakelung.

slop chest, Kleiderkiste; - *maker,* Matrosenschneider; - *room,* Kleiderkammer; - *shop,* K-d-laden.

slope of a stream, Stromgefälle.

sloped bank, steile Böschung.

slops, fertige Kleidungsstücke.

slot, 1. Bolzenloch; 2. Kerbe, Nut; - *hole,* Coulisse; - *hoop,* Rackband; - *link,* Spurcoulisse.

slow, to - down, die Fahrt verlangsamen; - *of Greenwich mean time,* nach der mittleren G.-Zeit zurückgehend; - *of sail,* langsam segelnd; - *to answer the helm,* dem Ruder nur langsam folgend.

sludge, schwimmende Eis- und Schneemassen; - *door,* Schlammlochdeckel; - *hole,* S-l-; - - *door,* S-l-deckel.

slue, überkanten; - *rope,* Seil

zum Drehen einer Spiere; - *round*, umdrehen.

sluer, Steuermann.

sluice, Schleuse: - *cock*, Schleusenhahn; - *master*, S-meister; - *valve*, S-ventil; - - *rod*, S-v-stange; - - *spindle*, S-v-spindel.

slush, 1. Schneewasser; 2. Stengenschmiere; - *barrel*, Schmierfaß; - *bucket*, S-gefaß; - *horn*, Fetthorn der Segelmacher; - *pot*, Schmiertopf; - *tub*, S-faß.

slushy, Schiffskoch.

smack,Schmack;-*boat*,Fischerschmack; - *man*, Schmackschiffer; - *sail*, S-segel.

small average, kleine Havarie; - *boat*, Jolle; - *bower*, Teuanker; - *carlings*, Balkfüllungen; - *coasting trade*, kleine Küstenfahrt; - *craft*, 1.kleinesFahrzeug;2.Fischergerät; - *damage club*, Klein-Havarieverband; - *eye of a crank*, Kurbelzapfen; - *gouge*, Stechgusche; *the - of an anchor*, der dünnste Teil eines Ankerschaftes; - *purchase*, kleines Gien; - *repairs*, kleine Reparaturen; - *sails*, kleine Segel; - *spur wheel*, kleines Spurrad; - - - *of steam winch*, k. Zahnrad der Dampfwinde;-*stores*, kleiner Proviant; - *stuff*, kleines Tauwerk.

smaller bend, das kleine Bergholz.

smart money,Schmerzensgeld; - *ticket*, Invalidenschein.

smashed, zerschmettert.

smelling, *ship - bottom*, das Schiff streifte den Grund.

smite a sail, ein Segel ausrücken.

smithers, Fetzen.

smith's tool, Schmiedewerkzeug; - *work*, S-dearbeit.

smithy, Schmiede.

smiting line, Rücker.

smoke arch, Rauchkasten; - *box*, R-kammer; - - *door*, R-k-tür;-*burner*,R-verbrenner; - *consumer*, R-verzehrer; - *consuming*, r-verzehrend; - - *furnace*, r-v-z-e Feuerbüchse; - *less coal*, r-lose Kohle; - *sail*, Rauchsegel.

smoking room, Rauchzimmer.

smooth, glatt; - *file*, Schlichtfeile; - *full*, gespannt voll (Segel); - *off*, abschlichten.

smotheration, Labskaus.

S. M. S. = *Shipwrecked Mariners' Society*, Gesellschaft zur Unterstützung schiffbrüchiger Seeleute.

smuggling trade, Schmuggelhandel.

snag,treibender ästiger Baumstamm; - *chamber* od. *room*, wasserdichte Abteilung im Bug.

snaggy, voller Baumstämme.

snake,schwichten; - *a seizing*, ein Bindsel kreuzen; - *line*, Schwichtleine; - *piece*, schräges Piekknie.

snaked seizing, Kreuzbindsel.

snap, Nietsetzer; - *block*, Kinnbacksblock; - *head rivet work*, die Schellkopfform der Nietung; - *off*, plötzlich abbrechen.

snape, zuschrägen.

snapping test, Zerreißprobe.

snatch, Lippe eines Blocks; - *a rope*, ein Tauende in einen Fußblock od. in eine Lippe einlegen; - *block*, Fußblock; - - *with tail*, Lotblock; - *cleat*,Lippklampe; - *sheave*, Scheibe mit Vorstecker.

snickersnee, Messerkampf.

sniffle valve, Luftauslaßventil.

sniffler, kurzer Sturm.

snifter, Schnäpschen.

snifting valve, Luftauslaßventil.

snipper snapper, Tropf.

snotter, Sprietstropp.

snottie, Kadett.

snow, Schnaue, Schnauschiff; - *drift*, Schneegestöber; - *mast*, Schnaumast; - *tail*, S-segel.

snub a *cable*, ein ablaufendes Tau plötzlich anhalten.

snubbed, plötzlich angehalten resp. zu Anker gebracht.

snubber, Kunstgriff beim Törnen.

snubbing *post*, Poller zum Törnen.

snug, 1. Knagge; 2. sauber, ordentlich; - *canvass*, kleine Segel; *everything* - *for a gale*, alles klar für einen Sturm; - *rig*, gute Takelung.

sny, leichte Biegung nach oben.

snying, gebogene Planke.

socket, 1. Sockel, Spur; 2. Hütchen der Kompaßnadel; - *and ball joint*, Kugeldichtung; - *of davit*, Davitspur.

soda cock, Sodahahn.

soft iron, weiches Eisen; - *plank*, bequemes Lager; - *solder*, Weichlot; - *tack* od. - *tommy*, weiches Weißbrot; - *wood*, weiches Holz.

soger, sich drücken, Drückeberger.

soil pipe, Klosettrohr.

solar corona, Sonnenring; - *eclipse*, S-finsternis; - *halo*, S-hof; - *time*, S-zeit.

solder, die Löte.

soldering iron, Lötkolben; - *ladle*, L-löffel; - *spirit*, L-spiritus.

soldier, Bückling; -'s *wind*, halber Wind.

sole, Sohle; - *of a bilge way*, Sohle des Schlagbettes; - *of the rudder*, S. des Ruders; - *piece of stern frame*, S. d. Schraubenrahmens; - *plate*, Fundamentsplatte; - - *bolt*, F.-bolzen.

solid hatch, massiver Lukendeckel; - *keel*, m. Kiel; - *packing for piston*, solide Kolbenpackung.

soot, Ruß.

sound, 1. Sund; 2. gesund; 3. loten (Grund); 4. peilen (Pumpen); 5. Dampfpfeifensignal; die D-pfeife ertönen lassen; - *signal*, Schallsignal; - *the whistle*, ein Dampfpfeifensignal geben.

soundage, Lotungsgebühr.

sounder, Tieflotungs-Apparat.

sounding, Grundprobe, Wassertiefe; - *apparatus*, Apparat zur G.; - *buoy*, Sondierungsboje; - *cap* od. *cover*, Peilrohrdeckel; - *lead*, Senkblei; - *line*, Tieflotleine; - *machine*, Lotapparat; - *pipe*, Peilrohr; - - *cap* od. *cover*, P.-deckel; - *pole* od. *rod* od. *stick*, Peilstock; - *tube*, P-rohr.

soundings, 1. lotbarer Grund; 2. Angabe der Wassertiefe; *to be in* -, auf lotbarem Grunde sein; *to go* od. *steer by* -, nach Lotungen steuern; *irregular* -, unregelmäßige L.; *regular* -, regelmäßige L.; *to strike* -, Grund werfen; *to take* -, loten.

soundless, nicht lotbar.

S. by E., Süd zum Osten; *S. b. W.*, S. z. Westen; *S. E. b. E.*, Südost z. Osten; *S. E. b. S.*, Südost z. Süden.

south, *to gain* od. *make* -, Süd gewinnen; - *east monsoon*, Südost-Monsun; - *east trades*, Südost-Passatwinde; - *west monsoon*, Südwest-Monsun; - *wester*, 1. Südwester; 2. Südwestwind.

southard, *southerly*, südlich.

southern amplitude, südliche Weite; - *hemisphere*, s. Halbkugel; - *light*, Südlicht.

southing, 1. südliche Richtung; 2. Breitenunterschied beim Fahren nach Süden.

southward, südwärts.

sow belly, Salzfleisch.

spacc, 1. Raum; 2. Spantenentfernung; 3. Seestrich; - *for steam*, Dampfraum.

spacing, Entfernung, Weite; - *of beams*, Balkenentfernung; - *of frames*, Spantenentfernung; - *of rivets*, Abstand der Nieten.

spales, Balkenverstärkung.

span, Toppreep; - *block*, T-block; *to - in the rigging*, die Wanten schwichten; - *lashing*,Laschung mit Spann; - *of the peak halliards*, Spann des Piekfalls; - *of the rigging*, Spannwant.

Spanish *burton*, Staggarnat; - *reef*, aut den Rand laufen lassen; - *windlass*, spanische Winde.

spank, 1. schlagen; 2. mit frischer Brise halbwinds segeln.

spanker, Besahn; - *boom*, B.-baum; - - *hoop*, B.-b-band; - - *topping lift*, B.-baum-Toppenant; - - - - *purchase*, B.-b-Dirktalje; - *brails*, B.-Geitaue; - *foot*, untere Teil des B.; - - *brail*, B.-Fußgeitau; - *gaff*, B.-gaffel; - *halliard*, B.-fall; - *in!* B. fest! - *inhaul*, B.-Einholer; - *inner peak brail*, B -gaffel-Innengeitau; - *middle brail*, B.-Mittelgeitau; - *out!* B. bei! - *outer peak brail*, B.-gaffel-Außengeitau; - *outhaul*, B.-Ausholer; - *peak brail*,B.-Gaffelgeitau; - *p. halliard*, B.-Piekfall; - *sheet*, B.-schote; - *tack*, B.-hals; - - *tracing line*, B.-h-Aufholer; - *throat brail*, B.-Brokgeitau ; - *t. halliard*, B.-Klaufall; - *topping lift*, B.-dirk; - *vang*, B.-gerde; - - *pendant*, B.-Gaffelgerdenschenkel.

spanking, kräftig; *to go -*, mit frischer Backstagsbrise segeln; - *breeze*, lebhafte Brise.

spanner, Schraubenschlüssel.

spar, Spiere; - *buoy*, Spierentonne; - *ceiling*, Wegerungslatten; *to - down*, Latten in die Wanten laschen; - *lashing*, Spierenlaschung.

spar deck, Spardeck; - - *beam*, S.-balken; - - - *angle bar*, S.-b-winkel; - - - *clamp*, S.-Unterbalkweger; - - - *hanging knee*, S.-balken-Hängeknie;

- - - *lodging knee*, horizontales Knie des S.-b-; - - - *shelf*, S.-Balkw* ger; - - - *stringer*, S.-Balkenstringer; - - - - *plate*, S.-B.-platte; *s. d. b. tie p.*, S.-balken-Lukenstringer; *s. d. hatch*, S.-luke; *s. d. hatchway coaming*, S.-Lukensüll; *s. d. rails and stanchions*, S.-geländer; *s. d. sheerstrake*, S.-Schergang; *s. d. ship*, S.-schiff; *s. d. side plating*, S.-Seitenbeplattung; *s. d. stanchion*, S.-Geländerstütze; *s. d. stringer*, S.-stringer; - - - *angle bar*, S.-s-winkel; - - - *plate*, S.-s-platte; *s. d. vessel*, S.-schiff; *s. d. waterway*, S.-Wassergang.

spare *anchor*, Reserveanker; - *bunker* od. - *coal b.*, R-s-kohlenbunker; - *gear*, R-s-teile; - *mast*, R-s-mast; - *propeller*, R-s-schraube; - *rigging* od. *ropes*, R-s-tauwerk; - *rudder*, R-s-ruder; - *sails*, R-s-segel; - *shackle*, R-s-schäkel; - *spars*, R-s-spiere; - *stores*, R-s-gut; - *stowage* od. *tonnage*, unbesetzter Schiffsraum; - *top mast*, R-s-stange; - *yard*, R-s-rahe.

spark *catcher*, Funkenfänger.

spars, Rundhölzer.

speak a *vessel*, ein Schiff ansprechen.

speaking *trumpet* od. *tube*. Sprachrohr.

special *survey*, 1. spezielle Aufsicht; 2. s. Besichtigung.

specific *gravity*, spezifische Schwere; - *heat*,Eigenwärme; - *weight*, spezifisches Gewicht.

specification, Beschreibung.

spectacle *clew* od. *clue*,Brillenlägel.

speed, Fahrt, Geschwindigkeit; - *controlling valve*, Fahrtkontrollventil; - *governor*, Maschinenregulator; - *indicator*,Geschwindigkeitsanzeiger; - *of the piston*, Kolbengeschwindigkeit; - *on trial*, Probefahrtgeschwindigkeit.

spell, 1. ablösen; 2. Schicht, Törn; - *below*, Törn zur Koje; - *on the wheel*, Törn am Ruder; - *the pump!* Pumpenmannschaft ablösen!

spelter solder, Schlaglot.

spencer, Gaffelsegel; - *gaff*, Schnausegelgaffel; - *mast*, Schnaumast.

spent, gebrochen.

spew, to - *oakum*, das Werg hervortreten lassen.

spherical segment, Kugelabschnitt; - *valve*, K-ventil.

spherograph, Sphärograph.

spider, Braßarm; - *band* od. *hoop*, 1. Belegnagelband; 2. Püttingsband.

spidereen frigate, märchenhafte Fregatte.

spigot of a cock, Halsrohr eines Hahns.

spike, Spiker, spikern, vernageln; - *bowsprit*, Bugspriet mit Klüverbaum in einem Stück; - *iron*, Spikereisen; - *of the windlass*, Spillspake; - *tackle*, Kantgien.

spile, Speiler.

spiling, Krümmung einer Planke.

spillage, Kehrling.

spilling, 1. verschütten; 2. Wind aus einem Segel nehmen; - *line*, Notgording.

spin a fair thread, Kleinigkeitskrämerei treiben; - *a long yarn*, Geschichten erzählen.

spindle, Spindel (der Drehbank); 2. Herz (eines hölzernen Mastes); 3. Pinne (des Gangspills); 4. Achse, Welle (des Steuerrades); 5. Axe, Spindel, Welle (des Ankerspills).

spindrift, dichter Sprühnebel.

spinnaker, Spinnaker; - *boom*, S.-baum; - *brace*, S.-brasse;

- *gear*. S.-geschirr; - *guy*, S.-baum-Achterholer; - *sheet*, S.-schote; - *tack*, S.-hals.

spiral buoy, Spierentonne; - *spring*, Spiralfeder.

spirit compass, Fluidkompaß; - *level*, Libelle; - *room*, Raum für geistige Getränke.

spirketting, spirkitting, Setzweger; - *bolt*, S.-Folzen; - *of forecastle*, S. der Back; - *of poop*, S. der Hütte; - *plate*, S.-platte.

spit, Spitze der Landspitze; - *fire jib*, Sturmklüver; - *head nightingale*, Bootsmann; - *kid*, Spucknapf.

splash board, Spritzbrett.

splice, spleissen, splissen, Splissung; - *the main brace!* Besahnschott an! od. Der Mannschaft ein Glas Schnaps! - *with whole strand*, Splissung mit vollen Duchten.

splicing fid, Splißhorn; - *hammer*, S-hammer; - *shackle*, S-schakel.

splinter, Splitter, zersplittern; - *netting*, Splitternetz.

split, Riß, zerreißen, bersten; - *crow*, Doppeladler; - *draught*, geteilter Zug; - *flag*, gespaltene Flagge; *to* - *out the blocks*. die Blöcke unter dem Schiff zersplittern; - *pillar*, geschleißte Stütze.

splitting blocks, obere Stapelblöcke.

spoke of a steering wheel, Steuerradspake.

spoken, gesprochene Schiffe.

sponge, Stahlbürste, bürsten; - *cloth*, Schwitztuch.

sponson, Radkastengallerie; - *beam*. äußerer R-k-balken; - *deck*, R-k-gallerie; - *rim*, R-k-träger.

spontaneous combustion, Selbstentzündung.

spontaneously developed fermentation, spontane Gärung.

spoom, spoon, lenzen.

spoon drift, Gischt.

spooning, lenzen.

spout, Wasserhose.

spray, Spritzwasser; - *board*, S-brett.

praying, Spritzer übernehmen.

spread, to - much cloth, breit getakelt; - *the awnings*, die Sonnensegel ausholen; *to make a - eagle of a man*, einen Matrosen zum Prügeln festbinden.

sprig, Düker; - *bolt*, Tackbolzen.

spring, 1. Spring, Sprung (Deck, Mast); 2. Feder; 3. Springtau; 4. Gezeit zur Zeit der Springflut; 5. *to clap a -*, Spring nehmen; *to - a butt*, sich am Plankenende lockern; *to - a leak*, leck springen; - *balance*, Federwage; - *beam*, äußerer Radkastenbalken; - *block*, Federblock; - *buffer*, F-stoßkissen; - *catch*, Sperrklinkensteuerung; - *forelock*, Federvorstecker; - *load*, F-belastung; - - *safety valve*, Sicherheitsventil mit Federbelastung; - *low water*, Springniedrigwasser; - *rope*, S-tau; - *safety valve*, Sicherheitsventil mit Federbelastung; - *stay*, Springstag; *to - the loof*, dem Winde näher kommen; - *tide*, Springflut; - *valve*, Federventil.

sprit, 1. Spriet; 2. Stützspiere des Mastkrans; - *sail*, Sprietsegel; - - *brace*, Brasse der blinden Rahe; - - *gaff*, Gaffel d. b. R.; - - *halliard*, Ausholer der Blinde; - - *sheet*, Schote d. B.; - - *topsail*, Schiebblinde; - - - *brace*, Brasse der S.; - - - *halliard*, Ausholer d. S.; - *sail yard*, blinde Rahe.

sprocket wheel, Kettentrommel.

sprockets, eine Reihe Stifte auf einem Rade.

spruce wood, Schwarzfichtenholz.

sprung, gesprungen; - *a leak*, ein Leck erhalten.

spunyarn, Schiemannsgarn; - *packing*, S.-packung; - *reel*, S.-mühle; - *winch*, S.-woid.

spur, 1. Ausläufer des Gebirges; 2. Stützspiere des Mastkrans; - *beam*, Balken der Radkastengallerie; - *bow*, Bug mit Sporn; - *horses*, Schlagständer; - *of a bulwark stay*, Strebe einer Relingstütze; - *of the beams*, Scherstock des Decks; - *of the bitts*, Betingsknie; - *of the cradle*, Schlittenständer; - *pinion*, Stirngetriebe; - *wheel*, S-rad.

spurling line, Übertragungsleine der Steuerradaxe auf den Ruderlage-Anzeiger.

spurn water, Wasserrinne auf Deck.

spurs of the bitts, Betingknie.

spy glass, Kieker.

squadron, Geschwader.

squall, Bö; - *with hail*, Hagelbö; - - *rain*, Regenbö; - - *snow*, Schneebö; - - *thunder and lightning*, Gewitterbö.

squally, böig.

square, to - away, die Rahen vierkant brassen; - *the course*, den Kurs stellen od. angeben; - *the dead eyes*, die Wanten od. Jungfern straken; - *the ratlines*, die Wanten nachweben; - *the yards*, die Rahen vierkant brassen; - - *by lifts and braces*, d. R. v. b. und toppen; - *the yards in*, die Luvbrassen einholen; - *up*, das Schiff stromgerecht legen; - *yards!* Brassen und toppen!

square, 1. vierkant; 2. Winkelmaß; - *body*, Mittelschiff; - - *frame*, Richtspant; - - *frames*, Mittschiffsspanten; - *bolt*, viereckiger Bolzen; - *bow*, vierkantiger Bug; - *file*, vierkantige Feile; - *foot*, Quadratfuß; - *fore sail*, Breitfock; - *frame*, Perpendikularspant; - - *saw*, Schülpsäge; - *head*, vierkantiger Bolzenkopf; - *headed bolt*, Diamantkopfbolzen; - *kentledge*, vierkantiges Ballasteisen; - *knee*, Winkelknie; - *knot*, Reffstich; - *of a sail*, Segelbreite; - *of the shank of an anchor*, Ankerstockschaft; - *ribbon*, Mittschiffssente; - *rig*, Rahtakelage; - *rigged*, mit Rahen getakelt; - *sail*, 1. Rahsegel; 2. Breitfock (Schoner und Einmaster); - - *boom*, B.-baum; - - *yard*, B.-rah; - *seam*, Quernaht; - *sennit*, Vierkantplatting; - *sluice*, Kastenschleuse; - *stern*, plattes Heck; - *timber*, 1. vierkantig behauenes Holz; 2. das gerade Spant; - *tuck*, Gillung; - *yards*, vierkant hängende Rahen; *the ship has very* - *yards*, das Schiff hat sehr breite Rahen.

squat, to -, sich mit dem Hinterteil festsetzen.

squeegee, squilgee, squillagee, squillager, Backschwabber resp. damit reinigen.

squirm, Tauverdrehung.

S-rounding, die S-Bucht eines Balkens.

stabber, Pricker.

stability, Stabilität; *an experiment to determine the* -, einen Krängungsversuch machen.

stack off the sheets, die Schoten auffieren.

staff, Stab, Stock.

stag, Klippe.

stage, 1. Stellage; 2. Landungssteg.

stagger under a press of sails, unter zu viel Segel arbeiten.

stairway, Treppe.

staith, Kohlenladegerüst.

stamp note, abgestempelter Passierschein für Waren.

stanch, dicht.

stanchion, Stütze, Geländerstütze; - *of the beam or deck*, Deckbalkenstütze; - *of the booms*, Barringstütze; - *of the rail*, Schanzkleidstütze; - *of the monkey rail* od. *of the nettings*, Finknetzstütze; - *socket*, Stützensockel; - *step*, Stützenspur.

stanchions and guard rods, Geländer; - *of steering gear*, Stützen des Steuergeräts.

stand, anliegen; - *after*, hinterherfahren; - *athwart the waves*, dwars See liegen; - *behind*, sich im Hintergrunde halten; - *by*, bereit stehen; Achtung! - *by the anchor!* Klar zum fallen lassen! - *clear*, klar bleiben; 10 Schritt vom Leibe! - *clear of the cable!* Anker klar! - *for the offing*, seewärts anliegen; - *from under!* Gebt Acht dort unten! - *in shore*, nach Land zu liegen; - *off*, seewärts anliegen; - *off and on*, in der Nähe der Küste ab und zu liegen; - *off shore*, vom Lande abliegen; - *on*, Kurs anliegen; - *out* od. - *out to sea*, herausliegen; auf hoher See sein; - *right under!* Packe Dich! - *seaward*, seewärts anliegen; - *to north*, Nord anliegen.

stand pipe, stehende Speiseröhre.

standard, 1. Gestell; 2. Ständer (des Steuergeräts); 3. Gestell (der Winde); - *against the riding bitts*, Betingsknie; - *barometer*, Normalbarometer; - *block*, der feste Block; - *compass*, Normalkompaß; - *knee*, 1. Betingsknie (eines Spills); 2. stehendes Knie (beim Bugband eines hölz. Schiffes); - - *of the gammoning piece* od. *of the head*, Scheggknie; - *lever*, Regulierhebel; - *pressure gauge*, Normalmanometer; - *weight*, N-m-gewicht.

standards of steering engine, Dampfsteuerapparat - Ständer; - *of the cable bitts*, Betingsknie.

*standing backstays,*die stehenden Pardunen; - *block*, der teste Block; - *bowsprit*, festes Bugspriet; - *in shore*, dem Lande zu halten; - *jib*, Klüfock; - - *downhaul*, K.-Niederholer; - - *halliard*, K.-fall; - - *sheet*, Binnen-Klüverschote; - - *stay*, Klüfockleiter; - *tack*, K-f-hals: - *part of a tackle*, stehender Part eines Takels; - *p. of the catfall*, s. P. des Kattfalls; - *rigging*, stehendes Gut; - - *water*, höchster oder niedrigster Wasserstand.

staple, Krampe; - *knee* od. *lodging knee*, Doppelknie; - *ropes*, Tauwerk aus bestem Hanf.

starboard, Steuerbord; - *anchor*, S.-Anker; *on - beam*, querab an S.; - *bilge suction valve*, S.-Lenzsaugventil; - *boiler*, S.-kessel; *on - bow*, querab am S.-bug; - *engine*, S.-Maschine; - *light*, S.-Licht; *on the - quarter*, querab an Steuerbordachter; - *side*, S.-Seite; *on - tack*, mit S.-halsen über Backbordbug; - *the helm!* Linksruder! - *watch*, Steuerbordwache.

starlight, starry, sternklar.

start, 1. Abfahrt; 2. Ort der letzten Peilung; 3. abfahren, anfangen; 4. anlassen, anschlagen, anspringen (Maschine); 5. sich begeben, lockern, gapen (Nieten u. Planken); 6. sich werfen (Holz); 7. springen (das Lösen des Ankers vom Grunde); - *a bolt*, einenBolzen austreiben;

a butt or butt end that starts, ein Plankenende gaapt; - *a cask*, ein Faß anbrechen; - *a rope*, ein Tau auffieren; - *a vessel from the stump*, ein Schiff ganz neu bauen resp. g. n. ausrüsten; - *bread*, Brot aus den Säcken in die Koje bringen; - *bulk*, zu löschen anfangen; - *the anchor*, den Anker lichten.

starter, Anlaßapparat; - *bolt*, Stempelbolzen.

starting cock, Anlaßhahn; - *engine*, A-l-maschine; - *gear*, A-l-getriebe; - *lever*, A-l-hebel; - *latitude*, abgefahrene Breite; - *longitude*, a. Länge; - *platform*, Maschinistenstand; - *punch*, Kettendorn; - *steam cylinder*, Anlaßmaschinenzylinder; - *valve*, A-l-ventil; - - *gear*, A-l-vgestänge; - - *handle*, A-l-vhandhabe; - - *pipe*, A-l-vrohr; - - *rod*, A-l-v-stange; - - *spindle*, A-l-v-spindel.

state barge, Staatsboot; - *room*, S-kabine.

station bill, Postenrolle; - *for stays*, klar zum Wenden.

stationary, to bring the ship - in the water, das Schiff zum Stillstand bringen.

staunch, hecht, dicht; *to - a leak*, ein Leck verstopfen.

stave a vessel, Löcher in die Schiffsseite hauen; - *and bundle a cask*, ein Faß aufschoven; - *the bottom of a cask*, einem Fasse den Boden einschlagen.

staves, Daubenholz.

stay, wenden, über Stag gehen, in den Wind bringen; - *a mast*, einen Mast stagen; - *a shroud with a shroud knot*, einen Wantknopf einschlagen.

stay, 1. Stag, Strebe, Stütze, Bock (verschiedene Stangen, Winkel etc.); 2. Anker, Stehbolzen (zur Versteifung von

Kesseln und Maschinen); 3. Stag (Tau zur Befestigung von Masten); 4. Leiter (Tau, an dem ein Segel gefahren wird); - *bolt*, Stehbolzen; - *collar*, Auge eines Stags.

stay foresail, Stagfock; - - *downhaul*, S.-Niederholer; - - *halliard*, S.-fall; - - *sheet*, S.-schote; - - *tack*, S.-hals.

stay gore, Staggillung; - *hole*, Gattchen am Stagliek; - *light*, Ankerlicht; - *nut*, Stehbolzenmutter; - *of the sheers*, Backstag; - *pin*, Steg im Kettengliede; - *rod*, Stehbolzen; - *rope*, Stagleik.

staysail, Stagsegel; - *downhaul*, S.-Niederholer; - *halliard*, S.-fall; - *sheet*, S.-schote; - - *pendant*, S.-Schotenschenkel; - *stay*, Stagsegelleiter; - - *tack*, S-s-hals.

stay tabling, Stag-kantensaum; - *tackle*, S-takel; - - *fall*, S-t-läufer; - - *pendants*, Hanger der Innentakel; - *tube*, Ankerrohr; - *whip*, Stagjolle.

staying of boiler, Kesselverankerung; - *of combustion chamber*, Stehbolzenversteifung der Feuerbüchse; *to miss* -, die Wendung versagen.

stays, to be in -, in der Wendung liegen; *to miss* -, die Wendung versagen.

steady! Recht so! Stützt das Ruder! *to* - *the vessel*, das Schiff gegen Überholen stützen.

steady breeze, beständige Brise; - *gale*, stehender Sturm; - *ship*, nicht schlingerndes Schiff.

steadying lines, Brassen der Heisstroppen.

steal ahead, ganz behutsam voraus fahren.

stealer, Aufbringer.

stealing strake, verlorener Gang.

steam away, abdampfen; - *back*,

zurückdampfen; - *down* hinunterdampfen; - *on*, weiterdampfen; - *over*, dampfen über; - *up*, hinaufdampfen.

steam, under own -, mit eigenem Dampf; - *to be kept handy*, Dampf aufhalten; - *admission passage*, Dampfeintrittsweg.

steam ash hoist, Dampfaschwinde; - - - *connecting rod*, D.-Pleuelstange; - - - - - *bolt*, D.-P.-bolzen; - - - - - *bottom end keep*, D.-Kurbelzapfen-Lagerschalendeckel; - - - - - - - *liner*, D.-Pleuelstangenfußfutter; *s. a. h. c. r. top end keep*, D.-Kreuzkopflagerschalendeckel; *s. a. h. crank pin bolt*, D.-Kurbelzapfenlagerbolzen; *s. a. h. c. p. brasses*, D.-K-b-z-l-schalen; *s. a. h. c. shaft*, D.-Kurbelwelle; - - - - - *bearing*, D.-K.-lager; - - - - - - *bolt*, D.-K.-l-bolzen; - - - - - - *brasses*, D.-K.-Lagerschalen; - - - - - - *keep*, D.-K.-Lagerdeckel; - - - - - - *bolt*, D.-K.-L.-bolzen; *s. a. h. crosshead bolt*, D.-Kreuzkopflager-Bolzen; *s. a. h. c. brasses*, D.-K.-schalen; *s. a. h. cylinder*, D.-zylinder; - - - - *cover*, D.-Z.-deckel; - - - - - *bolt*, D.-Z.-d-bolzen; *s. a. h. cylinder drain pipe*, D.-Z.-Entwässerungsrohr; *s. a. h. eccentric*, D.-Exzenter; - - - - *bolt*, D.-E.-bolzen; - - - - *brasses*, D.-E.-Lagerschalen; - - - - *rod*, D.-E.-stange; - - - - *sheave*, D.-E.-scheibe; - - - - *strap*, D.-E.-bügel; - - - - - *liner*, D.-E.-b-futter; *s. a. h. exhaust pipe*, D.-Dampfablaßrohr; *s. a. h. piston*, D.-Kolben; - - - - *rod*, D.-K.-stange; - - - - - *crosshead*, D.-K.-s-Kreuzkopf; - - - - - *stuffing box*, D.-K.-s-Stopfbüchse; - - - - - *gland*, D.-K.-s-S.-deckel; *s. a. h. slide valve*, D.-Schieber; *s. a. h. starting valve*,

D.-Anlaßventil; *s. a. h. stop
valve*, D.-Absperrventil; *s. a.
h. valve casing*, D.-Schieber-
kasten; - - - - - *door*, D.-S.-
deckel; *s. a. h. valve rod*, D.-
Schieberstange; - - - - -
stuffing box, D.-S.-Stopf-
büchse; - - - - - - - *gland*,
D.-S.-S.-deckel.
steam boat, Dampfboot; -
boiler, D.-kessel; - - *bursts*
od. *explodes* od. *flies into
pieces*, der D-k- platzt; - *box*,
D-büchse; - *bucket dredger*,
D-eimerbagger.
steam capstan, Dampfgang-
spill; - - *barrel*, D.-trommel;
- - *connecting rod*, D.-Pleuel-
stange; - - - - *bolt*, D.-P.-
bolzen; - - - - *bottom end
keep*, D.-Kurbelzapfen-La-
gerschalendeckel; *s. c. c. r.
b. e. liner*, D.-Pleuelstangen-
fußfutter; *s. c. c. r. top end
keep*, D.-Kreuzkopflager-
schalendeckel; *s. c. cover*,
D.-Überzug; *s. c. crank pin
bolt*, D.-Kurbelzapfen-Lager-
bolzen; *s. c. c. p. brasses*,
D.-K.-Lagerschalen; *s. c. c.
shaft*, D.-Kurbelwelle; *s. c.
c. shaft bearing*, D.-K.-lager;
- - - - - *bolt*, D.-K.-l-bolzen;
- - - - - *brasses*, D -K.-l-scha-
len; - - - - - *keep*, D.-K.-l-
deckel; - - - - - - *bolt*, D.-K.-
l-d-bolzen; *s. c. crosshead
bolt*, D.-Kreuzkopflagerbol-
zen; *s. c. c. brasses*, D.-K-k-
l-schalen; *s. c. cylinder*, D.-
zylinder; - - - *cover*, D.-Z.-
deckel; - - - - *bolt*, D.-Z.-d-
bolzen; *s. c. cylinder drain
pipe*, D.-Z.-Entwässerungs-
rohr; *s. c. eccentric*, D.-Ex-
zenter; - - - *bolt*, D.-E.-bol-
zen; - - - *brasses*, D.-E.-La-
gerschalen; - - - *rod*, D.-E.-
stange; - - - *sheave*, D.-E.-
scheibe; - - - *strap*, D.-E.-
bügel; - - - - *liner*, D.-E.-b.-
futter; *s. c. engine*, D.-ma-
schine; - - - *piston*, D.-kol-
ben; *s. c. exhaust pipe*, D.-

Dampfablaßrohr; *s. c. partner*, D.-fischung; *s. c. piston
rod*, D.-Kolbenstange; - - - -
crosshead, D.-K.-Kreuzkopf;
s. c. p. r. stuffing box, D.-
Kolbenstangen - Stopfbüch-
se; - - - - - - *gland*, D.-K.-S.-
deckel; *s. c. starting valve*,
D.-Anlaßventil; *s. c. slide
valve*, D.-Schieber; *s. c.
spindle*, D.-Spindel; - - -
collar, D.-S.-kragen; - - -
socket, D.-S.-spur; *s. c. steam
pipe*, D.-Dampfzuleitungs-
rohr; *s. c. stop valve*, D.-
Absperrventil; *s. c. valve
casing*, D.-Schieberkasten;
- - - - *door*, D.-S.-deckel; *s.
c. valve rod*, D.-Schieber-
stange; - - - - *stuffing box*,
D.-S.-Stopfbüchse; - - - - - -
gland, D.-S.-S.-deckel; *s. c.
whelp*, D.-rippe; - - - *chock*,
D.-Rippenkalb.

steam case od. *casing*, Dampfmantel; - *chest*, Schieberkasten; - - *cover* od. *door*,
S.-deckel; - - - *bolt*, S.-d-bol-
zen; - *coal*, Dampfkessel-
kohle; - *cock*, D-hahn; - -
for quenching fire, D-h- zum
Feuerlöschen; - *conduit*, D-
leitung.

steam crane, Dampfkran; - -
connecting rod, D.-Pleuel-
stange; - - - - *bolt*, D.-P.-
bolzen; - - - - *bottom end
keep*, D.-Kurbelzapfenlager-
schalendeckel; - - - - *b. e.
liner*, D.-Pleuelstangenfuß-
futter; - - - - *top end keep*,
D.-Kreuzkopf-Lagerschalen-
deckel; *s. c. crank pin bolt*,
D.- Kurbelzapfen - Lagerbolzen; *s. c. c. p. brasses*, D.-
K.-L-schalen; *s. c. c. shaft*,
D.-Kurbelwelle; - - - - *bearing*, D.-K.-lager; - - - - - *bolt*,
D.-K.-l-bolzen; - - - - *brasses*, D.-K.-l-schalen; *s. c.
crosshead bolt*, D.-Kreuz-
kopflagerbolzen; *s. c. c.
brasses*, D.-K-k-l-schalen; *s.*

c. cylinder, D.-zylinder; - - - *cover*, D.-Z.-deckel; - - - - *bolt*, D.-Z.-d-bolzen; *s. c. cylinder drain pipe*, D.-Z.-Entwässerungsrohr; *s. c. eccentric*, D -Exzenter; - - - *bolt*, D.-E.-bolzen; - - - *brasses*, D.-E.-Lagerschalen; - - - *rod*, D.-E.-stange; - - - *sheave*, D.-E.-scheibe; - - - *strap*, D.-E.-bügel; - - - - *liner*, D.-E.-b-futter; *s. c. engine crank shaft bearing keep*, D.-Kurbelwellenlagerdeckelbolzen; *s. c. e. piston*, D.-kolben; *s. c. exhaust pipe*, D.-Dampfablaßrohr; *s. c. piston rod*, D.-Kolbenstange; - - - - *crosshead*, D.-K.-Kreuzkopf; - - - - *stuffing box*, D.-Kolbenstangen-Stopfbüchse; - - - - - - *gland*, D.-K.-S.-dekkel; *s. c. post*, D.-arm; *s. c. crank shaft bearing keep*, D.-Kurbelwellenlagerdeckel; *s. c. slide valve*, D.-Schieber; *s. c. starting valve*, D.-Anlaßventil; *s. c. steam pipe*, D.-Dampfzuleitungsrohr; *s. c. stop valve*, D.-Absperrventil; *s. c. valve casing*, D.-Schieberkasten; - - - - *door*, D.-S.-deckel; *s. c. valve rod*, D.-Schieberstange; - - - - *stuffing box*, D.-S.-Stopfbüchse; - - - - - - *gland*, D.-S.-S.-deckel.

steam cylinder, Dampfzylinder; - *distributor*, D-verteiler; - *dome*, D-dom; - *dredger*, D-bagger; - *eccentric*, Einlaßexzenter; - *engine*, D-maschine; - - *indicator*, D-druckindikator; - *escape pipe*, D-abzugsrohr; - *exhaust passage*, D-austrittsweg; - *e. pipe*, D-ablaßrohr; - *e. port*, D-austrittskanal; - *ferry*, D-fähre; - *gauge*, D-spannungsmesser; - - *case*, Manometergehäuse; - - *cock*, M-n-m-hahn; - - *dial*, Zeigerblatt eines M-n-m-; - - *pipe*, M-n-m-rohr; - *generator*,

Dampferzeuger; - *governor*, Geschwindigkeitsmesser; - *heater*, Vorwärmer; - *heating*, Dampfheizung; - *indicator*, Kolbenmanometer; - *is on*, der Dampf ist angelassen; - *is up*, der volle D. i. a.; - *jacket*, D.-mantel; - *jet*, D-strahl; - - *apparatus*, D-s-apparat; - - *pump*, D-s-pumpe; - - *tube*, D-s-rohr; - *launch*, Dampfbarkasse; - *log*, Maschinistenjournal; - *navigation*, Dampfschifffahrt; - *ordered*, Befehl zum Dampfaufmachen; - *packet*, D.-paketboot; - - *communication*, Postdampferverbindung; - *passage*, Dampfweg; - *pile driver*, D-ramme; - *pinnace*, D-pinasse.

steam pipe, Dampfrohr; - - *bracket*, D.-stütze; - - *casing*, D.-mantel; - - *guards*, D.-Sicherungsvorrichtung; - - *safety valve*, D.-Sicherheitsventil; - - - - *load*, D.-S.-belastung; - - *studs*, D.-Stiftschrauben; - - *to electric light engine*, Elektrischlichtmaschinen - Dampfzuleitungsrohr; - - *to forced draught engine*, D-z-l-t-r-der Erzeugungsmaschine von künstl. Zug; - - *to refrigerating machine*, Eismaschinen-D-z-l-t-r-; - - *to reversing engine*, D-z-l-t-r-der Umsteuerungsmaschine; - - *to oil pump*, Ölpumpen-D-z-l-t-r-; - - *to steam ash hoist*, D-z-l-t-r- der Dampfaschwinde; - - *to steam capstan*, D-z-l-t-r- desDampfgangspills; - - *to steam crane*, D-z-l-t-r- des Dampfkrans; - - *to steam winch*, D-z-l-t-r-der Dampfwinde; - - *to steam windlass*, D-z-l-t-r-des Ankerspills; - - *to steering engine*, D-z-l-t-r- des Dampfsteuerapparats; - - *to turning engine*, D-z-l-t-r- der Drehvorrichtungsmaschine;

- - *to warping engine,* D-z-l-t-r- der Verholmaschine.
steam pipes, Dampfrohrleitung; - *piston,* Dampfkolben; - *port,* D-eintrittskanal; - - *of high pressure cylinder,* D-e-t-k- des Hochdruckzylinders; - - *of intermediate cylinder,* D-e-t-k- des Mitteldruckzylinders; - - *of low pressure cylinder,* D-e-t-k- des Niederdruckzylinders; - *power,* Dampfkraft; - *pressure,* D-spannung; - - *register,* Registriermanometer; - *propeller,* 1. Dampfschraube; 2. Schraubendampfer; - *propulsion,* Fortbewegung durch Dampf; - *pump,* D-pumpe (*see also* pump); - *ram,* D-ramme; - *reducing valve,* D-reduzierventil; - *regulator,* D-regulator; - *reversing gear,* D-umsteuerungsvorrichtung; - *room of boiler,* D-raum des Kessels; - *ship line,* D-schiffslinie; - *s. service,* Dampferdienst; - *sloop,* Dampfschaluppe; - *space,* D-raum; - *steering gear,* D-steuerapparat; - *s. wheel,* D-s-rad; - *tender,* kleiner Dampfleichter; - *tight,* dampfdicht; - *traffic,* Dampferverkehr; - *trap,* Wassersammler; - *fittings,* W.-garnitur; - *trawler,* Fischdampfer; - *trunnion,* Dampfzapfen; - *tug,* Schleppdampfer; - *turbine,* Dampfturbine; - *turning gear,* D-drehvorrichtung; - *valve,* D-ventil; - *vessel,* D-schiff; - *waste pipe,* D-abzugsrohr; - *way,* D-kanal; - *wharf,* D-schiffwerfte; - *whistle,* D-pfeife; - - *pipe,* D-p-rohr.
steam winch, Dampfwinde; - - *brake,* D-bremse; - - *connecting rod,* D.-Pleuelstange; - - - - *bolt,* D.-P.-bolzen; - - - - *bottom end keep,* D-Kurbelzapfen-Lagerschalendeckel;

- - - - *b. e. liner,* D.-Pleuelstangenfußfutter; - - - - *top end keep,* D.-Kreuzkopflagerschalendeckel; - - *cover,* D.-Überzug; - - *crank pin bolt,* D.-Kurbelzapfenlagerbolzen; - - *c. p. brasses,* D.-K-b-z-l-schalen; - - *c. shaft,* D.-Kurbelwelle; - - - - *bearing,* D.-K.-lager; - - - - - *bolt,* D.-K.-l-bolzen; - - - - - *brasses,* D.-K.-l-schalen; - - - - - *keep,* D.-K.-l-deckel; - - - - - - *bolt,* D.-K.-l-d-bolzen; - - *crosshead bolt,* D.-Kreuzkopf-Lagerbolzen; - - *c. brasses,* D.-K.-Lagerschalen; - - *cylinder,* D.-Zylinder; - - - *cover,* D.-Z.-deckel; - - - - *bolt,* D.-Z.-d-bolzen; - - *c. drain pipe,* D.-Z.-Entwässerungsrohr; - - *eccentric,* D.-Excenter; - - - *bolt,* D.-E.-bolzen; - - - *brasses,* D.-E.-Lagerschalen; - - - *rod,* D.-E.-stange; - - - *sheave,* D.-E.-scheibe; - - - *strap,* D.-E.-bügel; - - - *liner,* D.-E.-b-futter; - - - *exhaust pipe,* D.-Dampfablaßrohr; - - *pipe,* D.-rohr; - - - *cover,* D.-r-Schutzblech; - - *pipe stool,* D.-Rohrstuhl; - - *piston,* D.-Kolben; - - - *rod,* D.-K.-stange; - - - - *crosshead,* D.-K.-s-Kreuzkopf; - - - - *stuffing box,* D.-K.-s-Stopfbüchse; - - - - - - *gland,* D.-K.-s-S.-deckel; - - *slide valve,* D.-Schieber; - - *starting valve,* D.-Anlaßventil; - - *stay,* D.-Stehbolzen; - - *stop valve,* D.-Absperrventil; - - *valve casing,* D.-Schieberkasten; - - - - *door,* D.-S.-deckel; - - *valve rod,* D.-Schieberstange; - - - - *stuffing box,* D.-S.-Stopfbüchse; - - - - - - *gland,* D.-S.-S.-deckel.

steam windlass, Dampfankerspill (*see windlass*); - - *engine,* Ankerlichtmaschine; - *yacht,* Dampfjacht.

steamer, Dampfer.

steaming and sailing ship, Segeldampfschiff.

steel, Stahl; *stählern*, verstählen; - *boat*, stählernes Boot; - *boiler*, Stahlkessel; - *bolt*, stählerner Bolzen; - *casting*, Stahlfassonguß; - *deck*, stählernes Deck; - *mast*, s. Mast; - *piston*, Stahlkolben; - *vessel*, stählernes Schiff; - *wedge*, stählerner Keil; - *wire rigging*, Stahldrahttakelung; - *wire rope*, S-d-tau; - *works*, Stahlwerk; - *yard*, stählerne Rahe.

steeling strake, Splißgang.

steep tub, Frischbalje.

steeple engine, Maschine mit rückwirkenderPleuelstange.

steer as you go, geradezu steuern; - *by the sea*, nach dem Seegange s.; - *by the stars*, nach den Sternen s.; - *by the wind*, beim Winde s.; - *course*, Kurs s.; - *eastward*, ostwärts s.; - *for a point*, auf einen Punkt zusteuern; - *for the land*, auf das Land z.; - *in*, einsteuern; - *large*, schlecht s.; - *off*, abgieren; - *small*, gut steuern; - *the course*, in Kurs gehen; - *to the anchor*, auf den Anker zusteuern.

steerage, 1. Zwischendeck; 2. Steuerfähigkeit; - *accommodations*, Einrichtung für Zwischendecks-Passagiere; - *passenger*, Z.-Passagier; - *power*, Steuerfähigkeit; - *way*, 1. S.; 2. Kielwasser; *to have no - -*, keineFahrt haben.

steered course, gesteuerter Kurs.

steering, *nice -*, genaues Steuern.

steering apparatus, Steuerapparat; - *binnacle stand*, Steuer - Kompaßständer; - *chain*, S.-kette; - - *block*, S.-reepsblock; - *commands*, Ruderkommandos; - *compass*, Steuerkompaß.

steering engine, Dampfsteuerapparat; - - *bed plate*, D.-Grundplatte; - - *connecting rod*, D.-Pleuelstange; - - - - *bolt*, D.-P.-bolzen; - - - - *bottom end keep*, D.-Kurbelzapfen -Lagerschalendeckel; - - - - *b. e. liner*, D.-Pleuelstangenfußfutter; - - - - *top end keep*, D.-Kreuzkopflagerschalendeckel; - - *crank pin bolt*, D.-Kurbelzapfenlagerbolzen; - - *c. p. brasses*, D.-Kurbelzapfen-Lagerschalen; - - *crank shaft*, D.-Kurbelwelle; - - - - *bearing*, D.-Kurbelwellenlager; - - - - - *bolt*, D.-K.-bolzen; - - - - - *brasses*, D.-K.-schalen; - - - - *keep*, D.-K.-deckel; - - - - - *bolt*, D.-K.-d-bolzen; - - *crosshead bolt*, D.-Kreuzkopflagerbolzen; - - *c. brasses*, D.-K-k-l-schalen; - - *cylinder*, D.-Zylinder; - - - *cover*, D.-Z.-deckel; - - - - *bolt*, D.-Z.-d-bolzen; - - *cylinder drain pipe*, D.-Z.-Entwässerungsrohr; - - *eccentric*, D.-Exzenter; - - - *bolt*, D.-E.-bolzen; - - - *brasses*, D -E.-Lagerschalen; - - - *rod*, D.-E.-stange; - - - *sheave*, D.-E.-scheibe; - - - *strap*, D.-E.-bügel; - - - - *liner*, D.-E.-b-futter; - - *exhaust pipe*, D.-Ablaßrohr; - - *pipe*, D.-rohr; - - *p. cover*, D.-r-Schutzblech; - - *piston*, D.-Kolben; - - - *rod*, D -Kolbenstange; - - - - *crosshead*, D.-K.-Kreuzkopf; - - - - *stuffing box*, D.-Kolbenstangen-Stopfbüchse; - - - - - *gland*, D.-K.-S-deckel; - - *slide valve*, D.-Schieber; - - *standards*, D.-Ständer; - - *starting valve*, D.-Anlaßventil; - - *steam pipe*, D.-Dampfzuleitungsrohr; - *stop va ve*, D.-Absperrventil; - - *valve casing*, D -Schieberkasten; - - - - *door*, D.-S.-deckel; - - *valve rod*, D.-Schieberstange; - - - - *stuff-

ing box, D.-S.-Stopfbüchse;
- - - - - - gland, D.-S.-S-dekkel; - - worm, D.-schnecke.
steering gear, Steuergerät;
- - bracket, Stützplatte des S.; - indicator, Steuerindikator; - lantern, Kompaßlaterne; - machine, Dampfsteuerapparat (see also steering engine); - pin, Steuernagel; - point, S-strich; - oar, Steuerruder; - propeller, S-schraube; - quadrant. S-quadrant; - rod, Ruderstange; - - cover, R.-Schutzblech; - - leads, Führungsstaugen der Steuerung; - - stanchions, Ruderstangenstützen; - - stools, Steuerstangenstühle; - rods, Steuerstangen; - sail, Segel zur Unterstützung der Steuerung; - screw, Steuerschraube; - stanchions, Ruderstangen; - tackle, R-talje; - telegraph, Steuertelegraph; - wheel, S-rad; - - barrel, S-r-trommel; - - cover, S-r-bezug.
steerless, steuerlos.
steersman, Steuermann.
steersmate, Steuermannsmaat.
steeve, 1. neigen (Bugspriet); 2. trawen (d. h. Ladung durch Schrauben zusammenpressen); 3. Ladebaum zum Zusammenpressen der Ladung; 4. Erhöhungswinkel des Bugspriets.
steeving of cargo, Zusammenpressen von Ladung; - of the bowsprit, Erhöhungswinkel des Bugspriets.
stem, 1. buchen, einschreiben; 2. totsegeln; 3. Vordersteven; - deadwood, Vor-Totholz; - head, Stevenlauf; - knee, S-knie; - piece, Füllholz; - plate, Vorstevenplatte; - props, Stevenschoren; - rabbet, Spündung des Vorderstevens; - rivet, Vorderstevenniete; - shores, Stevenschoren.

stem, to - the current od. tide, wider den Strom segeln; - the water, das Wasser stauen.
stemson, Vorstevenknie; - bolt, V.-bolzen.
step, 1. Spur (unter einem Maste etc); 2. Sprosse, Tritt; to - a mast, einen Mast ins Spur fieren; - butted, treppenweise Verschießung der Planken; - of a capstan, Spillspur; - of a davit, Davitspur; - of a mast, Mastspur.
stepping, Einschnitte im Kiel für die Bauchstücke; - ken, Matrosentanzlokal; - line, innere Spannungslinie am Todholz.
stern, Heck; by the -, hinterlastig; to get a ship by the -, ein Schiff h. machen.
stern anchor, Heckanker; - board, der Gang über Steuer; - boat, Heckboot; - bush, Stevenrohrbüchse; - chase, Heckjagd; - chaser, Heckgeschütz; - davit, H-davit; - fast. hintere Landfeste; - flag, Heckflagge; - frame, 1. H-spant; 2. Schraubenrahmen; - gallery, Heckgalerie; - gland, Stevenrohr-Stopfbüchse; - - neck bush, S-v-r-Grundring; - hook, Heckband; - knee, Hinterstevenknie; - ladder, Heckleiter; - lay, hinterlastig; - light, Hecklicht; - line, hintere Verholleine; - most, achterst; the - - ship, das hinterste Schiff; - moulding od. ornament, Heckverzierung; - pipe, H-klüse; - planking, H-beplankung; - plating, H-beplattung; - port, hintere Ladepforte; - post, Hinterstoven; - - plate, H.-platte; - rabbet, Spündung des Hinterstevens; - - rivet, Hinterstevenniete; - pump, Heckpumpe; - rail, H-leiste; -

rope, Achterleine; - *rudder*, Heckruder; - *seats*, hintere Sitzbänke; - *shaft*, Schraubenschaft; - *sheets*, hintere Sitzbänke; - *thwart*, h. Ruderbank; - *timber*, Heckspant; - *tube*, Stevenrohr; - - *flange*, S.-flansch; - - *gland*, S.-Stopfbüchsendeckel; - - *nut*, S-v-r-mutter; - - *packing*, S-v-r-packung; - *way*, Fahrt über Steuer; *to have* - - *on* od. *to go* - -, F. ü. S. machen; - - *eccentric*, Rückwärtsexzenter; - - - *rod*, R.-stange; - - - *sheave*, R.-scheibe; - - - *strap*, R.-bügel; - *wheel*, Heckrad; - - *engine*, H.-dampfer-Maschine; - - *steamer*, H.-d-; - - *tug*, H.-Schleppdampfer; - *window*, Heckfenster.

sternsman. Steuermann.

sternson, Hinterstevenknie; - *bolt*, H.-bolzen.

sternwards, nach dem Heck zu.

stevedore, Stauer.

steward, Stuard, Proviantmeister; -*'s mate*, Proviantmeistersmaat; - *small stores*, Kajüten-Vorräte; - *stores*, Proviant.

stewardess, Stuardeß.

sticking candlestick, Schiffsleuchter.

stiff breeze, steife Brise; - *gale*, s. Sturm; - *vessel*, s. Schiff.

stiffen, versteifen.

stiffening, 1. versteifen; 2. Ballast resp. Ladung als B.; - *booms*, B.-bäume; - *order*, zollamtliche Erlaubnis zum Einnehmen von Ladung als B. vor gänzlicher Löschung der angebrachten Ladung; - *plate*, Versteifungsplatte.

stiffness, Steifheit.

still condenser, Kühlrohr.

stir the ground, den Grund aufwühlen.

stirrup, Springpferd; - *on the forefoot*, der Bügel über Vordersteven und Kiel.

stoak, verstopfen.

stock, Vorrat; - *of an anchor*, Ankerstock; - *shackle*, Stockschäkel; - *tackle*, Ankertauwerk; *to* - *the anchor*, den Anker stocken.

Stockholm pitch, schwedisches Pech; - *tar*, Holzteer.

stockless bower, stockloser Buganker.

stocks, Stapel; *on the* - *for repairs*, in Ausbesserung od. in Verzimmerung.

stokehold, Heizraum; - *bulkhead*, H.-schott; - - *angle bar*, H.-s-winkel; - *door*, H.-tür; - - *hinge*, H.-t-Scharnier; - *floor* od. *flooring*, H.-Flurplatten; - *ladder*, H.-leiter; - *plate*, H.-Flurplatte; - *platform*, H.-Plattform; - *ventilator*, H.-Ventilator.

stokehole see stokehold.

stoker, Heizer; -*'s place*, H.-stand; - *rod*, Schüreisen.

stoking, Feuerung.

stomach piece, Fisch des Vorderstevens.

stone ballast, Steinballast; - *colour paint*, Steinfarbe; - *wharf*, Steinbuhne.

stony bottom, steiniger Grund.

stood in for Cuxhaven, lagen nach C. an.

stool, 1. Stuhl, Unterschlag (der Pardunen); 2. Rüste (Planke am Hinterteil des Schiffes); - *of steam winch pipes*, Dampfwindenrohrstuhl.

stoop, übergehen, neigen.

stop, 1. stoppen, halten; 2. befestigen; - *a leak*, eine Leckstelle abdichten; - *a rope*, ein Tau befestigen; - *and reverse*, halt und rückwärts; - *the way*, die Fahrt stoppen; - *well*, gut s. (Tau, Trosse, Kette).

stop, Knagge; - *cleat*, Stoßklampe; - *cleats of rudder*, Ruderknaggen; - *cock*, Absperrhahn; - *motion*, Abstellvorrichtung; - *of the spring catch*, der 2te Sektor; - *valve*, Absperrventil; - - *box*, A.-gehäuse; - - *cover*, A.-deckel; - - *gear*, A.-gestänge; - - *gland*, A.-Stopfbüchsendekkel; - - *rod*, A.-stange; - - *spindle*, A.-spindel; - - *stuffing box*, A.-Stopfbüchse; - - *wheel*, A.-rad; - *water*, 1. Scheidenagel (in der Naht einer Kiellasche); 2. Gegenstrom; - *work*, Sperrkegelapparat.

stopped for engineer's purposes, stoppten wegen Maschinenreparaturen.

stopper, 1. stoppen (Tau); 2. abstoppen (Kette); 3. Törntau, Borg; *to clap on* od. *to make fast a* -, einen Stopper aufsetzen; *to take off a* -, e. S. abnehmen; - *bolt*, S.-bolzen; - *knot*, S.-knoten; - *of the anchor*, Porteurleine.

store, verproviantieren; - *bread*, Schiffszwieback; - *room*, Vorratskammer; - *ship*, Proviantschiff; - *twine*, zweidrähtiges Segelgarn.

stores, Vorräte; *to draw* -, V. einnehmen.

storm, Sturm; - *beaten*, vom S. gepeitscht; - *bird*, S.-vogel; - *blast*, S.-bö; - *breeder*, S.-wolke; - *card*, S.-rose; - *centre*, die ruhige Mitte eines Wirbelsturms; - *circle*, S.-rose; - *cone*, S.-kegelsignal; - *current*, durch S. verursachte Strömung; - *drum*, Zylinder als S.-signal; - *flag*, S.-flagge; - *flood*, S.-flut; - *fore staysail*, S.-Stagsegel; - *jib*, S.-klüver; - *kite*, Sturmdrachen - Rettungsapparat; - *mizen*, S.-Besahn; - *regions*, S.-region; - *sail*, S.-segel; - *scud*, niedrig ziehende S.-wolke; - *shattered*, vom S. zerschellt; - *signal*, S.-signal; - *spanker*, S.-besahn; - *stay*, S.-stag; - *sail*, S.-s-segel; - *swept*, vom S. gepeitscht; - *tossed*, vom S.

umhergeschleudert; - *trysail*, S.-Treisegel; - *warning*, S-warnung.

stormy, stürmisch.

stour, Treidelstange.

stove, 1. Ofen; 2. Kochflott (zum Biegen der Planken); - *in*, eingedrückt; eingeschlagen.

stow, 1. stauen; 2. festmachen, wegstauen (Anker, Segel); 3. aufrollen (Segel); - *away*, 1. verstauen; 2. sich verstecken.

stow wood, Stauholz.

stowage, 1. Stauung; 2. Staugeld; - *billets*, Stauholz; - *capacity*, Ladungsräumigkeit; - *certificate*, Stauungsattest; - *duties*, S-u-pflichten; - *goods*, Maßgüter; - *plan*, Stauungsplan.

stowaway, blinder Passagier.

stowed sail, festgemachtes Segel.

stower, Stauer.

stowing capacity, Ladungsräumigkeit; - *strake*, verlorener Gang.

straight ahead, recht voraus; - *brace*, Werkzeughalter; - *edge*, Richtscheit; - *of breadth*, das lange Flach des Schiffes; - *sheered*, ohne Spring gebaut; - *stem*, Stampfsteven; - *through cock*, Durchblashahn.

straighten, rechtmachen, richten; - *the sheer*, den Strohk gerade richten; - *up in the river*, sich im Flusse gerade legen.

strain, 1. sich begeben; 2. Druck, Spannung, Kraft, Zugspannung; - *bands*, Verstärkungsbänder; - *on the cable*, der Druck auf der Ankerkette; - *to bursting point*, bis zum Platzen angestrengt.

strainer, Saugesieb.

straining, 1. sich begeben; 2. Überanstrengung; - *power*, höchste Spannung.

straits, Meerenge, Straße.

strake, Gang, Strak (Platten-
od. Plankenreihe).
strand, 1. stranden, Strand;
2. Ducht (des Taues); 3. Kardeel (des kabelweise ge-
schlagenen Taues); 4. Draht-
stränge (eines Kabels); -
*authority,*Strandamt; - *right,*
S-recht.
stranded, 1. gestrandet; 2. gebrochene Ducht (im Tau);
- *goods,* Strandgut; - *rope,*
Tau mit gebrochener Ducht;
three or four - rope, 3 od. 4
schäftiges Tau.
stranding, Strandung; - *place,*
S.-stelle; - *right,* Strandrecht.
stranger, unbekanntes Schiff.
strap, 1. Bügel, Klammer; 2.
Riemen; 3. Stropp, stroppen;
to - a block, einen Block
stroppen; - *cable* od. *chain,*
Stroppkette; - *key,* Stellkeil.
stray line, Vorläufer der Logleine; - *mark,* Ende des
V. d. L.
streak see strake.
stream, 1. Strom; 2. S-anker;
- *anchor,* S-a.; - *buoy,* Mast-
boje; - *cable* od. *chain,* Strom-
ankerkette; - *current,* See-
strom; -*hawser,* Stromtrosse;
- *ice,* S-eis; - *the buoy,* die
Ankerboje auswerfen; - *the
log,* das Log a.
streamer, Wimpel.
strength, Festigkeit, Verband,
Verstärkuug.
strengthen, verstärken.
strengthening, Verstärkung.
stress, Gewalt; - *of weather,*
Unwetter, stürmisches
Wetter.
stretch, 1.ausrecken;2.strecken
(Segel); 3. prangen (beim
Winde mit starkem Segel-
druck segeln; - *out,* auslegen (beim Rudern); - - *to
sea,* nach See zuliegen.
stretch, Gang, Schlag (die zurückgelegte Strecke ohne
Wendung); - *rope,* Mittelliek
eines Sonnensegels.

stretcher, Fußlatte.
stretching *screw,* Spannschraube.
strike, 1. schlagen, treffen; 2.
Streik, streiken; *to - a sail,*
ein Segel streichen; - *aft,*
mit dem Fuße des Kiels auf
Grund stoßen; - *ahull,* vor
Topp und Takel treiben; -
amain, schnell die Segel
streichen; - *for anchorage,*
nach einem Ankerplatz
loten; - *soundings,* loten;
- *the bell,* Glasen schlagen;
-*the flag,*dieFlagge streichen;
- *the ground,* auf Grund
aufstoßen; - *the sails,* die
Segel streichen; - *the sand,*
auf eine Sandbank geraten;
- *the screw,* die Schraube
treffen; - *the ship,* das Schiff
t.; - *the topmast,* die Marsstenge streichen.
striking, stoßen, gegenstoßen.
string, Balkwäger.
stringer, Stringer; - *angle bar,*
S.-winkel; - *a. iron,* S.-w-
eisen; - *in the hold,* Raum-
stringer; -*plate,* 1. Stringerplatte; 2. Deckstringer; 3.
eiserner Balkwäger (unter
den Balken).
stringy bark, Eukalyptusholz.
strip, 1. abtakeln; 2. losneh-
men; 3. demontieren (Ma-
schine); - *me-naked,* Brannt-
wein.
stripped to the girtline, bis
auf die kahlen Untermasten
abgetakelt.
stroke, 1. Gang, Strak (Platten-
od. Plankenreihe); 2. Hub,
Kolbenhub; 3. Ruderschlag;
4. Vormann (beim Rudern);
- *down,* Kolbenniedergang;
- *forward,* der Hub vor-
wärts; - *oar,* Schlagriemen;
Vorruderer; - *up and down,*
Doppelhub.
strokesman, Vormann beim
Rudern.
strong back, Betingbalken; -
breeze, starke Brise; - *gale,*

s. Sturm; - *hold beam*, schwerer Raumbalken; - *ribbed*, stark gebaut.

strop, Stropp, bestroppen; *to - a block*, einen S. b.

stropped block, bestroppter Block.

struck a floating object, auf einen treibenden Gegenstand gestoßen; - *by a sea*, von einer See getroffen; - *the bar*, auf der Barre aufgestoßen; - *the bridge*, gegen die Brücke gestoßen.

structural strength, Baustärke.

strum, strum box, Saugekorb; *s. b. of bilge injection pipe*, S. des Bilge-Injektionsrohrs; *s. b. of b. pump suction pipe*, S. des Lenzpumpen-Saugerohrs.

stuck sail, das genähte Segel.

stud, stud bolt, Stiftschraube; - - *nut*, S.-mutter; - *link*, Kettenglied; - - *chain cable*, Ankerkette mit Stützen; - *linked chain*, Stegkette; - *of a chain cable*, Stütze eines Ankerkettengliedes; - *pin*, Stiftschraube; - - *nut*, S.-mutter.

studded chain, Ankerkette mit Stützen.

studding boom, Leesegelschiene.

studding sail, Leesegel; - - *boom*, L.-spiere; - - - *brace*, L.-Spierenbrasse; - - - *iron*, L.-S-bügel; *s. s. downhaul*, L.-Niederholer; *s. s. halliard*, L.-fall; - - - *bend*, L.-f-stich; *s. s. sheet*, L.-schote; *s. s. tack*, L.-hals; *s. s. yard*, L.-rahe.

studnsel = studding sail.

stuff, Reusel, Schmiere.

stuffed, vollgepfropft.

stuffing box, Stopfbüchse; - - *bulkhead*, Stopfbüchsenschott; - - - *angle bar*, S.-s-winkel; *s. b. flange*, S-b-flansch; *s. b. gland*, S-b-deckel; - - - *stud*, S-b-Stiftschraube;

s. b. round the rudder head, S-b- des Ruderkopfes.

stump, to start a vessel from the -, ein Schiff ganz neu bauen resp. ganz neu ausrüsten; - *mast*, niedriger Mast ohne Mastkorb; - *topgallant mast*, kurze Bramstenge.

subject to pay duty, zollpflichtig.

submarine cable, unterseeisches Kabel; - *lamp*, unter Wasser brennende Lampe; - *signals*, Unterwassersignale.

submerged, unter Wasser; ersoffen.

subpoena, Vorladung des Gerichts.

subsidy, Subvention.

substitute captain, Setzschiffer; - *for the first*, erste Wiederholungsflagge.

succour a mast, einen Mast verstärken.

suck, to -, saugen, lenz schlagen.

sucker, Sauger; - *rod*, Pumpenstange,

sucking, lenz schlagen; - *and forcing pump*, Saug- und Druckpumpe; - *jet pump*, Saugstrahlpumpe; - *pump*, Saugpumpe; - *tube*, Saugröhre; - *the monkey*, 1. durch einen Strohhalm saugen; 2. an einem Fasse oder einer Kokosnuß saugen.

suction, Sog, saugen, einsaugen; - *cock*, Saugehahn; - *connection*, S-anschluß; - *dredger*, S-bagger; - *lubricator*, S-schmierapparat; - *pipe*, S-rohr; - *pipes*, S-r-leitung; - *pump*, S-pumpe; - *space*, S-raum; - *tube*, S-rohr; - *valve*, S-ventil; - *v. box*, S-v-gehäuse; - *v. chest*, S-v-kasten; - *v. guard*, S-v-Hubbegrenzer; - *v. seat*, S-v-sitz.

sue = sew.

sugar loaf sea, krause See.

suit of sails, Stellsegel.
sulphur canister, Schwefel-
büchse; - *powder,* S-f-blüte.
summer sea marks, Sommer-
seezeichen.
sun rise, Sonnenaufgang; - *set,*
S-untergang; - *wake,* die
Strahlen der untergehenden
Sonne auf dem Wasser; *in
the -'s eye,* gerade auf die
S. zu.
sunk, gesunken, versenkt, in
den Grund gebohrt; - *bridge,*
versenktes Brückenhaus; -
forecastle, versenkte Back;
- *land,* Morast; - *poop,* versenkte Hütte; - *rock,* blinde
Klippe.
sunken ice, gesunkenes Eis; -
rock, blinde Klippe.
supercargo, 1. Cargadeur.
Superkargo; 2. Überfracht.
superheated, überhitzt; - *steam,*
überhitzter Dampf.
superheater, Überhitzer; -
coils, U.-schlangen; - *door,*
U.-tür: - *safety valve,* U.-
Sicherheitsventil; - *stop
valve,* U.-Absperrventil; -
test, U.-prüfung; - *tube,* U.-
rohr; - - *plate,* U.-r-wand.
superintend, beaufsichtigen; -
ance, Beaufsichtigung; - *ent,*
Beaufsichtiger; - - *of a Mercantile Marine Office,* Was-
serschout; - *ing engineer,*
Maschinen-Inspektor.
superstructure, Aufbau.
supplementary cock, Hülfs-
hahn; - *feed c.,* H-speisehahn.
supply, ergänzen, versorgen,
Vorrat; - *pipe,* Speiserohr;
- *steam,* Hinterdampf.
*supporter of the cat head,*Kran-
balkenknie.
supporters under the channels,
die Drücker unter den
Rüsten.
surf, Brandung; - *boat,* Brandungsboot: - *days,* Tage, an
denen starke B. herrscht.
surface, Fläche; - *blow off
cock,* Schaumhahn; - *b. o.*

pipe, S-rohr; - *b. o. valve,*
S-ventil; - *condensation,*
Oberflächen - Kondensation;
- *condenser,* O.-Kondensator;
- *condensing engine,* O.-K-d-
sationsmaschine; - *current,*
Oberströmung; - *of the sea,*
Meeresoberfläche.
surfman, Mitglied der Ret-
tungsmannschaft.
surge, 1. schricken, verfangen;
2. auf Grund stoßen; 3. Brandung; 4. große Welle, Sturzsee; 5. Rand der Spillbeklei-
dung; *to - a cable,* ein Tau
schnell abrollen lassen; -
the capstan, das Tau des
Gangspills lockern; *the - of
the whelps on a capstan,*
Rippen der Spillklampen.
surgeon, Schiffsarzt; - *'s mate,*
Lazarettgehülfe.
surging, 1. das Aufschricken;
2. branden, wogen; - *sea,*
wogende See; - *waves,*
brandende Wogen.
surmark, Kennzeichen an
Schiffshölzern.
surplus tonnage, Ladungsüberschuß.
survey, besichtigen, Besichtigung; - *on hatches,* Luken-
besichtigung; *to - the coast,*
die Küste aufnehmen.
surveying ship, Küstenver-
messungsschiff.
surveyor, Expert, Besichtiger,
Inspektor; - *of customs,*
Zollaufseher; - *of the port,*
Hafenmeister; - *of the shore,*
Strandvogt.
*suspected bill of health,*zweifel-
hafter Gesundheitspaß.
suspension of certificate, Pa-
tententziehung.
swab, aufschwabben, schwabbern, Schwabber; - *rope,*
Schwabberleine; - *washer,*
Gallionsgast.
swabber, Schwabbergast.
swage, Schlichthammer.
swallow, Schlund des Blocks;
- *tail,* das Split einer Flagge;

- - od. - - *scarf*, Schwalben-schwanz (d. h. Verbindung zweier Hölzer).

swamp, to -, vollaufen lassen.

swamped, vollgelaufen, voll-geschlagen.

swash, Untiefe einer Fluß-mündung; - *way* od. *swash-ing*, Fahrwasser über einer Bank.

swathe, Länge einer Welle.

sway, aufheißen; - *across*, kaien; - *aloft!* Bramstengen auf! - *away!* Heiß weg! - *down*, streichen.

swaying away on all top ropes, verschwenderisch leben.

sweat, schwitzen, Schweiß; *damaged by sweat*, schweiß-beschädigt; *to* - *the glass*, die Wachtuhr zu früh um-kehren, um die Wache zu verkürzen: - *the purser*, die Proviantkammer bestehlen.

sweep, fischen (nach verlore-nem Gegenstande); - *away*, lang rojen; - *the bottom*, dreggen; - *the coast*, der Küste entlang segeln; - *the deck*, das Deck abfegen; über d. D. wegfegen.

sweep, langer Riemen; - *of a coast*, Biegung einer Küste; - *of the tiller*, Leuwagen der Ruderpinne; - *of the vessel*, Rundung der Kimm; - *piece*, Schwingholz; -*rope*, Dregtau.

sweepings, Fegsel.

sweeps, lange Riemen.

sweetening cock, Wasserhahn im Unterraum.

swell, Dünung, Schwell; - *ing hammer*, Fußhammer.

swept, alles von Deck weg-geschlagen; *clean* -, besen-rein.

swift, 1. schwichten; 2. das Strecktau um die Gangspill-spaken legen.

swifter, 1. Schwichtleine; 2. Stoßtau (am Boot); *to* -, 1. die Wanttaue mit Takel od.

Gien ansetzen, schwichten; 2. ein Schiff kielholen.

swiftering-in line, Schwicht-leine.

swifters, hinteres Wantenpaar.

swifting tackle, Schwichtungs-talje.

swig, Takel mit nicht parallelen Tauen; - *off*, niederwuchten.

swimming belt, Schwimm-gürtel; - *bladder*, S-blase; - *mark*, Auswässerungslinie eines Schiffes.

swing, schwoien; - *clear*, klar s.; - *head to wind*, vor dem Winde aufdrehen; - *into the haven*, in den Hafeneinschnitt hineinschwenken; - *out a boat*, ein Boot ausschwingen; - *round the compass*, rund herum schwoien; *a* - *skylight*, ein bewegliches Oberlicht; *to* - *the right way*, den rechten Weg schwoien; - *the wrong way*, den verkehrten W. s.; - *the yards round*, umbrassen; - *to the tide*, mit dem Strome schwoien; - *to the wind*, mit dem Winde s.; - *with the tide*, vor dem Strome aufdrehen.

swinging, schwoien; - *berth*, Schwoiraum; - *boom*, Schwingbaum; - *space*, Schwoiraum; - *table*, Hänge-tisch; - *tray*, Schlingerbord.

switch, Schalter; - *board*, S.-brett.

swivel block, Wirbelblock; - *gun*, Schrotgewehr auf Dreh-gestell im Boote; - *hook*, Wirbelhaken; - *link*, Ketten-glied mit Wirbel; - *of a chain cable*, Ankerketten-wirbel.

swizzle, Grog.

sword mat, Schwertmatte.

sympiesometer, Sympieso-meter.

syphered joint, Übereinander-legen zweier Plankenenden.

T.

tabernacle, Mastbock.
table land, Hochplateau; - *shore,* flaches Vorland.
tables, Entwurf zum Bau eines Schiffes; - *of the sun,* Sonnentafeln; - - - -*'s declination,* Deklinationstabellen.
tabling, 1. Umschlag (Segelsaum); 2. Hakenlaschung; - *of timbers,* Hakenscherbe.
tachometer, Geschwindigkeitsmesser.
tack, to -, durch den Wind wenden, über Stag gehen; - *about,* umlegen; - *out,* ausmanövrieren.
tack, the -, 1. Bug, Hals; 2. Schlag, Gang (beim Lavieren u. Wenden); *to make a* -, einen Gang machen; - - - - *and half a* -, kurze und lange Gänge machen; *to hold* - *with,* Kurs halten mit; *on the opposite* -, über den andern Bug liegen; *on the port* -, mit Backbordhalsen über Steuerbordbug; *on the same* -, über denselben Bug liegen; *on the starboard* -, mit Steuerbordhalsen über Backbordbug.
tack block, Hals-block; - *cringle,* H-lägel; - *hook,* H-haken; - *knot,* H-knopf; - *lashing,* H-laschung; - *of a flag,* Flaggensteert; - - - *jib,* Klüverhals; - - - *lower studding sail,* Unterleesegelhals; - - - *royal,* Royalhals; - - - *spanker,* Besahnhals; - - - *staysail,* Stagsegelhals; - - - *studding sail,* Leesegelhals; - - - *topgallant sail,* Bramsegelhals; - - - *topsail,* Marssegelhals; - *piece,* Halsklampe; - *pin,* Coffeinnagel; - *tackle,* Halstalje; - *tracing line,* H-aufholer; - *wind,* Backstagswind.

tacking, Lavieren.
tackle, Takel, Talje, auftakeln; *to clap on a* -, ein Takel anschlagen; *to fleet a* -, ein Takel verfahren; *to frap a* -, ein Takel verzeisen.
tackle block, Takelblock; - *fall,* Taljeläufer; - *hook,* Takelhaken; - *upon* -, Takel auf Takel; - *will not purchase,* das Takel steht; - *with a tie,* spanisches Takel.
tackles, Halsen des Großsegels.
tackling, Takelwerk.
tacks and sheets! Auf Halsen! *to make long and short* - kurze und lange Gänge machen; *Up* - *and sheets!* Stich Halsen und Schoten auf!
taff rail, tafferel, Heckreling.
tail, Steert od. Tauende; - *block,* Steertblock; - *castle,* Hinterteil; - *end,* das hintere Ende; - - *shaft,* Schraubenwelle; - *jigger,* Steerttalje; - *key of propeller,* Schrauben-Querkeil; - *lashing,* Steerttau; - *of a gale,* Ende eines Sturmes; - *of a rope,* Steert; - *of a stream,* ruhiger Teil eines reißenden Stromes; - *piece of the piston rod,* Kolbenstangenende; - *rod,* Führungsstange; - - *gland,* F.-Stopfbüchsendeckel; - *rope,* Schlepptau; - *seizing,* Kattsteertbindsel; - *shaft,* Schraubenschaft; - *tackle,* Steerttalje; *to - to the tide* od. *to - up and down the stream,* mit dem verankerten Schiffe bei der Flut steigen und fallen; - *valve,* Schnüffelventil.
take aback, von vorn kommen; - *a bearing,* eine Peilung nehmen; - *aboard,* an Bord nehmen; - *a broad* od. *heavy*

sheer, weit ab scheren; - *a cast of lead,* das Lot werfen; - *an observation,* eine Höhe nehmen; - *and leave,* einholen und vorbeisegeln; - *charge of the deck,* das Deck versperren; - *charge of the ship,* die Schiffsführung übernehmen; - *down a yard,* eine Rahe herunternehmen; - *hold of,* festhalten; Faß an! Hol hier! - *in a reef,* ein Reff einstecken; - *in a sail,* ein Segel einnehmen; - *in cargo,* Ladung einnehmen; - *in the balance reef,* schwichtreffen; - *in the sails,* die Segel bergen; - *in the slack,* das Lose einholen; - *in tow,* in Schlepptau nehmen; - *off,* abnehmen; - *off the service from the rope,* dem Tau die Kleidung abnehmen; - *off the stopper,* den Stopper abnehmen; - *on board,* an Bord nehmen; - *out,* herausnehmen; - *the altitude,* die Höhe eines Gestirns messen; - *the blocks,* in das Trockendock gehen; - *the ground,* auf Grund geraten; - *the shine out of,* den Rang ablaufen; - *turns in a rope,* Törns eindrehen; - *t. out of a rope,* T. aus einem Tau drehen; - *t. or kinks out of a chain,* Kinken und Törns aus der Kette nehmen; - *water over,* Wasser übernehmen.

taken aback, die Segel back bekommen; back liegend.

taker on bottomry, Bodmereinehmer.

taking off, nachlassend.

tallant, Gilling.

tallow carrier, Talg-trage; - *cock,* T-hahn; - *cup,* T-napf; - *kettle,* T-kessel; - *spade,* T-spaten; - *syringe,* T-spritze; - *tank,* T-kasten; - *wood,* T-baumholz.

tally, 1. anschreiben; 2. anholen (Schoten); - *aft,* dicht anholen; - *on,* anholen; - *the coast,* an der Küste entlang segeln.

tally, Kerbholz; - *clerk* od. *man,* Taljemann.

tamarac wood, amerik. Lärchenholz.

tan a sail, ein Segel gerben.

tandem engine, Tandem-Maschine.

tangent, Berührungslinie; - *sailing,* Segeln nach Mittelbreite.

tank, Tank; - *filling pipe,* T-füllrohr; - *f. valve seat,* T-füll-Ventilsitz; - *f. v. spindle,* T-f-V-spindel; - *f. v. cover,* T-f-V-deckel; - *of a life boat,* Luftkasten eines Rettungsbootes; - *pipe,* Tankrohr; - *suction pipe,* T-saugerohr; - *s. valve,* T-Saugeventil; - *steamer,* T-dampfer; - *top,* T-decke; - *vessel,* T-schiff.

tap, 1. Gewindebohrer; 2. das Muttergewinde schneiden; - *a buoy,* das Wasser aus einer Boje laufen lassen; - *bolt,* Schraubenpfropfen; - *end of a cylinder,* Endfläche eines Zylinders; - *wrench,* Windeeisen.

taper bolt, konischer Bolzen.

tappet, Knagge; - *for distributing,* Steuerknagge.

tar, - down, labsalben, teeren.

tar, 1. Teer; 2. Matrose; *an old -,* ein alter Seebär; *to have a touch of a -,* etwas vom Seemann an sich haben; - *brush,* Teerquast; - *bucket,* T-pütze.

target practice, Schießübungen.

tarpaulin, tarpauling, 1. Persennig; 2. Matrosenhut; - *awning,* Nachtdecke; - *battens,* Schalkleisten; - *canvass,* geteertes Segeltuch; - *muster,* gemeinsame Beisteuer; - *nail,* Persennigspieker; - *phrases,* Matrosenwitze.

tarred rope, geteertes Tau; - *twine*, g. Segelgarn.
tarry, teerig.
tartan, Tartane.
task, 1. untersuchen, überholen; 2. aufbürden; 3. zur Rede stellen.
taught, steif, stramm, streng.
taunt masted. hochmastig; - *rigged*, hochgetakelt.
taut, steif, straff, streng.
tauten, steif od. straff machen.
tautness, Steifheit, Straffheit.
T-bulb beam, T-Wulstbalken; *T-bulb iron*, T-Wulsteisen.
tea clipper, Teeklipper.
teak wood, ostind. Eichenholz.
team boat, ein von Pferden gezogenes Fährboot.
tear, reißen, Riß; - *and wear*, 1. Abnutzung; 2. Schlittage (Taue, Segel).
tearing test, Zerreißprobe.
teaze, Werg auszupfen.
teeth cutting machine, Räderschneidezeug.
telegraph cable, Telegraphenkabel; - *cover*, Telegraph-Bezug; - *dial*, Zifferblatt eines Telegraphen; - *stand*, T.-stand; - *wire*, T.-draht.
telescope, Teleskop.
telescopic funnel, Teleskopschornstein.
tell-tale compass, Kajütskompaß; *t. t. of rudder*, Ruderlageanzeiger.
temper, adouzieren, härten.
temperate, gemäßigt.
tempered steel, gehärteter Stahl.
tempering test, Härtungsprobe.
tempest, Sturm; - *uous*, stürmisch.
templet, Schablone.
templete, Modellplatte.
temporary bulkhead, fliegendes Schott; - *deck*, Kuhbrücke; - *raft*, Notfloß; - *repairs*, notdürftige Reparaturen; - *rudder*, Notruder; - *seizing*, einfacher Bändsel.
tenacity, Zähigkeit.

tend, to -, beim Schwoien aufpassen.
T-ended connecting rod, T-förmige Plenelstange.
tending room, Schwoikreis.
tender, 1. Beiboot, Tender; 2. Submission; 3. empfindlich (Kompaß); 4. rank (Schiff); - *sided*, rank.
tenon, Zapfen; - *of the bowsprit*, Bugsprietzapfen.
tensible force, Spannkraft.
tensile strain, Zugtestigkeit; - *test*, Reckprobe.
tension, Spannung; - *of steam*, Dampfspannung.
term pieces, Verzierungen am Hukholz.
terminal pressure, Enddruck.
terms, Verzierungen am Hukholz.
terrestrial magnetism, Erdmagnetismus.
territorial waters, Seegebiet.
test, Probe, Prüfung, prüfen, proben; - *by steam pressure*, Dampfdruckprobe; - *by water p.*, Wasserdruckprobe; - *cock*, Probierhahn; - *hole*, P-b-loch; - *of double bottom*, Prüfung des Doppelbodens; - *of condenser*, Kondensator-Druckprobe; - *of superheater*, Überhitzer-D.; - *pressure*, Probedruck; - *valve*, Probierventil.
tested chain cable, geprüfte Ankerkette.
testing, Prüfung; - *of anchors*, Ankerprüfung; - *of chain cables*, Ankerkettenprüfung.
tew, schleppen, Schlepptau.
theoretical horse power, theoretische Pferdestärke.
there! Ho!
thick and thin block, Violinblock; - *garboard strake*, dicker Kielgang; - *squall*, geladene Bö; - *strakes of ceiling*, Kimmwegerung; - *stuff*, Bauchdielen; - *weather*, dickes Wetter; - *waterway*, Leibholz.

thickish, trübe, nebelig.
thief, Trinkbecher mit Leine.
thimble, Kausche; - *eye,* Kauschenloch; - *hook,* Haken mit Kausche.
thin waterway, Leibholzplanke.
third bower, der 3te Buganker; - *reef,* das 3te Reff; - - *band,* d. 3te R-band.
thoft, Ruderbank; - *fellow,* Mitruderer.
thole, Dolle, Ruderpflock; - *board,* R-d-klampe; - *pin,* R-d-dolle; - *plate,* R-d-platte; - *string,* Dollbaum.
Thornycroft stern, Thornycroftheck.
thorough put, durchgeschossen (Halsblock); - *repairs,* gründliche Reparaturen.
thowl see thole.
thrap, sorren.
thrashing, mühsam arbeiten.
thread a vessel, ein Schiff durch sehr enge Kanäle führen; - *of a screw,* Schraubengang; - *of oakum,* Wergzopf.
threatening appearance of the weather, drohende Luft.
three bladed propeller, dreiflügelige Schraube; - *crank engine,* Maschine mit drei Kurbeln; - *cylinder compound e.,* dreizylindrige Verbundmaschine; - *cylinder e.,* d. Maschine; - *deck rule,* Reglement für Dreidecker; - *d. ship* od. *vessel,* D.; - *decker,* D.; - *fold purchase,* Gien; - *forked,* dreizackig; - *mast fore and aft schooner,* Dreimast-Gaffelschoner; - *m. topsail s.,* D.-Toppsegelschoner; - *masted ship* od. - *master,* Dreimaster; - *mile limit,* Dreimeilengrenze; - *sided file,* dreikantige Feile; - *stranded rope,* dreischäftiges Tau; - *way cock,* Dreiwegehahn.
throat, Klauohr; - *bolt,* Hals-

bolzen; - *brail,* Brokgeitau; - *cringle,* Klauohrlägel; - *halliard,* Klaufall; - - *bolt,* K-bolzen; - *of a boom,* Klaue eines Baumes; - *of a gaff sail,* Klaubindsel; - *of a hook,* Hals eines Bugbandes; - *of a knee timber,* H. e. Knieholzes; - *of a sail,* Klauohr; - *of an anchor,* Ankerhals; - *seizing,* Augbindsel.
throttle, 1. drosseln; 2. Drosselklappe; - *expansion valve,* Drossel-Expansionsventil; - *valve,* Drosselklappe; - - *gear,* D.-gestänge; - - *handle,* D.-handhabe; - - *lever,* D.-Gestängehebel; - - *rod.* od. *spindle,* D.-spindel.
throttling of steam, Dampfdrosselung.
through bill of lading, Durchgangskonnossement; - *bolt,* Durchbolzen; - *butt bolt,* Durchbolzen in einem Stoß; - *fastening,* Durchverbolzung; - *key of propeller,* Schrauben-Querkeil; - *rate,* Durchgangsfracht; - *service,* direkter Verkehr.
throw, Hub; - *into gear,* einrücken; - *of the crank,* Kurbelhöhe; - *of the eccentric,* Exzentrikhub; - *of the lead,* der Wurf des Handlots; - *of the piston,* Kolbenhub; - *of the slide valve,* Schieberhub; *to - out of gear,* ausrücken.
thrown on her beam ends, zum Kentern liegen.
thrum, thrumb, 1. spicken; 2. Dromel; *to - a mat,* eine Matte bespicken.
thrummed mat, gespickte Matte; - *sail,* Futtermatte.
thrust, 1. Druck; 2. D.-lager, D.-l-welle; - *and tunnel shafting,* D.- und Tunnelwellenleitung; - *bearing,* D.-lager; - - *bolt,* D.-l-bolzen; - - - *nut,* D.-l-b-mutter; - *block,* D.-Lagerstuhl; - -

adjusting gear, D.-lager-Adjustiervorrichtung; - - keep, D.-l-Deckel; - - - bolt, D.-l-D-bolzen; - - - - nut, D.-l-D-b-mutter; - collar of a screw shaft, D.-ring einer Schraubenwelle; - liners, D.-Paßstücke; - of the propeller, Schraubendruck; - ring, Druckring; - shaft, Drucklagerwelle; - - collars, D.-ringe; - - flange, D.-flansch; - shoes, Drucklagerschuhe; - water service, Drucklager-Kühlvorrichtung.

thrusting block, Drucklagerstuhl.

thumb cleat, Hornklampe; - nut, Flügelmutter.

thunder cloud, Gewitterwolke; - squall, G-w-bö; - storm, G-w-sturm.

Thus! Very well thus! Recht so!

thwart, Ducht, Rojebank; - chocks, Duchtenschloß; - clamp, Duchtenknie; -hawse, quer vor dem Bug; - knee, Duchtenknie; - marks, Einsegelungsmarken; - ships, querschiffs; - ship bulkhead stringer, Querschottstringer; - ships coal bunker, Querschiffskohlenbunker; - ship piece in a hatchway, Quer-Scherstock einer Luke; - stanchion, Duchtenstütze; - stringer, Duchtenwäger.

thwarts of a boat, Ruderduchte.

tidal basin, Flut-dock; - chart, F-karte; - harbour, F-hafen; - light, Gezeitfeuer; - river, Gezeitfluß; - service, von der Flut abhängige Dampferverbindung; - stream, Gezeitstrom; - town, Stadt mit Ebbe und Flut; - train, ein von der F. abhängiger Zug; - valve, F-klappe; - wave, F-welle.

tide, Flut, Gezeit, Tide, Ebbe; the - changes, der Strom setzt um; - ebbs od. falls,

das Wasser läuft ab; - flows, es flutet; - gains, der Strom wird stärker; - gets slack, d. S. wird schwach; - gets stronger, d. S. w. stärker; - gets weaker, d. S. w. schwächer; - goes down od. out, die Flut geht: - is at its highest, die Flut ist am höchsten; - is at its lowest, es ist der niedrigste Ebbestand; - is coming in od. up, die Flut kommt herein; - is done od. slack, es ist Stauwasser; - makes, der Strom beginnt; - rises, das Wasser steigt; - runs out od. down, die Ebbe läuft; - serves, die Flut tritt ein; - slackens, der Strom läßt nach; - turns, d. S. kentert.

tide, to -, durch den Strom forttreiben; - away, die Flut läßt nach; - back, mit der F. zurücktreiben; - down, mit der Ebbe stromabwärts fahren; - it, die Flut zum Fahren benutzen; - up, mit der Flut stromaufwärts fahren.

tide ball, Gezeitball; - current, Flutstrom; - day, F-tag; - dial, F-messer; - duty, Hafenzoll; - gate, 1. Flutgatter; 2. Stromschnelle; - gauge, Flutmesser; - harbour, F-hafen; - hour, Hafenzeit; - light, Gezeitenfeuer; - lock, Schleuse; - meter od. pole, Pegel; - predictor, Instrument zur Vorausberechnung der Gezeiten; - rip, Stromkabbelung; - rock, bei Ebbe trockener Felsen; - rode, 1. stromgerecht; 2. mit dem Kopfe gegen den Strom verankert; - table, Fluttabelle; - wave, F-welle; - way, 1. Stromstrich; 2. dem Strome zugekehrt; - work, die während einer Gezeit zurückgelegte Distanz.

tides, at all -, bei Ebbe und Flut zugleich.

tie, to - two ropes together, zwei Taue aufeinander stekken.

tie, Drehreep; *- block,* D.-block; *- hole,* Hummergatt; *- plates,* Lukenstringer; *- rod,* Anker, Stehbolzen; *- tie,* Hängemattsnitzel.

tied up, zurückgehalten.

tier, 1. Reihe; 2. Lage; *- of a cable,* Bucht eines aufgeschossenen Taues; *- of beams,* Balkenlage; *- of plating,* Plattengang.

tierce beef, gesalzenes Rindfleisch in Fässern.

tierer, Ankertau-Aufschießer.

tight, dicht; *- and staunch,* d. und hecht.

tighten, - up, abdichten.

tightning key, Gegenkeil, Stellkeil.

tiller, Ruder-pinne; *- chain,* R-kette; *- cord,* R-reep; *- head,* Kopf der R-pinne; *- lines* od. *ropes,* R-schnur; *- sweep,* Leuwagen der R-pinne; *- wheel,* Steuerrad.

tilt, Bootzelt; *- boat,* mit Segeltuch bedecktes Boot; *- cloth,* S. zur B-bedeckung.

timber, 1. Holz, Bau- od. Nutzholz; 2. Auflanger, Inholz, Spant; *- and room* od. *space,* Inholz und Fach; *- dowel,* Verbindungszapfen; *- head,* Poller; *- hitch,* Zimmermannsstich; *to - - a rope,* ein Tauende mit einem Zimmermannsstich feststekken; *- mark* od. *marker,* Krabpasser; *- ship,* Holzschiff; *every - in her hull,* jeder Balken des Schiffes.

timbers of a ship, Rippenwerk eines Schiffes; *a pretty piece of -,* ein schmuckes Fahrzeug.

time ball, Zeitball; *- by chronometer,* Chronometerzeit; *- charter,* Zeitbefrachtung (für begrenzte Zeit); *- for loading,* Ladezeit; *- freight,*

Zeitfracht; *- of abandonment,* Abandonfrist; *- of service,* Fahrzeit; *- sight,* Sternhöhenmessung.

timenoguy, ausgespanntes Tau gegen Unklarwerden der Schote od. des Halses.

timoneer, Mann am Steuer.

tin shears, Blechschere.

tindel, ind. 2ter Bootsmann.

tinder, Funkentuch.

tip, 1. Kohlenkipper; 2. Kohlen einnehmen.

tipping, tippen, Kohlen einnehmen.

T-iron, T-eisen.

togged off like a tar, wie ein Matrose angezogen.

toggle, Knebel; *- bolt,* K.-bolzen.

togs, Kleider; *long -,* Zivilanzug.

tome off, abstützen.

tongs, Feuerzange.

tongue, 1. Klöppel (der Glocke); 2. Zunge (des Maststockes); *- of a packing ring,* Zunge eines Dichtungsringes; *- o land,* Landzunge; *- piece,* Füllstück.

tonnage, Tonnengehalt; *gross -,* Brutto-T.; *net -,* Netto-T.; *registered -,* festgestellte T.; *short -,* Ladungsmanko; *surplus -,* Ladungsüberschuß.

tonnage built, gebaute Tonnenzahl; *- deck,* Vermessungsdeck; *- dues,* Tonnengeld; *- law,* Vermessungsgesetz; *- space,* Vermessungsdeckraum; *- under deck,* Tonnengehalt unter Deck.

tons deadweight, Gewichtstonnen; *- measurement,* Raumtonnen; *- of displacement,* Tonnen Wasserverdrängung.

tool holder, Werkzeughalter.

toothed, gezahnt.

toothing, Verzahnung; *- plane,* Zahnhobel.

top, 1. auftoppen, toppen; 2. der Mars, Mastkorb; 3. Oberkante (eines Balkens); 4. Decke (des Tanks); 5. Deckel (des Zylinders); 6. Dom (des Kessels); - *and bottom ends*, die oberen und unteren Kurbelwellen-Lagerschalen: - *and butt*, die in England gebräuchliche Plankenverscherbung; - *and topgallant*, vollständig; - *block*, Stengewind-Reepsblock; - *braces*, Marsbrassen; - *brass*, obere Lagerschale; - *brim*, Marsrand; - *burton*, Stengetalje; - - *tackle*, Staggranat; - *chains*, Rahketten; - *clack of a valve*, Auslaßventil; - *cloth*, Bekleidung der Hängematten im Mars; - *end bolt*, Pleuelstangenkopf-Lagerbolzen; - - - *nut*, P.-L.-mutter; - *end brasses*, Pleuelstangen-Lagerschalen: - *end keep*, Deckelplatte des Kreuzkopflagers; - *end liner*, K-k-lagerfutter.

topgallant, 1. Bram-segel; 2. B-stenge; - *backstay*, B-pardune; - *bowline*, B-bulien; - *brace*, B-brasse; - *breeze*, Bramsegelbrise; - *bulwark*, Oberschanzkleid; - - *planking*, O.-Beplankung; - - *stanchion*, Monkeyrelingstütze; - *buntline*, Bram-Bauchgording; - *cap*, Bramstenge-Eselshaupt; - *clew line*, Bramgeitau; - *cross trees*, Dwarssahlingen der Bramstenge; - *foot rope*, Brampferd; - *forecastle*, die feste Back; - *futtock shrouds*, Brampüttingswanten; - *futtocks*, Brampüttingen; - *gale*, Bramsegelsturm; - *halliard* od. - *h. purchase*, Bramfall; - *leech line*, Bram-Nockgording; - *lift*, B.-Toppenaut; - *mast*, B.-stenge; - - *cap*, B.-s-Eselshaupt; - - *fid*, B.-s-Schloßholz; - - - *hole*, B.-s-S.-gatt; - *mast gale*, Bramsegelsturm; - *m. head*, Bramstengen-Topp· - *m. pole*, B.-

Flaggentopp; - *m. rope*, B.-Windreep; - *m. tripping line*, B.-Niederholer; - *netting*, Finkennetz; - *pole*, Bramstengen-Flaggentopp; - *poop*, Oberhütte; - *rail*, Finknetzreling; - *rigging*, 1. Bramgut; 2. B-stengewanten; - *royal*, Oberbramsegel; - *sail*, Bram-segel; - *sheet*, B-schote; - *shroud*, B-want; - *stay*, B-stag; - *staysail*, Bramstagsegel; - - *downhaul*, B.-Niederholer; - - *halliard*, B.-fall; - - *sheet*, B.-schote; - - *tack*, B.-hals; - *studding sail*, Bramleesegel; - - - *boom*, B.-spiere; - - - *downhaul*, B.-Niederholer; - - - *halliard*, B.-fall; - - - *sheet*, B.-schote; - - - *tack*, B.-hals; - - - *yard*, B.-rahe; - *trestle trees*, Bramstengen-Längssahling; - *tye*, Bramdrehreep; - *yard*, Bramrahe; - - *parrel*, Rack der B.; - - *rope*, B.-jolle.

top hamper, das unnütze Obergeschirr; - *hampered*, zu schwere obere Takelung; - *heavy*, 1. oberlastig; 2. betrunken; - *height*, Oberrand des Schiffes; - *honours*, Bramsegel; - *lantern* od. *light*, Topplicht; - *lining*, Stoßlappen; - - *of the top*, Marsbretter; - *of a sail*, Verdoppelung eines Segels; - *of the sheers*, Schere des Bocks; - *man*, Marsgast.

topmast, Marsstenge; - *backstay*, M.-pardune; - *cap*, Marsstenge-Eselshaupt; - *cross trees*, Dwarssahlingen der M.; - *fid*, M.-Schloßholz; - - *hole*, M.-S.-gatt; - *head*, Topp der M.; - *heel*, Hacke d. M.; - *hound*, M.-hummer; - *hounding*, M.-teil zwischen Untermast-Eselshaupt und Bramsahling; - *rigging*, 1. Marswanten: 2. Marsstengengut; - *shroud*, Stengewant; - *stay*, Marsstag; - *staysail*, Stenge-

Stagsegel; - - *downhaul*, S.
S.-Niederholer; - - *halliard*,
S.-S.-fall; - - *sheet*, S.-S.-
schote; - - *tack*, S-S.-hals;
- *studding sail*, Oberleesegel;
- - - *boom*, O.-spiere; - - -
downhaul, O.-Niederholer;
- - - *halliard*, O.-fall; - - -
sheet, O.-schote; - - - *tack*,
O.-hals; - - - *yard*, O.-rahe;
- *trestle trees*, Bram-Längssahling.
top *maul*, Mußkeule; - *netting*,
Marsnetz; - *of windsail*,
Kopf eines Windbeutels; -
of boiler, Dampfdom; - *of
deck*, Oberkante des Decks;
- *of double bottom* od. - *of
tank*, Tankdecke; - *of tunnel*,
Tunneldecke; - *plate of
steering gear*, Topplatte des
Steuergeräts; - *p. of piston*,
Kolbendeckel; - *rail*, Mars-
geländer; - *reef tackle*,
Marsrefftalje; - *rider*, Auflanger der Kattsporen; -
rim, Marsrand; - *rope*, Windreep.
topsail, 1. Marssegel; 2. Toppsegel (Schoner); - *bowline*,
Mars-bulien; - *brace*, 1. M-
brasse; 2. T.-brasse (Schoner);
- - *pendant*, 1. M-b-schenkel;
2. T.-b-s-; - *bunt line*, 1. M-
Bauchgording; 2. T.-B.(Schoner); - *clew line*, 1. M-geitau;
2. T.-g- (Schoner); - *foot
rope*, M-pferd; - *halliard* od.
- *h. purchase*, 1. M-fall; 2.
T.-f- (Schoner); - *h. rack*,
M-f-Gestell; - *lift*, 1. M-toppe-
nant; 2. T.-rahe-t- (Schoner);
- *reef tackle*, 1. M-refftalje;
2. T.-r-t- (Schoner); - *schooner*,
T.-schoner; - *sheet*, 1. M-
schote; 2. T.-s- (Schoner);
- - *bitts*, M-schotenpoller; -
tye, 1. M-drehreep; 2. T.-d-r-
(Schoner); - *yard*, 1. M-rahe;
2. T.-r- (Schoner); - - *foot
rope*, M-pferd; - - *parrel*,
Rack der M-rahe.
topsails over, kopfüber.
topside line, Sente der Ver-

teuning; - *planking*, Ober-
beplankung; - *plating*, obere
Plattengänge; - *stanchion*,
Relingstütze; - *strake*, obere
Seitengang.
topsides, die oberen Seitenteile eines Schiffes.
top *stay*, Borgstag; - *tackle*,
Stenge-Windreepstakel; - -
fall, S.-W-r-Gienläufer; - -
pendant, S.-W-r-hanger; -
tier, oberste Lage; - - *timber*,
oberer Auflanger; - - *hollow*,
Krümmung der obersten A.;
- - *line*, Toppsente; - - *of
forecastle*, Inholz der Back;
- - *of poop*, I. d. Hütte; - -
of raised quarter deck, I.
des erhöhten Quarterdecks;
- *valve*, Druckventil; - - *guard*,
D.-Hubbegrenzer; - - *seat*,
D.-sitz; - *weight*,Obergewicht;
- *whip*, Toppjolle.
Topas boy, ind. Decksjunge.
topping, Aufstopper; - *lift*,
Dirk; - - *block*, D.-block; - -
purchase, D.-talje; - - - *fall*,
D.-t-läufer; - *sea*, hochgehende See.
tormenter, tormentor, große
Fleischgabel.
Tornado, Wirbelsturm.
*torrential rain, torrents of
rain*, strömender Regen.
torrid zone, heiße Zone.
torsion, Zerdrehung.
tosh, die Kupferplatten vom
Schiffe stehlen.
toss the oars up! Riemen
hoch! - *in your o.!* R. ein!
tossing the vessel about, das
Schiff wurde hin- und hergeworfen.
total loss, Totalverlust; -
pressure, gänzlicher Druck.
touch a sail, das Segel flattern
lassen; - *and go*, 1. eine
riskante Sache; 2. Aufstoßen
und Untergehen ist Sache
eines Augenblicks; - *at a
port*, einen Hafen anlaufen;
- *the ground*, den Grund berühren; - *the wind*, dicht
an den Wind kommen; - *up*

a sail, ein Segel an der Rahe ausbessern.

touch, Seitenkante des Hecks; - *hole*, Ladegatt; - *wood*, Zunder, Zunderholz.

touching, raken; - *line*, Tangente.

tough, zähe; *a* - *yarn*, eine kaum glaubliche Geschichte.

tow, schleppen; - *ahead*, vorausschleppen; - *astern*, achteraus s.; - *in*, einschleppen; - *off*, abschleppen; - *out*, ausschleppen.

tow, Schleppzug; *in* -, im Schlepptau; - *boat*,Schlepper; - *line*, Schlepptau; - *path*, Leinpfad; - *rail*, Schleppbogen; - *rope*, S-tau.

towage, 1. Schleppen; 2. Schlepplohn.

towing bitts, Schlepp-betinge; - *bridle*, S-kette; - *hook*, S-haken; - *net*, S-netz; - *path*, Treidelpfad; - *post*, Poller für die Schlepptaue; - *rail*, S-bogen; - *rope*, S-tau; - *spring*, S-trosse; - *timber*, Poller für das S-tau.

T-pipe, Auslaßrohr; *T-plate*, eiserne Stütze.

tracing line, Aufholer.

track, 1. Route, Seeweg; 2. Fahrwasser; 3. treideln; - *boat*, Schleppboot; - *chart*, Segelkarte; - *road*, Treidelpfad; - *rope*, der Treil; - *scout*, Treckschute.

trackage, Treideln.

tracker, Treidler.

tracking, Ziehen am Seil.

trade, 1. Handel; 2. Fahrt nach X.; - *drift*, Passatdrift; - *winds*, Passatwinde.

trader, 1. Händler; 2. regelmäßiger Fahrer.

trades, Passatwinde.

trading to, fahren auf X.; - *port*, Handelshafen.

traffic of steamers, Dampferverkehr.

trail board, Gallionsbrett.

train tackle, Einholtalje.

training ship, Schulschiff; - *tackle*, Backstalje.

tramp, unregelmäßigerFahrer; - *owner*, Reeder von Schiffen in u. Fahrt.

transatlantic cable, transatlantisches Kabel; - *trade*, überseeischer Handel.

transfer elevator, Umladekran.

tranship, umladen; - *ment*, Umladung.

transire, Ausklarierungsschein.

transit duty, Durchgangszoll; - *traffic*, D-g-verkehr.

transmarine port, überseeischer Hafen; - *possession*, ü. Besitz; - *trade*, ü. Handel.

transmission, Übertragung; - *of heat*, Wärme-U.; - *of power*, Kraft-U.

transmitting shaft, Transmissionswelle.

transom, - *beam*, Heckbalken; - *bolt*, H.-bolzen; - *knee*, Heckknie; - *plate*, Heckbalkenplatte.

transport, Transportschiff; - *insurance*, T-p-versicherung.

transporting line, Verholleine

transship, umladen; - *ment*, Umladung.

transversal, quer; - *bulkhead*, Querschott; - *strength*, Querschiffsverband.

transverse, quer; - *frame*, Querspant.

trapezoidal sail, trapezoidisches Segel.

travel, 1. auf- und niedergehen; 2. Hubhöhe; - *of piston*, Kolbenhub.

traveller, 1. Bügel am Klüverbaum; 2. Leiter eines Stagsegels od. des Topplichtes; - *for the wheel chain*, Ausholring für die Ruderkette; - *horse* od. - *iron*, Leuwagen einer Schote; - *on a gaff*, Ausholring an einer Gaffel.

travelling backstay, das laufende Backstag; - *guy*, die laufende Geie; - *load*, die be-

wegliche Last; - *martingale*, das laufende Stampfstag.
traverse, 1. Koppelkurs; 2. Abtrift; *to work a -*, die Kurse koppeln; *to - a yard*, eine Rahe von vorn nach achtern brassen; - *board*, Stechkompaß; - *horse*, Jückstag; - *sailing*, Koppelkursrechnung; - *table*, Koppeltafel.
traversing nut, Spindelmutter.
trawl, 1. Grundschleppnetz; 2. mit G. fischen; *to set, to shoot* od. *throw the -*, das G. auslegen; - *beam*, Querbaum an der Mündung eines G.; - *head*, Klaue am Ende des G.-Querbalkens; - *net*, G.; - *warp*, Schlepptau eines G.
trawler, 1. Schleppfischer; 2. S.-Fahrzeug; - *man*, S.
trawling,Schleppnetzfischerei.
tread, Länge des Kiels.
treadle, Trittbrett (einer Drehbank).
treaty of navigation, Schifffahrtsvertrag.
treble block, dreischeibiger Block; - *ported slide valve*, Muschelschieber; - *reefed*, dreifach gerefft.
trebling, Extra-Beplankung des Bugs.
treenail, 1. Holznagel; 2. mit H. befestigen; - *wedge*, Deutel.
treenailing, Holznagelbefestigung.
trench the ballast by bulkheads, den Ballast abschotten.
trend, sich neigen; - *of the anchor*, Ankerhals.
trending, schiefe Richtung der Küste.
trennel, Holznagel.
trent see trend.
trestle trees, Längssahlings.
trestles, Schoren.
trial speed, Probefahrt-Geschwindigkeit; - *trip*, P.
triangular sail, dreieckiges Segel.

triatic stay, Toppreep.
Trice up! Lie out! Spieren auf! Leg aus!
tricing, aufholen; - *battens*, Leisten an Decksbalken zum Festmachen der Hängematten etc.; - *line*, Aufhoier.
trick, Dienstzeit des Mannes am Steuer (2 Stunden).
trident, Dreizack.
trigger, Stütze des Schloßpalles der Schlagbetten.
trim, 1. Trimm, trimmen (Ladung, Kohlen, Schiff); 2. Segelstellung; 3. schüren (Feuer); 4. putzen (Docht); 5. reddern, richtig stellen (Segel); *to - a boat*, ein Boot aufrichten; - *sharp*, scharf beim Winde brassen; - *the boat!* gerade das Boot! *in bad* od. *sad -*, schmutzig, unordentlich; *in bad, best, good, light, sad sailing -*, schlecht, bestens, gut, leicht, schlecht beladen; *in sailing -*, auf seinen Paß geladen; *out of sailing -*, aus dem Gleichgewicht.
trimmed two feet by the stern, zwei Fuß im Gatt liegen.
trimmer, Kohlentrimmer; -*'s lamp*, Trimmerlampe.
trimming shovel, Trimmerschaufel; - *tank*, Trimmtank; - *ventilators back to the wind*, die Ventilatoren wurden entgegengesetzt vom Winde gedreht.
trinket, Marssegel.
trip, 1. Fahrt, Ausfahrt; 2. Schlag beim Lavieren; *to - a mast*, einen Mast lüften; - *a yard*, eine Rahe kaien; - *an anchor*, einen Anker vom Grunde losmachen.
triple block, dreischeibiger Block; - *expansion engine*, dreifache Expansionsmaschine; - *ported slide valve*, Muschelschieber; - *riveting*, dreifache Nietung; - *sheaved block*, dreischeibiger Block.

triplets, drei Kettenglieder zwischen Ankertau und A-ring.

tripping line, Aufholer od. Niederholer; - *valve*, Kontaktventil.

tropic of cancer, Wendekreis des Krebses.

tropics, Wendekreise.

trough of the sea, Wellental.

truck, 1. Flaggenknopf; 2. Wantklotje.

true, rechtweisend; - *altitude*, wahre Höhe; - *bearings*, w. Peilung; - *course*, rechtweisender Kurs; - *distance*, der rechte Abstand; - *latitude*, wahre Breite; - *tide*, der gerade setzende Strom; - *time*, wahre Zeit; - *water*, richtige Wassertiefe.

trundle head, Trommel des Gangspills.

trunk, Koker; - *bulkhead*, Schacht-schott; - - *plate*, S-platte; - *cabin*, über und unter Deck liegende Kajüte; - *deck*, Kofferdeck; - - *beam*, K.-balken; - - - *angle bar*, K.-b-winkel; - - - *stringer*, K.-b-stringer; *t. d. guard rods*, K.-geländerstangen; *t. d. hatch*, K.-luke; *t. d. hatchway coaming*, K.-Lukensüll; *t. d. pillar*, K.-stütze; *t. d. plating* K.-beplattung; *t. d. rails and stanchions*, K.-geländer; *t. d. s.*, K.-g-stützen; *t. d. steamer*, K.-dampfer; *t. d. stringer*, K.-stringer; - - - *angle bar*, K.-s-winkel; - - - *inner a. b.*, Innenwinkel des K.-stringers; *t. d. waterway*, K.-Wassergang; - *engine*, Maschine mit hohler Kolbenstange; - *for skylight*, Oberlichtfenster; - *hatch*, Kofferdeckluke; - *piston*, Trunkkolben; - *screw*, Koker-schraube; - *side plating*, Kofferseitenbeplattung; - *ventilator*, Schachtventilator; - *way*, Koffergang.

trunnion, Schildzapfen; - *pipe*, S.-rohr.

truss, 1. steifen, stützen; 2. Rack; - *hoop*, R-band; - *parrel*, R-stropp; - *pendant*, R-kette; - *piece*, Füllholz; - *tackle*, R-talje; - *up*, ein Gaffelsegel schnell aufgeien.

try to gain the weather gauge, versuchen, luvwärts zu kommen.

trying, beiliegen.

trysail, Treisegel; - *boom*, T.-baum; - *brails*, T.-Geitaue; - *gaff*, T.-gaffel; - *halliard*, T.-fall; - *inhaul*, T.-Einholer; - *mast*, Schnaumast; - *outhaul*, T.-Ausholer; - *peak halliard*, T.-Piekfall; - *sheet*, T.-schote; - *tack*, T.-hals; - *throat halliard*, T.-Klaufall; - *vang*, T.-gerde.

tub, Balje.

tube, Rohr; - *brush*, R-bürste; - - *handle*, R-b-stange; - *compass*, Röhrenzirkel; - *expander*, Rohrdichter; - *fixing tools*, Werkzeug zum Rohreinsetzen; - *flue*, Feuerrohr; - *hole*, Rohrloch; - *mandrill*, R-pickhammer; - *packing*, R-packung; - *plate*, R-wand; - - *of condenser*, R-w- des Kondensators; - - *of superheater*, R-w- des Überhitzers; - *plug*, R-pfropfen; - *scraper*, R-kratzer; - *stopper*, R-pfropfen; - *stopper*, R-stopfstange; - - *nut*, R-ankermutter.

tubing, mit Röhren versehen; - *hammer*, Rohrhammer.

tubular, röhrenförmig; - *boiler*, Feuerrohrkessel.

tubulous boiler, Siederohrkessel.

tuck, Gillung; - *'s packing*, Tucksche Liderung.

tug, 1. hart rojen, ohne voraus zu kommen; 2. Schlepper; - *boat*, S.; *to tug at moorings*, an der Vertäuung schleppen.

tuggage, Schlepperlohn.

tulip wood, Tulpenholz.

tumble, to - home, sich nach innen neigen.

tumbler, Schlepphaken; *- of an anchor,* Schlipphaken; *-s,* Arme, auf denen der Rüstanker ruht.

tumbling, rollen.

tun buoy, Tonnenboje; *- for a b.,* Tonne für eine Boje.

tunnel, Tunnel; *- bearing,* T.-wellenlager; *- - bolt,* T.-w-l-bolzen; *- - - nut,* T.-w-l-b-mutter; *- bearing keep,* T.-l-deckel; *- cock,* T.-Kühlhahn; *- door,* T.-tür; *- flooring,* T.-Flurplatten; *- frames,* T.-spanten; *- plating,* T.-beplattung; *- recess,* T.-nische; *- shaft,* T.-welle; *- - bearing,* T.-Wellenlager; *- - - bolt,* T.-W.-bolzen; *t. s. coupling,* T.-Wellenkuppelung; *- bolt,* T.-W. bolzen; *t. s. flange,* T.-Wellenflansch; *t. s. journal,* T.-wellen-Lagerzapfen; *- shafting,* T.-Wellenleitung; *- ventilator,* T.-Ventilator; *- water service,* T.-wellen-Kühlvorrichtung; *- well,* T.-brunnen.

turbine, Turbine; *- engine,* T.-maschine; *- propulsion,* Fortbewegung durch T.; *- steamer,* Turbinendampfer; *- wheel,* T-b-rad.

turbulent, aufgeregt, kochend.

Turk's head, türk. Knoten.

turn, to -, lavieren; *- all hands up,* alle Mann auf Deck rufen; *- back into the port left,* in den Ausgangshafen zurückkehren; *- in,* zur Koje gehen; *- in a dead eye,* eine Jungfer einbinden; *- in the rigging,* die Wanten einbinden; *- off,* ablenken; *- out the watch,* die Wache purren; *- round,* umdrehen; *- to again,* die Arbeit wieder aufnehmen; *- to windward,* aufkreuzen; *- turtle,* umschlagen, kentern; *- up*

on the anchor, chain od. *rope,* am Anker, an der Kette od. an einem Tau auftörnen; *- up the watch,* die Wache purren; *- up the wheel,* das Ruder aufholen; *- windward,* den Wind abkneifen.

turn, Schlagtörn (eines Taues); *a - ahead,* einen Schlag vorwärts; *a - astern,* e. S. rückwärts; *the - in the cable* od. *hawse,* der Törn od. Rundtörn od. ganze Schlag in der Ankerkette; *- of a lashing,* der Törn einer Laschung; *- of a seizing,* d. T. eines Bindsels; *- of the bilge,* Rundung der Kimm; *- of the tide,* Stromwechsel.

turning buoy, Kursveränderungsboje.

turning engine, Drehvorrichtungsmaschine; *- - connecting rod,* D.-Pleuelstange; *- - - - bolt,* D.-P.-bolzen; *- - - bottom end keep,* D.-Kurbelzapfen-Lagerschalendekkel; *- - - - b. e. liner,* D.-Pleuelstangenfußfutter; *- - - top end keep,* D.-Kreuzkopflagerschalendeckel; *t. e. crank pin bolt,* D.-Kurbelzapfenlagerbolzen; *t. e. c. p. brasses,* D.-K-b-z-l-schalen; *t. e. c. shaft,* D.-Kurbelwelle; *- - - - bearing,* D.-Kurbelwellenlager; *- - - - - bolt,* D-K.-bolzen; *- - - - brasses,* D.-K.-schalen; *- - - - - keep,* D.-K.-deckel; *- - - - keep bolt,* D.-K.-d-bolzen; *t. e. crosshead bolt,* D.-Kreuzkopflagerbolzen; *t. e. c. brasses,* D.-K-k-l-schalen; *t. e. cylinder,* D.-Zylinder; *- - - cover,* D.-Z.-deckel; *- - - - bolt,* D.-Z.-d-bolzen; *t. e. cylinder drain pipe,* D.-Z.-Entwässerungsrohr; *t. e. eccentric,* D.-Exzenter; *- - - bolt,* D.-E.-bolzen; *- - - brasses,* D.-E.-Lagerschalen; *- - - rod,*

14*

D.-E.-stange; - - - *sheave*, D.-E.-scheibe; - - - *strap*, D.-E.-bügel; - - - - *liner*, D.-E.-b-futter; *t. e. exhaust pipe*, D.-Dampfablaßrohr; *t. e. piston*, D.-Kolben; - - - *rod*, D.-Kolbenstange; - - - - *crosshead*, D.-K.-Kreuzkopf; - - - - *stuffing box*, D.-K-b-s-Stopfbüchse; - - - - - - *gland*, D.-K-b-s-S.-deckel; *t. e. slide valve*, D.-Schieber; *t. e. starting valve*, D.-Anlaßventil; *t. e. steam pipe*, D.-Dampfzuleitungsrohr; *t. e. stop valve*, D.-Absperrventil; *t. e. valve casing*, D.-Schieberkasten; - - - - *door*, D.-S.-deckel; *t. e. v. rod*, D.-Schieberstange; - - - - *stuffing box*, D.-S.-Stopfbüchse; - - - - - - *gland*, D.-S.-S.-deckel.
turning fid, Dreh-knüppel; - *gear*, D-vorrichtung; - - *messenger*, D-v-r-Kabelaring; - - *worm*, D-v-r-schnecke; - *lathe*, Drehbank; - *valve*, D-ventil; - *wheel*, D-rad; - *wind*, scharfer Wind; - *worm wheel*, Drehvorrichtungsrad.
turpentine wood, Terpentinholz.
turret deck, Turmdeck; - - *beam*, T.-balken; - - - *angle bar*, T.-b-winkel; - - - *stringer*, T.-b-stringer; *t. d. guard rods*, T.-Geländerstangen; *t. d. hatches*, T.-luken; *t. d. hatchway coaming*, T.-l-süll; *t. d. pillar*, T.-stütze; *t. d. plating*, T.-beplattung; *t. d. rails and stanchions*, T.-geländer; *t. d. sheerstrake*, T.-Schergang; *t. d. stanchion*, T.-Geländerstütze; *t. d. steamer*, T.-dampfer; *t. d. stringer*, T.-stringer; - - - *angle bar*, T.-s-winkel; - - - *inner a. b.*, Innenwinkel des T.-s-; *t. d. waterway*, T.-Wassergang.
turret ship, Kriegsschiff mit Turmbatterien; - *side plating*, T-seitenbeplattung.

turtle back, - *deck*, Schildkrötendeck; - *peg*, Harpune für Schildkröten; - *turned*, umgeschlagen; - *twine*, drei-drähtiges Garn zu Schildkrötennetzen.
twain cloud, Haufenwolke.
tween deck, Zwischendeck; - *deck passenger*, Z.-passagier; - *decks ceiling*, Z.-wegerung.
twiddling line, Fangtau des Steuerrades.
twig a bowline, eine Bulien ausholen.
twin screw, Doppelschraube; - - *life boat*, D.-Rettungsboot; - - *saloon steamer*, D.-Salondampfer; - - *steamer*, D.-dampfer; - - *tug*, D.-Schleppdampfer; - *steamer*, Zwillingsdampfer.
twine, Segelgarn.
twist a cable, ein Kabeltau drehen; - *oakum into a thread*, Werg spinnen.
twisted oakum, gesponnenes Werg.
twisting force, Torsionskraft.
twixt deck, Zwischendeck.
two bladed propeller, zweiflügelige Schraube; - *blocks*, Block an Block; - *crank engine*, Maschine mit zwei Kurbeln; - *cylinder compound engine*, zweizylindrige Verbundmaschine; - *deck vessel*, Zweideck Schiff; - *fold block*, zweischeibiger Block; - - *purchase*, Vierläufer; - *half hitches*, doppelter Halbstich; - *masted*, zweimastig; - *throw crank shaft*, die Welle mit zwei Kurbeln; - *way cock*, Zweiwegehahn.
tye, Drehreep; - *block*, Drehreepsblock; - *hole*, Scheibgatt der Stenge; - *plates*, Lukenstringer; - *rod*, Stehbolzen; - *tye*, Hängematts-Nitzel.
typhoon, Taifun.

U.

ugly weather, drohendes Wetter.

ullage, ausgelaufene flüssige Ladung.

unanchor, losankern.

unballast, Ballast löschen; -ed, 1. ohne Ballast; 2. ungleichmäßig belastet.

unbank the fire, das Feuer wieder anschüren.

unbend, 1. abschlagen (Segel); 2. losmachen (Tau); 3. abstecken (Kette).

unbitt, von der Beting abnehmen.

unblockaded, unblockiert.

undecked vessel, ungedecktes Fahrzeug.

under bare poles, vor Topp und Takel; - *canvass*, unter Segel; - *current*, Unterströmung; - *foot*, unter dem Schiffe; - *freight*, 1. unterbefrachten; 2. unterverfrachten; - *freighter*, Afterverfrachter.

undermanned, zu schwach bemannt.

undermasted, zu leicht bemastet.

undermost, unterste.

under own steam, mit eigenem Dampf.

underrun, nachsehen und klaren.

under sail, unter Segel.

undersail, *to* -, längs der Küste fahren.

under sea, beigedreht.

underset, Unterstrom.

underside, Unterseite.

undershore, *to* -, abstützen.

undersparred, zu leicht bemastet.

under steam and sail, unter Dampf und Segel; - *the land*, unter Land; - *the lee*, unter Lee; - *the sea*, von Wellen begraben.

undertow, unregelmäßige Unterströmung.

underturns of a lashing, die unteren Törns einer doppelten Laschung; - - - *seizing*, d. u. T. eines d. Bindsels.

under way, in Fahrt; - - *lights*, die Lichter eines in der Fahrt begriffenen Schiffes; - *weigh*, über Steuer gehen.

underwriter, Assekuradeur; -'s *association*, Versicherungsverein; - *surveyor*, Besichtiger für die Versicherer.

underwriting, versichern.

undo a rope, ein Tau aufdrehen.

undock, aus dem Dock holen.

uneasy, unruhig.

unenclosed space, uneingeschlossener Raum.

unentered, unverzollt.

uneven keel, ungleichlastig.

unfathomable, unergründlich.

unfold, Segel beisetzen.

unfurl a flag, eine Flagge wehen lassen; - *the sails*, Segel losmachen.

unhailed, nicht angerufen.

unhang the rudder, das Ruder aushaken.

unhook, aushaken.

uniform pressure, gleichmäßiger Druck; - *temperature*, gleichmäßige Temperatur.

Union down, Notflagge; - *Jack*, engl. Nationalflagge.

unit, Einheit; - *of force*, Kraft-E.; - - *heat*, Wärme-E.; - - *weight*, Gewichts-E.; - - *work*, Arbeits-E.

universal joint, universale Dichtung; - *screw wrench*, Universal-Schraubenschlüssel.

unjacketed cylinder, Zylinder ohne Mantel.

unlace a bonnet, ein Bonnet abschlagen.

unlaid rope, ein aufgeschlagenes Tau.

unlash, losmachen.

unlaunched, nicht vom Stapel gelassen.

unlay a rope, ein Tau aufschlagen.

unload, ausladen.

unmanageable, manövrierunfähig.

unmanned, unbemannt.

unmoor, die Anker lichten.

unnavigable, nicht schiffbar.

unquenchable, unauslöschbar.

unreeving, ausscheren.

unrig, abtakeln.

unsafe anchorage, unsicherer Ankerplatz; - *port,* u. Hafen; - *road,* u. Reede.

unseamanlike, unseemännisch.

unseaworthiness, Seeuntüchtigkeit.

unseaworthy, seeuntüchtig.

unserve, entkleiden.

unserviceable, unbrauchbar.

unsettled, unbeständig.

unshackle, ausschäkeln.

unship, 1. abnehmen, herausnehmen; 2. ausschiffen; 3. aushängen (Ruder); 4. einlegen (Riemen).

unshore, entstützen.

unsling, eine Länge aushängen und abnehmen.

unsteady, veränderlich.

unstitch, auftrennen, trennen.

unstock, vom Stapel lassen.

unstow, umstauen; - *ed,* umgestaut.

unstrand, die Duchten aufdrehen.

unstropped block, unbestroppter Block.

untarred oakum, Dusse; - *rope,* ungeteertes Tau.

untie, abbinden.

untrustworthy bottom, altes wurmstichiges Fahrzeug.

untwist a rope, ein Tau aufdrehen; - *old ropes,* alte Taue auspflücken; - *the ends of the strands,* die Kabelgarne ausdrehen.

unwholesome ship, schlechtes Schiff.

up along, stromaufwärts; - *anchor,* Anker auf; - *and down,* auf und nieder (Anker, Flagge, Knie, Wind); - *and down bolts,* Bolzen, die abwechselnd von oben nach unten und umgekehrt geschlagen sind; - *a. d. stem,* Stampfsteven; - *a. d. stroke,* Kolbenspiel; *the wind is u. a. d.,* es regt sich kein Lüftchen; - *baats!* Boote heißen! - *courses!* Untersegel bergen! - *hands!* Enter auf! Gasten e. a.! - *helm!* Leewärts das Ruder! - *river barge,* Oberländerkahn; - *stream,* oberhalb im Strom; - *stroke,* Kolbenaufgang; - *tacks and sheets!* Halsen auf! - *the river,* stromaufwärts; - *with the helm!* das Ruder auf!

uphroe, 1. Spinnkopf; 2. S.-block

upmaking of the launching cradle, 1. Füllstücke der Schlagbetten; 2. Aufklotzen zum Stapellauf.

upper channel, Oberrüste; - *collar of a stay,* Stagauge; - *counter,* 1. Oberteil des Hecks; 2. Namenbrett; - *cringle of a sail,* Nocklägel eines Segels; - *deck,* Oberdeck.

upper deck beam, Oberdeckbalken; - - - *angle bar,* O.-winkel; - - - *clamp,* Oberdeck-Unterbalkweger; - - - *hanging knee,* Oberdeckbalken-Hängeknie; - - - *lodging knee,* Horizontales Knie des O.; - - - *shelf,* Oberdeck-Balkweger; - - - *stringer,* Oberdeckbalken - Stringer; - - - - *plate,* O.-S.-platte; *u. d. b. tie plate,* O.-Lukenstringer.

upper deck bolt, Oberdeckbolzen; *u. d. fastening,* O-d-befestigung; *u. d. hatch,* O-d-luke; *u. d. hatchway coaming,* O-d-lukensüll; *u. d.*

hook, O-d-band; *u. d. mast wedge*, O-d-mastkeil; *u. d. pillar*, O-d-stütze; *u. d. planking*, O-d-beplankung; *u. d. plating*, O-d-beplattung; *u. d. sheerstrake*, O-d-Schergang; *u. d. stanchion*, O-d-stütze; *u. d. stringer*, O-d-stringer; - - - *angle bar*, O-d-s-winkel; - - - *inner a. b.*, Innenwinkel des O-d-s-; - - - *plate*, O-d-s-platte; - - - *shell lugs*, kurze Stringerwinkel des O-d-; *u. d. waterway*, O-d-Wassergang.

upper false keel, Gegenkiel.

upper fore topgallant brace, Vor-Oberbram-brasse; *u. f. t. foot rope*, V-O-b-pferd; *u. f. t. sail*, V-O-b-segel; *u. f. t. yard*, V-O-b-rahe.

upper fore topsail, 1. Vor-Obermarssegel; 2. Vor-Obertoppsegel (Schoner); - - - *brace*, 1. V-O-m-brasse; 2. V-O-t-b-; - - - *b. pendant*, 1. V-O-m-Brassenschenkel; 2. V-O-t-B. (Schoner); - - - *foot rope*, 1. V-O-m-pferd; 2. V-O-t-p-(Schoner); - - - *yard*, 1. V-O-m-rahe; 2. V-O-t-rahe (Schoner).

upper futtock rider, Auflanger der Kattsporen; - *hold*, Oberraum.

upper jigger topgallant brace, Besahn-Oberbram-brasse; *u. j. t. sail*, B.-O-b-segel; *u. j. t. yard*, B.-O-b-rahe; *u. j. topsail*, B.-O-marssegel; - - - *brace*, B.-O-m-brasse; - - - - *pendant*, B.-O-m-b-schenkel; *u. j. t. foot rope*, B.-O-m-pferd; *u. j. t. yard*, B.-O-m-rahe.

upper keel, Oberkiel.

upper main topgallant brace, Groß-Oberbram-brasse; *u. m. t. foot rope*, G-O-b-pferd; *u. m. t. sail*. G-O-b-segel; *u. m. t. yard*, G-O-b-rahe.

upper main topsail, 1. Groß-Ober-marssegel; 2. G-O-topp-segel (Schoner); - - - *brace*, 1. G-O-m-brasse; 2. G-O-t-s-b-(Schoner); - - - *b. pendant*, G-O-m-Brassenschenkel; - - - *foot rope*, G-O-m-pferd; - - - *yard*, 1. G-O-m-rahe; 2. G-O-t-s-r- (Schoner).

upper mast, Stenge.

upper middle topgallant brace, Mittel-Oberbram-brasse; *u. m. t. foot rope*, M.-O-b-pferd; *u. m. t. sail*, M.-O-b-segel; *u. m. t. yard*, M.-O-b-rahe.

upper middle topsail, Mittel-Obermars-segel; - - - *brace*, M.-O-m-brasse; - - - *b. pendant*, M.-O-m-Brassenschenkel; - - - *foot rope*, M.-O-m-pferd; - - - *yard*, M.-O-m-rahe.

upper mizen topgallant brace, Kreuz-Oberbram-brasse; *u. m. t. foot rope*, K.-O-b-pferd; *u. m. t. sail*, K.-O-b-segel; *u. m. t. yard*, K.-O-b-rahe.

upper mizen topsail, Kreuz-Obermars-segel; - - - *brace*, K.-O-m-brasse; - - - *b. pendant*, K.-O-m-Brassenschenkel; - - - *foot rope*, K.-O-m-pferd; - - - *yard*, K.-O-m-rahe.

upper platform, Podest; - *pump box*, Pumpenschuh; - *rigging*, das obere stehende Gut; - *rounding*, Heck-bord; - - *of the stern*, H-geländer; - *sails*, Ober-segel; - *sheerstrake*, O-schergang; - *stern*, Heck; - - *timber*, H-spant; - *strake of a boat*, Schandeckelplanke; - *topgallant brace*, Oberbram-brasse; *u. t. sail*, O-b-segel; - *topsail*, 1. Ober-mars-segel; 2. Obertoppsegel (Schoner); - - *brace*, 1. O-m-brasse; 2. O-t-s-b- (Schoner); - - *yard*, O-m-rahe; - *tube*, Steigrohr; - *turns of a lashing*, die oberen Törns einer doppelten Laschung; *u. t. of a seizing*, d. o. T. eines d. Bindsels; - *turn of bilge keelson*, Kielschwein in der oberen Rundung der Kimm; - *valve*, Oberventil der Luftpumpe; - *waterway*, Setzweger; - *works*, Oberwerk; *to build* od. *to lay the u. w.*, das Oberschiff ausbauen; - *yards*, Oberrahen.

uprights, Ständer.

upset, umschlagen.

upstanders of the windlass, Haspelstützen.

upstream, stromaufwärts.

uptake, Rauchfang.

urge the fires, die Feuer schüren.

usage of the sea, Seegebrauch.

used up, aufgebraucht, ausgefahren.

useful effect, Nutzleistung.

uses and customs of the sea, Seegebräuche.

uvrou, 1. Spinnkopf; 2. S.- - block.

V.

vacillate, wanken.

vacuum, 1. Luftleere; 2. luftleerer Raum, Vacuum; - *gauge*, V.-messer; - - *pipe*, V.-m-rohr; - *indicator*, V.-m-; - *pipe*, V.-rohr; - *space*, V.-raum; - - *of condenser*, luftleerer Raum des Kondensators.

valances of an awning, Seitengarnitur eines Sonnensegels.

value insured, Versicherungswert.

valve, Ventil; - *balance piston*, Schieberabbalancierungskolben; - - - *cylinder*, Schutzkappe des S.; - *box*, Ventilkasten; - - *cover*, V.-deckel; - *bucket*, Kolben mit Ventil; - *casing*, Schieberkasten; - - *cover* od. *door*, S.-deckel; - - - *bolt*, S.-d-bolzen; - - - - *nut*, S.-d-b-mutter; - *casing escape valve load*, S.-Sicherheitsventilbelastung; - *chamber* od. *chest*, Schieberkasten; - - *door*, S.-deckel; - - - *bolt*, S.-d-bolzen; - *cock*, Drehventil; - *coupling*, Verschraubung mit Ventil; - *cover*, Ventildeckel; - *cylinder*, Steuerzylinder; - *face*, Schieberspiegel; - *gear*, äußere Steuerung; - *guard*, Hubbegrenzer; - *lever*, Ventil-hebel; - *lifter*, V.-heber; - *link*, Coulisse; - *load*, Ventilbelastung; - *motion*, äußere Steuerung; - *piston*, Ventilkolben; - *rod*, Schieberstange; - - *guide*, S.-führung; - - *link*, S.-gelenk; - - *stuffing box*, S.-Stopfbüchse; - - - - *gland*, S.-S.-deckel; - *seat*, Ventilsitz; - *shaft*, Schieberkurbelwelle; - *spindle*, Ventilspindel; - - *guide*, Schieberstangenführung; - *spring*, Ventilfeder; - *stem*, V.-scharnier.

valvelet, kleines Ventil.

vane, Windfahne; - *board*, Flügel-heckschere; - *spindle*, F-stange; - *stock*, F-heck.

vanes of a Jacob's staff, Läufer des Jakobstabs.

vang, Gerde; - *fall*, Gerdenläufer; - *pendant*, Gaffelgerdenschenkel.

vangee, Vorrichtung, um die Pumpen in Gang zu setzen.

variable, veränderlich; - *and unsteady*, v. in Richtung und Stärke; - *expansion*, veränderliche Expansion.

variables, the -, die Gegend der veränderlichen Winde.

variation, Mißweisung; - *chart*, M.-karte; - *compass*, Peilkompaß.

varnish, Lack, lackieren.
veer, 1. fieren, schricken (Tau); 2. umspringen (Wind); 3. halsen, wenden, drehen; - *about the northwest*, nach N. W. umspringen; - *aft*, raumen; - *aloft*, auf hissen; - *and haul*. 1. raumen und schralen (Wind); 2. fieren und holen (Tau); - *away*, ausstecken (Kette); - *no more!* Nicht mehr abfallen! - *out*, fieren.
veering, halsen; - *cable*, Luvkette.
vegetal tar, Holzteer.
velivolant, mit vollen Segeln.
velocity, Geschwindigkeit; - *of evaporation*, Verdampfungs-G.; - *of piston*, Kolben-G.
vent pipe, Abzugsrohr für Dampf.
ventilate, lüften.
ventilating arrangements, Ventilations-Einrichtung.
ventilator, Ventilator; - *coat*, V.-kragen; - *cover*, V.-kappe; - *cowl*, V.-kopf; - *flange*, V.-rohr; - *mouth*, V.-öffnung; - *socket*, V.-sockel.
ventilators trimmed back to wind, die Ventilatoren wurden vom Winde weggedreht.
vernal equinox, Frühlings-Äquinoctium.
versed frame, Gegenspant.
vertical air pump, vertikale Luftpumpe; - *bilge p.*, v. Lenzpumpe; - *centre plate keelson*, Mittelplattenkielschwein; - - - *angle bar*, M.-winkel; - *circulating pump*, vertikale Zirkulationspumpe; - *cylindrical boiler*, v. Zylinderkessel; - *deviation*, Höhenabweichung; - *direct acting engine*, direkt wirkende vertikale Maschine; - *drilling machine*, stehende Bohrmaschine; - *feed pump*, vertikale Speisepumpe; - *paddle wheel* od. - - - *with feathering paddles*, Schaufel-

rad mit beweglichen Schaufeln; - *steering engine*, vertikale Dampfsteuermaschine; - *through bolt*, v. Durchbolzen.
vessel, 1. Schiff; 2. Behälter, Gefäß; 3. Kessel; - *in distress*, Schiff in Not; - *of charge*, übertief geladenes Schiff; - *with very close timbers*, Schiff mit sehr dicht stehenden Inhölzern; - *with very wide t.*, S. m. s. weit auseinander s. I.
vessels spoken, gesprochene Schiffe.
veteran sailor, befahrener Seemann.
vice, Schraubstock; - *bench*, Feilbank; - *jaws*, Schraubstockbacken.
victual, verproviantieren; -*ler*, Verproviantierer; -*ling*, Verproviantierung; - - *bill*, Zolldeklaration für Schiffsproviant; - - *ship*, Proviantschiff; - - *stores*, Proviantvorrat.
vigia, Warnungszeichen für eine nicht genau bekannte Untiefe.
viol, Ankerwoit; - *block*, großer Block der A.
violent storm, fliegender Sturm.
visibility of distant objects, sehr durchsichtige Luft.
visible weather, sichtiges Wetter.
visitation and search, Durchsuchungsrecht.
vitry, *vittory*, leichte Segeltuchart.
voice pipe to engine, Sprachrohr zum Maschinenraum.
volicimeter, selbst registrierendes Log.
volt, Volt; - *meter*, V.-messer.
voluntary stranding, treiwillige Strandung.
vouch, to -, Streit verkünden; -*ee*, Gewährsmann; -*er*, *vouchor*, 1. Streitverkünder; 2. S-v-kündigung.

voyage home, Heimreise; - out, Ausreise. | voyol, Ankerwoit; - block, einscheibiger Block der A.

W.

wabble, to -, 1. wirr laufen (Wellen); 2. fliegen (Kompaß).

waft, to -, od. *with a -*, wehen lassen.

wages, Heuer; - *and maintenance*, H. und Unterhalt.

waggon shaped boiler, Wagenkessel.

waif, 1. herrenloses Gut; 2. kleine Flagge im Schau; - *pole*, Stange zur Befestigung eines Segeltuchsignals für Boote.

wainscoting, täfeln, verkleiden, Verkleidung.

waist, Kuhl (d. i. Mittschiffsteil des Decks); - *anchor*, Rüstanker; - *boat*, Decksboot; - *cloth*, 1. Schanzkleid von Segeltuch; 2. Bezug der Finknetzkasten mittschiffs; - *netting*, Finknetz an den Seiten der Kuhl; - *rail*, Relingsleiste bei den Rüsten; - *tree*, Reling des Finknetzes.

waisters, Kuhlgasten.

wait for the flood, die Flut abwarten.

wake, Kielwasser; *in the -*, im K.; *marks or objects are in the - of each other*, Marken oder Gegenstände sind in einer Linie oder decken sich; *to -*, waaken (d. i. über Wasser sein).

wales, Bergholz.

walk away with the anchor, mit dem Anker durchgehen; - *back the capstan*, das Gangspill mit Spaken zurückdrehen.

Walker's knot, Taljereepsknoten.

wall knot, Taljereepsknoten;

- - *with crown*, Fallreepsknoten; - *of a ship*, Bordwand; - *of a steam cylinder*, Zylindermantel; - *sided*, gerade aufsteigend.

walnut, Nußbaumholz.

walty, zum Kentern geneigt.

wane cloud, Schichtenwolke.

want of water, Wassermangel.

wap, wapp, 1. Wegweiserkaus; 2. das Borg auf einem Want.

ward room, Gesellschaftszimmer.

warm current, warmer Strom; - *water cistern*, Warmwasserzisterne.

warning signals, Warnungssignale.

warp, Warptrosse, warpen; - *a vessel*, ein Schiff verholen; - *down a river*, ein Schiff flußabwärts warpen; - *into dock*, in ein Dock holen; - *off*, abwarpen; - *out of dock*, aus einem Dock holen; - *up*, aufwarpen.

warpage, das Warpen.

warping, verholen, das Warpen; - *block*, Scherblock; - *buoy*, Verhol-boje; - *chock*, V-h-klampe; - *end*, 1. Außentrommel od. Windekopf; 2. Spillkopf.

warping engine, Verholmaschine; - - *connecting rod*, V.-Pleuelstange; - - - *bolt*, V.-P.-bolzen; - - - - *bottom end keep*, V.-Kurbelzapfen-Lagerschalendeckel; - - - - *b. e. liner*, V.-Pleuelstangenfußfutter; - - - - *top end keep*, V.-Kreuzkopflagerschalendeckel; *w. e. crank pin bolt*, V.-Kurbelzapfenlagerbolzen; *w. e. c. p. brasses,* V.-K-z-l-schalen; *w. e. c. shaft,* V.-Kurbelwelle; - - - - *bearing,* V.-Kurbelwellen-lager; - - - - *bolt,* V.-K.-bolzen; - - - - - *brasses,* V.-K.-schalen; - - - - - *keep,* V.-K.-deckel; - - - - *bolt.* V.-K.-d-bolzen; *w. e. crosshead bolt,* V.-Kreuzkopflagerbol-zen; *w. e. c. brasses,* V.-K-k-l-schalen; *w. e. cylinder,* V.-Zylinder; - - - *cover,* V.-Z.-deckel; - - - *bolt,* V.-Z.-d-bolzen; *w. e. cylinder drain pipe,* V.-Z.-Entwässe-rungsrohr; *w. e. eccentric,* V.-Exzenter; - - - *bolt.* V.-E.-bolzen; - - - *brasses,* V.-E.-Lagerschalen; - - - *rod,* V.-E.-stange; - - - *sheave,* V.-E.-scheibe; - - - *strap,* V.-E.-bügel; - - - - *liner,* V.-E.-b-futter; *w. e. exhaust pipe,* V.-Dampfablaßrohr; *w. e. piston,* V.-Kolben; - - - *rod,* V.-K.-stange; - - - - *cross-head,* V.-K-s-Kreuzkopf; - - - - *stuffing box,* V.-K-s-Stopf-büchse; - - - - - *gland,* V.-K-s-S.-deckel; *w. e. slide valve,* V.-schieber; *w. e. start-ing valve,* V.-Anlaßventil; *w. e. steam valve,* V.-Dampf-zuleitungsrohr; *w. e. stop valve.* V.-Absperrventil; *w. e. valve casing,* V.-Schieber-kasten; - - - - *door,* V.-S.-deckel; *w. e. v. rod,* V.-Schie-berstange; - - - - *stuffing box,* V.-S.-Stopfbüchse; - - - - - *gland,* V.-S.-S.-deckel.

warping hawser, Warptrosse; - *hook,* Haken am Anscher-pfahl; - *line,* Warptrosse; - *port,* Warppforte; - *post,* Anscherpfahl.

warrant, 1. Kaution; 2. Be-stallung; - *officer,* Deck-offizier.

warranty, Garantie.

wash boards, Setzborde; - - *under the lower cheeks of* the head, Blasebalken; - *deck bucket,* Pütze zum Deckwaschen; - *down,* ab-spülen; - *hand stand,* Wasch-tisch; - *overboard,* über Bord spülen; - *plates.* Schlinger-platten; - *port.* Wasserpfor-ten; - *rings,* Wasserfänger; - *strake,* Setzbord.

washer, Unterlagsscheibe.

washing plate, Schlingerplatte.

waste, Twist, Putzbaumwolle; - *board,* Setzbord; - *clothes,* Schanzkleid; - *deck pipe,* Deckabflußrohr; - *of a ship,* leerer Raum eines Schiffes; - *port of a valve,* Dampf-austritt eines Schiebers; - *steam,* verlorener Dampf; - - *pipe,* Dampfabzugsrohr; - *water,* Kondensationswas-ser; - - *pipe,* Auslaßrohr für überflüssiges Wasser.

watch. Wache; - *and* -, W. um W.; - *below.* Freiwache; - *bill,* Wachrolle; - *glass,* Wachtglas; - *pennant,* In-spektionswimpel; - *tackle,* Handtalje; *to - the glass,* auf das Wachtglas achten.

water, to - a vessel on the stocks, ein Schiff auf den Helgen vollpumpen.

water bailiff. Hafenmeister; - *ballast,* Wasserballast; - - *compartment,* W.-Komparti-ment; - - *tank,* W.-tank; - *bark.* Wasserboot; - *boards,* Setzbord; - *boat,* Wasser-boot; - *borne,* eben flott; - *bridge,* Wasserbrücke im Kessel; - *cask,* Wasserfaß; - - *chock.* Kopfholz; - *cat-cher,* Wassersammler; - - *fittings,* W.-Garnitur; - *chamber.* Zylinder; - *clerk,* Waterclerk; *W. C. = water closet,* Klosett; - *cock.* Was-serhahn; - *conduit,* W-lei-tung; - *course.* W-lauf; - *drawing crane,* Krankasten; - *for injection,* Einspritz-wasser; - *funnel,* Wassertrichter; - *gauge*, Wasserstands-anzeiger; - - *cock*, W-s-hahn; - - *column*, W-s-rohr; - - *glass*, W-s-glas; - - *lamp*, W-s-lampe; - - *pipe*, W-s-rohr; - *groin*, Stack; - *guards*, Zollbeamte; - *height indicator*, Wasserstandsanzeiger; - *hold of a ship*, Wasserraum; - *holes of the sprit sail*, Augen der Blinde; - *hose*, Schlauch; - *incrustation*, Kesselstein; - *jet*, Wasserstrahl; - *laid rope*, kabelweise geschlagenes Tau; - *leaving the ship*, das Wasser ebbte vom Schiffe weg; - *level*, W-stand; - - *indicator*, W-s-anzeiger; - *line*, W-linie; - - *model*, Schiffsmodell; - *logged ship*, auf seiner Ladung treibendes Schiff; - *man*, Jollenführer; - *mark*, Wassermarke; - - *post*, Pegel; - *measure*, Maßeinheit; - *outlet cock*, Wasserablaßhahn; - *pipe*, W-rohr, W-schlange; - *plane*, W-ebene; - *pressure*, W-druck; - *raised by a storm*, Sturmflut; - *sail*, Wassersegel; - *scoop*, Ösfaß. *water service*, Wasch- und Kühlwasser-Vorrichtung; - - *cock*, W. u. K.-hahn; - - - *for cleaning purposes*, Waschwasserhahn; - - - *for cooling p.*, Kühlwasserhahn; *w. s. f. cleaning p.*, Waschwasservorrichtung; *w. s. f. cooling p.*, Kühlvorrichtung; *w. s. for guides*, Gleitbahn-Kühlvorrichtung; *w. s. installation*, Wasch- u. Kühlwasser-Vorrichtung; *w. s. pipe*, Waschwasserrohr; - - - *for cleaning purposes*, Waschwasserrohr für Reinigungszwecke; - - - *for cooling p.*, Kühlwasserrohr. *water shot*, schräg im Strom vermoort; - *skeet*, Gießer; - *space*, Wasserraum; - *spout*, Wasserhose; - *supply pipe*, Speise-rohr; *w. s. pump*, S-

pumpe; - *tank*, Wassertank; - *test*, hydraulische Kesselprobe; - *tight*, wasserdicht; - - *bulkhead*, wasserdichtes Schott; - - *compartment*, w. Kompartiment; - - *door*, wasserdichte Tür; - - *frame*, Vollspant; - - *joint*, wasserdichte Gleitdichtung; - *trap*, Wassersammler; - *tube*, Siederohr; - - *boiler*, S.-kessel; - *valve*, Wasser-ventil; - *way*, W-gang; - - *bolt*, W-g-bolzen; - *wheel*, Schaufelrad. *watering place*, 1. Ort zum Wassereinnehmen; 2. Seebad. *waters*, Gewässer. *wave*, Welle; - *beaten*, wellengepeitscht; - *subduer*, Wellenberuhiger; - *tossed*, wellengepeitscht. *waveson*, schwimmendes Strandgut. *way*, Fahrt; - *aloft!* Gasten enter auf! *to give* -, tüchtig darauf los rudern; *to have fresh - through the water*, gute Fahrt haben; *to make* -, Fahrt voraus haben; *to lose* -, aus der Fahrt kommen; - *up!* Gasten enter auf! *under* -, in Fahrt; *to get under* -, abfahren. *way, the - of the frames*, der Weg bei den Spanten. *way reckoning*, Gissung. *ways*, Gleitbacken. *wear*, 1. vor dem Winde halsen; 2. sich abnutzen; - *and tear*, Abnutzung. *wearing surface*, Reibungsfläche. *weather, to* -, luvwärts vorbeisegeln; von oben holen; - *a gale*, einen Sturm aushalten; *How do you - the breeze?* Wie geht es? *We are making bad* -, wir halten den Sturm schlecht aus; *w. a. m. good w.*, w. h. d. S. gut a.; *to - upon a ship*, ein Schiff abdecken (d. i. ihm Luv abgewinnen).

weather anchor, Luvanker; - *backstay*, Luvpardune; - *beam*, luvwärts querab; - *beaten*, vom Wetter arg mitgenommen; *a - - sailor*, ein erfahrener Seemann; - *bitt*, 1. Luvbeting; 2. Törn um den Spillkopf; - *board of a boat*, Wasserbord; - *boards of raised quarter deck*, Schutzbretter des erhöhten Quarterdecks; - *borne*, von Wind und See getrieben; - *bound*, durch Unwetter zurückgehalten; - *bow*, Luvbug; *on the - -*, luvwärts voraus; - *bowline*, Luvbulien; - *brace*, Luvbrasse; - *brail*, Luvgeitau; - *breeder*, Sturmzeichen; - *buntline*, Luvbuggording; - *clearing up*, das Wetter klart auf; - *clewline*, Luvgeitau; - *cloth*, Schutzkleid; - *coil of a vessel*, der halbe Rundtörn eines Schiffes beim Umgehen des Windes; *to - coil*, aut dem andern Bug wenden; - *covers*, Schutzkleider; - *deck*, Wetterdeck; - *driven*, von Wind und See getrieben; - *earing*, Nockbindsel nach luvwärts; die Luvnock; - *eye*, das Ausgucken nach luvwärts; *Keep your - - open!* Gucke scharf nach luvwärts! - *forecast*, Wetterprognose; - *foresheet*, Luvfockschote.
weather gauge od. *gage, to try to gain the - -*, versuchen, luvwärts zu kommen; *to gain the - - of a ship*, einem Schiffe Luv abgewinnen; *to have the - -*, sich auf der Luvseite befinden; *to keep the - -*, Luv halten; *to strive for the - -*, Luv abzugewinnen trachten.
weather gull, Windgalle; - *gangway*, Luv-Laufplanke; - *glass*, Barometer; - *gleam*, ein heller Schein am Himmel, der schlechtes Wetter

andeutet; - *go*, ein Stück Regenbogen am Morgen, das gutes Wetter andeutet; - *head*, Neben-Regenbogen; - *helm*, Luvruder, luvgierig; - *lanyards*, Luvtaljereepen; - *leech*, Luvliek; - - *line*, Luvnockgording; - *lift*, Luv-Toppenant; - *line*, Windstrich; - *lurch*, nach luvwärts überholen; *to - out a gale*, einem Sturme widerstehen; - *quarter*, Windvierung an der Luvseite; *on the - -*, an der L. achter; - *reef tackle*, Luvrefftalje; - *rigging*, Luvwant; - *sheet*, Luvschote; - *shore*, L-küste; - *shrouds*, L-wanten; - *side*, L-seite; - *tack*, L-hals; - *tide*, luvwärts setzende Tide; - *tight*, wetterfest; - *wheel*, der an der Luvseite stehende Mann am Steuer; - *yard arm*, Luvnock.
weatherliness, Luvgierigkeit.
weatherly, to be -, luvgierig sein.
weathermost, am meisten luvwärts befindlich.
weather rolling, nach luvwärts rollend.
web eye of a crank, Kurbelwellenauge; - *frame*, Rahmenspant; - - *angle bar*, R.-winkel; - - *ship*, R.-schiff; - *of a crank shaft*, Kurbelarm; - *plate*, Stegplatte.
wedge, Keil, verkeilen; - *fid*, Schloßholz aus zwei stumpfen Keilen; - *for stowing*, Schichtkeil.
wedging, das Festkeilen.
weed, to -, die Takelung nach losem Kabelgarn absuchen.
weekly service, wöchentlicher Verkehr.
weep hole, Leckstelle.
weeping, tränen (lecken).
weigh, to - a sunken vessel, ein gesunkenes Schiff heben; - *down*, nieder drücken; dompen; - *the anchor*, den Anker lichten.

weigh, to get under -, die Anker lichten; - *bar.* Umsteuerungswelle; - *shaft,* U.; - - *arm,* Umsteuerungshebel; - - *brasses,* Umsteuerungswellen-Lagerschalen; - - *journal,* U.-Lagerzapfen; - - *lever,* Umsteuerungshebel.

weight of the hull, Eigengewicht.

weir, Wehr.

weld, Schweißung, schweißen; *to - together,* anschweißen.

weldable, schweißbar.

welding, Schweißung; - *heat,* Schweißhitze; - *steel,* schweißbarer Stahl.

well, 1. Brunnen; 2. Pumpensod; - *boat,* Fischerboot mit Fischkasten; - *cabin,* Kajüte unter Deck; - *deck,* Brunnendeck; - - *ship* od. *vessel* od. - *decker,* Welldeckschiff; - *down,* gut beladen; - *end,* Pumpenfuß; - *found,* gut ausgerüstet; - *hole,* Oesgatt eines Bootes; - *louden,* gut beladen; - *manned,* gut bemannt; - *of the centre board,* Brunnen des Kielschweins; - *room of a boat,* Oesgatt eines Bootes; - *smack,* Schmack; - *squared,* vollkantig; - *suction valve,* Brunnensaugventil; - *taught,* gut gestreckt.

wend a course, einen Kurs innehalten; - *a vessel,* das Vorderschiff nach der entgegengesetzten Richtung legen.

west by north, West zu Nord.

west coast trader, Westküstenfahrer; - *India t.,* Westindienfahrer; - *longitude,* westliche Länge; - *variation,* westliche Mißweisung.

westerly variation, westliche Mißweisung.

western amplitude, Abendamplitude; - *islands,* Azoren.

westing od. *westward,* westliche Richtung.

wet bottomed boiler, Kessel mit Wasserraum unter der Feuerung; - *dock,* 1. nasses Dock; 2. Hafenbassin; - *provisions,* nasser Proviant; - *steam,* feuchter Dampf.

whaleback steamer, Walrückendampfer.

whale boat, Wallfischboot.

whaler, Wallfischfahrer.

whap, Wegweiserkauß.

wharf, 1. Werfte; 2. Ladungsdamm, Kai.

wharfage, Kaigeld.

wharfinger, Kajenmeister.

wheel, Rad; - *arm,* R-arm; - *barrel,* Welle des Steuerrades; - *box,* Kappe des Steuergeräts; - *chain,* Ruderkette; - - *block,* R-d-k-nblock; - - - *springs,* R-d-k-nb-federn; - *cover,* Radüberzug; - *grating,* Ruder-grätings; - *house,* R-d-haus; - - *door,* R-d-h-tür; - - - *hinge,* R-d-h.-t-Scharnier; - *house window,* R-d-hfenster; - *rim,* Radkranz; - *rod,* Ruderstange; - *rope,* Steuerreep; - - *block,* S.-block.

whelp on wood lining, Klampe auf der Spillfütterung.

whelps, Spillklampen.

where away? in welcher Richtung? - *you bound to?* Wohin geht die Reise? - *you from?* Von woher kommen Sie?

wherry, Jolle; - *man,* J-nführer.

whiff, Windhauch.

whip, 1. Takelung; 2. Jollentau; 3. wippen; *to - cargo,* Ladung auswippen; *a - for discharging c.,* Wippe; - *of the throat brail,* Brohktalje; - *saw,* Fuchsschwanz; - *staff,* Kolder-stock; - - *hole,* K-gatt; *to - the end of a rope,* ein Ende takeln; - *upon* -, Klappläufer an einem Jollentau.

whipped end, das betakelte Ende.

whipper, Kohlenwipper.

whipping, 1. Takelung; 2. Bekleidung eines Taues; *to put a - on a rope*, eine Takelung auf ein Ende setzen; - *twine*, Takelgarn.

whips and falls for dressing ship, Fallen für Flaggengala.

whirl, dreifache Schiemannswoit; - *pool*, Strudel; - *wind*, Wirbelwind.

whiskers, blinde Rahe.

whistle, 1. Dampfpfeife; 2. Pfeife, pfeifen; - *buoy*, Heulboje; *to - for a wind*, pfeifen bis der Wind kommt; - *pipe*, Dampfpfeifenrohr; - - *cock*, D.-Hahn; - - *valve*, D.-ventil; - *signal*, Pfeifensignal; - *valve*, Dampfpfeifenventil.

white boot top, die weiß angestrichene Relingsleiste; - *caps*, die weißen Wellenköpfe; - *cordage*, das ungeteerte Tauwerk; - *heat*, Weißglut; - *horses*, die weißen Wellenköpfe; - *lead*, Bleiweiß; - *light*, weißes Licht; - *metal*, Weißmetall; - - *lining*, W.-garnitur; - *oak wood*, Weißeichenholz; - *oakum*, Werg von ungeteertem Tauwerk; - *pine wood*, Weymouthkieferholz; - *rope*, ungeteertes Tau; - *sea*, das weiße Meer; - *squall*, weiße Bö; - *twine*, ungeteertes Segelgarn; - *wash*, weißen; - *washing*, das Tünchen; - *water*, der weiße Schein der Brandung; - *zinc*, Zinkweiß.

whiting line, dreischäftige Sechsgarnleine.

whole effect, Totalleistung; - *gale*, ganzer Sturm.

wholesome ship, gutes Seeschiff.

whoodings, Plankenenden.

wick, Docht; - *holder*, D.-halter; - *trimmer*, D.-schere.

wild, 1. wild (Schiff, Kompaß); 2. offen (Reede).

wimble with a crooked handle, Umschlagbohrer.

winch, Winde, Winsch; - *bed plate*, Winden-Grundplatte; - *boiler*, W.-kessel; - *clutch*, W.-Kuppelungsklaue; - *cover*, W.-kappe; - *guards*, W.-Sicherungsvorrichtung; - *handle*, W.-schwengel; - *partner*, W.-Fischung; - *pipe cradles*, W.-rohrständer; - *standards*, W.-gestell; - *uprights*, W.-rohrständer.

winch see also steam *w*.

wind, to - a call, ein Signal mit der Bootsmannspfeife geben; - *a rope into a coil*, ein Tau aufschießen; - *away*, durch enges Fahrwasser steuern.

wind, Wind; - *ahead*, W. von vorn; - *bands*, W.-streifen; - *board*, W.-brett; - *bound*, durch ungünstigen W. aufgehalten; - *chart*, W.-karte; - *cloud*, W.-wolke; - *fall*, Fallwind; - *from abaft*, Afterwind; - *gall*, Windgalle; - *jammer*, W-jammerer (Segler); - *lipper*, die ersten kleinen Wellen; - *loved*, dem Winde sehr ausgesetzt; - *marker*, Windrichtungszeiger auf der Seekarte; - *mill pump*, Windmühlenpumpe; - *on the beam*, Dwarswind; - *on the quarter*, achterlicher Wind; - *right aft*, W. recht von hinten; - *rode*, auf dem W. liegend (d. i. mit dem Kopfe gegen den W. verankert sein); - *rose*, W.-rose; - *sail*, W.-sack, W.-segel; - - *hoops*, W.-s-bänder; *to trim the - -*, das W.-s- mit der Öffnung gegen den W. stellen; - *taught* od. *taut*, Windfang habend; - *tossed*, vom Wind hin- und hergeworfen; - *with west*, W. mit West.

wind, the - baffles, die Brise ist veränderlich; - *barks the*

sun, der Wind dreht sich der Sonne entgegen; - *becomes calm*, d. W. wird flauer; - *blows back again*, d. W. setzt wieder ein; - *comes from abaft*, es ist Afterwind; - *draws aft*, der Wind wird achterlicher; - *goes down*, d. W. lullt ein; - *has becalmed* od. *calmed*, d. W. mallt; - *has shifted*, d. W. ist umgesprungen; - *hauled forward*, d. W. schralte; - *is ahead*, d. W. kommt von vorn; - *is calming* oder c. *down*, d. W. wird schwächer; - *is shifting*, d. W. springt um; - *is slackening out*, d. W. nimmt ab; - *is straight up and down*, es ist Windstille; - *is up and down*, d. W. ist auf und nieder; - *keeps pace against the sun*, d. W. läuft von Westen durch Süden nach Osten; - *keeps with the sun*, d. W. dreht mit der Sonne; - *veers*, d. W. mallt.
windig butt, Krümmer; - *pendant*, Hanger eines Giens; - *tackle*, Gien; - - *fall*, G.-läufer.
windlass, Ankerspill; - *bars*, A.-spaken; - *bed plate*, A.-Grundplatte; - *bitts*, A.-Betinge; - *chocks*, A.-betten; - *end*, A.-kopf; - *brake* od. *break*, A.-bremse; - *clutch*, A.-Kuppelungsklaue; - *cylinder*, A.-zylinder; - *connecting rod*, A.-Pleuelstange; - - - *bolt*, A.-P.-bolzen; - - - *bottom end keep*, A.-Kurbelzapfen-Lagerschalendeckel; - - - *b. e. liner*, A.-Pleuelstangenfußfutter; - - *top end keep*, A.-Kreuzkopflagerschalendeckel; - *crank pin bolt*, A.-Kurbelzapfenlagerbolzen; - *c. p. brasses*, A.-K-z-l-schalen; - *c. shaft*, A.-Kurbelwelle; - - - *bearing*, A.-K.-lager; - - - - *bolt*, A.-K.-l-bolzen; - - - -

brasses, A.-K.-l-schalen; - - - - *keep*, A.-K.-l-deckel; - - - - - *bolt*, A.-K.-l-d-bolzen; - *crosshead bolt*, A.-Kreuzkopflagerbolzen; - *c. brasses*, A.-K-k-l-schalen; - *cylinder*, A.-Zylinder; - - *cover*, A.-Z.-deckel; - - - *bolt*, A.-Z.-d-bolzen; - *cylinder drain pipe*, A.-Z.-Entwässerungsrohr; - *eccentric*, A.-Exzenter; - - *bolt*, A.-E.-bolzen; - - *brasses*, A.-E.-Lagerschalen; - - *rod*, A.-E.-stange; - - *sheave*, A.-E.-scheibe; - - *strap*, A.-E.-bügel; - - - *liner*, A.-E.-b-futter; - *exhaust pipe*, A.-Dampfablaßrohr; - *friction gear*, A.-Friktionsgetriebe; - *gear*, A.-Zubehör; - *guard*, A.-Sicherung; - *head*, A.-kopf; - *lever*, A.-Handhebel; - *partner*, A.-Fischung; - *piston*, A.-Kolben; - - *rod*, A.-Kolbenstange; - - - *crosshead*, A.-K.-Kreuzkopf; - - - *stuffing box*, A.-Kolbenstange-Stopfbüchse; - - - - - *gland*, A.-K.-S.-deckel; - *slide valve*, A.-Schieber; - *starting valve*, A.-Anlaßventil; - *steam pipe*, A.-Dampfrohr; - *stop valve*, A.-Absperrventil; - *valve casing*, A.-Schieberkasten; - - - *door*, A.-S.-deckel; - *valve rod*, A.-Schieberstange; - - - *stuffing box*, A.-S.-Stopfbüchse; - - - - *gland*, A.-S.-S.-deckel.
windlass would not gripe the chain, das Ankerspill wollte die Kette nicht greifen.
window, Fenster; - *curtain*, F.-Vorhang; - *grating*, F.-Gräting; - *sill*, F-schwelle.
wind's eye, gerade gegen den Wind.
windward, luvwärts; *the -Islands*, die kleinen Antillen; - *set*, luvwärts setzende Strömung; - *tide*, der gegen den Wind setzende Strom.
wing, Schlag; - *and -*, 1. mit Leesegeln an beiden Seiten

(bei Rahtakelage); 2. beide Bäume abgefiert (bei Gaffeltakelage); - *feeder*, Wingfeeder; - *furnace*, Seiten-Feuerbüchse; - *girder of a double bottom*, Tankseitenplatte eines Doppelbodens; - *g. plate*, T.; - *house*, Seitenhaus; - *of the anchor fluke*, Ankerohr; - *of the paddle steamer*, Radkastendeck des Raddampfers; - *of the propeller*, Schraubenflügel; - *on* -, *see - and* -; - *passage*, Wallgang; - - *bulkhead*, W.-schott; -*pen*, Seitenbehälter für Eis, Salz etc.; - *stoppers*, Schwackenhalsen; - *transom*, Heckbalken; *to - up the ballast*, den Ballast hochstauen; - *wale*, Radkastengang.

wingers, kleine, an den Seiten verstaute Wasserfässer.

winter, to -. überwintern; - *quarters*, Winter-lager; - *sea marks*, W-seezeichen.

wire brush, Draht-bürste; - *drawing*, 1. D-ziehen; 2. Dampfdrosseln; - *netting*, Draht-netzwerk; - *nippers*, D-zange; - *packing*, D-pakkung; - *reel*, Tautrommel; - - *brake*, Drahttauwinden-Bremse; - - *frame*, D.-gestell; - - *handle*, D.-Schwengel; - - *stand* od. *standard*, D.-gestell; - *ridge rope*, Draht-Sonnensegelreep; - *rigging*, Draht-takelung; - *rope*, D-tau; - *runner*, D-mantel; -*winch*, D-tauwinde.

with the tide, mit dem Strom.

withe, Spierenbügel.

within hail od. - *hailing distance*, in Rufweite.

wood and -, 1. zwei Hölzer, die dicht aneinanderstoßen: 2. durchgeschlagene Holznägel; - *bending machine*, Holzbiegemaschine; - *casing*, Holzverkleidung; - *ends*, Plankenenden: - *ferrule*,

Holzring; - *flat*, zu einem Deck zusammengestellte Planken; - *hook*, Piekband; - *lining*, 1. Spillfütterung; 2. Holzverkleidung; - *lock*, Ruderschloß; - *sheathing*, Spikerhaut.

wooden block, hölzerner Block; - *boat*, hölzernes Boot; - *bucket*, Holzpütze; - *buoy*, Klotzboje; - *fender*, Holzfender; - *hook*, hölzernes Bugband; - *hoop*, h. Band; - *knee*, h. Knie; - *rail*, hölzerne Reeling; - *ship* od. *vessel*, h. Schiff; - *wedge*, Holzkeil; - *yard*, hölzerne Rahe.

woold, to -, bewuhlen.

woolder, Knebel zum Bewuhlen.

woolding, Wuhling.

work, to - a passage, seine Ueberfahrt abarbeiten; - *a ship*, mit einem Schiffe manövrieren; - - - *off*, ein Schiff abarbeiten; - *a traverse*, koppeln; - *double tides*, drei Tage Arbeit in zweien verrichten; - *loose*, sich lose arbeiten; - *out a day's way*, Kurs und Schiffsort während eines Etmals berechnen; - *to death*, jemand abschinden; - *to windward*, aufkreuzen; - *up the old iron*, Bestrafung durch unnütze Arbeit.

work, a - weather day, ein bequemer Liegetag.

working boat, Arbeitsboot; - *days*, Arbeitstage; - *parts*, funktionierende Teile; - *pressure*, Arbeitsdruck; - *sail*, Hauptsegel.

works, the ship - the oakum out, das Schiff kaut das Werg aus.

workshop, Werkstätte.

worm, 1. Wurm: 2 Schnecke (einer Schraube); *to - a rope*, ein Tau schladden; - *eaten*, wurmstichig; - *shaft*,

Schnecken-welle; - *wheel*, S-rad; - *rope*, Trensing.
worming, Trensing.
worn out broom, spanischer Besen.
wrain bolt, Setzbolzen; - *staff*, Zwinger.
wreck, to - a vessel od. - *off a v.*, 1. ein Wrack abbrechen; 2. e. W. plündern.
wreck, scheitern, Wrack, Strandgut, Schiffstrümmer; - *buoy*, Wrackboje; - *chart*, Strandungskarte; - *free*. dem Strandrechte nicht unterworfen; - *master*, Strandvogt; - *relieving steamer*, Bergungsdampfer.
wreckage, Wracktrümmer.
wrecked, gescheitert.

wrecker, 1. Berger, Wracker; 2. Strand-räuber; 3. S-wächter.
wrecking pump, Dampfpumpe zum Auspumpen eines Wracks.
wrench, Schraubenschlüssel.
wriggle, wriggen.
wring, to - a mast, einen Mast abdrehen; - *planks on a vessel*, Planken aufzwingen.
wring bolt, Zwingbolzen; - *staff*, Zwinger zum Antreiben der Planken.
wrong, to - a vessel, ein Schiff durch Wegnahme des Windes überholen.
wrought iron, Schmiedeeisen.
wrung heads, Kimm.

X.

xebec, Schebecke.

Y.

yacht, Jacht; - *race*, J.-wettfahrt; - *rig*, J.-zeug.
yachter, Führer einer Jacht.
yachting, Segelsport.
yachtish, jachtgemäß.
yachtsman, Jachtführer.
yachtship, die Kunst der Jachtführung.
yarage, Lenkbarkeit.
yard, 1. Rahe; 2. Werft; - *arm*, Rahnock; - - *and* - -, Nock an N.; - - *battens*, Stoßschalen; - - *chains*, Rahketten; - - *cleat*, Rahnockklampe; - - *gasket*, Beschlagzeising; - - *hoop*, Rahnockband; - - *iron*, Außen-Spierenbügel; - - *pendant*, Nocktakelhan-

ger; - - *tackle*, Außentakel; - - *whip*, Nockjolle; - *hoop*, Rahband; - *rope*, Rahjolle; - *sling*, Unterrahhanger; - *tackle*, Nocktakel; - - *pendant*, N.-hanger; - - *tricing line*, Rahtakel-Aufholer.
yards apeak, über Kreuz getoppte Rahen; - *are a-cockbill*, die Rahen sind getoppt; - *are square by the braces*, die Rahen sind rechtwinkelig gegen die Kielrichtung; *y. a. s. in the lifts*, d. R. sind vierkant in den Toppenanten.
yare, be - at the helm! Achtung beim Steuer!

Yarmouth mittens, schwielige Hände.

yarn, 1. Kabelgarn; 2. Ducht eines Seiles; 3. Geschichte.

yaul = yawl.

yawing, gieren.

yawl, Jolle mit kleinem Besahnmast.

yaws, the needle -, die Nadel schwankt hin und her.

Y. C. = Yacht Club.

yellow flag, Quarantäne-Flagge; *- Jack,* 1. Q. F.; 2. gelbe Fieber; *- metal,* Gelbmetall; *-- bolt,* Metallbolzen; *- pine wood,* Kalifornisches Föhrenholz.

yeoman, Gehülfe des Boots- oder Zimmermanns.

yew wood, Eibenbaumholz.

yield, to - a cable, ein Tau nachlassen.

yoke, 1. Joch (des Steuers); 2. Koulisse (des Handsteuergeräts); *- bolt,* Koulissenbolzen; *- line,* Steuerleine; *- of a boat rudder,* Bootsruderjochpinne; *- pin,* Jochnagel; *- rope,* Jochleine.

young flood od. *tide,* Vorflut; *- wind,* Anfang einer Brise.

youngster, 1. jüngster Offizier; 2. Jungmann.

Z.

zebeck, Schebecke.

zenith distance, Zenitdistanz.

zigzag bulkhead, Zickzackschott; *to steer a - course,* Schlangenlinien fahren; *- riveting,* Zickzacknietung.

zink boat, Zinkboot; *- sheathing,* Zinkhaut.

Z-iron, Z shaped iron, Z-eisen.

zodiac, Tierkreis.

zodiacal light, Tierkreislicht; *- signs,* Zeichen des Tierkreises.

Supplement.

bridge, 2. Sandrücken.

cap standard, Eselshauptständer.

duration, Zeitdauer der Fluttide.

erratic, abweichend.

haul a person over the coals, eine P. tadeln.

heaving, stampfen.

hoist, 4. Donkey.

logged, in's Journal eingetragen.

morse, to -, Morssignale geben.

slack off the sheets, die Schoten auffieren.

15*

VOLLSTÄNDIGES
NAUTISCHES
TASCHEN-WÖRTERBUCH
DEUTSCH-ENGLISCH und ENGLISCH-DEUTSCH
VON
JOHN BARTEN
Beeidigter Übersetzer und Dolmetscher,
Verfasser von „Deutsche und englische Sprüchwörter",
„Echo der englischen Umgangssprache" etc., etc.

TEIL II
DEUTSCH-ENGLISCH

DIETRICH REIMER (ERNST VOHSEN)
BERLIN

TEIL II
DEUTSCH-ENGLISCH.

A.

Aak, n., *the ake.*

Aap, m., *mizen stay sail.*

ab-und-an-stehen, *to stand off and on.*

Abandon, m., *the abandon;* - erklärung, f., *notice of abandonment;* - frist, f., *time of a-ment.*

Abandonnement, n., Abandonnierung, f., *abandonment.*

abandonnieren, *abandon.*

abandonniertes Wrack, n., *dead wreck.*

Abandonnist, m., *abandoner.*

abarbeiten, *work off;* - vom Legerwall, *w. o. the sea shore.*

abbäumen, *boom off.*

abbergen. *save, salve, recover.*

abbezahlen, *discharge, pay off.*

abbinden, *loosen, untie.*

abblasen, *blow off.*

Abblas-hahn, m., *blow off cock;* - rohr, n., *b. o. pipe;* - ventil, n., *b. o. valve;* - gehäuse, n., *b. o. v. box;* - spindel, f., *b. o. v. spindle.*

abblenden, *shut in.*

abbrechen, *break up (a ship).*

abbringen, *get off.*

Abbringungsarbeiten, *attempts to float the vessel.*

Abdampf, m., *exhaust steam;* - apparat, m., *evaporating apparatus.*

abdampfen, *steam away.*

Abdampfungskraft, f., *evaporating power.*

abdanken, *pay off.*

abdechseln, *dub (deck planking).*

abdecken, *to weather (upon another ship).*

abdeichen, Abdeichung, f., *diking.*

abdichten, *caulk, stop (a leak).*

Abend-amplitude, f., *western amplitude;* - schuß, m., *evening gun;* - wache, f., *e. watch;* - weite, f., *western amplitude.*

abfadmen, *fathom.*

abfahren, *proceed, sail, start.*

Abfahrt, f., *departure.*

Abfahrten, *sailings.*

Abfahrts-breite, f., *departed latitude;* - hafen, m., *port of sailing;* - länge, f., *departed longitude;* - punkt, m., *point of departure;* - signal, n., *Blue Peter;* - tage, *sailing dates.*

Abfall, m., *1. offal, refuse; 2. shakings (ropes, canvass);* - eisen, *scrap iron.*

abfallen, *1. cast (to port od. starboard); 2. fall off (to leeward);* ganz -, *pay round;* gern -, *to bear a slack helm;*

- lassen, *keep her off;* vom Winde -, *break off;* nicht -! *nothing off!*

Abfallstahl, m., *scrap steel.*

abfeiern, *cast off.*

abfertigen, Abfertigung, f., *despatch.*

abfieren, *run out, ease off;* - und holen, *veer and haul;* Halsen und Schoten -, *give up tacks and sheets.*

abflachen, *shoal.*

abflauen, *abate.*

Abfluß, m., *flow;* - hahn, m., *discharge cock.*

Abführung. f., *exhaustion.*

Abgaben, *dues.*

Abgangshafen, m., *port of sailing.*

abgeblendete Lichter, *lights shut in.*

abgedrängt, *broken from the course.*

abgefahrene Breite, f., *departed latitude;* - Länge. f., *d. longitude.*

abgehärtet, *weather hardened.*

abgescheuert, *chafed.*

abgeschlagen, *knocked off.*

abgeschlossenes Manometer, n., *closed manometer.*

abgeschnittener Dampf, m., *cut off steam.*

abgeschrägte Kante, f., *chamfered edge.*

abgesperrter Dampf, m., *cut off steam.*

abgetakelt, *unrigged;* - bis auf die kahlen Untermasten, *stripped to the girtline.*

abgieren, *sheer off.*

abhalten, *bear away (altering the course);* - auf, *bear down upon;* immer mehr -, *bear off gradually.*

Abhalttau. n., *launching fast.*

abhieven, *heave off.*

abholen, *warp off.*

abkeilen, *wedge.*

abkleiden, *take off the service of a rope,*

abkneifen, *ply to windward by boards.*

abkommen, *get off;* über Steuer vom Grunde -, *to back off from the ground.*

abkrabben, *to race timber.*

abkreuzen, *1. claw off (from a lee shore);* 2. *cut off (plates, &c.).*

Abkühlung, f., *cooling.*

abkuntjen, *chock.*

Ablader, m., *shipper.*

ablandig, abländisch, *land breeze.*

Ablaßvorrichtung, f., *blow-off gear.*

Ablauf, m., *launching (of a vessel);* - balken, m., *cradle;* - des Hinterstevens, *rake of the sternpost;* - des Vorderstevens, *r. o. t. stem;* - gerüst, m., *launching cradle;* - helgen, m., *l. slip;* - planken, *l. planks;* - rinnen, *scuppers;* - schlitten, m., *cradle.*

ablaufen lassen, *launch.*

ableichtern, Ableichterung, f., *lightening.*

ableiten, *lead off.*

Ableitung, f., *eduction.*

Ableitungs-gestell. n., - säule, f.. *exhaust column.*

Ablenkung der Magnetnadel, f., *local attraction.*

ablesen, *read.*

Ablieferungsschein, m., *delivery order.*

abliegen, *stand off.*

abliegender Gang, m., *outside strake.*

ablösen, *relieve.*

ablösender Arbeitergang, m., *relief gang.*

abmatten, *supply with dunnage mats.*

abmustern, *pay off.*

Abnahme der Materialstärke, f.. *deterioration of thickness.*

abnehmbare Ruderfingerling, m., *independent rudder pintle;* - Schraubenflügel, m., *movable propeller blade;* - Stütze, t., *m. pillar.*

abnehmen, *1. slackening out*

(of the wind); 2. *take off (hatches, stoppers, &c.)*; 3. *unship (propeller, rudder, &c.)*.
abnutzen, *wear out.*
Abnutzung. f., *wear and tear.*
abpallen, *chock.*
abpicken, *scale.*
abrauhen, *dress up.*
abreiben, *grind.*
abreiten, *ride out (a gale).*
abrosten, Abrostung, f., *rusting off.*
abrüsten, unrig.
Absatz, m., *offset.*
abschaken, *shift.*
abschäumen, *scum.*
Abschaum-hahn, m., *scum cock;* - ventil, n., *s. valve.*
abscheren, *sheer off;* -de Kraft, f., *sheering force.*
abscheuern, *scour;* den Boden eines Schiffes mit dem Besen -, *hog a vessel*
abschieben, *shove off.*
abschlachten, *break up (a vessel).*
abschlagen, *1. knock off; 2. unbend (a sail); 3. unlace (a bonnet).*
abschleppen, *tow off.*
Abschleppversuche, *attempts to tow her off.*
abschlichten, *smooth off;* das -, *dubbing.*
abschlieren, *surging.*
abschlippen, *slip off.*
abschnüren, *lay down (a vessel).*
abschotten, *1. partition off by bulkheads; 2. to trench (ballast).*
Abschottung, f., *compartment.*
abschricken, *check.*
abschroten, *parbuckle.*
abschwächen, *to deaden a blow.*
absegeln, *to get under sail.*
absenden, *despatch.*
Absender, m., *consigner.*
absetzen, *1. land (the pilot); 2. prick (the chart).*
Absetzer, m., *squillagee.*

absolute Druck, m., *absolute pressure;* - Gewicht, n., *a. weight;* - Kraft, f., *a. force, a. power.*
Absperr-hahn, m., *stop cock;* - schieber, m., *sliding stop valve;* - ventil, n., *stop v.;* - - deckel, m., *s. v. cover;* - - gehäuse, n., *s. v. box;* - - gestänge, n., *s. v. gear;* - - rad, n., *s. v. wheel;* - - spindel, f., *s. v. rod;* - - stopfbüchse, f., *s. v. stuffing box;* - - - deckel, m., *s. v. gland;* - vorrichtung, f., *closing gear.*
abspringen, *panting, starting.*
abspülen, *wash down.*
Abspülung durch die See, f., *breach of the sea.*
Abstand, m., *distance;* - von Mitte zu Mitte, *spacing;* seitlicher -, *lateral distance.*
abs*echen, *chip.*
Abstechmeißel, m., *chipping chisel.*
abstecken, *unbend.*
abstellen, *1. shut off (steam); 2. stop (engines).*
absteuern, *bear off.*
abstoppen, *stopper.*
abstoßen, *shove off.*
abstützen, *1. shore up, tome off; 2. prop (a vessel).*
abtakeln, *unrig.*
abteilen, *to partition off (by bulkheads).*
Abteilung, f., *1. compartment (of hold); 2. gang (of labourers).*
Abteilungsschott, n., *transversal bulkhead.*
abtreiben, *sagging (a considerable leeway).*
Abtrift, f., *leeway;* - haben, *to make l.;* wegen - verbesserter Kurs, *course corrected for l.*
Abtropfschale, f., *save-all.*
ab und an, *off and on.*
abwarpen, *warp off.*
abwartende Haltung beobachten, f., *take up a watching position.*
abwehren, *fend off.*

abweichen, *deviate.*
Abweichung, f., *leeway, drift;*
- vom Meridian der Abfahrt, *departure from the meridian from which the vessel sailed.*
Abweichungskompaß, m., *variation compass.*
Abweiser, m., *rubbing strake.*
Abweitung, f, *departure.*
abwerfen, *cast off.*
abwracken, *break up.*
abzeugen, *strip.*
abziehen. *grind.*
Abzweigrohr, n., *branch pipe.*
Accordarbeit. f., *contract work.*
Achse, f.. *axle.*
Achsen-büchse, f., *journal box;* - - Schmiervorrichtung, f., *j. b. lubricator;* - lager, n., *j. bearing.*
Acht, Gebt - dort unten! *Stand from under!*
achter, *aft.*
achteraus, *astern;* - gehen, *go a.;* - hieven, *heave a;* - holen, *haul a;* - sacken lassen, *drop a.;* - schleppen, *tow a.*
Achter-brassen, *after braces;* - deck, n., *a. deck;* - Gaffeltoppsegel, n., *mizen gaff topsail;* - galerie, f., *stern gallery;* - gangspill, n., *after capstan;* - geier, m., *gob line;* - holer, m., *back rope;* - - der Backspiere, *after guy;* - - des Stampfstocks, *gob line;* - klüver-Backstag. n., *after guy of the sprit sail gaff;* - knoten, m., *cat's paw;* - lastig, *by the stern;* - leine, f., *stern rope.*
achterlich, *abaft;* - gehen, holen od. räumen, *draw aft;* - von dwars, *abaft the beam.*
achterlicher als dwars, *abaft the beam.*
Achter-liek, n., *after leech rope;* - luke, f., *a. hatchway;* - luken, *a. hatches;* - - scherstock od. - - süll, m., *after hatchway coaming;* - pardune, f., *a. backstay;* - rahe, f., *a. yard;* - raum, m., *a.*

hold; - rund! *mainsail haul!* - schiff, n., *after body;* - segel. n., *after sails;* -seitentakel, n., *mizen tackle;* - springtau, n.. *back spring.*
achterst, *sternmost.*
Achter-steven, m., *stern post;* - stich, m., *figure-of-eightknot;* - treppe, f., *after ladder;* - wind, m., *following wind.*
Achterkant einer Rahe, f., *quarter of a yard.*
Achtung! *Stand by!* - beim Steuer! *Mind the helm!*
Achtungsverletzung, *disrespect.*
Adjustierer, m., *adjuster.*
Adjustierung. f., *adjustment.*
Admiral Elliots - Auge, n., *Elliot's eye.*
Admiralitäts-gericht, n., *Admiralty Court;* - karte, f., *A. Chart.*
adoucieren, *tempering.*
adoucierter Stahl, m., *annealed steel.*
adressiert an, *consigned to.*
ändern, *alter.*
Aenderung f., *alteration.*
Aequator, m., *equator;* den - passieren, *cross the line.*
Aequatorial-kalmen,*doldrums;* - strom, m., *equatorial current.*
Aequinoctial-kompaß. m.,*equinoctial compass;* - stürme, *e. storms.*
Aequinoctium, n., *equinox.*
Affidavit, n., *affidavit.*
Afteranker, m., *lower anchor.*
ahoi, *ahoy.*
Ahming, f., *draught marks;* die - machen, *to gauge the d.*
Ahornholz, n., *maple.*
ahull, *ahull.*
aichen, *gauge.*
Aichmeister, m., *gauger.*
Akazienholz, n., *locust.*
Aktionsradius, m., *radius of action.*
Alarm-apparat, m., *low water detector;* - ventil, n., *alarm valve.*

Algen. *sea weeds.*
Alle Mann auf Deck! *All hands on deck!*
alles back, *all aback;* - beigesetzt, *every stitch set;* - klar gelegt od. legen. *every rope an end;* - los! *Let go!* - von Deck geschlagen, *decks swept.*
alte Tauwerk. n., *junk;* - Vermessungsmethode, f., *old measurement.*
altersschwach, *crazy.*
Altweiberknoten, m., *granny's bend.*
Aluminium. n., *aluminium.*
am Backbord Bug, *on the port bow;* am Bug, *o. t. b.;* - Lee B., *o. t lee b.;* - Luv B., *o t. weather b.;* - Steuerbord B., *o. t. starboard b.*
am Grunde sitzend. *aground;* - Winde, *near the wind.*
Amboß, m., *anvil;* - abschroter, m., *a. chisel;* - horn, n, *a. horn;* - klotz od. stock, m., *a. block.*
Ammeral, m., *canvass bucket.*
Ampere. m., *ampere;* - messer, m., *amperemeter.*
amplitude, f., *amplitude.*
an Backbord achter, *on port quarter;* - - Bug, *o. p. bow;* - Bord. *on board;* - - kommen. *to board;* - Land, *on shore;* - - gehen, *go o. s.*
anbändseln, *to marry.*
Anbinde-block. m., *mooring block;* - pfahl, m., *m. post.*
anbohren, *scuttle.*
anbrassen, *brace up;* scharf -, *to point.*
Anderthalbmaster, m., *galeas.*
Aneinanderbolzen d. Spanten, n., *frame bolting.*
Anemometer, n., *anemometer.*
Aneroid Barometer, n, *aneroid barometer.*
anfangende Kirschrotglühhitze. f, *low cherry red heat.*
Anfangsdruck, m., *initial pressure.*
anfassen, *to lay hold of.*

Angabe der Wassertiefe, f., *sounding.*
Angebot, n.. *1. tender; 2. supply;* zu reichliches -, *an over s.*
angefressen, *pitted.*
angekommene Breite, f.. *latitude in;* - Länge, f., *longitude in;* - Schiffe. *arrivals.*
Angelhaken, m., *fish hook.*
Angellyholz, n., *angelly wood.*
angemessene Stärke, f., *adequate strength.*
angemustert für die Überfahrt, *shipped by the run.*
anhaken, *hook.*
anhalten, *stop.*
Anhang. m., *the tow;* im -, *in tow.*
anholen, die Baumschote -, *to haul over the booms;* die Großschote -, *t. h. the main sheet aft;* die Halsen -, *t. h. the tacks aboard;* die Luvklüverschoten -, *to flat in the jibs;* ein Tau -, *to tally on a rope.*
Anholpart eines Takels, f., *hauling part of a tackle.*
Anker, m.. *1. anchor (of the ship); 2. stay rod (of the boiler); 3. tie rod (of a winch).*
Anker, auf den - zusteuern, *to steer to the anchor;* - aufgehen, *to weigh a.;* den - hieven, *to heave up the a.;* den - stocken. *to stock the a.;* den - unter den Kranbalken bringen, *to cockbill the a.;* den - vom Bug abhalten. *to bear off the a.;* der - greift, *the a bites;* der - hängt vor dem Kran, *the a. is at the cat head;* der - ist auf und nieder. *the a. is apeak;* der - ist klar zum fallen lassen, *the a. is a-cockbill;* der - läßt los, *the a. is starting;* vor - gehen, *come to an a.;* vor - liegen, *lying at a.;* vor dem - treiben, *to be clubbing;* zu - gehen mit den Segeln im Topp, *to let go the a. with all sails set.*

Anker-arm, m., *anchor arm;* - aufwindebaum, m., *fish boom;* - auge, n., *eye of the anchor;* - bett. n., *a. bed;* - boje, f., *a. buoy;* - - reep. n., *a. b. rope;* - - wacht. *the b. watches;* - breite. f., *anchor crown;* - david. m., *a. david;* - - spur, f., *a. d. socket;* - deck, n., *a. deck;* - draggen, m., *a. drag;* - flügel, m., *palm of the a.;* - fütterung, f., *a. lining;* - gebühren od. - geld. *anchorage dues;* - geschirr, n., *ground tackle;* - grund. m., *anchorage;* guter - -. *good holding ground;* schlechter - -. *bad h. g.;* sicherer - -, *safe anchorage;* unsicherer - -, *unsafe anchorage;* - haken, m., *cat hook;* - hals, m., *neck of the anchor;* - hand, f., *palm of the a.;* - hieven, n., *a. heaving;* - katt, n., *cat tackle;* - kette, f., *chain cable;* - - mit Stege od. Stützen. *stud link c. c.;* - - ohne Stege. *short l. c. c.;* - kettenglied, n., od. - kettenschake. f., *l. of a. c. c.;* - kettenschäkel, m.. *shackle of a. c. c.;* - kettenwarrel, n.. od. - kettenwirbel, m., *swivel of a. c. c.;* - kippung, f., *fish of an anchor;* - klüse, f., *hawse hole;* - kran, m., *anchor crane;* - kreuz, n.. *a. cross;* - kugel mit Leine, f., *a. shot;* - laschnng, f., *a. lashing;* - licht, n., *riding light;* - lichten, *to weigh anchor.*
Ankerlichtmaschine, f, *steam windlass (See also Dampfspill and Ankerspill).*
Anker-mutter, f.. *stay nut;* - nuß. f., *anchor nut;* - ohr. n., *wing of the a. fluke;* - peilung. f., *a. bearings;* - platz, m., *see* - grund; den -platz verlegen, *to shift the berth;* - pünte, f., *bill od. peak of the anchor;* - rakete, f., *a. rocket;* - ring, m., *a. ring;* -rohr, n.,

stay tube; - röhrung od. - rührung, f., *puddening of an anchor ring;* - rute, f., *beam of an a ;* - schaar, f., *a. flue;* - schaft. m., *a. shaft;* - schäkel, m., *a. shackle;* - - bolzen, *a. s. bolt;* - schaufel, f., *a. fluke;* - scheuer, f., *bill board;* - schlipper, m., *anchor slipper;* - schmied, m., *a. smith;* - schmiede, f., *a. forge;* - schuh, m., *a. shoe;* - sorrung, f., *a. lashing;* - spaten, m., *a. fluke.*
Ankerspill, n., *windlass (See also Dampfspill);* - wollte die Kette nicht greifen, *w. would not gripe the chain;* das - zusammenschrauben, *to screw up the w.*
Anker-spitze, f., *anchor bill;* - sti h, m., *cable clinch;* - stock, m., *anchor stock;* - - band. n., *hoop of the a. s.;* - - bolzen, m., *a. s. bolt;* - - nägel, a. s. *tree nails;* - - nuß. f., a. s. *nut;* - - schaft, m., *a. shank square,* - - splint, m., *fore lock of the a. stock;* - talje, f., *a. s. tackle;* - taukrabber. *cable gripper;* - tausplissung, f., *the shot of a cable;* - tauwerk, m., *stock tackle;* - trosse, f., *cable;* - wache, f., *anchor watch;* - - halten, *to keep a. w.;* - woit, f., *viol;* - - block, m.. *v. block;* - zurrung. f., *anchor lashing.*
ankern, *anchor.*
ankreiden, *chalk down.*
anlanden. *landing.*
Anlaschbolzen, m., *scarf bolt.*
Anlaß-apparat, m., *starter;* - hahn, m., *starting cock;* - hebel, *s. lever;* - getriebe, n., s. *gear;* - maschine, f., *s. engine;* - schieber, m., od. - ventil, n., *s. valve;* - - gestänge, n., *s v. gear;* - - handhabe, f., *s. v. handle;* - - rohr, n., *s. v. pipe;* - - spindel, f., *s. v. spindle;* - - stange, f.. *s. v. rod.*

anlassen, *start.*
Anlauf des Vorderstevens, m., *fore foot.*
anlaufen, *call at.*
Anlegehafen, m., *port of call.*
anlegen, *1. come alongside; 2. das stehende Gut -, to place the standing rigging; 3. die Wanten -, t. p. t. shrouds on the masthead.*
anliegen nach Cuxhaven, *stand in for C.;* seewärts -, *s. off.*
anliegender Gang, m., *inside strake.*
anlieken, *to rope.*
anluven, *to round to.*
anmustern, *join, ship, sign the articles.*
Anordia, f., *anordia.*
anpassen, *fit.*
Anpassung, f., *adjusting.*
Anprall des Meeres, m., *the dashing and breaking of the sea.*
anreihen, *lace.*
anrufen, Anruf, m., *hail.*
Anscherpfahl, m., *warping post.*
Anschlag, m., *1. rabbet (of window, door); 2. bill posted up; 3. estimate (costs);* - bändsel od. bindsel, n., *rope-band;* - legel, m., *earing cringle;* - leine, f., *lacing;* - liek, n., *head rope.*
anschlagen, *1. start (engines); 2. clap on (tackle); 3. fetch (pump); 4. bend (sail); 5. sling (round a barrel).*
Anschluß, m., *connection.*
anschmiegen, *to hug (the land, wind).*
anschreiben, *tallying.*
anschweißen, *weld together.*
ansegeln, *1. make for (a port); 2. run foul of (a ship).*
Ansegelung, f., *1. collision; 2. calling at (a port); 3. beginning (regatta).*
Ansicht, f., *view.*
Anspannung, f., *strain.*
ansprechen, *speak (a vessel).*

anspringen, *start (engines).*
Anspruch, m., *claim;* - auf Bergelohn, *salvage c.*
Anstalt, f., *works.*
anstecken, *start (a cask).*
ansteuern, *stand for (a port).*
anstreichen, *to coat.*
Anstrich, m., *coating.*
Anteil haben, m., *to own a share.*
Anthracit, m., *anthracite.*
Antifriktionsmetall, n., *anti-friction metal.*
antreten, *enter (the service).*
Antriebswelle, f., *driving shaft.*
antun. *touch (a port).*
antworten, *to answer (a signal).*
anwärmen, *warm through.*
Anweisung, f., *allotment note.*
Anwendung, f., *appliance.*
Anzahl der Umdrehungen, f., *number of revolutions.*
Anzeichen, n., *appearance.*
anziehen. *screw down (packing, screw).*
Anziehungskraft, f., *attractive power.*
anzünden, *ignite.*
Anzündung, f., *ignition.*
Apparat, m., *apparatus.*
Arbeit, f., *work, workmanship.*
arbeiten, *1. work (men, machinery); 2. labour (ship); 3. work (a passage); 4. refuse to do duty (crew);* mühsam -, *thrashing (machinery).*
Arbeiter, m., *labourer.*
Arbeits-boot, n., *working boat;* - druck, m., *w. pressure;* - mann, *labourer;* - tage, *working days.*
Arcasse, f., *arcasse.*
Archipel, m., *archipelago.*
Areal des Mittelspants, n., *midship frame section.*
Arm eines Bugbandes, m., *arm of a hook.*
Armatur, f., *fittings.*
Arm-feile, f., *arm file;* - stopper, m., *compressor.*
armunklarer Anker, m., *anchor fouled by the flukes.*

Arsenal, n., *dock yard;* - arbeiter, m., *d. y. maty.*

Arzneikiste, f., *medicine chest.*

Asbest, m., *asbestos;* - liderung od. packung, f., *a. packing.*

Asch-davit, m., *ash davit;* - eimer, m., *a. bucket;* - ejector, m., *a. ejector;* - fall, m., *a. pit;* - - dämpfer, m., *a. p. damper;* - - tür, f., *a. p. door;* - - register, n., *a. p. damper;* - hahn, m., *a. cock;* - heiß. m., *a. hoist;* - - vorrichtung, f., *a. h. gear;* - kasten, m., *a. pan;* - sack, m., *a. bag;* - schlauch, m., *a. hose;* - schütte, f., *a. shoot.*

Asche ziehen, *draw ashes.*

Aschen-aufzug, m., *ash hoist;* - - vorrichtung, f., *a. h. gear;* - auslauf od. auswurf, m., *a. shoot. (See also* Asch-*).*

Asphalt, m., *asphalt.*

Assekuradeur, m., *underwriter.*

Assekuranz, f., *insurance;* - prämie, f., *i. premium;* - polize, f., *i. policy.*

astronomische Beobachtungen, *astronomical observations;* - Besteck, n., *ship's place by observation;* - Tag, m., *astronomical day;* - Zeit, f., *a. time.*

atlantische Fahrt, f., *Atlantic trade;* - Ozean. m., *A. Ocean.*

Atlasholz. n., *satin wood.*

Atmosphäre, f., *atmosphere.*

Atmosphärendruck, m., *atmospheric pressure.*

atmosphärische Linie, f., *atmospheric line;* - Maschine, f., *a. engine.*

Atomgewicht, n., *atomic weight.*

Aufbänken der Feuer, n., *banking the fires.*

Aufbau, m., Aufbauten, *deck erections;* mit einander verbundene -, *combined d. e.;* nicht m. e. v. A., *disconnected d. e.*

aufbojen, *to buoy up.*

aufbringen, *1. capture* od. *seize (a vessel); 2. hoist up (yards, masts); 3. bring up (with an anchor).*

Aufbringer, m., *1. captor (enemy); 2. steeler (a plank).*

Aufbug, m., *deck rising.*

auf das Ruder! *up with the helm!* - - - passen, *mind t. h.;* - dem Grunde sitzen, *to be aground;* - dem Kopfe liegen, *by the head;* - dem Winde l., *to be wind rode;* - den Rand laufen lassen, *to be Spanish reefed;* - den Strand l. l., *to beach;* - der Ausreise, *outward bound;* - der Höhe von, *abreast of;* - der Ladung treiben, *to be water logged;* - der Rückreise, *homeward bound.*

aufdrehen. *1. untwist (rope); 2. come to a stop; 3. swing to tide and wind; 4. bring the broadside to bear (coming abreast).*

Aufduning, f., *landfall.*

aufduven, *bear up.*

aufentern, *go aloft.*

Aufenthalt, m., *1. stay; 2. detention.*

auffahren, *run aground.*

Auffahrt einer Werft, f., *ramp.*

auffangen, *lash up.*

auffeuern, *fire up.*

auffieren, *1. slack off (sheets); 2. come up (tackle).*

auffliegen, *fly up.*

auffrischen, *to freshen.*

auffüllen, *line up (brasses).*

Aufgang, m., *1. up-stroke (of piston); 2. rising (of a star).*

aufgeben, *1. to ease (tacks); 2. abandon (a vessel).*

aufgebojet, *sewed.*

aufgebraucht, *used up.*

aufgebuckelt, *buckled.*

aufgedrehtes Tauende, n., *fag end.*

aufgegeit, *brailed up.*

aufgehalten, *delayed;* durch Wetter -, *weather bound;* d. Wind -, *wind b.*

aufgeien, *clew up (sails)*.
aufgelegt, *laid up*.
aufgenommen, nicht - auf der Karte, *chartless*.
aufgeputzt. *jaunty*.
aufgeschlammt. *silted up*.
aufgesetzte Schieberfläche, f., *false face*.
aufgetakelt, vollständig -, *completely rigged*.
aufgetrocknet, *dried up*.
aufgezeugt, *in prime kelter*.
auf gleicher Höhe mit, *flush with*; - Grund geraten, kommen od. laufen, *grounding*; - Halsen und Schoten! *Up tacks and sheets!*
aufheißen, *to hoist*.
aufheitern, *clear up*.
aufhieven, *heave up*.
aufhissen, *to veer aloft*.
auf hoher See, *on the high seas*
aufholen, *1. haul up; 2. round in (braces)*.
Aufholer. m., *tricing line*; - der Besahnbrohk, *girtline of the mizen brails*; - des oberen Rahetakels. *quarter tricing line*; - des unteren R., *bill t. l.*
aufkatten, *to cat*.
Aufkimmung einer Bodenwrange, f., *rise of a floor*.
aufklaren. *1. clear (deck, &c.); 2. c up (weather)*.
aufklotzen, *upmaking*.
Aufklotzung, f., *chock*; - bolzen, m., *deadwood bolt*.
aufknebeln, *put into a becket*.
aufkommen, *1. come up (the river); 2 spring up (wind)*; einem Schiffe -, *to come up with*; gegen den Strom -, *to stem the current*; mit dem Ruder -, *to ease her*.
aufkreuzen, *to beat up*; Schlag für S. -, *to ply by short boards*.
Aufkreuzer, m., *plyer*.
auf Kreuzung, *cruising*.
aufkürzen, *shorten*.

Auflage des Loches im Kreuz, f, *cross tail butt*.
auflandiger Wind, m., *wind from the sea*.
Auflanger, m., *futtock*; - der Kattsporen, *f. rider*.
auflaufen. *1. run aground; 2. run up (yards, &c)*; einem Schiffe -, *come up with another vessel*.
auflaufendes Wasser, n., *flowing water*.
Aufläufer, m., *ship's boy*.
auflavieren, *to gain to windward by backing*.
auflegen, *1. lay up (ship); 2. to place (standing rigging)*.
auflichten, *to prize*.
auflotsen, *to pilot up*.
aufluven. *to round to*.
aufmachen, *1. to rise (sea); 2. spring up (wind); 3. adjust (average)*.
aufnehmen, die Arbeit wieder -, *turn to again*.
aufpalmen, sich -, *climb hand over hand*.
aufpassen, *mind, watch, pay attention*.
aufpflücken, *to fag out*.
aufrichten, *1. to right (vessel); 2. to step (mast); 3. to trim (boat); 4. raise (frames)*.
Aufriß, m., *shear plan*.
aufrollen, *roll up (sail)*.
aufrühren, *stir the ground*.
auf See, *at sea*.
aufschießen lassen, *to forereach in stays*: gegen die Sonne -, *to coil against the sun*; mit der S. a., *t. c. with t. s.*; in Scheiben -, *to flemish*.
auf's neue, *anew*; - - ausbüchsen, *to rebush*: - - verankern, *to restay (boiler)*.
aufschlagen, *unlay (ropes)*.
Aufschlagwasser, n., *moving water*.
Aufschlepphelling, f., *slipway*.
aufschoven, *to stave and bundle a cask*.
aufschroten, *to parbuckle*.

aufschwellen, *to bouge.*

aufsegeln, *sail up.*

aufsetzen, *to set (rigging, watch, &c.);* die Schraube auf die Welle -, *to ship the propeller;* einen Stopper -, *to clap on a stopper.*

Aufsicht über, f., *the management of.*

aufsingen, *sing out.*

aufspeichern, *warehouse.*

aufstechen, *give up (tacks and sheets).*

Aufsteckschlüssel, m., *box spanner.*

Aufsteigen der Inhölzer, n., *rising of the timbers.*

aufstellen, *put up (boilers).*

aufstoßen, *bumping.*

auf Strand getrieben, *driven ashore;* - - laufen, *run a.;* - - setzen, *beach.*

aufstreifen, das stehende Gut -, *put the rigging on the mast head.*

aufstützen, *shore up.*

auftakeln, *rig.*

auftaljen, *bowse.*

auftoppen, *top.*

auftörnen, *1. come to a stop; 2. swing (to wind or tide); 3. turn up (on the anchor, chain or rope).*

auftrennen, *1. rip open (plates); 2. unstitch (sails).*

auftuchen, *duck up.*

auf und nieder, *1. the anchor is apeak; 2. the wind is up and down; 3. the flag is up a. d.;* - - - *stampfen, heaving and setting;* - - - *tanzen, bobbing.*

aufwallende See, f., *boiling sea.*

Aufwärter, m., *steward;* - in, f., *stewardess.*

aufweiten, *reeming.*

aufwickeln, *ball off.*

aufwinden, *to ground (a vessel).*

aufwuchten, *to prize.*

auf Zapfen drehendes Seitenfenster, n., *pivoted scuttle.*

aufzeisen, die Kette an das Kabelar -, *to nip the cable.*

Aufzeiser der Kette an das Kabelar, m., *nipper-man.*

aufzeugen, *to rig.*

Aufziehschlitten, m., *cradle.*

Aufzug, m., *lift.*

Aug-bindsel, n., *throat seizing;* - bolzen, m., *eye bolt;* - splissung, f., *e. splice.*

Auge, n., *1. eye (of backstays); 2. upper collar (of stays); 3. shaft hole (of propeller);* - zeising. m., *eye gasket.*

Augen, *see* Aug *and* Auge.

augenblickliche Hülfe, f., *immediate assistance.*

aus dem Dock holen, *to undock;* - - - kommen, *come out of dock;* - - Ruder laufen, *lose her steerage way;* - Sicht, *out of sight;* - und Rückfracht, f., *out and home freight;* - zweiter Hand, f., *second hand (vessel),*

ausbacken, *to beacon.*

Ausbau des Schafttunnels, m., *recess bulkhead of shaft tunnel.*

Ausbauchung, f., *belly (of sails).*

Ausbesserer, m., *repairer.*

ausbessern, *repair.*

Ausbesserung, f., *repairs.*

Ausblas-hahn, m., *blow-off cock;* - rohr, n., *b. o. pipe;* - - leitung, f., *b. o. pipes;* - ventil, n., *b. o. valve.*

ausbohren. *bore out.*

ausbojen. *to buoy.*

ausbooten, *to boat.*

ausbreiten, *ranging (a chain cable).*

ausbringen, *1. carry out (ropes, anchor); 2. rig out (booms).*

ausbüchsen, *rebush.*

Ausbucht, Ausbuchtung, f., *1. indentation (plates); 2. rounding-out (timber). 2. outward bend (river)*

Ausbugung. f., *bearding.*

Ausdehnung, f., *dilatation (heat).*

Ausdehnungs-kraft, f., - vermögen, n., *expansive force.*
ausdocken, *undock.*
ausdrehen, *untwist the ends of the strands (of rope yarn).*
auseinandernehmen, *open out (engines).*
ausfahren, *run out (hawsers, cables).*
ausfeuern, *to mark by beacons.*
Ausflug in See, m., *sea trip.*
Ausfluß, m., *1. eduction; 2. shoe (pipes);* - öffnung, f., *port of exit.*
Ausfracht, f., *out-freight.*
Ausfuhr, f., *export;* - artikel, m., *exports;* - dock, n., *export dock;* - erlaubnis, f., *permit of exportation;* - handel, m., *outwart trade;* - prämie, f., *bounty;* - zoll, m., *export duty.*
ausführen, 1. *to export (goods);* 2. *execute (orders).*
ausfüllen, *to line (brasses).*
ausgasen, *fumigate.*
Ausgasung, f., *fumigation.*
Ausgebaggertes, n., *dredgings.*
ausgebaucht, *bulged.*
ausgebrannteKohlen,*klinkers.*
ausgedoppt, *countersunk.*
ausgefahren, 1. *used up (materials);* 2. *run out (cables, hawsers).*
ausgehen, *die out (fires).*
ausgehende Ladung, f., *outward cargo;* - Stromkrümmung, f., *convex sinuosity.*
ausgehobenes Ruder, n., *unshipped rudder.*
ausgelaufene Flotte, f., *the fleet has run out.*
ausgenutzt, 1. *ill used;* 2. *used up.*
ausgereckt, *long jawed.*
ausgestemmter Block, m., *mortised block.*
ausgestoßenes Ruder, n., *unshipped rudder.*
ausgewittert, *seasoned (wood).*
ausgießen, das Lot mit Talg -, *to arm the lead;* die Lagerschalen -, *to line up the brasses.*

ausglühen, *annealing.*
Ausguck, m., *look out;* - halten, *keep l. o.;* - war gut besetzt, *a sharp l. o. was kept;* - brücke, f., *l. o. bridge;* - - geländer, n., *l. o. b. rails and stanchions;* - - scepter, n., *l. o. b. s.*
Ausgucksmann, m., *look-out-man.*
Ausguß. m., *discharge;* - hahn, m., *delivery cock;* - rohr, n., *discharge pipe;* - ventil, n., *d. valve box;* - - sitz, m., *d. v. seat;* - - spindel, f., *d. v. spindle.*
aushaken, *unhook.*
aushalten, *to weather out (a gale).*
aushängen, *unship (rudder).*
aushieven. *heave out.*
ausholen, 1. *to twig (a bowline);* 2. *haul out (the spanker);* gut -, *give way with a will (when rowing).*
Ausholer, m., *outhaul;* - der Blinde, *sprit sail halliard;* - der Schiebblinde, *s. s. top sail halliard.*
Aushol-ring, m., 1. *gaff traveller (of a gaff);* 2. *jib t. (of jib boom); 3. wheel chain t. (of w. c.);* - schlagen eines Nockbindsels, f., *outer turn of an earing.*
ausklarieren, *to clear outward.*
Ausklarierung, f., *outward clearance;* - schein, m., *transire.*
auskreuzen, 1. *beat out (of a river);* 2. *tack out (another vessel).*
auskuppeln, *disconnect.*
Auskuppelung, f., *disconnecting.*
ausladen, *discharge.*
ausländische Besatzung, f., *foreign crew;* - Fahrt, f., *f. going vessel;* - Gerichtshof, m., *f. court;* - Handel, m.. *f. trade;* - Seezeichen, *f. sea marks;* - Urteilsspruch, m., *f. judgment.*

auslangen, gut -, *give way with a will.*

Auslaß, m., *outlet.*

auslassen, *1. let off (steam); 2. hoist out (boat).*

Auslaß-hahn, m., *exhaust cock;* - rohr, n., *waste water pipe;* - ventil, n.. *outlet valve.*

Auslauf. m., *outlet.*

auslaufen, *1. set sail, leave; 2.* - lassen, *slip the chain.*

Ausläufer. m., *1. ship's boy; 2. spur (of a mountain); 3. branch (of sands).*

Ausleerungsrohr, n., *evacuation pipe.*

auslegen, *1. throw (trawl); 2. put (a buoy); 3. top over (booms); 4. lay out (on a yard); 5. ship (oars).*

Ausleger, m., *1. outrigger (boat); 2. o. of the cross trees: 3. spider (of main braces); 4. whisker (for spreading jib guys);* - stag, n., *boomkin shroud.*

ausliegende Krümmung, f., *outward bend.*

Auslieger *see* Ausleger.

auslochen, *punch.*

Auslöscben der Feuer, n., *drawing the fires.*

Auslö-e-haken, m., od. - vorrichtung, f., *detaching hook.*

ausloten, *examine the depth and quality of the ground.*

auslüften, *ventilate.*

Auslugger, m., *look-out man.*

ausmachen, *make out (lights, &c.).*

ausmanövrieren, *to tack out.*

Ausmündung, f., *1. mouth, disemboguement (canal); 2. shoe (of pipes).*

ausnehmen, *1. take out (reefs, cargo); 2. unship (rudder).*

ausösen, *baling.*

auspeitschen, *flog.*

auspflücken, *draw asunder.*

auspichen, *pay (seams).*

ausplüsen, *draw asunder.*

Auspuffmaschine, f., *non-condensing engine.*

auspumpen, *pump dry.*

ausrangieren, *disrate.*

ausräuchern, *fumigate.*

Ausräucherung, f., *fumigation.*

ausräumen, *rime out (rivet holes)*

Ausräumung, f., *countersink.*

ausrechnen, *to work (an observation).*

ausrecken, *stretch.*

ausreiben. *countersink.*

Ausreise, f., *outward passage.*

ausrichten, *straighten (plates and frames).*

Ausrichtung, f., *straightening.*

Ausrigger, m., *outrigger.*

ausrücken, *1. uncouple; 2. throw out of gear (machinery).*

Ausrückvorrichtung, f., *disengaging gear.*

ausrüsten, *fit out.*

Ausrüstung. f., *outfit;* -sgegenstände, *stores.*

Aussage, eidliche und schriftliche -, f., *affidavit.*

ausschäkeln, *unshackle.*

ausscheren, *1. sheer off (ship). 2. unreeve (rope).*

ausschieben, *rig out (boom).*

ausschießen, *1. come suddenly (from port or starboard); 2. n., the rake of the stem.*

ausschießender Steven, m., *raking stem.*

ausschiffen, *disembark;* n., *disembarkation.*

Ausschiftung, f., *disembarkation.*

Ausschlagpunze, f., *punch.*

ausschleppen, *tow out;* n., *towing out.*

Ausschnitt für einen Fingerling, m., *pintle score.*

Ausschuß, m., *refuse.*

ausschwingen, *swing out.*

aussegeln, *beat od. outsail.*

außen, *outside;* - barre, f., *outer bar;* - bekleidung, f.. *shell;* - beplankung, f., *outside planking;* - bords, *outboard;* - fall, m., *outer halliard;* - gang, m., *outside strake;* - hafen, m., *outer* harbour; - haut, f., *1. boiler shell;* 2. *outside plating (of ship);* - - niete, f.. *shell rivet;* - - nietung. f.. s. *riveting;* - - platten, *outside plating.*

Außenklüver, m., *flying jib;* - Backstag, n., *f. j. guy;* - baum, m., *f. j. boom;* - brille, f., *f. b. iron;* - bügel, m., *f. j. b. i.;* - domper, m., *f. martingale stay;* - fall, m., *f. jib halliard;* - geie, f., *f. j. boom guy;* - hals, m., *f. j. tack;* - leiter, f., *f. j. stay;* - niederholer, m., *f. j. downhaul;* - pferd, n., *f. j. boom foot rope;* - schote, f., *f. j. sheet;* - stampfstag, n., *f. j. boom stay.*

Außen-lager. n., *outer bearing;* - - der Radwelle, *paddle shaft outside bearing;* - liek, n., *after leech rope;* - mutter eines Kesselankers, f., *boiler stay outside nut;* - pfahl, m., *border pile;* - planke, f., *outside plank;* - schote, f., *outer sheet;* - seite, f., *outside;* - spierenbügel, m., *yard arm iron;* - stich. m.. *outside clinch;* - stoßplatte, f., *o butt strap;* - takel. n., *yard arm tackle;* - - auf! *Away with the yards!* - trommel, f., *warping end;* - winkel des Wasserlaufs, m., *gunwale angle bar.*

außer Betrieb, *1. stopped (engines);* 2. *out of gear (appliances);* - - setzung, f., *1. stopping (engines);* 2. *throwing out of gear (appliances);* - Dienst, *1. off duty (crew);* 2. *out of commission (vessel);* - europäischer Hafen, m., *non-European port;* - gewöhnliches Abtreiben, n., *sagging;* - halb lotbaren Grundes, *out of soundings;* - Hörweite od. Rufweite, *out of hailing distance;* - Schußweite, *out of shot range.*

äußere Barre, f., *outer bar;* - Beplattung, f.. *outside plating;* - Brille einer Leesegelspiere, f., *yard arm iron;* - Feuerbüchse, f.. *outside fire box;* - Kesselwandung, f., *shell plating of boiler;* - Klinsch, f., *outside clinch;* - Plattengang, m., *outer strake;* - Radkastenbalken, m , *spring beam;* - Riemenblatt, n.. *oar web;* - Rinnsteinwinkel, m., *gunwale angle bar;* - Schraubenwelle, f., *outer screw shaft;* - Sicherheitsventil, n., *external safety valve.*

äußere Steuerung. f., *valve gear;* - - des Hochdruckzylinders, *high pressure v. g.;* - - des Mitteldruckzylinders, *intermediate v. g.;* - - des Niederdruckzylinders, *low pressure v. g.*

äußerer Wassergang, m., *outer waterway.*

äußerste Boje, f., *outmost buoy;* - Breite, f., *extreme breadth;* - Länge, f., *e. length.*

aussetzen, *set out (boat).*

ausspannen. alle Segel -, *to let all sails out.*

ausstechen, ausstecken, *1. pay out (cable);* 2. *unbend (rope);* 3. *shake out (reefs).*

Ausströmung, f., *exhaustion.*

Ausströmungs-hahn, m., *exhaust port;* - öffnung, f., *eduction port;* - rohr, n., *escape pipe;* - vorrichtung, f.. *eduction gear.*

austreiben, *start (a bolt).*

Austrittskanal, m., *exhaust port.*

Aus- und Rückfracht, f., *out and home freight.*

Auswanderer, m., *emigrant;* - schiff, n., *e. ship.*

auswandern, *1. emigrate (to a foreign country);* 2. *shut in (lights).*

Auswanderung, f., *emigration;* - sbeamter, m., *e. officer;*

- kommissar, m., *e. commissioner.*
auswärts, *abroad;* nach - bestimmt, *outward bound.*
Auswässerung, f.. *free board;* - slinie, f.. *swimming mark (of vessel).*
ausweben, *rattle down.*
ausweichen, *keep clear (of a vessel).*
Ausweich-laterne, f., od. - licht, n., *right of way lamp;* - regeln, *rules of the road at sea.*
Ausweitung, f.. *countersink.*
auswendiger Druck, m., *external pressure.*
Auswerfer, m., *ejector.*
auswippen, *whip.*

Auswurf, m., *shoot;* - rohr, n., *discharge pipe.*
ausziehen, *drawing (the fires).*
automatisch, *automatic;* - schließendes Ventil, n., *alarm valve.*
Auszug aus dem Journal, m., *abstract of log.*
Auxiliar-dampf, m., *auxiliary steam;* - kraft, f., *a. s. power.*
Awningdeckschiff, n., *awning deck ship.*
Axe, f.. *1. axle (disc and wheel);* *2. spindle (windlass).*
Axiometer, m., *tell-tale of rudder.*
Axt, f., *hatchet.*
Azimut, m., *azimuth;* - Kompaß, m., *a. compass.*

B.

Baake, f., *beacon.*
Baas, m., *shipping master.*
Back, f., *1. forecastle (crew space);* *2. f. head (deck);* *3. mess (of crew);* *4. patter (for eating & drinking);* *5. saucer (of capstan);* *6. punt (for caulking);* feste -, *topgallant forecastle.*
back bekommen, die Segel - -, *to be taken aback;* - braß überall! *Lay all flat aback!* - brassen, *to brace a.;* ganz -! *Flat a.!* - halsen, *box hauling;* - holen, *to back;* - legen, *bring aback;* - liegen, *the sails are a.;* all - vorn! *all aback forward!*
Back-ältester, m., *captain of the mess;* - balkweger, m., *forecastle deck beam shelf.*
Backbord, n., *port;* nach - abfallen, *cast to p;* - achter, *on the p. quarter;* - bei - passieren, *pass port by port;* - das Ruder! *Starboard the helm!* - dwars, *on the port beam.*

Backbord Anker, m., *port anchor;* - Bilge, f., *p. bilge;* - - Saugventil, n., *p. b. suction valve;* - bug, m, *p. bow;* über - -, *on the starboard tack;* mit - halsen, *on the port tack;* - kessel, m., *p. boiler;* - laterne. f., - licht, n., *p. light;* - maschine, f., *p. engine;* - seite, f., *p. side;* - wache, f., *p. watch.*

Backdeck, n., *forecastle head;* - balken, m., *f. deck beam;* - - Hängeknie, n., *f. d. b. hanging knee;* - - Längsschiene, f., *f. d. b. tie plate;* - - Stringer, m., *f. d. b. stringer;* - - - platte, f., *f. d. b. s plate;* - - - winkel, m., *f. d. b. s. angle bar;* - befestigung, f., *f. d fastening;* - beplattung, f., *f. d. plating;* - stringer, m., *f. d. stringer;* - - platte, f., *f. d. s. plate;* - - winkel, m., *f. d. s. angle bar;* - stütze, f., *f. d. pillar;* - Wassergang, m., *f. d. waterway.*

Backe, f., 1. cheek (of blocks);
2. loof (of bow).
Backen. 1 bees (of bowsprit);
2. cheeks (of mast); 3. clamps
(of keelson); - knie, n.,
cheeks.
backen und füllen, back and
fill.
Back-gast, m., forecastle man;
- geländer, n., f. rails and
stanchions; - - stangen, f.
guard rods; - - stütze. f., f.
stanchion; - genosse, m.,
mess mate; - lasch, m., back-
lash; - leiter, f., forecastle
ladder; - Oberlicht, n., f. skylight; - reling, f., f. rail.
Backsbaum, m., swinging
boom.
Back-schafter, m., mess boy;
- schergang, m., forecastle
sheerstrake; - schicht machen, to do mess work; -
schott, n., f. bulkhead; -
schwabber, m., squillagee;
- Seitenbeplattung, f., forecastle side plating.
Backsmeister, m., captain of
the mess.
Back-spant, n., forecastle
frame; - spiere, f., swinging
boom; - - Achterholer, m.,
after guy of the s. b.; - - geie,
f., lower studding sail boom
guy.
Backsrolle, f., mess bill.
Backstag, n., back rope; - des
Butluvs, bumkin brace.
backstags, der Wind kommt
- ein, the wind is on the
quarter.
Backstags-brise, f., quarterly
breeze; - linie, f., quarter
line; - weise. on the q.; - -
segeln, quartering; - wind,
m., quarterly wind; mit - -
segeln, to lask.
Back-süll, m., forecastle
coaming; - - winkel, m., f.
c. angle bar; - tisch, m.,
mess table; - - ständer, m.,
crow foot of the m. t.; - ventilator, m., forecastle ventilator.

Badekammer, f., bath room.
Bagger, m., dredger; - eimer,
m., d. bucket; - haken, m.,
hand drag; - Konstruktor,
m., dredger constructor; -
leiter, f.. d. ladder; - löffel,
m , d. ladle; - prahm, m.,
hopper; - - mit Falltüren,
h. barge; - rinne, excavated
channel; - schute, f., ballast
lighter.
baggern, dredge.
Bagien see Kreuz.
Bagstag see Backstag.
Bahn. f., cloth (of a sail).
Bai. f., bay.
Bake, f, beacon.
Baken-boje, f., beacon buoy; -
geld, n., beaconnage; - klippe,
f., beaconed rock.
Balance, f., balance; - dock,
n., floating dock; - gewicht,
n., balance weight; - - des
Exzenters, back balance of
eccentric; - - des Schiebers,
b. b. of slide valve; - reff, n.,
balance reef; - - band, n., b.
r. band; - ruder, n., balance
rudder.
Balancier, m., 1. crosshead (of
windlass); 2. beam lever (of
beam engine); - axe, f., lever
shaft; - axenlager, n., rocking shaft bearing; - - deckel,
m., keep for r. s. b.; - - schalen, r. s. brasses; - bügel,
m., gimbal; - maschine, f.,
lever engine; - - mit schwingendem Hebel, grasshopper
e.; - spannen, luff timbers;
- spant, n., balance frame;
- träger, m., crosshead
bracket; - zapfen, m., beam
gudgeon; - - lager, n., pump
lever g. bearing.
Balane, f., balanid.
Balje, f., tub.
Balken, m., beam; - arm eines
Hängeknies, m., b. arm of
a hanging knee; - boje, f.,
stream buoy; - der Rad-
kastengalerie, spur beam; -
des erhöhten Quarterdecks,
raised quarter deck b.; - ende,

n., *b. end;* - entfernung, f., *spacing of beams;* - Hänge-knie, n., *beam hanging knee;* - kiel, m., *bar keel;* - klammern od. - klemmen, *beam grabs;* - knie, n., *b. knee;* - kopf, m., *b. end;* - lage, f., *tier of beams;* - laschung, f., *beam scarph;* - rost, m, *gridiron;* - schmiede, f., *beam forge;* - stich, m., *timber hitch;* - stringer, m., *beam stringer;* - - platte, f., *b. s. plate;* - verstärkung, f., *bales;* - winkel, m., *beam angle bar.*

Balk-füllungen, *small carlings;* - weger, m., *shelf piece;* - - bolzen, m., *s. bolt;* - - des erhöhten Quarterdecks, *raised quarter deck beam s.*

Ballast, *ballast;* - Abgaben, *ballastage;* - ausschießen, *to unballast;* - bäume, *stiffening booms;* mit - beladen, *to go in ballast;* - einschießen, *to b.;* - eisen, n., *kentledge;* - kleid, n., *port sail;* - korb, m., *ballast basket;* - kran, m., *b. crane;* - leichter, m. *b. lighter;* - liefern, *to provide b.;* - linie, f., *b. mark;* - löschen, *to discharge b.;* - mann, m., *b. master;* - mantje, n., *b. basket;* - pforte, f., *ballast port;* - pumpe, f., *b. pump* (see *also* Dampfballast-pumpe); - schaufel, f., *b. shovel;* - schießen, *to shoot b.;* - schlitten, m., *b. chest;* in - segeln, *to sail in b.,* - tank, m., *water b. tank;* - trimm-Wasserlinie, f., *b. trim water line;* in - zu-rückkommen, *to return in b.*

ballasten, *to ballast.*

Ballon, m., *ball (of a buoy);* - klüver, m., *balloon jib;* - segel, n., *b. sail;* - zum Sig-nalisieren, *signal ball.*

Balse, f., *balse.*

Banabaholz, n., *banaba.*

Band, n., *1. band* od. *ring (of spars); 2. hook (for stringer*

ends); *3. hoop (for booms, bowsprit, derricks, heels, masts, and yards);* - eisen, n., *hoop iron;* - stahl, m., *h. steel.*

Bändsel, n, *seizing;* ein - auf-setzen, *put on a s.;* ein - be-setzen, *secure the end of a s.;* - gut, n., *seizing stuff;* ein - kreuzen, *to snake a s.;* - leine, f., *point line;* -schraube, f., *rigging screw.*

Banjer = *Orlop.*

Bank, f., *bank (shoal);* - haken, m., *sail hook;* - hammer, m., *bench hammer.*

Baratterie, f., *barratry;* der - verdächtig, *barratrous;* wer - begeht, *barrator.*

Bark, f., *barque;* - rigged, *b. rigged;* - holz, n., *bends;* - schoner, *barkentine;* - segel, n., *main trysail;* - takelage, f., *barque rig.*

Barkasse, f., *launch.*

Barkune, f., *yuffer.*

Barnacles, *barnacles.*

Barometer, n., *barometer;* - Beobachtungen, *barometric observations;* - scala, f., *barometer scale;* - stand, m., *barometric height.*

Barre, f., *bar;* - hafen, m., *b. harbour;* die - kreuzen, *cross the b.*

Barring, f., *barring;* - balken, m., *skids;* - stütze, f., *stanchion of the booms.*

Bartnagel, m., *barb bolt.*

Basnerungsbrett, n., *monkey bulwark.*

Bastard-balken, m., *half beam;* - - winkel, m., *intermediate beam angle bar;* - feile, f., *bastard file;* - relingsbrett, n., *monkey bulwark.*

Bast, m., *coir;* - matte, f., *c. mat;* - tau, n., *c. rope.*

Batitinenholz, n., *batitinan.*

Batteriedeck, n., *gun deck.*

Bau, m., *construction;* - an-schlag, m., *builder's estimate;* - art, f., *build;* - material, n., *building material.*

Bauch, m., *belly (sails);* - band, n., *b. band;* - beschlagzeising, m., *bunt gasket;* - dennungen od. -dielen, *foot waling;* - frei, *bilge free,*
Bauchgording, f., *1. bunt line; 2. lower b. l. (of lower sail);* - block, m., *b. l. block;* - brille. f., *b. l. lizard;* - kleid, n., *b. l. cloth;* - lägel, m., *b. l. cringle.*
Bauch-stag, n., *belly guy;* - stück, n., *double floor timber:* - zeising, m., *breast gasket;* - talje, f., *bunt whip.*
bauen, *build.*
Bauer. m., *shipbuilder.*
Bauernknoten, m., *overhand*
Bauholz, n., *timber.* [knot.
Baum, m., *boom;* - bock, m., *crutch;* - brille, f., *boom iron;* - brücke, f.. *crutch;* - bügel, m., *boom iron;* - fock, f., *bentinck sail;* - - schote. f., *b. s. sheet;* - gabel, f., *boom crutch;* - geier, m.. *derrick guy;* - geld, n., *boomage;* - kragen, m., *saddle of a boom;* - krücke, f., *b. crutch;* - leesegel, n., *ringtail;* - schote, f., *boom sheet;* - - anholen, *to haul over the booms;* - stopper, m., *boom guy;* - - talje od. - talje, f., *b. tackle;* - tau, n., *capstan swifter;* - toppenant, f., *boom topping lift;* - - talje, f., *b. t. l. purchase;* - träger, m., *b. crutch.*
Baumeisters Zertifikat, n., *builder's certificate;* - vorschritt, f., *scheme of scantling.*
Bausch, in - und Bogen bedungene Fracht, f., *freight in a lump sum;* in B. u. B. befrachten, *to charter for a. l. s.*
Baustärke, f., *structural strength.*
Bearbeitung, f., *workmanship.*
beaufsichtigen, *to superintend.*
Beaufsichtiger, m., *superintendent.*

Beaufsichtigung, f., *superintendence.*
bebaken, *beacon.*
bedanken, *pay off.*
bedeckt. *overcast (sky).*
bedeckte Leichter, m.. *close lighter;* - Schute, f., *covered in barge.*
Beeting, f., *beting.*
befähigter Lotse, m., *licensed pilot.*
Betähigungsattest, n., *certificate of competency.*
befahrbar, *navigable;* nicht -, *unnavigable.*
befahren, den Atlantik -, *to navigate the Atlantic;* die See -, *to lead a sea-faring life;* - sein, *to be an able bodied sailor.*
Befehl, m., *order;* - über ein Schiff, *the command of a ship.*
befehlen, *command.*
Befehlshaber, m., *commander.*
befestigen, *fix, secure, make fast.*
Betestigung, f., *fastening (of a vessel).*
befeuern, *to beacon.*
Befeuerung, f., *beaconnage.*
befördern, *1. dispatch (ships); 2. carry (goods, passengers, &c.); 3.* zu Wasser -, *convey by water; 4. promote (in service).*
Beförderung, f., *dispatch (ships); 2. carriage (goods, passengers, &c.); 3. promotion (in service).*
Beförderuugsgeld, n., *dispatch money (for time saved).*
befrachtbar, *charterable.*
befrachten, *charter, fix, freight.*
Befrachter, m., *charterer.*
Befrachtung, f., *affreightment;* - geschäft, n., *chartering business.*
befugt. *competent.*
begeben, *1. strain, (ship, seams, bolts); 2. start (plates); 3. get adrift (boiler, flooring); 4. give way (booms); 5. repair (on board).*

Begebenheiten der Reise, *proceedings of the voyage.*
begegnen, *fall in with.*
begrenzt, *limited, confined.*
Begrenzungs-planke, f., *boundary plank;* - vorrichtung, f., *guard.*
behaltene Ankunft, f., *safe arrival;* - Kurs, m., *course corrected for leeway.*
Behälter, m., *vessel.*
beheimatet, *1. hailing from (persons); 2. port of registry (ships).*
Beheizung, f., *firing.*
Bei-anker, m., *back anchor;* - boot, n., *tender;* - dem Winder, m., *ship sailing by the wind;* - drehen, *heave to;* von selbst - -, *broach to;* - gedreht, *hove to;* - - liegen, *lie h. t.;* - Kontrakt, *by contract;* - holen, *to tally (sheets);* - holer, m., *bull rope;* - liegen, *hove to;* - - unter dicht gerefftem Großmarssegel, *to lie hove to under close reefed main topsail;* im Sturme gut und trocken - -, *lie steady and dry when hove to in the gale.*
Beil, n., *hatchet;* - brief, m., *builder's certificate.*
beiluven, *broach to.*
beim Winde, *by the wind.*
Bei-segel, n., *light sails;* - setzen, *set (sails);* alle Segel - -, *to crowd all sails;* - sitzer, m., *assessor.*
Beißzange, f., *cutting nippers.*
Beitel, m., *chisel.*
Beiträge zur großen Havarie, *average contributions.*
beitragspflichtige Werte, *contributory values.*
beizeisen, *stop.*
Bekaier, m., *downhaul.*
bekalmt, *becalmed.*
bekleiden, *serve (ropes).*
Bekleidung, f., *1. skin (of ships); 2. lagging (of boilers, cylinders); 3. lining (of frames, beams, cabins); 4. covers (of*

pipes); 5. serving (of ropes); - kissen, n., *pillow (of stays).*
bekniffen, *jammed, nipped.*
bekohlen, Bekohlung, f., *bunkering.* [*tude in.*
bekommene Länge, f., *longi-*
Bekrustung, f., *incrustation.*
beladen, *laden.*
Belastung, f., *load, (of safety valve).*
belegen, *belay (ropes, chains).*
Beleghölzer hinter den Masten, *knights.*
Beleg-klampe, f., *belaying cleat;* - knecht, m., *range;* - nagel, m., *belaying pin;* - nagelband, n., *spider hoop;* - poller, m., *mooring bitts;* - - hinter den Masten, *knights.*
belemmert, *encumbered.*
Belemmerung, f, *encumbrance.*
Beleuchtung, f., *lighting, light houses.*
bemallen, *bevelling.*
bemannen, *to man.*
bemannt, gut -, *well manned.*
Bemannung, f., *manning.*
bemasten, *to supply with masts.*
Bemastung, f., *masts and spars.*
benept, *beneaped.*
beobachtete Breite, f., *latitude by observation;* - Länge, f., *longitude by o.*
Beobachtung, f., *observation;* - ausrechnen, *to work an o.*
Beobachtungs-fehler, m., *error in observation;* - uhr, f, *job watch.*
beplanken, *to board, plank.*
Beplankung, f., *planking.*
Beplattung, f., *plating.*
bequem vor Anker liegen, *to ride easy.*
berechnen, Kurs u. Schiffsort während eines Etmals -, *to work out a day's work.*
Bergelohn, m., *salvage money.*
bergen, *1. salve, recover, save (cargo); 2. shorten in (sail); 3. Klüver -! Jibs downhaul!*

Berger, m., *1. salver (man); 2. wrecker (vessel).*
berggelbe Farbe, f., *umber paint.*
berghohe See, f., *mountainous sea.*
Bergholz, n., *bends;* das kleine -, *smaller b.;* - des Oberschifts, *quick wales.*
Bergung, f., *salvage;* -dampfer, m., *s. steamer;* - gesellschaft, f., *s. association;* -kontrakt, m., *s. agreement;* - kosten, *s. money;* - vergütung, f., *s. remuneration.*
bergwärts, *up the river.*
Bericht, m., *report;* -erstatten, *to r.*
berichten, *to report.*
bersten, *burst.*
berühren, den Grund -, *touch the ground.*
Berührungslinie, f., *touching line.*
Besahn, m., *1. mizen (barquentine, 3 mast fore and aft schooner, 3 m. topsail schooner); 2. jigger (4 & 5 mast barques); 3. spanker (barque, full rigged ship, 4 mast ship);* den - scharf anholen, *to haul the mizen sheets close aft;* den - übergehen lassen, *to shift the m.*
Besahn-ausholer, m., *1. mizen outhaul; 2. jigger o.;* -Bauchgording, f., *jigger bunt line;* - baum, m,, *j. boom;* --band, n., *spanker boom hoop;* --dirk, m., *1. mizen topping lift; 2. jigger t. l.;* ---talje, f., *1. mizen boom t. l. purchase; 2. jigger b. t. l. p.;* -baum-Toppenant, f., *1. mizen b. t. l.; 2. jigger b. t. l.;* ---talje, f., *1. mizen b. t. l. purchase; 2. jigger b. t. l. p.*
Besahnbram-Bauchgording, f., *jigger topgallant bunt line;* - brasse, f, *j. t. brace;* -Drehreep, n., *j. t. tie;* - fall, m., *j. t. halliard purchase;* - Geitau, n., *j. t. clew line;* - Längssahling, f., *j. t. trestle trees;* - Nockgording, f., *j. t. leech line;* - pardune, f., *1. mizen t. backstay; 2. jigger t. b.;* - Püttingswanten, *j. t. futtock shrouds;* - Rahe, f., *j. t. yard;* - schote, f., *j. t. sheet;* - segel, n., *j. t. sail;* - stag, n., *1. mizen t. stay; 2. jigger t. s.;* - - segel, n., *1. j. t. staysail; 2. mizen t. s.;* - - - fall, m., *1. m. t. s. halliard; 2. jigger t. s. h.;* - - - hals, m., *1. j. t. s. tack; 2. mizen t. s. t;* - - - leiter, f., *jigger t. s. stay;* - - - Niederholer, m., *1. j. t. s. downhaul; 2. mizen t. s. d.;* - - - schote, f., *1. m. t. s. sheet; 2. jigger t. s. s.*
Besahnbramstenge, f., *1. mizen topgallant mast; 2. jigger t. m.;* - Eselshaupt, n., *j. t. m. cap;* -Pardune, f., *1. j. t. backstay; 2. mizen t. b.;* -stag, n., *m. t. stay;* -wanten, *jigger t. rigging.*
Besahnbram - Toppenant, f., *jigger topgallant lift;* -want, n., *j. t. shroud;* - wanten, *j. t. rigging.*
Besahn-brasse, f., *1. mizen brace; 2. jigger brace;* -Brassenschenkel, m., *j. b. pendant;* - Brockgeitau, n., *spanker throat brail;* - bulin, f., *jigger bowline;* - Dempgording, f., *1. mizen brail; 2. jigger b.;* - dirk, *1. j. boom topping lift; 2. mizen b. t. l.;* - Einholer, m., *spanker inhaul;* - Ewer, m., *ketch barge;* - fall, m., *1. jigger halliard; 2. mizen h.;* - Fußgeitau, n., *spanker foot brail.*
Besahngaffel, f., *1. mizen gaff; 2. jigger g.;* - Außengeitau, n., *spanker outer brail;* -gerde, f., *1. mizen vang; 2. jigger vang;* - - schenkel, m., *1. j. v. pendant; 2. mizen v. p.;* -Innengeitau, n., *spanker inner peak brail;* - Toppsegel, n., *mizen gaff topsail;*

- - fall, m., *m. g. t. halliard;*
- - hals, m., *m. g. t. tack; -* -
Niederholer, m., *m. g. t.*
downhaul; - - schote, f., *m.*
g. t. sheet.

Besahn-geitau, n., *1. spanker*
brails; 2. jigger clew garnet,
- gerde, f., *1. mizen vang; 2.*
jigger vang; - hals, m., *1. j.*
tack; 2. mizen t.; - - Aufholer, *spanker tack tracing*
line; - - gording, f., *s. throat*
brails; - Klaufall, m., *mizen*
throat halliard.

Besahnmars, m., *1. mizen top;*
2. jigger top; - Bauchgording,
f., *j. topsail bunt line;* -
brasse, f., *j. t. brace;* - -
schenkel, m., *j. t. b. pendant;*
- Drehreep, n., *j. t. tie;* -
fall, m., *j. topsail halliard*
purchase; - Geitau, n., *j. t.*
clew line; - pferd, n., *j. t.*
foot rope; - rahe, f., *j. t.*
yard; - Refftalje, f., *j. t. reef*
tackle; - schote, f., *j. topsail*
sheet; - segel, n., *j. t.;* - -
schote, f., *j. t. sheet;* - stenge,
f., *j. topmast;* - - Eselshaupt,
n., *j. t. cap;* - Toppenant, f.,
j. topsail lift; - wanten, *j.*
topmast rigging.

Besahnmast, m., *1. mizen mast;*
2. jigger mast; - Dwarssahlinge, *1. j. m. cross trees;*
2. mizen m. c. t.; - Eselshaupt, n., *1. m. m. cap; 2.*
jigger mast cap; - Keile,
mizen mast wedges; - kragen,
m., *m. m. coat;* - Längs-
sahlinge, *1. m. m. trestle*
trees; 2. jigger mast t. t.;
- spur, f., *mizen mast step.*

Besahnmittel-Geitau, n, *span-*
ker middle brail; - Stagsegel, n., *1. mizen middle*
staysail; 2. jigger m. s.; - -
fall, m., *j. m. s. halliard;* - -
hals, m., *1. j. m. s. tack; 2.*
mizen m. s. t.; - - leiter, f.,
jigger middle s. stay; -
Niederholer, m., *1. j. m. stay-*
sail downhaul; 2. mizen m.

s. d.; - - schote, f., *1. m. m. s.*
sheet; 2. jigger m. m. s. s.

Besahn-Nagelbank, f., *mizen*
fife rail.

Besahn-Nockgording. f., *1.*
spanker outer peak brail; 2.
jigger leech line.

Besahnoberbram - brasse. f.,
upper jigger topgallant
brace; - rahe, f, *u. j. t. yard;*
- segel, n., *u. j. t. sail.*

Besahnobermars - brasse, f.,
upper jigger topsail brace;
- - schenkel, m., *u. j. t. b.*
pendant; - pferd, n., *u. j. t.*
foot rope; - rahe, f., *u. j. t.*
yard; - segel, n., *u. j. t.*

Besahn-pferd, n., *jigger yard*
foot rope; - Piekfall, m.,
mizen peak halliard; - Püttinge, *m. futtocks;* - - wanten,
jigger futtock shrouds; -
rahe, f., *1. mizen yard; 2.*
jigger y.; - - Toppenantstalje, f., *j. lift purchase;* -
Refftalje, f., *j. reef tackle.*

Besahnroyal, n., *jigger royal;*
- Bauchgording, f., *j. r. bunt*
line; - brasse, f., *j. r. brace;*
- fall, m., *j. r. halliard pur-*
chase; - Geitau, n., *j. r. clew*
line; - Längssahling, f., *j.*
topgallant trestle trees; -
Pardune, f., *j. royal backstay;*
- pferd, n., *j. r. foot rope;* -
rahe, f., *j. r. yard;* - schote,
f., *j. r. sheet;* - stag, n., *j. r.*
stay; - segel, n., *j. r. stay-*
sail; - - - fall, m., *j. r. s.*
halliard; - - - hals, m., *j. r.*
s. tack; - - - Niederholer, m.,
j. r. s. downhaul; - - - schote,
f., *j. r. s. sheet;* - stenge, f.,
1. mizen royal mast; 2. jigger
r. m.; - Toppenant, f., *j. r.*
lift.

Besahnrüste, f., *1. mizen chan-*
nel; 2. jigger c.; - eisen, n.,
1. j. c. plates; 2. mizen c. p.

Besahnscheisegel, n., *jigger*
skysail; - brasse, f., *j. s.*
brace; - fall, m., *j. s. halliard;*
- Geitau, n., *j. s. clew line;*

- Pardnne, f., *j. s. backstay*;
- pferd, n., *j. s. foot rope*;
- rahe. f., *j. s. yard*; - Schote,
f., *j. s. sheet*; - stag, n., *j. s.
stay*; - stenge, f., *j. s. mast*;
- Toppenant, f., *j. s. lift.*
Besahnschote, f., *1. mizen
sheet*; *2. jigger s.*; - anholen,
*splice the main brace (i. e.
to have a drink)*.
Besahnseitentakel, n., *mizen
tackle.*
Besahnstag, n., *1. mizen stay*;
2. jigger s.
Besahnstagsegel, n., *1. mizen
staysail*; *2. jigger s.*; - fall,
m., *1. j. s. halliard*; *2. mizen
s. h*; - hals, m., *1. m. s. tack*;
2. jigger s. t.; - leiter, f.,
mizen s. stay; - Niederholer,
m., *1. m. s. downhaul*; *2.
jigger s. d.*; - schote, f., *1. j.
s. sheet*; *2. mizen s. s.*; - -
schenkel, m., *1. m. s. s. pendant*; *2 jigger s. s. p.*
Besahnstenge. f., *1. mizen topmast*; *2. jigger t.*; - pardune,
f., *1. j. t. backstay*; *2. mizen
t. b.*; - stag, n., *1. m. t. stay*;
2. jigger t. s.
Besahnstengestagsegel, n., *1.
mizen topmast staysail*; *2.
jigger t s.*; - fall, m., *1. j. t.
s. halliard*; *2. mizen t. s. h.*;
- hals, m., *1. m. t. s. tack*; *2.
jigger t. s. t.*; - leiter, f.,
mizen topmast s. stay; -
Niederholer, m., *1. m. t. staysail downhaul*; *2. jigger t. s.
d.*; - schote. f., *1. j. t. s. sheet*;
2. mizen t. s. s.
Besahnstenge-want, n., *1. mizen
topmast shroud*; *2. jigger t.
s.*; - wanten, *1. j. t. rigging*:
2. mizen t. r.
Besahntoppenant, f., *jigger
lift.*
Besahnunterbram-brasse, f.,
lower jigger topgallant brace;
- rahe, f. *l. j. t. yard*; - segel,
n., *l. j t. sail.*
Besahnuntermars-brasse, f.,
lower jigger topsail brace;

- - schenkel, m., *l. j. t. b.
pendant*; - pferd, n., *l. j. t.
foot rope*; - rahe, f., *l. j. t.
yard*; - segel, n., *l. j. t.*
Besahn-want, n., *1. mizen
shroud*; *2. jigger s.*; - wanten,
1. j. rigging; *2. mizen r.*
Besan see Besahn.
besänftigen, *calming the sea.*
Besatzung. f, *crew*; - vervollständigen, *complete the complement of men*; genügende -,
well manned.
beschädigt. *damaged*; durch
auf Grund kommen -, *d.
through grounding*; durch
Kollision -, *d. t. collision*;
durch Raumschweiß -, *d. by
sweat in the hold*; infolge
schlechter Stauung -, *d.
through improper stowage*;
infolge stürmischer Witte-
rung -, *d. t. stress of weather*;
leicht -, *slightly d.*; stark -,
badly d.
Beschädigung, f., *damage*;
leichte -, *slight d.*; schwere
-, *serious d.*
Beschaffenheit, f., *condition,
state.*
beschicken, *to thrumb.*
Beschlag, m., *sheathing (of
ship's bottom)*; - aufheben,
raise the embargo; - belegen,
put under an e.; - blech. n.,
sheathing sheet; - der unteren Stengewantjungfer, *futtock plate*; - hammer, m.,
sheathing hammer; - leine, f.,
furling line; - nahme, f.,
seizure; - zeising, m., *furling gasket.*
beschlagen. *1. furl, hand (sails)*;
2. metalling (ship's bottom).
beschleunigende Kraft, f.,
accelerating force.
beschleunigte Bewegung, f.,
accelerated motion.
beschmartigen, *to parcel.*
beschmieren, *to coat.*
beschränkt, *confined, limited.*
Beschreibung, f., *specification,
description.*

Besegelung, f., *totality of sails*.

Besen, m., *broom*; - boje, f., *buoy with a broom*; - rein, *clean swept*.

besetzt, *embayed (in a bay)*; der Ausguck war gut -, *a good look-out was kept*; im Eise -, *ice bound*.

besichtigen, *survey*.

Besichtiger, m., *surveyor*.

Besichtigung, f., *survey*; - abhalten, *hold a s.*; - des Volkslogis, *inspection of the quarters*; - schein, m., *certificate of survey*.

besondere Verstärkung, f., *compensation*.

beständig, *1. steady (barometer, breeze)*; *2. settled (weather)*; *3. constant (pressure)*

Bestätter, m., *ship's husband*.

Besteck, n., *day's work* od. *reckoning*; - aufmachen, *to make up the d. w.*; gegißtes -, *dead r.*; - auszug, m., *track chart*; - macher, m., *pricker of the c.*; - versetzung, f., *error in dead reckoning*; mit dem - voraus sein, *to be astern of the r.*; m. d. B. zurück sein, *to be ahead of t. r.*

Bestimmungs-hafen, m., *port of destination*; - ort, m., d.

Bestmann, m., *first hand*.

bestricken, *to graft*.

bestroppen, *to strop*.

Betel, m., *1. chisel (tool)*; *2. betel (for chewing)*.

Beting, f., *1. carrick bitt (windlass)*; *2. jeer b. (masts)*; das Ankertau um die - legen od. schlingen, *to bitt*; d. A. von der - abnehmen, *to unbitt*; - balken, m., *strong back*; - bolzen, m., *bitt pin*; - hörner, *battledores*; - hut, m., od. - kappe, f., *bitt hood*; - klampe, f., *cheek of carrick bitt*; - knie, n., *standard knee*; - kopf, m., *bitt head*;

- schlag, m., *bitter*; - - abnehmen, *to unbitt*; - - nehmen, *to bitt*; - spanen, - spehnen, *bitt pins*; - spur, f., *step of the b. p.*; - steilen od. - stangen, b. p.; - stopfer. m., *claw stopper*; - stützen, *bitt pins*; - träger, m., *spur of the bitts*.

Betinge, *bitts*.

Betisholz, n., *betis*.

betonnen. *to buoy*.

Betonnung, f., *buoyage*.

Betriebs-kosten, *working expenses*; - kraft, f., *motive power*; - motor, m., *electric light engine*.

Betschiff. n., *bethel ship*.

Bettenstopper, m., *bitt stopper*.

Bettung der Helling, t., *frame of the stocks*; - des Bugspriets, *bed of the bowsprit*; - eines Trockendocks, *apron of a dry dock*.

Beule, f., *dint*.

beulen, *to dint*.

bewachsen, *foul*.

bewegende Kraft, f., *moving force*.

bewegliche Kiel, m., *sliding keel*; - Last, f., *travelling load*; - Radschaufel, f., *feathering float*; - Sand, m., *quick sand*; - Schaufel, f., *feathering paddle*.

bewegte See, f., *rough sea*.

Bewegung, f., *motion*; - mittelpunkt, m., *centre of m.*; - vorrichtung, f., *moving apparatus*.

bewölkt, *cloudy*.

bewuhlen, *to woold*.

Bezug, m., *cover*; - der Finknetzkasten mittschiffs, *waist cloth*.

Bibel, f., *bible*.

Bi-de-winner, m., *ship sailing by the wind*.

bidreien, *to heave to*.

biegen, *to bend*.

Biege-probe, f., *bending test*; - walze, f., *b. machine*.

biegsame Kuppelung, f., *flexible coupling*.

Biegung, f., *bend (in river).*
Biegungsmoment, m., *momentum of flexion.*
Biegzange, f., *plyers.*
Bildhauerarbeit, f., *or* Bildwerk, n., *ornaments.*
Bilge, f., *bilge*; - Außgußventil, n., *b. discharge valve*; - dekkel, m., *b. cap*; - Einlaß, m., *b. inlet*; - Flansch, m., *b. flange*; - Injektion, f., *b. injection*; - - hahn, m., *b. i. cock*; - - rohr, n., *b. i. pipe*; - - rohr Saugekorb, m., *strum box of b. i. p.*; - - ventil, n., *b. i. valve*; - - - deckel, m., *b. i. v. cover*; - - - gehäuse, n., *b. i. v. box*; - - - rohr, n., *b. i. v. pipe*; - - - - Schlammkasten, m., *b. i. v. mud box*; - I.-v-spindel, f., *b. i. v. spindle*; - I.-wasser, n., *b. i. water*; - rohr, n., *b. pipe*; - Saugeventil, n., *b. suction valve*; - wasser, n., *b. water.*
bilged, *bilged.*
Billen, *buttocks*; - beplankung, f., *buttock planking*; - planke, f., *b. plank*; - platte, f., *b. plate.*
Billet, n., *ticket.*
Billy-boy, m., *b. b.*
Binde-balken, m., *girder*; - bolzen, m., *binding bolt.*
Bindsel, n., Bindselung, f., *see* Bändsel.
Binnen-Achtersteven, m., *inner post*; - Beplankung, f., *inside planking*; - bords, *inboard*; - ende des Kranbalkens, n., *inner end of the cat head*; - fahrzeug, n., *inland vessel*; - fall, m., *inner halliard*; - fischerei, f., *inland fishery*; - hafen, m., *inner harbour*; - handel, m., *home trade*; - haut, f., *inside planking*; - Hintersteven, m., *inner stern post*; - klüver, m., *i. jib*; - - fall, m., *i. j. halliard*; - - hals, m., *i. j. tack*; - - leiter, f.,

i. j. stay; - - Niederholer, m., *i. j. downhaul*; - - schote, f., *i. j. sheet*; - meer, n., *inland sea*; - nock, f., *nock of a fore and aft sail*; - schifffahrt, f., *inland navigation*; - schote, f., *inner sheet*; - see, m., *lake*; - stich, m., *inside clinch*; - Vordersteven, m., *apron of the stem*; - - kalb, n., *dousing chock.*
Binsenmatte, f., *feather grass mat.*
Birkenholz, n., *birch wood.*
Birnen-boje, f., *can buoy*; - stahl, m., *bulb steel.*
bituminöse Kohle, f., *bituminous coal.*
Blackbuttholz, n., *black butt.*
Blase, f., *blister*; - balg, m., *bellows*; - balken, m., *wash boards under the lower cheeks of the head.*
Blasenstahl, m., *blister steel.*
Blas-hahn, m., *blast cock*; - rohr, n., *b. pipe.*
bläst, aus welchem Loche - der Wind? *How blows the wind?*
Blatt des Bugspriets, n., *fish of the bowsprit.*
blaue Farbe, f., *blue paint*; - Peter, m., *B. Peter.*
Blau-feuer, - licht, n., *blue light.*
Blech-schere, f., *tin shears*; - zange, f., *sheet iron tongs*; - zwickel, m., *gusset of a boiler.*
Blei-dichtung, f., *lead joint*; - draht, m., *l. wire*; - - dichtung, f., *l. w. joint*; - nagel, m., *1. scupper nail; 2. lead n.*; - platte, f., *sheet of lead*; - weiß, n., *white lead.*
Blend-laterne, f., *bull's eye*; - tür, f., *dead door.*
Bleuelstange *see* Pleuelstange.
Blick-feuer, n., *flashing light*; - signal, n., *f. signal.*
Blinde, f., *dead light*; - eines Seitenfensters, d. *door of a scuttle*; - fall, m., *spritsail*

halliard; - Hecktaschen, *quarter badges*; - Klippen, *sunken rocks*; - Passagier, m., *stow away*; - Rahe, f., *spritsail yard*; - - domper, m., *jumper of the s. gaff.*

Blindlaterne, f., *dark lantern.*

blind laufen, *racing (propeller)*; - schlagen, *1. r. (p)*; *2. flapping (sails).*

Blink, m., *blink*; - feuer, n., *flashing light*; - signal, n., *f. signal.*

Blitz-ableiter, m., *ligthening conductor*; - sektor, m., *flash sector.*

Block, m., *block*; - an -, *b. and b.*; - - - holen, *to haul two blocks*; - annähen, *to seize a block*; - backe, f., *cheek of a b.*; - bindsel, n., *b. seizing*; - boje, f., *wooden buoy*; - bolzen, m., *pin of a block*; - buchse, f., *bush of a b.*; - des Speckgiens, *cant b.*; - haken, m., *tackle hook*; - keepe, f., *score of a block*; - macher, m., *b. maker*; - - schuppen, m., *b. shed*; - mit Doppelkeep, *double scored b.*; - mit Eisenbeschlag, *iron stropped b.*; - mit Läufer, *b. and fall*; - mit Stropp im Gehäuse, *internal bound b.*; - nagel, m., *notch of a b.*; - scheibe, f., *sheave*; - - buchse, f., *bush of a block*; - stropp, m., *strap of a block*; - werk eines Schiffes, *the blocks of a ship.*

Blockade, f., *blockade*; - aufheben, *to raise a b.*; - brecher, m., *b. runner*; - bruch, m., *breach of the b.*; - durchbrechen, *to run the b.*; von der - befreien, *to disblockade.*

Bluegumholz, n., *blue gum.*

Blutflagge, f., *bloody ancient.*

Bö, f., *squall.*

Bock, m., *1. stay*; *2. boom crutch (of a boom)*; *3. bul-*

wark stay (of bulwark); *4. standard (of steering gear)*; *5. crane (of the lower topsail yard)*; *6. shears (apparatus of spars)*; - leiter, f., - schiff, n., *shears*; - spiere, *lower booms*; An die - -! *Hang on to the booms!* - stange, f, *sheer pole.*

Bocks-horn, n., - - bolzen, m., - ohr, n., *bolt with ring and hook.*

Boden, m., *1. bottom (of ship)*; *2. loft (for sails and rigging)*; *3. apron (of dry dock)*; - anstrich, m., *bottom coat*; - beplankung, f., *b. planking*; - beplattung, f., *b plating*; - beschlag, m., *b. sheathing*; - gang, m., *b. strake*; - hahn, m., *sea cock*; - mit runder Kimm, *kettle bottom*; - pflicht, f., *b. board*; - planke, f., *bottom plank*; - platte, f., *b. plate*; - plattform, f., *b. plank*; - spanten, *b. frames*; - spieker, m., *brad*; - stück, n., *floor timber*; - tank, m., *deep tank*; - ventil, n., *sea valve.*

Bodenwrangen. *floors*; - blech, n., *floor plate*; - des Hauptspants, *main f.*; - des Kreuzod. Mittel- od. Nullspants, *midship floor timbers*; - ende, n., *f. head*; - kalb, n., *f. h. chock*; - mit ungleichen Schenkeln, *long and short armed floors*; - platte, f., *floor plate*; - stücke, *intercostal floors.*

Bodmerei, f., *bottomry*; - brief, m., *b. bond*; - geber, m., *lender on b.*; - gelder, *b. money*; - nehmer, m., *borrower on b.*; - prämie, f., *b. premium*; - schuld, f., *b. loan*; - wechsel, m., *bill of b.*

Bogen, m., *1. arc (of sky)*; *2. tow rail (of tug)*; *3. bails (of boat awning)*; - block, m., *quarter block*; - feile, f., *bow file*; - kreuz über den

Niedergangsluken, n., *metal canopy*; - lampe od. - lichtlampe, f., *arc lamp*; - stück des Schraubenrahmens, n., *arch piece of stern frame.*

Böhnhase, m., *waterman.*

Bohr-block, m., *clave*; - loch, n., *bore hole*; ein - - besetzen, *to stem a hole*; - - messer, n., *fit rod*; - maschine, f., *boring or drilling machine*; - stock, m., *drill stand*; - stuhl, m., *boring frame*; - winde, f., *breast borer*; - wurm, m., *shipworm.*

böig. *squally.*

Boiklampe, f., *hanging clamp.*

Boje, f., *buoy*; die - ist blind, *the b. is below the water*; die - wacht, *t. b. is floating*; d. B. w. nicht, *t. b. does not watch*; - reep, n., *b. rope*; - - knoten od. - - stich, m., *b. r. knot*; - stropp, m., *b. sling.*

Bojen und Baken, *buoys and beacons*; - kasten, m., *carriers.*

bollen, *1. to reef the mizen*; *2. der -, sheer hulk.*

Boller, m., *bitts.*

Bollwerk, n., *1. bulwark (of ship)*; *2. pier (on shore).*

Bolten, m., *band or patches (of a sail)*; - und Stoßlappen, *linings.*

Bolzen, m., *bolt, pin*; - des Hintersteven-Reitknies, *sternson bolt*; - des Vorderstevenknies, *stemson b.*; - die abwechselnd von oben nach unten und umgekehrt geschlagen werden, *up and down bolts*; - eines Hängeknies, *hanging knee b.*; - eines horizontalen Knies, *lodging k. b.*; - von innen und außen, *in and out b.*; - zur Befestigung der Vorder- und Hinterenden der Außenbeplankung od. Wegerung, *hood end fastening.*

Bolzen-loch, n., *slot*; - mutter,

f., *bolt nut*; - schneidemaschine, f., *b. screwing machine*; - stift, m., *shackle b. pin.*

Bombardier-galiote, f., *bomb ketch*; - schiff, n., *floating battery.*

Bonnett, n., *bonnet*; - abschlagen, *unlace a b.*; - anschlagen, *lace a b.*

Boot, n., *boat*; Zu -! *Man the boat!*

Bootbauer, m., *boat builder.*

Bootdeck, n., *boat deck*; - balken, m., *b. d. beam*; - - stringer, m., *b. d. b. stringer*; - - winkel, m., *b. d. b. angle bar*; - geländer, n., *b. d. rails and stanchions*; - - stangen, *b. d. guard rods*; - - stütze, f., *b. d. stanchion*; - stringer, m., *b. d. stringer*; - - winkel, m., *b. d. beam s. angle bar*; - stütze, f., *b. d. pillar*; - wassergang, m., *b. d. waterway.*

Bootdrill, m., *boat drill.*

Boote aus! *out boats!* - heißen! *up boats!*

Boot-fender, m., *boat fender*; - führer, m., *1. waterman (in harbour)*; *2. coxswain (on board ship).*

Bootheißmaschine, f., *boat hoist engine*; - Absperrventil, n., *b. h. e. stop valve*; - Anlaßventil, n., *b. h. e. starting v.*; - Dampfabführungsrohr, n., *b. h. e. exhaust pipe*; - Dampfzuleitungsrohr, n., *b. h. e. steam p.*; - Exzenter, n., *b. h. e. eccentric*; - bolzen, m., *b. h. e. e. bolt*; - - bügel, m., *b. h. e. e. strap*; - - - futter, n., *b. h. e. e. s. liner*; - E-Lagerschalen, *b. h. e. e. brasses*; - E-scheibe, f., *b. h. e. e. sheave*; - E-stange, f., *b. h. e. e. rod*; - Kolben, m., *b. h. e. e. piston*; - - stange, f., *b. h. e. p. rod*; - - - Kreuzkopf, m., *b. h. e. p. r. crosshead*; - - - Stopfbüchse, f., *b. h. e. p. r. stuffing box*; - - - - deckel, m., *b. h. e. p. r. s. b. gland*; - Kreuzkopflagerbolzen, m., *b. h. e. crosshead bolt*; - K-k-l-schalen, *b. h. e. c. brasses*; - K-k-l-s-deckel, m., *b. h. e. connecting rod top end keep*: - Kurbelwelle, f., *b. h. e. crank shaft*; - - lager, n., *b. h. e. c. s. bearing*; - - - bolzen, m., *b. h. e. c. s. b. bolt*; - - - deckel, m., *b. h. e. c. s. bearing keep*; - - - - bolzen, m., *b. h. e. c. s. b. k. bolt*; - K-w-Lagerschalen, *b. h. e. c. s. bearing brasses*; - K-w-L.-Futter, n., *b. h. e. c. s. brasses liner*; - Kurbelzapfen-Lagerbolzen, m., *b. h. e. crank pin bolt*; - K-z-Lagerschalen, *b. h. e. c. p. brasses*; - K-z-L.-deckel, m., *b. h. e. connecting rod bottom end keep*; - Pleyelstange, f., *b. h. e. c. r.*; - - bolzen, m., *b. h. e. c. r. bolt*; - - fuß-Futter, n., *b. h. e. c. r. bottom end liner*; - Schieber, m., *b. h. e. slide valve*; - - kasten, m., *b. h. e. v. casing*; - - - deckel, m., *b. h. e. v. c. door*; - S-stange, f., *b. h. e. v. rod*; - S-s-Stopfbüchse, f., *b. h. e. v. r. stuffing box*; - S-s-S.-deckel, m., *b. h. e. v. r. s. b. gland*; - Zylinder, m., *b. h. e. cylinder*; - - deckel, m., *b. h. e. c. cover*; - - - bolzen, m., *b. h. e. c. c. bolt*; - Z.-Entwässerungsrohr, n., *b. h. e. cylinder drain pipe.*

Boot-regatta, f., *boat race.*
Boots-anker, m., *boat anchor*; - ausrüstungs-Gegenstände, *b. gear*; - beplankung, f., *b. planking*; - beplattung, *b. plating*; - bugmann, m., *foreman*; - bugsiertau, n., *guess rope*; - david, m., *b. davit*; - - spur, f., *b. d. socket*: - dienst, m., *b. duty*; - dolle, f., *thole pin*; - ducht, f., *thwart*; - galgen, m., *b.*

skids; - - ständer, m., *b. s. stanchion*; - gast, m., *boatman*; - geschirr, n., *boat gear*; - geschütz, n., *bow piece*; - hafen, m., *boat's creek*; - haken, m., *boat hook*; - kessel, m., *b. boiler*; - kiel, m., *b. keel*; - klampe, f., *b. chock*; - - ständer, m., *b. c. standard*; - kleid, n., *b. cover*; - kompaß, m., *b. compass*; - krabber, m., *b. gripe*; - laschung, f., *b. lashing*; - leiter, f., *entering ladder*; - mann, m., *boatswain*; - - gatt, n., *fore cock pit*; - - hellegatt, n., *boatswain's store room*; - kammer, f., *b. r.*; - - maat, m., *b. mate*; - - schaft, f., *boat's crew*; - - pfeife, f., *boatswain's call*; - - stuhl, m., *b. chair*; - - Vorratskammer, f., *b. locker*; - manöver, n., *boat manoeuvre*; - ösfaß, n., *b. baler*; - pfropfen, m., *b. plug*; - riemen, m., *b. oar*; - mast, m., *b. mast*; - ringe. *boat rings*; - rolle, f., *b. bill*; - ruder, n., *b. rudder*; - - dolle, f., *thole pin*; - - joch, n., *boat rudder yoke*; - - - leine, f., *yoke line of a b. r.*; - - - pinne, f., *y. of a b. r.*; - ruderpinne, f., *boat tiller*; - schuppen, m., *b. house*; - schwabber, m., *hand swab*; - segel, n., *boat sail*; - sorrung, f., *b. lashing*; - spanten, *b. frames*; - spill, n., *b. windlass*; - stander, m., *pendants of the lower booms*; - steuer, n., *b. rudder*; - steuerer, m., *coxswain*; - Stoßkissen, n., *boat pads*; - streichapparat, m., *b. lowering apparatus*; - stropp, m., *b. sling*; - takel, n., - talje, f., *b. tackle*; - tank, m., *b. tank*; - topping, n., *boat topping*; - überzug, m., *boat cover*; - werfte, f., *b. wharf*; - wimpel, m., *b. pennant*; - zelt, n., *b. tilt*; - zubehör, n., *b. gear*; - zurringe, *b. lashings.*

Bora, f., *bora*.

Bord, m., *1. board (of ship)*;
2. *board (distance of one
tack)*; - an -, *side by side*;
- - - schleppen, *to tow abreast*;
an - bleiben, *to keep afloat*;
- dienst, m., *duty on board
ship*; über - fallen od. gehen,
to fall over board; über -
gespült werden, *to be washed
o. b.*; - sessel, m., *folding
chair*; - telegraph.m., *ship's
telegraph*; - uhr, f., *s. clock*;
- wand, f., *s. side.*

Borg, m., *preventer stopper*; -
für stehendes Gut, *rigging s.*

Borg-bindsel, n., *preventers*;
- - des Bonnets, *preventer
of the bonnet*; - brasse, f.,
p. brace; - brohk, f., *p. brail*;
- geie, *p. guys*; - geitau, n.,
p. brail; - gerde, f., *p. vang*;
- hanger, m., *p. slings*; -
pardune, f., *p. backstay*; -
pardunen der Stengen, *travelling backstays*; - schote,
f., *preventer sheet*; - stag, n.,
p. stay; - stenge, f., *jury
mast*; - - windereep, n., *heel
rope*; - talje, f., *relieving
tackle*; - tau, n., *preventer
rope*; - toppenant, f., *p. lift*;
- want, n., *p. shroud*; - wanttau, n., *after swifter*; -
wasserstag, n., *preventer
bobstay*; - zeising eines
Gaffelsegels, m., *p. brail.*

Bossiereisen, n., *gouge.*

Bottler, m., *steward*; - ei, f.,
pantry.

brabbelnde See, f., *boiling
sea.*

brack, *brackish*; - wasser, n.,
b. water.

Bram-bauchgording, f., *topgallant bunt line*; - brasse,
f., *t. brace*; - bulien, f., *t.
bowline*; - drehreep, n., *t.
tye*; - fall, m., *topgallant
halliard*; - geitau, n., *t. clew
line*; - geschirr od. - gut, n.,
t. rigging; - Längssahling, f.,
topmast trestle trees.

Bramleesegel, n., *topgallant
studding sail*; - Außenschote,
f., *t. s. s. tack*; - Binnenschote, f., *t. s. s. sheet*; - fall,
m., *t. s. s. halliard*; - hals,
m., *t. s. s. tack*; - Niederholer, m., *t. s. s. downhaul*;
- rahe, f., *t. s. s. yard*; -
schote, f., *t. s. s. sheet*; -
spiere, f., *t. s. s. boom.*

Bram-Nockgording, f., *topgallant leech line*; - pardune, f., *t. backstay*; - pferd,
n., *t. foot rope*; - püttings,
t. futtocks; - - wanten, *t.
futtock shrouds*; - rahe, f.,
t. yard; - - jolle, f., *t. y.
rope*; - sahlingen, *t. cross
trees*; - schote, f., *t. sheet*;
- segel, n., *t. sail*; - - brise,
f., *t. breeze*; - - kühlte, f., od.
- - sturm, m., *t. gale*; - -
schote, f., *t. sheet.*

Bramstag, n., *topgallant stay*;
- segel, n., *t. staysail*; - -
fall, m., *t. s. halliard*; - -
hals, m., *t. s. tack*; - - Niederholer,m., *topgallant s. downhaul*; - - schote, f., *t. s.
sheet.*

Bramstenge, f., *topgallant
mast*; lange -, *long t. m.*;
kurze -, *short t. m.*; - Eselshaupt, n., *t. m. cap*; - jolle,
f., *t. m. rope*; - Niederholer,
m., *t. m. tripping line*; -
Pardune, f., *topgallant backstay*; - stag, n., *t. stay*; -
want, n., *t. rigging*; - Windreep, n., *t. mast rope*; - -
gatt, n., *sheave hole for top
rope in a t. m.*

Bramstengen auf! *Sway aloft !*
- Schloßholz, n., *topgallant
mast fid*; - - gatt, n., *t. m. f.
hole.*

Bram-toppenant, f., *topgallant
lift*; - tuch, n., *duck*; - want,
n., *topgallant shroud.*

Brand-balken, m.. *fire boom*;
- eisen, n., *curling iron*; -
herd, m., *seat of the fire*;
- holz, n., *billet wood*; -
rolle, f., *fire bill.*

branden, *to break (the sea)*.
Branden des Meeres, n.. *the dashing and breaking of the sea*.
brandende See, f., *surging sea*; - Wogen, *surging waves*.
Brandung, f., *1. breakers; 2. broken water* (bei Untiefen); - voraus, *breakers ahead*.
Brandungsboot, n., *surf boat*.
Brasse, f.. *brace*; - der blinden Rahe, *sprit sail b.*; - der Schiebblinde, *s. s. top sail b.*; - einer Unterrahe, *lower b.*
brassen, *to brace*; beim Winde -, *to haul the wind*; eine Rahe von vorn nach achtern -, *to traverse a yard*; in den Wind -, *to brace the sails in the wind*; übers Kreuz -, *or* - und toppen, *or* vierkant -, *to square the yards*.
Brassen anholen und festmachen, *to haul in and fasten the braces*; - arm, m., *spider*; - baum, m., *quarter bumkin*; - block, m., *brace block*; - der Heißstroppen, *steadying lines*; - der Rahen, *braces of the yard*; - schenkel, - ständer, m., *brace pendant*; - stroppe an den Rahnocken, *dog strips for the brace block*.
Bratspill, n., *windlass*; - beting, f., *carrick bitt*; kleines -, *fearn*.
brauchbar, *1. in gear; 2. serviceable (ropes, materials)*; nicht -, *1. out of gear; 2. unserviceable*.
Braunkohle, f., *lignite*.
Brause. f., *rose box*.
brausen, *roar*.
Brech-betel, m., *crooked chisel*; - deißel, m., *ripping adze*; - eisen, n., *slice*; - ihn aus! *Heave and aweigh!* - see, f., *overfall*; - stange, f., *crow bar*; - wasser, n., *breakwater*.

brechen, *1. break; 2. break up (ships); 3. part (chains, ropes)*.
brechend steif, *taught to part*.
Brecher, *breakers*.
Brefock *see* Breitfock.
breit getakelt, *broad rigged*.
breite Flach, n., *broad floor*.
Breite, f., *1. breadth (of ship); 2. scantling (of frames); 3. latitude (geographic)*; - des Querschiffsschenkels eines Spants, *moulding of a frame*; - machen, *to run down latitude*; - nach astronom. Beobachtung, *latitude by astronomic observation*.
Breiten-bestimmung, f., *determining the ship's latitude*; - gang, m., *black strake*; - grad, m., *degree of latitude*; - maßstab, m., *plain scale*; - parallelsegeln, n., *parallel sailing*; - unterschied, m., *difference in latitude*; - - beim Fahren nach Süden, *southing*.
Breitfock, f., *square fore sail*; - baum, m., *s. s. boom*; - rahe, f, *s. s. yard*.
breitseitig hieven, *to breast off*.
Brems-band, n., *brake hoop*; - federn, *b. springs*; - mutter, f., *screw b. nut*; - vorrichtung, f., *b.*
Bremse, f., *brake*; - hebel, m., *b. lever*.
brennbar, *inflammable*.
Brenn-eisen, n., *curling iron*; - holz, n., *billet wood*; - material, n., *combustibles*; - stoffe, *fuel*; - - verbrauch, m., *consumption of f.*
brennen, *breaming (ship's bottom)*.
Brigantine, f., *brigantine*.
Brigg, f., *brig*; - gaffel, f., *main trysail gaff*.
Briggbaum, m., *main boom*; - dirk, m., *main trysail boom topping lift*; - - talje, f., *m. t. b. t. l. purchase*; - Toppenant, f., *m. t. b. t. l.*;

- - talje, f., *m. t. b. t. l. pur-chase.*
Briggschoner, m., *brigantine.*
Briggsegel, n., *main trysail;*
- Ausholer, m., *m. t. outhaul;*
- baum, m., *m. t. boom;* -
dampgording, f., *m. t. brails;*
- Einholer, m., *m. t. inhaul;*
- fall, m., *m. t. halliard:* -
gaffel, f., *m. t. gaff;* - - gerde,
f., *m. t. vang;* - geitau, n.,
m. t. brail; - gerde, f., *m. t.*
vang; - hals, m., *m. t. tack;*
- schote, f., *m. t. sheet.*
Brigg-takelage, f., - zeug, n.,
brig rig.
Brille, f., *lizard.*
Brillenlägel, m., *spectacle*
clew.
Brillgatt, n., *hole of the privy.*
bringen, das Schiff an den
Wind -, *bring the ship to the*
wind; d. S. nach Dover -,
haul in for D.
Briquetten, *patent fuel.*
Brise, f., *breeze;* leichte -,
gentle b.; mäßige -, *moderate*
b.; frische -, *fresh b.;* starke
-, *strong b.,* die - setzt wieder ein, *the wind is blowing*
back again, die - springt
um, *the wind shifts;* die -
wird achterlicher, *t. w.*
draws aft.
Brodeln, n., *bubble of the sea.*
Brohk, f., *1. skin (of sails);*
2. span (rope and pulley);
3. throat brail (of mizen and
gaff sails); 4. - von Segeltuch, *coat;* 5. - im Hennegatt,
rudder coat; - nehmen beim
Segelfestmachen, *to gather*
up the skin.
Brohk-bolzen, m., *breeching*
bolt; - geitau, n., *throat*
brail; - loch, n., *breeching*
loop; - schäkel, m., *b. shackle;*
- talje, f., *whip of the throat*
brail; - welle, f., *breeching*
shaft.
Brok *see* Brohk.
Bronzegarnitur, f., *bronze*
metal lining.

Brook *see* Brohk.
Brot-back, f., *mess bowl;* -
kammer, f., - spind, n., *bread*
locker; - tonne, f., *b. barrel;*
- winner, m., *ringtail;* - - tall,
m., *r. halliard;* - spiere, f.,
r. boom.
Bruch, m., *1. fracture; 2. rup-*
ture (of shaft); 3. fall (of
deck); - kraft, f., *breaking*
strain; - moment, n., *hogg-*
ing moment; - probe, f.,
breaking test; - schaden, m.,
breakage; - spannung, f.,
breaking strain.
Bruch, frei von - außer im
Strandungsfalle, *free of*
breakage except in case of
stranding.
Brücke, f., *bridge.*
Brückendeck, n., *bridge deck;*
- balken, m., *b. d. beam;* - -
Längsschiene, f., od. - -
Lukenstringer, m., *b. d. b.*
tie plate; - - Stringer, m.,
b. d. b. stringer; - - - platte,
f., *b. d. b. s. plate;* - Balkenwinkel, m., *b. d. b. angle*
bar; - Beplattung, f., *b. d.*
plating; - stringer, m, *b. d.*
stringer; - - platte, f., *b. d.*
s. plate; - - winkel, m., *b.*
d. s. angle bar; - stütze, f.,
b. d. pillar; - Wassergang,
m., *b. d. waterway.*
Brücken - Frontschott, n.,
bridge break bulkhead; -
gang, m., *alley way of*
bridge; - geländer, n., *b.*
rails and stanchions; - -
stangen, *b. deck guard rods;*
- - stütze, f., *b. stanchion.*
Brückenhaus, n., *bridge house;*
- kajüte od. - kammer, f.,
b. cabin; - reling, f., *b. rail;*
- schott, n., *b. bulkhead;* -
Seitenbeplattung, f., *side*
plating of bridge; - Sonnensegel, n., *b. house awning;*
- spant, n., *b. h. frame;* -
süll. m., *b. h. coaming.*
Brücken-kleid, n., *bridge*
weather cloth; - leiter, f.,

b. ladder; - Schergang. m.,
b. sheerstrake; - schott, n.,
break bulkhead of bridge; -
Schutzbretter, *bridge weather boards*; - süllwinkel, m.,
*bridge house coaming angle
bar*; - treppe, f., *bridge
ladder*; - zelt, n., *b. awning.*
Brunnen, m., *well:* - des Kielschweins, *w. of the centre
board*; - Saugventil, n., *w.
suction valve.*
Brust-bohrer, m., or - leier,
f., *breast borer*; - leine, f.,
breast band; - platte, f., *b.
plate.*
Brutto-Fracht.f.,*gross freight*;
- Gewicht, n., *g. weight*; -
Tonnengehalt,m ,*g. tonnage.*
buchen für ein Trockendock,
to stem a vessel.
Buchenholz, n., *beechwood.*
Buchs-baumholz, n., *boxwood*;
- block, m., *bushed block.*
Büchse, f., *1. box; 2. bush (as
lining); 3. liner (inside a
steam cylinder or pump
chamber); 4. shell (of a
cock).*
Büchsen-Chronometer,m., *box
chronometer.*
Bucht, f., *1. creek (of river);
2. bight (of the sea and
rope): 3. fake (of a rope coil);
4. camber (middle of keel);
5. round (of a beam); 6. range
(of cable);* 7. - des Krummholzes, *the back sweep.*
Buchten des Kabels fangen
sich, *there are catch fakes
in the cable.*
Buchtsplissung, f, *bight splice.*
Buchtung, f., *rounding convexity, curvature.*
buckelt, *buckled.*
Buffer, m., *buffer*; - feder, f.,
b. spring.
Bug, m., *1. bow (of ship); 2.
tack(position of sails);* am -,
on the bow; am Backbord -,
o. t. port b.; am Lee -, *o. t.
lee b.;* am Luv -, *o. t. weather
b.;* am Steuerbord -, *o. t.*

starboard b.; - mit Stampfsteven, *bluff head*; das Schiff
trieb direkt vor unsern -,
she fell across our bow; über
dem andern - liegen, *to be
(stand) on the opposite tack*;
über demselben - liegen, *to
be on the same tack;* über
den anderen - gehen, *to
tack.*
Bug-anker, m., *bower anchor*;
- - ketten. *b. chain cable*;
- aufklotzung, f., *bow chock*;
- - platte, f., *b. c. plate*; -
band. n , *breast hook*; - -
bolzen, m , *b. h. bolt*; - beplankung, f., *bow planking*;
- beplattung, f., *b. plating*;
- bindsel, n., *breast gasket*;
- figur, f.. *figure head*; -
flagge, f.. *Jack*; - Füllstück,
n., *eking*; - gast, m.,*bowman* ;
- geschütz, n., *bow gun*;
- gording, f., *bunt line*; - -
block am Stag, m., *monkey
block*; - - kausche mit Steert,
f., - - sprut, f., - - wegweiser,
m., *bunt line span*; - holz,
n., *bow piece*; - klüsen,
hawse holes; - pforte, t,
bow port; - planke. f.. *b.
plank*; - platte, f, *b. plate*;
- propeller, m., *b. propeller*;
- pumpe, f., *b. pump*; - ruder,
n., *b. rudder.*
Bügel, m., *hoop, strap*; - arm,
m., *neck of h.*; - des Klüverbaums. *jib traveller*; - des
Mannlochdeckels, *bow of
manhole door*; - über Vordersteven und Kiel, *stirrup on
the forefoot.*
Bugsier-dampfer, m., *tug*; -
lohn, m., *towage*; - tau, n.,
tow rope.
bugsieren, *to tow.*
Bug-spitze, f, *head*; - split, f.,
glut (of sails).
Bugspriet, n., *bowsprit*; - einholen, *to run in the b.*; -
einsetzen, *to set up the b.*;
- ist geneigt. *the b. steeves*;
- und Klüverbaum aus einem

Stück, *spike b.*; - backen, *b. bees*; - band, n., *bowsprit hoop*; - Bettung, f., *b. bed*; - bügel, m., *bowsprit gammoning hoop*; - Eselshaupt, n., *b. cap*; - Fußzapfen, m., *b. heel tenon*; - Fischung, f., *b. bed*; - gasten, *bowsprit men*; - gut, n., *b. gear*; - Hausung, f., *b. housing*; - keil, m., *b. uedge*; - klampen, *b. cheeks*; - netz, n., *b. netting*; - spur, f., *b. step*; - steg, m., *bobstay*; - teil außerhalb des Stevens, m., *hounding of a bowsprit*; - violinen, *b. bees*; - wanten, *b. shrouds*; - wuhling, f., *b. gammoning*; - - scheren, *g. the b.*; - zapfen, m., *b. tenon*; - zurring, f., *b. rope gammoning*; - - scheren, *g. the b.*; - - gatt, n., *g. hole.*

Bug-stag, n., *bowsprit shroud*; - stopper, m., *bow cable stopper*; - stück, n., *1. hawse piece*; *2. bow gun*; - stücke der Kattspanten, *long top timbers*; - stücke mit den Klüsgatten, *bollard timbers*; - talje, f., *bunt whip*; - verzierung, f., *bow ornament*; - wasser, n., *b. waves*; - wegerung, f., *floor ceilings*: - wellen, *bow waves*; - zeising, m., *breast gasket*; - zelt, n., *forecastle awning.*

Buhne, f., *water groin.*

Buleine, Bulien, Bulin, Buline, f., *bowline*; - anholen, *to haul the b. tight*; - durchholen, *to take down the slack of the b.*; - in dem Mars festknebeln, *to stop the b.*; - los! *Let go the b.!* - schricken, *to check the b.*

Bulein-Hahnepot, f., *bowline bridle*; - Knebel, m., *b. toggle*; - legel, m., *b. cringle*; - spriet, n., *b. bridle.*

Bullauge, n., *bull's eye.*

Bullen, m., *sheer hulk*; - block, m., *careening block*; - tau, n., *guy of the main boom*; - des Fockhalses, *passaree.*

Bumbam, m., *gangway in scaffolding.*

Bumboot, n., *bumboat.*

Bunke, f., *bunk.*

Bunker, m., *bunker*; - kohlen einnehmen, *to take in b. coals*; - hafen, m., *bunkering port*; - lampe, f., *bunker lamp*; - platte, f., *b. plate*; - rohr, n., *b. pipe*; - spant, n., *b. frame*; - verkleidungen, *b. casings*; - wand, f., *b. bulkhead.*

bunkern, *to bunker.*

Bünn, f., *well.*

bürgerlicher Tag, m., *civil day.*

Busse, f., *cup (of capstan).*

buten *see* außen; - stich, m., *outside clinch.*

Butluv, m., *bumkin*; - stag, n., *b. stay.*

Butterland, n., *Cape-fly-away.*

Butzkopf, m., *bruise water.*

C.

See also K. and Z.

Caisson, m., *caissoon.*

Cargadeur, m., *supercargo.*

Casco, n., *hull*; - Versicherung, f., *insurance on hull and appurtenances.*

Cay, n., *key (a reef).*

Centerfeeder, m., *centre feeder.*

Cabotte, f., *anvil block.*

Champignonanker, m., *mushroom anchor.*

Charge, f., *rating.*

Chartepartie, f., *charterparty.*

chartern, *to charter.*

Chassemaree, m., *lugger.*

Chinafahrer, m., *China trader.*

Chronometer, m„ *chronometer*;
- gang, m., *daily rate of the
c.*; - kasten, m., - spind, n.,
c. chest; - zeit, f., *time by c.*
Chunam-Kitt, m., *chunam*.
circumferenzielle Dichtung, f.,
circumferential joint.
Cisterne, f., *hotwell*; - schiff,
n., *tank vessel*.
Cisternen-Ausgußöffnung, f.,
hotwell discharge orifice.
Coefficient, m., *coefficient*.
Communications-hahn, m.,
communication cock; - rohr,
n., *joint pipe*; - ventil, n.,
communication valve.
Compagnielotse, m., *company's
pilot*.
Compartiment, n., *compartment*.
Compensator, m., *expansion
joint*.

Compositschiff, n., *composite
vessel*.
Compound-Manometerrohr,n.,
compound gauge pipe; -
Maschine, f., *c. engine*.
Contre-brasse, f., *counter
brace*; - mutter, f, *lock nut*.
Convoy, m., *convoy*.
Cornischventil mit Doppel-
sitz, n., *Cornish double seat
valve*.
Cornwallkessel, m., *Cornish
boiler*.
Corrosion, f, *corrosion*.
Coulisse, f., *1. valve link*: 2.
link (of connecting gear); 3.
yoke (of steering gear).
Coulissen-bolzen. m , *yoke bolt*;
- stein, m., *link block*; -
Steuerung, f, *link motion*.
Cyklon, m., *cyclone*.

D.

Daal dat Roer! *Down the
helm!*
daalen, *to decline*.
Dachventil, n., *valve cock*.
Dallen, *dolphins*.
Damen-kajüte, f, *ladies cabin*;
- zimmer, n., *ladies room*.
Damm, m„ *embankment*.
dämmen, das Wasser -, *to
stem the water*.
dämpen, *to spill a sail*.
Dämpgording, f., *spilling line*.
Dampf, m., *steam*; - abblasen,
to blow off s.; - ablassen, *to
let off s.*; - abschließen, -
absperren, *to cut off s.*; abstellen, *to shut off s.*; - anlassen, *to put s. on*; - ist
angelassen, *the s. is on*; der
volle - i. a.; *the s. is up*; -
aufhalten, *to keep s. up*; -
aufmachen, *to get up s.*; - -
befohlen, *s. ordered*; mit
eigenem -, *under own s.*

Dampf-abführung, f., *ex-
haustion of steam*; - - rohr,
n., *s. exhaust pipe*.
Dampfabgangsrohr, n., *steam
waste pipe*; - des Sicherheitsventils, *safety valve
pipe*; - leitung, f., *steam
waste pipes*.
Dampf-ablaßrohr, n., *steam
exhaust pipe*; - abzugsrohr,
n., *s. escape p.*; - Ankerlichtmaschine *or* - Ankerspill *see* - spill.
Dampfaschwinde, f, *steam
ash hoist*; - Absperrventil,
n, *s. a. h. stop valve*; - Anlaßventil, n., *s. a. h. starting v.*; - Dampfabführungsrohr, n., *s. a. h. exhaust
pipe*; - Dampfzuleitungs-
rohr, n., *s. a. h. steam
pipe*; - Exzenter, n., *s. a. h.
eccentric*; - - bolzen. m , *s.
a. h. e. bolt*; - - bügel, m.,
s. a. h. e. strap; - - - Futter

od. Paßstück, n., *s. a. h. e.
s. liner*; - Exzenter-Lager-
schalen, *s. a. h. e. brasses*;
- E.-scheibe. f., *s. a. h. e.
sheave*; - E.-stange, f., *s. a.
h. e. rod*; - Kolben, m., *s. a.
h. piston*; - - stange, f, *s.
a. h. p. rod*; - - - Kreuzkopf, m., *s. a. h. p. r. crosshead*; - - - Stopfbüchse, f.,
s. a. h. p. r. stuffing box;
- - - - deckel, m., *s. a. h. p.
r. s. b. gland*; - Kreuzkopflager-bolzen, m., *s. a. h.
crosshead bolt*; - K-k-l-schalen, *s. a. h. c. brasses*; -
K-k-l-s-deckel, m., *s. a. h.
connecting rod top end keep*;
- Kurbelwelle, f., *s. a. h.
crank shaft*; - - lager, n.,
s. a. h. c. s. bearing; - - -
bolzen, m., *s. a. h. c. s. b.
bolt*; - - - deckel, m., *s. a.
h. c. s. bearing keep*; - - - -
bolzen, m., *s. a. h. c. s. b. k.
bolt*; - Kurbelwellenlagerschalen, *s. a. h. c. s. bearing
brasses*; - - Futter or Paßstück, n., *s. a. h. c. s.
brasses liner*; - Kurbel-
zapfenlager-bolzen, m., *s. a.
h. crank pin bolt*; - K-z-l-
schalen, *s. a. h. c. p. brasses*;
- K-z-l-s-deckel, m., *s. a. h.
connecting rod bottom end
keep*; - Pleuelstange, f., *s.
a. h. c. r.*; - - bolzen, m., *s.
a. h. c. r. bolt*; - - fuß-Futter
or Paßstück, n., *s. a. h. c.
r. bottom end liner*; - Schieber, m., *s. a. h. slide valve*;
- - kasten, m., *s. a. h. v.
casing*; - - - deckel, m., *s.
a. h. v. c. door*; - Schieberstange, f., *s. a. h. v. c. rod*;
- - Stopfbüchse, f., *s. a. h.
v. r. stuffing box*; - - - dekkel, m., *s. a. h. v. r. s. b.
gland*; - Zylinder, m., *s. a.
h. cylinder*; - - deckel, m.,
s. a. h. c. cover; - - - bolzen,
m., *s. a. h. c. c. bolt*; - Zylinder - Entwässerungsrohr,
n., *s. a. h. cylinder drain pipe.*

Dampf-Auslaßhahn, m., *blast
cock*; - Austritt eines Schiebers, m., *waste port of a
valve*; - Austrittskanal, m.,
steam exhaust port; - Aus-
trittsweg, m., *s. e. passage*;
- Ausströmung, f., *ex-
haustion of steam*; - bagger,
m., *hopper dredger.*
Dampfballastpumpe, f., *ballast donkey*; - Absperrventil, n., *b. d. stop valve*; -
Anlaßventil, n., *b. d. starting v.*; - Ausgußventil, n.,
b. d. discharge v.; - - spindel, f., *b. d. d. v. spindle*;
- Dampfabführungsrohr, n.,
b. d. exhaust pipe; - Dampfzuleitungsrohr. n., *b. d.
steam pipe*; - Druckraum,
m., *b. d. delivery space*;
- Druckventil, n., *b. d. d.
valve*; - - deckel, m., *b. d. d.
v. door*; - - sitz, m., *b.
donkey v. seat*; - Exzenter,
n., *b. d. eccentric*; - - bolzen,
m., *b. d. e. bolt*; - - bügel,
m., *b. d. e. strap*; - - - Futter
or Paßstück, n., *b. d. e. s.
liner*; - Exzenter - Lagerschalen, *b. d. e. brasses*; -
E.-scheibe, f., *b. d. e. sheave*;
- E.-stange, f., *b. d. e. rod*;
- Fußventil, n., *b. d. foot
valve*; - geschirr, n., *b. d.
gear*; - Kolben, m., *b. d.
bucket*; - - stange, f., *b. d.
piston rod*; - - - Kreuzkopf,
m., *b. d. p. r. crosshead*;
- - - Stopfbüchse, f., *b. d.
p. r. stuffing box*; - - - -
deckel, m., *b. d. p. r. s. b.
gland*; - Kolbenventil, n.,
b. d. bucket valve; - - sitz,
m., *b. d. b. v. seat*; - Kreuzkopflager-bolzen, m., *b. d.
crosshead bolt*; - K-k-l-schalen, *b. d. c. brasses*; - K-k-l-
s-deckel, m., *b. d. connecting
rod top end keep*; - Kurbelwelle, f., *b. d. crank shaft*;
- - lager, n, *b. d. c. s. bearing*; - - - deckel, m., *b. d. c.
s. b. keep*; - - - - bolzen, m.,

b. d. c. s. b. k. bolt; - K-b-w-Lagerschalen, *b. d. c. s. bearing brasses*; - K-b-w-L-s-Futter or Paßstück, n., *b. d. c. s. b. b. liner*; - Kurbelzapfenlager-bolzen, m., *b. d. crank pin bolt*; - K-z-l-schalen, *b. d. c. p. brasses*; - K-z-l-s-deckel, m., *b. d. connecting rod bottom end keep*; - Pleuelstange, f., *b. d. c. r.*; - - bolzen, m., *b. d. c. r. bolt*; - - fuß-Futter or Paßstück, n., *b. d. c. r. bottom end liner*; - Saugeraum, m., *b. d. suction space*; - Saugerohr, n., *b. d. suction pipe*; - Saugeventil, n., *b. d. s. valve*; - - deckel, m., *b. d. s. v. door*; - - sitz, m., *b. d. s. v. seat*; - Schieber, m., *b. d. slide valve*; - - kasten, m., *b. d. s. v. casing*; - - - deckel, m., *b. d. s. v. c. door*; - Schieberstange, f., *b. d. s. v. r. rod*; - - Stopfbüchse, f., *b. d. s. v. r. stuffing box*; - - - dekkel, m., *b. d. s. v. r. s. b. gland*; - Schwungrad, n., *b. d. fly wheel*; - ventil, n., *b. d. valve*; - - deckel, m., *b. d. v. door*; - - - sitz, m., *b. d. v. seat*; - Wendehahn, m., *b. d. master cock*; - Zylinder, m., *b. d. cylinder*; - - dekkel, m., *b. d. c. cover*; - - - bolzen, m., *b. d. c. c. bolt*; - Z.-Entwässerungsrohr, n., *b. d. cylinder drain pipe*.

Dampf-barkasse, f., - beiboot, n., *steam launch*; - - maschine, f., *s. l. engine*; - boot, n., *steamer*; - büchse, f., *steam box*; - dicht, *steam tight*; - dom, m., *s. dome*; - Drehvorrichtung, f., *s. turning gear*; - drosseln, *wire drawing*; - Drosselung, f., *throttling of steam*; - druck, m., *s. pressure*; - Indikator, m., *s. p. indicator*; - - messer, m., *s. p. gauge*; - - - hahn, m., *s. p. g. cock*;

- - - rohr, *s. p. g. pipe*; - Druckprobe, f, *s. p. test*; - D-regulator, m., *s. p. governor*; - einerbagger, m., *s. bucket dredger*; - einlaß-Exzenter, m., *s. eccentric*; - eintritt eines Schiebers, m., *port of a valve*.

Dampfeintrittskanal d. Hochdruckzylinders, m., *steam port of high pressure cylinder*; - des Mitteld-z-, *s. p. of intermediate p. c.*; - des Niederd-z-, *s. p. of low p. c.*; - des Zylinders, *s. p. of cylinder*.

Dampfeintrittsweg, m., *steam admission passage*.

dampfen über, *to steam over*.

dämpfen, *1. to damp (the fires); 2. to spill (a sail)*.

Dampf-entweichungsrohr, n , *steam escape pipe*; - entwickelung, f., *the getting up of steam*.

Dampfer mit Kühlvorrichtung, m., *refrigerating steamer*; - mit Ölfeuerung, *oiler*.

Dämpfer, m., *damper*.

Dampfer-dienst, m., *steam ship service*; - linie, f., *steam ship line*; - verkehr, m., *traffic of steamers*.

Dampf-erzeuger, m., *steam generator*; sofort wirkender - -, *instantaneous s. g.*; - erzeugung, f., *production of steam*; - fähre, f., *s. ferry*.

Dampffeuerspritze, f., *fire engine*; - Absperrventil, n., *f. e. stop valve*; - Anlaßventil, n., *f. e. starting v.*; - Dampf-abführungsrohr, n., *f. e. exhaust pipe*, -D-zuleitungsrohr, n , *f. e. steam pipe*; - Exzenter, n., *f. e. eccentric*; - - bolzen, m., *f. e. e. bolt*; - - bügel, m , *f. e. e. strap*; - - - Futter or Paßstück, n., *f. e. e. s. liner*; - E.-Lagerschalen, *f. e. e. brasses*; - E.-Scheibe, f., *f.*

e. e. sheave; - E.-stange, f., *f. e. e. rod*; - Kolben, m., *f. e. piston*; - - stange, f., *f. e. p. rod*; - - - Kreuzkopf, m., *f. e. p. r. crosshead*; - - - Stopfbüchse, f., *f. e. p. r. stuffing box*; - - - - dekkel, m., *f. e. p. r. s. b. gland*; - Kreuzkopf-Lagerbolzen, m., *f. e. crosshead bolt*; - - Lagerschalen, *f. e. c. brasses*; - - - deckel, m., *f. e. connecting rod top end keep*; - Kurbelwelle, t., *f. e. crank shaft*; - - lager, n., *f. e. c. s. bearing*; - - - bolzen, m., *f. e. c. s. b. bolt*; - - - deckel, m., *f. e. c. s. bearing keep*; - - - - bolzen, m., *f. e. c. s. b. k. bolt*; - Kurbelwellenlagerschalen, *f. e. c. s. bearing brasses*; - - deckel, m., *f. e. c. s. b. b. keep*; - - Futter or Paßstück, n., *f. e. c. s. b. b. liner*; - Kurbelzapfenlager-bolzen, m., *f. e. crank pin bolt*; - K-z-l-schalen, *f. e. c. p. brasses*; - K-z-l-s-deckel, m., *f. e. connecting rod bottom end keep*; - Pleuelstange, f., *f. e. c. r.*; - - bolzen, m., *f. e. c. r. bolt*; - - fuß-Futter or Paßstück, n., *f. e. c. r. bottom end liner*; - Schieber, m., *f. e. slide valve*; - - kasten, m., *f. e. v. casing*; - - - deckel, m., *f. e. v. c. door*; - Schieberstange, f., *f. e. v. rod*; - - Stopfbüchse, t., *f. e. v. r. stuffing box*; - - - deckel, m., *f. e. v. r. s. b. gland*; - Zylinder, m., *f. e. cylinder*; - - deckel, m., *f. e. cover*; - - - bolzen, m., *f. e. c. c. bolt*; - Z.-Entwässerungsrohr, n., *f. e. cylinder drain pipe*.

Dampfgangspill, n., *steam capstan*; - Absperrventil, n., *s. c. stop valve*; - Anlaßventil, n., *s. c. starting v.*; - Dampf-abführungsrohr, n., *s. c. exhaust pipe*; - D-zu-

leitungsrohr, n., *s. c. steam pipe*; - Exzenter, n., *s. c. eccentric*; - - bolzen, m., *s. c. e. bolt*; - - bügel, m., *s. c. e. strap*; - - - Futter or Paßstück, n., *s. c. e. s. liner*; - E.-Lagerschalen, *s. c. e. brasses*; - E.-Scheibe, f., *s. c. e. sheave*; - E.-stange, t., *s. c. e. rod*; - Kolben, m., *s. c. piston*; - - stange, f., *s. c. p. rod*; - - - Kreuzkopf, m., *s. c. p. r. crosshead*; - - - Stopfbüchse, f., *s. c. p. r. stuffing box*; - - - - dekkel, m., *s. c. p. r. s. b. gland*; - Kreuzkopf, m., *s. c. crosshead*; - - Lagerbolzen, m., *s. c. c. bolt*; - - Lagerschalen, *s. c. c. brasses*; - - - deckel, m., *s. c. connecting rod top end keep*; - Kurbelwelle, f., *s. c. crank shaft*; - - lager, n., *s. c. c. s. bearing*; - - - bolzen, m., *s. c. c. s. b. bolt*; - - - deckel, m., *s. c. c. s. bearing keep*; - - - - bolzen, m., *s. c. c. s. b. k. bolt*; - Kurbelwellenlagerschalen, *s. c. c. s. bearing brasses*; - - Futter or Paßstück, n., *s. c. c. s. brasses liner*; - Kurbelzapfenlager-bolzen, m., *s. c. crank pin bolt*; - K-z-l-schalen, *s. c. c. p. brasses*; - K-z-l-s-deckel, m., *s. c. connecting rod bottom end keep*; - Maschine, f., *s. c. engine*; - Pleuelstange, f., *s. c. connecting rod*; - - bolzen, m., *s. c. c. r. bolt*; - - fuß-Futter or Paßstück, n., *s. c. c. r. bottom end liner*; - Schieber, m., *s. c. slide valve*; - - kasten, m., *s. c. v. casing*; - - - deckel, m., *s. c. v. c. door*; - Schieberstange, f., *s. c. v. rod*; - - Stopfbüchse, f., *s. c. v. r. stuffing box*; - - - deckel, m., *s. c. v. r. s. b. gland*; - Zylinder, m., *s. c. cylinder*; - - deckel, m., *s.

c. c. cover; - - - bolzen, m., *s. c. c. c. bolt*; - Z.-Entwässerungsrohr, n., *s. c. cylinder drain pipe*.

Dampf-hahn, m., *steam cock*; - heizung, f., *s. heating*; - jacht, f., *s. yacht*; - kammer, f., *s. box*; - kanal, m., *s. way*; - kessel, m., *s. boiler*; - - explosion, f., *explosion of boiler*; - kesselkohle, *steam coal*; der - - platzt, [*the s. b. explodes*; - kesselrevision, f., *boiler inspection*; - kiste, f., *s. chest*; - klar sein, *to have s. up*; - kolbenliderung, f., *packing of the piston*; - kraft, f., *steam power*.

Dampfkran, m., *steam crane*; - Absperrventil, n., *s. c. stop valve*; - Anlaßventil, n., *s. c. starting v.*; - Dampfabführungsrohr, m., *s. c. exhaust pipe*; - D-zuleitungsrohr, n., *s. c. steam pipe*; - Exzenter, n., *s. c. eccentric*; - - bolzen, m., *s. c. e. bolt*; - - bügel, m., *s. c. e. strap*; - - - Futter or Paßstück, n., *s. c. e. s. liner*; - E.-Lagerschalen, *s. c. e. brasses*; - E.-scheibe, f., *s. c. e. sheave*; - E.-stange, f., *s. c. e. rod*; - Fundamentplatte or Grundp., f., *s. c. bed plate*; - Kolben, m., *s. c. piston*; - - stange, f., *s. c. p. rod*; - - - Kreuzkopf, m., *s. c. p. r. crosshead*; - - - - Stopfbüchse, f., *s. c. p. r. stuffing box*; - - - - deckel, m., *s. c. p. r. s. b. gland*; - Kreuzkopflagerbolzen, m., *s. c. crosshead bolt*; - K-k-l-schalen, *s. c. c. brasses*; - K-k-l-s-deckel, m., *s. c. connecting rod top end keep*; - Kurbelwelle, f., *s. c. crank shaft*; - - lager, n., *s. c. c. s. bearing*; - - - bolzen, m., *s. c. c. s. b. bolt*; - - - deckel, m., *s. c. c. s. bearing keep*; - - - - bolzen, m., *s. c. c. s. b. k.*

bolt; - Kurbelwellenlagerschalen, *s. c. c. s. bearing brasses*; - - Futter or Paßstück, n., *s. c. c. s. b. b. liner*; - Kurbelzapfenlagerbolzen, m., *s. c. crank pin bolt*; - K-z-l-schalen, *s. c. c. p. brasses*; - K-z-l-s-deckel, m., *s. c. connecting rod bottom end keep*; - Pleuelstange, f., *s. c. c. r.*; - - bolzen, m., *s. c. c. r. bolt*; - - Fuß-Futter or Paßstück, n., *s. c. c. r. bottom end liner*; - Schieber, m., *s. c. slide valve*; - - kasten, m., *s. c. v. casing*; - - - deckel, m., *s. c. v. c. door*; - Schieberstange, f., *s. c. v. rod*; - - Stopfbüchse, f., *s. c. v. r. stuffing box*; - - - deckel, m., *s. c. v. r. s. b. gland*; - Zylinder, m., *s. c. cylinder*; - - deckel, m., *s. c. c. cover*; - - - bolzen, m., *s. c. c. c. bolt*; - Z.-Entwässerungsrohr, n., *s. c. cylinder drain pipe*.

Dampf-kühlpumpe, f., *circulating pump engine*; - leitung, f., *steam conduit*; - lenzpumpe, f., *ballast donkey* (see also - ballastpumpe).

Dampfmantel, m., *cylinder jacket*; - des Hochdruckzylinders, *high pressure c. j.*; - des Mitteldruckzylinders, *intermediate c. j.*; - des Niederdruckzylinders, *low pressure c. j.*; - des Zylinders, *c. j.*; - Drainagehahn or - Entwässerungshahn, m., *jacket drain cock*; - rohr, n., *j. steam pipe*; - Sicherheitsventil, n., *j. safety valve*.

Dampf-maschine, f., *steam engine*; - öler. m., *impermeator*; - pfeife, f., *steam whistle*.

Dampfpfeifenrohr, n., *steam whistle pipe*; - hahn, m., *s. w. p. cock*; - ventil, n., *s. w. p. valve*.

Dampf - pfeifenventil , n.,
whistle valve; - pinasse, f.,
steam pinnace.
Dampfpumpe, f., *donkey pump*;
- Absperrventil, n., *d. p.
stop valve*; - Anlaßventil,
n., *d. p. starting v.*; - Ausgußventil, n., *d. p. discharge
v.*; - Dampf-abführungsrohr,
n., *d. p. exhaust pipe*; - D-
zuleitungsrohr. n., *d. p.
steam p.*; - Druckraum, m.,
d. p. delivery space; - Druckventil, n., *d. p. head valve*;
- - sitz, m., *d. p. h. v. seat*;
- Exzenter, m., *d. p. eccentric*;
- - bolzen, m., *d. p. e. bolt*;
- - bügel, m., *d. p. e. strap*;
- - - Futter or Paßstück, n.,
d. p. e. s. liner; - E.-Lager-
schalen, *d. p. e. brasses*;
- E.-scheibe, f., *d. p. e.
sheave*; - E.-Stange, f., *d. p.
e. rod*; - Fußventil, n., *d. p.
foot valve*; - Geschirr, n.,
d. p. gear; - Injektionsrohr,
n., *d. p. injection pipe*; -
I-j-ventil, n., *d. p. i. valve*;
- Kolben, m., *d. p. piston*;
- - ring, m., *d. p. p. ring*;
- - stange, f., *d. p. p. rod*;
- - - Kreuzkopf, m., *d. p. p.
r. crosshead*; - - - Stopfbüchse, f., *d. p. p. r. stuffing
box*; - - - - deckel, m., *d. p.
p. r s. b. gland*; - Kolbenventil, n., *d. p. bucket valve*;
- - sitz, m., *d. p. b. v. seat*;
- Kreuzkopf, m., *d. p. crosshead*; - - Lagerbolzen, m.,
d. p. c. bolt; - - Lagerschalen, *d. p. c. brasses*; - - -
deckel, m., *d. p. connecting
rod top end keep*; - Kurbelwelle, f., *d. p. crank shaft*;
- - lager, n., *d. p. c. s. bearing*; - - bolzen, m., *d. p. c.
s. b. bolt*; - - deckel, m., *d.
p. c. s. bearing keep*; - - -
bolzen, m., *d. p. c. s. b. k.
bolt*; - Kurbelwellenlagerschalen, *d. p. c. s. bearing
brasses*; - - Futter or Paßstück, n., *d. p. c. s. bearing*

liner; - Kurbelzapfenlager,
n., *d. p. c. pin bearing*; - -
bolzen, m., *d. p. c. p. bolt*;
- - schalen, *d. p. c. p. brasses*;
- - - deckel, m., *d. p. c. p. b.
keep*; - Pleuelstange, f., *d. p.
connecting rod*; - - bolzen,
m., *d. p. c. r. bolt*; - - fuß,
m., *d. p. c. r. bottom end*;
- - - Futter or Paßstück, n.,
d. p. c. r. b. e. liner; - Plunger, m., *d. p. plunger*; -
Sauge-hahnschlüssel, m., *d.
p. suction cock key*; - S-
raum, m., *d. p. s. space*; - S-
rohr, n., *d. p. suction pipe*;
- S-sieb, m., *d. p. s. rose
plate*; - S-ventil, n., *d. p. s.
valve*; - S-v-sitz, m., *d. p. s.
v. seat*; - Schieber, m., *d. p.
slide valve*; - - kasten, m.,
d. p. v. casing; - - - deckel,
m., *d. p. v. c. door*; - Schieberstange f., *d. p. v. rod*;
- - Stopfbüchse, f., *d. p. v.
r. stuffing box*; - - - deckel,
m., *d. p v. r. s. b. gland*;
- Schwungrad, n., *d. p. fly
wheel*; - Speiserohr, n., *d.
p. feed pipe*; - - ventil, n.,
d. p. check valve; - - - dekkel, m., *d. p. c. v. cover*; -
stange, f., *d. p. rod*; - Stopfbüchse, f., *d. p. stuffing box*;
- - deckel, m., *d. p. s. b.
gland*; - ventil, n., *d. p.
valve*; - - sitz, m., *d. p. v.
seat*; - Wendehahn, m., *d.
p. master cock*; - Zentral-
lagerständer, m., *d. p. centre
bearing standard*; - Zirkulationsrohr, n., *d. p. circulating pipe*; - Zylinder,
m., *d. p. cylinder*; - - deckel,
m., *d. p. c. cover*; - - bolzen,
m., *d p. c. c. bolt*; - - Entwässerungsrohr, n., *d. p.
cylinder drain pipe.*

Dampf-ramme, *steam pile
driver*; - raum, m., *s. space*;
- reduzierventil, n., *s. reducing valve*; - regulator. m.,
s. governor; - reservoir, m.,

1. s. chest; *2. receiver (of compound engine)*.
Dampfrohr, n., *steam pipe*; - flansch, m., *s. p. flange*; - leitung. f., *s. pipes*; - mantel, m., *s. pipe casing*; - Sicherheitsventil, n., *s. p. safety valve*; - - belastung, f., *s. p. s. v. load*; - Sicherungsvorrichtung, f, *s. p. guards*; - Stiftschraube, f., *s. p. stud*; - Stütze, f., *s. p. bracket*.
Dampf-schaluppe, f., *steam sloop*; - schiff, n., *steam ship*; - - fahrt, f., *s. navigation*; - - sagent, m., *s. ship agent*; - - sgesellschaft, f, *s. s. company*; - - sversicherungsverein, m., *s. s. assurance association*; - - swerft, f., *steam wharf*; - spannung, f., *s. pressure*; - - messer, m., *p. gauge.*
Dampfspeisepumpe, f., *feed donkey*; - Absperrventil, n., *f. d. stop valve*; - Anlaß-ventil, n., *f. d. starting v.*: - Ausgußventil, n., *f. d. discharge v.*; - Dampf-abführungsrohr, n., *f. d. exhaust pipe*; - D-zuleitungsrohr, n., *f. d. steam p.*; - dekkel, m., *f. d. cover*; - Druckraum, m., *f. d. delivery space*; - D-rohr, n., *f. d. d. pipe*; - Druckventil, n., *f. d. d. valve*; - - deckel, m., *f. d. d. v. door*; - - Hubbegrenzer, m., *f. d. top v. guard*; - - kasten, m., *f. d. delivery valve chest*; - - Klappenfänger, m., *f. d. d. v. guard*; - - sitz, m., *f. d. d. v. seat*; - eimer, m., *f. d. box*; - Einsatz, m., *f. d. liner*; - Exzenter, m., *f. d. eccentric*; - - bügel, m, *f. d. e. strap*; - - - Futter or Paßstück, n. *f. d. e. s. liner*; - E.-bolzen, m., *f. d. e. bolt*; - E.-Lagerschalen, *f. d. e. brasses*; - Exzenterscheibe, f., *f. d. e. sheave*; - E-z-stange, f., *f. d. e. rod*; - Fußventil, n., *f. d.*

foot valve; - Gelenk, n., *f. d. link*; - - Lagerschalen, *f. d. link brasses*; - Geschirr, n., *f. d. gear*; - Grundring, m., *f. d. neck bush*; - haken, m., *f. d. hook*; - hebel, m., *f. d. brake*; - Hubbegrenzung des Ventils, f., *f. d. valve guard*; - Kolben, m., *f. d. piston*; - - ring, m., *f. d. p. ring*; - - stange, f., *f. d. p. rod*; - - - Kreuzkopf, m., *f. d. p. r. crosshead*; - - - - Lagerschalendeckel, m., *f. d. connecting rod top end keep*; - Kolbenstangen-Stopfbüchse, f., *f. d. piston rod stuffing box*; - - - deckel, m., *f. d. p. r. s. b. gland*; - Kolbenventil, n., *f. d. bucket valve*; - - sitz, m., *f. d. b. v. seat*; - - Hubbegrenzer or Klappenfänger, m., *f. d. b. v. guard*; - Körper, m., *f. d. chamber*; - Kreuzkopf, m., *f. d. crosshead*; - - Lagerbolzen, m., *f. d. c. bolt*; - - L-schalen, *f. d. c. brasses*; - Kurbellager, n., *f. d. crank bearing*; - K-welle, f., *f. d. c. shaft*; - Kurbelwellenlager, n., *f. d. c. s. bearing*; - - bolzen, m., *f. d. c. s. b. bolt*; - - deckel, m., *f. d. c. s. bearing keep*; - - - bolzen, m., *f. d. c. s. b. k. bolt*; - - - schalen, *f. d. c. s. bearing brasses*; - - - - Futter or Paßstück, m., *f. d. c. s. brasses liner*; - Kurbelzapfenlager, n., *f. d. connecting rod bottom end*; - - bolzen, m., *f. d. crank pin bolt*; - - schalen, *f. d. c. p. brasses*; - - - deckel, m., *f. d. connecting rod bottom end keep*; - Mundstück, n., *f. d. nozzle*; - Peilstock, m., *f. d. sounding rod*; - Pleuelstange, f., *f. d. connecting rod*; - - bolzen, m., *f. d. c. r. bolt*; - - Lagerschalen, *f. d. c. r. top end brasses*; - - fuß-Futter or Paßstück, n., *f. d. c. r.*

bottom end liner; - Plunger, m., *f. d. plunger*; - Probier-hahn, m., *f. d. pet cock*; - Rücklaufventil, n., *f. d. relief valve*; - Saugeraum, m., *f. d. suction space*; - Sauge-rohr, n., *f. d. suction pipe*; - Saugeventil, n., *f. d. s. valve*; - - deckel, m., *f. d. s. v. door*; - - Hubbegrenzer, m., *f. d. foot valve guard*; - - kasten, m., *f. d. v. chest*; - - Klappenfänger, m., *f. d. suction valve guard*; - - sitz, m., *f. d. s. v. seat*; - Schieber, m., *f. d. slide valve*; - - kasten, m., *f. d. valve casing*; - - - deckel, m., *f. d. v. c. door*; - Schieberstange, f., *f. d. v. rod*; - - Stopfbüchse, f., *f. d. v. r. stuffing box*; - - - deckel, m., *f. d. v. r. s. b. gland*; - Schnürhahn, m., *f. d. pet cock*; - Schnürventil, n., *f. d. pet valve*; - Schraper, m., *f. d. scraper*; - Schuh, m., *f. d. bucket*; - Schwengel, m., *f. d. lever*; - Schwung-rad, n., *f. d. fly wheel*; - Sicherheitsventil, n., *f. d. escape valve*; - - belastung, f., *f. d. e. v. load*; - - spindel f., *f. d. e. v. spindle*; - stange, f., *f. d. rod*; - - Stopfbüchse, f., *f. d. r. stuffing box*; - Stopfbüchse, f., *f. d. s. b.*; - - deckel, m., *f. d. s. b. gland*; - Überlaufventil, n., *f. d. overflow valve*; - ventil, n., *f. d. v.*; - - deckel, m., *f. d. v. cover*; - - Hubbegrenzer, or - - Klappenfänger, m., *f. d. v. guard*; - - sitz, m., *f. d. v. seat*; - Wendehahn, m., *f. d. master cock*; - Windekessel, m., *f. d. air barrel*; - Zentral-lagerständer, m., *f. d. centre bearing standard*; - Zylinder, m., *f. d. cylinder*; - - deckel, m., *f. d. c. cover*; - - - bolzen, m., *f. d. c. c. bolt*; - Z.-Ent-wässerungsrohr, n., *f. d. cylinder drain pipe*.

Dampfspill, n., *steam windlass*;

- Absperrventil, n., *s. w. stop valve*; - Anlaßventil, n., *s. w. starting v.*; - Balancier, m., *s. w. crosshead*; - - träger, m., *s. w. c. bracket*; - Bremse, f., *s. w. brake*; - - federn, *s. w. b. springs*; - - mutter or - - scheibe, f., *s. w. screw brake nut*; - Dampf-ab-führungsrohr, n., *s. w. exhaust pipe*; - D-rohrflansch, m., *s. w. steam pipe flange*; - D-zuleitungsrohr, n., *s. w. s. p.*; - Exzenter, n., *s. w. eccentric*; - - bolzen, m., *s. w. e. bolt*; - - bügel, m., *s. w. e. strap*; - - - Futter or Paßstück, n., *s. w. e. s. liner*; - E-Lagerschalen, *s. w. e. bearing brasses*; - E.-scheibe, f., *s. w. e. sheave*; - E-stange, f., *s. w. e. rod*; - Fischung, f., *s. w. e. partner*; - Friktions-getriebe, n., *s. w. friction gear*; - Fundaments- or Grundplatte, f., *s. w. bed plate*; - Handhebel, m., *s. w. hand lever*; - Haupttriebrad, n., *s. w. main cone driving wheel*; - Ketten-ausrücker or K-austreiber, m., *s. w. cable reliever*; - K-scheibe, f., *s. w. c. lifter*; - Kolben, m., *s. w. piston*; - - stange, f., *s. w. p. rod*; - - - Kreuz-kopf, m., *s. w. p. r. crosshead*; - - - Stopfbüchse, f., *s. w. p. r. stuffing box*; - - - - deckel, m., *s. w. p. r. s. b. gland*; - kopf, m., *s. w. warping end*; - kranz, m., *s. w. cable holder*; - Kreuzkopf, m., *s. w. cross-head*; - - Lagerbolzen, m., *s. w. c. bolt*; - - Lagerschalen, *s. w. c. brasses*; - - - deckel, m., *s. w. connecting rod top end keep*; - K.-träger, m., *s. w. crosshead bracket*; - Kuppelungsklaue, f., *s. w. clutch*; - Kurbelwelle, f., *s. w. crank shaft*; - - lager, n., *s. w. c. s. bearing*; - - - bolzen, m., *s. w. c. s. b. bolt*; - - - deckel, m., *s. w. c. s. bearing keep*; - - - - bolzen, m., *s. w. c. s. b. k. bolt*; - Kurbelwellenlagerschalen, *s. w. c. s. bearing brasses*; - - Futter or Paßstück, n., *s. w. c. s. brasses liner*; - Kurbelzapfen, m., *s. w. crank pin*: - - Lagerbolzen, m., *s. w. c. p. bolt*; - - Lagerschalen, *s. w. c. p. brasses*; - - - deckel, m., *s. w. connecting rod bottom end keep*; - Mittelbeting, f., *s. w. centre bitt*; - - Wellenlager, n., *s. w. c. b. bearing*; - Mittelträger, m., *s. w. c. b.*; - Pall, n., or Palle, f., *s. w. pawl*; - - kasten, m., *s. w. p. box*; - - kranz, m., *s. w. p. rack*; - - ring, m., *s. w. p. rim*; - Pleuelstange, f., *s. w. connecting rod*; - - bolzen, m., *s. w. c. r. bolt*: - - fußFutter or Paßstück, n., *s. w. c. r. bottom end liner*; - Pumpenhebel, m., *s. w. hand lever*; - Rohrflansch, m., *s. w. steam pipe flange*; - Schieber, m., *s. w. slide valve*; - - kasten, m., *s. w. v. casing*; - - - deckel, m., *s. w. v. c. door*; - - - stange. f., *s. w. v. rod*; - - - - Stopfbüchse, f., *s. w. v. r. stuffing box*; - - - - - deckel, m., *s. w. r. s. b. gland*; - Seitenbeting, f., *s. w. side bitt*; - - Wellenlager, n., *s. w. s. b. bearing*; - Seitenlagerbock, m., *s. w. s. bitt*; - Sicherung, f., *s. w. guard*; - Stirnrad. n., *s. w. main cone driving wheel*; - Traverse, f., *s. w. crosshead*; - Verbindungsstange, f., *s. w. purchase rod*; - Welle, f., *s. w. main piece*: - - Lagerdeckel, m., 1. der Mittelbetinge, *s. w. centre bitt keep*; 2. der Seitenbetinge, *s. w. side b. k.*; - Zugstange, f., *s. w. connecting rod*; - Zylinder, m., *s. w. cylinder*; - - deckel, m., *s. w. c. cover*; - - - bolzen, m., *s. w. c. c. bolt*; - Z.-Entwässerungs-

rohr, n., *s. w. cylinder drain pipe.*

Dampfspritzenboot, n., *fire boat.*

Dampfsteuerapparat, m.,*steam steering engine*; - Absperrventil, n., *s. s. e. stop valve*; - Anlaßventil, n., *s. s. e. starting v.*; - Dampf-abführungsrohr, n., *s. s. e. exhaust pipe*; - D-zuleitungsrohr, n., *s. s. e. steam pipe*; - Exzenter, n., *s. s. e. eccentric*; - - bolzen, m., *s. s. e. e. bolt*; - - bügel, m., *s. s. e. e. strap*; - - - Futter or Paßstück, n., *s. s. e. e. liner*; - E.-Lagerschalen, *s. s. e. e. brasses*; - E.-scheibe, f., *s. s. e. e. sheave*; - E.-stange, f., *s. s. e. e. rod*; - Fundamentor Grundplatte, f., *s. s. e. bed plate*; - Hauptwelle, f., *s. s. e. main shaft*; - Hebel, m., *s. s. e. lever*; - Kettenscheibe u. Ruderkette, f., *s. s. e. messenger wheel and steering chain*; - Kolben, m., *s. s. e. piston*; - - stange, f., *s. s. e. p. rod*; - - - Kreuzkopf, m., *s. s. e. p. r. crosshead*; - - - Stopfbüchse, f., *s. s. e. p. r. stuffing box*; - - - - deckel, m., *s. s. e. p. r. s. b. gland*; - konisches Rad, n., 1. an der Schneckenwelle, *s. s. e. mitre wheel on worm shaft*; 2. an der Vorgelegewelle, *s. s. e. m. w. on transmitting shaft*; - Kreuzkopflager-bolzen, m., *s. s. e. crosshead bolt*; - K-k-lschalen, *s. s. e. c. brasses*; - K-k-l-s-deckel, m., *s. s. e. connecting rod top end keep*; - Kurbelscheibe. f., *s. s. e. crank disk*; - Kurbelwelle, f., *s. s. e. c. shaft*; - - lager, n., *s. s. e. c. bearing*; - - - bolzen. m., *s. s. e. c. s. b. bolt*; - - - deckel, m., *s. s. e. c. s. bearing keep*; - - - - bolzen, m., *s. s. e. c. s. b. k. bolt*; -

Kurbelwellenlagerschalen, *s.
s. e. c. s. bearing brasses*; - - Paßstück. n., *s. s. e. c. s.
brasses liner*; - Kurbelzapfen, m., *s. s. e. crank pin*; - - Lagerbolzen, m , *s. s. e. c. p.
bolt*; - - Lagerschalen, *s. s. e. c. p. brasses*; - - - deckel, m., *s. s. e. connecting rod bottom end keep*; - Leitblock, m., *s. s. e. guide pulley*; - Pleuelstange, f., *s. s. e. connecting rod*; - - bolzen, m., *s. s. e. c. r. bolt*; - - Futter or Paßstück, n., *s. s. e. c. r. bottom end liner*: - Schieber, m., *s. s. e. slide valve*; - - kasten, m., *s. s. e. v. casing*; - - - deckel, m., *s. s. e. v. c. door*; - Schieberstange, f., *s. s. e. v. rod*; - - Stopfbüchse, f., *s. s. e. v. r. stuffing box*; - - - deckel, m., *s. s. e. v. r. s. b. gland*; - Schnecke, f., *s. s. e. worm*; - - rad, n., *s. s. e. scroll wheel*; - Ständer. m., *s. s. e. standards*; - Stellschraube, f., *s. s. e. set screw*; - Stirnrad, n., *s. s. e. spur wheel*; - Stopfbüchse, f.. *s. s. e. stuffing box*; - Triebrad, n., *s. s. e. pinion*; - Umsteuerungswelle, f., *s. s. e. valve rod*; - Vorgelegewelle, f., *s. s. e. transmitting shaft*; - Windetrommel, f., *s. s. e. chain drum*; - Zylinder, m., *s. s. e. cylinder*; - - deckel, m., *s. s. e. c. cover*; - - - bolzen, m., *s. s. e. c. c. bolt*; - Z.-Entwässerungsrohr, n., *s. s. e. cylinder drain pipe.*

Dampfsteuermaschine *see* D-s-apparat.

Dampfsteuerrad, n., *steam steering wheel.*

Dampfsteuerung, f., *1. steering engine*; *2. s. by steam.*

Dampfstrahl, m., *steam jet*; - Apparat, m. *s. j. apparatus*; - Pumpe, f., *bilge injector*; - rohr, n., *steam jet*

tube; - Vorwärmer, m., *hydrokineter.*

Dampf-trawler, m., *steam trawler*; - trocknung, f., *drying of s.*; - trossenspill, n , *warping engine*; - turbine, f., *steam turbine*; - überspannung, f., *overpressure of s.*; - umsteuerungsmechanismus, m., *s. reversing gear*; - ventil, n., *s. valve*; - - sitz, m., *nozzle plate*; - verbrauch, m., *consumption of steam*; - verteiler, m., *s. distributor*; - verteilung, f., *distribution of s.*; - - rohr, n., *dristributing pipe*; - weg, m., *steam passage*; - widder, m., *s. ram.*

Dampfwinde, f., *steam winch*; - Absperrventil, n., *s. w. stop valve*; - anker, m., *s. w. stay*; - Anlaßventil, n., *s. w. starting valve*; - Außentrommel, f., *s. w. warping end*; - Bremse, f., *s. w. brake*; - - hebel, m., *s. w. b. lever*; - Dampf-abführungsrohr, n., *s. w. exhaust pipe*; - D-rohr or - D-zuführungsrohr, or D-zuleitungsrohr, n., *s. w. steam pipe*; - Drainagerohr, n., *s. w. drain pipe*; - Ein- und Ausrückhebel, m., *s. w. clutch lever*; - Entwässerungsrohr, n., *s. w. drain pipe*; - Exzenter, n., *s. w. eccentric*; - - bolzen, m., *s. w. e. bolt*; - - bügel, m., *s. w. e. strap*; - - - Futter or Paßstück, n., *s. w. e. s. liner*; - E.-Lagerschalen, *s. w. e. brasses*; - E-scheibe, f., *s. w. e. sheave*; - E.-stange, f., *s. w. e. rod*; - Exhaustrohr, n., *s. w. exhaust pipe*; - Fundamentsplatte, f., *s. w. bed plate*; - Gestell, n., *s. w. framing*; - Großes Stirnrad, n., *s. w. main spur wheel*; - Klauenhebel, m., *s. w. clutch lever*; - Kleines Stirnrad, n., *s. w. small spur wheel*; - Kolben, m., *s. w. piston*; - - stange, f., *s. w. p. rod*; - - - Kreuzkopf, m., *s. w. p. r. crosshead*; - - - Stopfbüchse, f., *s. w. p. r. stuffing box*; - - - - deckel, m., *s. w. p. r. s. b. gland*; - kopf, m., *s. w. warping end*; - Kreuzkopf, m., *s. w. crosshead*; - - Lagerbolzen, m., *s. w. top end bolt*; - - - mutter, f., *s. w. t. e. b. nut*; - Kreuzkopflagerschalen, *s. w. t. e. brasses*; - - deckel, m, *s. w. t. e. keep*; - Kuppelungsklaue, f., *s. w. clutch*; - Kurbelwelle, f., *s. w. crank shaft*; - - lager, n., *s. w. c. s. bearing*; - - - bolzen, m., *s. w. c. s. b. bolt*; - - - deckel, m., *s. w. c. s. bearing keep*; - - - - bolzen, m., *s. w. c. s. b. k. bolt*; - Kurbelwellenlagerschalen, *s. w. c. s. bearing brasses*; - - Futter or Paßstück, n., *s. w. c. s. b. liner*; - Kurbelzapfen, m., *s. w. crank pin*; - - lager, n., *s. w. connecting rod bottom end*; - - Lagerbolzen, m., *s. w. c. r. b. e. bolt*; - - - mutter, f., *s. w. c r. b. e. b. nut*; - Kurbelzapfenlagerschalen, *s. w. c. r. b. e. brasses*; - - deckel, m., *s. w. c. r. b. e. keep*; - Lagerdeckel, m., *s. w. bearing keep*; - Pleuelstange, f., *s. w. connecting rod*; - rohr, n., *s. w. pipe*; - - Schutzblech, n., *s. w. p. cover*; - schieber, m., *s. w. slide valve*; - - kasten, m., *s. w. v. casing*; - - - deckel, m., *s. w. v. c. door*; - Schieberstange, f., *s. w. v. rod*; - - Stopfbüchse, f., *s. w. v. r. stuffing box*; - - - deckel, m., *s. w. v. r. s. b. gland*; - Stehbolzen, m., *s. w. stay*; - Steuerungswelle, f., *s. w. weigh shaft*; - Stirnrad. n., *s. w. spur wheel*; - Stühle,

s. w. pipe stools; - Trommel, f., *s. w. barrel*; - - welle, f., *s. w. b. shaft*; - Überzug. m., *s. w. cover*; - Umsteuerungshebel, m., *s. w. reversing lever*; - Umsteuerungswelle, f., *s. w. weigh bar*; - welle, f., *s. w. engine shaft*; - Windeköpfe, *s. w. warping ends*; - Zahnkuppelung, f., *s. w. clutch*; - Zylinder, m., *s. w. cylinder*; - - deckel, m., *s. w. c. cover*; - - - bolzen, m., *s. w. c. c. bolt*.

Dampf-zapfen, m., *steam trunnion*; - zufuhrrohr, - zuführungsrohr, - zuleitungsrohr. n., *s. pipe*; - zylinder, m., *s. cylinder*.

Damm, m., *dam*.

Daniells Doppelhahn, m., *Daniell's stop cock*.

Daubenholz, n., *staves*.

Dauer, f., von kurzer -, *slatch (of a breeze)*; - proviant, m., *sea provisions*.

dauernde Kraft, f., *constant force*.

Daumkratt, f., *jack screw*.

David, Davit, m., *davit*; - Achterholer, m., *after guy of a d.*; - balken, m., *fish d.*; - geie, f., *d. guy*; - haken, m., *fish hook*; - halter, m., *d. collar*; - kran, m., *boat d.*; - - reeling, f., *d. rail*; - spur, f., *d. socket*; - stander, m., *d. topping lift*; - takel, n., - talje, f., *fish tackle*.

Davy, n., *davy*.

Dechsel, m., *adze*.

Deck, n., *deck*; das lose -, *the loose d.*; - abflußrohr, n., *waste d. pipe*; - aufbauten, *d. structures*; - balken, m., *d. beam*; - - knie, n., *arm beams*; - - Längsschiene, f., - - Lukenstringer, m., *deck beam tie plate*; - - Stringer, m., *d. b. stringer*; - - - platte, f., *d. b. s. plate*; - balkenstütze, f., *stanchion* of the beam; - b-Unter-schlag, m., central stringer; - b-U.-winkel, m., c. s. angle bar; - b-Unterzug, m., c. s.; - b-weger, m., deck beam shelf; - b-winkel, m., d. b. angle bar; - band, n., d. hook; - - bolzen, m., d. h. bolt; - bau, m., d. erection; - befestigung, f., d. fastening; - belag, m., d. flat; - beplankung, f., d. planking; - beplattung, f., d. plating; - besen, m., bear; - bolzen, m., deck bolt; - brett, n., covering board; - büchse für Backstaljenringe, f., box plate for training tackle bolts; - bugband, n., deck breast hook; - der Back, n., forecastle d.; - fenster, n., skylight; - bezug, m., s. cover; - - des Maschinenraums, engine room s.; - fläche des Schiebers, f., slide valve lap; - gebälk, n., deck framing; - gegenstände, d. stores; - glas, n., d. light; - haus, n., round house; - - fenster, n., deck h. window; - - süll, m., d. h. coaming; - - - winkel, m., d. h. c. angle bar; - installationen, d. fittings; - junge, m., d. boy; - klampen, arm cleats; - klüse, f., chain pipe; - ladung, - last, f., deck cargo; - - beherrschte das Deck, d. c. took full charge of the d.; - linie, f., d. line; - naht, f., d. seam; - niete, f., d. rivet; - passagier, m., d. passenger; - peilung, f., d. bearing; - persennige, d. tarpaulins; - pfropfen, m., d. dowel; - planke, f., d. plank; - platte, f., 1. d. plate (on deck); 2. rider p. (on frames); 3. keep (on brasses); - - der hinteren Rauchkammer, f., crown plate of combustion chamber; - salon, m., deck saloon; - schaden, m., d.

damage; - schrubber, m., d. scrubber; - schwabber, m., 1. swab (on mop); 2. main staysail; - - schote, f., s. sheet; - stopper, m., deck stopper; - stringer, m., d. stringer; - - platte, f., d. s. plate; - - winkel, m., d. s. angle bar; - stütze, f., d. pillar; - - mit Lippen, f., Samson post; - talje, f., d. tackle; - trockner, m., squillager; - Unterbalkweger, m., deck beam clamp; - verstützung, f., d. pillaring; - waschpumpe, f., d. wash pump; - waschschlauch, m., d. w. hose; - worp, n., d. transom; - wrange, f., d. transom.

Decke, f., 1. crown (of dome & tank); 2. top (of tank & tunnel); - der hinteren Rauchkammer, crown of combustion chamber.

Deckel, m., 1. cover (of cylinder); 2. door (of slide valve); 3. gland (of stuffing box); 4. keep (of bearings); 5. bush (as lining).

Deckelplatte des Kreuzkopflagers, f., top end keep; - des Kurbelzapfenlagers, bottom e. k.

Deckung eines Schiebers, f., lap of slide valve.

Deformierung, f., collapsing.

degradieren, disrate.

Dehnbarkeit, f., malleability.

Deich, m., embankment.

Deichsel, f., adze.

deinsen, to have sternway on.

Deklination, f., declination, variation; - karte, f, d. map; - kompaß, m., v. compass; - tabelle, f., table of the sun's d.

Delegation. f., allotment note.

demontieren, to open out, to strip.

Dempgording, f., brail; - block, m., b. block.

Deplacement, n., displacement; - berechnung, f., d. scale;

- Schwerpunkt, m., *centre of d.*; - Tonnen, *tons of d.*; - - gehalt, m., *d. tonnage*; - Überschuß, m., *reserve buoyancy.*
Depressionswinkel, m., *dip of the horizon.*
derde Hand, f., *watch tackle.*
Desaffourchage, f., *unmooring.*
Deutel, m., *treenail wedge.*
deutlich gemarkt, *ken speckled.*
Deviation, f., *deviation*; - beobachtung, f., *sight for d.*; - boje, f., *d. buoy.*
diagonal, *diagonal*; - gebaut, *d. built*; - anker, m., *d. stay*; - band, n, *d. tie plate*; - befestigung, f., *d. fastening*; - festigkeit, f., *d. strength*; - haut, f., *d. sheathing*; - knie, n., *d. knee*; - kraft, f., *resultant*; - linie eines Segels, f., *the line from clew to earing*; - planken, *diagonal planks*; - schiene, f.. *d. plate*; - spant, n., *d. frame*; - Spiekerhaut, f., *d. doubling*; - streber der Schlagbetten, m., *dagger piece*; oberster - - -, m., *dagger plank*; - verband, m., *diagonal system*; - verstärkung, f., *d. strengthening*; - Wegerung, f., *d. ceiling.*
diagonale Doppelhaut, f., *diagonal doubling*; - Platte, f., *diagonal plate*; - Spanten, *d. timbers*; - vom Schothorn zur Klau eines Gaffelsegels, f, *d. of a gaff sail*; - Zylinder, m.. *d. cylinder.*
Diagramm, n, *diagram.*
Diamant-knoten, m, *diamond knot*; - kopfbolzen, m., *square headed bolt*; - meißel, m.. *diamond pointed chisel*; - platte, f.. *d. plate.*
dicht, *tight*; - am Winde, *close hauled*; - anhalten, *to keep close to*; - beim Lande, *close to the land*; - gerefft, *close reefed*; - kalfatern, *to seal*; - machen, *1. to tighten*; *2. to close (a man-hole).*

Dichte, f., *density.*
Dichteisen, n., *caulking iron.*
dichten, *to tighten.*
dichter Mars, m., *close planked top.*
Dichtigkeit, f., *density (of steam).*
Dichtung, f., *1. joint (a junction)*; *2. packing (for tightening).*
Dichtungs-gummi, n., *rubber for packing*; - ring, m., *junk ring*; - winkel, m., *collar.*
Dick-dallen, *dolphins*; - zirkel, m., *callipers.*
Dicke, f.. *size (of chain cable)*; - Luft, f., *thick weather.*
dicker Kielgang, m.. *thick garboard strake*; - Nebel, m., *thick fog.*
dickes Wetter, n., *thick weather.*
Dienst, m., *duty*; - antreten, *to enter the service*; - frei, *off duty*; in - treten, *to enter the service*; - tuender Offizier, m., *officer on duty*; - vor dem Mast, *before the mast.*
Dies, m., *haze.*
diesig, *hazy.*
Differenzial Flaschenzug, m., *differential block*; - Manometer, n.. *d. manometer.*
Dingi, n., *dingy.*
dippen, *to dip (the flag).*
direkt wirkende Maschine, f., *direct acting engine*; - - vertikale Masch., *vertical d. a. e.*
direkte Wirkung, f., *direct acting.*
Dirk, m., *topping lift*; - block, m., *t. l. block*; - läufer, m., *derrick fall*; - talje, f., *t. l. purchase*; - taljenläufer, m., *t. l. p. fall.*
diskontinuierlich, *intermitting.*
Dispache, f., *average statement*; - einer Havarie grosse, *general a. s.*; - einer Havarie particulaire, *particular a. s.*

Dispacheur, m., *average ad-*dispachieren, *to adjust.*[*juster.*
Dispachierung, f., *adjustment.*
Dispositionsplan, m., *disposition plan.* [f., *d. freight.*
Distanz, f., *distance*; - fracht,
Dobelbohrer. m, *dowel borer.*
Docht, m., *wick*; - büchse, f., *lamp wick box*; - halter, m., - hülse, f., *wick holder.*
Dock, n., *dock*; - arbeiter, m , *docker*; - bänke, *d banks*; - behörde, f., *d. authorities*; - drempel, m., *d. sill*; - eingang, m., *d. entrance*; - geld, n., *d. dues*; - lotse, m., *d. pilot*; - meister, m., *d. master*; - ponton, m., *pontoon for careening ships*; - schleuse, f., *d. gate*; - sohle, f., *floor of a dock*; - stütze. f., *1. breast shore (if horizontal)*; *2. diagonal s. (if d.)*; *3. bilge s. (of bilge)*; - tor, n., *dock gate*; - winde, f., *d. block.*
Docke, f., *1. mandrel (of a lathe)*; *2. hank (of yarn).*
docken, *to dock*; das -, *docking.*
Dodshofd, n., *dead eyes.*
Doldrums, *doldrums.*
Dollbaum, m., *thole string.*
Dolle, f., *thole.*
Dollen-gatt, *or* - loch, n., *hole for a thole pin*; - platte, f., *thole plate*; - leiste, f., *thole stringer.*
Dom, m., *dome*; - decke, f., *crown of dome*; - hemd, n., *dome cover.*
dompen, *to martingale.*
Domper des Fischdavits, m., *fish martingale*; - kette, f., *crupper chain.*
Domptau, n., *lasher.*
Donkey, m., *1. hoist (on shore or river)*; *2. donkey (on board ship)*; - mann, m., *d. man.*
Doodshoofd, n., *heart*; - mit Einkerbungen für das Taljereep. *heart with scores for the laniard*; - mit glattem Gatt, *heart without scores.*
Dop der Kompaßnadel, m., *dab of a rhumb card.*

Doppelboden, m., *double bottom*; - mit Längsträgern auf gewöhnlichen Bodenwrangen, *double bottom on ordinary floors*; - nach dem Längsspanten- und Stützplatten - System, *cellular double bottom with continuous girders*; - nach dem Zellensystem, *cellular double bottom with continuous floors from centre girder to margin plate.*
Doppel-boot, n., *double boat*; - geschirr. n., *double gear*; - haken. m., *clip hook*; - haut, f., *doubling*; - hub, m., *up-and-down stroke*; - kausche, f., *double thimble*; - kessel, m., *double ended boiler*; - klinkerartiger Bau, m., *double klinker fashion*; - knie, n., *staple knee*; - leuchtfeuer. n.. *double light*; - Pfortenschieber, m., *double ported slide valve*; - Pfortenventil, n., *double ported valve*; - poller, m., *double bollard.*
Doppelschrauben-dampfer, m., *twin screw steamer*; - Salondampfer, m., *t. s. saloon steamer*; - Schleppdampfer, m., *t. s. tug*; - Schnelldampfer, m., *express t. s. steamer.*
Doppel-sitzventil, n., *double seat valve*; - spant, n., *double frame*; - splissung, f., *bight splice*; - steuerrad, n., *double steering wheel*; - stropp. m., *double strap*; mit - stropp versehen, *to double strap*; - Takelhaken, m., *match hook*; - T-eisen, n., *double T-iron*; - versicherung, f., *double insurance.*
Doppelung. f., *sheathing.*
Doppelwinkel-Kielschwein, n., *double angle bar keelson*; - Kimmkielschwein, n., *d. a. b. bilge keelson*; - Seitenkielschwein, n., *d. a. b. side keelson.*
doppelt einscheibige Talje, f., *gun tackle purchase*; - ge-

nietete Laschen od. Stoß-
bleche, *double riveted butt
straps*; - gerefft, *double
reefed*; - geschorenes Jollentau, n., *double whip*; - wirkend, *d. acting.*
Doppeltwirkende Luftpumpe,
f., *double acting air pump*;
- Maschine, f., *d. a. engine*;
- Pumpe, f., *d. a. pump*; -
Zirkulationspumpe, f., *d. a.
circulating pump.*
Doppelte Baggermaschine, f.,
double dredger; - Befestigung, f., *d. fastening*; -
Bodenwrangen, *long and
short armed floors*; - gekehrte
Winkel, *d. reversed angle
bars*; - Hahnepot, f., *d. crown
of a knot*; - Jolle, f., *d. whip*;
- Kurbel, f., *d. crank*; -
Marssegel, n., *d. topsails*, -
Naht, f., *flat seam*; - Nietung,
f., *d. riveting*; - Schrauben-
schneidekluppe, f., *screw
dies and stocks*; - Stoßplatte,
f., *d. butt strap*; - Stütze,
f., *split pillar*; - Winde, f.,
double purchase winch.
Doppelter Auflanger, m.,
double futtock; - Block, m.,
d. block; - Diamantknoten,
m., *d. diamond knot*; - Fallreepsknoten, m., *double wall
and crown knot*; - Flaggenstich, m., *d. bend*; - Hakenschlag, m., *d. black wall
hitch*; - Halbstich, m., *two
half hitches*; - Holländer,
m., *double black wall hitch*;
- Leibstich or - Pfahlstich,
m., *bowline upon the bight*;
- Schauermannsknoten, m.,
double wall knot; - Schotstich, m., *d. bend*; - Taljereepsknoten, m., *d. wall
knot*; - Wantknoten, m., *d.
shroud knot*; - Winkel, m., *d.
angle bar.*
Doppeltes Gangspill, n., *double
capstan*; - Jollentau, n., *d.
whip.*
Doppen, *round and hollow
cleats.*

Dorn, m., *drift.*
draggen, *to creep.*
Draht-bindsel, n., *seizing wire*;
- bürste, f., *wire brush*; -
liderung, f., *w. packing*; -
lose Telegraphie, f., *wireless
telegraphy*; - mantel, m., *wire
runner*; - netzwerk, n., *w.
netting*; - packung, f., *w.
packing*; - spiralfeder, f.,
spiral spring; - takelung,
f., *w. rigging*; - tau, n., *w.
rope*; - tauwinde, f., *w.
winch.*
Drahttauwinden-Bremse, f.,
wire reel brake; - Dreher,
m., *w. r. handle*; - Gestell,
n., *w. r. frame*; - Schwengel,
m., *w. r. handle.*
Draht-zange, f., *wire nippers*;
- ziehen, n., *w. drawing.*
Drainage-hahn, m., *drain
cock*; - hahnvorrichtung, f.,
d. c. gear; - rohr, n., *d. pipe*;
- - des Sicherheitsventils,
safety valve d. p.
draußen in See, *in the offing.*
Dreganker, Dregganker, m.,
grapnel.
dreggen, *to drag.*
Dreg-haken, m., *drag*; - tau,
n., *drag rope.*
Drehbank, f., *lathe*; - futter,
n., *chuck of a l.*; - gestell,
n., *l. frame*; - reitstock, m.,
popped head of a l.; - spindel, f., *spindle of a l.*
Dreh-baum, m., *crab bar*; -
bohrer, m., *drill*; - ewer,
m., *two mast barge*; - feuer,
n., *revolving light*; - knüppel,
m., *turning fid*; - ling, m.,
pinion; - rad, n., *turning
wheel.*
Drehreep, n., *tye*; - der Besahn Bramrahe, *jigger topgallant tye*; - der Besahn
Marsrahe, *j. topsail t.*; - der
Bramrahe, *topgallant t.*; -
der Großbramrahe, *main
t. t.*; - der Großmarsrahe,
m. topsail tye; - der Jigger-
Bramrahe, *jigger topgallant*

t.; - der Jigger Marsrahe, *j. topsail t.*; - der Kreuz-bramrahe, *mizen topgallant t.*; - der Kreuzmarsrahe, *m. topsail t.*; - der Mittelbram-rahe, *middle topgallant t.*; - der Mittelmarsrahe, *m. topsail t.*; - der Vorbram-rahe, *fore topgallant t.*; - der Vormarsrahe, *f. topsail t.*

Dreh-reepsblock, m., *tye block*; - reepsblock unter dem Stengentopp, m., *hanging block*; - reepsring, m., *sling hoop*; - schieber, m., *single ported slide valve*; - ventil, n., *turning valve.*

drehen, *to turn*; ein Tau zur vollen Härte -, *to give a full twisting to a rope.*

drehende Bewegung, f., *rotary motion.*

Dreher, m., *1. heaver; 2. rung (of steering wheel).*

dreht, der Wind - gegen die Sonne, *the wind keeps pace against the sun*; d. W. d. mit der S., *the wind is veering.*

Drehung, f., *rotation.*

Drehvorrichtung, f., *turning gear*; - Kabelaring, n., *turning gear messenger.*

Drehvorrichtungsmaschine, f., *turning engine*; - Absperr-ventil, n., *t. e. stop valve*; - Anlaßventil, n., *t. e. starting valve*; - Dampfab-führungsrohr, n., *t. e. exhaust pipe*; - Dampfzu-leitungsrohr, n., *t. e. steam pipe*; - Excenter, n., *t. e. eccentric*; - - bolzen, m., *t. e. e. bolt*; - - bügel, m., *t. e. e. strap*; - - - Paßstück, n., *t. e. e. s. liner*; - E.-lager-schalen, *t. e. e. brasses*; - E.-scheibe, f., *t. e. e. sheave*; - E.-stange, f., *t. e. e. rod*; - Kolben, m., *t. e. piston*; - - stange, f., *t. e. p. rod*; - - - Kreuzkopf, m., *t. e. p. r. crosshead*; - - - Stopf-

büchse, f., *t. e. p. r. stuffing box*; - - - - deckel, m., *t. e. p. r. s. b. gland*; - Kreuz-kopflagerbolzen, m., *t. e. crosshead bolt*; - Kreuzkopf-lagerschalen, *t. e. c. brasses*; - - deckel, m., *t. e. connecting rod top end keep*; - Kurbelwelle, f., *t. e. crank shaft*; - Kurbelwellenlager, n., *t. e. c. s. bearing*; - - bolzen, m., *t. e. c. s. b. bolt*; - - deckel, m., *t. e. c. s. bearing keep*; - - - bolzen, m., *t. e. c. s. b. k. bolt*; - Kurbelwellenlagerschalen, *t. e. c. s. bearing brasses*; - - Paßstück, n., *t. e. c. s. brasses liner*; - Kurbel-zapfenlagerbolzen, m., *t. e. crank pin bolt*; - Kurbel-zapfenlagerschalen, *t. e. c. p. brasses*; - - deckel, m., *t. e. connecting rod bottom end keep*; - Pleyelstange, f., *t. e. connecting rod*; - - bolzen, m., *t. e. c. r. bolt*; - - fuß-Paßstück, n., *t. e. c. r. bottom end liner*; - Schie-ber, m., *t. e. slide valve*; - - kasten, m., *t. e. valve casing*; - - - deckel, m., *t. e. v. c. door*; - Schieberstange, f., *t. e. valve rod*; - Stopf-büchse, f., *t. e. v. r. stuffing box*; - - - deckel, m., *t. e. v. r. s. b. gland*; - Zylinder, m., *t. e. cylinder*; - - deckel, m., *t. e. c. cover*; - - - bolzen, m., *t. e. c. c. bolt*; - Zylinder-Entwässerungsrohr, n., *t. e. cylinder drain pipe.*

Drehvorrichtungs - rad, n., *turning worm wheel*; - schnecke, f., *turning gear worm.*

Dreideckschiff, n., *three deck vessel.*

dreieckige Feile, f., *three sided file*; - Untersegel, *Bentincks.*

dreieckiges Segel, n., *triangular sail.*

Dreiecksblechanker, m., *gusset stay.*

dreifach genietete Laschen od. Stoßbleche, *triple riveted butt straps;* - gerefft, *triple reefed.*

dreifache Expansionsmaschine, f., *triple expansion engine;* - Nietung, f., *triple riveting.*

dreiflügelige Schraube, f., *three bladed propeller.*

Dreimast-Gaffelschoner, m., *three mast fore and aft schooner;* - Schoner or Toppsegelschoner, m., *three mast topsail schooner;* - Vor- und Hinter-Schoner, m., *three mast fore and aft schooner.*

Dreimaster, m., *1. three master; 2. cocked hat.*

Dreimeilengrenze, f., *three mile limit.*

dreischättiges Tau, n., *three stranded rope.*

dreischeibiger Block, m., *triple sheaved block.*

Dreiviertel Ebbe, f., *last quarter ebb.*

Dreiwegehahn, m., *three way cock.*

Dreizack, m., *trident.*

dreizackig, *three forked.*

Dreizylindrige Compoundmaschine, f., *three cylinder compound engine;* - Maschine, f., *three cylinder engine.*

Drempel, m., *sill.*

Drift, f., *drift;* - eis, n., *drift ice;* - strömung, f., *d. current;* - winkel, m., *d. angle.*

Drillbohrer, m., *drill.*

dritte Hand, f., *luff tackle.*

dritter Buganker, m., *third bower.*

drittes Reff, n., *third reef;* - Reffband, n., *t. r. band.*

Dromel, f., *thrum.*

Drossel-Expansionsventil, n., *throttle expansion valve;* - klappe, f., *t. valve;* - klappengestänge, n., *t. valve gear;* - - hebel, m., *t. v. lever;* - klappenspindel, f., *t. valve rod;* - ventil, n., *t. valve;* - ventil-Handhabe, f., *t. valve handle;* - ventilspindel, f., *t. valve spindle.*

drosseln, *to throttle.*

Drosselung, f., *throttling.*

Druck, m., *1. pressure (of steam); 2. thrust (of the shaft); 3. strain (on chain).*

Druck-Ansammlung, f., *accumulation of pressure;* - kraft, f., *compressive stress.*

Drucklager, n., *thrust bearing;* - Adjustiervorrichtung, f., *t. block adjusting gear;* - bolzenmutter, f., *thrust bearing bolt nut;* - deckel, m., *thrust block keep;* - deckelbolzen, m., *thrust block keep bolt;* - deckelbolzenmutter, f., *thrust block keep bolt nut;* - Kühlvorrichtung, f., *thrust water service;* - schuhe, *thrust shoes;* - stuhl, m., *thrust block;* - welle, f., *thrust shaft;* - wellenflansche, f., *thrust shaft flange;* - wellenringe, *thrust shaft collars.*

Druck-leitung, f., *delivery pipes;* - probe, f., *pressure test;* - pumpe, f., *force pump;* - raum, m., *delivery space;* - reduzierventil, n., *pressure reducing valve;* - reduzierventilgestänge, n., *regulating valve gear;* - reduzierventilspindel, f., *regulating valve spindle;* - reduzierventilstange, f., *regulating valve rod;* - ring, m., *1. guard ring (of piston); 2. thrust shaft collar (of propeller);* - rohr, n., *delivery pipe;* - rohrleitung, f., *delivery pipes;* - rohrschlauch, m., *delivery hose;* - scala, f., *scale of pressure;* - schraube, f., *set screw;* - steigerung, f., *increase of pressure;* - und Tunnelwellenleitung, f.,

18*

thrust and tunnel shafting; - ventil, n., top valve od. delivery valve; - ventilgehäuse, n., delivery valve chest; - ventil-Hubbegrenzer, m., delivery valve guard; - ventilkasten, m., delivery valve chest; - ventilklappenfänger, m., top valve guard; - ventilsitz, m., top valve seat; - verminderung, f., reduction of pressure; - zylinder-Liderungsring, m., pressure cylinder junk ring.

Drückeberger. m., skulker.

drückendes Wetter, n., sultry weather.

Drücker, m., supporter.

Drummel, f., thrum.

D-schieber, m., D-slide valve.

Dschunke, f., junk.

Dübel, m., dowel.

dübeln, doweling.

dublieren, to double (a cape).

Ducht, f., 1. strand (of a rope); 2. thwart (of a boat); 3. thwart (of a pontoon); - im Tau ist gebrochen, the rope is stranded.

Duchten, die - eines Taues drehen, to twist the strands of a rope; die - eines T. in die Schlagen eines anderen legen, to put the s. o. a r. into the lays of another; - knie, n., thwart clamp; - schloß, n., thwart chocks; - stütze, f., thwart stanchion; - wäger, m., t. stringer.

Dückdalben, dolphins.

Ducker, m., brad.

Düker, m., sprig.

Dülle, f., socket.

Dump, auf der - liegen, to lie balanced.

Dünen, downs.

Dungonholz, n., dungon.

Dunstkreis, m., atmosphere.

Dünung, f., swell; - von vorn, head swell.

Durchbefestigung, f., through fastening.

durch-blasen, to blow through.

Durchblas-hahn, m., blow through cock; - rohr, n., b. t. pipe; - ventil, n., b. t. valve.

durch-bogen, cambered; - bogener Kiel, m., cambered keel; - bolzen, m., through bolt; - bolzen in einem Stoß, through butt bolt; - bolzen und Holznägel, through fastenings; - brochenes Spant, n., lightened frame; - drehen durch den Wind, broaching; - drehen lassen, to let all sails come aback; - einanderbringen der Leitfeuer, to get the leading lights in a line: - fahrt, f., passage; - fracht or - gangsfracht, f., through rate; - gangs-Konnossement, n., through bill of lading; - gangszoll, m., transit duty; - gebogen, hogged; - gefallen, thorough put (said of a tack block); - gehen, coming home (of the anchor); - gehend von innen nach außen, in and out; - gehende Mittelkielplatte, f., centre through plate; - gehende Mittelkielschweinplatte, f., centre through plate keelson; - gehendes Konnossement, n., through bill of lading; - genähte Naht, f., monk seam; - gesackt, sagged; - geschossen, thorough put (said of a tack block); - laufende Bodenwrange, f., continuous floor; - löchert, holy; - messer, m., diameter; - sackmoment, n., sagging moment; - scheren, to reeve (rove, rove); - schlag, m., 1. punch (for making holes); 2. drift (for driving out bolts); - schlagen, racing (of engine); - schleusen, to pass through a lock; - schnitt, m., section: - schnittspunkt, m., point of intersection; - schnittsdruck, m., mean pressure; - schnittsgewicht, n., average weight;

- schnittslinie zwischen Gillung u. Heck, f., *margin between counter and stern*; - stoßen, *1. to punch*; *2. bumping (vessel)*; - suchungsrecht, n., *right of search*: - verbolzung, f., *through fastening*; - wandern, *to pass*.

Düse, f., *nozzle*.

düsig, *hazy*.

Dusse, f., *untarred oakum*.

Düwelshaken, m., *clip hook*.

D-ventil, n., *D-valve*.

dwars, *athwart*; - ab, *abeam*; - ab an Steuerbord, *on starboard*; - balken, m., *cross beam*; - feste, f., *breast rope*; - holz, n., *cross timber*; - latte, f., *cross pawl*; - leine, f., *cross line*; - liegen, *to lie across*; - nach Land zu treiben, *to drive bodily upon the coast*; - nach Lee zu abtreiben, *to drive bodily to leeward*; - naht, f., *butt seam*; - peilung, f., *cross bearing*.

Dwarssahling, f., *cross trees*; - der Bramstenge. *topgallant c. t.*; - der Großbramstenge, *main t. c. t.*; - der Groß-marsstenge, m. *topmast c. t.*; - der Jigger Bramstenge, *jigger topgallant c. t.*; - der Jigger Marsstenge, *j. topmast c. t.*; - der Kreuzbramstenge, *mizen topgallant c. t.*; - der Kreuzmarsstenge, m. *topmast c. t.*; - der Marsstenge, *t. c. t.*; - der Mittelbramstenge, *middle topgallant c. t.*; - der Mittelmarsstenge, m. *topmast c. t.*; - der Vorbramstenge, *fore topgallant c. t.*; - der Vormarsstenge, f. *topmast c. t.*

Dwars-schifts, *athwartships*; - schlagen. *broaching to*; - see, *athwart sea*; - see liegen, *to stand athwart the waves*; - strom, *athwart the stream*; - tau, n., *breast fast*: - wind, m., *wind on the beam*; - sich zum Winde halten, *to keep the broad side to the wind*.

Dweil, m., *mop*.

dynamische Leistung, f., *gross effect*.

Dynamo, m., *dynamo*; - meter, m., *dynamometer*; - metrisch, *dynamometrical*.

E.

Ebbe, f., *ebb*: - anker, m., *e. anchor*; - und Flut, *ebb and flood*; - strom, m., *ebb tide*.

ebben, *the tide is falling*.

ebbte, das Wasser - vom Schiffe weg, *the water left the ship*.

Ebene der Ladewasserlinie, f., *load water section*.

Ebenholz, n., *ebony*.

ebnen, *facing*.

Eck-anker, m., *gusset stay*; - pforte, f., *indented port*; die schräge - stütze, f., *gusset stay*.

Ecusson, m., *escutcheon*.

Effekt, m., *effect*.

effektive Kraft, f., *effective power*; - Pferdestärke, f., *e. horse power*.

Eibenbaumholz, n., *yew wood*.

eichen, *to gauge*.

Eichenholz, n., *oak*.

Eigenbewegung machen, f. *to make way of her own*.

eigene Hülfsmittel, *own resources*.

Eigen-gewicht, n., *dead weight*; - tümer, m., *owner*; - tumsrecht, n., *ownership*; - wärme, f., *specific heat*.

Eigner, m., *owner.*
Eiland, n., *island.*
einarmiger Anker, m., *one armed anchor.*
einbauen, neue Maschinen -, *to re-engine.*
Einbaum, m., *canoe, monoxyle.*
einbeulen, *to dint.*
Einbeulung, f., *denting, indentation.*
einbinden, *1. to secure (dead eyes); 2. to take in (a reef).*
einbooten, *to boat.*
einbrechen, *1. stave in (plates); 2. flat in (sails).*
Einbucht, Einbuchtung, f., *1. re-entering bend (of a river); 2. rounding-in (of spars & beams).*
Eindecker, m., *one deck vessel.*
Eindrückung, f., *collapsing.*
einfach wirkende Luftpumpe, f., *single acting air pump;* - - Maschine, f., *s. a. engine;* - - Pumpe, f., *s. a. pump;* - - Zirkulationspumpe, f., *s. a. circulating pump.*
einfache Baggermaschine, f., *single dredger;* - Befestigung, f., *s. fastening;* - Expansionsmaschine, f., *s. expansion engine;* - Havarie, f., *particular average;* - Nietung, f., *single riveting;* - Schraube, f., *s. thread screw;* - und doppelte Befestigung, f., *s. and double fastening.*
einfacher Bändsel, m., *temporary seizing;* - Block, m., *single block;* - Diamantknoten, m., *s. diamond knot;* - Fallreepsknoten, m., *s. wall and crown knot;* - Flaggenstich, m., *s. bend;* - Hakenschlag or - Holländer, m., *black wall hitch;* - Schauermannsknoten, m., *single wall knot;* - Schotstich, m., *common bend;* - Taljereepsknoten, m., *single wall knot;* - Wantknoten, m., *s. shroud knot;* - Winkelbalken, m., *s. angle beam.*

einfaches Bändsel, n., *temporary seizing;* - Gangspill, n., *single bodied capstan;* - Spant, n., *single frame.*
Einfahrt, f., *entrance.*
einfallen, stark von Steuerbord -, *to come suddenly strong from starboard.*
einfalzen, *to rabbet.*
einfieren, *to ease in.*
Einfuhr-dock, n., *import dock;* - waren, *imports;* - zoll, m., *import duty.*
einführen, den Topp der Stänge richtig zwischen die Schlinge -, *to point a topmast.*
Eingang, m., *entrance.*
Eingangs-hafen, m., *port of entry;* - zoll, m., *customs inwards.*
Eingeborener, m., *native.*
eingebrochen, eingedrückt, *stove in.*
eingefroren, *ice bound.*
eingehende Krümmung, f., *re-entering bend;* - Stromkrümmung, f., *re-entering sinuosity.*
eingeklemmt, *1. jammed; 2. nipped (by ice).*
eingeschlagen, *stove in.*
eingeschleppt, *towed in.*
eingeschlossen, *enclosed (space);* - vom Lande, *landlocked.*
eingeschoben, *intercostal.*
eingeschobene Bodenwrangenstücke, *intercostal floors;* - Kimmkielschweinplatte, f., *bilge i. keelson plate;* - Mittelkielschweinplatte, *middle line i. keelson plate;* - Platte, f., *i. plate;* - Seitenkielschweinplatte, f., *side i. keelson plate;* - Seitenstringerplatte, f., *side i. stringer plate.*
eingeschobenes Kielschwein, n, *intercostal keelson;* - Kimmkielschwein, f., *bilge i. k.;* - Mittelkielschwein, n., *middle line i. k.;* - Seitenkielschwein, n., *side i. k.*

eingestoßen, *stove in.*
eingetauchter Querriß des M.ttelspanten, m., *immersed midship section.*
eingezogene Bauchstücke, *rising floor timbers*; - Pforte, f., *indented port.*
eingreifen, *to gear together (cogged wheels).*
einhaken, *to hook.*
einhängen, *to ship.*
Einheit, f., *unit*; - der Arbeit or - der Leistung, *unit of work.*
einhieven, *1. to heave in; 2. to shorten in (the cable).*
einholen, *1. to haul in; 2. to rig in (a boom).*
Einholer, m., *inhaul*; - block, m., *i. block.*
Einholtalje, f., *train tackle.*
Einklarierung, f., *entry.*
einkluften, *to scarf up upon a stump.*
einkommen, *to enter.*
einkommende Fracht, f., *inward freight*; - Ladung, f., *i. cargo.*
einkreuzen, *to beat in.*
Einlagedichtung, f., *insertion cloth joint.*
Einlaß, m., - öffnung, f., *inlet*; - rohr, n., *i. pipe*; - ventil, n., *i. valve.*
einlassen, *to let down (a plate).*
einlaufen, *to put into port.*
einlaufendes Bugspriet, n., *running bowsprit.*
Einlauthafen, m., *port of entry.*
einlegen, *to unship (the oars)*; ein Tauende in eine Block- lippe -, *to snatch a rope.*
einlieken, *to rope (a sail).*
einlotsen, *to pilot in.*
einlullen, *to lull.*
einmal gerefft, *single reefed.*
einmannen, *to pass from man to man.*
einmausen, *to mouse (a hook).*
Einnahme laut Konnosse- ment, f., *intake as per bill of lading.*

einnehmen, *to take in (bunker coals, cargo, sails, &c.).*
Einplattenruder, n., *single plate rudder.*
einplattiges Kielschwein, n., *single plate keelson.*
einreffen, *to take in a reef.*
Einrichtung, f., *arrangement, accommodation, fittings.*
Einrichtungen für Passagiere, *accommodation for pas- sengers*; - - Zwischendecks- Passagiere, *steerage a.*
Einrichtungsgegenstände, *1. fittings; 2. furniture.*
einrücken, *to couple, to throw into gear.*
einrücken und ausrücken, *to couple and uncouple, to ship and unship.*
Ein- und Ausrückhebel, m., *clutch lever (of winch).*
Einsatz, m., *liner (of steam cylinder and pump chamber).*
Einsaugen, n., *suction.*
einschäkeln, *to shackle.*
einschalten, *to ship.*
einscheibiger Block, m., *single block.*
einscheren, *to reeve, rove, rove*; wieder -, *to rereeve.*
Einschiebebalken, m., *inter- costal beam.*
Einschiebsel, m., *intercostal.*
einschiffen, *to embark.*
Einschiffung, f., *embarcation.*
einschlagen, *to send in (a door, &c.).*
einschleifen, *to grind.*
einschleppen, *to tow in.*
einschneiden, *to engulf (a coast).*
Einschnitt, m., *1. groove; 2. stepping (in the keel).*
einschreiben für ein Trocken- dock, *to stem a vessel.*
einsegeln, *to enter.*
Einsegelungsmarken, *leading marks.*
einseitiger Aufsatzschlüssel, m.. *crow foot spanner.*
einsetzen, *to hoist in (a boat).*
Einsetzen der Flut, n., *the inset.*

einsetzende Strömung, f., *in-draught*.
Einspritz-handhabe, f., *injection handle*; - kondensator, m., *jet condenser*; - rohr, n., *jet injection pipe*; - strahl, m., *condensing jet*; - ung, f., *injection*; - ventil, n., *injection valve*; - vorrichtung, f., *injection gear*; - wasser, n., *waste water*.
einspünden, *to rabbet*.
einstecken, *to bend*; *to take in (a reef)*.
einsteuern, *to steer in for the river*.
Einströmen des Wassers, n., *inrush of water*.
Einströmung, f., *admission*.
Einströmungs-rohr, n., *inlet pipe*; - vorrichtung, f., *induction gear*.
eintauchen, *to dip*.
Eintauchung, f., *immersion*.
Eintauchungslinie, f., *floating line*.
eintörnen, *to turn in*.
eintreiben, *to drive*.
Eintreten der Flut, n., *the tide serves*.
Eintritt, m., *admission*.
Eintrittskanal, m.. *admission port*; - des Hochdruckzylinders, *high pressure cylinder a. p.*; - des Mitteldruckzylinders, *intermediate cylinder a. p.*; - des Niederdruckzylinders, *low pressure cylinder a. p.*; - des Schiebers, *slide valve a. p.*; - des Zylinders, *cylinder a p.*
Eintrittssteigerung, f., *initial pitch*.
Ein- und Ausrückhebel, m., *clutch lever*.
einwinden, *to heave*.
einzelne Kurbel, f., *single crank*.
Einzelschraubendampfer, m., *single screw steamer*.
einziehen, *1. to draw in*; *2. to rig in (a boom)*.

Eis-anker, m., *ice anchor*; - barre, f., *barrier of i.*; - berg, m., *i. berg*; - besetzter Hafen, m., *i. bound harbour*; - blink, m., *i. blink*; - brecher, m., *i. breaker*; - doppelung, f., *i. doubling*; - feld, n., *i. field*; - fender, m., *i. fender*; - flarde, f., *i. patch. i. isle*; - gang, m., *1. drifting of i.*; *2. ice lining (of bow)*; - hahn, m., *i. cock*; - haken, m., *i. claws*; - haut, f., *i. lining*; - höcker, m, *hummock of i.*; - kammer, f., *i. locker*; - karte, f., *i. chart*; - klausel. f., *i. clause*; - lotse, m., *i. master*; - maschine, f., *refrigerating machine*.
Eismaschinen - Absperrventil, n., *refrigerating machine stop valve*; - Anlaßventil, n., *r. m. starting valve*; - Dampfabführungsrohr, n., *r. m. exhaust pipe*; - Dampfzuleitungsrohr, n., *r. m. steam pipe*; - Exzenter, n., *r. m. eccentric*; - bolzen, m., *r. m. e. bolt*; - bügel, m., *r. m. e. strap*; - bügel-Paßstück, n., *r. m. e. s. liner*; - lagerschalen, *r. m. e. brasses*; - scheibe, f., *r. m. e. sheave*; - stange, f., *r. m. e. rod*; - kolben, m., *r. m. piston*; - stange, f., *r. m. p. rod*; - stangen-Kreuzkopf, m., *r. m. p. r. crosshead*; - stangen-Stopfbüchse, f., *r. m. p. r. stuffing box*; - Stopfbüchsendeckel, m., *r. m. p. r. s. b. gland*; - Kreuzkopf-Lagerbolzen, m., *r. m. crosshead bolt*; - Lagerschalen, *r. m. c. brasses*; - deckel, m., *r. m. connecting rod top end keep*; - Kurbelwelle, f., *r. m. crank shaft*; - Kurbelwellenlager, n.. *r. m. c. s. bearing*; - bolzen, m., *r. m. c. s. b. bolt*; - deckel, m., *r. m. c. s. bearing keep*; - deckelbolzen, m., *r. m.*

c. s. bearing keep bolt; - - schalen, *r. m. c. s. bearing brasses*; - - schalen-Paßstück, n., *r. m. c. s. brasses liner*; - Kurbelzapfenlagerbolzen, m., *r. m. crank pin bolt*; - Kurbelzapfenlagerschalen, *r. m. c. p. brasses*; - - deckel, m., *r. m. connecting rod bottom end keep*; - Pleyelstange, f., *r. m. connecting rod*; - - bolzen, m., *r. m. c. r. bolt*; - - fuß-Paßstück, n., *r. m. c. r. bottom end liner*; - Schieber, m., *r. m. slide valve*; - - kasten, m., *r. m. valve casing*; - - - deckel, m., *r. m. v. c. door*; - Schieberstange, f., *r. m. v. rod*; - Schieberstangen-Stopfbüchse, f., *r. m. v. r. stuffing box*; - - - deckel, m., *r. m. v. r. s. b. gland*; - Zylinder, m., *r. m. cylinder*; - - deckel, m., *r. m. c. cover*; - - bolzen, m., *r. m. cylinder bolt*; - - Entwässerungsrohr, n., *r. m. c. drain pipe*.

Eis-meer, n., *ice sea*; - raum, m., *i. room*; - region, f., *i. region*; - scholle, f., *i. floe*; - schutz, m., *bow grace*; - verstärkung, f., *i. doubling*; - wand, f., *barrier of i.*; - zange, f., *i. claws*.

Eisenbahn-fähre, f., *railway ferry*; - Liegeplatz, m., *r. berth*.

Eisen-ballast, m., *iron ballast*; - Befestigung, f., *iron fastening*; - beschlagen, *i. bound*; - block, m., *i. block*; - draht, m., *i. wire*; - drahttakelung, f., *i. wire rigging*; - fassonguß or - formguß, m., *i. casting*; - gestroppter Block, m., *i. strapped block*; - gießerei, f., *i. foundry*; - haken, m., *back hook*; - holz, n., *i. bark*; - hütte, f., *i. works*; - kitt, m., *rust putty*; - krank, *i. sick*; - mast, m.,

i. mast; - platte, f., *sheet of i.*; - stropp, m., *i. strap*; - verbolzung, f., *i. fastening*; - werk, n., *i. works*.

eiserne Klammer, f., *iron dog*; - Klampe auf der Spillfütterung, f., *i. whelp on windlass wood lining*; - Rahe. f., *i. yard*; - Reling, f., *i. rail*.

eiserner Block, m., *iron block*; - Bolzen, m., *i. bolt*; - Hammer, m., *i. hammer*; - Keil, m., *i. wedge*; - Kessel, m., *i. boiler*; - Kolben, m., *i. piston*; - Mast, m., *i. mast*.

eisernes Band, n., *iron hoop*; - Bugband, n., *i. hook*; - Boot, n., *i. boat*; - Deck, n., *i. deck*; - Knie, n., *i. knee*; - Rohr, n., *i. tube*; - Schanzkleid. n., *topside plating*; - Schiff, n., *i. vessel*; - Spant, n., *i. frame*.

Ejektor, m., *ejector*; - rohr, n., *e. pipe*.

Elastizität, f., *elasticity*.

Elektriker, m., *electrical engineer*.

elektrische Anlage, or - Einrichtung, f., *electric installation*; - Lichtmaschine, f., *e. light engine*.

elektrischer Strom, m., *electric current*.

elektrisches Kabel, n., *electric cable*.

Elektrischlichtmaschine, f., *electric light engine*; - Absperrventil, n., *e. l. e. stop valve*; - Anlaßventil, n., *e. l. e. starting valve*; - Dampfabführungsrohr, n., *e. l. e. exhaust pipe*; - Dampfzuleitungsrohr, n., *e. l. e. steam pipe*; - Exzenter, n., *e. l. e. eccentric*; - - bolzen, m., *e. l. e. e. bolt*; - - bügel, m., *e. l. e. e. strap*; - - - Paßstück, n., *e. l. e. e. s. liner*; - E.-Lagerschalen, *e. l. e. e. brasses*; - E.-scheibe, f., *e. l. e. e. sheave*; - E.-stange, f., *e. l. e. e. rod*; - Kolben, m., *e. l. e. piston*; - - stange, f., *e. l. e. p. rod*; - - - Kreuzkopf, m., *e. l. e. p. r. crosshead*; - - - Stopfbüchse, f., *e. l. e. p. r. stuffing box*; - - - - deckel, m., *e. l. e. p. r. s. b. gland*; - Kreuzkopflagerbolzen, m., *e. l. e. crosshead bolt*; - Kreuzkopflagerschalendeckel, m., *e. l. e. connecting rod top end keep*; - Kurbelwelle, f., *e. l. e. crank shaft*; - - lager, n., *e. l. e. c. s. bearing*; - - - bolzen, m., *e. l. e. c. s. b. bolt*; - - - deckelbolzen, m., *e. l. e. c. s. b. keep bolt*; - - - schalen, *e. l. e. c. s. bearing brasses*; - - - - Paßstück, n., *e. l. e. c. s. brasses liner*; - Kurbelzapfenlagerbolzen, m., *e. l. e. crank pin bolt*; - Kurbelzapfenlagerschalen, *e. l. e. c. p. brasses*; - - deckel, m., *e. l. e. connecting rod bottom end keep*; - Pleyelstange, f., *e. l. e. connecting rod*; - - bolzen, m., *e. l. e. c. r. bolt*; - - fuß-Paßstück, n., *e. l. e. c. r. bottom end liner*; - Schieber, m., *e. l. e. slide valve*; - - kasten, m., *e. l. e. valve casing*; - - - deckel, m., *e. l. e. v. c. door*; - Schieberstange, f., *e. l. e. valve rod*; - - Stopfbüchse, f., *e. l. e. v. r. stuffing box*; - - - deckel, m., *e. l. e. v. r. s. b. gland*; - Zylinder, m., *e. l. e. cylinder*; - - deckel, m., *e. l. e. c. cover*; - - - bolzen, m., *e. l. e. c. c. bolt*; - Z.-Entwässerungsrohr, n., *e. l. e. cylinder drain pipe*.

Elektromotor, m., *electromotor*.

Elektrotechnik, f., *electrical engineering*.

Elektrotechniker, m., *electrical engineer*.

Elevator, m., *elevator*.

Elger, m., *fish gig*.

Ellbogen in den Ketten, m., *elbow in the hawse*.

Ellbogen-hahn, m., *elbow cock*; - rohr, n., *e. pipe*.

Elliotauge, n., *Elliot's eye*.

elliptisch geformtes Heck, n., *elliptical stern*.

elliptischer Kessel, m., *elliptical boiler*.

Elmsfeuer, n., *Jack with a lantern*.

Embargo, m., *embargo*; - aufheben, *to take off an e.*

Empfänger, m., *receiver*.

Empfangsschein, m., *receipt*.

empfindlich, *tender (said of compass)*.

empfundene Wärme, f., *sensible heat*.

Ende eines Taues, n., *rope's end*; das obere und untere Ende eines Auflangers, *head and heel of a timber*.

Enden der Deckplanken, *deck ends*.

End-druck, m., *terminal pressure*; - ring, m., *ferrule*; - weise gestaute Fässer, *chine and chine stowed casks*; - zapfen, m., *end journal*.

Enge, f., *narrows*.

enges Fahrwasser, n., *narrow channel*.

englische Matte, f., *paunch mat*.

englischer Fallreepsknoten, m., *double diamond knot*; - Kanal, m., *English Channel*; - Schraubenschlüssel, m., *universal screw wrench*; - Wandknoten, m., *double shroud knot*.

entblößen, *to strip*.

enter auf! *way aloft!*

Enter-haken werfen or mit - haken festhalten, *to grapple*; - netz, n., *boarding netting*; - pieke, f., *half pike*.

entern (in das Takelwerk), *to go aloft*.

entfalten, *to display*.

entfernt, *distant*.

Entfernung, f., *1. distance*; *2. pitch (between two centres)*.

entgegenkommender Dampfer, m., *the steamer meeting us ends on.*

entgehen einer Gefahr, *to escape a danger.*

entkommen mit knapper Not, *to have a narrow escape.*

entkuppeln, *to disconnect.*

Entkuppelung, f., *disconnecting.*

Entkuppelungsvorrichtung, f., *disconnecting gear.*

entlang, *along*; - fahren, - laufen, *to run down (a coast).*

entlassen, *to discharge.*

Entlassung, f., E.-zeugnis, n., *discharge.*

entlasteter Dampfverteilungsschieber, m., *balanced slide valve*; - Kolbenschieber, m., *balanced piston valve.*

entlastetes Ventil, n., *balance valve.*

Entlastungs-hahn, m., *relief cock*; - rahmen, m., *relief frame*; - schieber, m., *balanced slide valve*; - ventil, n., *balance valve.*

entlöschen, *to discharge.*

Entlöschung, f., *discharge*; E.-skosten, *discharging expenses.*

entmastet, *dismasted.*

Entrepotdock. n., *bond dock.*

Entschädigungsklub, m., *indemnity club.*

entscheiden, *to arbitrate.*

Entstellung, f., *deformation.*

entstützen, *unshoring.*

Entwässerungshahn, m., *drain cock.*

Entwässerungsrohr, n., *drain pipe*; - des Sicherheitsventils, *safety valve drain pipe*; - des Zylinders, *cylinder d. p.*

Entweichung, f., *escape.*

Entwertung, f., *depreciation.*

Entwurf, m., *projected plan.*

Entziehung des Patents, f., *suspension of certificate.*

entzündbar, *inflammable.*

Ephemeriden, *ephemeris.*

Erbauer, m., *constructer.*

Erd-gürtel, m., *zone*; - pech, n., *asphalt.*

erfassen, *to catch.*

Erfolg, ohne - keine Zahlung, m., *no cure, no pay.*

erforderlicher Druck, m., *required pressure.*

Ergänzung, f, *supply.*

ergründlich, *fathomable.*

erhalten, *to preserve.*

Erhaltung, f., *preservation.*

erheben, *to rise.*

Erhebung, f., *loom (magnified appearance of distant objects).*

erhitzen, *to fire.*

erhitzt, *heated.*

Erhitzung, f., *heat (by friction).*

erhöhen, *to raise.*

erhöhte Temperatur, f., *increased temperature.*

erhöhtes Deck, n., *raised deck*; - Quarterdeck, *r. quarter deck*; - Quarterdeckgeländer, n., *r. q. d. rails and stanchions*; - Vorderdeck, n., *r. fore deck.*

Erhöhungswinkel, m., *steeve (of bowsprit).*

erkennen, *to make out.*

Erlaubnis zur Entlöschung, f., *discharging permit*; - schein, m., *permit.*

erleichtern, *to ease.*

Erleichterungslöcher, *manholes.*

Erneuern der Maschine, n., *to re-engine*; - der Zwingen, *to re-ferrule.*

erniedrigte Temperatur, f., *reduced temperature.*

erreichbarer Hafen, m., *approachable port.*

erreichen, *to fetch (a port).*

erreichte Breite, f., *latitude arrived at*; - Länge, f., *longitude a. a.*

Ersatzgegenstände, *spare gear.*

erschüttern, *to shake.*

Erschütterung, f., *concussion.*
ersetzen, *to make good.*
ersoffen, *submerged.*
erspähen, *to descry (land).*
erste Ebbe, f., *the beginning of the ebb*; - Wache, f., *first watch.*
Erstlingsreise, f., *maiden trip.*
erstrecken nach Süden, *trending away to the south-ward.*
Esbuchtung, f., *S-rounding.*
Eschenholz, n., *ash wood.*
Eselshaupt, n., *cap*; - der Marsstenge, *topmast c.*; - der Pardune, *c. backstay*; - des Untermastes, *lower mast c.*; - stütze, f., *c. shore.*
Etmal, n., *day's work.*
Eule fangen, *broaching to.*
Evaporator, m., *evaporator*; - deckel, m., *e. door*; - Gleichgewichtsventil, n., *e. equilibrium valve*; - Manometer, n., *e. pressure gauge*; - Probierhahn, m., *e. gauge cock*; - Schaumhahn, m., *e. brine cock*; - schlangen, *e. coils*; - schwimmer, m., *e. float*; - Sicherheitsventil-belastung, f., *e. escape valve load*; - Vacuummeter, m., *e. vacuum gauge*; - Wasser-standsglas, n., *e. gauge glass.*
Evolutionen unter Segel, *sailing evolutions.*
Ewer, m., *barge*; - führer, m, *b. master*; - knecht, m., *b. man*; - - lohn, m., *scullerage*; - haken, m., *barge hook.*
Excenter *see* Exzenter.
Exerciermast, m., *drill mast.*
Exerzierschiff, n., *drill ship.*
Exhaust-rohr, n., *1. eduction pipe*; *2. exhaust pipe (of winch)*; - zapfen, m., *exhaust trunnion.*
expandierender Dampf, m., *expansion steam.*
Expansion, f., *expansion.*
Expansions-dichtung, f., *expansion joint (see also -verdichtung)*; - exzenter,

n., *e. eccentric*; - kraft, f., *expansive power*; - luken or - lukendeckel, *expansion hatches*; - maschine, f., *e. engine*; - ring, m., *e. ring*; - rohrverbindung, f., *e. joint*; - schieber, m., *e. slide valve*; - - gestänge, n., *e. valve gear*; - - kolben, m., *e. valve piston*; - - stange, f., *e. v. rod*; - - - führung, f., *e. v. spindle guide*; - tanks, *e. tanks*; - ventil, n., *e. valve.*
Expansionsverdichtung, f., *expansion joint*; - rohr, n., *e. j. pipe*; - Sicherungsring, m., *e. j. safety collar*; - Sicherungsstift, m., *e. j. s. stud*; - Stopfbüchse, f., *e. j. stuffing box*; - - deckel, m., *e. j. s. b. gland*; - - stift, m., *e. j. s. b. stud.*
Expansionsvorrichtung, f., *expansion gear.*
Expansiv-dampf, m., *expansive steam*; - kraft, f., *e. force.*
Expedition, f., *1. dispatch (of vessels)*; *2. expedition (of discovery)*; *3. office.*
Expert, m., *expert* or *surveyor*; - für Versicherer, *underwriter s.*
explodierbar, *explosive*; nicht -, *inexplosive.*
explodieren, *to explode.*
Explosion, f., *explosion.*
Exporteur, m., *exporter.*
extra Liegetage, *demurrage.*
Extractor, m., *extractor.*
Exzenter, n., *eccentric*; - auge, n., *e. gab*; - Begrenzungs-knagge, f., *e. catch*; - bolzen, m., *e. bolt*; - - mutter, f., *e. b. nut*; - bügel, m., *e. strap*; - - bolzen, m., *e. s. bolt*; - - - mutter, f., *e. s. b. nut*; - Bügel-Paßstück, n., *e. s. liner*; - feder, f., *e. sheave feather*; - hub, m., *throw of the e.*; - keil, m., *e. key*; - - nute, f., *e. k. way*; - knagge, f., *e. catch*; - lagerschalen, *e. brasses*; - radius, m., *e.*

radius; - regulator, m., *e.*
governor; - ring, **m.**, *e.*
strap; - scheibe, f., *e. sheave*;
- - Druckschraube, f., *e. s.*
set screw; - - feder, f., *e. s.*
feather; - - Keilnute, f., *e.*
s. key way; - stange, f., *e.*
rod; - - auge, n., *e. r. gab*;
- - Ausrückung, f., *e. r.*

disengaging gear; - - gabel,
f., *e. r. fork*; - transmission,
f., *e. r. gear*; - vorrichtung,
f., *e. gear*; - weg, m., *e.*
throw; - welle, *e. shaft*; - -
lager, n., *e. s. bearing.*
Exzentrik *see* Exzenter.
exzentrische Bewegung, f.,
eccentric motion.

F.

Fach, n., *1. chamber (of tank)*;
2. panel (inserted board).
Fächerplatte, f., *gusset plate.*
Façon, f., façonnieren, *shape.*
Faden, m., fadmen, *fathom.*
fahrbar, *navigable.*
Fähre, f., *1. ferry*; *2. f. boat.*
fahren, *1. to lead (rigging)*;
2. to run (rope's end); *3. to*
sail (at sea); *4. to navigate*
(a ship); *5. to carry (sails)*;
6. to fly (a flag); zwischen
zwei Halsen - or mit offenen
H. -, *to coast*; mit drei
Strich in den Segeln -, *to*
sail with three points free.
Fahrensleute, *sea faring*
people.
Fahrensmann, m., *sea far-*
ing man.
Fahr-geld, n., *passage money*;
- kran, m., *portable crane*;
- loch, n., *man hole*; - plan,
m., *sailing list*; - rinne, f.,
1. channel (in river); *2. gat*
(between banks); - schein,
m., *ticket*; - stuhl, m., *lift*;
- wasser, n., *channel od.*
fairway; das - - abbaken,
to mark the channel by
beacons; - - boje, f., *fair-*
way buoy; das - - quer blok-
kieren, *to bridge the chan-*
nel; - - tiefe, f., *depth of*
water in the channel; - -
tonne, f., *leading buoy*; - -
zeichen, n., *channel marks*;
- zeug, n., *craft.*

fährt, das laufende Tauwerk
- gut, *the running rigging*
leads fair; das Schiff -
zwischen Goole und Ham-
burg, *the vessel runs between*
G. & H.
Fahrt, f., *1. speed (knots per*
hour); *2. way (progress*
through the water); *3. trip*
(short voyage); - achteraus,*to*
make sternway; - behalten,
to hold her way; aus der -
bringen, *to deaden her way*;
a. d. - kommen, *to lose way*;
in - kommen, *to gather up*
way; wieder in gute - kommen, *t. g. up fresh way*;
gute - haben, *to have fresh*
way through the water; -
machen, *to make headway*;
noch - voraus haben, *to*
have still headway on; in -,
under way; - stoppen, *to*
stop her way; - über den
Grund, *to make headway*
over the ground; - über
Steuer, *to make sternway*;
- verlieren, *to lose way*;
- voraus, *headway*; - - über
den Grund, *headway over*
the ground.
Fahrt-geschwindigkeit, f.,
speed; - - ändern, *to alter*
the s.; - - vermindern, *to*
slacken speed; - kontrollventil, n., *s. controlling*
valve.
Fall, m., *1. halliard (rope for*

hoisting); *2. halliard (purchase (tackle)*; *3. jeer (of lower yard)*; *4. haunch (of deck)*; *5. rake (of stem or sternpost)*; *6. rake (inclination of mast)*.
Fall-block, m., *halliard block*; - horn, n., *head of triangular sail*; - knüppel, m., *head stick*; - lappen, m., *head piece*; - netz des Klüverbaums, n., *jib netting*; - reep, n., *gangway*; - - gast, m., *side boy*; - - klampe, f., *gangway cleat*; - - knoten, m., *diamond knot*; - - leiter, f., *gangway ladder*; - - pforte, f., *gangway*; - - reling, f., *g. rail*; - - ständer, m., *side rope stanchion*; - - taue, *man ropes*; - - treppe, f., *accommodation ladder*; - ring, m., *sling hoop*; - stich, m., *fisherman's bend*; - Taljeläuter, m., *halliard purchase fall*; - wind, m., *gust of wind.*
fallen, *1. to drop (the anchor, &c.)*; *2. to fall aboard (of another vessel)*; *3. casting (falling off from the wind)*; *4. to hang (the mast)*; *5. falling (of barometer, tide water)*.
fallen lassen! *down!* fallen Fock! *down foresail!*
fallende Frachten, *declining freights*; - Tide, f., *falling tide.*
Fallwind. m., *eddy wind.*
falsche Tasche, f., *quarter badge.*
falscher Stich, m., *marling spike hitch.*
Falz, m., *rabbet.*
Familienzahlung, f., *allotment note.*
Fanal. n., *1. light*; *2. l. house*; - teuer. n., *l. h. fire.*
Fang-leine, f, *boat painter;* - - bolzen, m., *ring bolt for painter*; - reise, *catch*; - tau eines Steuerrades, n., *twiddling line.*

fangen, *1. to sling (a yard)*; *2. to hitch (the anchor buoy).*
Farbe, f., *paint*; - gang, m., *sheerstrake*; - - platte, f., *s. plate*; - pinsel or quast, m., *paint brush*; - schrubber, m., *p. scrubber.*
Farben-anstrich, m., *coat of paint*; - Kammertür, f., *p. locker door*; - lage, f., *coat of paint;* - öl, n., *p. oil*; - spind, n., *paint locker*; - - tür, f., *p. l. door*; - topf, m., *p. pot.*
Fase, f., *chamfered edge.*
Faß, ein - mit Kuntjes festlegen, *to chock a cask.*
Faßfloß, n., *raft of casks*;
Faßwindehaken, m., *can hook.*
Fasson, f, fassonnieren, *shape.*
Fasttag, m., *banian day.*
faule Küste, f., *foul shore.*
Fauten, *cunt lines (of a rope).*
Fautfracht, f., *dead freight.*
Feder, f., *spring*; - des Kolbenrings, *piston ring.*
Feder-belastung, f., *spring load*; - block, m., *s. block*; - bolzen, m., *hold fast*; - haken, m., *sister hook*; - stoßkissen, n., *spring buffer*; - stütze, f., *spring stay*; - ventil, n., *s. valve*; - vorstecker, m., *s. forelock*; - wage, f., *s. balance*; - wolken, *feather clouds.*
Federn der Fingerlinge, *pintle straps.*
Feeder, m., *feeder.*
fehl treten, *to miss one's footing.*
Fehler, m., *1. defect (of material, &c.) 2. error (calculation, &c.).*
fehlerhafte Konstruktion, f, *defective construction.*
fehlerhafter Kompaß, m., *defective compass.*
Feier-abend machen, *to knock off;* - tagsausflug, m., *holiday trip.*
Feil-bank, f., *vice bench*; -

kloben. or - kolben, m., hand vice; - spähne, *filings.*
Feile, f., *file.*
Feilenbürste, f., *file brush.*
Feineisen, n.. *refined iron.*
Fels-gestade, n., *cliff*; - spitze, f., *knag.*
Felsen-riff, m., *ledge of rocks*; - spitzen, *needles.*
felsiger Grund, m., *rocky bottom.*
Felucke or Feluke, f., *felucca.*
Fender, m., *fender*; - tau, n., *swifter.*
Fenster, n., *window*; - brett, n., *w. sill*; - gräting, f., *w. grating*; - loch, n., *scuttle*; - rahmen, m., *scuttle frame*; - scheibe, f., *pane*; - schwelle, f., *window sill*; - vorhang, m., *window curtain.*
Fernrohr, n., *spy-glass.*
Festblock, m., *standing block.*
feste Back, f., *topgallant forecastle*; - Expansion, f., *fixed expansion*: - Wegerung, f, *close ceiling.*
fester Block, m., *standing block*; - Schraubenflügel, m., *fixed propeller blade*; - Sektor, m., *fixed sector.*
festes Bugspriet, n., *standing bowsprit*; - Eis, n., *fast ice*; - Feuer, n., *fixed light*; - Licht, n., *shore light.*
festgeraakt, *fast aground.*
festgeraten, *to get aground.*
festhalten, *to hold on (a rope).*
Festigkeit, f., *strength.*
festkeilen. *to wedge.*
festkommen, *to run aground.*
Festland, n.. *1. main land, 2. continent.*
festlegen mit Kuntjes, *to chock.*
festmachen, *1. to hand (a sail); 2. to stow (the anchors); 3. to make fast (a ship).*
Festmachtau, n., *bow fast.*
festsitzen, *to be fast aground*; Signal beim -, *grounding signal.*
feststecken, *to hitch (a rope).*

feststehende Pumpe, f., *fixed pump*; - Radschaufel, f., *radial float.*
feststellen, *to ascertain.*
Fett, n., *grease*; - Backje des Kalfaterers, f., *caulker's grease box*: - faß, n., *slush barrel*; - gefäß, n., s. *bucket*; - horn, n., s. *horn*; - pütze, f., *slush bucket*; - schmiere, f., *slush.*
feuchter Dampf, m., *wet steam.*
feuchtes Wetter, n., *damp weather.*
Feudel, m., *clout.*
Feuer, n., *1. fire; 2. light*; - anzünden, *to light the fire*; - aufbänken, *to bank the f.*; - auslöschen or ausziehen, *to draw the f.*
Feuer-brücke, f., *furnace bridge*; - buch, n., *light house book*; - büchse, f., *f. flue*; - - decke f., or deckel, m., *furnace crown*; - - gase, f., *f. gases*; - drill, m., *fire drill*; - eimer, m., *fire bucket*; - fest, *fire proof*; - fester Stein, m., *fire brick*; - - Ton, m., *f. clay*; - geld, n., *light dues*; - haken, m., *fire picker*; - harke, f., *f. rake.*
Feuerkammer, f., *combustion chamber*; - decke, f., *crown of c. c.*; - - träger, *dog on crown of c. c.*; - Deckplatte, f., *crown plate of c. c.*; - Stehbolzen, m., *combustion chamber stay*; - - mutter, f., *c. c. s. nut*; - tür, f., *c. c. door.*
Feuer-kasten, m., - kiste, f., *1. see - büchse; 2. powder chest*; - korb, m., *beacon grate*; - krücke, f., *fire rake*; - lärm schlagen, *to beat the fire roll*: - linie, f., *line of fire*; - löschapparat, m., *fire extinguisher*; - löschen, *to quench the fire*; - raum, m., *fire box*; - rohr, n., *f. tube*; - - bürste, f.,

boiler tube brush; - - kessel, m., fire tube boiler; - - reiniger, m., flue cleaner; - - ring, m., boiler tube ferrule; - rolle, f., fire bill; - schaufel, f., firing shovel; - schiff, n., light vessel; - schirm, m., fire screen; - sichtig, clear; gut - -, lights visible in full range; - spieß, m., fire slice; - spritze, f., fire engine (see also Dampf-feuerspritze); - spritzenboot, n., fire boat; - spritzen-schlauch, m., fire hose; - station, f. station; - tür, f., furnace door; - - klinke, f., f. d. latch; - turm, m., light house; - türzarge, f., furnace front; - warte, f., beacon light house; - werker, m., gunner; - - maat, m., gunner's mate; - zange, f., tongs; - zarge, f., furnace front; - zug, m., flue.

Feuerung, f., firing.

Feuerungs-decke, f., fire place top; - raum, m., boiler furnace.

Feul, m., mop.

Fichtenholz, n., fir wood.

Fid, m., fid.

Fidley, f., fidley.

fieren, 1. to slack (a rope); langsam -, to slack handsomely; 2. to lower (a yard, barrel, &c.); 3. to flow (a stay sail sheet, &c.); - und holen, to veer and haul.

Fingerling, m., 1. pintle (of rudder); 2 tumbler (of cat head stopper); - bolzen, m., rudder pintle bolt; - feder, f., r. p. strap.

Finknetz, n., hammock nettings; - der Hütte, quarter n.; - des Mars, top n.; - kleid, n., hammock cloth; - reling, f., topgallant rail; - stütze, f., stanchion of the nettings.

Finsternis, f., eclipse.

Firnis, m., varnish.

Fisch des Decks, m., binding strake of the deck; - - Vor-derstevens, apron of the stem; - für die Pumpen, pump carlines.

Fisch-aufgeber, m., fish back; - block, m., f. tackle block; - dampfer, m., fishing steamer; - davit, m., fish davit; - - spur, f., f. d. socket; - dreg, m., f. drag; - gienläufer, m., f. tackle fall; - haken, m., f. hook; - kran, m., f. davit; - meister, m., master of fishery; - netz, n., fishing net; - reep, n., fish pendant; - schäkel, m., f. shackle; - - bolzen, m., f. s. bolt; - schwanzschraube, f., f. tail propeller; - segler, m., sailing trawler; - tag, m., banian day; - takel, n., f. tackle; - - block, m., f. t. block; - - hanger, m., f. t. pendant; - - läufer, m., f. t. fall.

fischen, 1. to fish (an anchor or mast); 2. to drag (for an anchor).

Fischer-boot, n., fishing vessel; - fahrzeug, n., fisherman; - flotte, f., fishing fleet; - grund, m., f. ground; - hafen, m., f. harbour; - knoten or - stich, m., fisherman's bend.

Fischerei, f., fishery; - gerät, n., fishing gear; - gerechtig-keit, f., privilege of fishing; - gesetz. n., fishery law; - grenze. f., fishing boundary; - grund, m., fishing ground; - polizei, f., fishery police; - recht, n., fishing privilege.

Fischung des Ruders or Fischungsplatte d. R., f., rudder partner plate.

Fischungen, partners.

Fjord, m., firth.

Fit or Fitt, f., fit rod.

fitten, to fit with the fit rod.

fixe Maschine, f., fixed engine.

fixes Rack, n., fixed parrel.

flach ansteigend, shelving; - bodig, flat bottomed; - in

den Wind segeln, *to sail head to wind*; - vor dem W. s., *to sail right before the wind*.

Flach, n., *1. floor (of the vessel)*; *2. flat (of the bottom of the vessel)*.

Flach-eisen, n., *flat iron*; - gänge, *planks of the bottom*; - kiel, m., *flush keel*; - kielschwein, n., *flat keelson*; - - platte, f., *f. k. plate*; - meißel, m., *flat chisel*; - weger or - wegerung, f., *floor ceiling*.

Fläche, f., *surface*.

flache Boden, m., *broad bottom (of vessel)*; - Kiel, m., *flat plate keel*; - - schwein, n., *flat plate keelson*; - - - platte, f., *flat keelson plate*; - Küste, f., *table shore*; - Stelle, f., *shoal*; - Wasser, n., *shallow water*.

Flächeninhalt, m., *area*; - der Schraubenflügel, *propeller blade area*; - des Mittelspants, *midship frame section*.

flacher werden, *to shoal*; - Wind, m., *large wind*.

Flackerlicht, n., *flare up light*.

Flage, f., *sudden squall*.

Flagge, f., *flag*; - deckt die Ladung, *the f. covers the cargo*; - erkennen, *to make out a f.*; - folgt dem Handel, *the f. follows the trade*; - im Schau, *f. with a waft*; die - streichen, *to lower the f.*

Flaggen-attest, n., *certificate of registry*; - fall, m., *signal halliard*; - gaffel, f., *monkey gaff*; - gala, f., *decorated with bunting*; - - über die Nocken, *dressed with up and down flags*; - - - - Toppen, *d. w. overall f.*; kleine Flaggengala, *dressed with mast head flags*; - karte, f., *flag chart*; - kasten, m., *flag chest*; - knopf, m., *mast head truck*;

- leine, f., *ensign halliard*; - - des Groß-Top, *pennant halliard*; - macher, m., *flag maker*; - parade, f., *hoisting and hauling down of colours*; - prüfungsrecht, n., *right of visit*; - sack, m., *flag bag*; - signal, n., *f. signal*; - spind, n., *signal locker*; - steert, m., *tack of the flag*; - stock, m., *flag staff*; - - auf dem Bugspriet, *jack staff*; - topp, m., *royal mast head*; - - der Bramstenge, *topgallant pole*; - - der Großscheisegelstenge, *main skysail p.*; - - der Kreuzroyalstenge, *mizen royal mast head*; - - der Kreuz-Scheisegelstenge, *mizen skysail pole*; - - der Royalstenge, *royal pole*; - - der Scheisegelstenge, *skysail p.*; - - der Vorroyalstenge, *fore royal mast head*; - - der Vor-Scheisegelstenge, *fore skysail pole*; - tuch, n., *bunting*; - zeugnis, n., *certificate of register*.

Flämisches Auge, n., *Flemish eye*.

Flammrohr, n., *flame tube*.

Flansch, m., or Flansche, f., *flange*; - zur Aufnahme des Injektionsrohrs, *f. for connection of injection pipe*.

Flanschendichtung, f., *flange joint*.

flappen, *to flap*.

Flaschen-boje, f., *nun buoy*; - post, f., *bottle post*; - zug, m., *gin block*.

flattern, *to flutter*.

flau werden, *to fall light*.

flaue Brise, f., *light breeze*; - Kühlte, f., *l. airs*.

Flaute, f., *fanning breeze*.

Flechting, f., *capelage*.

Flechtung, f., *capelage*; - aufsetzen, *to capeler*.

Flechtwerk um einen Mars, n., *top netting*.

Fleisch-back, f., *mess kid*; - schrank, m., *meat safe*; - ständer, m., *harness cask*.

Flieboot, n., *fly boat.*
fliegen, *to wabble (the compass)*; die Schoten - lassen, *to let the sheets fly.*
fliegende Brücke, f., *flying bridge*; - Holländer, m., *phantom ship*; - Schott, n., *temporary bulkhead;* - Schoten, *flying sheets*: - Sturm, m., *violent gale.*
Fliegenschrank, m., *meat safe.*
Flieger, m., *main middle staysail.*
Floß, n., *raft*; - brücke, f., *r. bridge*; - krampe, f., *r. dog.*
Flösser, m., *raftsman.*
floten, *to float.*
Flotille, f., *flotilla.*
flott bekommen, *to get afloat*; - halten, *to keep afloat*; - machen, *to float*; - sein, *to be afloat.*
Flotte, f., *fleet.*
Flotten-demonstration, f., *naval demonstration*; - parade or - schau, f., *naval review.*
Flucht, f., *flight (being the direction of a curve of a frame, &c.).*
Flügel, m., *1. vane (of bunting)*; *2. wing (of the anchor fluke)*; - hahn, m., *butterfly cock*; - heck, n., *vane stock*; - heckschere, f., *vane board*; - mutter, f., *thumb nut*; - pinne, f., *vane spindle*; - schere, f., *vane stock*; - spill, n., - spillstuhl, m., - stange, f., - stuhl, m., *vane spindle.*
Fluid-Kompaß, m., *spirit compass.*
Flur-platten, *floors*; - - der Maschinenkammer, *engine flooring*; - seute, f., *floor riband.*
Flushdeck, n., *flushdeck.*
Fluß-bett, n., *bed of the river*; - - sohle, f., *bottom of the river*; - dampfer, m., *river*

steamer; - delta, n., *river delta*; - fischerei, f., *river fishery*; - hafen, m., *river harbour*; - krümmung, f., *bend of the river*; - lotse, m., *river pilot*; - mündung, f., *mouth of the river*; - regatta, f., *river race*; - schiffahrt, f., *river navigation;* - transport-Versicherung, f., *river risk*; - ufer, n., *bank*; - und Kanal-Schiffahrt, f., *river and canal navigation*; - versicherung, f., *fluvial insurance.*
flüssige Heizmaterialien, *liquid fuel*; - Substanz, f., *fluid.*
Flüssigwerden,n.,*liquefaction.*
Flut, f., *flood*; Anfang der -, m., *setting tide*; halbe -, f., *half flood*; die - abwarten, *to wait for the f.*; die - beginnt, *the tide makes*; die - läßt nach, *t. t. slackens*: die - steigt, *t. t. rises*; die - tritt ein, *t. t. serves*; die - wird schwach, *t. t. gets slack*; - - - schwächer, *t. t. gets weaker*; - - - stärker, *t. t. gains*; - von Luv nach Lee setzend, *lee going tide*; von der - abhängig, *tidal.*
Flut-anker, m., *flood anchor*; - ball, m., *tide ball*; - deich, m., *fleet dike*; - dock, n., *tidal basin*; - hafen, m., *tidal harbour*; - höhe, f., *height of the tide*; - karte, f., *tidal chart*; - klappe, f., *tidal valve*; - marke, f., *high water mark*; - messer, m., *tide gauge*; - rinne auf den Watten, f., *passe*; - schleuse, f., *tide gate*; - tabelle, f., *tide table*; - tag, m., *tide day*; - tor, n., *flood gate*; - uhr, f., *tide dial*; - weg, m., *swash (of a bank)*; - welle, f., *tide wave*; - zeit, f., *flood tide.*
Fock, f., *fore sail*; an die - und Großbrassen! *lower*

braces and lifts! - Bauchgording, f., fore bunt line;
- brasse, f., fore brace; -
bulin, f., fore bowline; -
geitau, n., fore clew garnet;
- hals, m., fore tack; den
- - mit einem Bullentau
ausholen, to passaree; - -
block, m., fore tack block;
- hangertakel, n., fore mast
tackle; - kardeele, f., fore
gear; - leesegel, n., fore
studding sail; - mast, m.,
fore mast; - - Dwarssahling,
f., fore mast cross trees; - -
Eselshaupt, n., f. m. cap;
- - keile, f. m. wedges; - -
kragen, m., f. m. coat; - -
Längssahling, f., f. m. trestle
trees; - - hanger, m., f. m.
head pendant; - - spur, f.,
f. m. step; - Nockgording,
f., f. leech line; - pferd, n.,
f. foot rope; - rahe, f., f.
yard; - - takel, n., f. gear;
- - talje, f., f. lift purchase;
- refftalje, f., f. reef tackle;
- rüste, f., f. channel; - -
eisen, n., f. chain plates;
- schote, f , f. sheet; - seiten-
takel, n., f. pendant tackle;
- spiere, f., f. yard boom;
- stag, n., f. stay; - - segel,
n., f. s. sail; - stenge, f., f.
top mast; - - pardune, f., f.
t. m. backstay; - takel, n.,
f. tackle; - takelage, f., f.
rigging; - toppenant, f., f.
lift; - - talje, f., f. l. purchase;
- want, n., f. lower shroud;
- wanten, f. rigging.
Fock- see also Vor-.
Föhrenholz, n., red pine.
Forderung, f., claim.
Formation, f., formation.
Formstück, n., casting.
Fort-bewegung, f., propulsion;
- laufende See, f., following
sea; - legen, to shift; -
schaffung, f., conveyance.
Fracht, f., freight; - dampfer,
m., cargo steamer; - - linie,
f., line of cargo steamers;
- - verkehr, m., c. s. traffic;

- führer, m., carrier; - satz,
m., rate of freight; - schift,
n., cargo vessel; - verlust,
m., loss of freight; - versicherung, f., insurance of
freight; - - verein, m., freight
insurance association; - vertrag, m., contract of affreightment; - vorschuß, m., advance
on freight; - zulage, f,
additional f.; - zuschlag,
m., primage.
Fransen eines Sonnensegels,
valances of an awning.
französische Platting, f.,
French sennit.
französischerWantknoten, m.,
French shroud knot.
fräsen, to countersink.
Fräsmaschine, f., shaping
machine.
Fräsung, f., countersink.
Fregatte, f., frigate.
Fregattenschiff, n., full rigged
ship.
frei, clear weather; - von Beschädigung, außer im
Strandungsfalle, free of
damage except in case of
stranding; - von Bruch,
außer i. S., f. o. breakage e.
i. c. o. s.; - vom Lande
halten, to keep the offing;
- vom Schiffe bleiben!
lie off!
Frei-augen, holidays; - bord,
n., freeboard; - brief, m.,
bill of freedom; - gestellt,
optional; - hafen, m., free
port; - halten, to bear off;
- halter, m., fender; - handel,
m., free trade; - - brief, m.,
bill of sufferance; - hieven,
to heave off; - kommen von
einer Gefahr, to get clear of
a danger; - wache, f., watch
below; - wächter, m., idler.
freie Wärme, f., sensible heat.
freies Exzenter, n., loose
eccentric.
freiwillige Strandung, f.,
voluntary stranding.
fremde Flagge, f., foreign flag;
- Hafen, m., foreign port;

- Schiff, n., *f. vessel*; - See-leute, f., *sailors*; - Werft, f., *f. yard.*
Frequenz des Raumes, f., *crowding of the room.*
fressen, *to grind.*
Fretbohrer, m., *shipwright's whimble.*
Friedensflagge, f., *flag of truce.*
Friktion, f., *friction*; - des Kolbens, *f. of piston*; - des Schiebers, *f. of slide valve.*
Friktions-getriebe, n., *friction gear*; - kegel, m., *f. socket*; lösbare - - kuppelung, f., *f. s. coupling*; - kuppelung, f., *f. c.*; - - muff, m., *f. c. box*; - rad, n., *f. wheel*; - rollen, *f. rollers*; - scheibe, f., *f. plate.*
Frisch-balje, f., *meat tub*; - eisen, n., *bloom iron*; - wasser, n., *fresh water*; - - pumpe, f., *f. w. pump*; - - rohr, n., *f. w. pipe.*
frische Brise, f., *fresh breeze (of force 5)*; - Wetter, n., *fresh weather*; - Wind, m., *fresh gale (of force 8).*
Frittbohrer, m., *gimblet.*
Frontbalken, m., *breast beam*; - der Back, *b. b. of forecastle*; - der Hütte or Poop, *b. b. of poop*; - des erhöhten Quarterdecks, *b. b. of raised quarter deck.*
Front, in - linie, *formed abreast*; - reling, f., *front rail*; - schott, n., *front bulkhead*; - - der Back, *f. b. of forecastle*; - - der Hütte or Poop, *f. b. of poop*; - - der versenkten Back, *break bulkhead of sunk forecastle*; - - - - Brücke, *b. b. o. s. bridge*; - schott des erhöhten Quarterdecks, *b. b. of raised quarterdeck*; - - süll des erhöhten Quarterdecks, n., *coaming of r. q. bulkhead*; - wand, f., *front plate*; - - des Kessels, *f. p. of boiler.*

Frühjahrs-Äquinoctium, n., *vernal equinox*; - sturm, m., *gowk storm.*
Fuchs, m., *uptake*; - schwanz des Blockmachers, m., *whip saw of the block maker.*
Fuchsjes, *foxes.*
Fuge eines Kessels, f., *boiler seam*; - mit Überdeckungs-platten, *seam with butt straps.*
Fugen, in allen - krachen, *cracking in all joints.*
führen, alle Segel -, *to carry all sails.*
Fuhrlohn, m., *cartage.*
Führung, f., *1. management*; *2. guide (mechanical).*
Führung des Schieberventils, *t.. slide valve guide*; - - Schiffes haben, *to have charge of the ship*; - - - übernehmen, *to take c. o. t. s.*
Führungsauge der Abzugs-leine, n., *neck ring.*
Führungsstange, f., *guide rod*; - des Steuergeräts, *lead of the steering gear*; - Stopf-büchsendeckel, m., *tail rod gland*; - träger, m., *pump crosshead guide rod bracket.*
Füll-apparat, m., *feeding apparatus*; - blech, n., *liner*; - gang, m., *limber strake*; - holz, n., *stem piece*; - platte, f., *lining piece*; - rohr, n., *filling pipe*; - spant, n., *filling timber*; - streifen, m., *f. piece*; - stück, n., *eking piece*; - - der Schlag-betten. *upmaking of the launching cradle*; - - zwischen den Knien des Gallionsscheggs, *face piece.*
füllen. die Kessel -, *to fill the boilers.*
Füllstück des Bugs, n., *eking*; - des Gallions, n., *filling chocks of the cutwater.*
Füllung, f., *panel*; - des Wasserlaufs, *limber board.*
Füllungen, Reihe der -, *limber passage.*

Füllungs-balken, *planks between the wales*; - brett, n., *limber board*; - kette, f., *limber clearer*; - planke, f., *limber board*; - streifen. m., *filling piece*; - worp, f., *filling transom.*

Fundament, n., *1. sleeper (of bed plate)*; *2. bearer (of engine, &c.)*; - bolzen, *foundation bolt*; - platte, f., *bed plate*; - - bolzen, m., *b. p. holding down bolt*; - - - mutter, f, *foundation plate bolt nut*; - plattenpackung, f., *bed plate packing.*

Fünfmast-Bark, f., *five mast barque*; - Gaffelschoner, m., *f. m. fore and aft schooner;* - schoner, *f. m. s.*; - Vollschiff, n., *f. m. full rigged ship.*

Funkelfeuer, n., *scintillating light.*

Funken-fänger, m., *spark catcher*; - skala, f., *scale of sparks*; - spruch, m., *wireless telegraphy.*

Funktionieren, n., *function-ment.*

funktionieren, *to work*; nicht - wollen, *to refuse t. w.*

funktionierende Teile, *working parts.*

Fuß, m., *1. heel (of a mast)*; *2. well end (of a pump).*

Fuß-band, n., *foot band*; - block, m., *snatch block*; großer - -, *rouse about*; der - boden begab sich, *flooring got adrift*; - bolzen eines Strebers, m , *nog*; - brett, n., *bottom board*; - geitau, n., *foot brail*; - gillung, f., *foot gore*; - gräting, f., *foot grating*; - Hahnepot einer Hängematte, f, *foot clew of a hammock*; - halt, m., *footing*; - hammer, m., *swelling hammer*; - kette des Klüverbaums, f., *heel chain of the jib boom*; - knie, n., *heel knee*; - - bolzen, m., *h. k. bolt*; - laschung, f., *heel lashing*; - latte, f. *boat stretcher*; - leik or - liek, n., *foot rope*; - matte, f., *foot mat*; - reff, n., *bag reef*; - saum, m., *foot tabling*; - talje, f , *heel tackle*; - tritt, m., *step*; - ventil, n., *foot valve*; - zapfen, m., *heel pintle.*

Futter, n., *liner*; - blech, n., *liner of sheet iron*, - matte, f., *fother mat*; - segel, n., *thrummed sail*; - pappe, f, *sheathing paper.*

futtern, *to fother (a leak).*

Fütterung, f., *firlining*; - des Steuerruders, *back of the rudder.*

G.

Gaatche am Raaliek eines Segels, n., *head hole.*

Gabel, f., *1. jaw (of connecting rod)*; *2. gab (of eccentric)*; - glied. n., *fork link*; - hebel. m., *gab lever*; - schlüssel or - schraubenschlüssel, m., *fork wrench*; - stütze, f., *clutch.*

Gaffel, f., *gaff*; - Außengeitau, n., *outer peak brail*; - ende, n., *gaff end*; - flagge, f., *g.*

flag; - geer, f., *vang*; - geitau, n., *peak brail*; - gerde, f., *vang*; - gerdenschenkel, m , *vang pendant*; - innengeitau, n., *inner peak brail*; - klaue, f., *jaw of a gaff*; - leik or - liek, n., *head rope of a gaff sail*; - mick, f., *jaw of a gaff*; - nock, f., *gaff end*; - schiene, f., *patent jackstay of a gaff*; - Schoner, m., *fore and aft*

schooner; - segel, n., *gaff
sail*; - - baum, m., *g. s.
boom*; - stander, m., *peak
pendant*; - takelage, f.. *fore
and aft rig*; - toppsegel, n.,
gaff top sail; - - tall, m.,
gaff top sail halliard; - -
hals, m., *g. t. s. tack*; - -
Niederholer, m., *g. t. s.
downhaul*; - - schote, f., *g.
t. s. sheet.*
gahn achter! *main sail haul!
- vor! let go and haul!*
Galeasse, f., *galeas.*
Galeere, f., *galley.*
Galeerenknoten, m., *galley
hitch.*
Galgen, m., *skid beams*; - streber, m.. *gallows stanchion.*
Galleriebalken, m., *spur beam.*
Gallion, n., *cutwater*; - brett,
n., *head board*; - figur, f.,
figure head; - gast, m., *swab
washer*; - gräting, f., *head
grating*; - kleid, n., *head
cloth*; - knie, n., *bracket of
the head rail*; - krulle, f.,
fiddle figure head; - leiste,
f., *rail of the head*; obere
- -, *berthing rail*; - pumpe,
f., *head pump*; - puppe, f.,
bust head: - reling, f., *head
rails*; - schegg, n., *bobstay
piece.*
galvanisierter Bolzen, m.,
galvanised bolt; - Stahl, m.,
g. steel.
galvanisiertes Eisen, n.,
galvanised iron.
Gang, m., *1. allay way (under
deck); 2. board (when tacking); 3. strake (of plating);
4. working (of engine); 5.
rate (of chronometer); 6.
gang (of labourers)*; erster -
oberhalb des Bergholzes,
black strake.
Gänge, kurze und lange -
machen, *to make long and
short tacks.*
Gang-bord, m., *gangway*; -
spill, n., *capstan (see also
Dampf - -);* das - - ein-

winden, *to heave at the
capstan*; das - - zurück-
winden, *to come up with
the c.*; - - axe, f., *c. spindle*;
- - axenkragen, m., *c. s.
collar*; - - Fischung, f., *c.
partner*; - - kopf, m., *drum
head of a c.*; - - körper, m.,
c. barrel; - - pall, n., *c. pawl*;
- - Pallring, m., *c. p. rim*;
- - Pallstopper, m., *c. p.
head*; - - rippe, f., *c. whelp*;
- - rippenkalb, n., *c. w. chock*;
- - spake, f., *c. bar*; - - -
gat, or - - - loch, n., *c. b.
hole*; - - spindel, f., *c.
spindle*; - - - kragen, m.,
c. s. collar; - - - spur, f.,
c. s. socket; - spilltrommel,
f., *c. barrel*; - spillüberzug,
m., *c. cover*; - welle, f., *c.
barrel*; - way, f., *gangway*;
- wegzelt, n., *main deck
awning.*
Gänsehals eines Baumes, m.,
goose neck of a boom.
Ganzeisen, n., *pig iron.*
ganz versichert, *fully insured.*
ganze Fracht, f., *full freight*;
- Heuer, f., *f. pay*; - Kraft, f.,
full power.
gänzlicher Druck, m., *total
pressure.*
gapen, *to gape.*
Garantiemaschinist, m., *guarantee engineer.*
Garn, n., *twine.*
Garnat, n., *garnet.*
Garnier, n., *1. dunnage (for
protecting cargo); 2. ceiling
(planking of frames)*; - balken, m., *planks for the ceiling*; - holz, n., *dunnage
wood*; - latten, d. *battens*;
- matten, d. *mats*; - legen, *to
place the ceiling*; - planken,
d. *planks.*
garnieren, *1. to dunnage (for
protecting cargo); 2. to place
the ceiling (planking the
frames); 3. to line up (the
brasses)*; wieder garnieren,
to reline (brasses, sternbush).

Garnierung *see* Garnier.
Garnitur, f., *1. fittings(machine parts)*; *2. lining (covering of brasses)*.
Garnstropp, m., *selvagee strop*.
Gasboje, f., *gas buoy*.
Gase, *gases*.
Gasten. *hands*; - unter auf! *up hands*!
Gat or Gatt, n., *1. hole (in reef bands)*; *2. stern (of ship)*; *3. gat (channel between banks)*; - nadel, f., *large sail needle*.
Gatchen or Gattchen, *eyelet holes*; - am Raheliek, *head holes*; - am Stagliek, *stay holes*.
gebaut, *built*.
gebauter Mast, m., *built mast*.
geben, Kette -, *to give chain*.
geblieben, *lost (ship)*.
gebogene Planken, *snying*.
gebogenes Spant, n., *curved frame*.
geborgene Ladung, f., *saved cargo*.
geborsten, *cracked*.
gebrauchsunfähig, *1. disabled (ship)*; *2. unserviceable (rope, &c.)*.
gebrochen, *broken (cables, ropes)*; *2. carried away (masts, backstays, &c.)*; *3. fractured (metal)*.
gebrochene Deck, n., *deck with a break*; - Windstoß, m., *sudden squall of wind*.
Gebt acht dort unten! *Stand from under*!
Gebühren, *dues*.
gebundene Wärme, f., *latent heat*.
Geckstock, m., *handle of a pump*.
gedeckt, *decked*.
gedoppelt, *doubled*.
gedrehter Holznagel, m., *engine turned treenail*.
Geer or Geerde or Gerde, f., *vang*; - läufer, m., *v. fall*; - schenkel, m., *v. pendant*.
Geeter, m., *scoop*.

Gefahr, f., der - aussetzen, *to expose to danger*; einer - entgehen, *to escape a. d.*; einer - mit knapper Not entgehen, *to have a narrow escape*; in drohender - sein, *to be in an imminent danger*; Schiff in -, *vessel in distress*; - signal, n., *signal of distress*.
Gefahren d. Seefahrt, *dangers of the sea*.
gefährliche Klippe, f., *dangerous rock*; - Küste, f., *d. coast*.
Gefälle des Flusses, n., *fall of the river*.
Gefängnisschiff, n., *convict ship*.
Gefäß, n., *vessel*.
gefechts-klar, *clear for action*; - ruder, n., *action rudder*.
geflanschte Platte, f., *flanged plate*.
geflochtene Hanfliderung, f., *packing gasket*; - Tau, n., *plaited rope*.
Gefrierpunkt, m., *freezing point*.
gefrischter Stahl, m., *fined steel*.
gefüttertes Gat, n., *fairleader*.
gegabelte Pleyelstange, f., *forked connecting rod*.
Gegen-befehl, m., *counter order*; - brassen, *to counter-brace*; - dampf, m., *back steam*; - dampfer, m., *the steamer meeting end on*; - druck, m., *back pressure*; - forderung, f., *counter claim*; - gebraßt. *laid aback*; - gewicht, n., *balance weight*; - halter, m., *holding up hammer*; - keil, m., *tightening key*; - Kiel, m., *riding wood of a keel*; - kommer, m., *meeting vessel*; - kurbeln, *opposite cranks*; - lenker, m., *radius bar*; - welle, f., *radius shaft*; - liegen, *to be home*; - mutter, f., *check nut*; - passat, m., *anti trades*; - prallen, *to dash*;

- punze, f., *counter punch*;
- schein, m., *reciprocal bond*;
- see, f., *head sea*; - segler, m., *meeting vessel*; - seitig, *reciprocal*; - - zu gebrauchen, *reversible*; - signal, n., *counter signal*; - - wimpel, m., *answering pennant*; - spant, n., *reversed frame*; - stoßen, *striking*; - strömung, f., *eddy or counter current*; - über, *abreast*; - wind, m., *head wind*; - winkel, m., *reversed angle bar*; - wirkung, f., *reaction*.

gegißte Besteck, n., *dead reckoning*; - Breite, f., *latitude by d. r.*; - Länge, f., *longitude by d. r.*

gehämmertes Eisen, n., *beaten iron*.

Gehänge, n., *hinge*.

gehärteter Stahl, m., *tempered steel*.

Gehäuse, n., *1. box*; *2. shell (of a block)*; *3. chest (of valve)*.

gehen, über Stag -, *to go about*; an Bord -, *to go on board*.

gehorchen, dem Ruder zu - anfangen, *to gather steerage way*; d. R. gut g., *to answer her helm well*; d. R. nicht g., *to refuse t. a. h. h.*

Gehrunghshobel, m., *mitre plane*.

Gehülfe, m., *mate*.

Gei or Geie, f., eines Bocks, *guy of sheers*; - des Schwingbaums, *lower studding sail boom g.*

geiben, *to gybe*.

geien, *to brail up*.

Geitau, n., *1. brail (for gaff sails)*; *2. clew line (for upper square sails)*; *3. c. garnet (for lower s. s.)*.

Geitaublock, m., *1. brail block (for gaff sails)*; *2. clew line b. (for upper square sails)*; *3. c. garnet b. (for lower s. s.)*; - und Schotblock, *quarter b.*

Geisterschiff, n., *phantom ship*.

gekapzeist, *capsized*.

gekattet und gefischt, *catted and fished*.

gekehrter Winkel, m., *reversed angle bar*.

gekehrtes Spant, n., *reversed frame*; - Winkeleisen, n., *r. angle iron*.

geknickte Faser im Maste, f., *grain upset in the mast*.

gekochtes Leinöl, n., *boiled linseed oil*.

gekreuzte See, f., *cross sea*.

gekröpfte Welle, f., *crank*.

gekrümmt, *cambered*.

gekürzte Rationen, *short allowance*.

geladen, *laden*.

geladene Bö, f., *thick squall*.

Geländer, n., *rails and stanchions*; - stange, f., *guard rod*; - stütze, f., *stanchion*; - um einen Mars, *top rail*.

gelascht, *lashed*.

gelaufene Distanz, f., *distance run*.

Gelbgießerei, f., *brass foundry*.

Gelenk, n., *link*; - lagerdeckel, m., *keep for l. brasses*; - lagerschalen, *l. b.*; - ventil, n., *clack valve*.

gelichtet, der Anker ist -! *a-weigh, sir!*

gemarkt, *marked*; deutlich -, *ken speckled*.

gemäßigte Zone, f., *tempered zone*.

gemäßigtes Klima, n., *temperate climate*.

gemischte Dampf, m., *mixed steam*; - Holz, n., *m. timber*; - Ladung, f., *general cargo*.

genau östlich etc., *due east, &c.*

genaues Steuern, n., *nice steering*.

Generaldistanz, f., *distance made good*.

Generalkurs, m., *direct course*.

Genosse, m., *mate*.

gepanzert, *iron clad*.

gepeiltes Besteck, n., *ship's place by bearings.*

gepeitscht vom Sturme, *storm swept.*

gepreßter Holznagel, m., *compressed treenail.*

geprüfte Ankerkette, f., *tested chain cable.*

geprüfter Steuermann, m., *holding a mate's certificate.*

gepurrt, die Wache wurde -, *the watch was called to relief.*

gerade, 1. *true (course);* 2. *straight (rod, &c.);* - achter, *right astern;* - das Boot! *trim the boat!* - gegen die See, *head to sea;* - halten, *to keep steamer in position;* sich - legen, *to straighten up;* - im Winde, *head to wind.*

gerader Stoß, m., *direct impact.*

gerades Spant, n., *square body frame.*

Gerad-führung, f., *guide;* - führungsbacken des Kreuzkopfes, *slides of the crosshead;* - läufiger Kurs, m., *orthodromic course.*

Gerbstahl, m., *refined charcoal steel.*

gerefft, *reefed.*

gerichtet, *straightened.*

geringer Stahl, m., *common steel.*

Gerippe, n., *carcass (of a vessel).*

gerissen, *flawed.*

gerundeter Scheergang, m., *rounded gunwale.*

gesalzener Proviant, m., *salted provisions.*

Gesamtgewicht, n., *total weight.*

Gesangbuch, n., *holystone.*

gesättigter Dampf, m., *saturated steam.*

geschätzte Pferdekräfte, *estimated horse power.*

Gesche, f., *grab.*

gescheitert, *wrecked.*

geschifted, *shifted.*

Geschirr, n., *gear.*

geschleißte Stütze, f., *split pillar.*

geschleppt, *towed;* - werden, *to be in tow.*

geschlossene Brücke, f., *closed-in-bridge.*

Geschmeidigkeit, f., *ductility.*

geschmiedetes Balkenknie, n., *bracket end;* - Eisen, n., *forged iron.*

geschrammt, *scored.*

geschraubter Stehbolzen, m., *screwed stay.*

Geschützbank, f., *shot racks.*

geschützt, *sheltered.*

geschützte Reede, f., *sheltered road.*

Geschwader, n., *squadron.*

geschwellt, *rap full (sails).*

Geschwindigkeit, f., 1. *rate (of the current);* 2. *velocity (of piston and evaporation);* 3. *speed (of engines);* - vergrößern, *to increase the speed;* - vermindern, *to reduce t. s.;* - anzeiger, m., *speed indicator;* - messer, m., *tachometer.*

gesegelter Kompaßkurs, m., *compass made good.*

Gesellschaftsflagge, f., *burgee.*

Gesellschaftszimmer, n., *ward room.*

gesetzlich zulässige Waren, *lawful merchandise.*

Gesichts-feld, n., *field of view;* - punkt, m., *point of v.*

gespickte Matte, f., *thrummed mat.*

gesponnenes Werg, n., *twisted oakum.*

gesprochenes Schiff, n., *vessel spoken.*

gesprungen, 1. *started (anchor from the ground);* 2. *sprung (masts, spars);* 3. *sprung (a leak).*

Gestade, n., *beach.*

gestagt, zu viel - sein, *to hang forward.*

gestaltet, *shaped.*

Gestaltung, f., *formation.*

Gestänge, n., *gear.*

Gestell, n., *standard*; - mit Löchern, *rack*; - säge, f., *frame saw*; - wand, f., *1. jib stay (of engine)*; *2. framing (of winch)*.
gesteuerter Kurs, m., *steered course*.
Gestirnhöhe, f., *altitude of a star*.
gestoppten, mit - Rahen liegen, *to lie with yards apeak*.
gestoßen, *struck*.
gestrandet, *stranded*.
gestroppter Block, m., *stropped block*.
gesund, *1. healthy*; *2. sound (masts, &c.)*.
Gesundheits-paß, m., *bill of health*; - pflege, f., *ship's hygiene*.
gesunken, *sunk*.
getakelt, *rigged*; als Brigg -, *brig r.*; niedrig -, *low r.*; zu dick -, *overrigged*.
geteert, *tarred*.
geteilter Zug, m., *split draught*.
Getreide-heber, m., *grain elevator*; - schotten, *shifting boards*; - - stützen, *s. b. stanchions*; - wegerung, f., *grain ceiling*.
Getriebe, n., *1. gear (totality of parts)*; *2. pinion (of winch and toothed wheel)*.
getroffen, *struck*.
Geveling, f., *shifting board*.
Gewährsmann, m., *vouchee*.
gewalzte Platten, *rolled plates*.
gewaschen über Bord, *washed over board*.
Gewässer, *waters*.
gewebte Matte, f., *sword mat*.
Gewehrgestell, n., *arm rack*.
gewellte Feuerbüchse, f., *corrugated furnace*.
Gewichts-belastung, f., *dead weight load*; - einheit, f., *unit of weights*; - ersparnis, f., *saving of weight*; - kurve, f., *curve of w.*; - tonnen, *tons deadweight*; - verteilung, f., *distribution of weight*.

Gewinde-bohrer, m., *screw tap*; - kluppenbacken, *screw dies*; - schneideeisen, n., *screw plate*; - schneidkluppen, die; - stahl, m., *chasing tool*.
Gewitter, n., *thunder storm*; - bö, f., *t. squall*; - sturm, m., *t. storm*; - wolke, f., *t. cloud*.
gewöhnlicher Anker, m., *common anchor*; - Frachtdampfer, m., *ordinary cargo steamer*; - Knoten, m., *overhand knot*; - Wantknoten, m., *single shroud k.*
gewöhnliches Log, n., *common log*; - Spill, n., *c. windlass*; - Steuergerät, n., *c. steering gear*.
gewölbt, *cambered*.
geworfenes Gut, n., *jettison*.
gezahnt, *toothed*.
Gezeit, f., *tide*; - ball, m., *t. ball*; - bezüglich, *tidal*; - feuer, n., *tidal light*; - hafen, m., *tidal harbour*; - strom, m., *tidal stream*; - tabelle, f., *tide table*.
gezurrt, *lashed*.
Giek-baum, m., *spanker boom*; - - segel, n., *s. sail*; - tau, n., *topping lift*.
Gien, n., *purchase*; - block, m., *p. block*; - läufer, m., *p. fall*; - talje, f., *winding tackle p.*; - tau, n., *fall of a w. t.*
giepen, *to gype the ship*.
gieren, *to yaw*; - lassen, *to give her a sheer*.
Giertau der fliegenden Brücke, n., *moorings of the flying bridge*.
gießen, *1. to cast (metal)*; *2. to rain in torrents*.
Gießer, m., *scoop*.
Gießerei, f., *foundry*.
Gieß-löffel, m., *ladle*; - pfanne, f., *shank*.
Giffardscher Injektor, m., *injector of Giffard*.
Gig, f., *gig*.
Gigsgast, m., *light horseman*.

Gilling or Gillung, f., *1. counter (of the stern)*; *2. gore (of a sail)*; *3. gulleting (of the rudder)*; - holz, n., *counter timber*; - platte, f., *c. plate.*
Gischt, m., *spoon drift.*
Gissung, nach -, *by the log.*
Gitter, n., *guard (of a skylight)*; - schieber, m., *gridiron expansion valve*; - schott, n., *batten and space bulkhead*; - werk der Laterne, n., *lantern girdles.*
Glasen, *bells.*
glatt, *flush*; - deck, n., *f. deck*; - - machen, *to sweep the deck*; - - Schiff, n., *flush deck vessel.*
glatte Feuerbüchse, f., *plain furnace.*
Glatteis, n., *glazed frost.*
glätten, *to skim up.*
Gleich-förmigkeit, f., *equiformity*; - gewicht, n., *equibalance*; - - ventil, n., *equilibrium valve*; - heit, f., *identity*; - lastig, *even keel*; - - beladen, *laden on even keel*; - mäßige Temperatur, f., *uniform temperature*; - - Druck, m., *u. pressure*; - schenkelig, *equicrural*; - seitig, *equilateral*; - ung, f., *equation*; - weit entfernt, *equidistant*; - winkelig, *equiangular.*
Gleit-backe, f., *link block*; - bahn, f., *guide*; - bahnen-Kühlvorrichtung, f., *water service for guides*; - balken, *ways*; - block, m., *slide block (of a gaff)*; - dichtung, *sliding joint*; - planke einer Steuerkette, f., *slide board for steering chain*; - planken, *launching ways*; - reibung, f., *sliding friction*; - rohr einer Steuerkette, m., *slide box for steering chain*; - schiene einer Gaffel, f., *patent jackstay of a gaff*; - schuh, m., *guide block.*
gleitende Dichtung, f., *expansion joint.*

Glied-Durchmesser, m., *diameter of link.*
Gliederkessel, m., *sectional boiler.*
Gliedkette, f., *oval linked chain.*
Glocke, f., *bell.*
Glocken-arm, m., *bell crank*; - bezug, m., *b. cover*; - boje, f., *b. buoy*; - galgen, m., *belfry*; - kappe, f, *bell cover*; - klöppel, m., *b. clapper*; - signal, n., *b. signal*; - steert, m., or - tau, n., *b. rope*; - turmmaschine, f., *steeple engine*; - ventil, n., *cup valve*; - winkel, m., *bell crank.*
Glühlampe, f., *incandescent lamp.*
Gnadentage, *days of grace.*
Gobelung, f., *shifting boards.*
Golf, m., *gulf*; - strom, m., *g. stream.*
Gondel, f., *gondola.*
Gording, f., Gordingen, Gordungen, *leech lines.*
Gösch or Gösch-flagge, f., *Jack*; - stock, m., *J. staff.*
Graben, m., *drain.*
Grad, m., *degree*; - bogen, m., *protractor.*
grade *see* gerade.
Grainfeeder, m., *grainfeeder.*
Grant, m., *shingle.*
graphische Darstellung, f., *mapping out.*
Graphit, m., *graphite.*
Gratifikation, f., *gratuity.*
Gräting, f., *grating.*
Grau-Ulmenholz, n., *grey elm wood.*
Gravitationsgesetz, n., *law of gravitation.*
Greenheartholz, n., *greenheart wood.*
Greep, m., *gripe.*
greifen, *to gripe*; der Anker greift, *the anchor bites.*
Greifer, m., *grap.*
Grenadierblock, m., *monkey block.*
Grenze, f., *boundary.*
Greyhound, m., *greyhound.*

Griff, m., *handle*; - steuerrad, n., *hand steering wheel*.
grobe See, f., *rough sea*.
Groß - Aventürvertrag. m., *respondentia*; - Bauchgording, f., *main bunt line*.
Großbaum, m., *main boom*; - dirk, m.. *main topping lift*; - - talje, f., *main boom topping lift purchase*; - toppenant, f., *main boom topping lift*; - - talje, f., *m. b. t. l. purchase*.
Großboot, n., *long boat*.
Groß-Brambauchgording, f., *main topgallant bunt line*; - Brambrasse, f., *main topgallant brace*; - Bramdrehreep, n., *main topgallant tye*; - Bramfall, m., *main topgallant halliard*; - Bramgeitau, n., *main topgallant clew line*; - Bramlängssahlinge, *main topmast trestle trees*; - Bramleesegel, n., *main topgallant studding sail*: - - Außenschote f., *m. t. s. s. tack*; - - Binnenschote, f., *m. t. s. s. sheet*; - - fall. m., *m. t. s. s. halliard*; - - hals, m., *m. t. s. s. tack*; - - Niederholer, m., *m. t. s. s. downhaul*; - - schote, f., *m. t. s. s. sheet*; - - spiere, f., *m. t. s. s. boom*; - Bramnockgording, f., *m. t. leech line*; - Brampardune, f., *main topgallant backstay*; - Brampferd, n., *m. t. footrope*; - Brampüttings, *m. t. futtocks*; - - wanten, *m. t. futtock shrouds*; - Bramrahe, f., *m. t. yard*; - Bramsahling, f., *main topmast cross trees*; - Bramschote, f., *main topgallant sheet*; - Bramsegel, n., *m. t. sail*; - Bramstag, n., *m. t. stay*; - - segel, n., *m. t. s. sail*; - - - fall, m., *m. t. s. s. halliard*; - - - hals, m., *m. t. s. s. tack*; - - - leiter, f., *m. t. s. s. stay*; - - - Niederholer, m., *m. t. s. s. downhaul*; - - - schote, f., *m. t. s. s.*

sheet; - Bramstenge, f., *m. t. mast*; - - Eselshaupt, n., *m. t. m. cap*; - - pardune, f., *m. t. backstay*; - - stag, n., *m. t. stay*; - - wanten, *m. t. rigging*; - Bramtoppenant, f., *m. t. lift*; - Bramwant, n., *m. t. shroud*.
Groß-brasse, f., *main brace*; - - schenkel, m., *m. b. pendant*; - Bulin, f., *main bowline*: - butluv, m., *main bumkin*; - Dirk, m., *main boom topping lift*.
Groß-Gaffel, f., *main gaff*; - - gerde, f., *main vang*; - - - schenkel, m., *m. v. pendant*; - Gaffelsegel, n., *m. trysail*; - Gaffeltoppsegel, n, *m. gaff topsail*; - - fall, m., *m. g. t. halliard*; - - hals, m., *m. g. t. tack*; - - Niederholer, m., *m. g. topsail downhaul*; - - schote, f., *m. g. t. sheet*; - geitau, n., *main clew garnet*: · hals, m., *main tack*; - handel, m , *merchant trading*; - hangertakel, n., *main mast tackle*; - Klaufall, m., *main throat halliard*; - Klüver, m., *boom jib*; - - fall, m., *outer jib halliard*: - - hals, m., *outer jib tack*; - - leiter, f., *o. j. stay*; - - schote, f., *o. j. sheet*; - leesegel, n., *main studding sail*; - luke, f., *main hatch*; - lukendeckel, m., *m. h.*; - süll, m., *main hatchway coaming*.
Groß-mars, m., *main top*; - - Bauchgording. f., *main topsail buntline*; - - brasse, f., *main topsail brace*; - - - schenkel, m., *m. t. b. pendant*; - mars-Drehreep, n., *m. t. tye*; - - fall, m., *m. t. halliard purchase*; - - geitau. n., *m. t. clew line*; - - pardune, f., *m. topmast backstay*; - - pferd, n., *m. topsail foot rope*; - - püttings, *m. futtocks*; - - - wanten, *m. futtock shrouds*; - mars-rahe, f., *main topsail yard*; - - reff-

talje, f., *m. t. reef tackle*; - - schote, f., *m. t. sheet*; - - segel, n., *m. t.*; - - schote, f., *m. t. sheet*; - mars-stag, n., *m. topmast stay*; - - stenge. f., *m. topmast*; - - - Eselshaupt, n., *m. t. cap*; - mars-toppenant, f., *m. topsail lift*; - - wanten, *m. topmast shrouds*; - mast, m., *m. mast*; - - Dwarssahling, f., *m. m. cross trees*; - - Eselshaupt, n., *m. m. cap*; - - keile, *m. m. wedges*; - - kragen, m., *m. m. coat*; - - Längssahling, f., *m. m. trestle trees*; - - spur, f., *m. m. step*; - Mittelstagsegel, n., *main middle staysail*; - - fall, m., *m. m. s. halliard*; - - hals, m., *m. m. s. tack*; - - Niederholer, m., *m. m. s. downhaul*; - - schote, f., *m. m. s. sheet.*

Groß-Nockgording, f., *main leech line.*

Groß - Oberbrambrasse, f., *upper main topgallant brace*; - Oberbrampferd, n., *u. m. t. foot rope*; - Oberbramrahe, f., *u. m. t. yard*; - Oberbramsegel, n., *u. m. t. sail.*

Groß-Oberleesegel, n., *main topmast studding sail*; - - Außenschote, f., *m. t. s. s. tack*; - - Binnenschote, f., *m. t. s. s. sheet*; - - fall, m., *m. t. s. s. halliard*; - - hals, m., *m. t. s. s. tack*; - - Niederholer, m., *m. t. s. s. downhaul*; - - rahe, f., *m. t. s. s. yard*; - - schote, f., *m. t. s. s. sheet*; - - spiere, f., *m. t. s. s. boom.*

Groß-Obermarsbauchgording, *upper main topsail bunt line*; - Obermarsbrasse, f., *upper main topsail brace*; - - schenkel, m., *u. m. t. b. pendant*; - Obermarspferd, n., *u. m. t. foot rope*; - Obermarsrahe, f., *u. m. t.*

yard; - Obermarssegel, n., *u. m. t.*; - Obertoppsegel, n., *u. m. t.*; - - brasse, f., *u. m. t. brace*; - - rahe, f., *u. m. t. yard.*

Groß-pferd, n., *main foot rope*; - Piekfall, m., *main peak halliard*; - rahe, f., *m. yard*; - - toppenantstalje, f., *m. lift purchase*; - Refftalje, f., *m. reef tackle.*

Groß-Royal, n., *main royal*; - - Bauchgording, f., *m. r. bunt line*; - - brasse, f., *m. r. brace*; - - fall, m., *m. r. halliard*; - - geitau, n., *m. r. clew line*; - - Längssahling, f., *m. topgallant trestle trees*; - - Leesegel, n., *main royal studding sail*; - - - Außenschote, f., *m. r. s. s. tack*; - - - Binnenschote, f., *m. r. s. s. sheet*; - - - fall, m., *m. r. s. s. halliard*; - - - hals, m., *m. r. s. s. tack*; - - - Niederholer, m., *m. r. s. s. downhaul*; - - - rahe, f., *m. r. s. s. yard*; - - - schote, f., *m. r. s. s. sheet*; - - - spiere, f., *m. r. s. s. boom*; - Royal-Pardune, f., *m. r. backstay*; - - pferd, n., *m. r. foot rope*; - - rahe, f., *m. r. yard*; - - sahling, f., *main topgallant cross trees*; - - schote. f., *main royal sheet*; - - stag, n., *m. r. stay*; - - segel, n., *m. r. sail*; - - - fall, m., *m. r. s. s. halliard*; - - - hals, m., *m. r. s. s. tack*; - - - - leiter, f., *m. r. s. s. stay*; - - - - Niederholer, m., *m. r. s. s. downhaul*; - - - - schote, f., *m. r. s. s. sheet*; - Royal-Stenge, f., *m. r. mast*; - - - pardune, f., *m. r. backstay*; - - - stag, n., *m. r. stay*; - Royal-Toppenant, *m. r. lift.*

Groß-Rüste, f., *main channel*; - - eisen, n., *m. chain plates.*

Groß-Scheisegel, n., *main skysail*; - - brasse, f., *m. s. brace*;

- - fall, m., *m. s. halliard*;
- - geitau, n., *m. s. clew
line*; - - pardune, f., *m. s.
backstay*; - - pferd, n., *m. s.
foot rope*; - - rahe, f., *m. s.
yard*; - - schote, f., *m. s.
sheet*; - - stag, n., *m. s. stay*;
- - stenge, f., *m. s. mast*; - - -
pardune, f., *m. s. backstay*;
- - - stag, n., *m. s. stay*; -
Scheisegel-Toppenant, f., *m.
s. lift*.
Groß-schote, f., *main sheet*.
Groß-segel, n., *main sail*; - -
fall, m., *m. s. halliard*; - -
Gaffelgerde, f., *m. vang*; - -
Leitwagen, m., *m. sail horse*;
- - Refftalje, f., *main reef
tackle*; - - schote, f., *m. sheet*.
Groß-Seitentakel, n., *main
pendant tackle*; - spiere, f., *m.
yard boom*; - stag, n., *m.
stay*.
Groß-Stagsegel, n., *main staysail*; - - fall, m , *m. s. halliard*;
- - hals, m., *m. s. tack*; - -
leiter, f, *m. s. stay*; - -
Niederholer, m., *m. s. downhaul*; - - schote, f., *m. s.
sheet*; - - - schenkel, m., *m.
s. s. pendant*; - Stenge, f.,
m. topmast; - - pardune, f.,
m. t. backstay; - - stag, n.,
m. t. stay; - Stengestagsegel,
n., *m. t. staysail*; - - fall, m ,
m. t. s. halliard; - - hals,
m., *m. t. s. tack*; - - leiter,
f., *m. t. s. stay*; - - Niederholer, m., *m. t. s. downhaul*;
- - schote, f., *m. t. s. sheet*;
- Stengewanten, *main topmast shrouds*.
Groß-topp *see* - mars; - toppenant, *main lift*; - - talje, f.,
m. l. purchase.   [*man*.
Groß-toppgast, m., *main top*
Groß-Toppsegel, n., *main
topsail*; - - brasse, f., *m.
t. brace*; - - geitau, n., *m. t.
clew line*; - - rahe, f., *m.
topsail yard*.
Groß-Treisegel, n., *main
trysail*; - - Ausholer, m.,
m. t. outhaul; - - baum,

m., *m. t. boom*; - - Dempgordinge, *m. t. brails*; - -
Einholer, m., *m. t. inhaul*;
- - fall, m., *m. t. halliard*;
- - gaffel, f., *m. t. gaff*; - -
geitaue, *m. t. brails*; - - -
gerde, f., *m. t. vang*; - - -
schenkel, m., *m. v. pendant*;
- Treisegel-Hals, m., *m. t.
tack*; - - Klaufall, m., *m. t.
throat halliard*; - - Piekfall,
m., *m. t. peak halliard*; - -
schote, f., *m. t. sheet*.
Groß - Unterbrambrasse, f.,
lower main topgallant brace;
- Unterbrampferd, n., *l. m. t.
foot rope*; - Unterbramrahe,
f., *l. m. t. yard*; - Unterbramsegel, n., *l. m. t. sail*;
- Unterleesegel, n., *l. m.
studding sail*; - Untermars-
Bauchgording, f., *l. m. topsail
bunt line*; - Untermars-
brasse, f., *l. m. topsail brace*;
- - schenkel, m., *l. m. t. b.
pendant*; - Untermarspferd,
n., *l. m. t. foot rope*; - Untermarsrahe, f., *l. m. t. yard*;
- Untermarssegel, n., *l. m.
t.*; - Untertoppsegel, *l.
m. t.*; - - brasse, f., *l. m. t.
brace*; - - rahe, f., *l. m. t.
yard*; - wanten, *main rigging*.
große Bär, m., *Greater Bear*;
- Baum, m., *main boom*; -
Bergholz, n., *main bend*;
- Brambulin, f., *main topgallant bowline*; - Buganker,
m., *first bower*; - Dirk, m.,
boom topping lift; - Fahrt,
f., *distant trade*; - Gaffel,
f., *main gaff*; - - Toppsegel,
n., *club topsail*; - Gangspill,
n., *main capstan*; - Gien,
n., *main purchase*; - Hals,
m., *m. tack*; - Havarie, f.,
general average; - Klüver,
m., *standing jib*; - Küstenfahrt, f., *great coasting
trade*; - Leesegel, n., *main
studding sail*; - Lot, n.,
deep sea lead; - Luke, f.,
main hatch; - Marsbulin,

f., *main top bowline*; - Oberbramsegel, n., *main top-
gallant royal sail*; - Oberbramstenge, f., *m. t. r.
mast*; - Özean, m., *Pacific
Ocean*; - reparatur, f., *heavy
repairs*; - Rüste, f., *main
channel*; - Schote, f., *main
sheet*; - Seitentakel, n.,
main tackle; - Stenge, f.,
main topmast; - Stirnrad,
n., *main spur wheel*; - Takel,
n., *main tackle*; - Talje, f.,
main tackle; - Welle, f.,
surge; - Zahnrad, n., *main
spur wheel*.
Größe, f., *size (of cable, rope,
&c.)*.
größte Breite, f., *extreme
breadth*.
Grummetstropp, m., *grummet*.
Grund, m., *bottom* od. *ground*;
Fahrt voraus über den -,
headway over the g.; an or
auf - geraten, *to take the
g.*; am - sitzend, *aground*;
auf - setzen, *to ground*;
- brechseen, *bottom breakers*;
- dünung, f., *ground swell*;
- eis, n., *g. ice*; - farbe, f.,
priming; - geschirr, n., *g.
tackle*; - hahn, m., *bottom
blow off cock*; - kette, f., *g.
chain*; - log n., *g. log*; - los,
soundless; - netz, n., *trawl*;
- platte, f., *bed plate*; - -
bolzen, m., *holding down
bolt*; - - - mutter, f., *foundation plate bolt nut*; - ring,
m., *neck bush*; - - des Stevenrohrs, *stern gland neck bush*;
- schleppnetz, n., *trawl net*;
- see, f., *ground sea*; - sog,

m., *g. suction*; - stoß,
m., *running aground*; -
takelage, f., *ground tackle*;
- talje, f., *relieving tackle*;
- ventil, n., *blow down valve*;
- winkel am Zenterkiel, m.,
*bottom angle bars at the
centre keel*.
Gründe, *soundings*.
gründen, *to settle on the
ground*.
Gründen, auf den - sein, *to
be on the soundings*.
grüne Farbe, f., *green paint*;
- Licht, n., *g. light*.
Guijo-Holz, n., *guijo-wood*.
Gum-holz, n., *gum-wood*.
Gummi, n., *rubber*; - absetzer,
m., *squillager*; - dichtung,
f., *rubber joint*; - einlage, f.,
r. insertion; - liderung or
- packung, f., *r. packing*;
- puffer, m., *buffer*.
günstiger Wind, m., *fair
wind*.
Gunters Rechentafel, f.,
Gunter's scale.
Gunwale, f., *gunwale*.
Gürtellinie, f., *cordon line*.
Gurtplatte, f., *rider plate*.
Gurtungsplatte, f., *spirketting
plate*.
Guß-eisen, n., *cast iron*; -
stahl, m., *c. steel*; - - werk,
n., *c. s. works*; - stück, n.,
casting.
Güter, *goods*; - dampfer, m.,
cargo steamer; - schiff, n.,
c. vessel; - unterschlagung,
f., *plunderage*.
Güteverhältnis, n., *efficiency*.
gut machen, *to make good*.
Gutsche, f., *gouge*.

H.

Haarrauch, m., *haar*.
Hack-bolzen, m., *ragged bolt*;
- öse, f., *heel brace*.
Hacke, f., *heel (of rudder or
mast)*; - der Bramstenge,

topgallant mast h.; - der
Marsstenge, *topmast h*.
Hackenband, n., *heel hoop*.
Hackmatack-Holz, n., *hack-
matack wood*.

Hafen, m., *port, harbour,
haven*; - anker, m., *blind
anchor*; - barre, f., *harbour
bar*; - bassin, n., *wet dock*;
- baum, m., *boom of a harbour*; - - geld, n., *boomage*;
- behörde, f., *h. authorities*;
- damm, m., *jetty, quay wall,
pier*; - deck, n., *harbour
deck*; - - Geländerstütze, f.,
h. d. stanchion; - dienst, m.,
h. duty; - eingang, m., *h.
entrance*; - einschnitt, m.,
creek; - feuer, n., *harbour
light*; - gebrauch, m., *custom
of the port*; - geld, n., *h. dues*;
- kapitän, m., *h. master*;
- lotse, m., *h. pilot*; - meister,
m., *berthing master*; - ordnung, f., *port regulations*;
- polizei, f., *harbour police*;
- priel, m., *h. creek*; - schlängel, m., *h. boom*; - unkosten,
port charges; - verändern,
to shift ports; - zeit, f., *tide
hour*.

Haff, n., *backwater*.

Hagebuchenholz, n., *horn
beam wood*.

Hagel-bö, f., *hail squall*; -
körner, *h. stones*.

Hahn, m., *cock*; - ende, n., *tap
end*; - gehäuse, n., *box of a
cock*; - kegel, m., or - küken,
n., *plug of a cock*; - schlüssel,
m., *c. handle*; - steuerung,
f., *distributing mechanism
of cocks*; - stopfbüchsendeckel, m., *cock gland*.

Hahnepoot, f., *crow foot*; -
für die Bauchtalje der
Marssegel, *lifter up of a
topsail*; - und Sorraugen,
fork and lashing eye.

Haifischhaken, m., *shark hook*.

Hainbuchenholz, n., *horn
beam wood*.

Hakblock, m., *hook block*.

Haken, m., *hook*; - block, m.,
single block with a hook;
- bolzen, m., *hook bolt*; -
- keil, m., *gib*; - laschung,
f., or - scharf, n., or - scheibe,
f., *hook and butt scarph*; -

schlag, m., *blackwall hitch*;
- - machen, *to lay a bend
around the hook of a block*;
- stiel, m., *cant spar*; -
stropp, m., *can hook*; - und
Kausche, *thimble hook*.

Halb-Balanziermaschine, f.,
half beam engine; - balken.
m., *h. beam*; - - winkel, m.,
h. b. angle bar; - Dampf,
m., *h. speed*; - - achteraus,
h s. astern; - - voraus, *h. s.
ahead*; - deck, n., *h. deck*;
- insel, f., *peninsula*; - kreisartige Deviation, f., *semicircular deviation*; - kugel,
f., *hemisphere*; - messer, m.,
radius; - minutenglas, n.,
half minute glass; - rund
in der Segelducht, *half moon
in the mast thwart*; - eisen,
n., *h. round bar iron*; -
scheibe, f., *dead sheave*; -
schott, n., *partial bulkhead*;
- stahl, m., *half converted
steel*; - stich, m., *h. hitch*;
- stocks, *half staff high*; - -
geflaggt, *with the flag half
staff*; - überwölbte Hütte,
f., *half poop*; - Zeit-Besichti-
gung, f, *h. time survey*.

halbe Back, f., *monkey forecastle*; - Balken, m., *half
beam*; - Ebbe, f., *half ebb*;
- Flut, f., *h. flood*; - Gehalt,
n., or - Heuer, f., *h. pay*;
- Kraft rückwärts, *h. speed
astern*; - - vorwärts, *h. s.
ahead*; - Scheibe, f., *dead
sheave*; - Schlag rückwärts
or vorwärts, m., *half turn
astern* resp. *ahead*; - Stich,
m., *h. hitch*; - - und Zimmermannsstich, *h. h. and timber
h.*; - Törn rückwärts or
vorwärts, m., *h. turn astern*
resp. *ahead*; - Wind, m.,
leading wind.

halbrunde Bastardfeile, f., -
half round bastard file; -
Schlichtfeile, f., *h. r. smooth
f.*; - Eisen, n., *h. r. iron*.

Halbrundleiste, f., *half round
comber*.

Hals, m., *tack (of a sail)*; - eines Bugbandes, *throat of a hook*; - e. Klüvers, *tack of a jib*; - e. Knieholzes, *throat of a knee timber*; - autholer, m., *tack tracing line*; - bindsel eines Stagsegels, n., *tack of a staysail*; - block, *tack block*; - bolzen. m., *throat bolt*; - Dämpfgording or - gording, f., *throat brail*; - haken, m., *tack hook*; - horn, n., *tack*; - klampe, f., *tack piece*; - knopf, m., *tack knot*; - koppel, f., *men's harness for towing boats*; - lager, n., *davit collar*; - lägel, m., *tack cringle*; - laschung, f., *tack lashing*; - poller, m., *chess tree*; - rohr, n., *spigot (of a cock)*; - talje, f., *tack tackle*; - zapfen, m., *journal*.

Halszapfen der Balanzieraxe, m., *lever shaft journal*; - - Kurbelwelle, *crank s. j.*; - - Luftpumpentraverse, *air pump crosshead j.*; - - Pumpenbalanzieraxe, *pump lever shaft j.*; - - Pumpentraverse, *p. crosshead j.*; - - Traverse, *c. j.*; - - Welle, *shaft j.*; - - Zirkulationspumpentraverse, *circulation pump crosshead j.*

halsen, *tacking* oder *wearing*. Halsen auf! *up tacks and sheets!* - und Schoten aufstechen, *to give up tacks and sheets*.

Halt und rückwärts! *stop and reverse!*

halten, *to stop*.

halten, Hafenwache -, *to keep harbour watch*; Luv -, *to k. the luff*; Seewache -, *to k. sea watch*; die Steuerbordseite eines Flusses -, *to k. the starboard side of a river*; Wache -, *to k. watch*.

halten, sich auf dem Wasser halten, *to live on the water*; sich gut -, *to hold her own*;

s. g. am Winde -, *to h. h. wind*; sich hintenaus -. *to keep astern*; sich in Hörweite -, *to k. within hail*; sich in Signalweite -, *to k. w. signal distance*; sich unter Land -, *to k. the land aboard*; sich voraus -, *to k. ahead*.

Haltetau, n., *twiddling line (of steering wheel)*.

Hammer, m., *hammer*; - barkeit, f., *malleability*; - maschine, f., *inverted vertical engine.*

Hand über Hand klimmen, *to climb hand over hand*.

Hand-arbeit, f., *hand work*; - bagger, m., *hand drag*; - blasebalg, m., *hand bellows*; - bohrer, m., *h. drill*; - bohrmaschine, f., *h. d. machine*; - Drehvorrichtung, f., *h. turning gear*; - fit, f., *piercer*; - führer, m., *h. guide*; - geländer, n., *h. rails*; - geld, n., *advance*; - habe, f., *handle*; - haben, *to handle*; - - beim Schwoien, *to tend when swinging*; - habung, f., *management*; - haken, m., *hand hook*; - hammer, m., *bench hammer*; - hebel, m., *hand lever*; - kompaß, m., *dial compass*; - kran, m., *h. crane*; - lampe, f., *h. lamp*; - loch, n., *h. hole*; - - maschine, f., *h. punching machine*; - lot, n., *h. lead*; - - leine, f., *h. l. line*; - nietung, f., *h. riveting*; - pferde, *h. beckets*; - platte, f., *palm*; - pumpe, f., *h. pump*; - kolben, m., *h. p. bucket*; - - - ring, *h. p. b. ring*; - pumpenstange, f., *h. p. rod*; - pumpenventil, n., *h. p. valve*; - rad, n., *h. wheel*; - ruder, n., *h. wheel*; - säge, f., *h. saw*; - schellen, *h. cuffs*; - schere, f., *h. shears*; - schraubstock, m., *h. vice*; - segel, n., *h. sail*; - spake or - speiche, f., *h. spike*;

- steuer, n., *hand gear*; - - gerät, n., *h. steering gear*; - - rad, n., *h. s. wheel*; - steuerungshebel, m., *h. distributing lever*; - talje, f., *jigger*; - umsteuerungs- mechanismus, m., *h. revers- ing gear*; - umsteuerungsrad, n., *h. r. wheel*; - - bremse, f., *h. r. wheel brake*; - vorrich- tung, f., *h. gear.*

Handel, m., *trade*; - treibend, *trading.*

handelnd, *trading.*

Handels-angelegenheiten, *mer- cantile affairs*; - dampfer, m., *merchant steamer*; - flagge, f., *m. flag*; - flotte, f., *m. fleet*; - gesellschaft, f., *trading company*; - gesetz, n., *mercantile law*; - - buch, n., *commercial code*; - hafen, m., *trading port*; - kammer, f., *Chamber of Commerce*; - mann, m., *trader*; - marine, f., *mercan- tile marine*; - recht, n., *mercantile law*; - sachen, *m. affairs*; - schiff, n., *mer- chantman*; - - fahrtsgesetz, n., *merchant shipping act*; - verkehr, m., *traffic*; - ver- trag, m., *treaty of commerce.*

handiges Wetter, n., *handy weather.*

Händler, m., *trader.*

handliche Segel, *easy sails.*

handsames Wetter, n., *handy weather.*

Hanf-liderung or - packung, f., *hemp packing*; - schlauch, m., *canvas hose*; - tau, n., *hemp rope.*

Hängekiel, m., or Hängeknie, n., *hanging knee*; - der Hauptdeckbalken, *deck beam h. k.*; - der Oberdeck- balken, *upper d. b. h. k.*; - der Zwischendeckbalken, *lower d. b. h. k.*

Hänge-kompaß, m., *hanging compass*; - lampe, f., *h. lamp*; - matte, f., *hammock*;

- - Hahnepots, *h. clews*; - - steert, m., *h. lashing.*

Hängematts-decke, f., *ham- mock cloth*; - hahnepot, f., *h. clew*; - jolle, f., *h. gaunt line*; - nitzel, m., *tie tie*; - presennig, f., *hammock cloth*; - - steert, m., *h. lashing.*

Hanger, m., *pendant*; - der Backspiere, *p. of the lower booms*; - der Marsstengen, *burton p.*; - der Nocktakel, *yard tackle p.*; - der Wäsche- leinen, *clothes lines p.*; - des Backtisches, *crow foot of the mess table*; - des Groß- stagtakels, *main tackle p.*; - des Innentakels, *stay tackle p.*; - einer Unterrahe, *sling of a lower yard*; - eines Giens, *winding pendant.*

Hanger-band, n., *1. sling hoop (of a yard)*: *2. pendant hoop (of derrick)*; - block, m., *tackle pendant*; - ketten, *chain slings*; - ring, m., *pendant ring*; - stropp, m., *sling strop*; - stroppklampe, f., *sling cleat*; - takel, n., *mast tackle.*

Hängeschiene, f., *drag link.*

Hängpallen, *hanging pawls.*

hantieren, *to handle.*

Harke, f., *rake.*

Harmattan, m., *harmattan.*

Harpune, f., *1. harpoon (for fish)*; *2. turtle peg (for turtle).*

harpunieren, *to harpoon.*

Harpunierer, m., *harpooner.*

Harpunleine, f., *harpoon line.*

hart. *hard*; - am Winde lie- gen, *to sail near the wind*; - auf! *hard a-weather!* - auf's Steuer sein, *to be h. of steerage*; - Backbord, *h. a-port*; - bändsel, n., *throat seizing*; - brot, n., *biscuits*; - geschlagenes Tauwerk, n., *hard laid rope*; - gußstahl, m., *case hardened steel*; - in Lee! *hard a-lee!* - Steuer- bord! *h. a-starboard!*

hartes Holz, n., *hard wood*; - Tropenholz, n., *tropical h. w.*

härten, *to temper (tools)*.

Hartlot, n., *hard solder*.

hartlöten, *brazing*.

Härtungsprobe, f., *tempering test*.

Hartzinn, n., *pewter*.

häsig, *hazy*.

Haspelstützen, *upstanders of the windlass*.

Hauptabsperrventil, n., *main stop valve*; - spindel, f., *m. s. v. spindle*.

Hauptanker, m., *sheet anchor*.

Hauptausgußrohr, n., *main discharge pipe*.

Hauptausgußventil, n., *main discharge valve*; - deckel, m., *m. d. v. cover*; - sitz, m., *m. d. v. seat*; - spindel, f., *m. d. v. spindle*.

Hauptdampfrohr, n., *main steam pipe*; - leitung, f., *m. s. pipes*.

Hauptdampfventil, n., *main steam valve*.

Hauptdeck, n., *main deck*; - balken, m., *m. d. beam*; - - Hängeknie, n., *m. d. b. hanging knee*; - - Längsschiene, f., or - - Lukenstringer, m., *m. d. b. tie plate*; - - stringer, m., *m. d. b. stringer*; - - - platte, f., *m. d. b. s. plate*; - balkenwinkel, m., *m. d. b. angle bar*; - balkweger, m., *m. d. b. shelf*; - band, n., *m. d. hook*; - befestigung, f., *m. d. fastening*; - beplankung, f., *m. d. planking*; - beplattung, f., *m. d. plating*; - bolzen, m., *m. d. bolt*; - luke, f., or - Lukendeckel, m., *m. hatch*; - Lukenstringer, m., *deck beam tie plate*; - Lukensüll, m., *m. d. hatchway coaming*; - Mastkeile, *m. d. mast wedges*; - Scheergang, m., *m. d. sheerstrake*; - Setzweger, m., *m. d. spirketting*;

- Sonnensegel, n., *m. d. awning*; - stringer, m., *m. d. stringer*; - - platte, f., *m. d. s. plate*; - - winkel, m., *m. d. s. angle bar*; - stütze, f., *m. d. stanchion*; - Unterbalkweger, m., *m. d. beam clamp*; - Wassergang, m., *m. d. waterway*.

Haupt-einlaßventilsieb, n., *main injection valve rose plate*; - einspritzventilspindel, f., *m. i. v. spindle*.

Haupthalsblock, m., *main tack block*.

Hauptinjektions-rohr, n., *main injection pipe*; - ventil, n., *m. i. valve*; - - deckel, m., *m. i. v. cover*; - - spindel, f., *m. i. v. spindle*.

Haupt-kabel, n., *main cable*; - kessel, m., *m. boiler*; - kiel, m., *m. keel*; - kielschwein, n., *m. keelson*; - lagerdeckel, m., *m. bearing keep*; - nagel, m., *doubling nail*; - raum, m., *main hold*; - reeder, m., *principal owner*; - reparaturen, *thorough repairs*; - rumpf, m., *main body*; - - spanten, *m. b. frames*; - scheergang, m., *m. sheerstrake*; - schornstein, m., *m. funnel*; - sente, f., *breadth line*; - spant, n., *main frame*; - - balken, m., *main beam*; - - Querschnitt, or - - schnitt, m., *midship section*; - - Umfang von der Mittellinie der Oberkante des Kiels bis zum Oberdeckstringer, *girth from centre line at top of keel to weather deck stringer plate*; - speiserohr, n., *main feed pipe*; - - ventil, n., *m. check valve*; - triebrad, n., *m. cone driving wheel*; - ventil, n., *m. valve*; - welle, f., *m. shaft*; - - des Dampfsteuerapparates, *m. s. of steering engine*; - wind, m., *cardinal wind*.

Haus-boot, n., *house boat*; - reise, f., *passage home*.

Hause, zu - gehören, *to hail from*.

Hausung, f., *housing*.

Haut, f., *sheathing*; - spiker, m., s. *nail*.

Havarie, f., *casualty, average*; - akte, f., or - bond, m , *a. bond*; - gelder, *a. disbursement*; - grosse, f., *general a.*; - kontrakt, m., *a. agreement*; - kosten, *a. charges*; - - decken, *to settle the a.*; - leiden, *to suffer a.*; mit - einlaufen, *to put in in a damaged state*; - papiere, *average papers*; - particulaire, f., *particular a.*; - rechnung, f., *statement of a.*; - verteilung, f., *partition of a.*; - wird nur im Strandungsfalle vergütet, *a. will only be made good in case of stranding*.

havarierter Zustand, m., *damaged state*; in total havariertem Zustand, *in a crippled s.*

Hebe-baum, m., *heaver*; - daumen, m., *cam*; - rahmen, m., *banjo frame*; - versuch, m., *attempt to raise*; - vorrichtung, f., *lifting apparatus*; - zeug zurichten, *to raise a purchase*.

Hebel, m., *lever*; - des Drosselklappen - Gestänges, *throttle valve lever*; - des Kettenstoppers or - des Patentstoppers, *l. of the chain cable compressor*; - griff, m., *l. handle*.

heben, *to raise (a sunken vessel)*.

hebendes Segel, n., *lifting sail*.

hecht, *staunch*.

Heck, n., *stern*; - anker, m., s. *anchor*; - balken, m., *transom*; - - der Poop, *deck t. of poop*; der unterste - -, *helm port t.*; - - bolzen, m., *t. bolt*; - - knie, n., *t. knee*; - - platte f., *t. plate*; -

band, n., *stern hook*; - beplankung, f., *stern planking*; - beplattung, f., s. *plating*; - boog, m., *upper rounding*; - boot, n., *stern boat*; - bord, n., *upper rounding*; - davit, m., *stern davit*; - fenster, n., s. *port*; - flagge, f., s. *flag*; - galerie, f., s. *gallery*; - geländer, n., *taff rail*; - geschütz, n., *chase stern*; - klüse, f., *stern pipe*; - knie, n., *transom knee*; - laterne, f., *stern light*; - leiste, f., s. *rail*; unterste - -, *counter r.*; - leiter, f., *stern ladder*; - pfeiler, m., *side counter timber*; - pumpe, f., *stern pump*; - rad, n., s. *wheel*; - - dampfer, m., s. *w. steamer*; - - - maschine, f., s. *w. engine*; - rad-Schleppdampfer, m., s. *w. tug*; - reling, f., s. *rails*; - ruder, n., s. *rudder*; - spant, n., s. *frame*; - stütze, f., *side counter timber*; - verband, m., *stern framing*; - verzierung, f., *stern moulding*.

Heimats-hafen, m., *port of registry*; - wimpel, m , *homeward bounder*.

Heimreise, f., *voyage home*.

Heiß, m., *hoist (of flag, sail, or mast)*; - auf! *Sway away!* - luftmaschine, f., *hot air engine*; - maschine, f., *hoisting engine*; - vorrichtung, f., *h. gear*; - wasserheizung, f., *hot water heating*; - weg! *sway away!*

heiße Dampf, m., *heated steam*; - Klima, n., *hot climate*; - Wetter, n., *h. weather*; - Zone, f., *torrid zone*.

heissen, *to hoist*; weg -, *to h. away*.

Heiz-fläche, f., *heating surface*; - kraft, f., *h. power*; - materialien, *fuel*; - raum, m., *stoke hold*; - - Flurplatten, s. *h. platform*; - - leiter, f., s. *h. ladder*; - -

Plattform, f., s. *h. platform*;
- - schott, n., s. *h. bulkhead*;
- - - winkel, m., s. *h. b.
angle bar*; - raumtür, f., s. *h.
door*; - - Scharnier, n., s. *h.
d. hinge*; - raum-Ventilator,
m., s. *h. ventilator*; - vorrichtung, f., *heating apparatus*.
heizen einen Kessel, *to fire
a boiler.*
Heizer, m., *fireman.*
Heizung, f., *heating.*
Helgen, m., *building slip*; -
unter dem Schlagbett,
ground way.
Heling, m., *carrick bend.*
Heliograph, m., *heliograph.*
Hellegat, n., *store room.*
heller Teerfirnis, m., *bright
varnish.*
Helling, f., *slip*; - block, m.,
careening block.
Helm, m., *helm*; - holz or
- stock, m., *tiller.*
Hemisphere, f., *hemisphere.*
Hemlockholz, n., *hemlock
wood.*
Hemm-klampe des Ruders, f.,
rudder stops; - schraube,
f., *set screw.*
Hennegatt, n., *helm port.*
herab-gleiten, *to slip down*:
- lassen, *to lower*; ein Segel
- -, *to cut a sail.*
herausliegen, *to stand out.*
herausnehmen, *to unship, to
take out.*
Herbst-Äquinoktium, n., *autumnal equinox.*
Herd, m., *hearth*; - des Feuers,
seat of the fire; - des
Scheibengatts, *bottom of
the sheave hole.*
herfallen über uns, *to close
in on us.*
Herings-büse, f., *herring buss*;
- fischer, m., *h. smack*; -
fischerei, f., *h. fishery.*
herrenloser Fund, m., *waif.*
herum-brassen, *to brace about*:
- holen, *to veer*; - legen, *to
put about.*

herunter lassen, *to drop*; -
mit der Fock! *down fore-
sail!* - nehmen die Rahen,
to take down the yards.
Herz, n., *heart (of rope* or
mast): - bändsel, n., *throat
seizing*: - kausch der Bugsprietzurring, f., *gammon
plate*; - rad, n., *heart
wheel*: - ring der Bug-
sprietzurring, m., *gammon
ring*; - scheibe. f., *heart
wheel*; - sente, f., *breadth
line*: - förmiges Exzentrik,
n., *heart wheel.*
Heuer, f., *wages*; - amt, n.,
shipping office; - baas, m.,
s. *master*; - bureau, n., *s.
office*: - und Unterhalt im
Nothafen, *wages and maintenance in port of refuge*;
- vertrag, m., *articles*; - vorschuß, m., *advance money.*
heuern, *to hire.*
Heulboje, f., *whistle buoy.*
heulender Sturm, m, *harr.*
Hickoryholz, n., *hickory wood.*
Hiel, m, Hielung, f., *block
heel.*
Hiev mit Kraft! *Heave and
rally!* - pall! *H. and paul!*
hieven an einer Kette od.
einem Tau, *to heave upon
a chain or rope.*
Hilfe, f., *assistance.*
Hilfs-absperrventil, n., *intermediate stop valve*: - - spindel, f., *i. s. v. spindle*; - anlaßventil, n., *auxiliary starting valve*; - - rohr, n., *a. s.
v. pipe*: - besichtiger, m.,
assistant surveyor; - dampf,
m., *auxiliary steam*; - -
kraft, f., *a. s. power*; - -
pumpe, f., *a. s. pump*; - - rohr,
n., *a. s. pipe*; - - - leitung,
f., *a. s. pipes*; - dampfventil,
n, *a. s. valve*; - hahn, m.,
supplementary cock; - kessel, m., *donkey boiler*; -
Ablaßhahn, m., *d. blow down
cock*; - - Ausbau, m., *recess
bulkhead of donkey boiler*;
- - decke, f., *crown of d. b.*;

- - nische, f., *d. b. recess*;
- - Speiserohr, n., *d. b. feed
pipe*; - maschinen, *auxiliary
engines*; - mittel, n., *resource*;
- pumpe, f., *auxiliary pump*;
- rohr, n., *a. pipe;* - ruder,
n., *a. rudder*; - schieber, m.,
a. valve; - - Absperrventil,
n., *a. stop v.*; - - - gestänge,
n., *a. s. v. gear*; - schieber-ge-
stänge, n., *a. starting v. g.*; - -
spindel, f., *a. s. v. spindle*; - -
stange, f., *a. s. v. rod*; - schraube, f., *a. propeller*; - -
dampfer, m., *a. screw
steamer*; - spant, n., *assistant
frame*; - speisehahn, m.,
auxiliary feed cock; - Steuergerät, n., *a. steering gear*;
- takel, n., *tackle upon
tackle*; - ventil, n., *auxiliary
valve.*
hinauf-dampfen, *to steam up*;
- fahren, *to proceed up;* -
treiben mit der Tide, *to
drive up with the tide.*
hinfahren an der Küste, *to
range the coast*; - dicht a.
d. K., *to hug t. c.*
Hinfracht, f., *outward freight.*
hinhalten auf or zu, *to bear
down upon.*
Hinreise, f., *outward passage.*
hin- und hergehende Bewe-
gung, f., *alternative motion.*
hin und her schütteln, *to
fetch way.*
hinten, *aft*; - aus halten, *to
keep astern*; - aus holen,
to haul a.; - - sacken, *to
drop a.*; Schiff - -, *vessel a.*
hinter, *abaft*; - aus, *astern*;
- - gehen, *to go astern*; -
backen, *buttocks*; - brassen,
after braces; - Brunnen-
Saugventil, n., *after well
suction valve*; - dampf, m.,
supply steam; - deck, n.,
after deck; - ebbe, f., *end of
the ebb*; - Füll- und Saugventilkasten, m., *after tank
filling and suction box*; -
Gaffeltoppsegel, n., *mizen*

gaff topsail; - gangspill, n.,
after capstan; - herfahren,
to stand after; - kante, f.,
after leech; - kantspant, n., *a.
cant timber*; - klüse, f., *stern
pipe*; - ladeporte, f., *stern
port*; - lastig, *by the stern*;
- - machen, *to get a ship
by the stern*; - leik, n.,
after leech rope; - leine, f.,
stern rope; - luke, f., *after
hatch*; - - süll, m., *a. h.
coaming*; - pflicht, f., *a.
cuddy*; - piek, f., *a. peak*;
- - band, n., *crutch*; - - - bolzen, m., *c. bolt*; - piektank,
m., *after peak tank*; - - Saugeventil, n., *a. p. t. suction
valve*; - pforte, f., *stern
port*; - Plattform, f., *back
platform*; - rahe, f., *after
yard*; - raum, m., *a. hold*;
- säule, f., *back column*; -
schiff, n., *after body*; - segel,
a. sails; - Seitenauflanger,
m., *quarter timber*; - Steuergerät, n., *after steering
gear*; - Steven, m., *stern
post*; - - knie, n., *sternson*;
- - kniebolzen, m., *s. bolt*; - -
niete, f., *stern post rivet*;
- - platte, f., *s. p. plate*; - -
pumpe, f., *s. pump*; - tank,
m., *after tank*; - teil, m., *1.
after body (of ship); 2. rake
(of the rudder)*; - Todholz,
n., *after deadwood.*
hintere Aufklotzung, f., *after
deadwood*; - Deckel, m.,
after gland; - Doppelboden,
m., *double bottom aft*; -
Kreuzkopf u. Gleitplatten,
after crosshead and guides;
- Kurbelwelle, f., *after crank
shaft*; - Landfeste, f., *stern
fast*; - Propellersteven, m.,
heeling post; - Pumpen-
balanziergelenke, *back lever
links*; - Rauchkammer, f.,
combustion chamber; - Rohrwand des Kessels, f., *back
tube plate of boiler*; - Seitenfeste, f., *quarter fast*; -
Stirnwand des Kessels, f.,

back end plate of boiler;
- Verholleine, f., stern line.
hinterste Planken (Platten)
der Außenhaut (Innenhaut-)
Gänge, after hoods.
Hin- und Herwogen der See,
n., the rolling and tossing
of the sea.
hinunter-dampfen, to steam
down; - gleiten, to ride
down (a stay, &c.); - setzen,
sending; - treiben, to drop
down.
hissen, to hoist.
Hitze, f., heat; - gradmesser,
m., pyrometer.
Hitzwelle, f., heat wave.
Hobel, m., plane; - eisen, n.,
p. iron; - maschine, f., planing machine.
hobeln, to plane.
hoch am Winde liegen, to
sail near the wind; - und
trocken, high and dry.
Hochbootsmann, m., boats-
wain.
Hochdruck, m., high pressure;
- cylinder see - zylinder;
- dampf, m., h. p. steam;
- Exzenter, n., h. p. eccentric;
- - bolzen, m., h. p. e. bolt;
- - bügel, m., h. p. e. strap;
- - bügel-Paßstück, n., h. p. e.
s. liner; - - Lagerschalen, h.
p. e. brasses; - - scheibe, f.,
h. p. e. sheave; - - stange, f.,
h. p. e. rod; - - vorrichtung,
f., h. p. e. gear; - Geradführung, f., h. p. guide; -
gestänge or - getriebe, n.,
h. p. gear; - Gleitbahn, f.,
h. p. guide; - Gleitschuh, m.,
h. p. g. shoe; - kessel, m., h.
p. boiler.
Hochdruckkolben, m., high
pressure piston; - deckel,
m., h. p. p. gland; - Führungsstange, f., h. p. p.
guide rod; - Liderungsring,
m., h. p. p. packing ring;
- ring, m., h. p. p. ring; -
stange, f., h. p. p. rod; - -
Kreuzkopf, m., h. p. p. r.

crosshead; - - - führung, f.,
h. p. p. r. c. guide; - - -
gleitplatte, f., h. p. p. r. c. g.;
- - - Lagerschalen, h. p. p.
r. c. brasses; - stangen-Stopfbüchse, f., h. p. p. r. stuffing
box; - - - deckel, m., h. p. p.
r. s. b. gland.
Hochdruck - Kreuzkopflager -
bolzen, m., high pressure
crosshead bolt.
Hochdruck - Kreuzkopflager -
schalen, high pressure connecting rod top end; - -
deckel, m., h. p. c. r. t. e.
keep.
Hochdruck-Kurbelbacke, f.,
high pressure crank web.
Hochdruck-Kurbelwelle, f.,
high pressure crank shaft;
- - lager, n., h. p. c. s. bearing; - - - bolzen, m., h. p. c.
s. b. bolt; - - - deckel, m.,
h. p. c. s. bearing keep; - - - -
bolzen, m., h. p. c. s. b. k.
bolt; - - Lagerschalen, h. p.
c. s. bearing brasses; - - -
Paßstück, n., h. p. c. s.
brasses liner; - - Lager-
zapfen, m., h. p. c. s. journal.
Hochdruck-Kurbelzapfen, m.,
high pressure crank pin;
- - Lagerbolzen, m., h. p. c.
p. bolt; - - Lagerschalen, h.
p. c. p. brasses; - - - deckel,
m., h. p. connecting rod
bottom end keep.
Hochdruck-Leitung, f., high
pressure guide; - maschine,
f., h. p. engine; - Pleyelstange, f., h. p. connecting
rod; - - bolzen, m., h. p. c.
r. bolt; - - fuß-Paßstück, n.,
h. p. c. r. bottom end liner;
- receiverrohr, n., h. p.
receiver pipe; - rohr, n.,
h. p. tube; - Rückwärts-
bewegungs-Gleitplatten, h.
p. sternway guides.
Hochdruckschieber, m., high
pressure slide valve; - Abbalanzierungskolben, m., h.
p. v. balance piston; - kasten,
m., h. p. v. casing; - - dek-

kel, m., *h. p. v. c. door*;
- - Sicherheitsventilbe-
lastung, f., *h. p. v. c. escape
valve load*; - stange, f., *h. p.
v. rod*; - - führung, f., *h. p.
v. spindle guide*; - - Stopfbüchse, f., *h. p. v. rod stuffing box*; - - - deckel, m., *h.
p. v. r. s. b. gland.*

Hochdruck-Stopfbüchse, f.,
high pressure gland.

Hochdruckturbine, f., *high
pressure turbine*;-maschine,
f., *h. p. t. engine.*

Hochdruckzylinder, m., *high
pressure cylinder*: - Austrittskanal, m., *h. p. c. exhaust port*; - büchse, f., *h.
p. c. liner*; - deckel, m., *h.
p. c. cover*; - - bolzen, m., *h. p.
c. c. bolt*; - Drainagehahn,
m., *h. p. cylinder drain
cock*; - einsatz, m., *h. p. c.
liner*; - Entwässerungsrohr,
n., *h. p. c. drain pipe*; -
Kolbenstangen - Stopfbüchsendeckel, m., *h. p. c. piston
rod stuffing box gland*; -
mantel, m., *h. p. c. jacket*;
- Sicherheitsventil, n., *h. p.
c. escape valve*; - - feder, f.,
h. p. c. e. v. spring; - - belastung, f., *h. p. c. e. v. load*;
- - spindel, f., *h. p. c. e. v.
spindle*; - Stopfbüchsen-
deckel, m., *h. p. c. stuffing
box gland.*

hochgehende See, f., *topping
sea.*

hoch getakelt, *high rigged*;
- mastig, *taunt masted*; -
plateau, n., *table land*; -
seefischerei, f., *deep sea
fishing*; - und Niederdruck-
maschine, *compound engine.*

Hochwasser, n., *high water*;
- marke, f., *h. w. mark*; -
niveau, n., *h. w. level*; - zeit,
f., *time of h. w.*

Hock, n., *coop.*

Höcker, m., *hump.*

Höft, n., *jetty.*

Hofttau, n,, *swifter.*

hohe Bodenwrangen, *deep
floors*; - Breiten, *high latitudes*; - Fracht, f., *h. freight*:
- Land, n., *h. land*; - schmale
Heck, n., *pink stern*; - See,
f., *1. heavy sea*; *2. the main*;
die - - gewinnen, *to get sea
room*: - Spant, n., *deep
frame*; - Tank, m., *d. tank*;
- - kupfernes Verbindungsrohr, n., *d. t. copper bend.*

Höhe, f., *1. altitude (star or
sun)*; *2. height (barometer,
tween deck, above sea level)*;
auf der - von X., *off X.*;
eine - nehmen, *to take an
observation*; scheinbare -,
apparent altitude; wahre -,
true a.

Höhen-abweichung, f., *vertical deviation*; - kreis, m,
circle of altitude; - messer,
m., *altimeter*; - messung, f.,
altimetry; - rauch, m., *dust
haze*; - zirkel, m., *circle of
altitude.*

höher, nicht -! *no higher!*

Höhere Gewalt, f., *the Acts
of God*; - Nippflut, f., *deep
neap.*

Hohl-eisen, n., *gouge*; - kehl-
meißel, m., *round nose
chisel*; - kiel, m., *hollow
keel*; - klampe, f., *saddle
crutch*; - meißel, m., *hollow
chisel*; - welle, f., *h. shaft
(of engine)*; - zirkel, m., *inside callipers.*

hohle Säule, f., *hollow column*:
- See, f., *chopping sea*; -
Stütze, f., *hollow pillar*; -
Welle, f., *h. shaft (of engine).*

Hol steif! *Haul taught!*

holen, *rousing (on a rope)*;
das Schiff auf die Helgen -,
*to haul the ship on the
stocks.*

holender Part, m., *hauling
part of a tackle.*

Hohlklampe, f., *dumb snatch.*

Holz, n., *timber*; - biege-
maschine, f., *wood bending
machine*; - fender, m.,
wooden fender; - gattung,

f., *kind of timber*; - hafen eines Docks, m., *camber of a dock*; - hammer, m., *mallet*; - keil, m., *wooden wedge*; - kohle, f., *char coal*; - ladung, f., *cargo of timber*; - nagel, m., *treenail*; - - eines Strebers, *nog*; - - befestigung, f., *treenailing*; - pütze, f., *wooden bucket*; - ring, m., *w. ferrule*; - schraube, f., *short screw bolt*; - schuh, m., *clog*; - sorten, *kinds of wood*; - teer, m., *Stockholm tar*; - verkleidung, f., *wood lining*.

hölzerne Block, m., *wooden block*; - Band, n., *w. hoop*; - Boot, n., *w. boat*; - Bugband, n., *w. hook*; - Kausche, f., *bull's eye*; - Knie, n., *wooden knee*; - Mast, m., *w. mast*; - Rahe, f., *wooden yard*; - Reeling, f., *w. rail*.

Homogeneisen, n., *homogeneous iron*.

Honorarkonsul, m., *honorary consul*.

Hoofd, n., *foreland, jetty*; - tau, n., *swifter*.

Horizont, m., *horizon*; am - verschwinden, *to dip*.

Horizontalsteuer, n., *horizontal rudder*.

horizontale Dampfsteuermaschine, f., *horizontal steering engine*; - Durchbolzen, m., *h. through bolt*; - Knie, n., *h. knee*; - - platte, f., *gusset*; - Lenzpumpe, f., *horizontal bilge pump*; - Luftpumpe, f., *h. air p.*; - Maschine, f., *h. engine*; - Riß des Halbschiffes, m., *half breadth plan*; - Röhrenkessel, m., *horizontal tubular boiler*; - Speisepumpe, f., *h. feed pump*; - Trunkmaschine, f., *h. trunk engine*; - Zirkulationspumpe, f., *h. circulation pump*; - Zylinder, m., *h. cylinder*.

Horn, n., *peak (of a sail)*; - karte, f., *horn card*; - klampe,

f., *h. cleat*; - scheibe, f., *h. card*.

Hörner, *cusps (of the moon)*.

Hörweite, sich in - halten, *to keep within hail*.

Hosenboje, f., *breeches buoy*.

Hub, m., *stroke*; - rückwärts, *back s.*; - vorwärts, *forward s.*; - begrenzer, m., *valve guard*; - begrenzung, f., *travel guard (of steering gear)*; - höhe, f., *travel*; - länge, f., *length of stroke*; - wechsel, m., *change of s.*; - zähler, m., *counter*; - mit Zifferblatt, *dial c.*; - zählvorrichtng, f., *c. gear*.

Hufeisensplissung, f., *horse shoe splice*.

Hühnerhock, m., *hen coop*.

Huk, f., *hook*; - hölzer or - spannen or - spanten, *counter pieces*.

Huker, m., or - galeasse, f., *hooker*.

Hülfe see Hilfe.

Hülse, f., *boss*; - des Ruderstevens, *b. of stern post*; - der Schaftwelle, *propeller shaft liner*; - des Schraubenstevens, *boss of propeller post*.

Hülsen-platte, f., *boss plate*; - schlüssel, m., *box spanner*.

Hummer der Marsstenge, f., *foot of a topmast*; - gatt, n., *tie hole*.

Hunde-ende, n., *fag end*; - pünte, f., *point of a rope*; eine - - an ein Tau legen, *to point a rope*; - wache, f., *dog watch. (12—4 a. m.)*

Huon-Pineholz, n., *huon pine wood*.

Hurrarufen, n., *cheering*.

Hüsing, f., *houseline*.

Hütchen, n., *socket (of rhumb card)*.

Hütte, f., *poop*.

Hütten-balkweger, m., *poop deck beam shelf*.

Hüttendeck, n., *poop deck*; - balken, m., *p. d. beam*; - - Hängeknie, n., *p. d. b.*

hanging knee; - - Luken-stringer, m., *p. d. b. tie plate*; - - stringer, m., *p. d. b. stringer*; - - Stringerplatte, f., *p. d. b. s. plate*; - Balken-winkel, m., *p. d. b. angle bar*; - befestigung, f., *p. d. fastening*; - beplattung, f., *p. d. plating*; - stringer, m., *p. d. stringer*; - - platte, f., *p. d. s. plate*; - - winkel, m., *p. d. s. angle bar*; - Wassergang, m., *p. d. water-way*; - zelt, n., *p. awning.*
Hütten-geländer, n., *poop rails and stanchions*; - - stange, f., *p. guard rods*; - - stütze, f., *p. stanchion*; - leiter, f., *p. ladder*; - reling, f., *p. rail*; - Schergang, m., *p. sheer-strake*; - schott, n., *p. bulk-head*; - - süll, m., *coaming of p. b.*; - Schutzbretter, *p. weather boards*; - Seitenbe-plattung, f., *side plating of p.*; - Sonnensegel, n., *p. awning*; - spant, n., *p. frame*; - süll, m., *p. coaming*; - - winkel,

m., *p. c. angle bar*; - treppe, f., *p. ladder*; - wassergang, m., *p. waterway.*
Hydraulische Bagger, m., *hydraulic dredger*; - Dock, n., *screw dock*; - Druck, m., *hydraulic pressure*; - Hebe-apparat, m., *h. jack*; - Kessel-probe, f., *h. boiler test*; - Kran, m., *h. crane*; - Maschi-ne, f., *h. engine*; - Nietung, f., *h. riveting*; - Propeller, m., or - Schraube, f., *nautilus propeller.*
Hydro-graph, m., *hydro-grapher*; - graphie, f., *hydro-graphy*; - graphisches Amt, n., *hydrographical office*; - kineter, m., *hydrokineter*; - meter, m., *hydrometer*; - oxygengas, n., *hydro-oxygen-gas*; - statischer Druck, m., *hydrostatic pressure*; - statik, f., *hydrostatics.*
Hygienische Pumpe, f., *sani-tary pump*; - Rohr, n., *s. pipe.*

I.

Impermeator, m., *impermeator.*
Indikator, m., *indicator*; - diagramm, n., *i. diagram*; - feder, f., *i. spring*; - hahn, m., *i. cock*; - kolben, m., *i. piston*; - - feder, f., *i. p. spring*; - - stange, f., *i. p. rod*; - kurve, f., *diagram of the i.*; - papier, n., *i. card*; - - zylinder, m., *i. paper cylinder*; - rohr, n., *i. pipe*; - schnur, f., *i. cord*; - stift, m., *i. pencil*; - trommel, f., *i. barrel*; - zubehör, n., *i. gear*; - zylinder, m., *i. cylinder.*
indirekt wirkende Maschine, f., *indirect acting engine.*
indischer Ocean, m., *Indian Ocean.*

indizierte Druck, m., *indicated thrust*; - Kraft, f., *i. power*; - Pferdestärke, f., *i. horse power*; - Schraubendruck, m., *i. thrust of the propeller.*
Ineinandergehen der Lichter, n., *the opening out of the lights.*
Ingangsetzungsvorrichtung, f., *starting gear.*
Ingenieur, m., *engineer*; - wesen, n., *engineering.*
Inholz, n., *frame timber*; - der Back, *f. t. of forecastle*; - der Hütte or Poop, *f. t. of poop*; - des erhöhten Quarterdecks, *f. t. of raised quarter deck*; - mit einem Knick, *knuckle timber*; - und Fach, *timber and space.*

Inhölzer salzen, *to pickle the timbers.*
Inhölzern, mit schwachen - gebaut, *light timbered.*
Injektion, f., *injection.*
Injektions-hahn, m., *injection cock*; - rohr, n., *i. pipe*; - ventil, n., *i. valve*; - - deckel, m., *i. v. cover*; - - gehäuse, n., *i. v. box*; - - rohr, n., *i. v. pipe*; - - spindel, f., *i. v. spindle*; - wasser, n., *i. water.*
Injektor, m., *injector*; - Dampf-düse, f., *i. receiving pipe.*
Inklination, f., *dip*; - der Magnetnadel, *d. of the needle*; - der Schaufelräder, *d. o. t. paddle wheels.*
Inklinations-bussole, f., *dipping compass*; - nadel, f., *d. needle.*
Inkrustation, f., *incrustation.*
inländischer Hafen, m., *home port.*
Innen-Barre, f., *inner bar*; - Bekleidung, f., *i. skin*; - Beplankung, f., *inside planking*; - fall, m., *inner halliard*; - gang, m., *inside strake*; - kante einer Spündung, f., *back rabbet*; - lager der Radwelle, n., *paddle shaft inside bearing*; - mutter eines Kesselankers, f., *boiler stay inside nut*; - planke, f., *inside plank*; - reede, f., *inner roads*; - Schrauben-wellen, *i. screw shafts*; - Spierenbügel, m., *quarter iron of a yard*; - Stoßplatte, f., *inside butt strap*; - takel auf! *Away with the stays!* - Wassergang, m., *inner waterway.*
Innenwinkel des Deckstringers, m., *deck stringer angle bar*; - - Haupt-D., *main d. s. inner a. b.*; - - Koffer-D., *trunk d. s. i. a. b.*; - - Ober-D., *upper d. s. i. a. b.*; - - Orlop-D., *orlop d. s. i. a. b.*; - - Schatten-D., *shade d. s.*

i. a. b.; - - Schutz-D., *shelter d. s. i. a. b.*; - - Turm-D., *turret d. s. i. a. b.*; - - Unter-D., - - *Zwischen-D., lower d. s. i. a. b.*
Innenwinkel eines Längs-spants, m., *side stringer inner angle bar*; - - Orlop-deckstringers, *orlop deck stringer i. a. b.*; - - Piek-deckstringers, *panting d. s. i. a. b.*; - - Raumbalken-stringers, *hold beam s. i. a. b*; - - Seitenstringers, *side s. i. a. b.*; - - Stringers, *inner stringer a. b.*; - - Verstär-kungsbalkenstringers, *panting beam s. i. a. b.*; - - Wasser-laufs, *gutter i. a. b.*
innen, von - nach außen, *in and out.*
Innerboden, m., *inner bottom*; - Beplattung, f., *i. b. plating*; - Platte, f., *i. b. plate.*
innere Ausblasrohr, n., *internal blow down pipe*; - Brille einer Leesegelspiere, f., *quarter iron of a yard*; - Dampfrohr, n., *internal steam pipe*; - Deckung eines Schiebers, f., *exhaust lap*; - Feuerbüchse, f., *inside fire box*; - Feuerzug, m., *internal flue*; - Hülfsspeiserohr, n., *i. donkey feed pipe*; - Klinsch, f., *inside clinch*; - Platten-gang, m., *inner strake*; - Rinnsteinwinkel, m., *gutter angle bar*; - Rohr, n., *internal pipe*; - Schaumrohr, n., *i. scum p.*; - Schraubenwelle, f., *inner screw shaft*; - Sicherheitsventil, n., *internal safety valve*; - Speise-rohr, n., *i. feed pipe*; - Steuerung, f., *i. distributing mechanism*; - Stützbalken, *pales*; - Wasserstandsrohr, n., *internal water gauge pipe.*
Inspektionswinkel, m., *watch pennant.*
Inspektor, m., *surveyor.*

Installationen, *accommoda-tions*; - für Viehtransport, *cattle fittings*.
Intensität des Zuges, f., *intensity of draught*.
Interkostal, *intercostal*; - Kiel-schwein, n., *i. keelson*; - Kimm-K., *bilge i. k.*; - Kimmkielschweinplatte, f., *b. i. k. plate*; - Kimmkiel-schweinwinkel, m, *b. i. k. angle bar*; - Kimmstringer, m., *b. i. stringer*; - - winkel, m., *b. i. s. angle bar*; - Mittelkielschwein, n., *middle line i. keelson*; - - platte, f., *m. l. i. k. plate*; - - winkel, m., *m. l. i. k. angle bar*; - Platte, f., *i. plate*; - Seiten-kielschwein, n., *side i.*

keelson; - - platte, f., *s. i. k. plate*; - - winkel, m., *s. i. k. angle bar*; - Seitenstringer, m., *s. i. stringer*; - - platte, f., *s. i. s. plate*; - - winkel, m., *s. i. s. angle bar*; - Stringer, m., *i. stringer*.
internationales Signalbuch, n., *international code of sig-nals*.
Invalidenschein, m., *smart ticket*.
Inventar, n., *inventory*.
inwendiger Druck, m., *internal pressure*; - Schraubstahl, m., *inside screw tool*.
Ipilholz, n., *ipil wood*.
Isolierung des Kessels, f., *boiler composition*.
Isorachien, *cotidal lines*.

J.

Jacht, f., *yacht*; - führer, m., *yachtsman*; - mäßig, *yacht-ish*; - wettfahrt, f., *yacht race*; - zeug, n., *y. rigging*.
Jackstag, n., *jackstay*.
Jacke, f., *banian*.
Jagd machen auf, *to chase*.
Jagd-bolzen, m., *drift bolt*; - boot, n., *hunting skiff*.
Jageleine, f., *towing line*.
Jager, m., *jib topsail*; - hals, m., *j. t. tack*; - Niederholer, m., *j. t. downhaul*; - schote. f., *j. t. sheet*; - stock, m., *head boom*.
Jagleine, Jagtrosse, f., *tow rope*.
Jakarandaholz, n., *Brazilian rose wood*.
Jakobstab, m., *Jacob's staff*.
Jan Maat, *Jack Tar*.
Jarraholz, n., *jarrah timber*.
Jigger, m., *jigger*; - Ausholer, m., *j. outhaul*; - Bauch-gording, f., *j. bunt line*; - Bram-B., *j. topgallant b. l.*; - Brambrasse, f., *j. t. brace*; - Bramdrehreep, n., *j. t. tye*;

- Bramfall, m., *j. topgallant halliard*; - Bramgeitau, n., *j. t. clew line*; - Bram-längssahling, f., *j. t. trestle trees*; - Bramnockgording, f., *j. topgallant leech line*; - Brampardune, f., *j. t. backstay*; - Brampüttings-wanten, j. t. futtock shrouds; - Bramrahe, f., *j. t. yard*; - Bramsahling, f., *j. t. cross trees*; - Bramschote, f., *j. t. sheet*; - Bramsegel, n., *j. t. sail*; - Bramstag, m., *j. t. stay*; - - segel, n., *j. t. s. sail*; - - - fall, m., *j. t. s. s. halliard*; - - - hals, m., *j. t. s. s. tack*; - - - leiter, f., *j. t. s. s. stay*; - - - Nieder-holer, m., *j. t. staysail down-haul*; - - - schote, f., *j. t. s. sheet*; - Bramstenge, f., *j. t. mast*; - - Eselshaupt, n., *j. t. m. cap*; - - want, n., *j. t. shroud*; - - wanten, *j. t. rigging*; - Bramtoppenant, f., *j. t. lift*; - Bramwanten, *j. t. rigging*; - brasse, f., *j.*

brace; - - schenkel, m., j.
b. pendant; - bulin, f., j.
bowline; - fall, m.,j. halliard;
- gaffel, f., j. gaff; - - gerde,
f., j. vang; - - - schenkel,
m., j. v. pendant; - Gaffel-
toppsegel, n., j. gafftopsail;
- - fall, m., j. g. t. halliard;
- - hals, m., j. g. t. tack;
- - Niederholer, m., j. g topsail downhaul; - - schote,
f., j. g. t. sheet; - geitau, n,
j. brail; - gerde, f., j. vang;
- hals, m., j. tack; - Klaufall, m., j. throat halliard.
Jigger-mars, m., jigger top; - -
Bauchgording, f., j. topsail
bunt line; - - brasse, f., j. t.
brace; - - Brassenschenkel,
m., j. t. b. pendant; - - Drehreep, n., j. t. tye; - Marsfall,
m., j. topsail halliard; - Mars-
geitau, n., j. t. clew line;
- Marspferd, n., j. t. foot
rope; - Marsrahe, f., j. t.
yard; - Marsrefftalje, f., j.
t. reef tackle; - Marsschote,
f., j. topsail sheet; - Marssegel,
n., j. t.; - - schote, f., j. t.
sheet; - Marsstenge, f., j.
topmast; - - Eselshaupt, n.,
j. t. cap; - Marstoppenant,
f., j. topsail lift; - Marswanten, j. topmast rigging.
Jigger-mast, m., jigger mast; - -
Dwarssahling, f., j. m. cross
trees; - - Eselshaupt, n., j.
m. cap; - - Keile, j. m.
wedges; - - kragen, m., j. m.
coat; - - Längssahling, f.,
j. m. trestle trees.
Jigger-Mittelstagsegel, n.,
jigger middle staysail;
- - fall, m., j. m. s.
halliard; - - hals, m., j. m.
s. tack; - - Niederholer, m.,
j. m. s. downhaul; - - schote, f., j. m. s. sheet; - Nockgording, f., j. leech line.
Jigger-Oberbrambrasse, f., upper jigger topgallant brace;
- Oberbramrahe, f., u. j. t.
yard; - Oberbramsegel, n.,
u. j. t. sail; - Obermars-

brasse, f., u. j. topsail brace;
- - schenkel, m., u. j. t. b.
pendant; - Obermarspferd,
n., u. j. t. foot rope; - Obermarsrahe, f., u. j. t. yard;
- Obermarssegel, n., u. j. t.
Jigger-pferd, n., jigger foot
rope; - Piekfall, m., j. peak
halliard; - Püttingswanten,
j. futtocks; - rahe, f., j. yard;
- - Toppenantstalje, f., j.
lift purchase; - Refftalje, f.,
j. reef tackle.
Jigger-Royal, n., jigger
royal; - - Bauchgording,
f., j. r. bunt line; - - brasse,
f., j. r. brace; - - fall, m., j.
r. halliard; - - geitau. n., j.
r. clew line; - - Längs-
sahling, f., j. r. trestle trees;
- - pardune, f., j. r. backstay;
- - pferd, n., j. r. foot rope;
- - rahe, f., j. r. yard; - -
sahling, f., j. topgallant
cross trees; - - schote, f., j.
royal sheet; - - stag, n., j. r.
stay; - - - segel, n., j. r.
staysail; - - - - fall, m., j. r.
s. halliard; - - - - hals, m.,
j. r. s. tack; - - - - leiter, f.,
j. r. s. stay; - - - - Niederholer, m., j. r. staysail downhaul; - - - - schote, f., j. r. s.
sheet; - Royalstenge, f., j.
royal mast; - Royaltop-
penant, f., j. r. lift.
Jigger-rüste, f., jigger channel;
- Rüsteisen, n., j. chain
plates.
Jigger-Scheisegel, n., jigger
skysail; - - brasse, f., j. s.
brace; - - fall, m., j. s.
halliard; - - geitau, n., j.
s. clew line; - - - par-
dune, f., j. s. backstay; - -
pferd, n., j. s. foot rope;
- - rahe, f., j. s. yard; - -
schote, f., j. s. sheet; - - stag,
n., j. skysail stay; - - stenge,
f., j. skysail mast; - - toppenant, f., j. s. lift.
Jigger-schote, f., jigger sheet.
Jigger-stag, n., jigger stay; - -
segel, n., j. staysail; - - -

fall, m., *j. s. halliard*; - - -
hals, m., *j. s. tack*; - - -
leiter, f., *j. s. stay*; - - - Niederholer, m., *j. staysail
downhaul*; - - - schote, f., *j.
s.sheet*; - - - - schenkel, m.,
j. s. s. pendant.
Jigger-Stenge, f., *jigger topmast*; - - pardune, f., *j. topmast backstay*; - - stag, n.,
j. t. stay; - Stengestagsegel,
n., *j. t. staysail*; - - fall, m.,
j. t. s. halliard; - - hals, m.,
j. t. s. tack; - - leiter, f., *j.
t. s. stay*; - - Niederholer,
m., *j. t. staysail downhaul*;
- - schote, f., *j. t. s. sheet*; -
Stengewant, n., *j. t. shroud.*
Jigger-Toppenant, f., *jigger
lift*; - - talje, f., *j. lift purchase.*
Jigger-Unterbrambrasse, f.,
lower jigger topgallant brace;
- Unterbramrahe, f., *l. j. t.
yard*; - Unterbramsegel, n.,
l. j. t. sail.
Jigger-Untermarsbrasse, f., *l.
jigger topsail brace*; - -
schenkel, m., *l. j. t. b.
pendant*; - Untormarspferd,
n., *l. j. t. foot rope*; - Untermarsrahe, f., *l. j. t. yard*; -

Untermarssegel, n., *l. j. t.*;
- want, n., *j. shroud*; - wanten, *j. rigging.*
Joch-leine, f., *yoke rope*; -
nagel, m., *y. pin*; - stock,
m., *jack stay.*
Joll-boot, n., *jolly boat*; - tau,
n., *gant line*; - - block, m.,
girtline block.
Jolle, f., 1. *dingy (a boat)*; 2.
top rope.
Jollen-führer, m., *waterman*;
- tau, n., *single whip*; - -
des Klüverbaums, *heel rope
of the jib boom*; - - block
m., *girtline block.*
Journal, n., *log book*; in das
- eintragen, *to log* od. *to
enter into the log*; eine -
Eintragung, *an entry in the
log.*
Jückstag, n., *horse.*
Judasohr, n., *knight head.*
Juffer, Jungfer, f., *dead eye.*
Jungfern-block, m., *dead eye*;
große - -, *heart block*; -
reise, f., *maiden trip*; -
straken, *to square the dead
eyes.*
Jungmann, m., *youngster.*
Jutesack, m., *gunny bag.*

K.

Kaag, f., *a flat bottomed sailing vessel.*
Kaak, m., *a heavy squall of
wind.*
kabbelige See, f., *choppy sea.*
kabbeln, *to ripple.*
Kabbelsee, f., *turbulent sea.*
Kabbelung, f., *rippling.*
Kabel, n., *cable.*
Kabelar, m., *messenger*; - um
das Kabel legen, *to clap a
messenger on the cable*; -
kette, f., *m. chain*; - rad, n.,
m. wheel; - ring, m., *messenger*; - schäkel, m., *m.*

shackle; - zeising, m., *cable
nipper*; - zeisinge aufsetzen,
to pass the nippers.
Kabelgarn, n., *rope yarn*; -
ausschrapen, *to point out
r. y.*; - mit farbigem Herzgarn, *marking yarn*; - knoten or - stich, m., *rope yarn
knot*; - stropp, m., *selvagee.*
Kabel-gat, n., *cable tier*; -
jaufischerei, f., *cod fishery*;
- kleid, n., *cable serving*; -
länge, f., *cable length*; -
probe, f., *c. test*; - schiff, n.,
c. ship; - schlag, m., 1. *elbow*

in the hawse; 2. cable laid rope; - splissung, f., cable splice; - stich, m., hawser bend; - tau, n., best hawser; - - drehen, to twist a cable; - - splissung, f., cable splice; - verbindung, f, c. connection; - weise, cablewise; - - geschlagenes Tau, n., cable laid rope.

Kabestan, m., capstan.

Kabine, f., cabin.

Kabotage, f., coasting.

kahler Block, m., unstropped block.

Kahn, m., barge.

Kai, m., quay; - geld, n., quayage; - mauer, f., quay wall; - meister, m., wharfinger; - platz, m.. quay berth; - raum, m., quayage.

kaien, to sway across.

Kaier, m., brace of a lugsail yard.

Kaik, n., caique.

Kajak, n., kayak.

Kaje, f., see Kai.

Kajer, m., brace of a lugsail yard.

Kajüte, f., cabin; - einrichtung, f., c. fittings; - fenster, n., c. window; - fracht, f., c. freight; - fußboden, m., c. floor; - genosse, m., c. mate; - junge, m., c. boy; - kappe, f., c. companion; - kompaß, m., c. compass; - oberlicht, n., c. skylight; - - gräting, f., grating of c. s.; - ofen, m., c. stove; - passagier, m., c. passenger; - Schornstein, m., c. funnel; - tür, f., c. door; - treppe, f., companion ladder; - ventilator, m., cabin ventilator; - Vorräte, steward's small stores.

Kalb, n., (pl. Kalben), chock; - des Binnenvorderstevens, dousing c.

Kalfater, m., caulker; - arbeit, f., caulker's work; - bütte, f., caulking box; - eisen, n.,

c. iron; - faß, n., keeler; - floß, n., floating stage; - gasten, caulker screw; - hammer, m., caulking mallet; - kiste, f., caulking box; - meister, m., chief caulker; - stuhl, m., caulker's seat; - werg, n., oakum.

kalfatern, to caulk.

Kalfaterung, f., caulking.

Kaliber, n., size.

kalibrierte Kette, f., pitch chain.

kalifornisches Föhrenholz, n., yellow pine.

Kalmen, calms; - gürtel, m., calm belt; - - des Krebses, calms of cancer; - - des Steinbocks, calms of capricorn.

Kalorimeter, n., calorimeter·

Kalorin, f., calory.

kalt-gehämmertes Eisen, n., cold hammered iron; - meißel, m., cold chisel; - wasserprobe, f., hydraulic test; - wasserpumpe, f., cold water pump.

kalte Klima, n., cold climate; - Strom, m., cold current; - Wetter, n., c. weather; - Zone, f., frigid zone.

Kamel, n., air camel.

Kamm, m., 1. cog (of a wheel); 2. jackstay (of a yard); 3. fillings (between the head cheeks); 4. crest (of a wave).

Kammer, f., 1. . berth (for passengers and officers); 2. locker (for stores); 3. chamber (for machinery parts); - kessel, m., sectionnal boiler; - schleuse, f., chamber lock.

Kammrad, n., cog wheel.

Kammwellen, Neptune's sheep.

Kampanje, f., quarter deck cabin; - treppe, f, coach ladder.

Kanal, m., 1. canal; 2. Channel; (English Channel); 3. port (in cylinders and valves); - gebühren, - geld, n., canal dues; - lotse, m., Channel

pilot; - schiffahrt, f., *canal navigation*; - schleuse, f., *canal lock.*
Kanapee, n., *settee.*
Kanoe, n., *canoe.*
Kanonenboot, n., *gun boat.*
Kant-gien, n., *spike tackle*; - haken, m., *cant hook*; - ring, m., *ring of a cant hook*; - spant, n., *c. timber*; - - bolzen, m., *c. t. bolt.*
Kante, f., *leech (of a sail)*; - eines Stoßes, *butt edge.*
kanten, *to trim.*
Kantensaum, m., *leech tabling.*
Kanu, n., *canoe.*
Kap. n., *cape.*
Kaper, m., *privateer*; - brief, m., *letter of marque*; - ei, f., *privateering*; - schift, n., *privateer.*
kapern, *to capture.*
Kapitän, m., *master, captain*; - zur See, *captain of the fleet.*
Kapitänskammer, f., *captain's room.*
Kappe, f., *1. hood* or *cover*; *2. companion (of a cabin)*; - des Pfeilerhauptes, *capping of the cutwater*; - des Steuergeräts, *cover of steering gear.*
kappen, *to cut*; den Mast -, *to cut away the mast*; Trümmer, -, *t. c. a. wreck.*
Kapp-laken, n., *primage*; - naht, f., *round seam.*
kapzeisen, *to capsize.*
Karake, f,, *carac.*
Karavelle, f., *caravel.*
kardanisch, *Cardan's rule.*
Kardeel, n., *strand*; - block, m., *ram*; - stropp, m., *strops for the jeer blocks.*
Kardeelen, *jeers*; ein Tau in - zerlegen, *to unlay a rope.*
Kardinalstriche, *cardinal points.*
Kardusstock, m., *former.*
Karniseisen, n., *channel iron.*
Karriholz, n., *karri wood.*
Karte, f., *chart*; nicht auf der - aufgenommen, *chartless.*

Karten-haus, n., *chart house*; - - fenster, n., *c. h. window*; - - tür, f., *c. h. door*; - - - Scharnier, n., *c. h. d. hinge*; - kasten, m., *c. case*; - kiste, f., *c. chest.*
Karvbeil, n., *hatchet.*
karwehlartig gebaut, *carvel built.*
Kasko, n., *hull*; - versicherung, f., *insurance on hull and appurtenances.*
Kastanienholz, n., *chestnut wood.*
Kasten, m., *chest*; - des Schiebers, *steam chest*; - des Ventils, *valve chest*; der verschlossene - eines Sicherheitsventils, *locked up chamber*; - balken, m., *box beam*; - - winkel, m., *b. b. angle bar*; - kiel, m., *box keel*; - - schwein, n., *b. keelson*; - - - winkel, m., *b. k. angle bar*; - schleuse, f., *square sluice*; - schloß, n., *chest lock*; - schute, f., *covered-in-barge.*
Katt-anker, m., *back anchor*; - aufgeber, m., *cat back*; - block, m., *c. block*; - - haken, m., *c. hook*; - - steert, m., *back rope of a c. block*; - davit, m., *c. davit*; - - spur, f., *c. d. socket*; An das - fall! *Man the c. fall!* - gien, n., *c. tackle*; - haken, m., *c. hook*; - läufer, m., *c. fall*; - reep, n., *back rope of a c. block*; - spor, m., *floor rider*; - - eines Raumbalkens, *hold beam knee rider*; - - bolzen, m., *knee rider bolt*; - steert, m., *rat's tail*; - - bindsel, n., *tail seizing*; - stopper, m., *cat head stopper*; - takel, n., *c. tackle.*
katten, *to cat*; - und fischen, *to c. and fish.*
Katze, f., *cat*; - pfote, f., *cat's paw*; - rücken, m., *broken backed*; - schlupfloch, n., *cat hole.*

Kauriholz, n., *cowry wood*.

Kauffahrer, m., *merchantman*.

Kauffahrtei-flotte, f., *merchant fleet*; - schiff, n., *m. vessel*.

Kausche, f., *thimble*.

kaut, das Schiff - das Werg aus, *the ship works the oakum out*.

Kaution stellen, *to find bail*.

Kautschuk-liderung or - pak-kung, f., *rubber packing*; - ring, m., *r. ring*; - schlauch, m., *r. hose*.

Kavent, m., *bailee*.

Kavielnagel, m., *belaying pin*.

Keep, f., *score*.

Keepen, f., *lay of a rope*.

Kegel, m., *cone*; - boje, f., *can buoy*; - förmig, *conical*; - rad, n., *bevel wheel*; - ventil, n., *conical valve*; - zahnrad, n., *bevel wheel*.

Kehlhammer, m., *rounded hammer*.

Kehlung, f., *beading, moulding*.

Kehrling, m., *sweepings*.

Kehrtau des Schwingbaums, n., *lower studding sail boom guy*.

Keil, m., *wedge, cotter, key*; - band, n., *clasp hoop*; - loch, n., *key hole*; - nute, f., *k. way*; - - des Propellers, *propeller key way*; - stück, n., *filling timber*; - und Löse-keil, *gib and cotter*.

Kennung, f., or Kennzeichen, n., *character of a light*.

Kentering, f., *slackening of the tide*.

kentern, *to capsize*; - des Stromes, n., *turn of the tide*; zum - liegen, *to lie on the beam ends*.

kentert, der Strom -, *the tide turns*.

Kerbe, f., *score*.

Kerbholz, n., *tally*.

Kerkedortje, n., *bunt slab line*.

Kernpunkt, m., *centre mark*.

Kerzenstärke, f., *candle power*.

Kessel, m., *1. vessel (air v.)*; *2. boiler (steam)*; - der nur von einem Ende aus geheizt wird, *single ended b.*; - der unter Feuerung Wasser enthält, *wet bottomed b.*; - d. u. d. F. kein W. e., *dry b. b.*; - mit doppelter Feuerkammer, *double combustion chamber b.*; - mit einer Feuerröhre, *single flue b.*; - mit ovalen Enden, *egg ended b.*; - mit rückkehrender Flamme, *return flue b.*; - mit zwei Feuerröhren, *double f. b.*; - der platzt, *the b. bursts*.

Kessel-Abblashahn, m., *boiler blow out cock*; - anker, m., *boiler stay*; - - mutter, f., *b. s. nut*; - - Unterlegscheibe, f., *b. s. washer*; - - Verstärkungsscheibe, f., *b. s. w.*; - armatur, f., *b. mounting*; - bau, m., *b. making*; - - anstalt, f., *b. works*; - bekleidung, f., *b. lagging*; - besichtigung, f., *b. survey*; - bleche, *b. plates*; - druck, m., *b. pressure*; - - probe, f., *b. test*; - explosion, f., *b. explosion*; - fundament, n., *b. seating*; - garnitur, f., *b. mounting*; - Hauptabsperrventil, n., *b. main stop valve*; - hülle, f., *shell plating of b.*; - kielschwein, n., *b. seating*; - körper, m., *b. body*; - lager, n., *boiler bearer*; - - winkel, m., *b. b. angle bar*; - luke, f., *boiler hatch*; - mannloch, n., *man hole of b.*; - mantel, m., *boiler casing*; - platten, *b. plates*; - probe, f., *b. test*; - prüfung, f., *b. t.*; - raum, m., *b. space*; - - schott, n., *engine room forward bulkhead*; - reparatur, f., *boiler repairs*; - revision, f., *b. inspection*; - rohr, n., *b. tube*; - - ring, m., *b. t. ferrule*; - rost, m., *b. grate*; - schacht, m., *b. casing*; -

schmied, m., *b. maker*; - schwimmer, m., *b. float*; - Sicherheitsventil, n., *b. safety valve*; - - belastung, f., *b. s. v. load*; - stein, m., *b. scale*; - - ausschlagen, *to knock out b. s.*; - - bildung, f., *incrustation*; - stützen, *b. stays*; - teile, *b. parts*; - wandung, f., *shell plating of b.*; - wasser, n., *b. water*; - Werkstatt, f., *b. shop*.
Ketsch, f., *ketch*.
Kette, f., *chain*; - verlangen, *to ask cable*; - mit offenen Gliedern, *open linked chain*; Schiff an die - legen, *to put a seal on the mast*.
Ketten-ausrücker or - austreiber, m., *cable reliever*; - dorn, m., *starting punch*; - gang, m., *sprocket wheel*; - gerassel, n., *rattle of chains*; - glied, n., *stud link*; - - mit Wirbel, *swivel link*; - hahnepot der Vertäuungsbojen, f., *bridle chains*; - haken, m., *chain hook*; - hanger, m., *c. spans*; - im Kreuz, *cross in the hawse*; - kasten, m., *chain locker*; - krampe, f., *raft dog*; - ladeläufer, m., *chain cargo fall*; - länge, f., *length of chain cable*; - läufer und Blöcke, *chain runners and gins*; - nietung, f., *chain riveting*; - - stoß, m., *c. r. butt*; - pinne, f., *shackle bolt pin*; - probieramt, n., *chain proving house*; - pumpenaufsatz, m., *pump head*; - rack, n., *chain rack truss*; - rad, n., *sprocket wheel*; - reling, f., *chain rails*; - ring, m., *ring of a cant hook*; - scheibe, f., *chain sheave*; - - des Ankerspills, *cable holder*; - schleppschiffahrt, f., *chain towing*; - schlinge, f., *c. sling*; - stag, n., *bar*; - stich, m., *chain knot*; - stopper, m., *chain cable compressor*; - - der

Luke, *hatchway stopper*; - - hebel, m., *lever of the chain cable compressor*; - stropp, m., *chain sling*; - trommel, f., *chain drum*; - wirbel, m., *chain swivel*.
Kieferholz, n., *fir wood*.
Kieker, m., *spy glass*.
Kiel, m., *keel*; - bank, f., *gridiron*; - blöcke, *keel blocks*; - bolzen, m., *holding up bolt*; - boot, n., *keel boat*; - fuge, f., *rabbet*; - gang, m., *garboard strake*; - - bolzen, m., *g. bolt*; - - naht, f., *g. seam*; - - planke, f., *g. plank*; - - platte, f., *g. plate*; - geld, n., *keelage*; - gording, f., *gridiron*; - hacke, f., *skeg of a keel*; - höhe, f., *depth of the k.*; - holen, *careening*; - holplatz, m., *c. wharf*; - laschung, f., *keel scarph*; den - legen, *to set the k.*; - lichter, m., *pontoon for careening ships*; - linie, f., *middle line*; - niete, f., *keel rivet*; - oben, *bottom up*; - planke, f., *garboard strake*; - platten, *keel plates*; - raum, m., *hold*; - - wasser, n., *bilge water*; - recht, n., *keelage*; - schwein, n., *keelson*; - - bolzen, m., *keelson bolt*; - - im Doppelboden, *girder of double bottom*; - - in der oberen Rundung der Kimm, *upper turn of bilge keelson*; - - in der unteren R. d. K., *lower t. of b. k.*; - - kasten, m., *keelson casing*; - - laschen or - - laschung, f., *keelson scarph*; - - platte, f., *keelson plate*; - - sohle, f., *rider keelson*; - - winkel, m., *keelson angle bar*; - schwert, n., *centre board*; - - boot, n., *c. b. boat*; - sohle, f., *sole piece of stern frame*; - spündung, f., *keel rabbet*; - stück, n., *keel piece*; - - eines Hinterstevens, *k. p. of stern post*; - - eines Schraubenstevens, *k. p. of s. frame*;

- verscherbungsbolzen, m., *keel scarph bolt*; - wasser, n., *wake*; im - - folgen, *to follow in the wake*; - - formation, f., *order in line ahead*; - - linie, f., *line ahead*; - wegerungsbolzen, m., *limber strake bolt*; - wegerungsgang, m., *l. s.*; - wegerungsplanke, f., *futtock plank.*

Kieselgrund, m., *gravel ground.*

kilbrassen, *to keep the sails shivering.*

killen, *to shiver.*

Kimm, m., *1. bilge (of the ship)*; *2. horizon (apparent boundary of sea)*; - abstand der Sonne berechnen, *to shoot the sun*; - an - gestaut, *chime and chime stowed*; - beplankung, f., *bilge planking*; - beplattung, f., *b. plating*; - bolzen, m., *b. bolt*; - gang, m., *bilge strake*; - kiel, m., *b. keel*; - - schwein or - kolschwein, n., *b. keelson*; - - - winkel, m., *b. k. angle bar*; - kielwinkel, m., *b. keel a. b.*; - planke, f., *b. plank*; - platte, f., *b. plate*; - pumpe, f., *b. pump (see also* Lenzp.*)*; - spiegel, m., *horizon glass*; - stringer, m., *bilge stringer*; - - winkel, m., *b. s. angle bar*; - stütze, f., *bilge shore*; - - platte, f., *bracket frame*; - tiefe, f., *dip of the horizon*; - wasser, n., *bilge water*; - wegerung, f., *thick strakes of ceiling.*

Kimm- *see also* Bilge- *and* Lenz-.

Kimmung, f., *1. bilge (of ship)*; *2. mirage (of air).*

Kingston-ventil, n., *Kingston valve*; - spindel, f., *K. v. spindle.*

Kink, m., *kink*; kurze - im Tau, *nip.*

Kinken bekommen or bilden, *to kink*; sich aus den - stauen, *to get out of the*

twist; - in einer Trosse, *kink in a cable*; - und Törns aus der Kette nehmen, *to take the kinks and turns out of the cable*; voll von K., *kinky.*

Kinnbacken, m., *fore foot of the keel*; - block, m., *snatch block*; großer - -, *rouse about.*

Kippleine, f., *shank painter.*

Kirchenschiff, n., *Bethel ship.*

Kirschrotglühhitze, f., *cherry red heat.*

Kissen, n., *bolster*; - der Betinge, *lining of the bitts*; - des Bugspriets, *pillow of the bowsprit.*

Kits, f., *ketch.*

Kitt, m., *putty.*

Klabautermann, m., *bogy man.*

Klamei-eisen, n., *horsing iron*; - hammer, m., *reeming beetle.*

Klameien, *1. to horse up (to drive in oakum)*; *2. cross chocks (carlings between the beams).*

Klammer, f., *brace.*

Klampblock. m., *clump block.*

Klampe, f., *cleat*; - der Schlagbettung, *dog c.*

Klapp-bolzen, m., *preventer bolt*; - boot, n., *folding boat*; - läufer, m., *whip*; - - an einem Jollentau, *w. upon w.*; - stuhl, m., *folding chair.*

Klappe, f., *flap.*

Klappen des Ruders, n., *thumping*; gegen ein anderes Schiff -, *to fall aboard another vessel*; - fänger, m., *valve guard*; - fenster, n., *port sash*; - ventil, n., *clack valve*; - wirbel, m., *valve stem.*

Klappern, n., *jarring (of engine).*

klar, alles -, *all clear*; - bei der Schote stehen, *to stand c. by the sheet*; - Deck machen, *to c. the decks*; - fahren or - kommen, *to get c.*; *to go c.*; - fahrende

Taue, *c. ropes*; - halten, *to keep c.*; - laufende Taue, *c. ropes*; - - Takelung, f., *rendering*; das Gangspill - machen, *to rig the capstan*; das Schiff - machen, *to clear for action*; ein Tau - machen, *to see a rope c.*; - schwoien, *to swing c.*; - zum Fallen lassen, *1. to be a-cock-bill*; *2. Stand by the anchor!* - zum Wenden! *Ready about!*

klare Ketten, *clear hawse.*

klaren, *to clear (the land, chains, tackle, &c.).*

klares Fahrwasser, n., *clear and open channel.*

klarieren, *to clear at the custom house.*

Klasse, f., *class.*

Klassifikation, f., *classification*; - schein, m., *certificate of character.*

klassifizieren, *to class.*

Klatsch, m., *galley news.*

Klaue, f., *1. jaw (of the gaff)*; *2. throat (of a boom)*; *3. claw (of the grapnel)*; - am Ende des Schleppnetz-Querbalkens, *trawl head.*

Klauen-hebel, m., *clutch lever*; - kuppelung, f., *c. coupling.*

Klau-fall, m., *throat halliard*; - - bolzen, m., *t. h. bolt*; - horn, n., *neck of a gaff sail*; - ohr, n., *throat of a sail*; - - legel, m., *t. cringle*; - stopper, m., *claw stopper.*

kleeden, *to serve.*

Kleid, n., *1. cover*; *2. cloth (of a sail)*; - keule, *serving mallet*; - span, m., *s. board.*

kleiden, *to serve.*

Kleiderkammer, f., *slop room.*

Kleidung, f., *serving (of a rope).*

kleine Bär, m., *dog's tail*; - Boot, n., *dingy*; - Flaggengala, f., *to dress with mast head flags*; - Gangspill, n., *jeer capstan*; - Küstenfahrt, f., *small coasting trade*; - Luke, f., *scuttle*; - Repara-

tur, f., *small repairs*; - Segel, *s. sails*; - Stirnrad, n., *s. spur wheel*; - Zahnrad, n., *s. spur wheel.*

Klemmfutter, n., *elastic chuck.*

Klick des Ruders, n., *back piece of rudder.*

Klima, n., *climate.*

Klimmstag, n., *man rope.*

Klink-bolzen, m., *rivet bolt*; - ring, m., *clinch ring.*

Klinke, f., *latch.*

klinken, *to clinch.*

klinkerartig gebaut, *clincher built.*

Klinsch, m., *clinch.*

Klippe, f., *rock*; bei halber Tide bedeckte od. trockene -, *half tide r.*; blinde -, *blind r.*; mit dem Wasser gleiche -, *lurking r.*; sichtbare -, *r. above water*: steil aufsteigende -, *r. steep to*; wachende -, *lurking r.*

Klippeninsel, f., *rock island.*

Klipper, m., *clipper*; - steven, m., *c. stem.*

Kloben, m., *running block*; - schraube, f., *shackle jack.*

Klopf-keule, f., *mallet*: - see, f., *sea breach*; - zurring, f., *muzzle lashing.*

klopfen, *to knock.*

Kloset, n., *W. C.*; - rohr, n., *W. C. pipe*; - tür, f., *W. C. door.*

Klotje, n., *truck*; flache -, *shroud t.*; Rack -, *parrel t.*

Klotzboje, f., *spar buoy.*

klubholen, *to clubhaul.*

Klüfock, f., *standing jib*; - fall, m., *s. j. halliard*; - hals, m., *s. j. tack*; - leiter, f., *s. j. stay*; - niederhoher, m., *s. j. downhaul*; - schote, f., *s. j. sheet.*

Kluft, f., *angular notch.*

Klumpblock, m., *clump block.*

Klüse, f., *hawse hole.*

Klüsen, die See bricht durch die -, *hawse fallen*; - back, f., *naval hood*; - backe, f., *hawse bolster*; - band, n., *h. chock*; - deckel, m., *h. flap*: - fütterung, f., *h. box* - loch, n., *h. hole*; - pfropfen, m., *hawse plug; -* rohr, n., *h. pipe*; - - deckel, m., *h. p. cover*; - - flansch, m., *h. p. flange*; - säcke, *h. bags*; - schott, n., *bulkhead of the manger*; - stopper, m., *bow cable stopper.*

Klüsholz, n., *hawse timber.*

Klüver, m., *jib*; - backstag, n., *j. guy*; - baum, m., *j. boom*; - - band, n., *j. b. hoop*; - - netz, n., *j. b. netting*; - bei! *Clear away the j.!* - domper, m., *martingale stay*; - fall, m., *jib halliard*; - gast, m., *j. man*; - geie, f., *j. boom guy*; - hals, m., *1. j. tack*; *2. outer j. t. (schooner)*; - holz, n., *head stick*; - kleid, n., *jib cover*; - kopf, m., *j. head*; - legel, m., *j. hank*; - leiter, f., *j. stay*; - niederholer, m., *j. downhaul*; an die - -! *Jibs downhaul!* - pferd, n., *j. boom foot rope*; - schote, f., *j. b. sheet*; - schoten anholen! *Flat in the jibs!* - - los! *Ease off the j.!* - - schenkel, m., *jib sheet pendant*; - - Steuerbord! *Haul aft jibs starboard sheets!* - setzen! *Clear away the jibs!* - stag, n., *jib stay*; - stampfstag, n., *j. boom s.*; - toppsegel, n., *j. topsail*; - - hals, m., *j. t. tack*; - - Niederholer, m., *j. t. downhaul*; - - schote, f., *j. t. sheet.*

Knagge, f., *catch, stop, tappet.*

Knallgas, n., *oxyhydrogen gas.*

knapper Wind, m., *scant wind.*

knarren, *to jar.*

Knäuel, m., *ball.*

Knebel, m., *toggle*; - zum Bewuhlen, *woolder*; - bolzen, m., *toggle bolt*; - stropp, m., *becket.*

Knechte, *jeers.*

Kneif, n., *knife*; - bindsel, n. *lashing for wringing two cables together*; - stek or stich, m., *rolling hitch*; - zange, f., *cutting nippers.*

kneifen, *to hug the wind.*

Knepeling, m., *blinder Matrose.*

Knick, m., *nip (of a rope)*; - stag, n., *spring stay.*

Knie, n., *knee*; - auf dem Todholz, *dead wood k.*; - bleche, *k. plates*; - bolzen, m., *k. bolt*; - des Steuerapparats, *k. of steering gear*; - holz, n., *k. timber*; - kattspor, f., *k. rider*; - platte, f., *knee plate*; - rohr, n., *elbow pipe.*

Knief, n., *knife.*

Knopf, *1. buoy rope knot (of rope)*; *2. acorn (of vane)*; - stopper, m., *knotted stopper.*

Knoten, m., *1. knot (of rope)*; *2. knot (of speed)*; - stopper, m., *knotted stopper.*

Knüppel, m., *bar*; - einer Bootsleiter, *rounds*; - holz, n., *billet wood.*

Knüttel am Kopfe der Hängematte, m., *head clue.*

Koch, m., *cook*; - flott, n., *stove*; - gerät, n., *mess kit*; - geschirr, n., *cooking utensils*; - haus, n., *galley*; - - herd, m., *g. stove*; - - tür, f., *g. door*; - maat, m., *cook's mate*; - punkt, m., *boiling point.*

kochende See, f., *boiling sea.*

Kochspumpe, f., *hand pump.*

Koefficient, m., *coefficient.*

Kofainnagel, Koffeinnagel, Koffeljenagel, m., *belaying pin*; - band, n., *spider hoop.*

Koffer-damm, m., *cofferdam*; - dampfer, m., *trunk deck steamer*; - deck, n., *t. d.*; - - balken, m., *t. d. beam*; - - balkenstringer, m., *t. d. b. stringer*; - - balkenwinkel, m., *t. d. b. angle bar*; - - beplattung, f., *t. d. plating*;

- - geländer, n., *t. d. rails and stanchions*; - - geländerstangen, *t. d. guard rods*; - - geländerstützen, *t. d. stanchions*; - - luken, *t. d. hatches*; - - lukendeckel, m., *t. deck hatch*; - - lukensüll, m., *t. d. h. coaming*; - deck-Stringer, m., *t. d. stringer*; - - - winkel, m., *t. d. s. angle bar*; - deckstütze, f., *t. d. pillar*; - deck-Wassergang, m., *t. d. waterway*; - gang, m., *t. way*; - kessel, m., *rectangular boiler*; - seitenbeplattung, f., *trunk side plating.*

Kohlen-blende, f., *anthracite coal*; - bunker, m., *c. bunker*; - - loch, n., *c. b. opening*; - - platte, f., *c. b. plate*; - - rohr, n., *c. b. pipe*; - - spant, n., *b. frame*; - - stag, n., *coal b. stay*; - - tür, f., *c. b. door*; - - Versteifungswinkel, m., *c. b. stays*; - - wand, f., *c. b. bulkhead*; - dampfer, m., *collier*; - depot, n., *coaling depot*; - - lampe, f., *miner's lamp*; - einnehmen, *to coal*; - exporteur, m., *c. exporter*; - fahrer, m., *collier*; - gesellschaft, f., *coal company*; - hammer, m., *c. hammer*; - hulk, n., *hulk*; - - mit Böcken, *sheer h.*; - kipper, m., *tip*; - ladeplatz, m., *coal tip*; - leichter, m., *c. barge*; - loch, n., *c. bunker opening*; - - deckel or - - verschluß, m., *c. b. lid*; - löschrad, n., *c. gin*; - luke, f., - - deckel, m., *coaling hatch*; - maß, n., *coal measure*; - oxyd, n., *carbonic oxide*; - pfanne, f., *cage*; - pforte, f., *coaling port*; - platz, m., *coal jetty*; - presenning, f., *c. screen*; - raum, m., *c. hold*; - - lampe, f., *bunker lamp*; - sack, m., *coal bag*; - schaufel, f., *c. shovel*; - schiff, n., *collier*; - schirm, m., *coal screen*; - schlingen, *c. gins*; - station, f., *coaling port*; -

staub, m., *c. dust*; - teer, m., *coal tar*; - träger, m., *c. heaver*; - trimmer, m., *trimmer*; - verbrauch, m., *consumption of coal*; - vorrat, m., *supply of coal*; - werft, f., *c. wharf*; - wipper, m., *c. whipper.*

Koje, f., *bunk*; zur - gehen, *to turn in.*

Koker, m., *rudder trunk*; - deckel, m., or platte, f., *horse shoe plate*; - schraube, f., *trunk screw.*

Kolben, m., *1. piston; 2. bucket (of a pump); 3. forcer (of forcing pump)*; - mit Metall-Liderung, *metallic piston*; - mit Ventil, *valve bucket.*

Kolben-aufgang, m., *up-stroke*; - bewegung, f., *motion of piston*; - deckel, m., *piston cover*; - - bolzen, m., *p. c. bolt*; - - handhabe, f., *p. c. eye bolt*; - durchmesser, m., *diameter of piston*; - Expansionsventil, n., *p. expansion valve*; - feder, f., *p. spring*; - fläche, f., *area of p.*; - geschwindigkeit, f., *velocity of p.*; - hub, m., *p. stroke*; - - vorwärts, *the fore s. of the p.*; - kitt, m., *p. paste*; - körper, m., *p. body*; - liderung, f., *p. packing*; - manometer, n., *steam indicator*; - mastic, m., *piston paste*; - mutter, f., *p. nut*; - nabe, f., *p. boss*; - niedergang, m., *down stroke*; - öse, f., *piston eye*; - packung, f., *p. packing*; - pumpe, f., *p. pump*; - reibung, f., *friction of piston*; - ring, m., *piston packing ring*; - ringe schlichten, *to face the p. p. rings*; - rohr, n., *barrel of the pump*; - schieber, m., *piston valve*; - - Austrittskanal, m., *p. v. exhaust port*; - - deckel, m., *p. v. cover*; - - Eintrittskanal, m., *p. v. steam port*; - - Füllstück, n., *p. v. tongue piece*;

- - stange, f., *p. v. spindle*;
- - - Stopfbüchsendeckel, m., *p. v. s. gland*; - schieber-Stopfbüchse, f., *p. v. stuffing box*; - schieberzunge, f., *p. v. tongue piece*; - schlag, m., *piston stroke*; - schraube, f., *junk ring bolt*; - spiel, n., *up and down stroke*; - stange, f., *piston rod*; - - ende, n., *tail piece*; - - führung, f., *piston rod guide*; - - Kreuzkopf, m., *p. r. crosshead*; - - K-k-führung or - - K-k-gleitplatte, f., *p. r. c. guide*; - - mutter, f., *p. r. nut*; - - packung, f., *p. r. packing*; - - Stopfbüchse, f., *p. r. stuffing box*; - - - deckel, m., *p. r. s. b. gland*; - ventil, n., *bucket valve*; - - Klappenfänger, m., *b. v. guard*; - - Metall-Liderung, f., *piston valve packing ring*; - - sitz, m., *piston valve seat*.

Kolder-gatt, n., *whip staff hole*; - stock, m., *w. s.*

Koljer, m., *collier*.

kollidieren, *to collide*.

Kollision, f., *collision*.

Kollisions-matte, f., *collision mat*; - pflaster, n., *c. pad*; - riß, m., *breach made by the c.*; - schott, n., *c. bulkhead*; - - winkel, m., *c. b. angle bar*.

Kolonial-hafen, m., *colonial port*; - handel, m., *c. trade*.

Kolschwinn see Kielschwein.

kombiniertes Druck- und Vakuum-Manometer, n., *compound gauge*; - Steuergerät, n., *combined steering gear*.

Kombüse, f., *1. galley*; *2. g. stove*; - schornstein, m., *g. funnel*; - tür, f., *g. door*; - - Scharnier, n., *g. d. hinge*.

Kommandant, m., *commander*.

kommandieren, *to command*.

Kommando, n., *command*; - bank, f., *conning bench* - brücke, f., *pilot bridge*; - -
geländer, n., *p. b. rails and stanchions*; - - - stütze, f., *p. b. s.*

Kommodor, m., *commodore*; - stander, m., *broad pennant*.

Komm und hilf hier! *Bear a hand here!*

Kommunikations-hahn, m., *communication cock*; - rohr, n., *joint pipe*; - ventil, n., *communication valve*.

Kompagnie, f., *company*; - dampfer, m., *c. steamer*; - lotse, m., *c. pilot*; - signal, n., *c. signal*.

Kompartiment, n., *compartment*.

Kompaß, m., *compass*; - Adjustierer, m., *c. adjuster*; - bezug, m., *binnacle cover*; - bügel, m., *gimbal of a compass*; - deviation, f., *local attraction*; - dose, f., *kettle of the compass*; - fehler, m., *compass error*; - fliegt, the *c. gets wild*; - gehäuse, n., *c. bowl*; - häuschen, n., *binnacle*; - hütchen, n., *rhumb card socket*; - ist wild, the *c. is wild*; - Journal, n., *deviation book*; - kurs, m., *compass course steered*; - lichter, f., *binnacle lamps*; - linie, f., *rhumb lines*; - mörser, m., *compass bowl*; - nadel, f., *c. needle*; - peilung, f., *c. bearing*; - pinne, f., *pivot of a c.*; - ringe, *gimbal of a c.*; - rose, f., *rhumb card*; - säule, f., *binnacle stand*; - signal, n., *c. signal*; - ständer, m., *binnacle stand*; - stativ, n., *compass stand*; - strich, m., *point*; - uhr, f., *dial compass*.

Komplement des Kurses, n., *complement of the course*.

Kompoundmaschine mitOberflächenkondensation, f., *compound engine with surface condensation*.

kondemniert, *condemned*.

Kondensation, f., condensation; - durch Einspritzung, c. by injection; - fläche, f., condensing surface; - maschine, f., condensing engine; - röhren-Dichtungsringe, condenser ferrules; - wasser, n., circulating water.
Kondensator, m., condenser; - deckel, m., c. door; - - Bolzenmutter, f., c. d. bolt nut; hintere - - Verbindung, f., after c. d. joint; - druckprobe, f., c. test; - hahn, m., c. cock; - Mannloch, n., c. manhole; - prüfung, f., c. test; - rohr, n., c. tube; - - dichtung or - - packung, f., c. t. packing; - - ring, m., c. t. ferrule; - wasser, n., circulating pump water.
Kondenser see Kondensator.
kondensierter Dampf, m., condensed steam.
konisch, conical.
konischer Bolzen, m., taper bolt; - Keil, m., cottar.
konisches Getriebe, n., bevel gear; - Pendel, n., conical pendulum; - Rad, n., bevel wheel; - Ventil, n., conical valve.
Konnossement, n., bill of lading.
Konservierung, f., preservation.
Konsignant, m., consigner.
Konsignatar, m., consignee.
Konsignateur, m., consigner.
konsignieren, to consign.
konstante Kraft, f., constant force.
konstanter Druck, m., constant pressure.
konstatieren, den erlittenen Schaden -, to ascertain the damage sustained.
Konstruktion, f., construction; - breite, f., moulded breadth; - material, n., building material.
konstruktiver Totalverlust, m., constructive total loss.

Konstruktor, m., constructer.
Kontaktventil, n., tripping valve.
Konterbande, f., contraband.
Konterbrasse, f., counter brace.
Kontrahent, m., contractor.
Kontroll-Manometer, n., standard pressure gauge; - Ventil, n., controlling valve.
kontrollieren, to control.
Konus, m., 1. cone; 2. plug (of a cock); - ventil, n., conical valve.
Kopf, m., head (of anchor, pier, sail, ship, tiller); - der Dampfwinde, steam winch warping end; - der Ruderpinne, tiller head; - des Ankerspills, windlass w. e.; - des Hafendamms, pier head; - des Spills, windlass warping end; das Schiff liegt auf dem -, the ship is by the h.
Kopf-bolzen, m., fender bolt; - ende der Hängematte, head clue; - - der Pleyelstange, connecting rod top end; - gillung, f., head gore; - holz, n., water cask chock; - hölzer, gauntree; - lägel, m. head cringle; - laschung der Spieren eines Bocks, f., sheer lashing; - platte der Feuerbüchse, f., dead plate of furnace; - saum, m., head tabling; - see, f., h. sea; - seite eines Radzahnes, f., face of a tooth of a wheel; - tau, n., stay of the sheers; - über, topsails over; - - sinken, to founder head down; - zurring, f., muzzle lashing.
Koppel-kurs, m., compound course; - - rechnung, f., traverse sailing; - tafel, f., t. table.
koppeln, to work a traverse.
Korallen-fischerboot, n., coral boat; - riff, n., c. reef.
Korbbake, f., Jack in the basket.

Kork, m., *cork*; - boje, f., *c. buoy*; - fender, m., *c. fender*; - weste, f., *c. jacket*.
Körner, m., *centre punch*; - punkt, m., *c. mark*.
Körper, m., *barrel* od. *body*.
Korrespondenzreeder, m., *managing owner*.
Korvette, f., *corvet*.
Kosten für das Ableichtern eines gestrandeten Schiffes und folgliche Schäden, *expenses for lightening a ship when ashore and consequent damage*; K. im Nothafen, e. *at port of refuge*.
Kovainnagel, Koviennagel, m., *belaying pin*.
krabben, *to race timber*.
Krabber, m., *racing knife*.
Krabpasser, m., *timber marker*.
krachen, in allen Fugen -, *cracking in all joints*.
Kraft, f., *force* od. *power*; es steht viele - auf den Ketten, *there is much strain on the cables*: - der Fahrt, *speed*; - einheit, f., *unit of force*; - entwickelung, f., *deployment of force*; - leistung, f., *effect*; - messer, m., *dynamometer*; - moment, m., *momentum of force*; - übertragung, f., *transmission of power*; - verlust, m., *loss of power*.
Kragen, m., *1. coat (of masts, pumps, and rudder)*; *2. grommet (of royal mast)*; *3.* - am Unterende eines Stags, *lower collar of a stay*; *4.* - im Hennegatt, *rudder coat*; *5.* - über den Augen des stehenden Gutes, *hood over the eyes of the standing rigging*.
Krähennest, n., *crow's nest*.
Krahn see Kran.
Krampe, f., *cramp* od. *staple*.
Kramstücken, pl., *hamper*.
Kran, m., *crane*; - arm, m., *c. post*; - ausleger, m., *whisker*; - balken, m., *cat head*;

den Anker am - - verholen, *to c. h. the anchor*; - - dücker, m., *c. h. knee*; - - knie, n., *supporter of c. h.*; - - steert, m., *c. tail*; - - stütze, f., *c. head bracket*; - balksweise, *on the bow*; - baum, m., *crane post*; - - zapfen, m., *c. p. pivot*; - gestell, n., *c. framing*; - handhabe, f., *c. handle*; - kasten, m., *water drawing c.*; - kette, f., *c. chain*; - leine, f., *boom topping lift*; - - block, m., *topping lift block*; - leiter, f., *crane peg ladder*; - mit Ausleger, *derrick c.*; - säule, f., *c. post*; - - pinne, f., *c. p. pin*; - schnabel, m., *outrigger of a c.*; - ständer, m., *c. post*; - trommel, f., *c. barrel*.
krängen, *to heel*.
Krängung, eine starke - geben, *to make a boot topping*; - fehler, m., *heeling error*; - messer, m., *nauropometer*; - versuch machen, *to try to determine the stability*.
Kranken-koje, f., *sick berth*; - liste, f., *sick list*; Mannschaft der - -, *main yard men*; - messe, f., *sick mess*; - schein, m., *sick ticket*; - schiff, n., *hospital ship*; - wärter, m., *sick berth attendant*.
Kranz, m., *rim*.
kränzen, *to give topping*.
Kratzeisen, n., *meaking iron*.
Kratzer, m., *tube scraper*.
kräuseln, *to ripple*.
Kräuselung, f., *ripples*.
Kräuselwasser, n., *bobble*.
Kravelle, f., *carling*.
Kreidestriche, *chalks*.
Kreisteil, m., *circular sector*.
Kreuz see also Besahn; - anker, m., *diagonal stay*; - bändsel, n., *racking*; Bauchgording, f., *crossjack bunt line*; - betinge, *topsail sheet bitts*; - bindsel, n., *cross seizing*.

Kreuzbram-Bauchgording, f., *mizen topgallant bunt line*; - brasse, f., *m. t. brace*; - Drehreep, n., *m. t. tye*; - fall, m., *m. topgallant halliard*; - Geitau, n., *m. t. clew line*; - Längssahling, f., *m. topmast trestle trees*; - Nockgording, f., *m. topgallant leech line*; - pardune, f., *m. t. backstay*; - pferd, n., *m. t. foot rope*; - püttings, *m. t. futtocks*; - - wanten, *m. t. futtock shrouds*; - rahe, f., *m. t. yard*; - sahling, f., *m. topmast cross trees*; - schote, f., *m. topgallant sheet*; - segel, n., *m. topgallant sail*; - stag, n., *m. t. stay*; - - segel, n., *m. t. staysail*; - - - fall, m., *m. t. s. halliard*; - - - hals, m., *m. t. s. tack*; - - - leiter, f., *m. t. s. stay*; - - - Niederholer, m., *m. t. staysail downhaul*; - - - schote, f., *m. t. s. sheet*; - stenge, f., *m. t. mast*; - - Eselshaupt, n., *m. t. m. cap*; - - pardune, f., *m. t. backstay*; - - stag, n., *m. t. stay*; - - want, n., *m. t. rigging*; - Toppenant, f., *m. t. lift*; - wanten, *m. t. rigging*.

Kreuz-brasse, f., *crossjack brace*; - - schenkel, m., *c. b. pendant*; - bulin, f., *c. bowline*; - fahrt, f., *cruise*; - geitau, n., *crossjack clew garnet*; - hahn, m., *four way cock*; - hals, m., *crossjack tack*; - holz, n., *kevel*; - klampe, f., *kevel*; - klampen für Halsen und Schoten, *belaying cleats for tacks and sheets*; - knoten, m., *carrick bend*.

Kreuzkopf, m., *crosshead*; - führung, f., *c. guide*; - Gleitplatte, f., *c. g.*; - Halszapfen, m., *c. journal*; - Lagerbolzen, m., *c. bolt*; - - mutter, f., *c. b. nut*; - Lagerfutter, n., *top end liner*; - Lagerschalen, *crosshead*

brasses; - - deckel, *connecting rod top end keep*; - träger, m., *crosshead bracket*.

Kreuzmars, m., *mizen top*; - Bauchgording, f., *m. t. sail bunt line*; - brasse, f., *m. t. s. brace*; - - schenkel, m., *m. t. s. brace pendant*; - Drehreep, n., *m. t. s. tye*; - fall, m., *m. t. s. halliard*; - geitau, n., *m. t. s. clew line*; - pardune, f., *m. topmast backstay*; - pferd, n., *m. topsail foot rope*; - püttings, *mizen futtocks*; - - wanten, *m. futtock shrouds*; - rahe, f., *m. topsail yard*; - Refftalje, f., *m. t. reef tackle*; - schote, f., *m. t. sheet*; - segel, n., *m. topsail*; - - schote, f., *m. t. sheet*; - stag, *m. topmast stay*; - stenge, n., f., *m. topmast*; - Eselshaupt, n., *m. t. cap*; - toppenant, f., *m. topsail lift*; - want, n., *m. topmast shroud*; - wanten, *m. topmast rigging*.

Kreuzmast, m., *mizen mast*; - Dwarssahling, f., *m. m. cross trees*; - Eselshaupt, n., *m. m. cap*; - keile, *m. m. wedges*; - kragen, m., *m. m. coat*; - Längssahling, f., *m. m. trestle trees*; - spur, f., *m. m. step*.

Kreuzmeißel, m., *cross cut chisel*.

Kreuz-Mittelstagsegel, n., *mizen middle staysail*; - - fall, m., *m. m. s. halliard*; - - hals, m., *m. m. s. tack*; - - Niederholer, m., *m. m. s. downhaul*; - - schote, f., *m. m. s. sheet*.

Kreuz-Nagelbank, f., *mizen fife rail*; - Nockgording, f., *crossjack leech line*.

Kreuz-Oberbram-brasse, f., *upper mizen topgallant brace*; - - pferd, n., *u. m. t. foot rope*; - - rahe, f., *u. m. t. yard*; - - segel, n., *u. m. t. sail*.

Kreuz-Obermars-brasse, f., *upper mizen topsail brace*; - - - schenkel, m., *u. m. t. b. pendant*; - - pferd, n., *u. m. t. foot rope*; - - rahe, f., *u. m. t. yard*; - - segel, n, *u. m. t.*

Kreuzpeilung, f., *cross bearing.*

Kreuz-pferd, n., *crossjack yard foot rope*; - rahe, f., *c. y.*; - - Toppenantstalje, f., *c. lift purchase*; - reefe der Blinde, *cross reefs*; - refftalje, f., *crossjack reef tackle.*

Kreuzroyal, n., *mizen royal*; - Bauchgording, f., *m. r. bunt line*; - brasse, f., *m. r. brace*; - fall, m., *m. r. halliard*; - geitau, n., *m. r. clew line*; - Längssahling, f., *m. topgallant trestle trees*; - pardune, f., *m. royal backstay*; - pferd, n., *m. r. foot rope*; - rahe, f., *m. r. yard*; - sahling, f., *m. topgallant cross trees*; - schote, f., *m. royal sheet*; - stag, n., *m. r. stay*; - - segel, n., *m. r. s. sail*; - - - fall, m., *m. r. s. s. halliard*; - - - hals, m., *m. r. s. s. tack*; - - - leiter, f., *m. r. s. s. stay*; - - - Niederholer, m., *m. r. s. s. downhaul*; - - - schote, f., *m. r. s. s. sheet*; - stenge, f., *m. r. r. mast*; - - pardune, f., *m. r. backstay*; - - stag, n., *m. r. stay*; - topp, m., *m. r. mast head*; - Toppenant, f., *m. r. lift.*

Kreuzrüste, f., *mizen channel*; - eisen, n., *m. chain plates.*

Kreuzscheisegel, n., *mizen skysail*; - brasse, f., *m. s. brace*; - fall, m., *m. s. halliard*; - geitau, n., *m. s. clew line*; - pardune, f., *m. s. backstay*; - pferd, n., *m. s. foot rope*; - rahe, f., *m. s. yard*; - schote, f., *m. s. sheet*; - stag, n., *m. skysail stay*; - stenge, f., *m. skysail mast*; - - pardune, f., *m. s. backstay*;

- - stag, n., *m. s. stay*; - Toppenant, f., *m. skysail lift.*

Kreuz-schote, f., *crossjack sheet*; - see, f., *cross sea*; - segel, n., *crossjack*; - - bulien, f., *mizen top bowline*; - - Nockgording, f., *crossjack leech line*; - - Refftalje, f., *c. reef tackle*; - seitig verlascht, *cross lashed*; - sorrung, f., *racking*; - spahn, m., *cross spale*; - spant, n., *dead flat.*

Kreuzstag, n, *mizen stay*; - segel, n., *m. s. sail*; - - fall, m., *m. s. s. halliard*; - - hals, m., *m. s. s. tack*; - - leiter, f., *m. s. s. stay*; - - Niederholer, m., *m. staysail downhaul*; - - schote, f., *m. s. sheet*; - - - schenkel, m., *m. s. s. pendant.*

Kreuzstange, f., *cross bar (of the piston).*

Kreuzstenge, f., *mizen topmast*; - Eselshaupt, n., *m. t. cap*; - pardune, f., *m. t. backstay*; - stag, n., *m. t. stay*; - - segel, n., *m. t. s. sail*; - - fall, m., *m. t. s. s. halliard*; - - - hals, m., *m. t. s. s. tack*; - - - leiter. f., *m. t. s. s. stay*; - - - Niederholer, m., *m. t. staysail downhaul*; - - - schote, f., *m. t. s. sheet*; - want, n., *m. t. shroud*; - wanten, *m. t. rigging.*

Kreuz-stich, m., *carrick bend*; - tau, n., *cross hawser*; - topp, m., *mizen top*; - toppenant, f., *crossjack lift*; - toppsgasten, *mizen top men*; - törns, *cross turns.*

Kreuz-Unterbram-brasse, f., *lower mizen topgallant brace*; - - pferd, n., *l. m. t. foot rope*; - - rahe, f., *l. m. t. yard*; - - segel, n., *l. m. t. sail.*

Kreuz-Untermars-brasse, f., *lower mizen topsail brace*;

- - - schenkel, m., *l. m. t. b.
pendant*; - U-m-pferd, n., *l.
m. t. foot rope*; - U-m-rahe,
f., *l. m. t. yard*; - U-m-segel,
n., *l. m. t.*
Kreuz-want, n., *mizen shroud*;
- wanten, *mizen rigging.*
kreuzen, *to cruise*; hin und
her -, *to beat about*; unter
kleinen Segeln -, *to lie by*;
die Barre -, *to cross the
bar*; vor unserm Bug -, *to
cross our bow*; ein Bindsel -,
to cross a seizing.
Kreuzer, m., *1. cruiser (vessel)*;
2. beating wind.
Kreuzung, f., *cross turns*; -
legen, *to scaze.*
Kriegs-flotte, f., *navy*; - konterbande, f., *contraband of
war*; - schiff, n., *man of war.*
krimpen, *backing (the wind
shifting against the sun).*
Krippe, f., *water groin.*
Krone, f., *crown (knot).*
Kronrad, n., *crown wheel.*
Krücke, f., *fire rake.*
Krückstag, n., *flag staff stay.*
krümmen, *to bend*; stärker -,
to quicken.
Krümmer, m., *1. elbow (of a
pipe)*; *2. winding butt (of
the bow)*; - rohr, n., *elbow
pipe.*
Krummholz, n., *knee timber.*
Krümmung, f., *1. curve*; *2.
bend (of a river)*; - der
obersten Auflanger, *top
timber hollow*; - des Krummholzes, *the back sweep.*
Krummzapfen, m., *crank.*
Krüppel-spill, n., *crab windlass*; - winde, f., *c. winch.*
kubischer Inhalt, m., *cubic
capacity.*
Küchen-geschirr, n., *cooking
utensils*; - junge, m., *Jack-
nasty-face*; - maat, m., *cook's
mate*; - meister, m., *jerker.*
Kücken, n., *plug (of a cock).*
Kufenschlitten, m., *bilge ways.*
Kuff, f., *galliot*; - ähnlich gebaut, *Dutch built.*

Kugel-abschnitt, m., *segment
of a sphere*; - dichtung, f.,
socket and ball joint; -
lampe, f., *ball lamp*; - laterne,
f., *globe lantern*; - segment,
n., *spherical segment*; - ventil, n., *ball valve*; - zapfen,
m., *b. gudgeon.*
Kuh-brücke, f., *temporary
deck*; - fuß, m., *crow bar*;
- - mit einem Schäkel,
shackle crow; - schwanz,
m., *fag end*; - schwänze in
der Takelung, *Irish pen-
nants.*
Kuhl, f., *waist*; - gasten,
waisters.
Kühl-apparat, m., *refrigerator*;
- balje, f., *match tub*; - fläche,
f., *cooling surface (of the
condenser)*; - gefäß, n.,
refrigerator; - hahn, m.,
*water service cock for cool-
ing purposes*; - raum, m.,
refrigerating chamber; -
rohr, n., *cooling pipe*; - -
ring, m., *condenser tube
ferrule*; - segel, n., *windsail*;
- vorrichtung, f., *water
service for cooling purposes*;
- wasserhahn, m., *w. s. cock
f. c. p.*; - wasserrohr, n.,
*w. s. pipe for cooling pur-
poses.*
Kühlte, f., *breeze (up to
force 7).*
Küken, n., *plug (of a cock).*
Kulisse, f., *link.*
Kumme, f., *bowl (of wood).*
künstlicher Hafen, m., *artificial harbour*; - Horizont,
m., *a. horizon*; - Zug, m., *a.
draught.*
Kuntje, n., *stowage quoin.*
Kupfer, n., *copper*; - befestigung, f., *c. fastening*; - beschlag, m., *c. sheathing*;
- blech, n., *sheathing c.*;
- - dichtung, f., *c. sheet
joint*; - bodig, *c. bottomed*;
- bolzen, m., *c. bolt*; - draht,
m., *c. wire*; - - dichtung, f.,
c. w. joint; - fest, *c. fastened*;

- hammer, m., *c. hammer*;
- haut, f., *c. sheathing*; eine
- - geben, *to sheathe with c.*;
- platte, f., *c. sheet*; - schmied,
m., *c. smith*; - verbolzung,
f., *c. fastening*.
kupfern, *to copper*.
kuppeln, *to couple*.
Kuppelstange, f., *drag bar*.
Kuppelung, f., *coupling*; -
bolzen, m., *1. c. bolt*; *2. drop
bolt (of the windlass)*; - -
mutter, f., *crosshead bolt
nut*; - flansch, m., *coupling
flange*; - hebel, m., *c. lever*;
- hülse, f., *c. box*; - klaue,
f., *clutch*; - muff, m., *coupling box*; - stange, f., *c. bar*.
Kurbel, f., *1. crank*; *2. lever (of
a winch)*; - achse, f., *crank
axle*; - arm, m., *c. lever*; -
auge, n., *eye of a crank*; -
grube, f., *c. pit*; - höhe, f.,
throw of a crank; - nabe,
f., *c. boss*; - scheibe, f., *c.
disk*; - wange, f., *c. web*;
- welle, f., *c. shaft*; - - und
Lauflager, *c. s. and tunnel
bearing*.
Kurbelwellen-auge, n., *web
eye of a crank shaft*; -
flansch, m., *crank shaft
flange*; - keilnute, f., *c. s.
key way*; - Kühlvorrichtung,
f., *c. s. water service*; -
Kupplung, f., *c. s. coupling*;
- - bolzen, m., *c. s. c. bolt*;
- lager, n., *crank shaft bearing*; - - bolzen, m., *c. s. b.
bolt*; - - bolzenmutter, f., *c.
s. b. b. nut*; - - deckel, m.,
c. s. bearing keep; - - -
bolzen, m., *c. s. b. k. bolt*;
- - - - mutter, f., *c. s. b. k.
b. nut*; - lagerschalen, *c.
s. brasses*; die oberen und
unteren - -, *top and bottom
ends*; - - Paßstück, n., *crank
shaft brasses liner*; - Lagerzapfen, m., *c. s. journal*.
Kurbelzapfen, m., *crank pin*;
- lagerbolzen, m., *c. p. bolt*;
- - mutter, f., *bottom end*

bolt nut; - Lagerschalen,
crank pin brasses; - - deckel,
m., *connecting rod bottom
end keep*.
Kurs, m., *course*; den - ändern, *to alter the c.*; den -
angeben, *to square the c.*; -
anliegen, *to lie the c.*; den -
festsetzen, *to fix the c.*; in
- gehen, *to steer the c.*; -
halten mit, *to hold tack
with*; den - setzen, *to shape
the course*; wieder auf -
setzen, *to keep ship away
again*; den - stellen, *to square
the course*; den - verbessern,
to correct the c.; den - verfolgen, *to stand on*.
Kurs-feuer, n., *principal light*;
- karte, f., *pilot chart*; -
linie, f., *course*; - messer,
m., *dromoscope*; - winkel,
m., *course angle*.
Kurve, f., *curve*; - lineal, n.,
c. templet; - vergrößern, *to
quicken*.
kurze Bramstenge, f., *stump
topgallant mast*; - D-schieber, m., *short D-slide valve*;
- Gänge, *short boards*; -
Gegenwinkel, m., *lug piece*;
- Hütte or - Poop, f., *short
poop*; - Reise, f., *s. trip*; -
Riemen, m., *double banked
oar*; - Schläge, *short boards*;
- Schraubenwelle, f., *adjusting length of shafting*; -
See, f., *short sea*; - Stringer-
winkel, *shell lugs*; - Tunnelwelle, f., *adjusting length of
shafting*; - Wellenstück, n.,
adjusting shaft; - Winkel
des Hauptdeckstringers,
*main deck stringer shell
lugs*; - - des Orlopdeckstringers, *orlop d. s. s. l.*;
- - des Raumbalkenstringers,
hold beam s. s. l.; - - des
Unterdeckstringers, *lower d.
s. s. l.*; - - des Zwischendeckstringers, *middle s. s. l.*
kurz-hieven, *to heave short*;
- splissung, f., *short splice*;
- Stag hieven, *to heave short*.

Küste, f., *coast*; - beleuchtung, f., *c. lighting*; - dampfer, m., *coasting steamer*; - fahrer, m., *coaster*; - fahrt, f., *coasting trade*; - fahrzeug, n., *coaster*; - feuer, n., *shore light*; - fischerei, f., *coast fishery*; - gebiet, n., *c. jurisdiction*; - handel, m., *coasting trade*; - kabel, n., *sea coast cable*; - karte, f., *coast chart*; - linie eines Fluß-delta, f., *base of a river delta*; - lotse, m., *coasting pilot*; - telegraph, m., *semaphore*; - vermessung, f., *coast survey*; - wache, f., *coast guard*; - wächter, m., *c. waiter.*

Kuttenknoten, m., *granny's knot.*

Kutter, m., *cutter*; - brigg, f., *c. brig*; - läufer, m., *c. fall*; - zeug, n., *c. rigging.*

Kuttsplissung, f., *cont splice*

L.

laag, *low.*

labsalben, *to pay with tar.*

Labskaus, n., *smotheration.*

Ladebaum, m., *derrick*; - band, n., *d. hoop*; - Doppelhanger, m., *d. span*; - gei, f., *d. guy*; - holer, m., *gilguy*; - stander, m., *derrick pendant.*

Lade-bord, m., *skids*; - brief, m., *bill of lading*; - buch, n., *cargo book*; - compartiment, n., *c. compartment*; - fähigkeit, f., *capacity*; - geschirr, n., *loading gear*; - hafen, m., *port of loading*; - haken, m., *cargo hook*; - kette, f., *c. chain*; - kosten, *loading expenses*; - kran, m., *loading and discharging crane*; - linie, f., *load line*; - luke, f., *cargo hatch*; - pforte, f., *c. port*; - platz, m., *loading berth*; - raum, m., *cargo hold*; - schlitten, m., *skids*; - stag, n., *triatic stay*; - tage, *loading days*; - takel, n., *garnet*; - wasserlinie, f., *load line*; - zeit, f., *time for loading.*

laden, *to load.*

Ladung, f., *cargo*; gemischte -, *miscellaneous c.*; in - liegen, *to be in loading*; - beteiligte, *parties interested in the cargo*; - empfänger, *receivers of the cargo*; - empfangsschein, m., *mate's receipt*; - hafen, m., *loading port*; - interessenten, *part owners of the cargo*; - manifest, n., *manifest of the c.*; - manko, n., *short tonnage*; - räumigkeit, f., *stowage capacity*; - überschuß, m., *surplus tonnage*; - versicherung, f., *cargo insurance.*

Lagan, m., *lagan.*

Lage, f., *1. tier (goods, &c.)*; *2. coat (of paint).*

Lägel, n., *cringle*; - mit Steert, *reef span.*

Lager, n., *1. bearing (of machinery parts)*; *2. bearer (support for engines, &c.)* *3. sleeper (of bed plate)*; *4. banjo (of propeller)*; *5. warehouse*; - aufseher, m., *warehouse-man*; - block, m., *pedestal*; - bock, m., *plumber block*; - bolzen, m., *bearing bolt*; - mutter, f., *b. b. nut*; - büchse, f., *journal box*; - deckel, m., *bearing keep*; - - der Mittelbetinge, *centre bitt keep*; - - der Pumpenbalancieraxe, *keep for pump lever shaft brasses*; - - der Seitenbetinge, *side bitt keep*;

- deckelbolzen, m., *keep bolt*; - - mutter, f., *k. b. nut*;
- schalen, *brasses*; obere - -, *top b.*; untere - -, *bottom b.*;
- - auffüllen, *to line up the brasses*; - stelle, f., *bearing;*
- stuhl, m., *block*; - - or - träger eines Schaufelrades, m., *paddle wheel bracket*;
- wall, m., *lee shore*; - weiß- metall, n., *white metal*; - zapfen, m., *journal*; - - der Balancieraxe, *rocking shaft j.*; - - der Tunnelwelle, *tunnel s. j.*; - - der Um- steuerungswelle, *weigh s. j.*; - - der Welle. *s. j.*
lagern, *to warehouse.*
Lagune, f., *lagoon.*
Lamellenbremse, f., *plate compressor.*
Lampe, f., *lamp*; - cylinder, m., *l. glass*; - docht, m., *l. wick*; - fall, m., *l. halyard*; - glas, n., *l. glass*; - raum, m., *l. room*; - schere, f., *l. scissors*; - trimmer, *l. trimmer*; - zylinder, m., *l. glass.*
Lampisterie, f., *lamp locker*; - tür, f., *l. l. door.*
Land, n., *shore*; - anker, m., *s. anchor*; - antun, *to make the land*; - blink, m., *land blink*; - brise, f., *l. breeze*; - dwars in Lee. *l. on the lee beam*; - eis, n., *land ice*; - enge, f., *isthmus*; - feste, f., *shore fast*; - feuer, n., *s. light*; - in Sicht, *land in sight*; - in S. bekommen, *to dis- cover l.*; an - kommen, *to get ashore*; - machen, *to make the land*; - marken, *land marks*; - maschinist, m., *superintending engineer*; - ratte, *long shore lubber*; - seefahrzeug, n., *lake craft*; über -, *by land*; vom - ab, *off the land*; - wärts, *inshore.*
landen, *to land.*
Landung, f., *landing*; - be- scheinigung, f., *l. certificate*;

- boot, n., *flat bottomed boat*; - brücke, f., *landing stage*; - - einer Fähre, *floating wharf of a flying bridge*; - damm, m., *jetty*; - gerüst, n., *skeleton pier*; - kosten, *landing charges*; - platz, m., *landing place.*
lange Fahrt, f., *distant trade*; - Flach, n., *long floor*; - Gänge, *l. boards*; - Hütte or - Poop, f., *l. poop*; - Rahen, *square yards*; - Riemen, *single banked oars*; - Schläge, *long boards*; - See, f., *l. sea.*
Länge, f., 1. eines Schiffes, *length*; äußerste -, *extreme l.*; - in der Höhe der Lade- linie, *l. on load line*; - zwischen den Perpendikeln, *l. between perpendiculars*; der - nach, *lengthway*; 2. geographische -, *longitude*; - nach astronomischer Be- obachtung, *l. by astronomic observation*; 3. - und Tiefe der Flagge, *the fly and hoist of the flag.*
Längen - durchschnitt, m., *longitudinal section*; - uhr, f., *longitude watch*; - unter- schied, m., *difference of longitude.*
langer D-schieber, m., *long D-slide valve.*
länger, ein Schiff - machen, *to lengthen a ship.*
Langhalsen, *barnacles.*
längs, *along*; - band, n., *tie plate*; - bramsahlings, *top- mast trestle trees*; - der Kaje vertäut, *moored along the quay*; - der Küste, *along the shore*; - festigkeit, f., *longitudinal strength*; - naht, f., *1. longitudinal seam*; 2. *landing edge (of a plate)*; - - nietung, f., *edge riveting*; - platte, f., *tie plate.*
Längssahling, f., *trestle trees*; - der Bramstenge, *topgallant t. t.*; - der Großbramstenge,

main t. t. t.; - der Groß-marsstenge, *main topmast trestle trees*; - der Kreuz-bramstenge, *mizen top-gallant t. t.*; - der Kreuz-marsstenge, *m. topmast t. t.*; - der Marsstenge, *topmast t. t.*; - der Mittelbramstenge, *middle topgallant t. t.*; - der Mittelmarsstenge, *middle topmast t. t.*; - der Vorbram-stenge, *fore topgallant trestle trees*; - der Vormars-stenge, *fore topmast t. t.*; - des Untermastes, *lower t. t.*

Längs-schiene, f., *tie plate*; - - der Brückendeckbalken, *bridge deck beam t. p.*; - schiffs, *fore and aft*; - schott, n., *longitudinal bulkhead*; - - stringer, m., *l. b. stringer*; - seits, *alongside*; - - holen, *to haul a.*; - - kommen, *to come a.*; - - legen, *to lay a.*; - - liegen, *to lie a.*; - - schleppen, *to tow abreast*; - spannung, f., *longitudinal strain*; - spant, n., *l. frame*; - träger, m., *1. fore and after (of a hatchway)*; *2. longitudinal girder (of the double bottom)*; - verband, m., *longitudinal strength*; - verbindung, f., *web plate*; - verstärkung f., *longitudinal strengthening*; - winkel-eisen, n., *girder*.

Langsahling der Radwelle, f., *paddle bearer*.

langsam, *ease her!* - beim Wenden, *slack in stays*; - fieren, *to slack handsomely*; - rückwärts! *slow astern!* - vorwärts! *s. ahead!* so - wie möglich, *dead slow*.

langsamer gehen lassen, *to ease the engines*.

Lang-scherbe, f., *long scarf*; - schotten, *lengthwise built bulkheads*; - splissung, f., *long splice*; - strähnig, *l. skeined*.

lang- und kurzarmige Boden-

wrangen, *long and short armed floors*.

Lappen, m., *doublings*; alle - bei haben, *to have all sails set*.

lappsalben, *to pay with tar*.

Lärchenholz, n., *larch wood*; amerikanisches -, *hackma-tack*.

Lasch, m., *1. scarph*; *2. butt strap (of double bottom)*; - bolzen, m., *butt bolt*.

laschen, *1. to lash (ropes and chains)*; *2. to scarph (timber and metal)*.

Laschung, f., *lashing (ropes and chains)*; *2. scarph (timber and metal)*; - einer ge-fischten Spiere etc., *lashing around a fished spar*; - mit gewöhnlichen Bindseln, *l. by flat seizing*; - mit Spann, *span l.*; - zweier Augen aufeinander, *l. of two eyes*; - zwischen Vordersteven nnd Kiel, *boxing of stem and keel*.

Laßt laufen! *Let go!* - die Segel rasch nieder! *Let go amain!*

Last, das Schiff liegt mehrere Fuß aus der Last, *the ship has sewed several feet*; d. S. ist 2 F. a. d. Last gehoben, *t. s. is s. up 2 feet*.

Lastgeld, n., *lastage*.

Lastigkeit, f., *burthen*; - haben, *to bear water*.

lateinische Rahe, f., *Lateen yard*; - Segel, n., *L. sail*.

latente Wärme, f., *latent heat*.

Laterne, f., *lantern*; - eisen, n., *l. braces*; - kammer, f., *light room*; - kasten, m., *sidelight screens*; - - stützen, *s. s. stanchions*; - signal, n., *lantern signal*; - turm, m., *light house*.

Latte, f., *batten*.

Latten der Rüsten, *laths of the chain wales*; - kiste, f., *crate*; - klampe, f., *batten*

cleat; - verschlag, m., crate;
- wegerung, f., batten and
space ceiling.
Lauf-brücke, f., bridge of
boards; - kran, m., overhead
travelling crane; - lager, n.,
tunnel bearing; - planke, f.,
gangway; - rolle, f., roller;
- stag, n., man rope.
laufen, alle Segel mit einem
Male - lassen, to let everything run; ein Segel einer
Bö wegen - lassen, to lower
a sail for a squall; auf
Strand -, to run ashore;
unklar -, to run foul; zu
weit - beim Aufsuchen des
Ankerplatzes, to overshoot.
laufende Auge, n., running
eye; - Block, m., r. block;
- Ende, n., r. end; - Frachten, current rates; - Fuß, m.,
foot run; - Gewicht, n.,
sliding weight; - Gut, n.,
running rigging; das - -
fährt gut, the r. r. leads
fair; - Knoten, m., running
hitch; - Ladetage, r. days;
- Leibstich, m., r. bowline;
- Part eines Takels, r. part
of a tackle; - Pfahlstich,
m., r. bowline; - Tage, r.
days; - Tauwerk, n., r. rigging; der - Teil eines Takels,
the leading part of a tackle.
Läufer, m., fall (rope); 2.
runner (a tout); - des
Jakobstabes, vane of a
Jacob's staff; - des Speckgiens, cant fall.
Läutewerk zum Anzeigen
eines Lecks, n., leak alarm.
lavieren, to work to windward.
Lazarett, n., lazaret.
lebender Ballast, m., live
lumber.
lebendes Werk, n., quickwork.
Lebensboje, f., live buoy.
lebhaft werden, to freshen.
Leck, n., leak; - abdichten,
to staunch a l.; - bekommen
or springen, to spring a l.;

- hat sich zugezogen, the l.
has been stopped acciden-
tally; - stopfen, to stop a l.;
leckes Schiff etc., leaky ship,
&c.
Leckage, f., leakage.
lecken, to leak.
Leck-sucher, m., leakage
finder; - tuch, n., fother mat;
mit dem - - stopfen, to
fother.
Leder-reep, n., hide rope; -
schlauch, m., leather hose;
- tau, n., hide rope.
Lee, in -, under the lee; Das
Ruder in -! Put the helm
alee! mit dem Winde von -
ein, by the lee; sich in - befinden, to have the lee gauge;
in - voraus, on the l. bow;
Querab nach -, on the l.
beam.
Lee-anker, m., l. anchor;
- boot, n., l. boat; - brasse,
f., l. brace; - bulin, f., l.
bowline; - geitau, n., l. brail;
- gierig, the ship carries a
lee helm; - küste, f., l. shore;
- nock, f., l. arm; - ruder,
n., l. helm; Nicht soviel - -
geben! Don't give so much
l. h.! viel - - verlangen, to
bear a slack h.; - schote, f.,
lee sheet.
Leesegel, n., studding sail;
- Außenschote, f., s. s. tack;
- Binnenschote, f., s. s. sheet;
- fall, m., s. s. halliard; - -
block, m., jewel block; - -
stich, m., studding sail
halliard bend; - hals, m., s.
s. tack; - Niederholer, m., s.
s. downhaul; - rahe, f., s. s.
yard; - schote, f., s. s. sheet;
- spiere, f., s. s. boom; - -
brasse, f., s. s. b. brace; - -
bügel, m., s. s. boom iron;
- - talje, f., s. s. b. jigger.
Lee-seite, f., lee side; - tide, f.,
l. tide; - wärts, leeward; -
weg, m., leeway; - zeit, f., l.
tide.
leer, empty; - pumpen, to
pump dry.

leeren, *to empty.*
Leg aus! *lie out!* Leg ein!
l. in!
Legel, n., *cringle*; - mit Steert,
reef span (see also Lägel).
legen, *to abate (gale)*; das
Ruder über -, *to shift the
helm*; das R. nach Steuerbord -, *to port the h.*; ein
Deck -, *to lay a deck*; einen
Kiel -, *to lay a keel.*
Legerwall, m, *lee shore.*
legierter Stahl, m., *alloyed
steel.*
Leguan, m., *dolphin.*
Lehmgrund, m., *clayey bottom.*
Lehnbrett, n., *back board.*
Lehrling, m., *apprentice.*
Leibholz, n., *waterway*; -
planke, f., *inner w.*
Leibstich, m., *bowline hitch.*
leicht beladen, *lightly laden*;
- bemannt, *light handed*; -
bewegte See, f., *slightly
rough sea*; - matrose, m.,
ordinary seaman; - schmelzbarer Tropfen, m., *fusible
plug*; - verderbliche Güter,
perishable goods.
leichte Beschädigung, f.,
slight damage; - Bö, f.,
light squall; - Brise, f.,
gentle breeze; - Güter, *light
goods*; - Regen, m., *l. rain*;
- Segel, n., *l. sails*; - tuch,
n., *duck*; - Wasserlinie, f.,
light water line; - Zug, m.,
l. airs.
Leichter, m., *lighter*; - führer,
m., *lighterman*; - geld, n.,
lighterage; - mann, m.,
lighterman.
leichtern, *to lighten.*
Leik, n., *bolt rope*; - garn, n.,
b. r. yarn; - Leine, f., *b. r.
line*; - nadel, f., *b. r. needle.*
Leim, m., *glue*; - topf, m., *glue
pot.*
Leine, f., *line.*
Leinöl, n., *linseed oil.*
Leinpfad, m., *tow path.*
Leiste, f., *comber*; - zur Bekleidung der Schottenfugen,
ribband of the bulkheads.

Leisten der Farbenstreifen
anmerken od. straaken, *to
line a vessel*; - mit Zwischenräumen, *batten and space.*
Leistung, f., *effect.*
Leistungsfähigkeit, f., *efficiency.*
Leit-block, m., *1. guide pulley*;
*2. nine pin block (round the
masts)*; - bügel, m., *backstay
traveller (of the topsail tye)*;
- feuer, n., *leading lights*;
- linie, f., *l. line*; - marken,
leading marks; - ring, m.,
head ring; - rolle, f., *guide
pulley*; - spindel, f., *leading
screw*; - stange des Parallelogramms, f., *parallel motion
radius bar.*
leiten, *to lead.*
Leiter, f., *1. ladder (steps)*; *2.
stay (of staysail).*
Leitung, f., *1. conduit (pipes)*;
2. guide (for directing a rod);
*3. management (of engines,
&c.).*
Leitungs-draht, m., *electric
cable*; - fähigkeit, f., or -
vermögen, n., *conductibility.*
Leitwagen, m., *lee fange.*
Lenktau, n., *bridle cable.*
lenßen, *see* lenzen.
Lenz-druckrohr, n., *bilge
discharge pipe*; - - leitung,
f., *b. delivery pipes*; - ejector, m., *b. ejector*; - hahn,
m., *b. cock*; - kasten, m., *b.
valve box*; - pforte, f.,
scupper.
Lenzpumpe, f., *bilge pump*;
- Ausgußrohr, n., *b. p. discharge pipe*; - Ausgußventil,
n., *b. p. d. valve*; - - deckel,
m., *b. p. d. v. cover*; - Aus-
gußventilspindel, f., *b. p. d.
v. spindle*; - Balancier, m.,
b. p. lever; - deckel, m., *b. p.
cover*; - Druckraum, m., *b.
p. delivery space*; - Druckrohr, n., *b. p. discharge
pipe*; - Druckventil, n., *b. p.
top valve*; - - Hubbegrenzer,
m., *b. p. t. v. guard*; - -

kasten, m, *b. p. delivery
valve chest*; - - Klappenfänger, m., *b. p. d. v. guard*;
- - sitz, m., *b. p. top valve
seat*; - Einsatz, m., *b. p.
liner*; - Fußventil, n., *b. p.
foot valve*; - Gelenk, n., *b.
p. link*; - - lagerschalen, *b.
p. l. brasses*; - Grundring,
m., *b. p. neck bush*; - Kolben, m., *b. p. bucket*; - - ring,
m., *b. p. b. ring*; - - stange,
f., *b. p. b. rod*; - - ventil, n.,
b. p. b. valve; - - - sitz, m.,
b. p. b. v. seat; - Körper,
m., *b. p. chamber*; - Plunger,
m., *b. p. plunger*; - Probierhahn, m., *b. p. pet cock*;
- Rücklauf- or - Rückflußventil, n., *b. p. relief valve*;
- Saugeraum, m., *b. p. suction
space*; - Saugerohr, n., *b. p.
suction pipe*; - - Saugekorb,
m., *b. p. suction pipe strum
box*; - Saugeventil, n., *b. p.
suction valve*; - - Hubbegrenzer, m., *b. p. foot valve guard*;
- - kasten, m., *b. p. suction
valve chest*; - - Klappenfänger, m., *b. p. s. v. guard*;
- - sitz, m., *b. p. s. v. seat*;
- Schnürhahn, m., *b. p. pet
cock*; - Schnürventil, n., *b. p.
p. valve*; - stange, f., *b. pump
rod*; - - Stopfbüchse, f., *b.
p. r. stuffing box*; - Stopfbüchse, f., *b. p. s. b.*; - ventil, n., *b. p. valve*; - - deckel,
m., *b. p. v. cover*; - - Hubbegrenzer or - Klappen-
fänger, m., *b. p. v. guard*;
- - sitz, m., *b. p. v. seat*;
- - vorrichtung, f., *b. p. v.
gear*; - Windkessel, m., *b.
p. air vessel*; - Zylinder, m.,
b. p. cylinder.
lenzpumpen, *to free a vessel.*
Lenz-raum, m., *bilge*; - rohrleitung, f., *b. pipes*; - sauge-
rohrleitung, f., *b. suction
pipe*; - schlagen, *sucking*;
- ventil, n., *bilge suction
valve*; - - kasten, m., *b. v.
box.*

lenzen, *1. to scud (while sailing); 2. to free a vessel
(from water); gut -, to
behave well when scudding.*
letzte Ebbzeit, f., *the lowest
of the ebb.*
Leucht-bake, f., *light beacon*;
- boje, f., *gas buoy*; - feuer,
n., *beacon*; - - Behörde, f.,
lighthouse board; - - buch,
n., *l. book*; - kraft, f., *candle
power*; - tonne, f., *gas buoy*;
- turm, m., *light house*; - -
wächter, m., *l. h. keeper.*
Leuwagen, m., *1. sweep (of
the tiller); 2. lee fange (of
a sheet).*
Levanter, m., *Levanter.*
Libelle, f., *spirit level.*
Licht, n., *light*; - blitzsignal,
n., *flashing l.*; - klampe, f.,
snatch cleat; - pforte, f.,
light port; - signal, n., *optic
signal.*
lichten, *1. to lighten (a vessel);
2. to weigh (anything); den
Anker -, to weigh anchor.*
Lichter, m., *lighter*; - führer
or - mann, m., *l. man.*
lidern, *to pack.*
Liderung, f., *packing*; - deckel,
m., *packing washer*; - drang
heraus, *p. gave out*; - feder,
f., *piston spring*; - ring, m.,
packing ring; - scheibe, f.,
p. washer; - schraube, f.,
p. bolt.
Liege-geld, n., *demurrage*;
- platz, m., *berth*; - tage, *lay
days.*
liegen, *to lie*; Wie - wir an?
How does she -? auf dem
Strome -, *to ride to the tide*;
auf dem Wind -, *to r. t. the
wind*; bequem vor Anker -,
to r. easy; mit dem Schandeckel im Wasser -, *to heel
gunwale to*; nach Cux-
haven zu -, *to stand in
for C.*; nach Land zu -, *t. s.
in shore*; zwischen Wind
und Strom -, *to ride between
wind and tide.*

22*

liegende Bohrmaschine, f., *horizontal drilling machine.*

Lieger des Gallions, m., *gammoning piece.*

Liegt ab! *Put off!*

Liek *see* Leik.

Ligan, m., *ligan.*

Linie, f., *line (equator, steamers, &c.).*

Linien-schiff, n., *line of battle ship*; - taufe, f., *ducking.*

linksdrehende or linksgehende Schraube, f., *left handed propeller.*

linksgeschlagenes Tau, n., *left handed rope.*

Linksruder, n., *starboard.*

Lipp-block, m., *snatch block*; - klampe, f., *s. cleat.*

Lippe, f., *snatch*; - einer Laschung, *lip of a scarph.*

Lippen *see* Lipp.

Liquid Kompaß, m., *spirit compass.*

Lißleine, f., *lacing*; - eines Bonnets, *lasket of a bonnet.*

Litzung, f., *lacing.*

Loch, n., *hole*; - beitel, m., *mortise chisel*; - dorn, m., *drift*; - im Kreuz, *cross tail hole*; - maschine, f., *punching machine*; - taster, m., *inside callipers.*

lochen, *to punch.*

locker werden, *to start.*

Log, n., *log*; - auswerfen, *to stream the* -; - einholen, *to haul in the* -; - stellen, *to set the* -; - wieder stellen, *to reset the l.*

Log-brett, n., *log ship*; - buch, n., *l. book*; - glas, n., *l. glass*; - leine, f., *l. line*; - rolle, f., *l. reel*; - scheit or - schiff, n., *l. ship*; - schraube, f., *rotator*; - tafel, f., *log slate.*

Loggat, n., *limber hole.*

loggen, *to heave the log.*

Logger, m., *lugger.*

Logis, n., *crew space*; - kappe, f., *c. s. companion*; - Oberlicht, n., *crew s. skylight*; - - gräting, f., *grating of c. s. s.*;

- ofen, m., *c. space stove*; - schornstein, m., *c. space funnel*; - tür, f., *c. s. door.*

Lohntag, m., *pay day.*

lorchen or lörken, *to blow.*

los! *let go amain!* - ankern, *to unanchor*; - arbeiten, *to work loose*; - brechen, *to break adrift*; - eisen, *to dig out of the ice*; - gerissen vom Leik, *blown from the bolt rope*; - haken, m., *to unhook*; - hieven, *to dislodge (the anchor)*; - kaufen, *to ransom*; - machen, *1. to unlash; 2. to unbend (a rope); 3. to unfurl (a sail)*; - nehmen, *to strip*; - nieten, *unrivet*; - reißen, *to dislodge*; - überall! *let go everywhere!* - werfen, *1. to unmoor (from wharf); 2. to cast off (tug).*

lösbare Friktionskegelkupplung, f., *friction socket coupling*; - Kuppelung, f., *loose coupling.*

Lösch-bord, n., *skids*; - geld, n., *discharging expenses*; - geschirr, n., *d. gear*; - hafen, m., *port of discharge*; - haken, m., *can hook*; - platz, m., *discharging berth*; - rad, n., *cargo gin*; - tage, *discharging days.*

löschen, *to discharge (the cargo)*; - von Brand an Bord eines Schiffes, n., *extinguishing fire on board ship.*

Löschungshafen, m., *port of discharge.*

Loshaken, m., *can hook.*

lose, *1. loose (machinery); 2. slack (rope); das* -, *the loose part; das* - einholen, *to haul in the slack*; - Außenklüverbaum, m., *the loose flying jib boom*; - Deck, n., *preventer deck*; - Excenter, n., *loose eccenter*; - Fockstag, n., *fore preventer stay*; - geben, *1. to slack (ropes); 2. to flow (sheets)*; - Kiel, m., *false keel*; - Ladung, f., *cargo in bulk*; - Leikstopfen, m., *fod-dering*; - Oberbramsegel, n., *the loose royal*; - Rad, n., *l. wheel*; - schrauben, *to slack back*; - Wegerung, f., *loose ceiling*.

lösen, *1. to take off (stoppers)*; *2. to loosen (key, screw, sail)*.

Loskiel, m., *false keel*.

lossen, *to discharge*.

Lot, n., *1. solder (for solder-ing)*; *2. lead (for sounding)*; - apparat, m., *sounding machine*; auf - barem Grun-de sein, *to be in soundings*; nicht - bar, *soundless*; - blei, n., *sounding lead*; - block, m., *notch block*; - brook, m., *horse*; - leine, f., *lead line*; - leinbalje, f., *l. l. tub*; - recht, *perpendicular*; - wer-fen, *to heave the lead*; - wurf, m., *a cast of lead*.

Löte, f., *solder*.

löten, *1. to braze (iron)*; *2. to solder (other metal)*.

loten, *to sound*; fortwährend -, *to cast the lead continually*.

Löt-kolben, m., *soldering iron*; - löffel, m., *s. ladle*; - spiri-tus, m., *s. spirit*.

Lotse, m., *pilot*.

Lotsen-anweisung, f., *pilot's orders*; - aspirant, m., *ap-prentice pilot*; - boot, n., *pilot boat*; - fahrwasser, n., *p. waters*; - flagge, f., *p. flag*; - gebühr, f., or - geld, n., *pilo-tage*; - - ausgehend, *p. out-ward*; - - einkommend, *p. inward*; - kommandeur, m., *pilot master*; - kunde, f., *pilo-tage*; - lehrling, m., *appren-tice p.*; - signal, n., *p. signal*; - station, f., *p. station*; - ver-setzdampfer, m., *p. steamer*; - wesen, n., *pilotage*; Bureau für das - -, *pilot office*; - zwang, m., *compulsory pilo-tage*.

lotsen, *to pilot*; auf -, *to p. up*; auf und nieder -, *to p. in and out*; aus -, *to p. out*;

ein -, *to p. in*; nieder -, *to p. down*.

Lotungen vornehmen, *to take soundings*; nach L. steuern, *to steer by s.*

Lotungsgebühr, f., *soundage*.

loxodromische Kurs, m., *loxodromic course*; - Linie, f., *rhumb line*.

Luft-auslaßventil, n., *snifting valve*; - dicht verschließen, *to close hermetically*; - druck, m., *air pressure*; - ejektor, m., *a. ejector*; - ein-lassen, *to admit air*; - ein-laßventil, n., *internal safety valve*; - gang, m., *air course*; - hahn, m., *a. cock*; - heizung, f., *hot air heating*; - kasten, m., *1. air chamber*; *2. tank (of life boat)*; - leere, f., *vacuum*; - - messer, m., *v. gauge*; - leerer Raum, m., *vacuum space*; - - - des Kondensators, *v. s. of con-denser*; - loch, n., *air hole*; - messer, m., *pneumatometer*; - pforte, f., *air port*.

Luftpumpe, f., *air pump*; - Ausguß, m., *a. p. orifice*; - Balancier, m., *a. p. lever*; - deckel, m., *a. p. cover*; - Drainagehahn, m., *a. p. drain cock*; - Druckraum, m., *a. p. hotwell*; - - Ausgußöffnung, f., *a. p. h. discharge orifice*; - ventil, n., *a. p. top valve*; - - - Hubbegrenzer, m., *a. p. t. v. guard*; - - - Klappenfänger, m., *a. p. delivery valve guard*; - - - sitz, m., *a. p. top valve seat*; - Druckraum-Verbindungen, *a. p. delivery space connections*; - Einsatz, m., *a. p. liner*; - Fußventil, n., *a. p. foot valve*; - gelenk, n., *a. p. link*; - lager-schalen, *a. p. l. brasses*; - Grundring, m., *a. p. neck bush*; - Halszapfen der Balancierachse, m., *a. p. lever shaft journal*; - der Traverse, m., *a. p. crosshead journal*; - Kolben, m., *a. p.*

bucket; - - ring, m., a. p. b.
ring; - - ventil, n., a. p. b.
valve; - - - Hubbegrenzer
or Klappenfänger, m., a. p.
b. v. guard; - - - sitz, m., a.
p. b. v. seat; - Körper, m.,
a. p. chamber; - - deckel,
m., a. p. c. door; - Kreuzkopf,
m., a. p. crosshead; - Luftauslaßventil or Luftventil,
n., a. p. air valve; - Mannloch, n., a. p. man hole; -
Pleyelstange, f., a. p. connecting rod; - plunger, m., a. p.
plunger; - Probierhahn, m.,
a. p. pet cock; - Rückfluß-
or Rücklaufventil, n., a. p.
relief valve; - Saugeraum, m.,
a. p. suction space; - Saugerohr, n., a. p. suction pipe;
- Saugeventil, n., a. p. s.
valve; - - Hubbegrenzer, m.,
a. p. foot valve guard; - -
Klappenfänger, m., a. p.
suction v. g.; - - sitz, m., a.
p. s. v. seat; - Schnürhahn,
m., a. p. pet cock; - Sicherheitsventil, n., a. p. escape
valve; - stange, f., a. p. rod;
- - Stopfbüchse, f., a. p. r.
stuffing box; - Stopfbüchse,
f., a. p. s. b.; - - deckel, m.,
a. p. s. b. gland; - Traverse,
f., a. p. crosshead; - Überlaufrohr, n., a. p. overflow
pipe; - Überlaufventil, n.,
a. p. o. valve; - - deckel, m.,
a. p. o. v. cover; - - feder, f.,
a. p. o. v. spring; - - sitz, m.,
a. p. o. v. seat; - - spindel,
f., a. p. o. v. spindle; - ventil,
n., a. p. v.; - - Hubbegrenzer
or Klappenfänger, m., a. p.
v. guard; - - sitz, m., a. p. v.
seat; - Vorrichtung, f., a. p.
gear; - Zylinder, m., a. p.
barrel.
Luft-rohr, n., air pipe; - sack,
m., wind sail; - - bänder,
w. s. hoops; - - kette, f.,
alhydic chain; - spalt im
inneren Plankengang, m.,
air strake; - spiegelung, f.,
mirage; - trockenes Holz,

n., seasoned wood; - ventil,
n., air valve; - - deckel, m.,
a. v. cover; - - des Kessels,
n., a. v. of boiler; - - gehäuse,
n., a. v. box.
Lüftchen, n., es regte sich
kein -, there was no breeze
stirring.
lüften, to ventilate, to air, to
lift (the hatches).
Lüft-vorrichtung, f., easing
gear.
Lugger, m., lugger; - fock, f.,
lug foresail; - segel, n., lug
sail; - - rahe, f., lug yard.
Lugswinkel, aperture angle
bars.
Luitwagen, m., lee fange.
Luk- see Luken-.
Luke, f., 1. hatch; 2. hood (of
fishing boat); die - bedecken,
to cover the hatch; - lüften,
to lift t. h.; - öffnen, to
open t. h.; - schließen, to
close down t. h.; - ver-
schalken, to batten d. t. h.
Luken, hatches; - balken, m.,
hatch beam; - - winkel, m.,
h. b. angle bar; - besichtigung, f., survey on hatches;
- bügel, m., hatch bar; -
deckel, m., h.; - eisen, n., h.
iron; - gräting, f., h. grating;
- haus, n., h. house; - kappe,
f., hatchway companion; - -
Schutzvorrichtung, f., hatch
house protectors; - karbe, f.,
hatchway coaming; - koker,
m., h. bulkhead; - latte, f.,
port flange; - leiter, f., pillar
ladder; - marker, m., gutter
ledge; - netz, n., hatchway
netting; - öffnung, f., h.; -
rahmen, m., hatch frame; -
ring, m., h. ring; - rippe, f.,
h. carling; - schalken, t. h.
battens; - - klampen, h. batten
cleats; - scherstock, m., h.
carling; - schlinge, f., h. c.;
- schlüssel, m., h. c.; - stange,
f., h. bar; - stopper, m.,
hatchway stopper; - stringer,
m., beam tie plate; - stützen,
hatch stanchions; - süll, m.,

hatchway coaming; - - winkel, m., *h. c. angle bar.*
lullen or luren, *to lull.*
Lunten-kiste, f., *match chest;* - stock, m., *m. staff.*
lüstert, das Schiff - gut auf das Steuer, *the ship answers the helm readily.*
Lust-fahrt, f., *pleasure trip;* - fahrzeug, n., *p. boat.*
Luv, f., *1. weather (direction of wind); 2. luff! (order for the helm);* einem Schiffe - abgewinnen, *to gain the weather gauge of a ship;* - anker, m., *w. anchor;* - baum, m., *outrigger;* - bäume, *luff timbers;* sich in - befinden, *to have the w. gauge;* - brasse, f., *weather brace;* - - einholen, *to square the yards in;* - buggording, f., *weather bunt line;* - bulin, f., *w. bowline;* - fockschote, f., *w. fore sheet;* - geitau, n., *w. brail;* - gewinnen, *to gain the w. gauge;* - gierig sein, *to be weatherly;* - gierigkeit, f., *weatherliness;* - hals, m., *weather tack;* - halten, *to keep the luff;* - halter, m., *plier;* - kette, f., *veering cable;* - küste, f., *weather*

shore; - Laufplanke, f., *w. gangway;* - liek, n., *w. leech;* - nock, f., *w. earing;* - - gording, f., *w. leech line;* - pardune, f., *w. backstay;* - refftalje, f., *w. reef tackle;* - ruder, n., *w. helm;* - schote, f., *w. sheet;* - seite, f., *w. side;* sich auf der - - befinden, *to have the w. gauge;* - spant, n., *luff frame;* - taljereep, n., *weather laniard;* - toppenant, f., *w. lift;* - verlieren, *to lose the w. gauge;* - wanten, *w. rigging.*

luvwärts, *a-weather;* ganz - das Ruder! *hard a-weather!* - halten, *to keep the luff;* - querab, *weather beam;* - setzende Gezeit, f., *w. tide;* - - Strömung, f., *windward set;* - voraus, *on the weather bow;* - vorbeisegeln, *to weather;* - zu kommen suchen, *to try to gain the w. gauge.*

Luv-Windvierung, f., *weather quarter;* - zum wenden! *Ready about!*
luven, in den Wind -, *to luff round;* in die See -, *to ease a vessel.*

M.

Maat, m., *mate.*
magnetisch, *magnetic.*
magnetische Pole, *magnetic poles;* - Kurs, m., *m. course.*
Magnetnadel, f., *compass needle.*
Mahagoniholz, n., *mahogany.*
mahlen, *to fray, grind, wear out.*
Mahlstrom, m., *whirlpool.*
Maker, m., *maul.*
malen, *to give a coat of paint.*
Malgang, m., *paint strake.*
Mall, f., *mould;* - boden, m.,

m. *loft floor;* - breite, f., *moulding;* - - eines Hinterstevens, *m. of a stern post;* - brett, n., *bevelling board;* - brief, m., *building contract;* - kante, f., *moulding edge.*
mallen, *1. to mould (wood, &c.); 2. to be unsteady (wind).*
Mallung, f., *1. moulding (wood, &c.); 2. unsteadiness (wind).*
Mangachapuy-holz, n., *mangachapuy.*
Mangel haben an, *to be short of.*

m., *topsail sheet bitts*; - segel, n., *t.*; - - fall, m., *t. halliard*; - - reffen, *to reef topsails*; - - schote, f., *topsail sheet*; - stag, n., *topmast stay*; - stenge, f., *t.*; - - bänder, *hoops on the topmast*; - - Eselshaupt, n., *t. cap*; - - hummer, m., *t. hound*; - - pardune, f., *t. backstay*; - - Schloßholz, n., *t. fid*; - - - gat, n., *t. f. hold*; - stengestag, n., *t. stay*; - stengeteil, m., *t. hounding*; - stengewanten, *t. rigging*; - toppenant, f., *topsail lift*; - want, n., *topmast shroud*; - wanten, *topmast rigging*.
Maschine des Dampfankerspills, f., *steam windlass engine*; - mit Balancier in winkelmäßiger Bewegung, *bell crank e.*; - mit einfach. Balancier, *single beam e.*; - - - Kurbel, *one crank e.*; - mit rückwirkender Pleyelstange, *steeple e.*; - mit zwei Kurbeln, *two crank e.*; - - 3 -, *three c. e.*; - - 4 -, *four c. e.*; - - 5 -, *five c. e.*; - mit hohler Kolbenstange, *trunk e.*; - mit oben liegendem Balancier, *overhead beam e.*; - mit rückwirkender Pleyelstange, *return connecting rod e.*; - mit umgekehrten Zylindern, *overhead cylinder e.*; - ohne Expansion, *non expansive e.*; - zum Drehen der Schiffsmaschine, *turning e.*; - zur Erzeugung von künstlichem Zug, *forced draught e.*
Maschinen-arbeit, f., *machine work*; - bau, m., *constrution of machinery*; - - anstalt, f., *engine works*; - - Ingenieur, m., *mechanical engineer*; - Besichtiger, m., *engineer surveyor*; - Besichtigung, f., *engine survey*; - bruch, m., *engines broken down*; - defekt, m., *engines defect*; - depot, n., *engineer's store room*; - formguß, m., *engine*

casting; - fundament, n., *e. sleepers*; - garnitur, f., *e. fittings*; - havarie, f., *engines broken down*; - indikator, m., *engine indicator*; - Ingenieur, m., *engineer*; - Inspektor, m., *superintending e.*; - kammer, f., *engine room*; - kommandos, *engine commands*; - kraft, f., *e. power*; - lager, n., *e. sleepers*; - - winkel, m., *e. seating angle bar*; - lampe, f., *e. room lamp*; - luke, f., *1. e. hatchway*; *2. crank h. (of paddle boat)*; - manöver, *engine movements*; - nietung, f., *e. riveting*; - Oberlicht, n., *engine room skylight*; - - gräting, f., *e. r. s. grating*; - öl, n., *e. oil*; - personal, n., *e. room complement*; - pumpen-Speiseventil, n., *main feed check valve*; - putzbaumwolle, f., *cotton waste*; - raum, m., *engine room*; - - brunnen, m, *e. r. well*; - - flurplatten, *e. r. flooring*; - - geländer, n., *e. guard rail*; - - Journal, n., *engineer's log book*; - - lampe, f., *engine room lamp*; - - leiter, f., *e. r. ladder*; - - Plattform, f., *e. r. platform*; - - Podest, m., *e. r. upper p.*; - - schott, n., *e. r. bulkhead*; - - süll, m., *e. r. coaming*; - - tür, f., *e. r. door*; - - tür-Scharnier, n., *e. r. d. hinge*; - - uhr, f., *e. r. clock*; - ventilator, m., *e. r. ventilator*; - - Werkzeug, n., *e. r. tools*; - regulator, m., *speed governor*; - reparatur, f., *e. repairs*; - schaden, m., *damage to machinery*; - - beim Abbringen eines Schiffes, *d. t. m. in refloating a ship*; - schmiedestück, n., *engine forging*; - schmierer, m., *greaser*; - schmieröl, n., *lubricating oil*; - schlosser, m., *fitter*; - schottwinkel, m., *engine room bulkhead angle*

bar; - tagebuch, n., *engineer's log book*; - teile, f., *engine parts*; - telegraph, m., *e. room telegraph*; - Werkstatt, f., *engine shop*.
Maschinerie, f., *machinery*.
Maschinist, m., *engineer*.
Maschinisten-Assistent, m., *assistant engineer*; - Journal, n., *engineer's log*; - kammer, f., *e. berth*; - maat, m., *assistant engineer*; - messe, f., *engineer's mess room*; - patent, n., *e. certificate*; - stand, m., *lower platform*.
Maß-güter, *measure goods*; - stab, m., *scale*.
mäßige Brise, f., *moderate breeze*; - Wind, m., *m. wind*.
massiver Kiel, m., *solid keel*; - Lukendeckel, m., *s. hatch*.
Mast, m., *mast*; - aus einem Stück, *single tree m.*; - backe, f., *m. cheek*; - balken, m., *m. beam*; - - winkel, m., *m. b. angle bar*; - band, n., *m. hoop*; - bauer, m., *m. maker*; - baumstütze, f., *m. prop for careening*; - bock, m., *tabernacle*; - bügel, m., *m. hoop*; - ducht, f., *main thwart*; - Eselshaupt, n., *mast cap*; - fisch, m., *or - fischung, f., m. partner*; - fischungskalben, m., *m. p. chock*; - fischungsplatte, f., *m. p. plate*; - Fußzapfen, m., *m. heel tenon*; - gabel, f., *lumber iron*; - gien, n., *main purchase*; - gillung, f., *mast gore*; - hafen, m., *m. pond*; - hausung, f., *m. housing*; - holz, n., *hand mast piece*; - hummer, m., *mast hound*; - kante, *fore leech*; - - saum, m., *mast tabling*; - keile, f., *m. wedges*; - klampe, f., *m. cleat*; - knecht, m., *topsail sheet bitt;* - koker, m., *mast trunk*; - korb, m., *crow's nest*; - kragen, m., *mast coat*; - kran, m., *masting sheers*; - liek, n., *fore leech rope*; - loch, n., *mast hole*;

- - in der Segelducht, *half moon in the mast thwart*; - reifen, m., *mast hoop*; - schlinge, f., *or - schlüssel, m., mast carling*; - spur, f., *m. step*; - stumpf, m., *stump of a m.*; - stütze, f., *1. outrigger*; *2. mast prop (for careening)*; - takelhanger, m., *m. head pendant*; - takelläufer, m., *m. tackle fall*; - teil, m., *m. hounding*; - top, m., *m. head*; - - deckel, m., *m. cover*; - - winkel, m., *m. h. angle*; - - zapfen, m., *m. h. tenon*; vor dem -, *before the m.*; - zapfen, m., *m. tenon*.
Masten- *see* Mast.
Mastix, m., *mastic*.
Materialstärke, f., *scantling*.
Matrose, m., *sailor*.
Matrosen-gepäck, n., *kit*; - jacke, f., *pea jacket*; - kiste, f., *sailor's chest*; - makler, m., *crimp*; - presser, m., *pressman*; - quartierschiff, n., *receiving ship*; - sack, m., *sailor's bag*; - schneider, m., *slop maker*; - suppe, f., *skilligolee*; - tanzlokal, n., *stepping ken*.
Matte, f., *mat*.
Mauerwerk der Feuerbüchse, n., *brickwork of furnace*.
Maulbeerbaumholz, n., *mulberry wood*.
Maulstich, m., *midshipman's hitch*.
Maus, eine - aufsetzen, *to raise a mouse*.
mausen, *to mouse*.
Mausing or Mausung, f., *mousing*.
Maximaldruck, m., *maximum pressure*.
mechanische Kraft or Leistung, f., *mechanical power*.
Medizinkiste, f., *medicine chest*.
Meer, n., *sea*; - busen, m., *gulf*; - enge, f., *straits*; - wasser, n., *sea water*; - - Destillierapparat, m., *fresh water condenser*.

Meeres-arm, m., *inlet*; - boden, m., *bottom of the sea*; - horizont, m., *sea line*; - oberfläche, f., *surface of the sea*; - spiegel, m., *level of the sea*; - strömung, f., *sea current*; - tiefe, f., *depth of the s.*; - ufer, n., *s. shore*.

Mehl-bank or - koje, f., *flour binn*; - tonne, f., *f. barrel*.

mehrfache Expansion, f., *multiple expansion*; - - maschine, f., *m. e. engine*.

mehrscheibiger Block, m., *block with several sheaves*.

Meißel, m., *chisel*.

Meisterschafts-rennen, n., *race championship*; - rudern, n., *rowing c.*

melden, *to report*; sich - bei, *to r. oneself to.*

Meldung, f., *report*.

Mennige. f., *red lead*; - kittdichtung, f., *r. l. joint*.

Meridian, m., *meridian*; - distanz, t., *meridional distance*; - kreis, m., *meridian circle*; - teil, m., *meridional part*; - zeichen, n., *meridian mark*.

Merlspieker, m., *ketch barge*.

Meß-brief, m., *certificate of tonnage*; - instrument, n., *gauge*; - stab, m., *metestick*.

Messe, f., *mess room (see also Messen-).*

messen, *to gauge*.

Messen-geschirr, n., *mess trap*; - - kasten, m., *m. chest*; - kappe, f., *messroom companion*; - oberlicht, n., *m. skylight*; - - gräting, f., *m. s. grating*; - ofen, m., *m. stove*; - Schornstein, m., *m. funnel*; - tür, f., *m. door*; - - Scharnier, n., *m. d. hinge*; - ventilator, m., *m. ventilator*.

Messing, n., *brass*; - band, n., *brass hoop*; - draht, m., *b. wire*; - rohr, n., *b. tube*; - platte, f., *sheet of b.*

metacentrische Höhe, f., *metacentric height*.

Metacentrum, n., *metacentre*.

Metall, n., *metal*; - befestigung, f., *m. fastening*; - beschlag, m., *m. sheathing*; - bolzen, m., *m. bolt*; - büchse, f., *brass bush*; - dichtung, f., *metallic joint*; - draht, m., *metallic wire*; - - gaze und Mennigkittdichtung, f., *gauze wire and red lead joint*; - garnitur, f., *metal lining*; - haut, f., *m. sheathing*; - - anlegen, *to lay on a m. sheathing*; neue - - anlegen, *remetalling*; - Liderung, f., *metallic packing*; - Packung, f., *m. p.*; - platte, f., *sheet of metal*; - ring, m., *brass ferrule*; - rohr, n., *brass tube*; - verbolzung, f., *metal fastening*.

metallene Scheibe, f., *metal sheave*.

meteorologische Beobachtungen, *meteorological observations*.

Meuterei, f., *mutiny*.

Meuterer, m., *mutineer*.

meutern, *mutinying*.

mieten, *to hire*.

Mieter, m., *freighter*.

mildes Klima, n., *mild climate*; - Wetter, n., *m. weather*.

Minimaldruck, m., *minimum pressure*.

Minium, n., *red lead*.

Mirage, f., *looming*.

Mire, f., *cairn*.

Miß-gissung, f., *error of the dead reckoning*; - weisender Gesamtkurs, m., *compass course*; - weisender Kurs, m., *magnetic course*; - weisung, f., *variation*; östliche - -, *east v.*; westliche - -, *west v.*; - - beobachtung, f., *sight for v.*

Mist, m., *mist*.

mistig, *misty*.

mit Backbordhalsen, *on the port tack*; - Beschlag belegen, *to embargo*; - Dampf fahren, *to steam*; - der Feile ebnen, *to skim up*; - der

Stoßmaschine gemachtes Nietenloch, *punched rivet hole*; - einander verbundene Aufbauten, *combined deck erections*; nicht - - - -, *disconnected d. e.*; - eins, *amain*; - Elektrizität getrieben, *driven by electricity*; - fahrer or - fahrender Dampfer, m., *companying steamer*; - gehen, *dragging (an anchor)*; - Gewalt niederholen, *to ride down*; - Hülfe von Schleppern, *with the assistance of tugs*; - knapper Not entkommen, *to have a narrow escape*; - Kraft hieven, *to heave astrain*; - Metall beschlagen, *metalling*; - neuen Kesseln versehen, *re-boilering*; - - Maschinen -, *to be re-engined*; - reeder, m., *part owner*; - Röhren versehen, *tubing*; - Sandstein scheuern, *to holystone*; - schleppen, *dragging*; - segeln, *to sail on the same tack*; - segler, m., *consort*; - starkem Segeldruck beim Winde segeln, *to stretch*; - Steuerbordhalsen, *on the starboard tack*; - Übersetzung wirkende Maschine, *geared engine*; - Weißmetall ausfüllen, *to line with white metal.*

Mittags-besteck, n., *day's work*; - höhe, f., *meridian altitude.*

Mitte des Fahrwassers, *mid channel.*

Mittel, n., *means*; - band, n., *belly band*; - bändsel, n., *quarter seizing*; - Bauchgording, f., *middle bunt line*; - beting, f., *centre bitt*; - - Wellenlager, n., *c. b. bearing*; - Bilgesaugventil, n., *c. bilge suction valve.*

Mittelbram-Bauchgording, f., *middle topgallant bunt line*; - brasse, f., *m. t. brace*; - Drehreep, n., *m. t. tye*; - fall, m., *m. topgallant halliard*;

- geitau, n., *m. t. clew line*; - Längssahling, f., *m. topmast trestle trees*; - Nockgording, f., *m. topgallant leech line*; - pardune, f., *m. t. backstay*; - pferd, n., *m. t. foot rope*; - püttings, *m. t. futtocks*; - - wanten, *m. t. futtock shrouds*; - rahe, f., *m. t. yard*; - sahling, f., *m. topmast cross trees*; - schote, f., *m. topgallant sheet*; - segel, n., *m. topgallant sail*; - stag, n., *m. t. stay*; - - segel, n., *m. t. staysail*; - - - hals, m., *m. t. s. tack*; - - - leiter, f., *m. t. s. stay*; - - - Niederholer, m., *m. t. staysail downhaul*; - - - schote, f., *m. t. s. sheet*; - stenge, f., *m. t. mast*; - - Eselshaupt, n., *m. t. cap*; - - pardune, f., *m. t. backstay*; - - stag, n., *m. t. stay*; - - wanten, *m. t. rigging*; - toppenant, f., *m. t. lift*; - wanten, *m. t. rigging.*

Mittelbrasse, f., *middle brace*; - schenkel, m., *m. b. pendant.*

Mittelbreite Rechnung, f., *middle latitude sailing*; - Segeln, n., *tangent sailing.*

Mittelbulin, f., *middle bowline.*

Mitteldeck, n., *middle deck*; - balkenwinkel, m., *m. d. beam angle bar*; - luke, f., *m. d. hatchway*; - - süll, m., *m. d. h. coaming.*

Mitteldruck, m., *medium pressure*; - Absperrventil, n., *intermediate pressure stop valve*; - - gestänge, n., *i. p. s. v. gear*; - Anlaßventil, n., *i. p. starting v.*; - Exzenter, n., *i. p. eccenter*; - - bolzen, m., *i. p. e. bolt*; - - bügel, m., *i. p. e. strap*; - - bügel-Paßstück, n., *i. p. e. s. liner*; - - Lagerschalen, *i. p. e. brasses*; - - scheibe, f., *i. p. e. sheave*; - - stange, f., *i. p. e. rod*; - - vorrichtung, f., *i. p. e. gear*; - Geradführung, f., *i. p. guide*; - gestänge or - getriebe, n., *i. p. gear*; - Gleitbahn, f., or - Gleitschuh, m., *i. p. guide*; - kessel, m., *i. p. boiler*; - kolben, m., *i. p. piston*; - - Führungsstange, f., *i. p. p. guide rod*; - - Kurbelwange, f., *i. p. p. crank web*; - - Liderungsring or - - ring, m., *i. p. p. packing ring*; - - stange, f., *i. pressure piston rod*; - - - Kreuzkopf, m., *i. p. p. r. crosshead*; - - - - führung or gleitplatte, f., *i. p. p. r. c. guide*; - - - - Lagerschalen, *i. p. p. r. c. brasses*; - Kolbenstange-Stopfbüchse, f., *i. p. p. r. stuffing box*; - Kreuzkopflagerbolzen, m., *i. pressure crosshead bolt*; - Kreuzkopflagerschalendeckel, m., *i. p. connecting rod top end keep*; - Kurbelbacke, f., *i. p. crank web*; - Kurbelwelle, f., *i. p. c. shaft*; - - lager, n., *i. p. c. s. bearing*; - - - bolzen, m., *i. p. c. s. b. bolt*; - - - deckel, m., *i. p. c. s. bearing keep*; - - - - bolzen, m., *i. p. c. s. b. k. bolt*; - Kurbelwellenlagerschalen, *i. p. c. s. bearing brasses*; - - Paßstück, n., *i. p. c. s. brasses liner*; - Kurbelwellen-Lagerzapfen, m., *i. p. c. s. journal*; - Kurbelzapfen, m., *i. p. crank pin*; - Kurbelzapfenlagerbolzen, m., *i. p. c. p. bolt*; - Kurbelzapfenlagerschalen, *i. p. c. p. brasses*; - - deckel, m., *i. p. connecting rod bottom end keep*; - Leitung, f., *i. p. guide*; - Maschine, f., *i. p. engine*; - Pleyelstange, f., *i. p. connecting rod*; - - bolzen, m., *i. p. c. r. bolt*; - - fuß-Paßstück, n., *i. p. c. r. bottom end liner*; - Receiverrohr, n., *i. p. receiver pipe*; - schieber, m., *i. p. slide valve*; - - Abbalancierungskolben, m., *i. p. valve balance piston*; - - kasten, m., *i. p. v. casing*; - - - deckel, m., *i. p. v. c.

door; - - - Sicherheitsventilbelastung, f., *i. p. v. c. escape valve load*; - Schieberstange, f., *i. p. valve rod*; - - führung, f., *i. p. v. spindle guide*; - - Stopfbüchse, f., *i. p. v. rod stuffing box*; - - - deckel, m., *i. p. v. r. s. b. gland*; - Stopfbüchse, f., *i. p. s. b.*; - turbine, f., *i. p. turbine*; - - Maschine, f., *i. p. t. engine*; - Zylinder, m, *i. p. cylinder*; - - Austrittskanal, m., *i. p. c. exhaust port*; - - büchse, f., *i. p. c. liner*; - - deckel, m., *i. p. c. cover*; - - deckelbolzen, m., *i. p. c. c. bolt*; - - Drainagehahn, m., *i. p. cylinder drain cock*; - - einsatz, m., *i. p. cylinder liner*; - - Entwässerungsrohr, n., *i. p. c. drain pipe*; - - Kolbenstangen - Stopfbüchsendeckel, m., *i. p. piston rod stuffing box gland*; - - mantel, m., *i. p. c. jacket*; - - Sicherheitsventil, n., *i. p. c. escape valve*; - - - belastung, f., *i. p. c. e. v. load*; - - - feder, f., *i. p. c. e. v. spring*; - - - spindel, f., *i. p. c. e. v. spindle*; - Zylinder-Stopfbüchsendeckel, m., *i. p. c. stuffing box gland*.
Mittel-geie, f., *belly guy*; - - tau, n., *middle clew garnet*; - hals, m., *m. tack*; - hangertakel, n., *m. mast tackle*; - Heckspant, n., *horn timber*; - Kastenkielschwein, n., *middle line box keelson*; - Kielplatte, f., *m. l. centre through plate keel and keelson*; - Kielschwein, n., *m. l. keelson*; - - winkel, m., *m. l. k. angle bar*; - klüver, m., *m. jib*; - - fall, m., *m. j. halliard*; - Längsschott, n, *m. line bulkhead*; - liek, n., *m. rope (of an awning)*; - linie, f., *m. line*.
Mittelmars, m., *middle top*; - Bauchgording, f., *m. top-*

sail *bunt line*; - brasse, f.,
m. t. *brace*; - - schenkel,
m., *m. t. b. pendant*: - Drehreep, n., *m. t. tye*; - fall, m.,
m. topsail halliard; - geitau,
n., *m. t. clew line*; - pardune,
f., *m. topmast backstay*; -
pferd, n., *m. topsail foot
rope*; - püttings, *m. futtocks*:
- - wanten, *m. futtock
shrouds*; - rahe, f., *m. topsail
yard*; - refftalje, f., *m. t.
reef tackle*; - schote, f., *m.
topsail sheet*; - segel, n., *m. t.*;
- - schote, f., *m. t. sheet*; -
stag, n., *m. topmast stay*; -
stenge, f., *m. t.*; - - Eselshaupt, n., *m. t. cap*; - toppenant, f., *m. t. lift*; - want,
n., *m. t. shroud*; - wanten,
m. t. rigging.

Mittelmast, m., *middle mast*;
- Dwarssahling, f., *m. m.
cross trees*; - Eselshaupt, n.,
m. m. cap; - keile, *m. m.
wedges*; - Längssahling, f.,
m. m. trestle trees.

Mittelmeerkarte, f., *chart of
the Mediterranean.*

Mittelmittelstagsegel, n.,
middle middle staysail; -
fall, m., *m. m. s. halliard*;
- hals, m., *m. m. s. tack*; -
Niederholer, m., *m. m. s.
downhaul*; - schote, f., *m.
m. s. sheet.*

Mittel-naht, f., *monk seam*; -
Nockgording, f., *middle
leech line.*

Mitteloberbram-brasse, f.,
*upper middle topgallant
brace*; - pferd, n., *u. m. t.
foot rope*; - rahe, f., *u. m.
t. yard*; - segel, n., *u. m. t.
sail.*

Mittelobermars-brasse, f., *upper middle topsail brace*;
- - schenkel, m., *u. m. t. b.
pendant*; - pferd, n., *u. m. t.
foot rope*; - rahe, f., *u. m. t.
yard*; - segel, n., *u. m. t.*

Mittelpferd, n., *middle yard
foot rope.*

Mittelplatte, f., *centre plate*;
- kiel, m., *plate keel*; - -
schwein, n., *middle line
centre through plate keelson*:
- - - winkel, m., *vertical
centre plate keelson angle
bar*; - kiel und Kielschwein,
*middle line centre through
plate keel and keelson.*

Mittel-plattform, f., *middle
platform*; - punkt, m., *centre*;
vom - - abweichend, *centrifugal*; - - der Drehung, *centre
of giration*; - - der Wirkung,
c. *of action*: - rahe, f., *middle
yard*; - - Toppenautstalje,
f., *m. lift purchase*; - Refftalje, f., *m. reef tackle*; -
Roststabträger or - Rostträ-
ger, m., *centre bearer of
fire bars.*

Mittelroyal, n., *middle royal*;
- Bauchgording, f., *m. r.
bunt line*; - brasse, f., *m. r.
brace*; - fall, m., *m. r. halliard*;
- geitau, n., *m. r. clew line*;
- Längssahling, f., *m. r.
trestle trees*; - pardune, f.,
m. r. backstay; - pferd, n.,
m. r. foot rope; - rahe, f.,
m. r. yard; - sahling, f., *m.
r. cross trees*; - schote, f.,
m. r. sheet; - stag, n., *m. r.
stay*; - - segel, n., *m. r. s.
sail*; - - - hals, m., *m. r. s. s.
tack*; - - - leiter, f., *m. r. s.
s. stay*; - - - Niederholer,
m., *m. r. staysail downhaul*;
- - - schote, f., *m. r. s. sheet*;
- stenge, f., *m. r. mast*; - -
pardune, f., *m. r. backstay*;
- - stag, n., *m. r. stay*; -
toppenant, f., *m. r. lift.*

Mittelscheisegel, n., *middle
skysail*; - brasse, f., *m. s.
brace*; - fall, m., *m. s. halliard*;
- geitau, n., *m. s. clew line*;
- pardune, f., *m. s. backstay*;
- pferd, n., *m. s. foot rope*;
- rahe, f., *m. s. yard*; -
schote, f., *m. s. sheet*; - stag,
n., *m. skysail stay*; - stenge,
f., *m. skysail mast*; - - pardune, f., *m. s. backstay*; - -

stag, n., *m. s. stay*; - top-penant, f., *m. skysail lift.*

Mittel-schiff, n., *square body*; - schote, f., *middle sheet*; - schwert, n., *centre board*; - segel, n., *middle sail*; - - schote, f., *m. sheet*; - seiten-takel, n., *m. pendant tackle*; - spant, n., *midship frame.*

Mittelstag, n., *middle stay*; - segel, n., *m. staysail*; - - fall, m., *m. s. halliard*; - - hals, m., *m. s. tack*; - - leiter, f., *m. s. stay*; - - Nieder-holer, m., *m. staysail down-haul*; - - schote, f., *m. s. sheet*; - - - schenkel, m., *m. s. s. pendant.*

Mittelstenge, f., *middle top-mast*; - pardune, f., *m. t. backstay*; - stag, n., *m. t. stay*; - -segel, n., *m. t. stay-sail*; - - - fall, m., *m. t. s. halliard*; - - - hals, m., *m. t. s. tack*; - - - leiter, f., *m. t. s. stay*; - - - Niederholer, m., *m. t. staysail downhaul*; - - - schote, f., *m. t. s. sheet*; - want, n., *m. t. shroud*; - wanten, m., *t. rigging.*

mittelster Gilge, m., or mit-telste Heckstütze, f., *middle timber.*

Mittelstück des Spills, n., *main piece of the windlass.*

Mittel-toppenant, f., *middle lift*; - - talje, f., *m. l. pur-chase*; - träger, m., *1. centre girder (of double bottom)*; *2. c. bitt (of windlass)*; - - platte, f., *c. girder plate*; - - winkel, m., *c. g. angle bar.*

Mittelunterbram-brasse, f., *lower middle topgallant brace*; - pferd, n., *l. m. t. foot rope*; - rahe, f., *l. m. t. yard*; - segel, n., *l. m. t. sail.*

Mitteluntermars-brasse, f., *lower middle topsail brace*; - - schenkel, m., *l. m. t. b. pendant*; - pferd, n., *l. m. t. foot rope*; - rahe, f., *l. m. t. yard*; - segel, n., *l. m. t.*

Mittel-wache, f., *middle watch* (12—4 a. m.); - want, n., *m. shroud*; - wanten, *m. rigg-ing*; - Zwischendeck, n., *middle tween decks.*

mitten im Fahrwasser, *mid channel.*

Mitternachts-sonne, f., *mid-night sun*; - weite, f., *northern amplitude.*

Mittlandsee, f., *Mediterranean.*

mittlere Heckbalken, m., *middle transom*; - Heck-stütze, f., *m. timber*; - Tief-gang, m., *mean draught*; - Zeit, f., *m. time.*

mittschiffs, *midships*; - balken, m., *midship beam*; - Boden-wrangen, *flats*; - das Ruder! *midships the helm!* od. *helm a-midship!* - hoher Tank, m., *midship deep tank*; - Katsporen, *breadth riders*; - linie, f., *central line*; - sente, f., *square ribbon*; - spant, n., *midship frame*; - spanten, *square body frames*; - stütze, f., *middle line pillar.*

Modell, n., *model*; - tiefe, f., *moulded depth.*

Moderator, m., *regulator.*

Moderbank, f., *mud bank.*

Moderprahmboot, n., *mud boat.*

mojes Wetter, n., *fine weather.*

Moker, m., *iron maul.*

Molaveholz, n., *molave wood.*

Mole, f., or Molo, m., *break-water.*

Molekulargewicht, n., *mole-cular weight.*

Molenfeuer, n., *pierhead light.*

Moment, m., *momentum.*

Monats-charter, m., *monthly charter*; - geld, n., *m. wages*; - weise befrachten, *to charter by the month.*

Mond-aufgang, m., *moon rise*; - distanz, f., *lunar distance*; - finsternis, f., *l. eclipse*; - gucker, m., *moon sail*; - - brasse, f., *m. s. brace*; - - schote, f., *m. s. sheet*; - helle

Nacht, f., *moonlight night;*
- hof, m., *lunar halo;* - reiter,
m., *moon raker;* - ring, m.,
lunar corona; - segel, n., *moon
sail;* - tafeln, *lunar tables.*
Monkeyreling, f,, *monkey rail;*
- stütze, f., *topgallant bulwark stanchion.*
Monsun, m., *monsoon;* -
drift, f., m. *drift;* - wechsel,
m., *change of m.*
Monteur, m., *fitter.*
montieren, *to erect.*
Montierungswerkstätten, f..
erecting shop.
Mooringsketten, *chain moorings.*
Morsomsche Vermessungs-
methode, f., *new measurement.*
Morastbank, f., *mud bank.*
Morgen-amplitude, f., *eastern
amplitude;* - grauen, n.,
dawn; - schuß, m., *morning
gun;* - wache, f., *morning
watch* (4—8 a. m.); - weite,
f., *eastern amplitude.*
Morraholz, n., *morra wood.*
Mörser zum Abfeuern von
Raketen mit Rettungsleinen,
m., *life mortar.*
Morungsaulholz, n., *morung
saul wood.*
Motor. m., *motor.*
Mouillage, m., *anchorage.*
Mucke, f., *mug.*

Mudbauk, f., *mud bank.*
Mudderprahm, m., *mud lighter.*
muddern, *to make foul water.*
Muffenkupplung, f., *box
coupling.*
Mugge, f., *mug.*
Mühle, f., *reel.*
Mündung, f., *1. estuary (of
river);* 2. *orifice (of pipe).*
Mundstück, n., *nozzle.*
muren, *to moor.*
Muschel, f., *mushroom;* - grund,
m., *shelly ground;* - schieber,
m., *treble ported slide valve;*
- ventil, n., *retaining valve;*
- ventilator, m., *mushroom
ventilator.*
Mußkeule, f., *commander.*
mustern, *to ship.*
Musterrolle, f., *articles.*
Musterungsamt, n., *shipping
office.*
Mutter, f., *1. nut;* 2. - des
Stevenrohrs, *stern tube nut;*
- bohrer, m., *screw tap;* -
bolzen, m., *nut bolt;* - fräsmaschine, f., *n. shaping
machine;* - gewinde, n.,
female thread; das - - schneiden, *to tap;* - schlüssel, m.,
nut wrench; - schraube, f.,
screw nut.
Muttern und Unterlagsschei-
ben der Kesselanker, *boiler
stay nuts and washers.*

N.

Nabe, f., *boss;* - eines Schaufelrades, *centre piece of a
paddle wheel.*
Nachenfähre, f., *sculler boat.*
Nacherklärung, f., *additional
declaration.*
nachgeben, *1. to give to (the
wind);* 2. *to ease (the helm);*
3. *to give out (machinery).*
nachlassen, *1. yielding (a
rope);* 2. *abating (wind).*

Nachmittagswache, f., *after-
noon watch* (12—4 p. m.).
nachschlagen, die Nähte -,
to overhaul the seams.
nachstecken, *to pay out.*
Nacht-arbeit, f., *night work;*
- dienst, m., *n. service;* -
glas, n., *night glass;* - haus,
n., *binnacle;* - - lampe, f.,
b. lamp; - - Überzug, m.,
b. cover; - - Untersatz, m.,

b. stand; - klarschiff, *night quarters*; - marke, f., *n. mark*; - schicht, f., *n. work*; - signal, n., *n. signal*; - teleskop. n., *n. glass*; - wache, f., *n. watch* (8—12 p. m.); - wimpel, m., *n. pennant.*

Nachverklarung, f., *to extend protest* oder *extension of p.*

Nackenschlag, m., *blackwall hitch.*

Nadel, f., *needle*; die - schwankt hin und her, *the n. yaws.*

Nagel, m., *nail; -* bank, f., *1. pin rail*; *2. fife r. (round masts or pumps)*; - bohrer, m., *gimblet*; - gat, n., *pin hole*; - keil, m., *treenail wedge*; - kopf, m., *pin's head.*

Näh-beutel, m., *ditty bag*; - nadel, f., *seaming needle.*

nahe bei, *close to.*

nähern, sich dem Lande -, *to near the land.*

Naht, f., *seam*; eine - dicht machen, *to close a s.*; - haken, m., *rave hook*; - kante, f., *bevelled edge of a plank*; - loses Rohr, n., *seamless tube (of boiler)*; - streifen, m., *landing edge*; die - - lockerten sich, *the landing edges of the plates started.*

Nähte untersuchen, *to examine the seams*; - zum Dichten öffnen, *to ream.*

Nähungen des Ankertaues, *breaking stoppers.*

Namenbrett, n., *name board.*

Narraholz, n., *narra wood.*

Nase, f., *fillet (of crank shaft).*

nasse Dampf, m., *wet steam*; - Dock, n., *w. dock*; - Proviant, m., *w. provisions*; - Wetter, n., *w. weather.*

National-flagge, f., *colours*; - wimpel, m., *national pennant.*

Naturereignisse, *acts of God.*

natürlicher Hafen, m., *natural harbour.*

Nautik, f., *nautical science.*

nautische Ausdrücke, *nautical terms*; - Beisitzer, m., *n. assessor*; - Buchhandlung, f., *n. stationery*; - Instrumente, *n. instruments*; - Jahrbuch, n., or - Kalender, m., *n. almanac*; - Sachverständige, m., *n. surveyor*; - Tag, m., *n. day*; - Zeit, f., *n. time.*

Navigation, f., *navigation*; - Instrument, n., *n. instrument*; - Offizier, m., *navigator*; - schule, f., *navigation school*; - zimmer, n., *chart room.*

Navigator, m., *navigator.*

navigieren, *to navigate.*

Nebel, m., *fog*; - alarmsignal, n., f. *alarm*; - bank, f., f. *bank*; - glocke, f., f. *bell*; - horn, n., f. *horn*; - land, n., *Cape-fly-away*; - schicht, f., *fog bank*; - schwaden, m., f. *showers*; - signal, n., f. *signal*; - - horn, n., f. *horn.*

nebelig, *foggy.*

Neben-kielgang, m., *outer garboard strake*; - Regenbogen, m., *weather head*; - speisehahn, m., *supplementary feed cock*; - Wassergang, m., *inner waterway.*

Neer f., or - strom, m., *eddy water.*

negativer Slip, m., *negative slip.*

Neigung, f., *rake (of a mast)*; - winkel, m., *angle of inclination.*

Nennwert, m., *nominal value.*

Netto-Fracht, f., *net freight*; - Gewicht, n., *n. weight*; - Raumgehalt or - Tonnengehalt, m., *n. tonnage.*

Netz über einem Wasserbehälter, n., *quilting*; - um einen Mars, *top netting.*

Netz-fischerei, f., *net fishery*; - werk, n., *netting.*

neu bemasten, *to remast*; - verbolzen, *to rebolt*; - vernageln, *to re-treenail.*

neutrale Flagge, f., *neutral flag*; - Schiff, n., *n. bottom.*

Nichtleiter, m., *non-conductor.*

Niederbucht der Hölzer, f., *the round down of the timbers*; - des Decks, *the fall of the deck*; - eines Deckbalkens, *the round down of a beam.*
Niederdruck, m., *low pressure*; - Absperrventil, n., *l. p. stop valve*; - - gestänge, n., *l. p. s. v. gear*; - Anlaßventil, n., *l. p. starting valve*; - dampf, m., *l. p. steam*; - Excenter, n., *l. p. eccenter*; - - bolzen, m., *l. p. e. bolt*; - - bügel, m., *l. p. e. strap*; - - bügel-Paß-stück, n., *l. p. e. s. liner*; - - Lagerschalen, *l. p. e. brasses*; - - scheibe, f., *l. p. e. sheave*; - - stange, f., *l. p. e. rod*; - - vorrichtung, f., *l. p. e. gear*; - Geradführung, f., *l. p. guide*; - gestänge or - getriebe, n., *l. p. gear*; - Gleitbahn, f., *or - Gleitschuh*, m., *l. p. guide shoe*; - kessel, m., *l. p. boiler.*
Niederdruckkolben, m., *low pressure piston*; - Führungs-stange, f., *l. p. p. guide rod*; - Kurbelwange, f., *l. p. p. crank web*; - Liderungsring or - Ring, m., *l. p. p. packing ring*; - stange, f., *l. pressure piston rod*; - - Kreuzkopf, m., *l. p. p. r. crosshead*; - - - führung or - - - Gleitplatte, f., *l. p. p. r. c. guide*; - - - lagerschalen, *l. p. p. r. c. brasses*; - stange-Stopf-büchse, f., *l. p. p. r. stuffing box*; - - - deckel, m., *l. p. p. r. s. b. gland.*
Niederdruck-Kreuzkopflager-bolzen, m., *low pressure crosshead bolt*; - Kreuzkopf-lagerschalendeckel, m., *l. p. connecting rod top end keep*; - Kurbelbacke, f., *l. p. crank web.*
Niederdruckkurbelwelle, f., *low pressure crank shaft*; - lager, n., *l. p. c. s. bearing*; - - bolzen, m., *l. p. c. s. b. bolt*; - - deckel, m., *l. p. c.*

s. bearing keep; - - bolzen, m., *l. p. c. s. b. k. bolt*; - - schalen, *l. p. c. s. bearing brasses*; - - - Paßstück, n., *l. p. c. s. brasses liner*; - Lagerzapfen, m., *l. p. c. s. journal.*
Niederdruckkurbelzapfen, m., *low pressure crank pin*; - lager, n., *l. p. c. p. bearing*; - - bolzen, m., *l. p. c. p. bolt*; - - schalen, *l. p. c. p. brasses*; - - - deckel, m., *l. p. connecting rod bottom end keep.*
Niederdruck-Leitung, f., *low pressure guide*; - Maschine, f., *l. p. engine*; - Pleyel-stange, f., *l. p. connecting rod*; - - bolzen, m., *l. p. c. r. bolt*; - fuß-Paßstück, n., *l. p. c. r. bottom end liner*; - Receiverrohr, n., *l. p. receiver pipe.*
Niederdruckschieber, m., *low pressure slide valve*; - Ab-balancierungskolben, m., *l. p. valve balance piston*; - kasten, m., *l. p. v. casing*; - - deckel, m., *l. p. v. c. door*; - - Sicherheitsventil-belastung, f., *l. p. v. c. escape valve load*; - stange, f., *l. p. valve rod*; - - führung, f., *l. p. v. spindle guide*; - - Stopfbüchse, f., *l. p. valve rod stuffing box*; - - - deckel, m., *l. p. v. r. s. b. gland.*
Niederdruck-Stopfbüchse, f., *low pressure stuffing box*; - turbine, f., *l. p. turbine*; - - maschine, f., *l. p. t. engine.*
Niederdruckzylinder, m., *low pressure cylinder*; - Austrittskanal, m., *l. p. c. exhaust port*; - büchse, f., *l. p. c. liner*; - deckel, m., *l. p. c. cover*; - - bolzen, m., *l. p. c. c. bolt*; - Drainage-hahn, m., *l. p. cylinder drain cock*; - einsatz, m., *l. p. c. liner*; - Entwässerungs-rohr, n., *l. p. c. drain pipe*; - Kolbenstange, f., *l. p. c.*

piston rod; - - Stopfbüchsendeckel, m., *l. p. c. p. r. stuffing box gland*; - Mantel, m.,
l. p. c. jacket; - Sicherheitsventil, n., *l. p. c. escape valve*;
- - belastung, f., *l. p. c. e. v.
load*; - - feder, f., *l. p. c. e.
v. spring*; - - spindel, f., *l.
p. c. e. v. spindle*; - Stopfbüchsendeckel, m., *l. p. c.
stuffing box gland.*

Niedergang, m., *1. down
stroke (of piston); 2. companion way (to cabins); 3.
ladder (to fire room).*

Niedergangskappe, f., *companion.*

nieder-geknickt, *settled down
(mast)*; - gleiten, *to slip
down*; - hieven, *to heave
down*; - holen, *to haul
down*; - holer, m., *downhaul*;
- - block, m., *d. block*; - -
des Fliegers, *middle staysail d.*; - - des großen Klüvers, *outer jib d.*; - lassen,
to lower; - lotsen, *to pilot
down*; - schlag, m., *1. saline
deposit; 2. sediment (of
boiler)*; - setzen, *to set
down*; - wuchten, *to swig off.*

niedrig getakelt, *low rigged*;
- Wasser, n., *l. water*; - -
linie, f., *l. w. mark*; - -stands-
zeichen, n., *l. w. m.*

niedrige Breiten, *low latitudes*;
- küste, f., *l. shore*; - Zwischendeck, n., *l. between
decks.*

niedriger, nicht -, *nothing off!*

niet- und nagelfest, *clinched
and riveted.*

Niet-blech, n., *river plate*; -
durchmesser, m., *diameter
of rivet*; - eisen, n., *riveting
punch*; - hammer, m., *r.
hammer*; - kloben, m., *screw
stock*; - kopfmacher, m., *rivet
stamp*; - loch, n., *r. hole*; -
maschine, f., *riveting machine*; - presse, f., *r. m.*; -
punze, f., *r. punch*; - reihe,
f., *row of rivets*; - setzer,

m., *rivet stamp*; - stahl, m.,
r. steel; - stempel, m., *r.
stamp.*

Niete, f., *rivet.*

nieten, *to rivet*; - abstand, m.,
spacing of rivets; - loch, n.,
rivet hole; - - mit der Stoßmaschine gemacht, *punched
r. h.*; - reihe, f., *row of
rivets*; - schaft, m., *rivet
shank*; - stahl, m., *r. steel.*

Nieter, m., *riveter.*

Nietung, f., *riveting.*

Nippel, m., *nipple.*

Nipp-flut or - gezeit, f., *neap
tide*; - tide, f., *dead neap*;
- zeit, f., *n. tide.*

Nische, f., *recess*; - des Hülfskessels, *donkey boiler r.*

Nitzel, m., *knittle.*

Nock, f., *yard arm*; - an -,
y. a. and y. a.; - band, n.,
y. a. hoop; - bändsel or -
bindsel, n., *earing*; - - um
die Rahe nehmen, *to pass
an e.*; - gording, f., *leech
line*; - - block, m., *l. l. block*;
- horn, n., *earing*; - - kausche, f., *e. thimble*; - jolle,
f., *yard arm whip*; - klampe,
f., *y. a. cleat*; - lägel, m.,
earing cringle; - lappen der
Gaffelsegel, *peak piece*; -
ohr, n., *earing*; - - lägel, m.,
e. cringle; - - mutt, m., *e. c.*;
- pferd, n., *Flemish horse*;
- takel, n., *yard tackle*; - -
hanger, m., *y. arm pendant*;
- - schenkel, m., *y. tackle
pendant*; - zeising, m., *y. arm
gasket.*

Nominalkraft, f., *nominal
power.*

nominelle Pferdestärke, f.,
nominal horse power.

Nord gewinnen, *to gain northing.*

Norder, m., *norther oder heavy
gale from the north*, - breite,
f., *northern latitude*; - sonne, f., *midnight sun.*

nordisch, *northern.*

nördliche Abweichung, f.,

northing; - Breite, f., *latitude north*; - Halbkugel, f., *northern hemisphere*; - Polarkreis, m., *arctic circle.*
Nordlicht, n., *polar light.*
Nordost-Monsun, m., *north east monsoon*; - Passat, m., *n. e. trades*; - - drift. m., *n. e. t. drift*; - wind, m., *n. e. wind.*
N. O. zu O., *N. E. by E.*
Nordostering, m., *easterly variation.*
Nordpol-Expedition, f., *north pole expedition*; - fahrt, f., *n. p. trip.*
Nord-seekarte, f., *north sea chart*; - stern, m., *polar star*; - westering, m., *westerly variation*; - west-Monsun, m., *north west monsoon*; - west-Wind, m., *n. w. wind*; - wind, m., *n. wind.*
Normal-barometer, n., *standard barometer*; - druck, m., *normal pressure*; - geschwindigkeit, f., *proper speed*; - gewicht, n., *standard weight*; - kompaß, m., *s. compass*; - Manometer, n., *s. pressure gauge.*
Normale, die - auf der Flursente, *floor sweep*; - Druck, m., *normal thrust.*
Normann, m., *norman.*
notarieller Verkaufs-Kontrakt, m., *certificate of sale.*
Not, f., *distress*; - flagge, f., *flag of d.*; - floß, n., *temporary raft*; - gording, f., *spilling line*; - hafen, m., *port of distress*; - injektion, f., *bilge injection*; - - hahn, m.,

jet injection cock; - - ventil, n., *j. i. valve*; - kante, f., *bevelling edge*; - ketten, *auxiliary chains*; - lampen, *danger lamps*; - leidende Seeleute, *distressed seamen*; - mast, m., *jury mast*; - reparatur, f., *temporary repairs*; - ruder, n., *jury rudder*; - schraube, f., *j. propeller*; - schuß, m., *shot of distress*; - signal, n., *signal of d.*; - stenge, f., *jury topmast*; - stek or - stich, m., *harness hitch*; - takelage, f., *jury rigging*; - talje, f., *relieving tackle*; - wanttau, n., *swifter.*
Null-punkt, m., *freezing point*; - spant, n., *midship frame.*
Nüstergat, n., *limber hole.*
Nuß, f., *boss*; - baumholz, n., *walnut*; - des Ruderstevens, *boss of stern post*; - des Schraubenstevens, *b. of propeller p.*; - platte, f., *b. plate*; - schale, f., *cockle shell.*
Nut, f., *groove, rabbet*; - eisen or - hobeleisen, n., *plough bit*; - maschine, f., *grooving machine*; - stoßmaschine, f., *key groove m.*
nuten, *to groove.*
nutz-bare Hitze, f., *available heat*; - effekt, m., *useful effect*; - kraft, f., *actual power*; - last, f., *travelling load*; - leistung, f., *useful effect*; - lose Leistung, f., *lost e.*
nützlicher Effekt, m., *useful effect.*
Nutzungswert, m., *efficiency.*

O.

Obacht, f., *superintendence.*
oben, *aloft*; - bindsel, n., *upper seizing*; von - bis unten mit Segeln bedeckt,

low and aloft; - geladen, *stowed at the top*; - hütte, f., *top gallant poop*; - in der Takelage, *aloft*; - liegender Zylinder, m., *inverted cylinder*; - platte, f., *face plate*; - schwerer als unten, *top weight*; - werk, n., *upper work*.

Ober-Auflanger, m., *top timber*; - Beplankung, f., *topside planking*; - block, m., *jack block*; - bordwände, *topside planking*.

Oberbram-brasse, f., *upper topgallant brace*; - pardune, f., *royal backstay*; - rahe, f., *r. yard*; - segel, n., *r.*; - stenge, f., *r. mast*.

Oberbram *see also* Royal.

Oberdeck, n., *upper deck*; - balken, m., *u. d. beam*; - - Hängeknie, n., *u. d. b. hanging knee*; - - Längsschiene, f., or - - Lukenstringer, m., *u. d. b. tie plate*; - - stringer, m., *u. d. b. stringer*; - - - platte, f., *u. d. b. s. plate*; - balkenwinkel, m., *u. d. b. angle bar*; - Balkweger, m., *u. d. b. shelf*; - band, n., *u. d. hook*; - befestigung, f., *u. d. fastening*; - Beplankung, f., *u. d. planking*; - Beplattung, f., *u. d. plating*; - bolzen, m., *u. d. bolt*; - luke, f., *u. d. hatchway*; - - deckel, m., *u. d. hatch*; - - stringer, m., *u. d. beam tie plate*; - - süll, m., *u. d. hatchway coaming*; - Mastkeile, *u. d. mast wedges*; - Schergang, m., *u. d. sheerstrake*; - stringer, m., *u. d. stringer*; - - platte, f., *u. d. s. plate*; - - winkel, m., *u. d. s. angle bar*; - stütze, f., *u. d. stanchion*; - Unterbalkweger, m., *u. d. beam clamp*; - Wassergang, m., *u. d. waterway*.

obere Bordwände, *topside planking*; - Gallionsleiste or - Gallionsreling, f., *berthing rail*; - Gut, n., *upper rigging*; - Lagerschale, f., *top brass*; - Marstallblock, m., *fly block*; - Plattengänge,

topside plating; - Seite, f., *upper side*; - Seitenteile, *topsides*; - stehende Gut, n., *upper rigging*; - Wegerung, f., *ceiling of the tween decks*.

Ober-ende einer Bodenwrange, n., *floor heads*; - fläche, f., *surface*; - - Kondensation, f., *s. condensation*; - - - Maschine, f., *s. condensing engine*; - Flächen Kondensator or Kondenser, m., *s. condenser*; - flächenströmung entgegen, *underset*; - halb, *above*; - hals eines Schraatsegels, m., *nock of a fore and aft sail*; - heckbalken, m., *counter transom*; - heizraum, m., *fidley*; - holz, n., *top timber*; - hütte, f., *topgallant poop*; - kante der Bodenwrangen und des Todholzes, f., *cutting down line*; - kante eines Balkens, f., *top of a beam*; - kiel, m., *upper keel*; - - schwein, n., *rider keelson*; - kreuz-Bramstenge, f., *mizen royal mast*; - länderkahn, m., *up-river barge*; - leesegel, n., *topmast studding sail*; - - Außenschote, f., *t. s. s. tack*; - - Binnenschote, f., *t. s. s. sheet*; - - fall, m., *t. studding sail halliard*; - - hals, m., *t. s. s. tack*; - - Niederholer, m., *t. s. s. downhaul*; - - rahe, f., *t. s. s. yard*; - - schote, f., *t. s. s. sheet*; - - spiere, f., *t. studding sail boom*; - leik, n., *head leech*; - licht, m., *skylight*; - - bezug, m., *s. cover*; - - der Back, *forecastle s.*; - - der Messe, *mess room s.*; - - des Mannschaftsraums, *crew space s.*; - - gräting, f., *skylight grating*; - - süll, m., *s. coaming*; - lotse, m., *head pilot*; - marsbrasse, f., *upper topsail brace*; - marsrahe, f., *u. t. yard*; - marssegel, n., *u. t.*; - rahen, *u. yards*; -

raum, m., u. *hold*; - Rüste, f., u. *channel*; - Schanzkleid, n., *topgallant bulwark*; - Beplankung, f., *t. b. planking*; - - Reling, f., *monkey rail*; - Schergang, m., *upper sheerstrake*; - segel, n., u. *sails*; - Seitengang, m., *topside strake*; - steuermann, m., *master*; - strom, m., or - strömung, f., *surface current*; - toppsegel, n., *upper topsail*; - - brasse, f., *u. t. brace*; - - rahe, f., *u. t. yard*; - ventil, n., *top valve*; - werk, n., *upper works*; - Zahlmeister, m., *shore purser*; - zolldirektion, f., *commissioners of customs*; - Zwischendeck, n., *upper tween decks.*

obere Seite, f., *upper side.*

oberste Balkwäger, m., *deck shelf*; - Gallionsknie, f., *gammon knee*; - Lage, f., *top tier*; - Plattengang, m., *paint streak.*

Observation, f., *observation*; - Journal, n., *journal of observations.*

observierte Breite, f., *latitude by observation*; - Länge, f., *longitude by o.*

Ocean, m., *ocean.*

Ochsenauge, n., *bull's eye.*

Octant, m., *octant.*

öffnen, 1. *to open (cylinder, pumps, hatches)*; 2. *to open out (engines).*

Oeffnung, f., *aperture.*

Oehr, n., *eyelet hole.*

Oel, n., *oil*; - baumholz, n., *olive wood*; - behälter, m., *oil tank*; - büchse, f., *o. box*; - dicht, *o. tight*; - fänger, m., *save-all*; - farbe, f., *oil paint*; - hahn, m., *o. cock*; - kanne, f., *o. can*; - loch, n., *o. hole*; - maß, n., *o. measure*; - nute, f., *o. groove.*

Oelpumpe, f., *oil pump*; - Absperrventil, n., *o. p. stop*

valve; - Anlaßventil, n., *o. p. starting valve*; - Ausgußventil, n., *o. p. discharge v.*; - Dampfabführungsrohr, n., *o. p. exhaust pump*; - Dampfzuführungsrohr or Dampfzuleitungsrohr, n., *o. p. steam pipe*; - Druckraum, m., *o. p. delivery space*; - Druckventil, n., *o. p. d. valve*; - - sitz, m., *o. p. d. v. seat*; - Excenter, n., *o. p. eccentric*; - - bolzen, m., *o. p. e. bolt*; - - bügel, m., *o. p. e. strap*; - - - Paßstück, n., *o. p. e. s. liner*; - Excenterlagerschalen, *o. p. e. brasses*; - Excenterscheibe, f., *o. p. e. sheave*; - Excenterstange, f., *o. p. e. rod*; - Fußventil, n., *o. p. foot valve*; - Kolben, m., *o. p. piston*; - Kolbenstange, f., *o. p. p. rod*; - - Kreuzkopf, m., *o. p. p. r. crosshead*; - - Stopfbüchse, f., *o. p. r. stuffing box*; - - - deckel, m., *o. p. p. r. s. b. gland*; - Kolbenventil, n., *o. pump bucket valve*; - - sitz, m., *o. p. b. v. seat*; - Kreuzkopflagerbolzen, m., *o. p. crosshead bolt*; - Kreuzkopflagerschalen, *o. p. c. brasses*; - - deckel, m., *o. p. connecting rod top end keep*; - Kurbelwelle, f., *o. p. crank shaft*; - - lager, n., *o. p. c. s. bearing*; - - - bolzen, m., *o. p. c. s. b. bolt*; - - - deckel, m., *o. p. c. s. bearing keep*; - - - - bolzen, m., *o. p. c. s. b. k. bolt*; - Kurbelwellenlagerschalen, *o. p. c. s. brasses*; - - deckel, m., *o. p. c. s. bearing keep*; - - Paßstück, n., *o. p. c. s. brasses liner*; - Kurbelzapfenlagerbolzen, m., *o. p. c. s. pin bolt*; - Kurbelzapfenlagerschalen, *o. p. c. s. p. brasses*; - - deckel, m., *o. p. connecting rod bottom end keep*; - Pleyelstange, f., *o. p. connecting rod*; - - bolzen, m., *o. p. c. r. bolt*; - - fuß-Paßstück, n., *o. p. c. r. bottom end liner;* - Saugeraum, m., *o. p. suction space*; - Saugerohr, n., *o. p. s. pipe*; - Saugeventil, n., *o. p. s. valve*; - - sitz, m., *o. p. s. v. seat*; - Schieber, m., *o. p. slide valve*; - - kasten, m., *o. p. s. v. casing*; - - - deckel, m., *o. p. v. c. door*; - Schieberstange, f., *o. p. v. rod*; - - Stopfbüchse, f., *o. p. v. r. stuffing box*; - - - deckel, m., *o. p. v. r. s. b. gland*; - ventil, n., *o. p. valve*; - - sitz, m., *o. p. v. seat*; - Zylinder, m., *o. p. cylinder*; - - deckel, m., *o. p. c. cover*; - - - bolzen, m., *o. p. c. c. bolt*; - Zylinder-Entwässerungsrohr, n., *o. p. cylinder drain pipe.*

Oel-rohr, n., *oil pipe*; - sack, m., *o. bag*; - sammler, m., *o. receiver*; - sieb, m., *o. sieve*; - spritze, f., *syringe for lubricating*; - tank, m., *oil tank*; - trichter, m., *o. funnel*; - tropfschale, f., *drip pan*; - verbrauch, m., *consumption of oil*; - zeug, n., *o. skin.*

ölen, *to lubricate.*

Oes-faß, n., *scoop*; - gat, n., *well hole.*

östliche Länge, f., *east longitude.*

Ofen, m., *stove.*

offen, eine Marke von einer anderen - bekommen, *to open a bearing*; wir bekamen die Feuer von Dover -, *we opened the lights of D.*; eine Einsegelung - bekommen, *to open the entrance of a port.*

offene Brücke, f., *open bridge house*; - Fahrzeug, n., *undecked vessel*; - Manometer, n., *open manometer*; - Musterrolle, f., *running agreement*; - Naht, f., *open seam*; - Polize, f., *o. policy*; - Reede, f.,

o. road; - See, f., *the main*; - Wasser, n., *open water*; - Wegerung, f., *cargo battens.*

offizielles Journal, n., *official log book.*

Offiziers-kammer, f., *officer's berth*; - Messe, f., *o. mess room.*

Ohr-bummeln, *dead men*; - holz, n., *knight head*; - spant, n., *foremost frame.*

Oktant, m., *octant.*

optische Telegraph, m., *semaphore.*

Order für-, *for orders*; - hafen, m., *port for o.*

Ordnung, f., in -, *in gear*; nicht in -, *out of gear*; alles in bester -, *all a-taunto*; in - bringen, *to regulate.*

Oregon - Fichtenholz, n., *Oregon pine wood.*

Orkan, m., *hurricane*; - artig, *of h. force*; vom - schwer mitgenommen, *to be h. swept.*

Orlopdeck, n., *orlop deck*; - balken, m., *o. d. beam*; - - Längsschiene, f., or - - Lukenstringer, m., *o. d. b. tie plate*; - - stringer, m., *o. d. b. stringer*; - - - platte, f., *o. d. b. s. plate*; - Balkenwinkel, m., *o. d. b. angle bar*; - Längsschiene, f., *o. d. beam tie plate*; - luke, f., *o. d. hatchway*; - - deckel, m., *o. d. hatch*; - - stringer, m., *o. d. beam tie plate*; - - süll, m., *o. d. hatchway coaming*; - Mastkeile, *o. d. mast wedges*; - stringer, m., *o. d. stringer*; - - platte, f., *o. d. s. plate*; - - winkel, m., *o. d. s. angle bar*; - stütze, f., *o. d. pillar.*

Orlopstringer, m., *orlop stringer.*

Ort und Stelle, f., *on the spot.*

orthodromischer Kurs, m., *orthodromic course.*

örtliche Ablenkung, f., *local attraction.*

Orts-bestimmung, f., *finding*

the ship's place; - meridian, m., meridian of a place.

oscillierende Hebel, m., rocking lever; - Maschine, f., oscillating engine; - Welle, f., rocking shaft; - Zylinder, m., oscillating cylinder.

Ost-indienfahrer, m., East India Trader; - seefahrt, f., Baltic trade; - seekarte, f., Baltic chart; - wind, m., east wind.

östliche Mißweisung, f., easterly variation.

P.

paajen, to tar.
Paal, m., pole; - stek, m., bow-
Paard, n., horse. [line knot.
Paarhölzer, couples.
Packeis, n., pack ice.
packen, to pack.
Packhaus, n., warehouse; - aufseher, m., w. man.
Packung, f., packing; - bolzen, m., p. bolt; - messer, n., p. knife; - ring des Schiebers, m., slide valve p. ring; - stock, m., p. stick; - zieher, m., p. drawer.
Paddel, m., paddle.
paddeln, to paddle.
Paketboot, n., steam packet.
Palinurus, m., palinurus.
Pall, n., pawl; - beting, f., p. bitt; - hieven, to heave p.; - kasten, m., p. box: - klampen, p. cleats; - kranz, m., p. rack; - pfosten, m., p. bitt; - - des Schlittens, p. of the cradle; - ring, m., p. rim; - setzen, to p.; - stütze, f., p. bitt; - winden, to p. the capstan.
Palle, f., pawl.
Pallen, pawls; die - niederlassen, to lower the p.
Pampero, m., pampero.
Pannier, n., the banner.
panting, panting.
Pantry, f., pantry; - tür, f., p. door; - - Scharnier, n., p. d. hinge.
Panzer, m., armour; - bolzen, m., a. bolt; - platte, f., a. plate; - träger, m., a. shelf.

Papagei-mast, m., jigger mast: - stock, m., iron horse of the head.
Papennaht, f., monk seam.
Pappedichtung, f., mill board joint.
Paraffin, n., paraffin.
Parallel-bewegung, f., parallel motion; - führung, f., guides; - gestängen-Glieder, parallel motion links; - stange, f., p. bar.
Parallelogramm, n., parallel motion; - welle, f., p. m. shaft; - - lager, n., p. m. s. bearing.
Pard, n., foot rope.
Pardenhanger, m., stirrup.
Pardune, f., backstay.
Parlamentär-flagge, f., flag of truce; - schiff, n., cartel ship.
Part eines Reffzeisings, m., leg of a reef point.
Parten, 1. parts (of a tackle); 2. outer turns (of a seizing).
Partie, f., parcel.
Paß aufs Ruder! Mind the helm! auf seinen - geladen sein, to be in her sailing trim.
Passage arbeiten, f., to work a passage; - billet, n., passenger ticket; - geld, n., passage money; - luke, f., booby hatch; - preise, passenger rates.
Passagier, m., passenger; - aufzug, m., p. lift; - dampfer,

m., *p. steamer*; - gesetz, n., *p. act*; - Installationen, *p. accommodations*: - kammer, f., *p. room*; - makler, m., *p. broker*; - schiff, n., *p. vessel*.

Passat, m., *trades*; - drift, f., *trade drift*; - wind, m., *t. wind*.

passen, *to fit*; passende Hitze, f., *available heat*.

passieren, *to pass*; die Linie -, *to cross the line*; in Lee -, *to pass to leeward*; Steuerbord bei S. -, *to p. starboard to s.*; vor dem Bug -, *to cross the bow*.

Passierzettel, m., *transire*.

Paßstück, n., *liner*.

Patent, n., *certificate*; - anker, m., *patent anchor*; - für große Fahrt, *certificate of competency for distant trade*; - Jackstag, n., *patent jackstay (of a gaff)*; - liderung, f., *p. packing*; - Log, n., *p. log*; - lotse, m., *branch pilot*; - Marssegel, n., *patent topsail*; - Schäkel, m., *p. shackle*; - scheibe, f., *multiplying sheave*; - spill, n., *patent windlass*; - Steuergerät, n., *p. steering gear*; - stopper, m., *chain cable controller*; - - hebel, m., *lever of the chain cable compressor*; - Toppsegel, n., *patent topsail*.

Pavillon, m., *casing*; - des Maschinenraums, *engine c.*

Pech, n., *pitch*; - faß, n., *p. barrel*; - grapen, m., *p. pot*; - kelle, f., or - löffel, m., *pitch ladle*; - Quast, m., *p. mop*; - tannenholz, n., *pitch pine*; - topf, m., *pitch pot*; - werg, n., *pitch tow*.

Peerd, n., *foot rope*.

Pegel, m., *water mark post*.

Peil-baake, f., *bearing beacon*; - kompaß, m., *b. compass*; - rohr, n., *sounding pipe*; - - deckel, m., *s. p. cover*; - stange, f., *s. rod*; - stock,

m., *1. s. r. (for tanks or wells)*; *2. s. stick (for shallow water)*; *3. gauge rod (for pumps*.

peilen, *1. to sound (pumps, tanks, wells)*; *2. to take a bearing (by compass)*; das Land -, *to set the land*; die Sonne -, *to observe the sun's amplitude*.

peilt, Dover - N. O., *Dover bears N. E.*

Peilung. f., *bearing*; eine - auf die Karte übertragen, *to lay down a bearing on the chart*; In welcher - liegt der Hafen? *How does the harbour bear?* eine - nehmen, *to take a bearing*; wahre -, *true bearings*.

Peilungslinie, f., *line of bearing*.

peitschender Regen, m., *driving rain*.

Penter *see* Davits.

pentern, *to fish*.

periodische Besichtigung, f., *periodical survey*: - Winde, *anniversary winds*.

perkussive Kraft, f., *percussive force*.

Perpendikularspant, n., *square frame*.

Persennig, f., *tarpaulin*; - leisten, *battens of the t.*; - nagel, m., *scupper nail*; - spieker, m., *tarpaulin nail*.

Perturleine or Perturlien, f., *cat head stopper*.

Petroleum, n., *petroleum*; - dicht, *oil tight*; - transportschiff, n., *oil carrying vessel*; - werft, f., *petroleum wharf*.

Petschen, *sweeps*.

Pfahl. m., *bollard*; - ausheber, m., *pile withdrawer*; - gruppe, f., *dolphins*; - kompaß, m., *pole compass*; - mast, m., *p. mast*; - ramme. f., *pile driver*; - stich, m., *bowline hitch*.

Pfand, n., *mortgage*; - brief, m., *certificate of m.*; - recht, n., *lien*; - schuldner, m., *mortgager.*

Pfanne, f., *1. pan (for cooking)*; *2. saucer (of capstan)*; offene -, *socket.*

Pfannen, *bearing brasses (of engines)*; - deckel, m., *gland (of a plumber block).*

Pfeife, f., *whistle.*

Pfeifensignal, n., *whistle signal.*

Pferde, *foot ropes*; - kraft, f., *horse power*; - leine, f., *heavy warp*; - stall, m., *horse box*; - stärke, f., *h. power.*

Pfiff, m., *blast (on the steam whistle).*

Pflicht, *cuddy (of a barge)*; - anker, m., *sheet anchor.*

Pforte, f., *port*; - deckel, m., *p. lid*; - - gehänge, n., *p. l. hinge*; - drempel, m., *p. sill*; - gehänge, n., *p. flap hinges*; - hanger, m., *p. pendant*; - hebel, m., *p. bar*; - klappe, f., *p. flap*; - öffnungen, *p. holes*; - rahmen, m., *p. frame*: - ring, m., *p. shackle*; - talje, f., *p. tackle*; - tau, n., *p. rope.*

Pfort-laken, n., *kersey*; - luke, f., *eye of a ship*; - segel, n., *port sail*; - talje, f., *p. tackle.*

Pfriem, m., *bodkin.*

Pfropfen, m., *plug*; - loch, n., *p. hole.*

Piassavabesen, m., *coir broom.*

Pick-hammer, m., *scaling hammer*; - werkzeug, n., *s. tools.*

Piedestal, n., *pedestal.*

Piejacke, f., *pea jacket.*

Piek, f., *peak (of gaff and ship)*; - balkenstringer, m., *panting beam stringer*; - balkenwinkel, m., *panting beam angle bar*; - band, n., *hook of the run*; - deck, n., *panting deck*; - - balkenstringer, m., *p. d. beam stringer*; - - - platte, f., *p. d. b. s. plate*; - deckstringer, m., *p. d. stringer*; - - platte,

f., *p. d. s. plate*; - - winkel, m., *p. d. s. angle bar*; - fall, m., *peak halliard*; - - ständer, m., *p. pendant*; - hölzer, *crotches*; schräges - knie, n., *snake piece*; - lappen, m., *peak piece (of gaff sail)*; - legel, m., *peak cringle*; - leine, f., *peak line*; - Niederholer, m., *p. downhaul*; - ohr, n., *p. of a gaff sail*; - pforte, f., *raft port*; - schott, n., *peak bulkhead*; - - winkel, m., *p. b. angle bar*; - spant, n., *p. frame*; - stock, m., *rising floor timber*; - stringer, m., *panting stringer*; - stück, n., *cant floor*; - stücke, *deep floor*; - tank, m., *peak tank*; - tau, n., *topping lift*; - Versteifungsbalken, m., *panting beam.*

Pilz-anker, m., *mushroom anchor*; - förmiges Ventil, n., *m. valve.*

Pinasse, f., *pinnace.*

Pink or Pinke, f., *pink ship.*

Pinkompaß, m., *traverse board.*

Pinkschiff, n., *pink ship.*

Pinne, f., *1. tiller (of rudder)*; *2. spindle (of capstan)*; *3. pin (of shackle bolt)*; *4. centre pin (of compass)*; *5. pin (of block).*

Pinnkompaß, m., *traverse board.*

Piraterie, f., *piracy.*

Piroge, f., *pirogue.*

Pitting, f., *pitting.*

Plan, m., *plan (of ship)*: - karte, f., *plane chart*; - scheibe, f., *face plate (of a lathe)*; - schiffahrt, f., or - segeln, n., *plane sailing*; - zeichnung, f., *plan drawing.*

Planiglob, m., *globular chart.*

Planken gaapen, *planks starting*; - schicht, f., *layer of planking*; - schraube, f., *planking screw*; - stoß, m., *butt of a plank.*

plastisches Metall, n., *plastic metal.*

Platanenholz, n., *plane tree wood.*

Plate, f., *sand.*

Platt-bindsel, n., *rounding seizing;* - bindselung, f., *flat s.;* - form, f., *platform;* - - Gräting, f., *p. grating;* - fuß, m., *dog watch* (6—8 *p. m.*); - gat, n.. *square stern;* - hoofd, n., or - Kopf, m., *scupper nail;* - köpfige Niete, f., *flush head rivet;* - scheibe, f., *flat scarf;* - werfen, *to feather (an oar);*

Platte, f., *plate;* - für den Schäkel der Bugsprietzurring, *gammon plate;* - Naht, f., *flat seam.*

Platten eines gerundeten Schergangs, *rounded gunwale plating;* - eisen, n., *plate iron;* - gang, m., *strake;* - kiel, m., *plate keel;* - panzerung, f., *p. armour;* - spant, n., *web frame;* - - winkel, m., *w. f. angle bar;* - stahl, m., *plate steel;* - stoß, m., *butt of a plate;* - stringer, m., *plate stringer;* - zunge, f., *tongue of a plate.*

plattes Heck, n., *square stern.*

Platting, f., *plaited rope* or *sennit;* gewöhnliche -, *common s.;* - auge, n., *sennit eye;* - leine, f., *common s.*

platzen, *to burst;* bis zum - anstrengen, *to strain to bursting point.*

Pläuel- or Pleuel- or Pleyel-kopflagerbolzen, m., *connecting rod top end bolt;* - - mutter, f.. *c. r. t. e. b. nut;* - stange, f., *c. r.;* - - bolzen, m., *c. r. bolt;* - - - mutter, f., *c. r. b. nut;* - stangenfuß, m., *c. r. bottom end;* - - Paß-stück, n., *c. r. b. e. liner;* - stangeugabel, f., *c. r. jaw;* - stangenkeil, m., *c. r. key;* - stangenkopf, m., *c. r. top end;* - stangenkreuz, n., *cross tail;* - stangenlager, u., *connecting rod bearing;* - -

schalen, *c. r. top end brasses;* - stangen-Paßstück, n., *c. r. liner;* - stangenzapfen, m., *c. r. gudgeon.*

Plump, m., *dipper.*

Plunger, m., *plunger;* - pumpe, f., *p. pump.*

pneumatische Transmission, f., *pneumatic transmission;* - Werkzeug, n., *p. tool.*

Pockholz-lager, n., *lignum vitae bearing;* - scheibe, f., *l. v. sheave;* - streifen, m., *l. v. strips.*

Podest, m., *upper platform.*

Pogaier, m., *downhaul.*

Poker, m., *poker.*

Pol, m., *pole.*

Polar-achse, f., *polar axis;* - distanz, f., *p. distance;* - eis, n., *p. ice;* - forschung, f., *p. exploring;* - kreis, m., *p. circle;* - linie, f., *p. line;* - stern, m., *lode star.*

Police, f., *policy.*

Polierhammer, m., *polishing hammer.*

Poller, m., *1. bitts (for belaying); 2. timber head (of top timber); 3. towing post (for t. ropes); 4. mooring pall (on shore).*

Ponton, m.. *pontoon;* - brücke, f., *bridge of boats;* - kran, m., *pontoon crane.*

Poop, f., *identical with* Hütte.

Porteurleine, f., *cat head stopper;* - kette, f., *c. h. s. chain.*

portugiesisches Segel, n., *sliding gunter sail.*

Positions-laternen or P-lichter, *side lights.*

positiver Slip, m., *real slip.*

Post, f., *mail;* - dampfer, m., *m. steamer;* - - Verbindung, f., *m. s. communication;* - dienst, m., *m. service;* - einnehmen, *to pick up the m.;* - flagge, f., *m. flag.*

Posten, m., *rating (on board ship);* - rolle, f., *station bill.*

Pottlot, n., *black lead.*

Prahm, m., *praam*.
praien, *to hail*.
Praktika, f., *pratique*.
Prämie, f., *1. premium (on insurance)*; *2. bounty (on import and export)*.
prangen, *to carry a press of sail*.
preien, *to hail*.
preimen, *to prime*.
Presenning, f., see Persennig.
pressen, *1. to impress (seamen)*; *2. to crowd sails*.
Preß-gang, m., *press gang*; - geld, n., *impress money*; - kohlen, *patent fuel*; - schraube, f., *set screw*.
Preventer, m., *preventer*.
Pricke, f., *perch*.
Pricker, m., *pricker*; - stange, f., *p. bar*.
Priel, m., *creek*.
priemen, *to prime*.
Prise, f., *prize*; als gute - erklären, *to condemn as lawful p.*; - auf hoher See, *maritime p*.
Prisen-geld, n., *prize money*; - gericht, n., *p. court*; - güter, *p. goods*; - prozeß, m., *p. cause*; - reglement, n., *adjudication of prizes*.
Privatwerft, f., *private yard*.
Probe, f., *test*; - druck, m., *t. pressure*; - fahrt, f., *trial trip*; - - geschwindigkeit, f., *trial speed*.
Probenstecher, m., *sampling stick*.
probieren, *to test*.
Probier-glas, n., *essaying glass*; - hahn, m., *gauge cock*; - loch, n., *test hole*; - ventil, n., *t. valve*.
probierte Ankerkette, f., *tested chain cable*.
Profil, n., *scantling*.
Promenadendeck, n., *promenade deck*; - balken, m., *p. d. beam*; - - stringer, m., *p. d. b. stringer*; - - winkel, m., *p. d. b. angle bar*; - geländer, n., *p. d. rails and*

stanchions; - - stangen, *p. d. guard rods*; - - stützen, *p. d. stanchion*; - stringer, m., *p. d. stringer*; - stützen, *p. d. pillars*; - Wassergang, m., *p. d. waterway*.
Propeller, m., *propeller*; - rahmen, m., *p. frame*; - schraube, f., *p.*; - steven, m., *p. post*; - - auge, n., *shaft hole of propeller*; - - niete, f., *p. post rivet*.
Propulsion, f., *propulsion*; - durch Dampf, *steam p.*; - d. Elektrizität, *electric p.*; - mittelst Schaufelräder, *paddle p.*; - m. Schrauben, *screw propulsion*; - m. Turbinen, *turbine p*.
Propulsionskraft, f., *propelling power*.
Protest, m., *protest*.
Proviant, m., *provisions*; - ausgaberaum, m., *p. issue room*; - boot, m., *p. boat*; - kammer, f., *provisions room*; - liste, f., *p. list*; - mangel, m., *short of p.*; - meister, m., *purser*; - - maat, m., *nipcheese*; - Steward, m., *purser's steward*; - raum, m., *store room*; - schiff, n., *store ship*; - vorrat, m., *supply of provisions*.
prüfen, *to test*.
Prüfung, f., *test*; - der Anker, *anchor t.*; - der Ankerketten, *chain cable t.*; - des Doppelbodens, *t. of double bottom*; - durch Anschlagen, *hammer t*.
Prüfungs-kraft or - spannung, f., *proof strain*.
Prügel mit dem Tauende, f., *colting*.
prügeln, *to lick*.
Puddelstahl, m., *puddled steel*.
Puffer, m., *buffer*; - feder, f., *b. spring*.
Puhutukawaholz, n., *puhutukawa wood*.
pull, *to pull*; einen - holen, *to give a jerk*.

pullen, *to pull.*

Pulley, f., *pulley.*

Pulsometer, n., *pulsometer.*

Pultfeuerung, f., *firing with back flame.*

Pulver-flagge, f., *powder flag;* - kammer, f., *p. room.*

Pump- *see* Pumpen.

Pumpe, f., *pump;* die - anschlagen or ansaugen lassen, *to fetch the p.;* - arbeitet schwer, *p. thrashing heavily;* - faßt, *p. is fetched;* - - nicht, *p. does not fetch;* - klaren, *to free the p.;* - lorcht, *the p. blows;* - schlägt lenz, *the p. is dry.*

pumpen, *to pump;* - back, f., *p. cistern;* - bagger, m., *p. dredger.*

Pumpenbalancier, m., *pump lever;* - axe, f., *p. rocking shaft;* - axenlager, n., *p. r. s. bearing;* - axenzapfen, m., *p. centre gudgeon;* - gelenk, n., *p. lever link;* - - deckel, m., *p. l. l. keep;* - Lagerschalen, *p. lever brasses;* - Lagerzapfen, m., *p. l. gudgeon;* - Zapfenlager, n., *p. l. g. bearing;* - - deckel, m., *p. l. g. b. keep;* - - schalen, *p. l. g. brasses.*

Pumpen-bockständer, m., *fulcrum of pumps;* - bohrer, m., *pump bit;* - bolzen, m., *p. bolt;* - brunnen, m., *p. well;* - büchse, f., *p. liner;* - daal, n., *p. dale;* - deckel, m., *p. cover;* - - bolzenmutter, f., *p. c. bolt nut;* - eimer, m., *p. box;* - einsatz, m., *p. chamber liner;* - fischung, f., *p. partner;* - gatt, n., *side hole of a pump;* - gelenk, n., *p. link;* - - lagerschalen, *p. l. brasses;* - gerät, n., *p. gear;* - haken, m., *p. hook;* - hammer, m., *p. hammer;* - hebel, m., 1. *hand lever (of windlass);* 2. *pump lever (of pump);* - hub, m., *p. lift;* - kammer, f., *p. room;* - kappe,

f., *p. hood;* - kasten, m., *p. well;* - kessel, m., *p. kettle;* - kette, f., *p. chain;* - kolben, m., *p. bucket;* - - ring, m., *p. b. ring;* - - stange, f., *p. b. rod;* - korb, m., *p. kettle;* - körper, m., *p. chamber;* - kragen, m., *p. coat;* - Kreuzkopf, m., *p. crosshead;* - - Führungsstange, f., *p. c. guide rod;* - - - träger, m., *p. c. g. r. bracket;* - Kurbellager, n., *p. crank bearing;* - Kurbelwelle, f., *p. shaft;* - leder, n., *p. leather;* - mick, f., *p. cheeks;* - peilstock, m., *p. sounding rod;* - pleyellagerschalen, *p. connecting rod top end brasses;* - pleyelstange, f., *p. c. r.;* - rinne, f., *p. dale;* - rohr, n., *p. pipe;* - schraper, m., *p. scraper;* - schuh, m., *p. suck;* - schwengel, m., *p. handle;* - sonde, f., *p. gauge;* - sood, n., *p. well;* - spiker, m., *p. tack;* - spill, n., *windlass;* - ständer, m., *fulcrum of p.;* - stange, f., *p. rod;* - stiefel, m., *p. body;* - stock, m., *p. staff;* - Stopfbüchse, f., *p. stuffing box;* - deckel, m., *p. s. b. gland;* - stütze, f., *p. cheeks;* - tiegel, m., *p. coat tack;* - ventil, n., *p. valve;* - vorrichtung, f., *p. gear;* - zylinder, m., *p. cylinder.*

Punkt, m., *point;* - ieren, *to dot a line.*

Pünte, f., *the end od. the point (of a sail or rope);* - des Ankers, *the peak od. the bill (of the anchor).*

Pup *identical with* Hütte.

Puppenblock, m., *shoe block.*

purren, die Wache -, *to call the watch to relief.*

Pütting des Parduns, f., *backstay plate.*

Püttingen or Püttings, *futtocks;* - band, n., *spider hoop;* - bolzen, m., *chain* bolt; der untere - -, *preventer c. b.*; - eisen, n., *chain plate*; - halter, m., *preventer plate*; - kette, f., *futtock chain*; - klappe, f., *preventer chain plate*; - -bolzen, m., *preventer bolt*; - ring, m., *futtock rider*; - - kette, f., *neck lace*; - taue, *cat harpings*; - wanten, *futtock shrouds*.

Putz-baumwolle, f., *cotton waste*; - tuch, n., *sponge cloth*.
Pütze, f., *bucket*; - zum Deckwaschen, *wash deck b.*
Pützengestell, n., *bucket rack*.
putzen, 1. *to polish or dress up*; 2. *to scour (metal)*; 3. *to trim (the wick of a lamp)*.
Pyrometer, n., *pyrometer*.

Q.

Quadrant, m., *quadrant*; - bogen, m., *q. arc.*
Quai see Kai.
Quarantäne, f., *quarantine*; - arzt, m., *health officer*; - beamter, m., *quarantine o.*; aus der - entlassen, *to discharge from q.*; - flagge, f., *q. flag*; - hafen, m., *q. harbour*; - station, f., *q. station.*
Quarter-block, m., *quarter block*; - deck, n., *q. deck*; - - reling, f., *q. rail*; - - schott, n., *break bulkhead of raised quarter deck.*
Quartiermeister, m., *quartermaster.*
Quast, m., *brush.*
Quatze, f., *seine fishing boat.*
Quecksilber-Barometer, n., *mercurial barometer*; - Manometer, m., *m. gauge.*
quer, *athwart* od. *transverse.*
Quer ab, *on the beam*; - - an Steuerbord, *on the starboard b.*; - - in das Fahrwasser kommen, *to reach across the channel*; - - nach Lee, *on the lee beam*; - - nach Luvward, *o. t. weather b.*
quer auf or - über or - vor liegen, *to lie across.*
quer vor dem Bug, *athwart hawse.*
Quer-balken, m., *cross bitt*; - baum des Schleppnetzes, m., *trawl beam*; - bram-

salings, *topmast cross trees*; - durchschnitt, m., *cross section*; - feste, f., *breast fast*; - festigkeit, f., *transversal strength*; - halse, f., *cross hawser*; - haupt, n., *crosshead*; - holen, *to bring to the broadside*; - holz, n., *cross beam*; - keil, m., 1. *cross key (of coupling)*; 2. *cotter (of propeller)*; - leine, f., *cross line*; - naht, f., *butt seam*; - sahling, f., *cross trees*; - scherstock, m., *c. coaming*; - - in einer Luke, *thwartship piece in a hatchway.*
querschiffs, *athwartship*; - bunker, m., *cross bunker*; - gestaut, *aburton*; - kohlenbunker, m., *thwartships coal bunker*; - liegendes Stück des Luksülls, *headledge*; - liegende Süllplatte, f., *headledge plate*; - schenkelbreite eines Spants, *moulding of a frame*; - verband, m., *transversal strength.*
Quer-schlagen, n., *falling across*; - schnitt, m., *midship section*; - - des Mittelspants, m., *frame s.*; - schott, n., *transversal bulkhead*; - - des Doppelbodens, *end plate of double bottom*; - - stringer, m., *thwartship bulkhead stringer*; - spant, n.,

transverse frame; - steg des Ruderrahmens, *rudder stay*; - stück, n., *headledge (of a hatchway coaming)*; - verbindung, f., *lateral fastening*; - vor dem Bug, *athwart*

hawse; - wand, f., *partition*; - wind, m., *cross wind*; - winkeleisen, n., *transverse angle iron*.

Quirlanker, m., *grapnel*.

R.

Raa *see* Rah.
Rabatteisen, n., *making iron*.
Rack, n., *parrel (of a yard)*; 2. *bend (of river)*; - band, n., *truss hoop (of yard and mast)*; - kette, f., *t. pendant*; - klampe, f., *parrel cleat*; - klotje, n., *p. truck*; - stropp, m., *truss parrel*; - talje, f., *truss tackle*; - - aufholer, m., *parrel halliard*; - tau, n., *jaw rope*; - tonne, f., *barrel of a parrel*.
Rad, n., *wheel*; - arm, m., *paddle w. arm*; - bezug, m., *w. cover*; - boden, m., *flooring of water wheels*; - dampfer, m., *paddle steamer*; - - maschine, f., *p. wheel engine*; - Frachtdampfer, m., *p. cargo steamer;* - gehäuse, n., *p. box*; - Passagierdampfer, m., *p. passenger steamer*; - Salondampfer, m., *paddle saloon s.*
Radkasten, m., *paddle box*; - anbau, m., *p. b. annex*; - balken, m., *p. beam*; - boot, n., *p. box boat*; - deck, n., *p. deck*; - Galerie, f., *sponson deck*; - kajüte, f., *paddle box cabin*; - knie, n., *joggle of the p. b.;* - strebe or - stütze, f., *p. b. stay*; - träger, m., *p. beam*.
Rad-kranz, m., *wheel rim*; - - des Schaufelrades, *paddle w. r.;* - nabe, f., *boss of a wheel;* - propeller, m., *paddle wheel propeller*; - ring, m., *paddle ring*; - schaufel, f.,

p. wheel float; - schlepper, m., *paddle tug*; - überzug, m., *wheel cover*; - welle, f., *paddle shaft*; - - lager, n., *p. s. bearing;* - zahn, m., *cog of a wheel.*
Räderschneidzeug, n., *teeth cutting machine.*
Radial-Bohrmaschine, f., *radial drilling machine.*
Radius, m., *radius*; - der größten Breite, *lower breadth sweep*; - des Schaufelrades, *paddle wheel radius.*
Rae *see* Rah.
raffinierter Stahl, m., *refined charcoal steel.*
Rah, f., *yard*; - an -, *y. arm and y. arm*; - arm, m., *quarter of a yard*; - band, n., *y. hoop*; - bändsel or - bindsel, n., *rope band*; - stek, m., *roband hitch*; - hanger, m., *jeers*; - jolle, f., *yard rope;* - ketten, *y. chains*; - leik or - liek, n., *head rope*; - nock, f., *yard arm*; - - band, n., *y. a. hoop*; - - klampe, *y. a. cleat*; - segel, n., *square sail*; - stücke, *arm pieces of the yard*; - großes - takel, n., *main jeers*; - takelage, f., *square rig*; - takel-Aufholer, m., *yard tackle tricing line*; - takelblock, m., *jeer block.*
Rahe *see* Rah.
Rahen mit Ketten fangen, *to secure the yards with chains*; - über Kreuz getoppt, *y. apeak*; mit - getakelt, *square*

rigged; - vierkant toppen und brassen, *to square the yards by lifts and braces.*
Rahmenspant, f., *web frame*; - schiff, n., *w. f. ship*; - winkel, m., *w. f. angle bar.*
Rahmwerk, n., *framing*; - des Radgehäuses, *paddle box f.*
Raisonneur, m., *growler.*
raken, *touching.*
Rakete, f., *rocket*; - leine, f., *shot line*; - signal, n., *rocket signal*; - werfen, *to fire a rocket.*
Ramme, f., *pile driver.*
Rampe, f., *ramp.*
ramponieren, *to damage.*
Rand, m., *rim (of wheel and top)*; - dichtung, f., *faucet joint*; - planke, f., *margin plank*; - platte, f., *wing girder plate*; - somholz, n., *fashion timber.*
Rang, m., *rating*; - abzeichen, n., *distinguishing mark.*
rank, *crank.*
Rankenfüßer, *barnacles.*
Rankheit, f., *crankiness.*
Ransomholz or Ransunholz, n., *fashion timber.*
Ranzion, f., *ransom*; - kontrakt, m., *r. bill.*
Rapport, m., *report.*
Raselung, f., *ripple.*
rasieren, *raze.*
rasiertes Schiff, n., *razee.*
Raspel, f., *rasp.*
rasseln, *to jar.*
Ration, f., *allowance*; - faß, n., *harness cask*; - netz, n., *garland.*
Ratschbohrer, m., or Ratsche, f., *ratchet drill.*
Rattenschwanz, m., *round file.*
Raubfahl, m., *bottom pile.*
Rauch, m., *smoke*; - fang, m., *uptake*; - kammer, f., 1. vordere, *smoke box*; 2. hintere, *combustion chamber*; - - Stehbolzen, m., *c. c. stays*; - kammertür, f., or - kastendeckel, m., *smoke box door*; - lose Kohle, f., *smokeless*

coal; - segel, n., *smoke sail*; - verbrenner, m., *s. burner*; - verzehrende Feuerbüchse, f., *s. consuming furnace*; - verzehrer, m., *s. consumer*; - zimmer, n., *smoking room.*
räuchern, *to fumigate.*
Räucherung, f., *fumigation.*
Rauhfrost, m., *silver thaw.*
Raum, m., *1. room*; *2. space (for machinery)*; *3. hold (for cargo)*; *4. large (wind).*
Raumbalken, m., *hold beam*; - Hängeknie, n., *h. b. hanging knee*; - Setzweger, m., *h. b. spirketting*; - stringer, m., *h. b. stringer*; - - platte, f., *h. b. stringer plate*; - - winkel, m., *h. b. s. angle bar*; - Unterbalkweger, m., *h. b. clamp*; - Wassergang, m., *h. b. waterway*; - winkel, m., *h. b. angle bar.*
Raum-balkweger, m., *hold beam shelf*; - deck, n., *lower orlop deck*; - - balken, *l. o. d. beam*; - - stringerwinkel, m., *l. o. d. stringer angle bar*; - gehalt, m., *capacity*; - haken, m., *cargo hook*; - ladung, f., *bottom cargo*; - lampe, f., *c. lamp*; - laufen, *the wind draws aft*; - leiter, f., *hold ladder*; - plattenstringerwinkel, m., *orlop stringer angle bar*; - schots segeln, *to sail with flowing sheets*; - segeln, *to run full*; - stringer, m., *hold stringer*; - - winkel, m., *h. s. angle bar*; - stütze, f., *h. stanchion*; - tiefe, f., *depth of h.*; - tonnen, *tons measurement*; - treppe, f., *hold ladder*; - Unterbalkweger, m., *h. beam clamps*; - ventilator, m., *h. ventilator*; - weger, m., or - wegerung, f., *h. ceiling*; - wind, m., *leading wind.*
Räumahle, f., *rimer.*
räumen or raumen, *to veer aft.*
räumen und schralen, *to veer and haul.*

Räumigkeit, f., *measurement capacity.*
Räumte, f., *sea room.*
Raventuch, n., *ravenduck.*
Rawissen, *clamps.*
Reaktions Dampfer, m., *jet propelled steamer*; - Maschine, f., *j. p. engine.*
Receiver, m., *receiver*; - Manometer, n., *r. gauge*; - rohr, n., *r. pipe.*
recht achteraus, *right astern*; - auf die Nase, *right in one's teeth;* - dwars, *r. abeam*; - hinten aus, *r. astern*; - in den Wind, *r. in the wind's eye*; - machen, *to straighten*; den Vordersteven im Platz - -, *t. s. the stem in its place*; die Spanten - -, *t. s. the frames*; - so! *Steady!* - von vorn, *dead on end*; - voraus, *right ahead*; - weisend, *true course*; - weisender Gesamtkurs, *total t. c.*; die Rahen sind - winkelig gegen die Kielrichtung, *the yards are square by the braces*; - winkeliges Knie, n., *square knee.*
rechter Abstand, m., *true distance*; - Winkel, m., *right angle.*
rechtsdrehende or rechtsgängige Schraube, f., *right handed propeller.*
rechtsgeschlagenes Tau, n., *right handed rope.*
Rechtsruder, n., *to port the helm.*
rechtwinkelig, *rectangular.*
Recken, n., *rack.*
Reck-kraft, f., *tensile strain*; - probe, f., *t. test.*
reclassieren, *to reclass.*
Reclassification, f., *reclassification.*
Redderbrett, n., *well cover.*
reddern, *to trim (sails).*
Ree (i. e. Ruder in Lee)! *Ready about!*
Reede, f., *road*; ein Schiff auf die - legen, *to lay a vessel in the r.*

Reeder, m., *ship owner.*
Reederei, f., *shipping business*: - flagge, f., *burgee*; - Schutzverband, m., *Protection Club of Shipowners*; - verein, m., S. *Association*; - Vertrag, m., *Agreement of Ownership.*
Reef, n., *reef.*
Reefe, Reefe! *On deck to reef!*
reefen, *to reef.*
Reeling see Reling.
Reep, n., *rope*; - schläger, m., *r. maker*; - - arbeit, f., *r. m. work*; - schlägerei, f., *ropery.*
Rees, n., or Reester, n., *lace*; ein R. auf die Naht setzen, *to prick the seams.*
Reff, n., *reef*: - aufholer, m., *r. burton*; - band, n., *r. band*; - bändsel, n., *r. points*; - bindsel, n., *r. earing*; - gat, n., *eyelet hole*; - hanger, m., *reef pendant*; - - klampe, f., *r. p. cleat*; - klampe, f., *reefing cleat*; - knebelsteert, m., *r. becket*; - knoten, m., *reef knot*; - knüttel, m., *r. points*; - legel, m., *r. cringle*; - leine, f., *r. line*; - - an der Achterkant der Segel, *slab r. l.*; - seisings, *r. points*; - stich, m., *square knot*; - talje, f., *reef tackle*; - - block, m., *r. t. block*; - - lappen, m., *r. t. patch*; - - legel, m., *r. t. cringle*; - zeising, m., *r. point*; - zeisinge in ein Segel nähen, *to point a sail*; - zeisingsknebel, m., *reef becket toggle.*
Reffe losmachen, *to let out the reefs.*
reffen, *to reef.*
Regatta, f., *race*; - verein, m., *yacht club.*
Regeling see Reling.
Regelkompaß, m., *standard compass.*
regelmäßig fahren, *to ply.*
regelmäßige Fahrer, m., *regular trader*; - Linie, f., *r. line.*
Regen, m., *rain*; - bö, f., *r. squall*; - bog en, m., *r. bow*; - böig, *showery*; - messer, m.,

ombrometer; - schauer, m., *rain shower*; - wolke, f., *r. cloud*; - zeit, f., *rainy season*.
Regierungs-dampfer, m., *government steamer*; - schlepper, m., *g. tug*.
Region, f., *region*; - der Windstillen, *r. of calms*.
Register, n., *damper (machinery)*; - buch, n., *register book*; - Tonnage, f., *r. tonnage*; - vorrichtung, f., *damper gear*; - Zertifikat, n., *certificate of registry*.
Registriermanometer, n., *steam pressure register*.
Reglement für Dreideckschiffe, *three-deck rule*.
regnerisch, *showery*.
Regulator, m., *governor*; - feder, f., *g. spring*; - kugeln, *g. balls*; - stange, f., *g. rod*; - steuerung, f., *g. valve gear*.
regulierbar, *adjustable*.
regulieren, *to adjust*.
Regulier-hebel, m., *standard lever*; - rad, n., *regulating wheel*; - schraube, f., *r. screw*; - ventil, n., *r. valve*.
regulierte Expansion, f., *governor cut off*.
Regulierung der Dampfverteilung, f., *regulating of the steam distribution*.
Rehling *see* Reling.
Reib-ahle, f., *rimer*; - holz, n., 1. *wooden fender*; 2. *rubbing strake*.
Reibung, f., *friction*; - fläche, f., *wearing surface*; - widerstand, m., *frictional resistance*.
Reichs-flagge, f., *national pennant*; - kommissar, m., *Imperial Commissioner*; - postdampfer, m., *Royal Mail Steamer*.
Reif, m., *hoar frost*.
Reifen, m., *hoop*.
Reihe, f., *tier*.
Reihleine, f., 1. *lacing (of a sail)*; 2. *lask (of a bonnet)*.
Rein-eisen, n., *refined iron*.

reine Gesundheitspaß, m., *clean bill of health*; - Grund, m., *c. bottom*; - Konossement, n., *c. bill of lading*; - Küste, f., *c. coast*; - Luft, f., *pure air*.
reinigen, 1. *to clean (boiler and engines)*; 2. *to sponge (with steel brush and sponge)*.
Reinigungs-kette, f., *limber chain*; - öffnung, f., *mud hole*; - ventil, n., *blow through valve*.
Reise, reise! *(a call) Rise, rise!*
Reise, f., *voyage, passage, trip*; lange -, *long passage*; schnelle -, *quick p.*
Reise-begebenheiten, *occurrences during the voyage*; - kosten, *travelling expenses*; - paß, m., *passport*; - unkosten, *travelling expenses*.
Reiß ihn aus! *heave and a-weigh!*
Reißbogen, m., *curve templet*.
reiten, *riding*; schwer vor Anker -, *to ride hard*; zwischen Wind und Strom -, *t. r. between wind and tide*.
Reitknie des Hinterstevens, n., *sternson*; - - des Vorderstevens, *stemson*.
reklassifizieren, *to reclassify*.
Reklassifikation, f., *reclassification*.
Reling, f., *rail, main rail*; - an der Kuhl, *waist rail*; - der Back, *forecastle r.*; - der Brücke, *bridge r.*; - des erhöhten Quarterdecks, *raised quarter deck r.*; - des Finknetzes, *topgallant rail*; - des Gallions, *head r.*; - der Hütte, *poop r.*; - des Schanzkleides, *roughtree r.*; - um einen Mars, *top rail*.
Relings-brett, n., *quarter rail (of q. deck)*; - stütze, f., *bulwark stanchion*; - winkel, m., *b. angle bar*.
Remen, m., *oar*.
Renn-boot, n., *race boat*; - jacht, f., *r. yacht*.

Renommierschiff, n., *crack vessel.*

Reparatur, f., *repairs;* - am Schiffsrumpf, *r. to the hull;* große -, *heavy r.;* vollständige -, *permanent r.;* vorläufige -, *temporary r.*

Reparatur-Dock, n., *repairing dock;* - fonds, m., *r. fund;* - kosten, *cost of repairs;* - Werkstatt, f., *repairing shop.*

reparieren, *to repair.*

Repsöl, n., *colza oil.*

Reserve-anker, m., *spare anchor;* - bunker, m., *s. bunker;* - gerde, f., *preventer vang;* - gut, n., *spare stores;* - Kohlenbunker, m., *s. coal bunker;* - mast, m., *s. mast;* - rahe, f., *s. yard;* - ruder, n., *s. rudder;* - schäkel, m., *s. shackle;* - schraube, f., *s. propeller;* - schwimmfähigkeit, f., *reserve buoyancy;* - segel, *spare sails;* - spiere, f., *s. spar;* - talje, f., *relieving tackle;* - tau, n., *spare rope;* - teile, *s. gear;* - Versicherungsfonds, m., *reserve insurance fund.*

Respekttage, *days of grace.*

Resultante, f., *resultant.*

Retarder, m., *retarder.*

Retentionsrecht, n., *lien.*

Retour-billet, n., *return ticket;* - dampfregulator, m., *exhaust regulator.*

retten, *to save.*

rettlos, *disabled.*

Rettungs-apparat, m., *life saving apparatus;* - bake, f., *refuge beacon;* - boje, f., *life buoy;* die - - werfen, *to let go the l. b.;* - boot, n., *l. boat;* - dienst, m., *l. saving service;* - floß, n., *l. s. raft;* - gerät, n., *l. s. apparatus;* - geschoß, n., *life shot;* - gig, f., *l. gig;* - gürtel, m., *l. belt;* - jacke, f., *l. jacket;* - kutter, m., *l. cutter;* - leine, f., *l. line;* - - kasten, m., *faking box;* - mittel, n.,

resource; - pfeil mit Leine, m., *life arrow;* - ringkiste, f., *life belt box;* - signal, n., *l. signal;* - station, f., *l. boat station;* - wagen, m., *l. car.*

Reusel, n., *stuff.*

Revers, m., *reciprocal bond;* - spant, n., *reversed frame.*

Revidieren und Instandsetzen, n., *overhauling.*

Revier, n., *river;* - lotse, m., *r. pilot.*

Rhede, Rheder see Reede etc.

Richt-feuer, n., *guiding light;* - scheit, n., *straight edge;* - spant, n., *square body frame.*

richten, *to straighten.*

Richtungs-bake, f., *range beacon;* - feuer, n., *r. lights;* - linie, f., *leading line;* - marke, f., *l. mark.*

Ricker, m., *fancy line.*

riefig, *scored.*

Riegel, m., *dog;* - bolzen, m., *d. stay.*

Riemen, m., *1. strap; 2. oar;* - außenbords außer dem Blatt, *oar web;* kurze -, *double banked oar;* lange -, *single b. o.;* - aus! *out oars!* auf den - liegen, *to lie on the oars;* die - gebrauchen, *to ply the o.*

Riemen-blatt, n., *oar blade* - griff, m., *or* - heft, n., *o handle.* ;

Riff, n., *reef;* das aus or vorliegende -, *fringing reef;* - kette, f., *barrier of reefs.*

Riffelplatte, f., *chequered plate.*

Rille, f., *groove.*

Ring, m., *1. ring; 2. bush (inserted as lining); 3. collar (on shaft and engine parts); 4. band (on spars); 5. hoop (of a yard);* - bolzen, m., *ring bolt;* - kette, f., *oval linked chain;* - legel, m., *clue ring;* - stopper, m., *r. stopper.*

Rinne, f., *1. gutter (a channel); 2. groove (of a pulley); 3. bilge ways (of a bilge); 4.*

24*

navigable way (schiftbare
R.).
Rinneneisen, n., *channel iron.*
Rinnstein, m., *gutter.*
Rippe der Spillklampen, f.,
*surge of the whelps on a
capstan*; - eines Bootes,
boat frame; - zwischen den
Deckbalken, *ledge between
the beams.*
Riß, m., *1. crack, flaw, split
(of metal); 2. shakes (of
wood); 3. plan (of a ship).*
rissig, *1. cracked, flawed (of
metal); 2. chinked (of wood).*
Robbenfänger, m., *sealer.*
Rodger Anker, m., *Rodger's
anchor.*
Roh-eisen, n., *cast iron, pig
i.*; - produkte, *raw material*;
- stahl, m., *r. steel.*
roher Gußstahl, m., *raw cast
steel.*
rohes Oel, n., *raw oil.*
Rohr, n., *1. tube (of boiler); 2.
pipe (of steam & water)*; -
anker, m., *stay tube*; - - für
ein leckes -, *tube stopper*;
- - mutter, f., *t. s. nut*; -
bürste, f., *tube brush*; - -
stange, f., *t. b. handle*;
dichter, m., *t. expander*; -
dichtung, f., *t. packing*;
- flansch, m., *pipe flange*;
- hammer, m., *tubing hammer*; - kratzer, m., *tube
scraper*; - leitung, f., *pipes*;
- loch, n., *tube hole*; - pak-
kung, f., *t. packing*; - pfropfen, m., *t. plug*; - pickhammer,
m., *tube mandrill*; - plan,
m., *plan of the pipes*; -
platte, f., *tube plate*; -
schraper, m., *t. scraper*; -
stopfstange, f., *t. stopper*; -
stöpsel, m., *tube plug*; -
stütze, f., *pipe bracket*; -
walze, f., *tube expander*; -
wand, f., *t. plate.*
Rohre or Röhren, *pipes.*
röhrenförmig, *tubular.*
Röhren-kessel, m., *flue boiler*;
- kondensator, m., *external
condenser*; - pfropf, m., *tube*

stopper; - verbindung, f.,
pipe connections; - zirkel,
m., *tube compass.*
Rohstahl, m., *raw steel.*
Roje-gabel, f., *row lock*; -
klampe, f., *thole board*; -
leiste, f., *t. stringer*; - pforte,
f., *row port*; - platte, f.,
thole plate.
rojen, *to row*; alle zugleich -,
to r. all at once; kurzen
Schlag -, *to r. short stroke*;
lang -, *to sweep away*;
langen Schlag -, *to row long
stroke*; stehend -, *to r. standing*; trocken -, *to r. dry.*
Rojer, m., *oarsman.*
Rolle, f., *1. reel (for winding
ropes on); 2. bolt (of canvas);
3. coil (of rope)*; lose -, *loose
pulley*; - der Ankerkette,
chain lifter; - des Kolderstocks, *rowel.*
Roll-bank, f., *roller of the
cable*; - stich, m., *rolling
hitch*; - takel, n., or - talje,
f., *r. tackle.*
rollen, *rolling*; - nach der
Leeseite, n., *lee lurch*; - - -
Luvseite, *weather roll.*
rollende Reibung, f., *rolling
friction.*
Roller, *roller.*
Rosen-bindselung, f., *rose
seizing*; - holz, n., *r. wood*;
- kreuzung, f., *r. knot*; -
laschung or - zurring, f., *r.
lashing.*
Roßbreiten, *horse latitudes.*
Rost, m., *1. rust (on metals);
2. fire grate*; - dichtung, f.,
rust putty joint; - fläche, f.,
grate surface; - kitt, m.,
rust putty; - - dichtung, f.,
r. p. joint; - schieber, m.,
gridiron valve; - schutz-
anstrich, m., *rust preventive*;
- schwelle, f., *grating beam*;
- sicher, *rust proof*; - stab,
m., *fire bar*; - - träger, m.,
furnace bar bearer; - träger,
m., *fire b. b.*
Röster-mars, m., *grated top*;
- werk, n., *grating.*

Rostwerk, n., *grating.*
Rotation, f., *revolution*; - pumpe, f., *rotary pump.*
Rot-glühhitze or - glut, f., *red heat*; - tannenholz, n., *r. pine.*
rote Faden, m., *rogues yarn*; - Farbe, f., *red paint*; - Licht, n., *r. light.*
rotierende Bewegung, f., *rotary motion*; - Maschine, f., *r. engine.*
Route, f., *track.*
rowen, *to row. See also rojen.*
Royal, n., *royal*; - bauchgording, t., *r. bunt line*; - brasse, f.. *r. brace*; - fall, m., *r. halliard*; - geitau, n.. *r. clew line*; - Längssahling, f., *topgallant trestle trees.*
Royalleesegel, n., *royal studding sail*; - Außenschote, f., *r. s. s. tack*; - Binnenschote, f., *r. s. s. sheet*; - fall, m., *r. s. s. halliard*; - Niederholer, m., *r. s. s. downhaul*; - rahe, f., *r. s. s. yard*; - schote, f., *r. s. s. sheet*; - spiere, f., *r. s. s. boom.*
Royal-pardune, f., *royal backstay*; - pferd, n., *r. foot rope*; - rahe, f., *r. yard*; - - jolle, f., *r. y. rope*; - - Niederholer, m., *r. y. tripping line*; - sahling, f., *topgallant cross trees*; - schote, f., *r. sheet*; das lose - segel, n., *loose royal*; - stag, n.. *r. stay.*
Royalstagsegel, n., *royal staysail*; - fall, m., *r. s. halliard*; - hals, m., *r. s. tack*; - Niederholer, m., *r. s. downhaul*; - schote, f., *r. s. sheet.*
Royalstenge, f., *royal mast*; - pardune, f., *r. backstay*; - Schloßholz, n., *r. mast fid*; - - gat, n., *r. m. f. hole*; - stag, n., *r. stay.*
Royal-top, m., *royal mast head*; - toppenant, f., *r. lift*; - wanten, *r. rigging.*
Rüböl, n., *colza oil.*

Rückansicht, f., *back view.*
Rücken, m., *1. rudder frame (of rudder)*; *2. ridge (of an awning)*; - brett, n., *back board*; - knie der Gallionsfigur, n., *lacing*; - stück des Gallions, n., *independent piece.*
Rücker, m., *smiting line.*
Rück-fahrschein, m., *return ticket*; - flußventil, n., *return valve*; - fracht, f., *homeward freight*; - gehende Bewegung, f., *astern motion*; - halttau, n., *check rope*; - kehr, f., *return*; - ladung, f., *homeward cargo*; - lauf der Welle, m., *backwater*; - laufender Zug, m., *reverting (in boiler)*; - laufventil, n., *relief valve*; - leine, f., *snotter*; - reise, f., *return voyage*; - schlagventil, n., *r. valve*; - ständige Heuer, f., *arrears*; - strömung, f., *eddy water*; - versicherung, f., *re-insurance*; - wand der Feuerkammer, f., *back plate of combustion chamber*; - - des Kessels, f., *b. p. of boiler.*
rückwärts, *astern or backwards*; -! *Back her!* - bewegung, f., *astern motion*; - exzenter, n., *go astern eccentric*; - - bügel, m., *sternway e.*; - scheibe, f., *s. e. sheave*; - - stange, f., *s. e. rod*; - gehen, *to go astern*; - geradführung, f., *a. way guides.*
rückwirkende Pleyelstange, f., *return connecting rod.*
Rückwirkung, f., *reaction.*
Rückzoll, m., *drawback.*
Ruder, n., *helm or rudder*; das - an Bord gelegt, *helm on board*; das - auf! *up with the h.!* das - auflegen, *to put up the h.*; dem - folgen, *to answer the h.*; das - hart an Bord legen, *to put the h. hard on board*; das - hart Backbord legen, *to put the h. h. a-starboard*; - - - Steuerbord -, *to p. t. h. h.*

a-port: das - in der Mitte, *helm amidships*: das - in Lee legen, *to put the h.* alee; das - mittschiffs legen, *to right the h.*; das - überlegen, *to shift the h.*; das - wurde nach Luv gelegt or aufgeholt, *the helm was put up*; fest gebundenes -, *h. lashed*; das - stützen, *to meet the helm.*

Ruder-achse, f., *axis of the rudder*; - arme, r. *arms*; - bank, f., *bank of oars*; - beplattung, f., *rudder plating*; - beschlag, m., *r. pintles and straps*; - blatt, n., *1. back piece (of rudder)*; *2. blade (of an oar)*; - büchsen, *rudder bushes*; - druck, m., *r. pressure*; - ducht, f., *thwart*; - fingerling, m., *rudder pintle*; - Fischungsplatte, f., *r. head plate*; - fläche, f., *r. surface*; - gabel, f., *row lock*; - gänger, or - gast, m., *helmsman*; - gräting, f., *wheel grating*; - griff, m., *handle of an oar*; - hacke, f., *skeg (of the keel)*; - haken, m., *rudder pintle*; - haus, n., *wheel house*; - - fenster, n., *w. h. window*; - - tür, f., *w. h. door*; - - - scharnier, n., *w. h. d. hinge*; - herz, n., *main piece of rudder*; - horn, n., *preventer tiller*; - in Lee! *Down the helm!* - kette, f., *1. steering chain (of s. engine)*; *2. rudder pendants (of sailing ship)*; - - block, m., *wheel chain block*; - - - federn, w. *c. b. springs*; - klicks, m., *cheek (of rudder)*; - klub, m., *rowing club*; - knagge, f., *stop cleats of rudder*; - koker, m., *r. trunk*; Wer hat die - kommandos gegeben? *Who gave the steering commands?* Wer beaufsichtigte die Ausführung der - kommandos? *Who was conning?* - kopf, m., *rudder head*; - - band, n., *r. h. hoop*; - - deckel, m., *r. head*

gland; - kragen, m., *r. coat*; - lage, f., *position of the r.*; - - Anzeiger, m., *tell tale of the r.*; - lager, n., *r. carriage*; - leinkette, f., *r. pendant chain*; - leitung, f., *r. leads*; - lichter, *r. breeching*; - mall, n., *r. mould*; - mann, m., *helmsman*; - manöver, n., *wheel manoeuvre*; - mittschiffs legen, *to right the helm*; - nägel, *rudder nails*; - niete, f., *r. rivet*; - öse, f., *r. gudgeon*; - pflock, m., *thole*; - loch, n., *t. pin hole*; - pfosten, m., *rudder main piece*; - pinne, f., *r. tiller*; - quadrant, m., *quadrant t.*; - radwelle, f., *paddle shaft*; - rahmen, m., *rudder frame*; - - Quersteg, m., or - - strebe, f., *rudder stay*; - reep, n., *tiller rope*; - rennen, n., *rowing match*; - schaft, m., *rudder main piece*; - schere, f., *rudder gudgeon*; - - bolzen, m., *r. g. bolt*; - schlag, m., *stroke*; - schloß, n., *wood lock*; - schmiegen, *feathers of the rudder braces*; - smann, m., *helmsman*; - spiker, m., *rudder nail*; - stamm, m., *main piece of r.*; - stangen, *steering rods*; - - Schutzblech, n., *s. r. cover*; - steven, m., *stern post*; - - hülse, f., or - - nuß, f., *boss of s. p.*; - stiel, m., *handle of an oar*; - stopper, m., *rudder stops*; - strebe, f., *rudder arms*; - stropp, m., *rudder strap*; - talje, f., *r. tackle*; - törn, m., *the spell on the wheel*; - träger, m., *dumb chalder*; - trichter, m., *rudder trunk*; - turn, m., *the spell on the wheel*; - verband or - verein, m., *rowing club*; - zapfen, m., *rudder pintle*; - zeiger, m., *tell tale of the r.*

rudern see rojen.

rufen, *1. to hail (a ship)*; *2. to call (the watch).*

Rufer, m., *speaking trumpet.*
Rufweite, f., *hail;* innerhalb -, *within hail.*
ruhig, 1. *smooth* (sea); 2. *easy* (*engines*).
Rumpf, m., *hull.*
rumschmeißen,   to   heave *about.*
rund achter! *mainsail haul;* - brassen, *to haul round;* achter und vorn zugleich - brassen, *to h. off all;* - vorne! *Let go and haul!*
Rund-Charter,   m.,   *round charter;* - gat, n., *r. stern;* - hölzer, *spars;* - platting, f., *round sennit;* - reise, f., *r. voyage;* - - Befrachtung, f., *r. charter;* - - polize, f., *r. policy;* - schlag, m., *r. turn;* - törn in den Ketten, m., *r. turn in the hawse.*
runde Auge, n., *half a crown;* - Feile, f., *round file;* - Heck, n., *r. stern;* - Naht, f., *r. seam;* - Platting, f., *r. sennit.*
runden, *to round.*

Rundung der Kimm, f., *turn of the bilge;* die untere - d. Kimm, *lower t. of the b.*
Rusche, in -, *in bulk.*
Ruse, in - befrachten, *to charter for a lump sum.*
Ruß, m., *soot.*
Rüst-anker, m., *waist anchor;* - balken, *channel boards;* - bolzen, m., *c. bolt;* - eisen, n., *chain plate;* - klampe der Pardune, f., *backstay stool;* - leine, f., *shank painter;* - - kette, f., *s. p. chain;* - leiste, f., *channel rail;* - stütze, f., *c. support.*
Rüste, f., *channel;* - der Pardune, *backstay stool.*
Rüsten-bergholz, n., *channel wales;* - knie, n., *c. knee;* - stütze, f., *c. support;* - träger, m., *c. knee.*
Rüstung, f., *tackle.*
Rute, f., *Lateen yard.*
Rutensegel, n., *Lateen sail.*
rutschender Ballast, m., *shifting ballast.*

S.

Saadholz or Saatholz, n., *bilge keelson.*
sach-gemäß, *proper;* - kenner, or - kundiger, m., *expert;* - kundiges Gutachten, n., *professional opinion;* - verständiger, m., *expert.*
sacht, *gently.*
Sack-gestelle, *bag racks;* - moment, n., *sagging moment;* - stich, m., *overhand knot.*
sacken, 1. *declining* (*of the sun*); 2. *dropping astern* (*sinking*); 3. *driving to leeward;* 4. *to make a sternboard* (*going astern*).
Sägefeile, f., *saw file.*
Sahling, f., *trestle trees.*
Salinometer, m., *salinometer;* - hahn, m., *s. cock.*

Salon, m., *saloon;* - dampfer, m., *s. steamer;* - einrichtung, f., *s. accommodations.*
Salut schießen, *to fire a salute.*
Salz-abblashahn, m., *scum cock;* - abblasventil, n., *brine valve;* - ansatz, m., *saline deposit;* - gehaltmesser, m., *salinometer;* - hahn, m., *brine cock;* - loch, n., *mud hole;* - niederschlag, m., *saline deposit;* - pfropfen, m., *salt stop;* - rohr, n., *brine pipe;* - ventil, n., *b. valve;* - - deckel, m., *b. v. cover;* - - gehäuse, n., *b. v. box;* - wasser, n., *b.;* - - aus dem Kessel entfernen, *brining;* - - pumpe, f., *brine pump.*

Sammeltank, m., *auxiliary exhaust tank.*

Sampan. m., *sampan.*

Sand-ballast, m., *sand ballast*; - bank, f., *s. bank*; - glas, n., *s. glass*; - grund, m., *sandy bottom*; - pumpenbagger, m., *sand pump dredger*; - räumer, m., *drag boat*; - rücken, m., *sand ridge*; - stein, m., *holystone*; mit - - scheuern, *to h.*; - strook, m., *thick garboard strake*; - uhr, f., *hour glass*; - zunge, f., *sand spit.*

Sanitäts-amt, n., *Board of Health*; - beamter, m., *H. Officer*; - paß, m., *bill of h.*

sanker Körper, m., *a body heavier than water.*

Sardellenfischerei, f., *sardine fishery.*

Sargassomeer, n., *Sargasso Sea.*

Sattel, m., *saddle (of the jib boom)*; - rücken-Bunkerluke, f., *saddle back bunker hatchway.*

sättigen, *to saturate.*

Sättigung, f., *saturation.*

Sattlung, f., *hound.*

Saug-klappe, f., *suction valve*; - kolben, m., *v. piston*; - pumpe, f., *suction pump*; - strahlpumpe, f., *sucking jet p.*; - und Druckpumpe, f., *s. and forcing p.*

Sauge-anschluß, m., *suction connection*; - bagger, m., *s. dredger*; - hahn, m., *s. cock*; - korb, m., *strum box*; - raum, m., *suction space*; - rohr, n., *s. pipe*; - - leitung, f., *s. pipes*; - schmierapparat. m., *s. lubricator*; - sieb, m., *strainer*; - ventil, n., *suction valve*; - - gehäuse, n., *s. v. box*; - - Hubbegrenzer, m., *foot v. guard*; - - kasten, m., *suction valve chest*; - - Klappenfänger, m., *s. v. guard*; - - sitz, m., *s. v. seat.*

saugen, *to suck*; das -, *suction.*

Sauger, m., *sucker.*

Säuger, m., *hanks (of a sail).*

Säule, f., *standard*; - der Heckgalerie, *ballustre.*

Saum, m., *tabling*; - tau, n., *tack (of a flag).*

S-Bucht or S-Buchtung or S-förmige B., f., *S-rounding.*

Scaphander-Apparat, m., *scaphander.*

Scepter, n., *stanchion*; - tau, n., *man rope.*

Schabeisen. n., or Schaber, m., *scraper.*

Schablone, f., *templet.*

Schacht, m., 1. *trunk bulkhead*; 2. *casing (round engine parts, funnel, &c.)*; - des Kesselraums, *boiler c.*; - des Maschinenraums, *engine c.*; - luke, f., *trunk hatchway*; - platte, f., *t. bulkhead plate*; - schott, n., *t. b.*; - ventilator. m., *t. ventilator.*

Schaden, m., *damage*; - durch Seewurf u. Aufopferung zur Rettung aus gemeinsamer Gefahr, *d. by jettison and sacrifice for common safety*; - mit Interessen, *d. and cost*; - natürlicher Art, *natural defect*; - od. Verlust an Segeln, *d. to or loss of sails.*

Schaden-Bericht, m., *damage report*; - Besichtigung, f., *d. survey*; - ersatz, m., *indemnity*; - feststellung, f., *damage survey*; - gutmachen, *to make good d.*; - reparatur, f., *d. repairs.*

schaffen, *to eat.*

Schafhock, m., *sheep pen.*

Schafschinken, m., *shoulder of mutton sail.*

Schafstall, m., *sheep pen.*

Schaft, m., 1. *shank (of a rivet)*; 2. *lace piece (of the cutwater)*; 3. *loom (of an oar)*; - welle, f., *propeller shaft*; - - flansch, m., *p. s. flange*; - - mutter, f., *p. s. nut.*

Schäkel, m., *shackle*; - bolzen, m., *shackle bolt*; - der Bug-

sprietzurring, *gammon s.*;
- Kette, m., *one length of chain cable.*

schäkeln, *to shackle.*

Schakenkette, f., *oval linked chain.*

schalken, *to batten down.*

Schalk-leiste, f., *hatch batten*; - - klampen, *h. b. cleats*; - persennig, f., *hatchway tarpaulin.*

Schall, m., *blast* or *sound*; - signal, n., *s. signal.*

Schalstück, n., *side piece.*

Schalter, m., *switch (of electric lighting)*; - brett, n., *s. board.*

Schalung, f., *rubbing paunch (of a mast).*

Schaluppe, f., *1. sloop*; *2. jolly boat (of a ship)*; *3.* kleine -, *yawl*; *4.* große -, *barge*; - tau, n., *boat rope.*

Schamfielleiste, f., *chafing batton.*

schamfielt, *chafed.*

Schamfielung, f., *chafing gear*; - latte, f., *Scotchman*; - matte, f., *chafing mat.*

Schandeck, n., or Schandeckel, m., *1. planksheer, covering board*; *2. gunwale (of a boat)*; - gang, m., *black strake*; - leiste, f., *planksheer rail*; - planke, f., *upper strake*; mit dem - zu Wasser liegen, *to lie gunwale.*

Schanzenschott, n., *bulkhead of the quarter deck.*

Schanzkleid, n., *bulwark*; das lose -, *the loose b.*; - von Segeltuch, *waist cloth.*

Schanzkleid-Beplankung, f., *bulwark planking*; innere - bretter, *quick work of the top sides*; - netzwerk, n., *bulwark netting*; - pforte, f., *b. port*; - platte, f., *b. plate*; - reling, f., *roughtree rail*; - stütze, f., *1. bulwark stanchion (of iron)*; *2. roughtree s. (of wood)*; - winkel, m., *bulwark angle bar.*

scharf anbrassen, *to brace up sharp.*

Scharf des Vorschiffes, n., *entrance of the vessel.*

scharfe Boden, m., *sharp floor*; - Bug, m., *s. bow.*

Scharfeisen, n., *reeming iron.*

Scharnier, n., *hinge*; - bolzen, m., *h. bolt*; - stift, m., *h. pin*; - ventil, n., *hanging valve.*

Scharstock, Schärstock, m., *binding strake (see also* Scherstock).

Schattendeck, n., *shade deck.*

Schattendeckbalken, m., *shade deck beam*; - Längsschiene, f., or - Lukenstringer, m., *s. d. b. tie plate*; - stringer, m., *s. d. b. stringer*; - - platte, f., *s. d. b. s. plate*; - winkel, m., *s. d. b. angle bar.*

Schattendeckgeländer, n., *shade deck rails and stanchions*; - stützen, *s. d. s.*

Schattendeck-luke, f., *shade deck hatch*; - - süll, n., *s. d. hatchway coaming*; - schiff, n., *s. d. ship*; - stringer, m., *s. d. stringer*; - - platte, f., *s. d. stringer plate*; - - winkel, m., *s. d. s. angle bar*; - stütze, f., *s. d. pillar*; - Wassergang, m., *s. d. waterway.*

Schattenrisse, *sketch blocks.*

Schau, Flagge im -, *flag with a waft.*

schaueriges Wetter, n., *showery weather.*

Schauerkleid, n., *weather cloth.*

Schauermann, m., *longshore man*; - knoten, m., *wall knot.*

Schaufel, f., *1. shovel (for coal, &c.)*; *2. paddle (of p. boat)*; - bolzen, m., *hook bolt*; - lenker, m., *paddle float connecting rod*; - nagel, m., *p. bolt*; - platte, f., *boarding plate*; - rad, n., *paddle wheel*; - - arm, m., *p. w. arm*; - - mit feststehenden Schaufeln, *radial p. w.*; - - mit verstell-

baren S., *feathering p. w.*;
- - nabe, f., *p. w. boss*; - raum, m., *shovelling flat*; - ruder, n., *sweeps.*
Schauke, f., *punt.*
Schaum, m., *scum*; - hahn, m., *s. cock*; - löffel, m., *s. dish*; - rohr, n., *surface blow off pipe*; - sammler, m., *foam collector*; - ventil, n., *brine valve.*
schaurig. *showery.*
Schebecke, f., *xebeck*; - segel, n., *settie sail.*
Scheggknie, n., *standard knee of the head.*
Scheibe, f., *1. disc*; *2. sheave (of a block)*; *3. fixed block (in the bulwark)*; *4.* lose -, *loose pulley*; *5.* - mit Vorstecker, *snatch sheave.*
Scheiben-gat, n., *sheave hole*; - klampe, f., *cheek block*; - loch, n., *sheave hole*; - - nagel or - nagel, m., *s. h. pin*; - schießen, n., *target practice*; - ventil, n., *disc valve.*
Scheide-nagel, m., *stopwater*; - platte, f., *diaphragm plate.*
Scheilicht, n., *skylight*; - Persennig, f., *s. cover.*
scheinbar, *apparent*; - Distanz, f., *a. distance*; - Höhe, f., *a. altitude*; - Slip, m., *apparent slip*; - Zeit, f., *a. time.*
Scheinwerfer, m., *search light.*
Scheisegel, n., *skysail*; - brasse, f., *s. brace*; - fall, m., *s. halliard*; - geitau, n., *s. clew line*; - pardune, f., *s. backstay*; - pferd, n., *s. foot rope*; - rahe, f., *s. yard*; - schote, f., *s. sheet*; - stag, n., *skysail stay*; - stenge, f., *s. mast*; - - pardune, f., *s. backstay*; - - stag, n., *s. stay*; - toppenant, f., *skysail lift.*
Scheitel-punkt, m., *zenith*; - winkel, m., *opposite angle.*
scheitern, *to wreck.*
Schellkopfform der Nietung, f., *snap head rivet work.*
Schelpen, *shells.*

Schenkel, m., *1. pendant (of standing rigging)*; *2. leg (of compasses)*; *3.* - eines Stagauges, *leg of the fork of a stay*; - haken, m., *can hook.*
Scherben, *scarfs*; - verschießen, *to shift the s.*
Scher-block, m., *warping block*; - brett, n., *fairleader*; - eisen, n., *reeming iron.*
Schere, f., *kevel (a special cleat)*; - des Bocks, f., *top of the sheers.*
Schergang, m., *sheerstrake*; - der Back, *forecastle s.*; - der Brücke, *bridge s.*; - der Hütte or Poop, *poop s.*; - des erhöhten Quarterdecks, *raised quarter deck s.*; - platte, f., *s. plate.*
Scher-holz, n., *chuck*; - kraft, f., *shearing force*; - latte, f., *fairleader batten*; - leine, f., *reeving line*; - leinen eines Hahnpoots, *crowfoot lines*; - maschine, f., *shearing machine*; - sente, f., *breadth line*; - spannsenten, *diagonal ribbands*; - spanten, *chief frames*; - stock, m., *1. hatchway coaming (of hatch)*; *2. half beam (of deck)*; - stück, n., *arris piece*; - tau an der Brücke, n., *brace cable.*
scheren, *1. to reeve (rope or tackle)*; *2. to sheer (vessel)*; *3. to split (sail or boom)*; - lassen, *to give a sheer.*
Scheuer-lappen, m., *clout*; - leiste, f., *rubbing strake*; - prahm, m., *copper punt*; - stein, m., *holystone.*
scheuern, *to scour.*
Schicht antreten, t., *to begin the shift*; - machen, *to knock off.*
Schicht-arbeit, f., *day work*; - arbeiter, m., *d. worker*; - keil, m., *wedge for stowing.*
Schichtenwolke, f., *wane cloud.*
Schiebbalken, m., *shifting*

beam; - winkel, m., *s. b. angle bar.*

Schiebblinde, f., *sprit sail top sail.*

schieben, *to shove.*

Schieber, m., *slide valve;* - Abbalancierungskolben, m., v. *balance piston:* - Austrittskanal, m., *slide v. exhaust port;* - bahn or - brücke, f., *slide bridge;* - Entlastungsring, m., *s. valve packing ring;* - feder, f., *s. v. spring;* - fläche, f., *slide v. face;* - - des Zylinders, *cylinder face;* - gleitfläche, f., *valve face;* - hub, m., *slide v. travel;* - kasten, m., *valve casing;* - - deckel, m., *v. c. door;* - - - bolzen, m., *v. c. d. bolt;* - - - - mutter, f., *v. c. d. b. nut;* - kasten-Sicherheitsventilbelastung, f., *v. c. escape valve load;* - keil, m., *sliding keel;* - kurbelwelle, f., *valve shaft;* - lappen, m., *slide valve face;* - Regulierung, f., *setting of the slide valves;* - reibung, f., *friction of the slide valve;* - spiegel, m., *1. v. face; 2. cylinder f. (of cylinder);* - stange, f., *valve rod;* - - bolzen, m., *v. r. bolt;* - - führung, f., *v. r. guide;* - - - stütze, f., *v. r. g. bracket;* - - - träger-Lagerschalen, *v. spindle g. b. brasses;* - stangengegenmutter, f., *v. s. check nut;* - stangenmutter, f., *v. s. nut;* - stangenpakkung, f., *v. rod packing;* - stangenstopfbüchse, f., *v. r. stuffing box;* - - deckel, m., *v. r. s. b. gland;* - steuerung, f., *distributing mechanism of slide valves;* - überdekkung, f., *lap of slide valve;* - Umsteuerungsvorrichtung, f., *s. v. reversing gear;* - verschluß, m., *sliding stop valve;* - voreilung, f., *lead of slide v.;* - weg, m., *s. v. travel.*

Schiebe-stange, f., *setting pole;* - tür, f., *sliding door.*

Schiebstenge, f., *sliding gunter.*

Schieds-richter, m., *arbitrator;* - richterliches Verfahren, n., *arbitration;* - spruch, m., *a. award.*

schief, *1. crooked, inclined; 2. lapsided (owing to a list).*

Schief-betel, m., *crooked chisel;* - knie, n., *dagger knee.*

schiefer Stoß, m., *oblique impact (by collision).*

Schiemann, m., *boatswain's mate.*

schiemannen, *to overhaul the rigging.*

Schiemanns-arbeit, f., *boatswain's work;* - garn, n., *spun yarn;* - - mühle, f., *s. y. reel;* - - packung, f., *s. y. packing;* - gasten, *boatswain's crew;* - winde or - woid, f., *spun yarn winch.*

Schiene, f., *rider.*

Schiertuch, n., *Russian sheeting.*

Schieß-gatt, n., or - scharte, f., *loop hole.*

Schiff, n., *ship, vessel;* - auf die Bank holen or legen, *to put a v. on the beach;* - auf Stapelklötze stellen, *to p. a v. on the blocks;* - in Not, *v. in distress;* - mit sämtlichem Zubehör und Ausrüstung, *make, rigging, and apparel of a v.;* - mit teilweisem Sturmdeck, *partial awning deck v.*

Schiff-abbrecher, m., *ship breaker;* - fahrt, f., *shipping.*

Schiffahrts-abgaben, *port charges;* - akte, f., *shipping bill;* - angelegenheiten, *s. affairs;* - betrieb, m., *s. trade;* - gesetz, n., *navigation law;* - - buch, n., *maritime code;* - - gebung, f., *maritime legislation;* - kanal, m., *canal;* - kunde, f., *navigation;* - prämie, f., *n. bounty;*

- schule, f., *naval school*; - vertrag, m., *navigation treaty*.

schiff-bar, *navigable*; - bare Rinne, f., *n. way*; - bau, m., *ship building*; - bauer, m., *s. builder*; - bruch, m., *ship wreck*; - - erleiden, *to s. w.*; - brüchig, *s. wrecked*; Gesellschaft zur Unterstützung - brüchiger Seeleute, f., *s. w. mariners society*.

Schiffer, m., *skipper*; - knoten, m., *clove hitch*; - patent, n., *master's certificate*.

Schiffersgatt, n., *master's store room*.

Schiffs-agent, m., *ship agent*; - art, f., *s. shape*; - arzt, m., *ship's surgeon*; - ausbesserer, m., *ship repairer*; - ausdrücke, *nautical terms*; - bau-Architekt, m., *naval architect*; - bauer, m., *ship-builder*; - bauhof, m., *dock yard*; - bauholz, n., *sea timber*; - bau-Ingenieur, m., *naval architect*; - baukunst, f., *n. architecture*; - bauschule, f., *n. school*; - bauwerft, f., *ship building yard*; - besatzung, f., *ship's crew*; - besichtiger, m., *surveyor*; - blech, n., *ship plate*; - boden, m., *ship's bottom*; - breite, f., *s. breadth*; - certifikat, n., *certificate of registry*; - dienst, m., *ship's service*; - eigner, m., *ship owner*; - expert, m., *s. surveyor*; - formguß, m., *ship casting*; - führer, m., *s. master*; - führung haben or leiten, *to direct the navigation of the s.*; - gelegenheit, f., *shipping opportunity*; - gerät, n., *apparel*; - gerippe, n., *framing*; - glocke, f., *ship's bell*; - händler, m., *ship chandler*; - hobel, m., *compass plane*; - hygiene, f., *ship's hygiene*; - Inspektor, m., *s. husband*; - journal, n., *log book*; - junge, m., *ship's*

boy; - kamerad, m., *ship mate*; - kapitän, m., *s. master*; - kessel, m., *marine boiler*; - koch, m., *ship's cook*; - klasse, f., *class of a vessel*; - klassifikation, f., *ship's classification*; - kompaß, m., *mariner's compass*; - körper, m., *ship's body*; - kran, m., *ship's crane*; - kratze, f., *ship scraper*; - kurs, m., *steered course*; - länge, f., *ship's length*; - leim, m., *marine glue*; - leuchter, m., *sticking candlestick*; - lieger, m., *ship keeper*; - maat, m., *ship mate*; - makler, m., *s. broker*; - maschine, f., *main engine*; - maschinen-Regulator, m., *marine governor*; - mäßig, *ship shape*; - modell, n., *ship's model*; - - Versuchsstation, f., *s. m. trying station*; - nachrichten, *shipping news*; - ort, m., *ship's position by dead reckoning*; - - nach der Seekarte feststellen, *to set down the s. p. on the chart*; - papiere, *s. papers*; - part, m., *s. part*; - pech, n., *common black pitch*; - plan, m., *plan of a vessel*; - platte, f., *ship plate*; - polize, f., *sea policy*; - polizei, f., *board's police*; - rat, m., *consultation*; - reeder, m., *ship owner*; - register, n., *ship's register*; - rumpf, m., *hull*; - schinder, m., *ship breaker*; - schmied, m., *ship's smith*; - schmiede, f., *portable forge*; - - stück, n., *ship forging*; - schnabel, m., *beak*; - schreiber, m., *captain's clerk*; - seite, f., *ship's side*; - tagebuch, n., *log book*; - takelage. f., *ship rig*; - trümmer, *wreckage*; - uhr, f., *ship's clock*; - unfall, m., *casualty*; - unterbaumeister, m., *assistant shipwright*; - utensilien, *marine stores*; - verkauf, m., *ship's sale*; - vermessung, f., *measurement of the vessel*; - vorräte, *ship stores*; - wand, f., *ship's side*; - werft, f., *ship building yard*; - wurm, m., *sea worm*; - zeit, f., *ship's time*; - zertifikat, n., *certificate of registry*; - zettel, m., *shipping note*; - zimmermann, m., *ship's carpenter*; - zubehör und Vorräte als Heizmittel verbraucht, *ship's materials and stores burnt for fuel*; - zugkessel, m., *marine flue boiler*; - zwieback, m., *biscuits.*

schiften, *to shift*; -, n., *shifting.*

Schild-anker, m., *mud anchor*; - krötendeck, n., *turtle deck*; - patt, n., *cheek block*; - zapfen, m., *trunnion*; - - rohr, n., *t. pipe.*

Schillen, *slabs.*

Schirm, m., *screen.*

Schlacke, f., *cinder.*

schlacken, *to slack.*

schladden, *to worm.*

Schladding, f., *keckling.*

Schläf, m., *furring.*

Schlaf-baas, m., *boarding master*; - koje, f., *sleeping berth*; - stelle, f., *boarding house.*

schlaff, *slack.*

Schlag, m., *1. hitch (bending a rope); 2. lay (of a rope); 3. stretch (when tacking); 4. wing (tweendeck sides); 5. turn (of propeller); 6. knock (in cylinder); 7. dead rising (of a ship from fore to aft).*

Schlag 8 Glasen! *Strike 8 bells!* - für -, *hank for hank*; - halten, *to keep stroke*; - rudern, *to pull even stroke*; langen - -, *to pull long s.*; kurzen - -, *t. p. short s.*; - über den Haken, *midshipman's hitch.*

Schlagbetten, *cradles.*

Schlagbettungsstrebe, f., *dog shore.*

Schlag-bug, m., *good board*; einen guten - - machen, *to make a g. b.*; - holz, n., *pointer*; - keil, m., *1. slice; 2. launching wedges*; - leine, f., *carpenter's chalk line*; - lot, n., *hard solder*; - probe, f., *fall proof*; - pumpe, f., *bilge pump*; - pütze, f., *draw bucket*; - remen, m., *stroke oar*; - seite nach Steuerbord, f., *list to starboard*; mit einer - - gebaut or ein Schlagseiter, *lapsider*; - törn, m., *turn (in a rope)*; - wasser, n., *bilge water*; - - bretter, *wash boards*; - - Einspritzung, f., *bilge injection*; - - platte, f., *1. wash plate (between floors); 2. dash plate (machinery).*

Schläge, kurze und lange - machen, *to make short and long tacks*; mehr - als zu essen bekommen, *to find monkey's allowance.*

Schlagen, die oberen - eines Bindsels, *outer turns of a seizing.*

schlagen, *1. flapping (sails); 2. beating (another vessel); 3. striking (bell); 4. to lay (a rope).*

Schlamm, m., *mud, silt*; - ausblaseventil, n., *mud cock*; - boot, n., *m. hopper*; - hahn, m., *sediment cock*; - harke, f., *mud rake*; - kasten, m., *m. box*; - - deckel, m., *m. b. door*; - - dichtung, f., *m. b. joint*; - krücke, f., *m. rake*; - loch, n., *sludge hole*; - - deckel, m., *s. h. door*; - - riegel, m., *dog of s. h. d.*; - löffel, m., *scum dish*; - rohr, n., *s. pipe*; - sammler, m., *sediment collector*; - schaufel, f., *mud shovel*; - tür, f., *m. hole.*

Schlamm, im - festsitzen, *to stick in the mud.*

schlammig, *muddy.*

Schlange, f., *pointer*; zweite -, *clamp.*

Schlängel, m., *floating boom.*

Schlangen, *coils (for heating or cooling)*; - bolzen, m., *pointer bolt*; - linien fahren, *to steer a zigzag course.*

Schlapp-gording or - leine, f., *slab line.*

schlarren, *to keckle.*

Schlarring, f., *keckling.*

Schlauch, m., *hose*; - mundstück, n., *nozzle of a h.*; - verschraubungsschlüssel, m., *h. wrench.*

schlechtes Wetter, n., *foul weather.*

Schleep, f., *sledge.*

Schleich-handel, m., *smuggling trade*; - lotse, m., *waterman.*

Schleif-knoten, m., *slip knot*; - stein, m., *grindstone.*

schleifen, *to grind.* ✦

schleifender Anker, m., *dragging anchor.*

Schlepp-betinge, *towing bitts*; - bogen, m., *tow rail*; - dampfer, m., *tug*; - geld, n., *towage*; - haken, m., *towing hook*; - holz, n., *drogue*; - kette, f., *towing bridle*; - lohn, m., *towage*; - netz, n., *drag*; - pforte, f., *hawser port*; - poller, m., *towing bitts*; - sack, m., *drag*; - segel, n., *drift sail*; - tau, n., *tow rope*; - - eines Schleppnetzes, *trawl warp*; im - -, *in tow*; in - - nehmen, *to take in t.*; - verbindung, f., *t. connection*; - versuche, *towing attempts*; - wagen, m., *cradle*; - zug, m., *the tow.*

schleppen, *to tow.*

Schleppen, n., *towage.*

Schlepper, m., *tug*; - boot, n., *boat of t.*; - kette, f., *towing bridle.*

Schleten, m., *parrel rib.*

Schleuse, f., *sluice.*

Schleusen-einsatz or - fall, m., *tide lock*; - geld, n.,

lockage; - hahn, m., *sluice cock*; - kammer, f., *lock chamber*; - meister, m., *sluice master*; - pforte, f., *dock gate*; - schieber, m., *sluice valve*; - tor, n., or - tür, f., *dock gate*; - ventil, n., *sluice valve*; - - spindel, f., *s. v. spindle*; - - stange, f., *s. v. rod*; - wächter, m., *dock gate man*; - zoll, m., *lockage.*

Schlicht-feile, f., *flat file*; - hammer, m., *swage*; - werkzeug, n., *finishing tools.*

schlichte Bastardfeile, f., *flat bastard file.*

schlichten, *facing*; das Schiff -, *to give the ship her sheer*; einen Streit -, *to arbitrate.*

Schlick, m., *silt*; durch - verstopft, *silted*; im - festsitzen, *to stick in the mud*; - grund, m., *muddy bottom.*

schlieren, *to slip, to surge.*

Schließ-bolzen, *joint bolts*; - haken, m., *catch*; - knie des Gallions, n., *cheek of the head*; - kopf, m., *rivet point.*

schließen, *to close.*

Schlinge, f., *1. carling (timber between beams)*; *2. sling (for holding cargo).*

Schlinger-blech, n., *washing plate*; - block, m., *fly block*; - bord, n., *swinging tray*; - bretter, s. *trays*; - kiel, m., *rolling chock*; - lampe, f., *hanging lamp*; - leiste, f., *swinging tray*; - pardune, f., *shifting backstay*; - platten, *wash plates*; - schlagbug, m., *bungling board*; - stag, n., *second preventer stay*; - stock, m., *pump handle.*

schlingern, *rolling*; die Masten über Bord -, *the masts r. over board*; nicht -, *steady.*

Schlingknoten, m., *slipping knot.*

Schlipp-bindsel, n., *tie*; - haken, m., *slip hook, tumbler*;

- - des Ankers, *anchor tumbler*; - planken, *the ways laid on the blocks*; - schäkel, m., *slip shackle*; - stopper, m., *slip stopper*; - tau, n., *slip rope*; - zeisinge, *breaking stoppers*.

schlippen lassen, *to slip*.

Schlittage, f., *wear and tear*.

Schlitten, m., 1. *cradle (on a slip)*; 2. bilge *ways*; - balken or - kufen, *b. w.*; - ständer, *spurs of the cradle*; - stützen, *poppets*.

Schloi-knie, n., *cheek of the head*; - schoren, *stem props*.

Schlossen, *hail stones*.

Schloß, n., *lasket (of the bonnet)*; - band, n., *truss hoop*; - bolzen, m., *drop bolt*; - holz, n., 1. *fid*; 2. *topmast fid (of t. m.)*; - gat, n., *fid hole*.

Schlot, m., *chimney*; - holt, m., *land lubber*.

Schlüffe, *passages (of the bunkers)*.

Schlund, m., *swallow (of a block)*.

Schlünge, f., *brad*.

Schlup, f., *sloop*.

schlüpferig, *slippery*.

Schlupfhafen, m., *cove*.

Schlüssel, m., 1. *lasket (of the bonnet)*; 2. *carling (between deck and hold beams)*; 3. *key (for machinery and lock)*; 4. - des Zahnrades, *key of the cog wheel*; 5. - mit Doppelenden, *double ended spanner*; - bart, m., *k. bit*; - brett, n., *k. rack*; - schaft, m., *k. shank*.

Schluß-paket, n., *pile for armour plate*; - triebrad, n., *clutch pinion*.

Schmack, f., *smack*.

schmale Platte, f., *narrow plate*.

Schmarting, f., *parcelling*; mit - belegen, *p.*; - Streifen, m., *p. upon a seam*; - tuch, n., *p. canvass*.

Schmelz-barkeit, f., *fusibility*; - punkt, m., *melting point*; - stahl, m., *natural steel*; - topf, m., *melting pot*.

schmelzen, *to melt*.

Schmerzensgeld, n., *smart money*.

Schmetterlings-klappe, f., or - schieber, m., or - ventil, n., *butterfly valve*.

schmiedbarer Eisenguß, m., *annealed cast iron*.

Schmiede, f., *forge*; - arbeit, f., *iron work*; - eisen, n., *wrought i.*; - hammer, m., *sledge hammer*; - maschine, f., *forging machine*; - stück, n., *f.*; - werkzeug, n., *smith's tool*; - zange, f., *forge tongs*.

schmieden, *to forge*.

Schmiegen der Fingerlinge und Ruderhaken, *feathers of the pintles and rudder braces*.

Schmier-apparat, m., *oil cup*; - bäume, *boat fenders*; - büchse, f., *grease cup*; - faß, n., *slush barrel*; - fett, n., *s.*; - gefäß, n., *oil cup*; - - des Lagers, *bearing o. c.*; - - eines Zylinders, *cylinder o. c.*; - geld, n., *charges for paying a ship*; - gelder or Schweigegeld, *palm oil*; - gording, f., *preventer leach line*; - hahn, m., *grease cock*; - horn, n., *slush horn*; - kanne, f., *oil feeder*; - keile, *launching wedges*; - loch, n., *oil hole*; - mittel, n., *grease*; - nute, f., *oil track*; - öl, n., *lubricating oil*; - - rohr, n., *o. pipe*; - planken, *launching ways*; - rack, n., *jaw rope*; - reep, n., *reef pendant*; - - klampe, f., *r. p. cleat*; - rohr, n, *oil pipe*; - topf, m., *slush bucket*; - vorrichtung, f., *lubricator*.

Schmiere, f., *grease*.

schmieren, *to lubricate*; -, n., *lubrication*.

Schmierer, m., *greaser*.

schmierig, 1. *greasy*; 2. *gloomy* (*air*).
Schmirgel, m., *emery*; - feile, f., - holz, n., e. *stick*; - leinewand, f., e. *cloth*; - papier, n., e. *paper*; - - kasten, m., e. p. *box*; - pulver, n., e. *powder*; - tuch, n., e. *cloth.*
Schmokewer, m., *steamer.*
Schmuggel, m., *smuggling*; - handel, m., s. *trade*; - waren, *contraband goods.*
Schmutt, m., *drizzling rain.*
Schmutz-ansetzung verhindernder Anstrich, m., *anti fouling paint*; - ventil, n., *mud cock.*
schmutziger Boden, m., *foul bottom.*
Schnabel, m., *nose* (*of a ship*).
Schnäpper des Feuertür-riegels, m., *catch of the furnace door latch.*
Schnarch-klappe, f., or - ventil, n., *sniffle valve.*
Schnaue, f., or Schnau-schiff, n., *snow*; - mast, m., s. *mast*; - segel, n., s. *sail*; - - gaftel, f., *snow gaff.*
Schnecke, f., *worm.*
Schnecken-rad, n., *worm wheel*; - welle, f., *worm shaft.*
Schnee, m., *snow*; - bö, f., s. *squall*; - gestöber, n., *snow drift*; eisiger - sturm, m., *blizzard*; - wehe, f., *snow drift.*
Schneid-bohrer, m., *screw tap*; - eisen, n., - stahl, m., *cutter.*
Schnell-dampfer, m., *fast steamer*; - lot, n., *soft solder*; - segler, m., *clipper.*
Schnigge, f., *small sailing craft.*
Schnittpunkt, m., *point of intersection.*
Schnitzwerk, n., *carved work.*
Schnüffelventil, n., *pet valve.*
Schnür-boden, m., *mould loft floor*; - hahn, m., *pet cock*: - leine, f., *lacing*; - löcher, l. *holes*; - ventil, n., *pet valve.*

Schoner, m., *schooner*; - bark, f., *barquentine*; - brigg, f., *brigantine*; - mast, m., *fore and aft rigged mast.*
Schonersegel, n., *fore sail*; - baum, m., *f. s. boom*; - fall, m., *f. s. halliard*; - gaffel, f., *f. s. gaff*; - - gerde, f., *boom f. s. vang*; - - - schenkel, m., *fore vang pendant*; - gerde, f., *f. v.*; - hals, m., *fore tack*: - klaufall, m., *boom fore sail throat halliard*; - piekfall, m., *b. f. s. peak h.*; - schote, f., *b. f. s. sheet.*
Schoner-takelage, f., or - zeug, n., *schooner rigging.*
Schöpfeimer, m., *boat scoop.*
Schore, f., *shore.*
schoren, *to prop up.*
Schornstein. m., *funnel*; - des Hülfskessels, *donkey f.*; - band, n., *f. rig*; - blasrohr, n., *blast pipe of f.*; - dämpfer, m., *f. damper*; - kappe, f., *f. hood*; - kragen, m., *f. cape*; - licht, n., *f. light*; - mantel, m., *f. casing*; - register, n., *f. damper*; - ring, m., *f. ring*; - stag, n., *f. stay*; - stelling, f., *f. stage*; - umbau, m., *boiler casing*; - zeichen, n., *funnel mark*; - zug, m., *f. draught.*
Schot or Schote, f., *sheet*; - block, m., s. *block*; - der Blinde, *sprit sail s.*; - gatt, n., *sheet hole*; - gording, f., *foot brail*; - horn, n., *clew*; - - der Fock, *goose wing*; - - legel, n., *clew cringle*; - - leik, n., *clew rope*; - - ring, m., *c. ring*; - klampe, f., *sheet cleat*; - knecht, m., *topsail sheet bitt*; - liek, n., *foot rope*; - poller, m., *sheet bitts*; - rahe-Toppsegel, n., *jackyard topsail*; - stek or - stich, m., *sheet bend*; - stopper, m., s. *stopper*; - strak or - strok, m., *girt-strain of a staysail.*

Schoten *see also* Schot; die - der Untersegel an Bord holen, *to haul the sheets aft.*
Schott, n., *bulkhead*; - Begrenzungswinkel, m., *b. boundary angle bar*; - der Back, *forecastle bulkhead*; - der Hütte or Poop, *poop b.*; - Füllblech, n., or - Füllplatte, f., *b. liner*; - platte, f., *b. plate*; - platten, f., *b. plating*; - spant, n., *b. frame*; - stringer, m., *b. stringer*; - winkel, m., *b. angle bar.*
Schotten, *bulkheads.*
Schottschmann, m., *Scotchman.*
Schove, f., *fagot, sheaf.*
Schraatsegel, n., *fore and aft sail.*
schräge, *aslant*; - geschnittene Kleider, *gores*; - Piekknie, n., *pointer.*
Schrägen, *goring cloths.*
Schräg-holz, n., mit Scheibe im Schanzkleide, *fixed block*; - kante, f., *chamfered edge*; - liegende Maschine, f., *diagonal engine*; - maß, n., *bevel*; - segel, n., *fore and aft sails*; - stück *see* - holz.
schralen, *scanting.*
schrammen, *to score*; entlang -, *to scrape along.*
Schrap-eisen or - messer, n., *scraping iron.*
schrapen, *to scrape.*
Schraper, m., *scraper.*
Schrapp, m., *race on timber.*
schrappen, *to scrape.*
Schrapper, m., *scraper.*
Schratsegel, n., *fore and aft sails.*
Schraub-band, n., *screw hoop*; - stahl, m., *s. tool*; - stock, m., *s. vice*; - - backen, *v. jaws*; - zwinge, f., *clamp.*
Schraube, f., *1. screw; 2. propeller (of steamer only)*; - mit festen Flügeln, *fixed blade p.*; - mit verstellbaren F., *feathering p.*; - schlug blind, *engines were racing.*

Schraube abnehmen, *to unship the propeller*; - auf die Welle setzen, *to ship the p.*
Schrauben-bock, m., *propeller shaft stay*; - bohrer, m., *screw tap*; - bolzen, m., *screw bolt*; - - mit Splint, *junk ring eye bolt*; - - mutter, f., *screw bolt nut*; - - steg, m., *s. b. stay*; - bremse, f., *s. brake*; - brunnen, m., *s. well*; - bügel, m., *s. shackle*; - dampfer, m., *s. steamer*; - druck, m., *thrust of the propeller*; - durchmesser, m., *diameter of propeller*; - flügel, m., *p. blade*; - - flansch, m., *p. b. flange*; - Frachtdampfer, m., *screw cargo steamer*; - gang, m., *thread of a screw*; - gat, n., *shaft hole of a propeller*; - heberahmen, m., *banjo frame*; - hebevorrichtung, f., *screw lifting gear*; - keilnute, f., *propeller key way*; - kloben, m., *screw vice pinchers*; - längskeil, m., *longitudinal key of propeller*; - mutter, f., *nut, propeller nut*; - - blech, n., *rivet plate*; - nabe, f., *propeller boss*; - nagel, m., *clincher nail*; - Passagierdampfer, m., *screw passenger steamer*; - pfropfen, m., *tap bolt*; - propeller, m., *propeller*; - querkeil, m., *tail key of p.*; - rahmen, m., *p. frame*; - rettungsboot, n., *screw life boat*; - ruder, n., *s. rudder*; - Salondampfer, m., *s. saloon steamer*; - Salon- u. Frachtdampfer, m., *s. s. and cargo s.*; - schaft, m., *propeller shaft*; - schiffsmaschine, f., *screw steam engine*; - schleppdampfer, m., *screw tug*; - schlüssel, m., *s. wrench*; - schneidmaschine, f., *s. cutting machine*; - steven, m., *propeller post*; - - auge, n., *shaft hole of propeller*; - - hülse, f., *boss of p. post*; - -

knie, n., *keel piece of stern frame*; - - niete, f., *propeller post rivet*; - - nuß, f., *boss of p. p.*; - tunnel, m., *screw alley*; - wasser, n., *back wash of the propeller*; - welle, f., *tail end shaft*; - - bock, m., *propeller shaft stay*; - - gang, m., *screw alley*; - - hülse, f., *propeller shaft sleeve*; - - keilnute, f., *p. s. key way*; - - lager, n., *pillow block*; - - mutter, f., *propeller shaft nut*; - - tunnel, m., *p. s. tunnel*; - winde, f., *jack screw*; - zieher, m., *s. driver.*

Schrickel, m., or Schricktau, n., *check rope.*

schricken, *1. to check (a rope); 2. to surge (a rope round a windlass).*

Schrobhobel, m., *jack plane.*

Schrot-eisen, n., *ripping chisel*; - meißel, m., *hot chisel*; - tau, n., *parbuckle.*

schrubben, *to scrub.*

Schrubber, m., *scrubber.*

Schrubhobel, m., *jack plane.*

Schubstange, f., *driving rod.*

Schuh, m., *1. block (of machinery); 2. saddle (of the jib boom)*; - block, m., *shoe block*; - planke, f., *s. piece.*

Schuhe unter den Schlagbetten, *launching ways.*

Schuldfrage, f., *the question of the fact.*

schulen, der Wind läuft -, *it is a dead calm.*

Schul-kledje, n., *weather cloth*; - schiff, n., *training ship.*

schülp-artiger Grund, m., *shelly ground*; - säge, f., *square frame saw.*

Schulterblock, m., *shoulder block.*

Schuner, m., *see* Schoner.

Schuppen, m., *shed.*

Schür-eisen, n., *poker*; - haken, m., *fire picker*; - loch, n., *stoke hold*; - platte der

Feuerbüchse, f., *dead plate of furnace.*

schüren, die Feuer -, *to urge the fires.*

schurren über den Grund, *to scrape the ground.*

Schute, f., *barge.*

Schuten-führer, m., *bargemaster*; - führersknecht, m., *bargeman.*

Schütte, f., *shoot.*

schütteln, *1. to shake; 2. to wabble (the compass)*; hin und her -, *to fetch way.*

Schutz, m., *shelter*; - anstrich, m., *anti corrosive paint*; - bleche der Dampfrohre, *guard plates of steam pipes*; - bretter, *weather boards*; - brief, m., *safe conduct.*

Schutzdeck, n., *shelter deck*; - balken, m., *s. d. beam*; - - Längsschiene, f., or - - Lukenstringer, m., *s. d. b. tie plate*; - - stringer, m., *s. d. b. stringer*; - - platte, f., *s. d. b. s. plate*; - balkenwinkel, m., *s. d. b. angle bar*; - Geländer, n., *s. d. rails and stanchions*; - stützen, *s. d. s.*; - Luke, f., *s. d. hatchway*; - - süll, m., *s. d. h. coaming*; - Schergang, m., *s. d. sheerstrake*; - schiff, n., *s. d. ship*; - stringer, m., *s. d. stringer*; - - platte, f., *s. d. s. plate*; - - winkel, m., *s. d. s. angle bar*; - stütze, f., *s. d. pillar*; - Wassergang, m., *s. d. waterway.*

Schutz-deckel, m., *dead light*; - gitter, n., *grating*; - - des Oberlichts, *skylight grating*; - hafen, m., *harbour of refuge.*

Schutzkappe des Hochdruckschieber Abbalancierungskolbens, f., *high pressure valve balance piston cylinder*; - - Mitteldrucks.Abb.-k., *intermediate p. v. b. p. c.*; - - Niederdrucks. Abb.-k., *low p. v. b. p. c.*; - - Schieber-Abb.-k., *v. b. p. c.*

Schutz-kleid, n., *weather cloth*; - - der Brücke, *bridge w. c.*; - marke, f., *trade mark*; - platte, f., *baffle plate (of fire door)*; - schott, n., *screen bulkhead*; - suchend einlaufen, *to put in for shelter*; - vorrichtung, f., *guard*; - wände, *screens*.

Schwabber, m., *swab*; - gast, m,, *swabber*; - leine, f., *swab rope*.

schwabbern, *to swab*.

Schwackenhalsen, *wing stoppers*.

schwaien *see* schwoien.

Schwalbennest, n., *crow's nest*.

Schwalbenschwanz, m., *dove tail*; - platte, f., *d. t. plate*; - verbindung, f., *dovetailing*.

Schwalpe, f., *fish front*.

Schwanenhals, m., *1. goose neck (of a boom); 2. crooked tiller*.

Schwangde, f., *rounding-in*.

Schwanz-block, m., *tail block*; - talje, f., *train tackle*; - welle, f., *tail shaft*.

Schwarte, f., *slab*.

Schwarz-birkenholz, n., *black birch*; - Fichtenholz, n., *spruce*; - meerfahrer, m., *Black Sea trader*; - meerfahrt, f., *B. S. trade*; - wallnußholz, n., *black walnut*.

schwarzer Teerfirnis, m., *black varnish*.

Schweberklappe, f., *suction valve*.

schwedisches Pech, n., *Stockholm pitch*.

Schwefel, m., *sulphur*; - blüte, f., *s. powder*; - büchse, f., *s. canister*.

schweien *see* schwoien.

Schweifstock, m., *anvil horn*.

Schweine-hock or - stall, m., *pig pen*.

Schweinsrücken, m., *anchor chock*.

schweiß-bar, *weldable*; - hitze, f., *welding heat*; - latten, *spar ceiling*.

schweißen, *to weld*.

Schweißung, f., *weld*; - bei Überlappung, *lap w.*

Schwell, m., *swell*.

Schwelle, f., *sill*.

schwellende Segel, *bellying sails*.

Schwellung, f., *belly (of a sail)*.

Schwengel, m., *handle*.

schwer beschädigt, *1. badly damaged; 2. disabled (engines)*.

Schwere, f., *gravity*.

schwere Beschädigung, f., *serious damage*; - Buganker, m., *best bower*; - Raumbalken, m., *strong hold beam*.

Schwer-gut, n., *dead weight*; - punkt, m., *centre of gravity*; - takel, n., *1. einer Unterrahe, jeer; 2. der Fockrahe, fore j.; 3. der Großrahe, main j.*

Schwert, n., *lee board*; - brunnen, m., *centre board well*; - matte, f,. *sword mat*.

Schwesterschiff, n., *sister ship*.

Schwicht-leinen von den Pardunen nach dem Mars, *crane lines*; - reff, n., *balance reef*; - reffband, n., *b. r. band*; - reffen, *to take in the balance r.*; - takel, n., *swifting tackle*; - tau der Gangspillspaken, n., *capstan swifter*.

schwichten, *to swift*.

Schwichtung or - leine or - hahnepoot, f., *cat harpings*; - latte, f., *futtock staff*; - ring, m., *f. rider*; - talje, f., *swifting tackle*.

schwielige Hand, f., *Yarmouth mittens*.

Schwimm-blase, f., *swimming bladder*; - dock, n., *floating dock*; - fähigkeit, f., *buoyancy*; - gürtel, m., *life belt*; - - kiste, f., *l. b. box*; - kasten, m., *caissoon*; - körper, m., *floating body*; - kraft, f.,

buoyancy; - kran, m., *floating crane*; - netz, n., *drag net*.
Schwimmen, n., *flotation*.
schwimmender Körper, m., *floating body*; - Kran, m., *crane bridge*; - Wellenbrecher, m., *floating breakwater*.
Schwimmer, m., *float*.
Schwinden, n., *shrinkage*.
Schwing-baum, m., *swinging boom*; - holz, n., *sweep piece*.
Schwingung, f., *oscillation*; - mittelpunkt, m., *centre of o.*
schwitzen, *to weep*.
Schwitztuch, n., *sponge cloth*.
Schwoi-kreis, m., *tending room*; - raum, m., *swinging space*.
schwoien, *to swing*; den rechten Weg -, *to s. the right way*; den verkehrten W. -, *t. s. t. wrong w.*; in den Hafen ein -, *t. s. into the port*; vor dem Strome -, *t. s. with the tide*; v. d. Winde -, *t. s. head to wind*.
schwül und feucht, *muggy*.
Schwund, m., *shrinkage*.
Schwung-kraft, f., *centrifugal power*; - rad, n., *fly wheel*; - kugelregulator, m., *governor of Watt*; - zapfenrohr, n., *trunnion pipe*.
Scirocco, m., *sirocco*.
See, f., *sea*; in -, *at s.*; in - bleiben, *to keep afloat*; in - gehen or stechen, *to put to s.*; - halten, *to keep the s.*; - nimmt zu, *s. is making*; übernehmen, *to ship a s.*; - von vorne, *head s.*; von - zurückkommen nach Ausgangshafen, *to turn back*.
See-amt, n., *Admiralty Court*; - anker, m., *sea anchor*; - ansicht, f., *s. view*; - arsenal, n., *dock yard*; - ausflug, m., *sea excursion*; - aussicht, f., *s. view*; - auswurf, m., *wreck*; -

bagger, m., *hopper dredger*; - beben, n., *sea quake*; - berufsgenossenschaft, f., *Marine Co-operative Association*; - beute, f., *prize*; - brief, m., *certificate of registry*; - brise, f., *sea breeze*; - dampfer, m., *sea going steamer*; - deich, m., *sea wall*; - dienst, m., *maritime service*; - fahrende Nation, f., *sea faring nation*; - fahrer, m., *sailor*; - fahrsbuch, n., *sailor's book*; - fahrt, f., *sea trip*; - fest, *seaworthy*; - festigkeit, f., *seaworthiness*; - fischerei, f., *sea fishery*; - verein, m., *association of s. f.*; - füße haben, *to have s. legs* - gang, m., *s.*; - - nimmt zu, *s. is making*; dementsprechender - -, *corresponding s.*; - gatt, n., *gat*; - gatten, *fair ways*; - gebiet, n., *territorial waters*; - gebrauch, m., *usage of the sea*; - gefahren, *s. risks*; - gehend, *s. going*; - gericht, n., *naval court*; - - barkeit, f., *maritime jurisdiction*; - gesicht, n., *loom*; - gestade, n., *sea shore*; - hafen, m., *s. port*; - hahn, m., *s. cock*; - haltend, *seaworthy*; - handel, m., *shipping trade*; - injektion, f., *sea injection*; - - ventil, n., *s. i. valve*; - - wasser, n., *s. i. water*; - kabel, n., *submarine cable*; - kadett, m., *midshipman*; - karte, f., *chart*; - kennung, f., *intelligence of the soundings and leading marks of the sea*; - kiste, f., *sailor's chest*; - klar, *ready for sea*; - krank, *s. sick*; - - heit, f., *s. sickness*; - krieg, m., *naval war*; - leuchte, f., *sea light*; - leute, seamen; - lotse, m., *sea pilot*; - löwe, m., *jack tar*; - macht, f., *maritime power*; - mann, m., *sailor*.
Seemanns-amt, n., *mercantile marine office*; - ausdruck,

m., *sea term*; - brauch, m., *sailor fashion*; - gang, m., *deep sea roll*; - geschichte, f., *sailor's yarn*; - haus or - heim, n., *sailor's home*; - schaft, f., *seamanship*; - sprache, f., *sailor's parlance*.
See-mauer, f.. *sea wall*; - meile, f., *nautical mile*; - not, f., *distress at sea*; - paß, m., *certificate of registry*; - pfandrecht, n., *maritime lien*; - protest, m., *sea protest*; - raub, m., *piracy*; - räuber, m., or - - schiff, n., *pirate*; - rauch, m., *sea roke*; - raum, m., *s. room*; - recht, n., *merchant shipping act*; - regatta, f.. *sea race*; - reise, f., *voyage*; - sack, m., *kit*; - schaden, m., *sea damage*; - schiff, n., *s. going vessel*; - - fahrt, f., *s. navigation*; - schiffsverkehr, m., *maritime traffic*; - schlepper, m., *sea going tug*; - schleuse, f., *s. gate*; - stadt, f., *maritime town*; - stage, *man ropes*; - stiefel, *sea boots*; - strand, m., *s. shore*; - straßenordnung, f., *rules of the road at sea*; - straßenrecht, n., *right of way*; - strich, m., *part of sea*; - strom, m., *stream current*; - tag, m., *sea day*; - tage, *passage days*; - taktik, f., *naval tactics*; - tang, m., *sea weeds*; - transport. m., *s. carriage*; - trift, f., or - triftige Gegenstände, *sea drift*; - tüchtig, *s. worthy*; - keit, f., *s. worthiness*; - ufer, n., *s. shore*; - uhr, f., *chronometer*; - unfähig, *disabled*; - untüchtig, *unseaworthy*; - - keit, f., *unseaworthiness*; - Usancen, *uses and customs of the sea*; - ventil, n., *s. valve*; - verbindungen, *s. connections*; - verkehr, m.. *s. traffic*.
Seeversicherung, f., *marine insurance*; - bedingungen,

m. i. clauses; - kontrakt, m., *m. i. contract*; - recht, n., *m. i. law*.
See-vorräte, *sea stores*; - wache halten, f., *to keep s. watch*; - wärts, *seaward*; - - anlegen, *to stand for the offing*; - wasser, n., *sea water*; - - kasten, m., *s. w. tank*; - wechsel, m., *bottomry bond to order*; - weg, m., *track*; - wesen, n., *maritime affairs*; - wind, m., *sea wind*; - wissenschaft, f., *naval science*; - wurf, m., *jettison*; - wurm, m.. *sea worm*; - zeichen, n., *sea mark*.
Seele, f., *heart (of a rope)*.
Seelenverkäufer, m., *crimp*.
Segel, n., *sail*; - age, f., *set of sails*; - anweisungen, *sailing directions*; - balken, m., *midship beam*; - bezug, m.. *sail cover*; - boden, m., *s. loft*; - boot, n., *sailing boat*; - breite, f., *square of a sail*; mit starkem - druck beim Winde segeln, *stretching*; - ducht, f., *main thwart*; - exerzieren, n., *sail drill*; - fahrzeug, n., *sailing craft*; - fertig, *ready for sea*; - - machen, *to get under way*; - fläche, f.. *area of sails*; - garn, n., *twine*; - haken, m., *sail hook*; - handbuch, n., *pilot*; - handschuh, m., *palm*; mittlere - höhe, f., *mean height of a sail*; - jacht, f., *sailing yacht*; - kammer, f.. *sail room*; - karte, f.. *track chart*; - kleid, n., *cloth*; - koje, f., *sail locker*; - - tür, f., *s. l. door*.
Segelmacher, m.. *sail maker*; - haken, m., *s. hook*; - maat, m., *sailmaker's mate*; - splissung, f., *sailmaker's splice*; - Werkstatt, f., *sail loft*.
Segel-nadel, f.. *sail needle*; - order, f., *sailing orders*; - ordnung, f., *order of s.*; - plan, m., *plan of sails*; - pressen, *carrying a press of s.*; -

punkt, m., *centre of effort
of the sails*; - riß, m., *plan
of s.*; - schiff, n., *sailing
vessel*; - - fahrt, f., *s. navigation*; - - linie, f., *s. ship
line*; - sport, m., *yachting*;
- stellung, f., *trim of the
sails*; - streichen, *to clew
down*; - stropp, m., *grommet
of a stay*; - systemschwer-
punkt, m., *centre of effort
of the sails*; - takel, n., *sail
tackle*; - taktik, f., *sailing
tactics*; - tragen, *to bear
sails*; - trimmer, m., *sail
trimmer*; - trocknen, *to
loose sails to dry*; - tuch, n.,
canvass; geteertes - -, *tarpaulin c.*; - - pütze, f., *c. bucket*;
- - schlauch, m., *c. hose*;
unter - gehen, *to get under
weigh*; - unterschlagen, *to
make up sails*; - vertragen,
to bear sails; - wechseln, *to
shift sails*; - wehen lassen,
to unfurl the sails; - yacht,
f., *sailing yacht.*
segeln, *to sail*; im größten
Kreise -, *great circle sailing*; mit halbem (Backstags-
winde) Winde -, *to sail
with the wind abeam*; beim
Winde -, *t. s. by the wind*;
vor dem Winde -, *t. s. before
the wind*; nach vergrößerter
Breite -, *Mercator's sailing.*
Segen des Strandes, m., *godsend.*
Segler, m., *sailing craft*; -
verband, m., *s. yacht club.*
Sehweite, f., *distance of
vision.*
seicht, *shallow*; seichter werden, *to shoal.*
Seiher für Pumpenrohr, m.,
rose sponge.
Seite, f., *1. side (of the ship)*;
2. *gauge (of the ship and
wind)*; auf der - liegend,
logged.
Seiten-ansicht, f., *side view*;
- arm, m., *side arm (of a
hanging knee)*; - balancier,

m., *s. lever*; - - maschine, f.,
s. l. engine; - Beplattung, f.,
s. plating; - - der Back, *s.
p. of forecastle*; - beting,
m., *s. bitt*; - - Wellenlager,
n., *s. b. bearing*; - boot, n.,
s. boat; - bunker, m., *s.
bunker*; - fenster, n., *s. light*;
- Feuerbüchse, f., *wing furnace*; - füllung, f., *air course
board*; - galerie, *side gallery*;
- gang der Back, *side strake
of forecastle*; - - der Brücke,
s. s. of bridge; - - der Hütte
or Poop, *s. s. of poop*; - garnitur, f., *valances (of an awning)*; - hanger, m., *1. quarter
boat*; 2. *mast head pendant*;
- - der Untermasten, *lower
pendants*; - haus, n., *wing
house*; - höhe, f., *moulded
depth*; - kielschwein, n., *side
keelson*; - - bolzen, m., *s. k.
bolt*; - - winkel, m., *s. k.
angle bar*; - kleid, n., *curtain
(of an awning)*; - kohlenbunker, m., *s. coal bunker*;
- lagerbock, m., *s. bitt*;
laterne, f., *s. light*; - - schir-
me, *s. l. screens*; - leiter, f.,
s. ladder; - lichter, *s. lights*;
- liek, m., *leech rope*; - pardune, f., *breast backstay*; -
pforte am Heck, f., *quarter
port*; - platte des Kiels, f.,
side bar of the keel; - - kiel,
m., *s. b. k.*; - Pleyelstange,
f., *s. connecting rod*; - - des
Kolbenkreuzes, *cross tail
strap*; - rechte Dicke, f.,
siding; - riß, m., *shear plan*;
- schenkel eines Vertikal-
knies. m., *side arm of a
hanging knee*; - schwert, n.,
s. lee board; - stoß, m.,
oblique impact; - stringer,
m., *side stringer*; - - winkel,
m., *s. s. angle bar*; - stütze,
f., *quarter pillar*; - stützen
des Hecks, *q. pieces*; - takel,
n., *pendant tackle*; - talje,
f., *side t.*; - tau einer Sturmtreppe, n., *limmer*; - träger,
m., *side girder*; - - platte,

f., *s. g. plate*; - - winkel, m., *s. g. angle bar*; - Verdoppelungsband, n., *leech lining*; - wand der Feuerkammer, f., *side plate of combustion chamber*; - wandungen der Feuerbüchse, *fire box sides*; - zelt, n., *curtain of an awning.*

seizen, *to seize.*

Sektionsdock, n., *sectional dock.*

Sektor, m., *sector*; - der Hebelsteuerung, *eccentric catch*; erster - - -, *driver of the spring c.*; zweiter - - -, *stop o. t. s. c.*

Selbst-auslösung, f., *stop motion*; - entzündung, f., *spontaneous combustion*; - öler, m., *self-acting lubricator*; - schließendes Ventil, n., *non-return valve*; - schmierendes Lager, n., *self-lubricating bearing*; - speisender Kessel, m., *automatically feeding boiler*; - speisung, f., *automatic f.*; - tätig, *automatic, self-acting.*

selbsttätige Feuerbüchse, f., *self-feeding furnace*; - Schmiervorrichtung, f., *s. acting lubricator*; - Speisevorrichtung, f., *s. a. feed apparatus*; - Umsteuerungsvorrichtung, f., *automatic reversing gear*; - Hammer, m., *a. hammer.*

Selbst-verbrennung, f., *spontaneous combustion*; - wirkend, *self-acting*; - - Feuerung, f., *s. a. stoker*; - - Speiseröhre, f., *feed head.*

Semaphor, m., *semaphor.*

Senk-blei, n., *sounding lead*; - kasten, m., *caissoon.*

Senkung, f., *immersion.*

Sente, f., *ribband*; - der Schneidungen, *floor ribbon*; - des Scharfs, *rising line*; - der Verteuning, *top side line*; - mit Schmiege, *harpin*; - ohne S., *ribband.*

Senten im Spannriß, *diagonal lines*; - linie auf dem Wasserpaßriß, f., *ribbon line*; - nagel, m., *ribbing nail*; - riß, m., *floor plan.*

Separations-schott, n., *shifting board*; - tuch, n., *separation cloth.*

Serving, f., *platting.*

Sessel, m., *chair.*

Settiesegel, n., *settie sail.*

Setz-bolzen, m., *wrain bolt*; - bord, n., *wash board*; - eisen, n., *hot chisel*; - schiffer, m., *acting captain*; - stange, f., *setting pole*; - wage, f., *carpenter's level*; - weger, m., *spirketting*; - - bolzen, m., *s. bolt*; - - platte, f., *s. plate.*

setzen. Segel -. *to set sail*; ein Schiff auf Strand -, *to force a ship on shore.*

setzt, Wohin - die Ebbe? *How will the ebb set?* der Strom - nach West, *the current sets westward.*

Sextant, m., *sextant.*

sichere Ankerplatz, m., *safe anchorage*; - Hafen, m., *s. port*; - Reede, f., *s. road.*

Sicherheits-bolzen, m., *lock bolt*; - - für eine Gangspillspake, *capstan bar pin*; - lampe, f., *safety lamp*; - pfropfen, m., *fusible plug (in boiler)*; - pinne, f., *safety pin*; - schloß, n., *s. lock.*

Sicherheitsventil, n., *escape valve*; inneres -, *reserve v.*; - mit Federbelastung, *spring safety v.*; - mit Gewichtsbelastung, *dead weight safety v.*; - mit Hebel, *lever s v.*; - mit verschlossenem Kasten, *locked up s. v.*

Sicherheitsventil-belastung, f., *safety valve load*; - deckel, m., *s. v. cover*; - feder, f., *s. v. spring*; - gehäuse, n., *check valve box*; - hebel, m., *safety valve lever*; - kasten, m., *s. v. box*; - regulierung, f., *setting* of the safety valves; - rohr, n., safety valve pipe; - sitz, m., s. v. seat; - spindel, f., escape valve spindle; - vor- richtung, f., safety valve gear.

sichern, to secure.

Sicherung, f., 1. safety device; 2. guard (of steam windlass).

Sicherungs-ring, m., safety ring; - stift, m., s. stud; - vorrichtung, f., guard.

Sicht, f., sight; aus -, out of s.; aus - verlieren, to lose s. of; in - bekommen, to catch s. of; in - von, in s. of.

sichten, to sight.

sichtig, clear.

Sichtweite, f., sighting dis- tance.

sickern, to weep.

Siede-punkt, m., boiling point; - rohr, n., water tube; - - kessel, m., w. t. boiler.

Sieden, n., boiling.

Signal, n., signal; - bake, f., s. beacon; - beantworten, to answer the s.; - buch, n., s. code; - - staben, s. letters; - fackel, f., s. torch; - feuer, n., s. light; - flagge, f., s. flag; - glocke, f., s. bell; - kasten, m., s. chest; - laterne, f., s. lantern; - nummer, f., s. number; - pfeife, f., s. whistle; - rakete, f., sky rocket; - stange, f., perch; - station, f., signal station; sich in - weite halten, to keep within signal distance; - wimpel, m., pendant.

Signalisierungsballon, m., sig- nal ball.

Simonspfosten, m., Samson's post.

Singelgrund, m., gravel ground.

sinken, to sink, to founder.

sinkendem, in - Zustande, in a foundering state.

Sirene, f., siren.

Sirocco, m., sirocco.

Sitter, m., half floor.

Sitz, m., seat; - eines Hahnes, s. of a cock.

Sitzer, m., half floor.

Skiff, n., skiff.

Sklaven-handel, m., slave trade; - schiff, n., slaver.

slip see schlipp.

S. M. S., H. M. S.

Smutje, m., cook.

Sockel, m., socket.

Sodahahn, m., soda cock.

Sog, m., 1. run (i. e. a vessel's bottom aft); 2. dead water (i. e. the eddy round the stern post); - brüstung, f., diminishing a ship on fore- castle and stern downwards.

Sohle, f., 1. heel (of the rudder); 2. sole piece (of the stern frame); 3. sole (of the bilge way).

Soldaten-gat or - loch, n., lubber's hole.

solide Kolbenpackung, f., solid packing for piston.

Sommer-fahrten, summer navigation; - seezeichen, s. sea marks.

sondieren, to sound.

Sondiermaschine, f., sounding machine.

Sondierungs-boje, f., sounding buoy; - rohr, n., s. pipe.

Sonne, die - peilen, to observe the sun's amplitude.

Sonnen-aufgang, m., sun rise; - deck, n., bridge deck; - - balken, m., b. d. beam; - finsternis, f., solar eclipse; - hof, m., s. halo; - höhe, f., altitude of the sun; - mes- ser, m., back staff; - linie, f., line; - ring, m., solar corona.

Sonnensegel, n., awning; - ausholen, to spread the awnings; - band, n., awning hoop; - baum, m., a. boom; - kleid, n., a. curtain; - reep, n., ridge rope of an a.; - Seitengarnitur, f., awning valances; - Seitenkleid, n., a. curtain; - strebe, f., a. stretcher; - stütze, f., a. stanchion; - - am Heck, quarter a. s.

Sonnen-tafeln, *tables of the sun*; - zeit, f., *apparent time*; - zelt, n., *awning*.

Sorg-ketten, *rudder chains*; - klampe, f., *hollow cleat*; - leinen, *rudder pendants*; - leinkette, f., *r. pendant chain*.

Sorr-kette, f., *lashing chain*; - tau, n., *l. rope*.

Sorrung, f., *lashing*; - zweier Augen eines Taues an ein- ander, *parrel l.*

Spaken, *bars*; - einlegen, *to rig the capstan*; - löcher, *holes in the head of the c.*; - reep, n., *c. swifter*; - - nehmen, *to swift the c.*

spanische Besen, m., *hog*; - Takel, n., *tackle with a tie*; - Winde. f., *Spanish windlass.*

Spann des Piekfalls, n., *span of the peak halliards*; - holz für Taue, n., *rack bar*; - kraft, f., *tensile force*; - Pardunen, *pair of backstays*; - säge, f., *frame saw*; - schraube, f., *1. stretching screw*; *2. regulating screw (of a steering chain)*; - vor- richtung, f., *regulating device*; - want, n., *pair of shrouds.*

Spannung, f., *pressure*; ab- solute -, *absolute p.*; höchste -, *straining power*; über- große -, *strain*; zu große -, *excessive s.*; - bis zum Platzen, *strain to bursting point*; - in der Schotstrak, *girt strain of a staysail.*

Spannungslinie am Todholz, f., *stepping line.*

Spant, n., *frame*; - bolzen. m., *f. bolt*; - der Back, *forecastle f.*; - des erhöhten Quarter- decks, *raised quarter deck frame*; - Füllstreifen, f. *liners*; - niete, f., *f. rivet*; - umfang, m., *girth of a ship*; - winkel, m., *frame angle bar.*

Spanten aufsetzen, *to erect the frames*; - entfernung, f.,

spacing of frames; - gelascht durch Ueberlappung, *lapped f.*; - riß, m., *body plan*; das Schiff steht in -, *the vessel is in frames.*

Spardeck, n., *spar deck.*

Spardeckbalken, m., *spar deck beam*; - Hängeknie, n., *s. d. b. hanging knee*; - Längs- schiene, f., or - Lukenstrin- ger, m., *s. d. b. tie plate*; - stringer, m., *s. d. b. stringer*; - - platte, f., *s. d. b. s. plate*; - weger, m., *s. d. b. shelf*; - winkel, m., *s. d. b. angle bar.*

Spardeck-geländer, n., *spar deck rails and stanchions*; - - stützen, *s. d. stanchions*; - luke, f., *s. d. hatchway*; - - süll, m., *s. d. h. coaming*; - schergang, m., *s. d. sheer- strake*; - schiff, n., *s. d. ship*; - Seitenbeplattung, f., *s. d. side plating*; - stringer, m., *s. d. stringer*; - - platte, f., *s. d. s. plate*; - - winkel, m., *s. d. s. angle bar*; - Unter- balkweger, m., *s. d. beam clamp*; - Wassergang, m., *s. d. waterway.*

Sparograph, m., *spherograph.*

special *see* spezial.

Spediteur, m., *forwarding agent.*

Speicher, m., *warehouse.*

Speigat, n., *scupper*; - klappe, f., *s. valve*; - leder, n., *s. leather*; - pflock, m., *s. plug*; - rohr, n., *s. pipe.*

Speil or Speiler, m., *skewer.*

Speise-apparat, m., *feeding apparatus*; - hahn, m., *feed cock*; - pumpe (*see also Dampfspeisep.*) *feed pump*; - rohr, n., *f. pipe*; - - leitung, f., *f. pipes*; - salon, m., *din- ing room*; - ventil, n., *feed check valve*; - - deckel, m., *f. v. cover*; - - gehäuse, n., *f. v. box*; - vorrichtung, f., *feeding means*; - wasser, n., *feed water*; - - behälter, m., *f. w. tank*; - - filter-Sicherheitsventilbelastung, f., *f. w. filter escape valve load*; - - vorwärmer, m., *f. w. heater*; - - - Dampfzuleitungsrohr, n., *f. w. h. steam pipe*; - - - deckel, m., *f. w. h. door*; - - - schlange, f., *f. w. h. coils.*

speisen, *1. to feed (a boiler)*; 2. das Lot -, *to arm the lead.*

Speisung, f., *1. feeding (of a boiler)*; *2. arming (of the lead).*

Spell, m., 1. am Ruder, *spell on the wheel*; 2. zur Koje, *s. below.*

Sperr-haken, m., *ratchet*; - kegel, m., *hanging pawls*; - - apparat, m., *stop work*; - klinke, f., *ratchet*; - - steuerung, f., *spring catch*; - rad, n., *ratchet wheel.*

sperren, *1. to shut (a harbour)*; 2. *to put an embargo on (a ship).*

Spezial-Aufsicht or - Besichtigung, f., *special survey.*

spezifische Druck, m., *steam pressure*; - Gewicht, n., *specific weight*; - Schwere, f., *s. gravity*; - Wärme, f., *s. heat.*

spicken, *to thrum (a mat or sail).*

Spiegel-heck, n., *square stern*; - Leuchtapparat, m., *catoptric illuminating apparatus*; - Oktant, m., *reflecting quadrant*; - spant, n., *stern frame.*

Spieker, m., *spike*; - back, f., *s. box*; - eisen, n., *s. iron*; - haut, f., *wood sheathing*; - - auf dem Bergholz, *boot topping*; einem Schiffe eine - - geben, *to sheathe a ship with boards*; - pinne, f., *spile.*

spiekern, *to spike.*

Spiekerung, f., *nailing.*

Spiel, n., *play*; - kragen, m., *mast collar*; - raum, m., *1. to fetch way (things not suffi-*

ciently secured); *2. clearance (of piston)*; *3. play (of piston rod)*; - - geben, *to loosen (screws, &c.).*

Spielen, n., das - des Segels, *the lift of a sail*; - im Winde, *to flutter.*

Spiere, f., *spar, boom*; - brasse, f., *b. brace*; - brille, f., *boom iron*; - des Brotwinners, *ring tail boom*; - steert, m., *heel lashing.*

Spieren auf! Leg aus! *Trice up!* - aus! *Rig out the booms!* - bügel, m., *boom iron*; - laschung, f., *spar lashing*; - stich, m., *fisherman's bend*; - tonne, f., *spar tun buoy.*

Spießruten laufen, *to run the gauntlet.*

Spiker *see* Spieker.

Spill, n., *windlass*; An's -! *Man the capstan!* - beting, f., *carrick bitt*; - fütterung, f., *wood lining on main piece*; - klampe, f., *whelps*; - klötze, *mooring chocks*; - kopf, m., *windlass warping end*; - kranz, m., *1. purchase rim (of windlass)*; *2. cable lifter (of steam windlass)*; - palle, f., *drop pawl (of capstan)*; - spake, f., *hand spike*; - - gat, n., *pigeon hole*; - spur, f., *step of a capstan*; - stamm, m., *main piece.*

Spillage, f., *spillage.*

Spind, n., *locker.*

Spindel, f., *1. spindle*; *2. screw (of steering gear)*; - boje, f., *nun buoy*; - mutter, f., *traversing nut.*

Spinnaker, m., *spinnaker*; - baum, m., *s. boom*; - - Achterholer, m., *s. guy*; - brasse, f., *s. brace*; - geschirr, n., *s. gear*; - hals, m., *s. tack*; - schote, f., *s. sheet.*

Spinnkopf, m., *crowfoot*; - block, m., *c. dead eye.*

Spint, m., *sap wood.*

Spiralfeder, f., *spiral spring.*

Spirituslast, f., *spirit room.*
Spitz-boje, f., *nun buoy*; - docke, f., *sliding head of a lathe*; - hammer, m., *mandril.*
Spitze, f., *point*; - des Krummholzes, *bill of a knee timber.*
spitzer Winkel, m., *acute angle.*
spitzwinkelig, *acute angled.*
Spleiss, n., *see* Splissung.
spleissen, *to splice.*
Splint, m., *1. key (wedge for machinery); 2. bar pin (for capstan); 3. sap (of wood);* - bolzen, m., *key bolt;* - dorn, m., *starting punch;* - gat, n., *eye in a forelock bolt;* - mit Federn, *spring f.*
splissen, *to splice.*
Spliss-gang, m., *drop strake;* - hammer, m., *splicing hammer;* - horn, n., *s. fid;* - schäkel, m., *s. shackle.*
Splissung, f., *splice;* - mit verjüngten Duchten, *tapered s.;* - mit vollen D., *s. with whole strand.*
Split, m., *swallow tail (of a flag);* - Flagge, f., *split flag.*
Splitter, m., *splinter;* - netz, n., *s. netting.*
splittern, *to splinter.*
Splittflagge, f., *burgee.*
Sponung or Sponnung, f., *rabbet.*
Sporn, m., *ram;* - spitze, f., *point of the r.*
Sprachrohr, n., *1. speaking trumpet; 2. voice pipe (to engine room).*
Spreelatte or Spreizlatte, f., *sheer batten.*
Sprengkiste, f., *powder chest.*
Sprett, n., *sprit.*
Spriet, f., *sprit;* - block, m., *dead eye of the crowfoot;* - latte, f., *sheer batten;* - segel, n., *sprit sail;* - - brasse, f., *s. s. brace;* - - gaffel, f., *s. s. gaff;* - stropp, m., *snotter;* - tau, n., *spirit sail rope;* - wurst, f., *futtock staff.*

Spring, m., *1. spring (rope); 2. sheer (of a ship);* viel - geben, *to quicken the sheer;* mit wenig -, *straight sheered;* - flut or - gezeit, f., *spring tide;* - luke, f., *scuttle cap;* - Niedrigwasser, n., *spring low water;* - pferd, n., *stirrup;* - stag, n., *spring stay;* - stock, m., *balk staff;* - stropp, m., *stirrup;* - tau, n., *spring;* - zeit, f., *s. tide.*
Spritz-brett, n., *spray board;* - see, f., or - wasser, n., *spray;* - wasser übernehmen, *spraying.*
Spritze, f., *syringe.*
Spritzer übernehmen, *spraying.*
Spritzung, f., *lipper.*
Sprosse, f., *step (of a ladder).*
Sprühregen, m., *drizzling rain.*
Sprung, m., *1. crack (of a metal part); 2. round (of a beam); 3. sheer (of a ship).*
Sprut, m., *lizard.*
Sprute, f., *bridle (of the bowline).*
Spund, m., *1. bung (of a cask); 2. fur (for filling up a hole in a plank, &c.).*
Spündung, f., *rabbet;* - des Hinterstevens, *stern post r.;* - des Vorderstevens, *stem r.*
Spunt, m., *furr (in a plank, &c.)*
Spur, f., *1. socket (of a davit); 2. step (bed of a mast, &c.); 3. saucer (of the capstan); 4. gorge (of a pulley);* - coulisse, f., *slot link;* - lager, n., *socket;* - - eines Davits, *davit socket.*
Staats-pützen, *state buckets;* - räume, *s. rooms.*
Stab, m., *1. bar; 2. staff (of a flag);* - eisen, n., *bar iron.*
Stabilität, f., *stability.*
Stachelnaht, f., *garnet.*
Stack, n., *groin.*
Staffelformation, f., *order in quarter line.*
Stag, n., *stay;* - eines Untermastes, *lower s.;* über - gehen, *to put about;* - auge, n., *eye*

of a stay; - block, m., *heart*; großer - -, *dead block*.
Stagfock, f., *fore staysail*; - fall, m., *f. s. halliard*; - hals, m., *f. s. tack*; - leiter, f., *f. s. stay;* - Niederholer, m., *f. staysail downhaul*; - schote, f., *f. staysail sheet*.
Stag-garnat, n., *Spanish burton*; - gilling or - gillung, f., *stay gore*; - jolle, f., *s. whip*; - kante, f., *fore leech*; - - saum, m., *stay tabling*; - kragen, m., *collar of a stay*; - liek, m., *head rope*; - matte, f., *breeches mat*; - maus, f., *mouse of the stay*; - ring, m., *grommet of a stay*.
Stagsegel, n., *staysail*; - fall, m., *s. halliard*; - hals, m., *s. tack*; - Niederholer, m., *s. downhaul*; - schote, f., *s. sheet*; - - schenkel, m., *s. s. pendant*.
Stag-takel, n., *stay tackle*; - - läufer, m., *s. t. fall*; - - schenkel, m., *s. t. pendant*; - talje, f., *garnet*; - weise, *astay*.
stagen, *1. to put about (a ship)*; *2. to stay (a mast)*.
Stahl-draht, m., *steel wire*; - - takelung, f., *s. w. rigging*; - - tau, n., *s. w. rope*; - faconguß or - formguß, m., *s. casting*; - gießerei, f., *s. foundry*; - hammer, m., *s. hammer*; - kessel, m., *s. boiler*; - kolben, m., *s. piston*; - mast, m., *s. mast*; - platte, f., *sheet of s.*; - werk, n., *steel institute*.
stählerne Bolzen, m., *steel bolt*; - Boot, n., *s. boat*; - Deck, n., *s. deck*; - Keil, m., *s. wedge*; - Kolben, m., *s. piston*; - Mast, m., *s. mast*; - Rahe, f., *s. yard*; - Rohr, n., *s. tube*; - Schiff, n., *s. vessel*.
Staken, m., *setting pole*.
Stall, m., *pen*.
Stampf-stag, n., *dolphin striker*; - steven, m., *straight stem*; - stock, m., *martingale*;

- - Achterholer, m., *m. back rope*; - - band, n., *m. boom hoop*; - - geie, f., *m. guy*; - - stag, n., *m. stay*.
stampfen, *pitching*; auf und nieder -, *heaving and setting*.
Stampfer, m., *ram*.
Stand des Wassers, m., *water level*.
Stander, m., *pendant*; - des Stagtakels, *mast head p.*
Ständer, m., *1. uprights*; *2. column (of cylinder)*; *3. standard (of steering engine)*; - der Schlagbetten, *sliding bilge block*; - der Waschjollen, *clothes lines pendants*; - des Backtisches, *crow foot of the mess table*.
Stange, f., *bar, rod*.
Stänge *see* Stenge.
Stangen-bohrer, m., *auger*; - coulisse, f., *bar link*; - eisen, n., *b. iron*; - kiel, m., *b. keel*.
stanzen, *to punch*.
Stanzmaschine, f., *shaping machine*.
Stapel, m., *stocks*; auf - legen, *to put on the s.*; - blöcke, *launching ways*; obere - -, *splitting blocks*; - keile, *launching wedges*; - klotz, m., *l. block*; - lauf, m., *launch*; vom - laufen lassen, *lauching*.
starke Brise, f., *strong breeze*; - Wind, m., *s. wind*.
Stärke, f., *1. power*; *2. intensity (of draught)*; *3. force (of wind)*.
Staubregen, m., *drizzling rain*.
Stauchwegerung, f., *floor head ceiling*.
Stau-damm, m., *dam*; - geld, n., *stowage*; - holz, n., *dunnage wood*; mit - - garniert und mit Matten unterlegt, *laid out with dunnage wood and mats*; - keil, m., *quoin for stowing*; - kosten, *stowage*; - lücken, *broken s.*; - wasser, n., *1. slack water (of the tide)*; *2. back-*

water (*of the sluice*); - wehr, f., *weir.*

stauen, *1. to stow (cargo); 2. to trim (ballast); 3. to stem (water).*

Stauer, m., *stevedore.*

Stauung, f., *stowage;* - attest, n., *certificate of s.;* - pflichten, s. *duties;* - plan, m., s. *plan.*

Stech-bolzen, m., *reef earing;* - eisen, n., *stoker's rod;* - güdse, f., *small gouge;* - heber, m., *sampling tube;* - kompaß, m., *traverse board;* - maschine, f., *punching machine.*

Steck-bolzen, m., *reef earing;* - - um die Rahe nehmen, *to pass an e.;* - pumpe, f., *hand pump;* - schoren, *bottom props;* - zirkel, m., *compasses with shifting points.*

stecken, Kette -, *paying out more chain;* zwei Taue aufeinander -, *to bend two ropes together.*

Steckenboje, f., *buoy with a broom.*

Steek-pumpe f., *hand pump;* - schoren, *bottom props.*

Steert, m., *1. tail (of a rope); 2. nipper (of a stopper);* - block, m., *tail block;* - stopper, m., *pointed stopper;* - talje, f., *tail jigger;* - tau, n., *1. heel lashing (of a studding sail boom); 2. lanyard (of a buoy);* - - mit Kauschen für Buggordinge, *lizards.*

Steg, m., *1. gangboard; 2. stud (of chain cable link);* - kette, f., *stud linked chain;* - platte, f., *web plate.*

Stehbolzen, m., *1. stay bolt; 2. s. rod (of boiler); 3. s. (of combustion chamber); 4. tie rod (of winch);* - mutter, f., *stay nut;* - - der hinteren Rauchkammer, *combustion chamber s. n.;* - versteifung, f., *staying (of a c. c.).*

stehen, *to grow (i. e. the chain);* unter dem Schiffsboden -, *to g. underneath the bottom;* wie ein Stengstag -, *to g. a short stay;* zum Springen steif -, *to g. exceedingly;* bereit -, *to stand by.*

stehende Bohrmaschine, f., *vertical drilling machine;* - Eis, n., *fast ice;* - Gut, n., *standing rigging;* das - - auflegen or aufstreifen or überstreifen, *to put the r. on the masthead;* - Knie, n., *standard knee;* - Liek, n., *leech rope;* - Pardunen, *standing back stays;* - Part eines Takels, m., s. *part of a tackle;* - Speiseröhre, f., s. *pipe;* - Tauwerk, n., s. *rigging;* - Wind, m., *settled wind;* - Zapfen, m., *pivot.*

Stehleik, n., *leech rope.*

stehlen, die Segel - einander den Wind, *the sails overlap each other.*

steif, *1. rigid; stiff (a vessel); 2. taught (a rope);* - hieven, *to heave taught;* - holen, *to haul tight;* - geholt, *hand t.;* - machen, *to tauten.*

steife Brise, f., *stiff breeze;* - Kühlte, f., or - Wind, m., s. *wind.*

Steifheit, f., *1. rigidity; 2. tautness (of a rope); 3. stiffness (of a vessel).*

steigen, *to rise.*

Steigen, n., *rising (of freights, stars, and tide);* - und Fallen, *rise and fall (of river).*

Steigrohr, n., *rising main.*

Steigung, f., *pitch (of rivets, propeller, teeth, threads, &c.).*

steile Küste, f., *bold coast;* - Vorland, n., *bluff.*

Stein, m., *block (of machinery);* - ballast, m., *stone ballast;* - buhne, f., s. *wharf;* - eichenholz, n., *live oak;* - farbe, f., *stone colour paint;* - kohle, *steam coal;* - ulmenholz, n., *rock elm wood.*

steiniger Grund, m., *stony bottom.*

Stek, m., *bend.*

Stellage, f., *stage.*

Stell-bares Winkelmaß, n., *bevel*; - bolzen, m., *check bolt*; - Flaggen, *set of flags*; - keil, m., *tightening key*; - mutter, f., *check nut*; - schraube, f., *adjusting screw*; - Segel, *set of sails*; - stift, m., *check pin*; - vertreter, *substitute*; - vertretender Besichtiger, m., *assistant surveyor.*

stellen, 1. *to set (the log)*; 2. *to trim (the sails).*

Stelling, f., *stage.*

Stellung, f., 1. *stage (for painting, &c.)*; 2. *rating (as per articles).*

Stemm - Werkzeug, n., or Stemmer, m., *caulking tools.*

Stempelbolzen, m., *starting bolt.*

Stenge, f., *topmast*; - pardune, f., *t. backstay*; - schmiere, f., *slush*; - stag, n., *topmast stay.*

Stengestagsegel, n., *topmast staysail*; - fall, m., *t. s. halliard*; - hals, m., *t. s. tack*; - Niederholer, m., *t. s. downhaul*; - schote, f., *t. s. sheet.*

Stenge-talje, f., *top burton*; - want, n., *topmast shroud*; - - block or - - Violinblock, m., *sister block*; - wanten, *topmast rigging.*

Stengewindreep, n., *top rope*; - block, m., *t. block*; - Gienläufer, m., *t. tackle fall*; - hanger or - stander, m., *t. t. pendant*; - takel, n., *t. t. tackle.*

Stern-büchse, f., *stern bush*; - gucker, m., *moon raker*; - höhenmessung, f., *time sight*; - jahr, n., *sideral year*; - rohr, n., *stern tube*; - tag, m., *sideral day*; - warte, f., *observatory*; - zeit, f., *sideral time.*

Stert *see* Steert.

Steuer, n., *rudder*; Wie gehorcht das Schiff dem -? *How does she carry her helm?* Es gehorcht dem - gut, *She answers her helm readily*; aus dem - laufen, *to lose her steerage way*; kein - im Schiff, *becalmed*; über - gehen, *to go astern.*

Steuer-apparat, m., *steering apparatus*; - barkeit, f., *manageableness*; - bord, *starboard*; - - anker, m., s. *anchor*; - - Bilgesaugeventil, n., s. *bilge suction valve*; - - bug, m., *starboard bow*; über - - - mit Backbordhalsen, *on the port tack*; - bord das Ruder! *Port the helm!* mit - bordhalsen über Backbordbug, *on the starboard tack*; - bord Kessel, m., s. *boiler*; - bord Licht, n., s. *light*; - bord Maschine, f., s. *engine*; - bord Seite, f., s. *side*; - bord Wache, f., s. *watch*; - fähigkeit or - fahrt, f., *manageableness, steerage way*; die - - or - - verlieren, *to lose her s. w.*; - gerät, n., *steering gear*; - hahn, m., *valve cock*; - haus, n., *wheel house*; - indikator, m., *steering indicator*; - kette, f., *wheel chain*; - knagge, f., *tappet for distributing*; - kompaß, m., *steering compass*; - - ständer, m., *s. c. stand*; - lastigkeit, f., *trim*; - leine eines Bootes, f., *yoke line of a boat rudder*; - los, *helmless*; - mann, m., *mate*; - - kammer, f., *mate's room*; - - kunde or - - kunst, f., *navigation*; - - maat, m., *quartermaster*; - - patent, n., *mate's certificate*; - - Quittung, f., *m. receipt*; - maschine (*see also* Dampfsteuerapparat) *steering engine*; - nagel, m., s. *pin*; - quadrant, m., *s. quadrant*; - rad, n., *s. wheel*; - - bezug, m., *s. w. cover*; - - kranz, m., *rim of s. w.*; - - nabe, f., *boss of s. w.*; - - spake, or - - speiche, f., *spoke of s. w.*; - reep, n., *tiller rope*; - - block, m., *wheel rope block*: - ruder, n., *rudder*; - stangen, *steering rods*: - - schutzblech, n., *s. rod cover*; - - stühle, *s. r. stools*; - strich im Kompaßgehäuse, m., *Lubber's point*; - telegraph, m., *steering telegraph*; - vermögen, n., *steerage*; - welle, f., *reversing shaft*.

steuern, *to steer*; beim Winde -, *t. s. by the wind*; geradezu -, *s. as you go*; gut -, *t. s. well*; Kurs -, *t. s. course*; nach dem Anker zu -, *t. s. to the anchor*; n. d. Seegange -, *t. s. by the sea*; nach der Leeseite eines anderen Schiffes -, *to bear under the lee*; nach den Sternen -, *t. steer by the stars*; westwärts -, *t. s. westward*.

steuert, Wie - das Schiff? *How does she carry her helm?* es - gut, *she is steering well*.

Steuerung, f., *distributing mechanism*; - von Stephenson, *link motion*.

Steuerungs-hahn, m., *distributing cock*; - hebel, m., *d. lever*; - stange, f., *reversing rod*; - welle, f., *weigh bar*.

Steurer, m., *helmsman*.

Steven, m., *1. stem (fore)*; *2. stern post (aft)*; - anlauf, m., *gripe*; - knie, n., *gammon knee*; - lauf, m., *fore foot*; - platte, f., *stem plate*; - rohr, n., *stern tube*; - - büchse, f., *s. bush*; - - flansch, m., *s. tube flange*; - - packung, f., *s. t. packing*; - - welle, f., *propeller shaft*; - stütze, f., *prop of the stem*.

Stewardskammer, f., *steward's room*.

Stich, m., *bend (of a rope)*; -

auf Halsen und Schoten! *Up tacks and sheets!*

Stiel, m., *handle*; - boje, f., *stream buoy*; - meißel, m., *round chisel*.

Stiffening, f., *stiffening (cargo or ballast for keeping the vessel upright)*.

Stift, m., *pin*; - eines Schäkelbolzens, *shackle bolt pin*; - schraube, f., *stud bolt*; - - der Schraubennabe, *propeller s. b.*; - - mutter, f., *s. b. nut*; - - - der Schraubennabe, *propeller s. b. n.*

still, *calm*.

Stille, f., *calm*; von - überfallen, *becalmed*.

Stillengürtel, m., *calms*.

Stiller Ocean, m., *Pacific Ocean*.

Stillstand, m., das Schiff zum - bringen, *to bring the ship stationary in the water*.

Stillwasser, n., *lowest of the ebb*.

Stirn-fläche eines Radzahnes, f., *face of a tooth of a wheel*; - getriebe, n., *spur pinion*; - rad, n., *1. spur wheel*; *2. main cone driving w. (of steam windlass)*; - zapfen, m., *gudgeon*.

Stocher, m., *poker*.

Stock, m., *staff*; - finster, *pitch dark*; - lägel, m., *upper cringle*; - loser Buganker, m., *stockless bower*; - pferd, n., *Flemish horse*; - schäkel, m., *stock shackle*; - unklarer Anker, m., *anchor fouled by the stock*.

stöhnen, *to creak*.

Stopfbüchse, f., *stuffing box*; - der Schraubenwelle, *propeller shaft s. b.*; - des Ruderkopfes, *s. b. round rudder head*; - des Stevenrohrs, *stern gland*; hintere - des S., *after s. g.*; - deckel, m., *stuffing box gland*; - - des Stevenrohrs, *stern tube g.*; - flansch, m., *stuffing box flange*; - liderung or -

packung, f., *gland packing*;
- reiniger, m., *p. worm*; -
ring, m., *neck ring of a
stuffing box*; - schott, n.,
s. b. bulkhead; - - winkel,
m., *s. b. b. angle bar*; -
Sicherungsstift, m., *gland
safety stud*; - stift, m., *g.
stud*; - - schraube, f., *stuffing
box g. s.*
Stopf-eisen, n., *chinsing iron*;
- matte, f., or - tuch, n.,
fother mat.
stopfen, *to chinse (by chinsing
iron).*
Stopp-bindsel, n., *tie*; - stück,
n., *furring*; - vorrichtung des
Ankerspills, f., *compressors
of the windlass.*
stoppen, *to stop*; ein Tau -,
to hold on a rope; gut -, *to
stop well (rope, hawser, &c).*
Stopper, m., *preventer stopper*;
einen - aufsetzen, *to nip*; -
bolzen, m., *stopper bolt*; -
ende, n., *nipper*; - Hand-
speichenbüchse, f., *box plate
for stop bar*; - knoten, m.,
stopper knot; - stek, m.,
magnus hitch; - talje, f.,
guy tackle; - - des Besanbaums, *lazy g. of the mizzen
boom.*
störende Kraft, f., *perturbating power.*
Stoß, m., *1. impact (of collision); 2. butt (of planks and
plates)*; der dichte -, *close
butt*; *3. jerk (in cylinder)*;
- blech, n., *butt strap*; -
bolzen, m., *b. bolt*; - durchbolzen, m., *butt through bolt*;
- eisen, n., *billiard*; - fuge,
f., *butt seam*; - geerden,
preventer vangs; - kalb, n.,
butt chock; - kante, f., *b.
edge (of a plate)*; - keile,
launching wedges; - kissen,
n., *1. buffer (for machinery);
2. puddening (for any other
purpose)*; - klampe, f., *stop
cleat*; - kraft, f., *percussive
force*; - lappen, m., *top
lining*; - matte, f., *rigging

mat; - nietung, f., *butt riveting*; - platte, f., *b. strap*; -
polster, n., *spring buffer*;
- schale, f., *rubbing paunch*;
- schalen, *yard battens*; -
schweißung, f., *butt weld*;
- see, f., *head sea*; - talje,
f., *rolling tackle*; - - stropp,
m., *quarter strop*; - - tau,
n., *rolling rope*; - tau,
n., *swifter*; - verbindung, f.,
butt joint; - vernietung, f.,
b. riveting; - verteilung, f.,
shift of butts; - weger, m.,
thick strakes of ceiling; -
wind, m., *gust of wind*; -
winkel, m., *butt strap angle
bar*; mittelst - - gelaschtes
Spant, n., *butted frame.*
stoßen, *striking.*
Stößt ab! *Shove off!*
Straffheit, f., *tautness.*
straff, *taut*; - machen, *to
tauten.*
Strahl, m., *jet (of water or
steam)*; - pumpe, f., *j. pump*;
- schaufelrad, n., *radial
paddle wheel.*
strahlende Wärme, f., *radiating heat.*
Strahlung, f., *radiation.*
Strähne, f., *hank.*
Strak, f., *1. strake (of plating);
2. band (on the reef tackle).*
stramm, *taut.*
Strand, m., *beach*; - amt, n.,
strand office; - batterie, f.,
shore battery; - behörde, f.,
strand authorities; - dieb, m.,
longshore thief; - gut, n.,
godsend; - läufer, m., *land-
lubber*; - raub, m., *plunder-
ing goods from a wreck*; -
räuber, m., *wrecker*; - recht,
n., *strand right*; - richter,
m., *arbitrator of averages*;
- see, m., *lagoon*; - steine,
boulders; - vogt, m., *wreck
master.*
stranden, *stranding.*
Strandungs-fall, m., *case of
stranding*; - karte, f., *wreck
chart*; - ordnung, f., *law of
salvage*; - ort or - platz, m.,

or - stelle, f., *place of stranding*.

Straßenordnung, f., *the rules of the road*.

Strauchbake, f., *perch*.

Strebe, f., *stay, shore*; - des Ruderrahmens, *rudder stay*; - einer Relingsstütze, *spur of a bulwark stay*.

Streber-Backstag, n., *after guy of the sprit sail guy*.

Streck-barkeit, f., *malleability*; - bug, m., *good board*; einen guten - - machen, *to make a g. b.*; - eisen, n., *rolled iron*; - kette, f., *ridge chain (of an awning)*; - tau, n., 1. *r. c. (of an a.)*; 2. *lee fang (for lacing a bonnet)*; 3. *life buoy line (for life saving)*.

streichen, 1. *to strike (the flag, the mast)*; 2. mit den Riemen -, *to hold water*; m. d. R. rückwärts -, *to back water*.

Streicht die Rahe! *Down the yard!* - schnell die Segel! *Strike amain!*

streifen, *grazing (a vessel)*.

streifender Schlag, m., *grazing blow*.

Streik, m., *strike*.

streiken, *to strike*.

Streit verkünden, *to vouch*; - verkünder, m., *voucher*.

Strich, m., *point*; - kompaß, m., *steering compass*; - rose, f., 1. *point*; 2. *flower of the winds*.

Stringer, m., 1. *stringer*; 2. band (of the reefing tackle); - platte, f., *stringer plate*; - - eines Wetterdecks, *gunwale p.*: - winkel, m., *stringer angle bar*; - - eisen, n., *s. a. iron*.

Strohk, m., *sheer (of a ship)*; - leine, f., *ram line*.

Strok, m., 1. *sheer (of a ship)*; 2. band (on the reef tackle).

Strom, m., 1. *river* od. *stream*; 2. *current (of air, electricity, water)*; der - kentert, *the tide turns*; wider den -

segeln, *to stem the tide*: gegen den -, *against the tide*; mit dem -, *with the t.*

strom-abwärts, *down the river*; - anker, m., *stream anchor*; - - kette, f., *s. cable*; - aufwärts, *up the river*; - enge, f., *narrow channel*: - gefälle, n., *slope of the stream*; - gerecht legen, *to square up*; - kabbelung, f., *race tide rip*; - karte, f., *current chart*; - kenterung, f., *turn of the tide*; - mündung f., *mouth of the river*; - polizei, f., *river police*; - recht liegen, *to be tide rode*; - regulierung, f., *river regulating*; - richtung, f., *setting of the current*; - rinne, f., *channel*; - rippling, m., *tide rip*; - schnelle, f., *rapid*; - segeln, n., *current sailing*; - stille, f., *calm of current*; - strecke, f., *reach*; - strich, m., *tide way*; - strudel, m., *whirlpool of the current*; - trosse, f., *stream hawser*; - versetzung, f., *drift*; wegen - - verbesserter Kurs, *course corrected for current*: - wechsel, m., *turn of the tide*; - welle, f. *tide rip*.

Strömler, m., *stream ice*.

Strömung, f., *current*; die - ausgleichen, *to counteract the c.*

Stropp, m., 1. *strop*; 2. *sling (attached to crane or derrick)*; - am Unterende eines Stags, *lower collar of a stay*; - rack, n., *parrel with short and long leg*; - tau, n., *strap cable*.

stroppen, *to strap (a block)*.

Stroppen, *quarter slings (of a yard)*; 2. *strop (of a block)*.

Strudel, m., *whirlpool*.

Stück-arbeit, f., *piece work*; - güter, *general cargo*.

Stücke, in - schlagen, *to smash to pieces*.

Stückpforten, *gun ports*; - klappe, f., *half port*.

Stufen, *rounds* (*of a boat's ladder*).
Stufscherbe, f., *butt scarf*.
Stuhl, m., *stool*; - eines Schaufelrades, *paddle wheel bracket*.
Stülpluke, f., *hatch cover*.
stümpern, *to botch*.
Stumpfbolzen, m., *dump bolt*; - Befestigung, f., *d. b. fastening*.
stumpfer Winkel, m., *obtuse angle*.
Stundenwinkel, m., *horary angle*.
Sturm, m., 1. *gale* (*force 7—10*); 2. *storm* (*force 11*); den - gut anshalten, *to make good weather*; den - schlecht aushalten, *to m. bad w.*
Sturm-besan, m., *storm mizen*; - bö aus heiterem Himmel, f., *white squall*; - - mit viel Regen od. Schnee, *thick s.*; - - mit Wolkenansammlung, *arched s.*; - deck, n., *awning deck*.
Sturmdeckbalken, m., *awning deck beam*; - Längsschiene, f., or - Lukenstringer, m., *a. d. b. tie plate*; - stringer, m., *a. d. b. stringer*; - - platte, f., *a. d. b. s. plate*; - winkel, m., *a. d. b. angle bar*.
Sturmdeck-geländer, n., *awning deck rail and stanchions*; - - stütze, f., *a. d. s.*; - luke, f., *a. d. hatchway*; - - süll, m., *a. d. h. coaming*; - Schergang, m., *a. d. sheerstrake*; - schiff, n., *a. d. ship*; - Seitenbeplattung, f., *a. d. side plating*; - stringer, m., *a. d. stringer*; - - platte, f., *a. d. s. plate*; - - winkel, m., *a. d. s. angle bar*; - stütze, f., *a. d. pillar*; - Wassergang, m., *a. d. waterway*.
Sturm-drachen, m., *storm kite*; - flagge, f., *s. flag*; - flut, f., *s. flood*; - fock, f., or - - segel, n., *fore staysail*; - kegelsignal, n., *storm cone*;

- klüver, m., *s. jib*; - - fall, n., *fore topmast staysail halliard*; - laterne, f., *hurricane deck lamp*; - leiter, f., *rope ladder*; - region, f., *storm region*; - rose, f., *storm card*; - segel, n., *s. sail*; - signal, n., *storm signal*; - - Zylinder, m., *storm drum*; - stag, n., *s. stay*; - - segel, n., *s. s. sail*; - warnung, f., *storm warning*; - wolke, f., or - zeichen, n., *s. breeder*.
stürmisch, *gusty, rough, stormy, tempestuous*.
Stürze, f., *shoot*.
stürzen, sich -, *to engulf* (*a river*).
Sturz-güter, *goods laden in bulk*; - see, f., *breaker*; hinten überkommende - -, *pooping sea*; - weise, *in bulk*.
Stütz! *Meet her*; - balken, m., *shifting beam*; innere - - der Spanten, *pales*; - haken, m., *hinge hook*; - klammern, *boiler braces*; - platte, f., *bracket*; - - des Steuergeräts, *steering gear b.*; - - unter einem Fingerling, *dumb chalder*; - punkt, m., *fulcrum* (*of a lever*).
Stütze, f., 1. *stanchion, stay, prop*; 2. *pillar* (*principally for the support of decks*); 3. *fulcrum* (*of a lever*); 4. *stud* (*of a chain cable link*); 5. *bracket* (*of the head rail*); fast senkrecht stehende -, *proppet*.
stützen, 1. *to meet the helm, to steady the ship*; 2. *to flap* (*backstays in case of broken masts*).
Stützen-fuß, m., *heel of a pillar*; - kopf, m., *p. head*; - leiter, f., *p. ladder*; - sockel, m., or - spur, f., *stanchion socket*.
Stuufbolzen or Stuvbolzen, m., *dump bolt*.
Submission, f., *tender*.
Subvention, f., *subsidy*.

Süd gewinnen or - machen, *to gain south.*

südlich, *southerly.*

südliche Breite, f., *latitude south*; - Eismeer, n., *Antarctic Ocean*; - Halbkugel, f., *southern hemisphere*; - Weite, f., *s. amplitude.*

Südlicht, n., *southern light.*

Südost Monsun, m., *south east monsoon*; - Passat, m., *s. e. trades*; - - drift, m., *s. e. t. drift*; - Wind, m., *s. e. wind*; S. O. zu O., *S. E. by E.*

Südpol-Expedition, f., *South Pole Expedition.*

südwärts, *southward.*

Süd-West-Monsun, m., *south west monsoon.*

Südwester, m., *southwester.*

Süll, m., *coaming*; - des Back-schotts, *c. of forecastle bulkhead*; - des Quarterdeck-schotts, *c. of raised quarter deck b.*; - platte, f., *c. plate*; - - des Maschinenraum-schachts, *c. p. of trunk bulkhead*; - - des Oberlichts, *skylight c.*; - winkel, m., *c. angle bar.*

Sund, m., *sound.*

Supercargo, m., *supercargo.*

Surf, m., *surf.*

Süßwasser, n., *fresh water*; - pumpe, f., *f. w. pump.*

Suut, der - des Schiffes von vorn bis hinten, *the dead rising.*

Swabber, m., *swab.*

Swell, m., *swell.*

System-Schwerpunkt, m., *centre of gravity.*

T.

tabellarische Übersicht, f., *tabular synopsis.*

Tabelle, f., *table.*

Tackbolzen, m., *sprig bolt.*

Tacken, *1. sprigs (of a bolt)*; *2. arms (of a knee).*

Tafeleis, n., *ice floes.*

täfeln, *to wainscot.*

Täfelung, f., or Täfelwerk, n., *wainscotting.*

Tag-arbeit, f., *day work*; - der Einklarierung, m., *day of entry*; - dienst, m., *d. service*; - licht, n., *d. light*; - signal, n., *d. signal*; - wache, f., *morning watch.*

Tagebuch, n., *log book.*

Tage in See, *passage days.*

Tages-anbruch, m., *day break*; - schicht, f., *d. work.*

täglicher Anker, m., *second bower.*

Taifun, m., *typhoon.*

Takel, n., *purchase*; das - steht, *the tackle will not p.*; ein - anbringen or aufsetzen, *to raise a p.*; - auf -, *tackle upon t.*

Takelage, f., *rigging*; - arbeiten, *r. works.*

Takel-boden, m., *rigging loft*; - block, m., *purchase block*; - garn, n., *whipping twine*; - haken, m., *tackle hook*; - läufer, m., *purchase fall*; - werk, n., *rigging*; - - statt, f., *r. loft.*

Takeler, m., *rigger.*

Takelung, f., *rigging (of a ship)*; *2. whip (of a rope).*

Takt beim Rudern, *to pull stroke.*

Tal-fahrt, f., *passage down the river*; - wärts, *d. t. r.*

Talg-baumholz, n., *tallow wood*; - behälter or - kasten, m., *t. tank*; - hahn, m., *tallow cock*; - kessel, m., *t. kettle*; - napf, m., *t. cup*; - spaten, m., *t. spade*; - spritze, f., *t. syringe*; - trage, f., *t. carrier.*

Talje, f., *tackle*; - auf -, *luff upon l.*; - aus einem ein- und zweischeibigem Block, *l. tackle*; - block, m., *tackle block*; - haken, m., *t. hook*; - läufer, m., *t. fall*; - mann, m., *tally clerk*; - reep, n., *lanyard*; - - bindsel, n., *l. seizing*; - - der Pardunen, *backstay l.*; - - der Wanten, *shroud l.*; - - knoten, m., *Matthew Walker knot*; - - matte, f., *lanyard mat.*

taljen, *to bowse.*

Tamaracholz, n., *tamarac wood.*

Tamp, n., *rope's end.*

Tandem-Maschine, f., *tandem engine.*

Tangente, f., *touching line.*

Tank, m., *tank*; - dampfer, m., *t. vessel*; - decke, f., *crown of t.*; - deckenplatte, f., *inner bottom plate*; - fach, n., *chamber of a tank*; - füllrohr, n., *t. filling pipe*; - füllventil, n., *t. f. valve*; - - deckel, m., *t. f. v. cover*; - - sitz, m., *t. f. v. seat*; - - spindel, f., *t. f. v. spindle*; - rohr, n., *t. pipe*; - saugerohr, n., *t. suction pipe*; - saugeventil, n., *t. s. valve*; - schiff, n., *t. vessel*; - seitenplatte, f., *margin plate*; - seitenwinkel, m., *tank side angle bar*; - topp, m., *top of tank*; - - platte, f., *inner bottom plate.*

Tannenholz, n., *fir wood.*

tanzen, auf und nieder -, *to be bobbing.*

Tartane, f., *tartan.*

Tasche, f., *shredding.*

Taschen-bunker, m., *pocket bunker*; - fernrohr, n., *kenning glass.*

Taster, m., *callipers.*

Tätigkeit der Schraube, f., *action of the propeller.*

Tau, n., *rope*; an einem - holen or trecken or ziehen, *to pull on a r.*; - mit einem

Katsteert, *pointed laid r.*; - zum Fieren, *check r.*

Tau-bucht, f., *bight (of a rope)*; - ducht, f., *strand (of a rope)*; - fender, m., *rope fender*; - gestroppter Block, m., *r. stropped block*; - haken, m., *cable hook*; - kabelar, m., *rope messenger*; - kragen, m., *garland*; - kranz, m., *grommet*; - matte, f., *rope mat*; - packung, f., *r. packing*; - raum, m., *swallow (of a block)*; - stopper, m., *rope stopper*; - stropp, m., *r. strop*; - trommel, f., *wire winch*; - werk, n., *cordage*; - - rolle, f., *fake (of a coil of rope)*; - wulst, m., *puddening.*

tauchen, *diving.*

Taucher, m., *diver*; - anzug, m., *diving suit*; - glocke, f., *d. bell*; - kasten, m., *d. case*; - kolben, m., *plunger piston*; - rüstung, f., *scaphander.*

Tauchung, f., 1. *immersion (of the ship)*; 2. *dip (of the paddle wheels).*

tauen, *to tow.*

taufen, 1. *to name (a ship)*; 2. *to duck (when passing the line).*

tanglich, *fit.*

Tausendbein, n., *rack.*

Teakholz or Teckholz, n., *teak wood.*

Teer, m., *tar*; - bütte. f., *t. bucket*; - faß, n., *t. barrel*; - firnis, m., *black varnish*; heller - -, *bright v.*; - hanf, m., *coats*; - jacke, f., *Jack Tar*; - kleid or - tuch, n., *tarpaulin*; - pütze, f., *tar bucket*; - quast, m., *t. brush*; - werg, n., *coats.*

teeren, 1. *to tar*; 2. *to pay (the bottom).*

teerig, *tarry.*

Teers, Teersje or Teertsje, f., *toggle.*

Teifun, m., *typhoon.*

Teile und Zubehör, *parts and fittings.*

teilweise Doppelboden, m., *part double bottom*; - eisernes Deck, n., *partial iron deck*; - versichert, *partly insured.*
Teilzirkel, m., *divider.*
T-eisen, n., *T-iron.*
Telegraphen-bezug, m., *telegraph cover*; - draht, m., *t. wire*: - kabel, n., *t. cable*; - stativ, n., *t. stand.*
Teleskop, n., *telescope*; - Schornstein, m., *telescopic funnel.*
Teller-bort, n., *drain board*; - ventil, n., *cup valve.*
Temperatur, f., *temperature.*
temporäre Reparatur, f., *temporary repairs.*
Tender, m., *tender.*
Terpentin, n., *turpentine*; - baumholz, n., *t. wood.*
Teuanker, m., *small bower.*
Teufelsklaue, f., *sling dogs.*
T-förmige Pleyelstange, f., *T-ended connecting rod.*
thanen, *to tan.*
theoretische Kraft, f., *theoretical power*; - Pferdestärke, f., *t. horse p.*
Thermometer, n., *thermometer.*
Thinghamholz, n., *thingham wood.*
Thornycroftheck, n., *Thornycroft stern.*
Tjalk, f., *small cuff.*
Tide, f., *1. shift (day's work)*; *2. tide*; die - beginnt, *the t. makes*; die - kentert, *t. t. turns*; die - läßt nach, *t. t. slackens*; die - läuft ab, *t. t. falls*; die - läuft aus, *t. t. runs out*; die - setzt um, *t. t. changes*; die - steigt, *t. t. rises*; die - wird schwach, *t. t. gets slack*; die - - schwächer, *t. t. g. weaker*; die - - stärker, *t. t. gains.*
tief-beladen, *deeply laden*; - gebaut, *deep in the hold*; - gehend, *of d. draught*; - gehendes Schiff, n., *deep going ship*; zu - gehend, *drawing too much water*; 25

Fuß - gehendes Schiff, *she is drawing 25 feet of water*; - geladen, *deep laden.*
Tiefe, f., *1. depth (ship and water)*; *2. drop (sail)*; *3. moulding (floor)*; - von der Oberkante des Kiels biz zur Oberkante des Oberdeckbalkens, *depth from top of keel to top of weather deck beam.*
Tiefgang, m., *draught*; den - aichen or abmarken, *to mark the d.*; - messer, m., *instrument for measuring the draught.*
Tief-ladelinie, f., *load water line*; - lot, n., *deep sea load*; - - leine, f., *d. s. lead line*; - lotungsapparat, m., *sounder*; - seefischerei, f., *d. s. fishery*; - seeforschung, f., *d. s. exploring*; - seekabel, n., *d. s. cable*; - seelotung, f., *d. s. sounding*; - wasserlinie, f., *d. water line*; - wasserlot, n., *d. sea lead.*
Tiegelgußstahl, m., *crucible steel.*
Tier, m., *tier.*
Tippen, n., *tipping.*
Timmerstich, m., *timber hitch.*
Tischtuch, n., *mess cloth.*
Todesfall, m., *casualty.*
Tod-holz, n., *deadwood*; - - bolzen, m., *d. bolt*; - punkt, m., *dead point*; - wasser, n., *d. water.*
Ton, m., *1. sound (of the bell, &c.)*; *2. blast (of the steam whistle).*
Tonnagegeld, n., *tonnage dues.*
Tonne, f., *1. barrel*; *2. buoy (water mark)*; *3. ton (measure).*
Tonnen, *tons*; - boje, f., *tun buoy*; - floß, n., *raft of casks*; - gehalt, m., *tonnage*; - - unter Deck, *t. under deck*; - geld, n., *t. dues*; - und Bakengeld, n., *buoy and beacon dues*; - linie, f., or - strich, m., *inside the line of the buoys*; - rack, n., *barrel*

parrel; - zahl gebaut, tonnage built.
Topf, m., bucket.
Topp, m., mast head; - des Fockmastes, fore m. h.; - des Großmastes, main m. h.; - des Jiggermastes, jigger mast h.; - des Kreuzmastes, mizen m. h.; - der Marsstenge, topmast h.; - der Vorstenge, fore t. h.; vor - und Takel, under bare poles.
Topp-auflanger, m., top timber; - band, n., mast head hoop; - block, m., span block; - gast, m., top man; - jolle, f., t. whip; - ketten, t. chains; - licht, n., mast head light; - platte, f., 1. rider plate (of keelson); 2. top p. (of steering gear); - reep, n., top rope.
Toppsegel, n., topsail; - Bauchgording, f., t. bunt line; - brasse, f., t. brace; - - schenkel, m., t. b. pendant; - Drehreep, n., t. tye; - fall, m., topsail halliard; - Geitau, n., t. clew line; - mit Schotrahe, jackyarder; - rahe, f., topsail yard; - Refftalje, f., t. reef tackle; - Schoner, m., t. schooner; - schote, f., t. sheet.
Topp-sente, f., top timber line; - tau, n., or - talje, f., top rope; - wimpel, m., narrow pennant; - winkel am Zenterkiel, m., top angle bars at the centre keel.
toppen, to top.
Toppen, über die - geflaggt, to dress with overall flags.
Toppenant, f., topping lift; - block, m., l. block; - der Marsrahe or - der Toppsegelrahe, topsail l.; - gien, n., top tackle; - talje, f., lift purchase; - - block, m., l. p. block; - - läufer, m., l. p. fall.
Torfbagger, m., peat drag.
Törn, m., 1. turn (of a lashing or seizing); 2. spell (period

of employment); - am Ruder, spell on the wheel; - zur Koje, spell below.
törnen, to turn.
Törn-holz, n., raft; - tau, n., check rope.
Törns ausdrehen, to take turns out; - eindrehen, to t. t. in a rope; die oberen - einer doppelten Laschung or eines doppelten Bindsels, upper turns of a lashing od. seizing.
Torsion, f., torsion.
Torsionskraft, f., twisting force.
Total-druck, m., total pressure; - effekt, m., whole effect; - leistung, f., gross e.; - verlust, m., total loss.
tote Gewicht, n., dead weight; - Punkt, m., d. point; - Scheibe, f., dumb sheave; - Scheibengat, n., half s. hole; - Werk, n., dead work.
totenstill or Totenstille, f., dead calm.
totsegeln, to outsail; to stem the tide.
Tour, f., trip, excursion; - dampfer, m., e. steamer.
Tracht, f., burthen.
Track, m., track; - karte, f., t. chart.
Trag-balken, m., girder; - fähigkeit, f., burthen; - lager, n., tunnel bearing; - - bolzen, m., pillow block bolt.
tragen, to carry.
Träger, m., 1. bracket (of valve rod and crosshead guide); 2. girder (of double bottom); 3. dog (of man hole door and crown plate); - bolzen, m., dog stay; - Kielschwein, n., middle line vertical plate keelson; - platte, f., girder plate; - winkel, m., g. angle bar.
Trägheitsmoment, n., momentum of inertia.
trägt 1200 Tonnen, carries 1200 tons.
tränen, to weep.

Traljeschott, n., *bulkhead of gratings.*

Tramp, m., *tramp;* - dampfer, m., *t. steamer.*

Tranfahrt, f., *fish oil trade.*

transatlantischeDampferlinie, f., *Transatlantic steamer line;* - Handel, m., *T. trade;* - Kabel, n., *T. cable.*

Transit, m., *transit;* - güter, *t. goods;* - verkehr, m., *t. traffic.*

Transmission, f., *motion;* - welle, f., *transmitting shaft.*

Transomplatte, f., *transom plate.*

Transport, m., *transport;* - kosten, *cartage;* - schiff, n., *transport;* - versicherung, f., *t. insurance.*

transportieren, *to convey;* - per Schiff, *to carry by bottom.*

trapezoidisches Segel, n., *trapezoidal sail.*

Trauerflagge, f., *flag half mast.*

traven, *to steeve.*

Traverse, f., *crosshead;* - des Ankerspills, *windlass c.;* - der Luftpumpe, *air pump c.;* - des Steuergeräts, *steering apparatus c.;* - der Zirkulationspumpe, *circulation pump c.*

trawen, *to steeve.*

Trawldampfer, m., *steam trawler.*

Treck-säge, f., *cross cut;* - schute, f., *track scout.*

Treffpunkt, m., *point of impact (of a collision).*

Treib-anker, m., *driving anchor;* - bake, f., *floating beacon;* - band, n., *drift hoop;* - eis, n., *floating ice;* - gut, n., *flotsam;* - hammer, m., *chasing hammer;* - kette, f., *messenger chain;* - kraft, f., *moving power;* - land, n., *Cape-fly-away;* - netzfischer, m., *drifter;* - fischerei, f., *drift fishery;* - rad, n., *driving wheel;* - sand, m., *shift-ing sand;* - segel, n., *drag sail.*

treiben, *to drive;* auf Strand -, *to d. ashore;* gegen ein anderes Schiff -, *to fall aboard another vessel;* sich - lassen, *to keep dodging;* vor schleppendem Anker -, *to be clubbing;* zum - liegen, *to lie ahull.*

treibend, *adrift;* auf seiner Ladung -, *water logged.*

treibende Gegenstände, *floating objects;* - Wracktrümmer, f. *wreckage.*

treibendes Eis, n., *drift ice.*

Treiber, m., *lug mizen;* - fall, m., *driver halliard;* - mast, m., *jigger mast;* - rahe, f., *driver yard;* - Toppsegel, n., *lug mizen topsail.*

Treidel-pfad, m., *tow path;* - stange, f., *stour.*

treideln, *1. to track (at sea); 2. to tow (on the river).*

Treidler, m., *hobbler.*

Treisegel, n., *trysail;* - Ausholer, m., *t. outhaul;* - baum, m., *t. boom;* - Dempgordinge, *t. brails;* - Einholer, m., *t. inhaul;* - fall, n., *t. halliard;* - gaffel, f., *t. gaff;* - - gerde, f., *t. vang;* - geitaue, *t. brails;* - gerde, f., *t. vang;* - hals, m., *t. tack;* - Klaufall, m., *t. throat halliard;* - Piekfall, m., *t. peak h.;* - schote, f., *t. sheet.*

Trempel, m., *sill.*

trennen, *to unstitch.*

Trennungs-platte, f., *division plate;* - rippe des Kondensators, f., *d. p. of condenser.*

trensen, *to worm.*

Trensgarn, n., *pointing line.*

Trensing, f., *worming;* - ausfüllen, *to back the w.*

Treppe, f., *ladder;* - der Back, *forecastle ladder;* - zum erhöhten Quarterdeck, *raised quarter deck l.*

treppenweise Verschießung, f., *step butted.*

Treul or Treut, f., *clinch* Trichter, m., *funnel*. [*ring*. Trieb-kraft, f., *moving force*; - rad, n., *driving wheel*; - welle, f., *d. shaft*; - werk, n., *gear*.

triftig, *1. drifting, adrift, to get* or *to break adrift* (*said of a ship*); *2. anchor dragging* od. *a. brought home* (*said of ship and anchor*); *3. dragging her moorings* (*said of ship and m.*).

Trift-holz und Schaum, *scum of the sea*; - strom, m., *drift current*; - strömung, f., *surface current*; - winkel, m., *drift angle*.

Trimm, m., *trim*; in gutem -, *in good t.*; aus dem - or nicht im -, *out of t.*; - tank, m., *trimming tank*.

trimmen, *to trim.*

Trimmer, m., *trimmer*; - lampe, f., *t. lamp*; - schaufel, f., *trimming shovel.*

Trink-kanne, f., *monkey*; - wasser-Destillierapparat, m., *fresh water condenser*; - wassertonne, f., *scuttle cask.*

Tripel or Tripelstein, m., *rotten stone.*

Trissen der Blinden, *spritsail braces.*

Tritt, m., *step* (*of a ladder*); - brett, n., *treadle* (*of a lathe*); - klampen, *side steps*; - leiter, f., *step ladder.*

trocken fallen bei Niedrigwasser, *to fall dry at low water*; das Schiff ist 2 Fuß - gefallen, *the ship is sewed up two feet.*

Trocken-dock, n., *dry dock*; - fäule, f., *d. rot.*

trockene Kondensation, f., *dry condensation*; - Proviant, m., *d. provisions.*

trockener Dampf, m., *dry steam.*

trocknen, *to dry* (*the sails*).

Troier, blauer -, m., *Jersey frock.*

Trombe, f., *waterspout.*

Trommel, f., *1. barrel* (*of winch, steam w., and steering gear*); *2. trundle head* (*of windlass*); - welle, f., *barrel shaft* (*of winch and steam w.*).

Trompete, f., *cat's paw*; - stek or - stich, m., *sheep shank.*

Tromptau, n., *lasher.*

Tropfstelle, f., *weep hole.*

Trosse, f., *hawser.*

Trossenstich, m., *half hitch and seizing.*

trossweise geschlagenes Tau, n., *hawser laid rope.*

Troyer, m., *Jersey.*

trübe, *gloomy.*

Trümmer, *wreckage.*

Trunkdeck see Kofferdeck.

Trunk-kolben, m., *trunk piston*; - maschine, f., *t. engine*; - seitenbeplattung, f., *trunk side plating*; - zapfen, m., *trunnions*; - - des oscillierenden Zylinders, *oscillating cylinder trunnions*; - - des Zylinders, *c. t.*

Trupp Arbeiter, m., *gang of labourers.*

Tucksche Liderung, f., *Tuck's packing.*

Tüg, n., *rigging.*

Tulpenbaumholz, n., *tulip wood.*

Tunnel, m., *tunnel*; - beplattung, f., *t. plating*; - brunnen, m., *t. well*; - decke, f., *top of t.*; - flurplatten, *tunnel flooring*; - kammer or - nische, f., *t. recess*; - spanten, *t. frames*; - tür, f., *t. door*; - Ventilator, m., *t. ventilator*; - welle, f., *t. shaft*; - - flansch, m., *t. s. flange*; - - Kühlhahn, m., *t. cock*; - - Kühlvorrichtung, f., *t. water service*; - - Kuppelung, f., *t. shaft coupling*; - - - bolzen, m., *t. s. c. bolt*; - wellenlager, n., *t. s. bearing*; - - bolzen, m., *t. s. b. bolt*; - - - mutter, f., *t. s. b. b. nut*; - wellenlagerdeckel, m., *t. bearing keep*; - - bolzen, m., *plummer block*

keep bolt;- - -mutter, f., *p. b.*
k. b. nut; - wellenlagerzapfen,
m., *tunnel shaft journal*; -
wellenleitung, f., *t. shafting*.
Tür, f., *door*; - schwelle, f., *d.
sill*.
Turbine, f., *turbine*.
Turbinen-dampfer, m., *turbine
steamer*; - elektrischer Motor, m., *turbo electric motor*;
- Luft- und Zirkulations-
pumpe, f., *turbine air and
circulating pump*; - maschine, f., *t. engine*: - rad, n., *t.
wheel*.
Türkenkopf or türkischer
Knoten, m., *Turk's head*.
Turmdeck, n., *turret deck*; -
balken, m., *t. d. beam*; - -
stringer, m., *t. d. b. stringer*;
- - winkel, m., *t. d. b. angle
bar*; - beplattung, f., *t. d.
plating*; - dampfer, m., *t. d.
steamer*; - geländer, n., *t. d.
rails and stanchions*; - -

stangen, *t. d. guard rods*;
- - stütze, f., *t. d. stanchion*;
- luke, f., *t. d. hatchway*;
- - deckel, m., *t. d. hatch*; - -
süll, m., *t. d. hatchway
coaming*; - schergang. m.,
t. d. sheerstrake; - stringer,
m., *t. d. stringer*; - - winkel,
m., *t. d. s. angle bar*; -
stütze, f., *t. d. pillar*; -
Wassergang, m., *t. d. waterway*.
Turm-maschine, f., *steeple
engine*; - seitenbeplattung,
f.. *turret side plating*.
tuten, *to blow the whistle*.
Twille, f., *cant floor*.
T-Winkel, m., or - - maß, n.,
T-square; - Wulstbalken,
m., *T-bulb-beam*; - Wulst-
eisen, n., *T-bulb-iron*.
Twist, m., *cotton waste*.
Typ, m., *type*; Typenschiff,
n., *t. vessel*.
Typhun, m., *typhoon*.

U.

über achtern auf der Leeseite,
on the lee quarter.
Ueberall! Ueberall! *All hands
up!*
über Backbordbug, *on the
starboard tack*; - Bord, *over
board*; - - geschlagen, *carried away*; - den rechten
Bug fallen, *casting the right
way*; - den verkehrten B. f.,
c. t. wrong w.; - Kraft angestrengt, *strained*; - Stag
gehen, *to put about*; - Steuer
gehen, *to go astern*; - -
halsen, *box hauling*; - Steuerbordbug, *on the port tack*.
Ueber-anstrengung, f., *straining*; durch - - beschädigt,
strained; - blattung, f., *lap
seam*; - deckung des Schiebers, f., *lap of slide valve*;
- druck, m., or - - spannung,
f., *effective pressure*; - fahrt,

f., *passage*; lange - -, *long p.*;
kurze or schnelle - -, *quick p.*;
für die - - angemustert, *shipped by the run*; - - geld, n.,
passage money; - - stelle,
f., *ferry*; - fall, m., *clamp
(of a boat mast)*; - fällig,
overdue; - flüssiger Dampf,
m., *waste steam*; - fluten, *to
flood*; - gegangen, *shifted
(cargo)*; - gehen, 1. *shifting
(of cargo)*; 2. *to gybe (of a
boom)*; - gewicht, *overweight*;
- hängen, n., *rake (of a mast)*;
achter - -, *to hang aft*; -
hängend, *lapsiding (a listing
ship)*.
überhängende Kurbel, f.,
overhung crank; - Schaufelrad, n., *o. paddle wheel*;
- Steven, m., *raking stem*.
überheizt, *superheated*.
Ueberhitzer, m., *superheater*;

- Absperrventil, n., *s. stop valve*; - Druckprobe or - prüfung, f., *test of superheater*; - rohr, n., *s. tube*; - schlangen, *s. coils*; - Sicherheitsventil, n., *s. safety valve*; - tür, f., *s. door.*

über-hitzt, *superheated*; - hitzter Dampf, m., *s. steam.*

Ueberhitzung, f., *overheating of steam*; - rohr, n., *o. pipe.*

überholen, *1. to overhaul (i. e. inspecting ship or any part of her)*; *2. to fleet (i. e. changing a tackle)*; *3. to overhaul (another ship)*; *4. lurching (i. e. sudden movement of a ship)*; 5. - nach der Leeseite, *lee lurch*; - nach der Luvseite, *weather lurch.*

überholte Ankerkette, f., *range of a chain cable.*

über-kanten, *to slue*; - laden, *1. overladen (with cargo)*; *2. overpressed (with sails)*; - ladener Dampf, m., *wet steam*; - lappen, *to lap over*; - lappte Stöße, *lap butts*; - lappung, f., *overlap (of plating)*; - - dichtung, f., *lap joint*; - lasten, *to overfreight.*

Ueberlauf-rohr, n., *overflow pipe*; - ventil, n., *o. valve*; - - feder, f., *o. v. spring*; - - sitz, m., *o. v. seat*; - - spindel, f., *o. v. spindle.*

überlaufen. die Distanz -, *to overrun the log.*

über-legen, *to shift (the helm)*; - liegen, *to heel*; - liegetage, *days of demurrage*; - maß in Luken, n., *excess of hatchway*; - mäßiger Druck, m., *excessive pressure*; - mastet, *overmasted*; - nehmen, *to ship (cargo, water, &c.)*; - schießen, *1. to overshoot (when seeking anchorage)*; *2. to lap over (plates)*; 3. das - - zweier Enden von Planken, *the shift of two butts*; - schiffen, *to tranship, transhipment*; - schwemmen, *1.*

to flood (decks); 2. *to overflow (pipes)*; - schwemmung, f., *flowage.*

überseeisch, *transmarine.*

überseeische Produkte, *transmarine products*; - Verbindungen, *t. connections.*

überseeischer Besitz, m., *transmarine possession*; - Hafen, m., *t. port*; - Handel, m., *t. trade.*

über-segeln, *to pass right over a vessel od. to run down a. v.*; - setzen, *to ferry over (by ferry boat)*; - setzung wirkende Maschine, f., *geared engine*; - spänig, *cross grained*; - Stag gehen, *to put about*; - streifen, *to put the rigging on the masthead*; - strömen, *to overflow*; - strömrohr, n., *o. pipe*; - strömung, f., *flowage*; - takelt, *over rigged*; - tragen, *to consign*; - tragung, f., *transmission*; - - des Schiffsbauplans in natürlicher Größe auf dem Mallboden, *the laying down*; - treffen, *to take the shine out of*; - triebener Druck, m., *excessive pressure*; - versichert, *over insured*; - weben, *to graft*; - wintern, *to winter*; - winterung, f., *wintering*; - wölbte Hütte, f., *full poop*; - zeit, f., *overtime*; - zug, m., *cover.*

Uebungsgeschwader, n., *evolutionary squadron.*

Ufer, n., *shore*; - damm, m., *pier*; - geld, n., *shore dues*; - mauer, f., *river wall.*

Uhrbord, m., *traverse board.*

Ulmenholz, n., *elm wood.*

Umbau, m., *1. casing*; *2. rebuilding.*

umbrandet, *billow beaten.*

umbrassen, *to swing the yards round.*

umdrehen, *1. to slue round (the ship)*; *2. to reverse (engines).*

Umdrehung, f., *revolution*; -s geschwindigkeit, f., *rotary speed.*

Umfang, m., *size (of a rope).*

Umfangsnaht f., *circumferential seam.*

umgebaut, *rebuilt.*

umgekehrter Winkel, m., *reversed angle bar*; - Zylinder, m., *inverted cylinder.*

umgekippt, *overturned (boat).*

umgesprungen, *shifted (wind, cargo).*

umgürten mit Tauen, *to frap.*

Umgürtung, f., *frappings.*

umhergeschleudert vom Sturm, *storm tossed.*

umhergeworfen vom Seegange, *sea tossed.*

Umhüllung einer Nische, f., *recess bulkhead.*

umkehren, *to reverse.*

Umkehrstange, f., *reversing rod.*

umladen, *to tranship.*

Umlade-hafen, m., *port of transhipment*; - kran, m., *transfer elevator.*

Umladung, f., *transhipment.*

umlaufende Winde, *baffling winds.*

umlaufender Strom, m., *shifting current.*

umlegen, *1. to tack (the ship)*; *2. to shift (the helm, jibs).*

umschiffen, *to double.*

Umschiffer, m., *doubler.*

Umschlag, m., *tabling (of sails)*; - bohrer, m., *wimble with a crooked handle.*

umschlagen, *1. to capsize (a boat)*; *2. to relay (a rope)*; *3. to veer (wind).*

umschmeißen, *to bring the helm round.*

umsegeln, *to round (a cape)*; eine Landspitze vorsichtig -, *to haul round a point.*

Umsegelung, f., *circumnavigation.*

Umsegler, m., *doubler.*

Umsetzen, n., *change (of the tide).*

umspringender Wind, m., *shifting wind.*

umstauen, *to restow.*

Umstauer, m., *rummager.*

Umstauung, f., *rummage, restowage.*

umsteuerbar, *reversible.*

umsteuern, *to reverse.*

Umsteuerung, f., *reversing motion*; - kulisse, f., *r. link*; - hebel, m., *r. lever.*

Umsteuerungsmaschine, f., *reversing engine*; - Absperrventil, n., *r. e. stop valve*; - Anlaßventil, n., *r. e. starting valve*; - - handhabe, f., *r. e. s. v. handle*; - Coulisse, f., *r. e. slide valve*; - - stein, m., *r. e. link block*; - Dampfabführungsrohr, n., *r. e. exhaust pipe*; - D-zuleitungsrohr, n., *r. e. steam pipe*; - Excenter, n., *r. e. eccentric*; - - bolzen, m., *r. e. e. bolt*; - - bügel, m., *r. e. e. strap*; - - - bolzen, m., *r. e. e. s. bolt*; - - - Paßstück, n., *r. e. e. s. liner*; - Excenter-Lagerschalen, *r. e. e. brasses*; - E.-scheibe, f., *r. e. e. sheave*; - E.-stange, f., *r. e. e. rod*; - Exhaustrohr, n., *r. e. eduction pipe*; - Handrad, n., *r. e. worm wheel*; - Hängeschiene, f., *r. e. drag link*; - Hebel, m., *r. e. weigh shaft lever*; - Kolben, m., *r. e. piston*; - - stange, f., *r. e. p. rod*; - - - Kreuzkopf, m., *r. e. p. r. crosshead*; - - - Stopfbüchse, f., *r. e. p. r. stuffing box*; - - - - deckel, m., *r. e. p. r. s. b. gland*; - Kreuzkopflagerbolzen, m., *r. e. crosshead bolt*; - Kreuzkopf lagerschalen, *r. e. c. brasses*; - - deckel, m., *r. e. connecting rod top end keep*; - Kulisse, f., *r. e. slide valve*; - - stein, m., *r. e. link block*; - Kurbelwelle, f., *r. e. crank shaft*; - - lager, n., *r. e. c. s. bearing*; - - - bolzen, m., *r. e. c. s. b. bolt*; - - - deckel, m.,

r. e. c. s. bearing keep; - - - -
bolzen, m., *r. e. c. s. b. k. bolt*;
- Kurbelwellenlagerschalen,
r. e. c. s. bearing brasses;
- - Paßstück, n., *r. e. c. s.
brasses liner*; - Kurbel-
zapfenlager, n., *r. e. c. pin
bearing*; - - bolzen, m., *r. e.
c. p. bolt*; - - schalen, *r. e.
c. p. brasses*; - - - deckel,
m., *r. e. connecting rod bottom end keep*; - Pleyelstange,
f., *r. e. c. r.*; - - bolzen, m.,
r. e. c. r. bolt; - - fuß-Paßstück, n., *r. e. bottom end
liner*; - Rad, n., *r. e. wheel*;
- Schieber, m., *r. e. slide
valve*; - - kasten, m., *r. e. v.
casing*; - - - deckel, m., *r. e.
v. c. door*; - Schieberstange,
f., *r. e. v. rod*; - - stopfbüchse, f., *r. e. v. r. stuffing
box*; - - - deckel, m, *r. e. v.
r. s. b. gland*; - spindel, f.,
r. e. shaft; - Spurkulisse,
f., *r. e. slot link*; - Wellen-
lagerschalen, *r. e. weigh
shaft brasses*; - Zugstange,
f., *r. e. drag link*; - Zylinder,
m., *r. e. cylinder*; - - deckel,
m., *r. e. c. cover*; - - - bolzen, m., *r. e. c. c. bolt*; - Zylinder - Entwässerungsrohr,
n., *r. e. cylinder drain pipe.*
Umsteuerungs - Mechanismus,
m., *reversing gear*; - rad, n.,
r. worm wheel; - schnecke,
f., *r. worm*; - spindel, f., *r.
shaft*; - turbine, f., *r. turbine*; - vorrichtung, f., *r.
gear*; - welle, f., *weigh shaft;*
- - lagerschalen, *w. s. brasses.*
um-takeln, *to rig anew*; -
wandeln, *to convert*; - wech-
selnd, *reciprocating*; - wenden, *to boxhaul*; - wickeln
or - wuhlen, *to muffle.*
un-auslöschbar, *inextinguishable*; - auslöschlich, *unquenchable*; - befahren, *raw
(sailor)*; - bearbeitete Spiere,
f., *rough tree spar.*
unbehauene Holz, n., *rough
timber*; - Mast, m., *hand

mast piece; - Spiere, f., *rough
tree spar.*
un-bemannt, *unmanned*; - besetzter Schiffsraum, m.,
spare tonnage; - beständig,
unsettled (weather); - bestroppter Block, m., *unstropped block*; - biegsam, *rigid*;
- brauchbar, *1. disabled (engine); 2. unserviceable (ropes,
gear, boats, &c.)*; - dicht,
leaky; - eigentliche Bodmerei, f., *respondentia*; -
eingeschlossener Raum, m.,
unenclosed space; - ergründlich, *fathomless*; - explodier-
barer Kessel, m., *inexplosive
boiler*; - fall, m., *casualty*;
- fälle auf See, *casualties at
sea*; - gedecktes Fahrzeug,
n., *undecked craft*; - genügend bemannt, *short-
handed*; - geschützter Ankerplatz, m., *exposed anchorage*;
- gestaltet, *shapeless*; - gestaut, *unstowed*; - gestüm,
tempestuous (weather); - geteertes Segelgarn, n., *white
twine*; - - Tau, n., *w. rope*;
- - - werk, n., *w. cordage*;
- gleichlastig, *uneven keel*;
- gleichschenkelige Bodenwrange, f., *long and short
armed floors*; - gleichseitig,
lapsided; - handiges Wetter,
n., *heavy weather.*
universale Dichtung, f., *universal joint.*
Universal-schlüssel, m., *monkey spanner*; - Schraubenschlüssel, m., *universal screw
wrench.*
unklar, *1. foul (anchor); 2.
choked (pumps)*; - kommen,
to foul (another vessel); -
laufendes Tau, n., *foul running rope.*
unklare Anker, m., *foul
anchor*; - - platz, m., *f. berth*;
- Fahrwasser, n., *channel
full of banks od. rocks*; -
Ketten, *foul hawse*; - Lage,
f., *precarious position.*
unpassierbar, *impassible.*

unregelmäßig bewegte See, f., *confused sea.*

unregelmäßige Fahrer, m., *tramp;* - Strom, m., *cross tide.*

unreine Gesundheitspaß, m., *foul bill of health;* - Grund, m., *f. bottom;* - Küste, f., *f. coast;* - Luft, f., *f. air.*

un-ruhige See, f., *disturbed sea;* - schmelzbar, *infusible;* - schweißbarer Stahl, m., *harsh steel;* - seemännisch, *unseamanlike.*

unsichere Ankerplatz, m., *unsafe anchorage;* - Hafen, m., *u. port;* - Reede, f., *u. road.*

unsichtig, *misty.*

unsichtiges Wetter, n., *1. misty weather; 2. view obscured.*

un-sinkbar, *insubmersible;* - stetig, *unsettled (weather);* - tauglich, *unserviceable.*

Unterbalkweger, m., *clamp;* - der Back, *c. of forecastle;* - der Hütte or Poop, *c. of poop;* - des erhöhten Quarterdecks, *c. of raised quarterdeck;* - bolzen, *c. bolt.*

unterbefrachten, *to underfreight.*

Unterbram-brasse, f., *lower topgallant brace;* - segel, n., *l. t. sail.*

unterbrochenes Deck, n., *break;* - Feuer, n., *intermitting light.*

Unter-bunker, m., *hold bunker;* - deck, n., *lower deck.*

unter Dampf, *under steam.*

Unterdeckbalken, m., *lower deck beam;* - Hängeknie, n., *l. d. b. hanging knee;* - Kattspor, m., *l. d. b. k. rider;* - Längsschiene, f., or - Lukenstringer, m., *l. d. b. tie plate;* - stringer, m., *l. d. b. stringer;* - - platte, f., *l. d. b. s. plate;* - winkel, m., *l. d. b. angle bar.*

Unterdeck-Balkweger, m., *lower deck beam shelf;* - band, n., *l. d. hook;* - Beplankung, f., *l. d. planking;* - Befestigung, f., *l. d. fastening;* - bolzen, m., *l. d. bolt;* - Längsschiene, f., *l. d. beam tie plate;* - Luke, f., *l. d. hatchway;* - - deckel, m., *l. d. hatch;* - - stringer, m., *l. d. beam tie plate;* - - süll, m., *l. d. hatchway coaming;* - Mastkeile, *l. d. mast wedges;* - Setzweger, m., *l. d. spirketting;* - stringer, m., *l. d. stringer;* - - platte, f., *l. d. s. plate;* - - winkel, m., *l. d. s. angle bar;* - stütze, f., *l. d. stanchion;* - Unterbalkweger, m., *l. d. beam clamp;* - Wassergang, m., *l. d. waterway.*

unter dem Schiffe, *underfoot;* - dem Werte versichert, *under-insured.*

untere Gallionsleiste, f., *main rail;* - Lagerschale, f., *bottom brass;* - Püttingsbolzen, m., *preventer chain bolt;* - Seite, f., *under side.*

unteren Auflanger der Kantspanten, *the half timbers in the cant body.*

Unterende eines Inholzes, n., *the heel of a timber.*

Unter-frachtvertrag, m., *contract of recharter;* - gang, m., *foundering;* - garniert, *dunnaged;* - gegangen, *foundered;* - gehen, *to founder;* unter Segel - -, *to f. under sails;* vor Anker - -, *t. f. at anchor;* - gewicht, *underweight;* - haltungskosten, *expense of maintenance;* - kiel, m., *lower keel;* - lage, f., *glut (of a handspike);* - lagsstreifen, m., *liner;* - Land, *under the land;* dicht - - bleiben, *to keep close u. t. l.;* - Lee, *u. t. lee.*

Unterleesegel, n., *lower studding sail;* - Aufholer, m., *l. s. s. tripping line;* - Außenschote, f., *l. s. s. tack;* - Binnenschote, f., *l. s. s. sheet;* - fall, n., *l. s. s. halliard;* - hals, m.

l. s. s. *tack*; - Innenfall, n., l. s. s. *inner halliard*; - rahe, f., l. s. s. *yard*; - schote, f., l. s. s. *sheet*; - spiere, f., l. s. s. *boom*.

Unter-legscheibe, f., *washer*; - liek, n., *foot rope*.

Untermars-brasse, f., *lower topsail brace*; - rahe, f., l. t. *yard*; - segel, n., l. t.; - - Jackstag, n., l. t. *jackstay*.

Untermast, m., *lower mast*; - Dwarssahling, f., l. m. *cross trees*; - Eselshaupt, n., l. m. *cap*; - hummer, m., l. m. *hound*; - Längssahling, f., l. m. *trestle trees*.

Unterrahe, f., *lower yard*; - Toppenant, f., l. *lift*.

Unterraum, m., *lower hold*; - balken, m., l. h. *beam*.

Unterreff, n., *bag reef*; - talje, f., *lower reef tackle*.

Unter-rüste, f., *lower channel*; - scheidungssignal, n., *distinguishing signal*; - scheidungswimpel, m., d. *pennant*; - schiff, n., *hull*; - schlag, m., *stringer*; - schlagen, 1. *to bend (a sail)*; 2. *to embezzle (fraudulently)*; 3. *to dunnage (when stowing)*; - schlagung, f., *embezzlement*; - seeboot, n., *submarine boat*; - seeisch, *submarine*; - segel, 1. *under sail*; 2. *courses*; die - -aufgeien, *to haul up the c.*; - - bei! or die - - beisetzen, c. *ready for setting*; - - bleiben, *to keep under sail*; - - gehen, *to go u. s.*; - seite, f., *underside*; - strom, m., *underset*; - strömung, f., *under current*; - suchen und ausbessern, *to overhaul*; - tauchen, *diving*

(*with the bow*); - teil der Gillung, m., *lower counter*; - Zwischendeck, n., *lower tweendecks*.

unterst, *undermost*.

unterste Heckleiste, f., *counter rail*.

Untertoppenant, f., *lower lift*; - talje, f., l. l. *purchase*; - - läufer, m., l. l. p. *fall*.

Untertoppsegel, n., *lower topsail*; - brasse, f., l. t. *brace*; - rahe, f., l. t. *yard*.

unterversichert, *under-insured*.

Unterwant or - tau, n., *lower shroud*.

Unterwanten, *lower rigging*.

Unterwasser-glocke, f., *submarine bell*; - signale, s. *signals*; - teile, *sea connections*.

unterwegs, *underway*.

untief, *shallow*.

Untiefe, f., *shallow water*.

Untiefen, *shelves*.

ununterbrochen, *flush with*.

unvermeidliche Seeschäden, *perils of the sea*.

unversichert, *uninsured*.

Unwetter, n., *stress of weather*.

Up dat Roer! *Up with the helm!*

up un dal, *apeak*.

Urlaub, m., *liberty*; - an Land zu gehen, l.; - überschreiten, *to break l.*

Urlauber, m., *liberty man*.

Urlaubs-paß, m., *liberty ticket*; - tag, m., l. *day*.

Usanz, f., *customs and uses (of sea or port)*; - gemäß, *according to the usual practice*.

Utensilien, *utensils*; - kasten, m., *ditty box*.

V.

Vakuum, n., *vacuum*; - messer, m., v. *gauge*; - - rohr, n., v. g. *pipe*; - meter, n., v. g.; - raum, m., v. *space*; - rohr, n., v. *pipe*; - - des Zylinders, *cylinder v. p.*

Venatikaholz, n., *vanatica wood*.

Ventil, n., *valve*; - anschlag, m., *v. guard*; - belastung, f., *v. load*; - deckel, m., *v. cover*; - feder, f., *v. spring*; - gegengewicht, n., *slide v. balance*; - gehäuse, n., *v. box*; - hebel, m., *v. lever*; - heber, m., *v. lifter*; - hubbegrenzer, m., *v. guard*; - kasten. m., *v. box*; - - deckel, m., *v. b. cover*; - kegel, m., *v. cone*; - klappenfänger, m., *v. guard*; - kolben, m., *v. piston*; - scharnier, n., *v. stem*; - sitz, m., *v. seat*; - spindel, f., *v. spindle*; - steuerung, f., *distributing mechanism of valves*; - stütze, f., *valve guard*.

Ventilations - Einrichtungen, *ventilating arrangements*; - maschine, f., *electrical ventilating motor*.

Ventilator, m., *ventilator*; - dülle, f., *v. socket*; - kappe, f., or - kopf, m., *v. cowl*; - kragen, m., *v. coat*; - öffnung, f., *v. mouth*; - rohr, n., *v. flange*; - sockel, m., *v. socket*.

Ventilatoren vom Winde wegdrehen, *trimming ventilators back to wind*.

veränderliche Expansion, f., *variable expansion*; - Wetter, n., *v. weather*.

veränderte Breite, f., *variation of latitude*; - Länge, f., *v. of longitude*.

verankern, 1. *to moor (the vessel)*; 2. *to grapple (the boiler)*.

Verankerung, f., 1. *mooring (of vessel)*; 2. *staying (of boiler)*.

Verankerungsdrähte, *anchoring wires*.

Verband, m., *strength (ship and connections)*; wichtige - teile, *material fastenings*.

verbessert, *improved*.

verbesserte Abstand, m., *corrected distance*; - Breite, f.,

c. latitude; - Kurs wegen Abtrift, m., *course corrected for leeway*; - - - Stromversetzung, *c. c. f. current*; - Länge, f., *corrected longitude*.

Verbesserung, f., *improvement*.

verbeulen, *to dint*.

Verbeulung, f., *dinting*.

verbinden, *to connect, to joint*; das stehende Gut verbinden, *to fleet the dead eyes of the standing rigging*.

Verbindlichkeit, f., *warranty*.

Verbindung, f., *joint* oder *connection*; - herstellen, *to establish a c.*

Verbindungs-blech, n., *tie plate*; - bolzen, m., *holding bolt*; - brücke, f., *flying bridge*; - - geländer, n., *f. b. rails and stanchions*; - - - stützen, *f. b. s.*; - dock, n., *junction dock*; - gang, m., *binding strake*; - getriebe, n., *connecting gear*; - platte, f., *c. plate*; - rohr, n., *joint pipe*; - - des hohen Tanks. *deep tank copper bend*; - schäkel, m., *joining shackle*; - stange, f., *purchase rod*; - teile, *connecting parts*; - trosse, f., *c. rope*; - welle, f., *intermediate shaft*; - winkel, m., *bosom piece*; - zapfen, m., *butt dowel*; *joint dowel*.

verbolzen, *to bolt*.

Verbolzung, f., *fastening*.

verbotener Handel, m., *clandestine trade*.

Verbrauch, m., *consumption*.

verbrauchen, *to consume*.

Verbrennung, f., *combustion*; - raum, m., *furnace*.

verbunden, *connected*.

verbundener Dampf, m., *combined steam*.

Verbundmaschine, f., *compound engine*.

Vercharterer, m., *charterer*.

verchartern, *to charter*.

verdampfen, *to evaporate*.

Verdampfung, f., *evaporation*; - apparat, m., *evaporating*

apparatus; - fähigkeit, f.,
evaporative power; - geschwindigkeit, f., *velocity of
evaporation*; - wärme, f.,
evaporative heat.
Verdeck, n., *deck.*
Verdichtung, f., *joint.*
Verdoppelung, f., *top lining
(of a sail)*; - am Rahliek,
head lining; - am Mastliek,
mast l.
Verdoppelungen auf ein Segel
setzen, *to put tabling on a
sail.*
Verdoppelungs-band,n.,*lining*;
- gang, m., *doubling strake*;
- nagel, m., *d. nail*; - platte,
f., *d. plate.*
verdrehen, *to distort.*
Verdrehung, f., *distortion.*
verdübeln, *to dowel.*
verdunkeln, die Kimm -, *to
dusk the horizon.*
Verdünnung, f., *rarefaction.*
verfahren, *to overhaul (a
tackle).*
verfangen, *1. to relieve (the
man at the wheel)*; *2. to surge
(a rope round the windlass).*
verfault, *decayed (mast, boom,
&c.).*
verfehlen, *to miss.*
verfolgen, *1. to chase (a ship)*;
2. den Kurs -, *to stand on.*
verfolgendes Schiff, n., *chaser.*
verfolgtes Schiff, n., *chase.*
Verfolgung, f., *chase.*
verfrachten, *to freight, to fix,
to let.*
Verfrachter, m., *freighter.*
vergeben, nichts -! *Nothing
to lose!*
vergießen mit Blei, *to run in
lead.*
vergissen, *to make errors in
the dead reckoning.*
Vergnügungs-dampfer, m., *excursion steamer*; - reise, f.,
pleasure trip.
vergrößerter Breite, nach - -
segeln, *Mercator's sailing.*
Vergütung, f., *allowance*;
bounty; *indemnity*; gegen -,

for a consideration; - für
durch Aufopferung ver-
lorene oder beschädigte
Ladung, *amount to be made
good for cargo lost* or *damaged by sacrifice*; - für beschädigte Güter, *allowance
for damaged goods*; - für
Bruchschaden, *a. for breakage.*
verhäuten, *to sheathe a ship.*
verheuern, *to ship.*
Verhol-boje, f., *warping buoy*;
- klampe, f., *w. chock*; - leine
or - trosse, f., *hauling line.*
Verholmaschine, f., *warping
engine*; - Absperrventil, n.,
w. e. stop valve; - Anlaßventil, n., *w. e. starting v.*;
- Dampfabführungsrohr, n.,
w. e. exhaust v.; - D-zuleitungsrohr, n., *w. e. steam
pipe*; - Exzenter, n., *w. e.
eccentric*; - - bolzen, m., *w.
e. e. bolt*; - - bügel, m., *w. e.
e. strap*; - - - Paßstück, n.,
w. e. e. s. liner; - Exzenter-
Lagerschalen, *w. e. e. brasses*;
- E.-scheibe, f., *w. e. e. sheave*;
- E.-stange, f., *w. e. e. rod*; -
Kabelaring, m., *w. e.
messenger*; - Kolben, m., *w.
e. piston*; - - stange, f., *w. e.
p. rod*; - - - Kreuzkopf, m.,
w. e. p. r. crosshead; - - -
Stopfbüchse, f., *w. e. p. r.
stuffing box*; - - - - deckel,
m., *w. e. p. r. s. b. gland*; -
Kreuzkopf, m., *w. e. crosshead*; - - lagerbolzen, m.,
w. e. c. bolt; - - lagerschalen,
w. e. c. brasses; - - - deckel,
m., *w. e. connecting rod top
end keep*; - Kurbelwelle, f.,
w. e. crank shaft; - - lager,
n., *w. e. c. s. bearing*; - - -
bolzen, m., *w. e. c. s. b. bolt*;
- - - deckel, m., *w. e. c. s.
bearing keep*; - - - - bolzen,
m., *w. e. c. s. b. k. bolt*; -
Kurbelwellenlagerschalen,
w. e. c. s. bearing brasses;
- - Paßstück, n., *w. e. c. s.*

brasses liner;- Kurbelzapfen, m., *w. e. c. pin*: - - lagerbolzen, m., *w. e. c. p. bolt*; - - lagerschalen, *w. e. c. p. brasses*; - - - deckel, m., *w. e. connecting rod bottom end keep*; - Pleyelstange, f., *w. e. c. r.*; - - bolzen, m., *w. e. c. r. bolt*; - - fuß-Paßstück, n., *w. e. c. r. bottom end liner*; - Schieber, m., *w. e. slide valve*; - - kasten, m., *w. e. v. casing*; - - - deckel, m., *w. e. v. c. door*; - Schieberstange, f., *w. e. v. rod*; - - Stopfbüchse, f., *w. e. v. r. stuffing box*; - - - deckel, m., *w. e. v. r. s. b. gland*; - Zylinder, m., *w. e. cylinder*; - - deckel, m., *w. e. c. cover*; - - - bolzen, m., *w. e. c. c. bolt*; - Zylinder-Entwässerungsrohr, n., *w. e. cylinder drain pipe*.

verholen, *to haul, to warp*.

Verjüngungsplanken, *diminishing planks*.

verkatten, *to back (an anchor)*.

verkattet und gefischt, *catted and fished*.

Verkaufs-akt, m., *bill of sale*; - wert, m., *market value*.

Verkehr, m., *1. traffic, 2. service*; direkter -, *through service*; regelmäßiger -, *regular s.*; täglicher -, *daily s.*

Verkehrserlaubnis, f., *pratique*.

verkehrt liegender Zylinder, m., *inverted cylinder*.

verkehrte Auflanger, m., *top timber*; - Seite, f., *wrong side*.

verkeilen, *to wedge*.

verkitten, *to putty up*.

Verklarung belegen, *to extend protest*.

verkleiden, *1. to secure with woodwork; 2. to wainscot (walls and ceilings)*.

Verklicker, m., *dog vane*.

verklinkern, *to clinch (a bolt)*.

Verkrustung, f., *incrustation*.

verkürzen, *to shorten*.

Verkürzung, f., *shortening*.

Verladungs-dokumente, *shipping documents*; - kosten or - spesen, s. *charges*.

verlängern, *to lengthen (a ship)*.

Verlängerung, f., *1. lengthening (of a ship); 2. continuation (of classification)*; - rohr, n., *extension pipe*.

verlaschen, *1. to lash (cargo); 2. to scarf (rails, bars)*.

Verlaschung, f., *1. lashing (of cargo); 2. scarf (of keel pieces, rails)*.

verlassen, *to abandon*.

verlassene Breite, f., *departed latitude*; - Länge, f., *d. longitude*; - Schiff, n., *derelict*.

verlegen, *to change (the berth)*.

verlieren aus dem Gesicht, *to lose sight of*; nichts -! *nothing to lose!*

verlorener Dampf, m., *waste steam*; - Effect, m., *lost effect*; - Gang, m., *drop strake*.

Verlustbuch, n., *loss book*.

vermehrter Tiefgang, m., *increased draught*.

vermeiden, *to avoid (a collision)*.

vermessen, *to gauge*.

Vermessungs-deck, n., *tonnage deck*; - gesetz, n., *t. law*; - tiefe, f., *depth for t.*

vermieten, *to let*.

vermindern, *to ease*.

vermindert, *reduced*.

Verminderung des Schieberhubes, f., *notching-up*.

vermißt, *missing (vessel)*.

vermuren, *to moor*.

vermutlicher Verlust, m., *presumptive loss*.

vernichtet, *gone*.

vernieten, *to rivet*.

Vernietung, f., *riveting*; - der Ueberlappungen der Längsnähte, *edge riveting*.

verpacken, *to pack*.

verpechen, *to pay (a seam)*.

verpfänden, *to mortgage*.

Verpfändung, f., *mortgaging; hypothecation*.

verpflichten, *to covenant.*

verpinnen, *to indent with a pin.*

verproviantieren, *to draw stores; to victual.*

Verproviantierer, m., *victualler.*

verproviantiert sein, *to be victualled.*

Verproviantierung, f., *victualling.*

verringern, *to shorten (sails, cable).*

versacken, *to founder.*

versagen, *to refuse.*

versanden, *sanding up.*

versatztes Zapfenloch, n., *indented mortise.*

verschalen, *1. to fish (a mast); 2. to secure with woodwork.*

verschalken, *to batten down.*

Verschalung, *1. clamp (of mast, yard); 2. girdle (of wales).*

verschanzen, *to barricade.*

Verschanzung, f., *bulwark.*

Verscharterer, m., *charterer, freighter.*

verschartern, *to charter.*

verscherben, *to scarph.*

Verscherbungsbolzen, m., *scarph bolt.*

Verschiffung, f., *shipment;* - anzeige, f., *advice of s.;* - gewicht, n., *shipping weight.*

Verschlagbretter, *bulkhead boards.*

verschlagen, *1. driven out of one's course; 2. blown over (a squall): 3. boarded off (with boards).*

verschlammt, *silted.*

verschlingen, *to engulf (a ship).*

Verschlüsse, *manhole doors.*

Verschlußponton, m., *pontoon for careening ships.*

verschollen, *missing.*

Verschraubung mit Ventil, f., *valve coupling.*

Verschuß der Planken, m., *shifting of planks.*

verschwinden am Horizont, *to dip.*

versegeln, *1. to sail to another port; 2. to carry away (upon the shore).*

versehen mit, *to supply with.*

Versenkkasten, m., *caissoon.*

versenkte Back, f., *sunk forecastle;* - Brücke, f., or - Brückenhaus, n., *s. bridge;* - Niete, f., *countersunk rivet;* - Poop, f., *sunk poop;* - Vernietung, f., *flush riveting.*

versetzbare Pumpe, f., *portable pump;* - Stütze, f., *movable stanchion.*

Versetzdampfer, m., *pilot steamer.*

versetzen, *1. to change the berth (of the anchor); 2. to convey (the pilot).*

versetzt, *1. carried away (by current); 2. set adrift (flooring).*

Versicherer, m., *insurer; underwriter.*

versichern, *1. to insure (by insurance); 2. to secure (hatches, cargo).*

Versicherte, m., *insured.*

Versicherung auf Gegenseitigkeit, f., *mutual insurance;* - auf Zeit, *time i.;* - gegen Seegefahr, *i. against sea risk.*

Versicherungswert, m., *value insured.*

versperren, *1. to choke (the entrance of a harbour); 2. to take charge (of the deck).*

verstagen, *to stay in the wrong way.*

verstählen, *to steel.*

verstärkter Längsverband, m., *additional longitudinal strength;* - Verband, m., *a. s.*

Verstärkung, f., *additional strength;* - balken, m., *panting beam;* - -Stringerwinkel, m., *p. b. stringer angle bar;* - band, n., *lining;* - - eines Sonnensegelrückens, *ridge l. of an awning;* - leiste, f., *false rail;* - ring, m., *compensation ring;* - scheibe, f., *washer.*

verstauen, *to stow.*

Verstauer, m., *stevedore.*

versteifen, *to stiffen.*

Versteifungs-platte, f., *stiffening plate;* - stange, f., *tie rod;* - winkel, m., *stiffening angle bar.*

verstellbare Radschaufel, f., *feathering float;* - Schraubenflügel, m., *detachable propeller blade;* - Schraubenschlüssel, m., *shifting spanner.*

verstemmen, *caulking.*

Verstemmer, m., *caulking tool.*

verstopfen, *1. to plug up (a hole); 2. to chinse (by chinsing iron).*

verstopft, *1. silted up (by silt); 2. choked (pumps, limbers, &c. by dirt).*

Verstützung, f., *pillaring.*

Versuchsstempel, m., *proof mark.*

versunkenes Land, n., *drowned land.*

Vertäu-anker, m., *mooring anchor;* - boje, f., *m. buoy;* - gegenstände, *moorings;* - kette, f., *mooring chain;* - klüse, f., or - Klüsenrohr, n., *m. pipe;* - pfahl, m., *m. post;* - poller, m., *m. bitts;* - ring, m., *m. ring;* - schäkel, m., *m. shackle;* - wirbel, m., *m. swivel.*

vertäuen, *to moor;* - mit zwei Ankern voraus, *mooring with two anchors ahead.*

Vertäuer, m., *moorings.*

Vertäuung, f., *mooring;* die - bis auf eine Trosse einziehen, *to single up the ship.*

Vertäuungen, *moorings.*

Vertäuungs-arbeiten, *mooring works;* - klüse, f., - klüsenrohr, n., *m. pipe;* - knoten, m., *m. bend;* - poller, m., *m. bitts;* - tau, n., *m. rope.*

verteunen, *to build the upper works.*

Verteunung, f., *upper works;* - sente, f., *fife rail.*

Vertiefung, f., *deepening.*

vertikale Dampfsteuermaschine, f., *vertical steering engine;* - Durchbolzen, m., *v. through bolt;* - Gurtplatte, f., *face plate;* - Kielschwein, n., *single plate keelson;* - Lenzpumpe, f., *vertical bilge pump;* - Luftpumpe, f., *v. air p.;* - Maschine, f., *inverted vertical cylinder engine;* - Mittelkielschwein, n., *middle line single plate keelson;* - Mittelplatte, f., *centre vertical plate;* - Platte, f., *v. p.;* - Speisepumpe, f., *vertical feed pump;* - Zirkulationspumpe, f., *v. circulating p.;* - Zylinderkessel, m., *v. cylindrical boiler.*

Vertikalknie, n., *hanging knee.*

vertreiben, *to carry away.*

verunglücken, *to perish.*

Verunstaltung, f., *deformation.*

Veruntreuung, f., *embezzlement.*

verweht, *driven from the right course.*

verwirrt machen, *to badger.*

Verwirrung, f., *derangement.*

verzahnen, *to tooth.*

Verzahnung, f., *toothing.*

verzapfen, *1. to caulk (the deck); 2. to mortise.*

Verzapfung, f., *mortising;* doppelte -, *connecting by double tenon and mortise joint.*

verzäunen, *to build the upper works.*

Verzäunung, f., *upper works;* - sente, f., *fife rail.*

verzehrend, *consuming.*

verzeisen, *1. to seize; 2. to frap (a tackle).*

verzerren, *to distort.*

Verzerrung, f., *distortion.*

Verzierung, f., *1. ornament; 2. term pieces (on counter pieces);* - leiste, f., *1. moulding; 2. friezing (on rails); 3. cable moulding (cable shaped).*

27*

Verzimmerung, in -, *on the stocks for repairs.*

verzinktes Eisen, n., *galvanized iron.*

verzögerte Bewegung, f., *decreasing motion.*

Verzögerung der Flut, f., *retard of the tide.*

Vieh-begleiter, m., *cattle man*; - transportdampfer, m., *c. steamer*; - verschläge, *c. fittings.*

vielröhriger Kessel, m., *multi-tubular boiler.*

Vier-deckschiff, n., *four deck vessel*; - drähtiges Schiemannsgarn, n., *f. thread spun yarn.*

viereckige Bolzen, m., *square bolt*; - Platting, f., *s. sennit.*

vieren, *to veer.*

vierfache Expansionsmaschine, f., *quadruple expansion engine*; - Nietung, f., *q. riveting.*

vierflügelige Schraube, f., *four bladed propeller.*

vierkant, *square*; - brassen, *to square the yards*; - des Ankerschaftes, n., *the square of the shank of an anchor*; - getakelt, *broad rigged*; - machen, *to square*; - toppen und brassen, *to s. the yards by lifts and braces*; die Rahen sind - in den Toppenanten, *the yards are s. in the lifts.*

vierkantige Ballasteisen, n., *square kentledge*; - Feile, f., *s. file*; - Holz, n., *s. timber*; - Platting, f., *s. sennit*; - Schiff, n., *bruise water.*

Vier-läufer, m., *twofold purchase*; - mast Bark, f., *four mast barque*; - - Schiff, n., *f. m. ship*; - ruderer or -ruderig, *f. oared*; - schäftiges Tau, n., *f. stranded rope*; - - werk, n., *f. cant*; - scheibiger Block, m., *f. sheave block*; - strichpeilung, f., *f. point bearing.*

Viertel Ebbe, f., *first quarter ebb*; - Kompaßstrich, m., *a q. point*; - kreisartige Deviation, f., *quadrantal deviation.*

vierter Buganker, m., *fourth bower.*

Vierwegehahn, m., *four way cock.*

Vierzylindrige Compound-Maschine, f., *four cylinder compound engine.*

Violinblock, m., *fiddle block.*

Violinen des Bugspriets, *the bee blocks of the bowsprit.*

Volkslogis, n., *crew space.*

voll, *bluff (build of a vessel)*; gut -, *clean full (the sails)*; - befahren, *able bodied (sailor)*; - brassen, *to fill*; - Dampf achteraus, *full speed astern*; - - voraus, *f. s. ahead*; - druck, m., *f. pressure*; - - Maschine, f., *non-expansive engine*; - gebaut, *full bottomed*; hinten - -, *very f. aft*; - gelaufen, *swamped*; - gepfropft, *chock full*; - geschlagen, *swamped*; - getakelt, *full rigged*; - halten! *Keep her f.!* - - zum Wenden! *F. for stays!* - handiges Wetter, n., *strong breeze*; - hart geschlagen, *full twisted*; - kantig, *well squared*; - laufen, 1. *filling with water*; 2. *to swamp*; einen Tank - - lassen, *to run up a tank*; - lotse, m., *first class pilot*; - mast, m., *mast with top and topgallant trees*; - matrose, m., *an A. B.*; - pumpen, *to water (a vessel)*; - schiff, n., *full rigged ship*; - - takelage, f., *ship rig*; - schlagen, *to swamp*; - spant, n., *water tight frame*; - ständige Reparatur, f., *permanent repairs*; gut - stehen, *to belly out*; - und bei! *Full and by!* - Wasser, *water logged.*

volle Back, f., *topgallant forecastle*; - Bug, m., *bluff bow*; - Fracht, f., *full freight*; -

Hütte, f., *f. poop*; - Kraft, f., *f. power*; - - achteraus, or - - rückwärts, *f. speed astern*; - - vorwärts, *f. s. ahead*; - Ladung, f., *f. cargo*; - Poop, f., *f. poop*.

vollen, mit - Segeln fahren, *to go a main pace*.

voller Klippen und Sandbänke, *shelvy*.

Völligkeitsgrad, m., *coëfficient of fineness*.

Volt, n., *volt*; - ameter, m., *voltameter*; - messer, m., *voltmeter*.

von unnern! *Stand from under!*

Vor- *see also* Fock-.

voransegeln, *to take the lead·*

voraus, recht -, *right ahead*; ein Schiff -, *a ship a.*; - gang, m., *a. motion*; - gehen, *to go a.*; - hieven, *to heave a.*; - holen, *to haul a.*; - holer des Toppreeps, m., *guy of the cargo pendant*; - schießen, *to shoot ahead*; - schleppen, *to tow ahead*; die Riemen gut - werfen, *to bend to the oars*.

Vorbaum, m., *fore boom*; - dirk, m., *f. b. topping lift*; - - talje, f., *f. b. t. l. purchase*; - toppenant, f., *f. b. t. l.*; - - talje, f., *f. b. t. l. purchase*.

vorbei-fahren or - segeln, *to pass*; - - so dicht wie möglich, *to p. as close as is safe*.

Vorbram-Bauchgording, f., *fore topgallant bunt line*; - brasse, f., *f. t. brace*; - bulien, f., *f. t. bowline*; - Drehreep, n., *f. t. tye*; - fall, n., *f. topgallant halliard*; - Geitau, n., *f. t. clew line*; - Längssahling, f., *f. topmast trestle trees*; - Leesegel, n., *f. topgallant studding sail*; - - Außenschote, f., *f. t. s. s. tack*; - - Binnenschote, f., *f. topgallant s. s. sheet*; - - fall, n., *f. t. s. s. halliard*; - - hals, m., *f. t. s. s. tack*; - - Nieder-

holer, m., *f. topgallant s. s. downhaul*; - - rahe, f., *f. t. s. s. yard*; - - schote, f., *f. t. s. s. sheet*; - - spiere, f., *f. t. s. s. boom*; - Nockgording, f., *f. t. leech line*: - pardune, f., *f. t. backstay*; - pferd, n., *f. t. foot rope*; - püttings, *f. t. futtocks*; - - wanten, *f. t. futtock shrouds*; - rahe, f., *f. t. yard*; - sahling, f., *fore topmast crosstrees*; - Schote, f., *f. topgallant sheet*; - sail, n., *f. t. sail*; - stag, n., *f.t.stay*; - - segel, n., *f. t. s. sail*; - stenge, f., *f. t. mast*; - - Eselshaupt, n., *f. t. m. cap*; - - Pardune, f., *f. t. backstay*; - - stag, n., *f. t. stay*; - - wanten, *f. t. rigging*; - Toppenant, f., *f. t. lift*; - wanten, *f. t. rigging*.

Vorbrassen, *fore braces*; - schenkel, m., *f. brace pendant*.

Vordeck or Vorderdeck, n., *fore deck*.

vor dem Winde, *before the wind*.

Vordemwinder, m., *vessel sailing before the wind*.

Vorder-balanzierspant, n., *luff frame*; - brunnen-Saugventil, n., *forward well suction valve*; - ende, n., *head of a vessel*; - ende eines Berg; holzganges, n., *ribband line- geie, f., *fore guy*; - geschirr, n., *f. rigging*; - kajüte, f., *f. cabin*; - lastig, *too much by the head*; - Pardune, f., *foremost backstay*; - pflicht, f., *fore cuddy*; - piekdeck, n. *f. peak deck*; - säule, f., *front column!* - schiff, n., *fore body*; - schott, n., *break of the poop*; - steven, m., *stem*; - - pumpe, f., *bow pump*; - wand der Hütte, f., *break of the poop*.

vordere Doppelboden, m., *double bottom forward*; - Festmachtau, n. *bow fast*;

- Kurbelwelle, f., *forward crank shaft*; - Landfeste, f., *bow fast*; - Pumpenbalanziergelenke, *front lever links*; - Rauchkammer, f., *smoke box*; - Rohrwand des Kessels, f., *front tube plate of boiler*; - Stirnwand, f., *front plate*; - - des Kessels, *f. p. of boiler*; - Teil des Schiffsrumpfs, m., *cant body forward*; - Verholleine, f., *head rope*.

vorderste Planken or Platten der Außen- od. Innenhaut-Gänge, *fore hoods*.

Vor-dirk, m., *fore topping lift*; - dock, n., *basin*; - ebbe, f., *first quarter ebb*: - eilung des Schiebers, f., *lead of slide valve*; - feile, f., *bastard file*; - flut, f., *young flood*.

Vorgaffel, f., *fore gaff*; - gerde, f., *f. vang*; - - schenkel, m., *f. v. pendant*; - segel, n., *f. trysail*.

Vorgaffeltoppsegel, n., *fore gaff topsail*; - fall, n., *f. g. t. halliard*; - hals, m., *f. g. t. tack*; - Niederholer, m., *f. g. topsail downhaul*; - schote, f., *f. g. t. sheet*.

Vor-gänge während der Reise, *the proceedings during the voyage*; - gebirge, n., *promontory*; - gelege, n., *gearing*; - - welle, f., *transmitting shaft*; - geschirr, n., *head gear*; - halter, m., *holding-up hammer*; - handener Druck, m., *actual pressure*; - hang, m., *screen*; - hängeschloß, n., *padlock*; - herrschende Winde, *prevailing winds*; die Marsschoten vorholen, *to haul the topsail sheets home*; - kajüte, f., *lobby*; - kante, f., *fore leech*: - kantspant, n., *f. cant timber*: - kehrtau, n., *fore guy*; - klaufall, m., *f. throat halliard*; - land, n., *foreland*; - laß, m., *fore runnings*; - lastig, *by the head*; - - be-

laden, *laden b. t. h.*; - lauf, m., *fore runnings*; - - or - läufer, m., *stray line (of the log line)*; - lauf zum Vordersteven, *fore foot*; - leesegel, n., *fore studding sail*; - leik, n., *f. leech rope*.

vorlich gehen, *to draw ahead*; - holen, *t. d. forward*; - von dwars, *before the beam*.

vorlicher, zwei Strich - als dwars, *two points before the beam*; - Wind, m., *head wind*.

Vor-liek, n., *fore leech rope*; - leine, f., *bow rope*; - luke, f., *fore hatch*; - - deckel, f. *hatches*; - - süll, m., *f. hatchway coaming*; - mann beim Rudern, m., *strokesman*.

Vormars, m., *fore top*; - Bauchgording, f., *f. topsail buntline*; - brasse, f., *f. t. brace*; - - schenkel, m., *f. t. b. pendant*; - bulien, f., *f. t. bowline*; - Drehreep, n., *f. t. tye*; - fall, n., *f. topsail halliard*; - Geitau, n., *f. t. clew line*; - leesegelfall, n., *f. topmast studding sail halliard*; - Pardune, f., *f. t. backstay*; - pferd, n., *f. topsail foot rope*; - püttings, *fore futtocks*; - - wanten, *fore futtock shrouds*; - rahe, f., *fore topsail yard*; - Refftalje, f., *f. t. reef tackle*; - schote, f., *f. topsail sheet*; - segel, n., *f. t.*; - - schote, f., *f. t. sheet*; - stag, n., *f. topmast stay*; - stenge, f., *f. t.*; - - Eselshaupt, n., *f. t. cap*; - Toppenant, f., *f. topsail lift*; - want, n., *f. topmast shroud*; - wanten, *f. t. rigging*.

Vormittagswache, f., *forenoon watch*.

Voroberbram-brasse, f., *upper fore topgallant brace*; - pferd, n., *u. f. t. foot rope*; - rahe, f., *u. fore t. yard*; - segel, n., *u. f. t. sail*.

Voroberleesegel, n., *fore topmast studding sail*; - Außenschote, f., *f. t. s. s. tack*; - Binnenschote, f., *f. t. s. s. sheet*; - fall, n., *f. t. studding sail halliard*; - hals, m., *f. t. s. tack*; - Niederholer, m., *f. t. s. s. downhaul*; - rahe, f., *f. t. s. s. yard*; - schote, f., *f. t. s. s. sheet*; - spiere, f., *f. t. studding sail boom.*

Vorobermars - Bauchgording, f., *upper fore topsail bunt line*; - brasse, f., *upper fore topsail brace*; - - schenkel, m., *u. f. t. b. pendant*; - pferd, n., *u. f. t. foot rope*; - rahe, f., *u. fore t. yard*; - segel, n., *u. f. t.*; - - schote, f., *u. f. t. sheet.*

Vorobertoppsegel, n., *upper fore topsail*; - brasse, f., *u. f. t. brace*; - rahe, f., *u. f. t. yard.*

Vorpflicht, f., *fore cuddy.*

Vorpiek, f., *fore peak*; - fall, n., *f. p. halliard*; - tank, m., *f. p. tank*; - - Saugeventil, n., *f. p. t. suction valve.*

Vor-propeller, m., *bow propeller*; - rahen, *fore topsail yards*; - rat, m., *supply*; - räte, *provisions*; - - für die Kajüte, *steward's small stores*; - ratskammer, f., *store room*; - raum, m., *fore hold.*

Vorrichtung, f., *gear*; - zur Entlastung des Sicherheitsventils, *easing g.*

Vorroyal, n., *fore royal*; - Bauchgording, f., *f. r. bunt line*; - brasse, f., *f. r. brace*; - bulien, f., *f. r. bowline*; - fall, n., *f. r. halliard*; - geitau, n., *f. r. clew line*; - Längssahling, f., *f. topgallant trestle trees.*

Vorroyalleesegel, n., *fore royal studding sail*; - Außenschote, f.,*f. r. s.s. tack*; - Binnenschote, f., *f. r. s. s. sheet*; - fall, n., *f. r. s. s. halliard*; - hals, m., *f. r. s.*

s. tack; - Niederholer, m., *f. r. s. s. downhaul*; - rahe, f., *f. r. s. s. yard*; - schote, f., *f. r. s. s. sheet*; - spiere, f., *f. r. s. s. boom.*

Vorroyal-pardune, f., *fore royal backstay*; - pferd, n., *f. r. foot rope*; - rahe, f., *f. r. yard*; - sahling, f., *f. topgallant cross trees*; - schote, f., *f. royal sheet*; - stag, n., *f. r. stay*; - - segel, n., *f. r. staysail*; - stenge, f., *f. r. mast*; - - Pardune, f., *f. r. backstay*; - - stag, n., *f. r. stay*; - Toppenant, f., *f. r. lift*; - want, n., *f. r. rigging.*

Vorscheisegel, n., *fore skysail*; - brasse, f., *f. s. brace*; - fall, n., *f. s. halliard*; - geitau, n., *f. s. clew line*; - pardune, f., *f. s. backstay*; - pferd, n., *f. s. foot rope*; - rahe, f., *f. s. yard*; - schote, f., *f. s. sheet*; - stag, n., *f. skysail stay*; - stenge, f., *f. skysail mast*; - - pardune, f., *f. s. backstay*; - - stag, n., *f. s. stay*; - Toppenant, f., *f. skysail lift.*

Vorschießen der Buttenden, n., *shift of the butt ends.*

Vor-schiff, n., *bow, prow*; - schlaghammer, m., *sledge hammer*; - schleppendem Anker treiben, *to be clubbing*; - schoten, *1. head sheets*; *2. to sheet home*; - schrift, f., *rule*; - schriftsmäßige Lichter, *regulation lights*; - schuß, m., *advance*; - - anweisung, f., *a. note*; - segel, *head sails*; - spannen, *to make fast*; - spill, n., *jeer capstan*; - springende Bug, m., *flaring bow*; - stagsegel, n., *foretop staysail*; - stand eines Seemannsamts, m., *Superintendent of a Mercantile Marine Office*; - stange, f., *fore topmast*; - steckstift, m., *pin.*

Vorstenge, f., *fore topmast*; - pardune, f., *f. t. backstay.*

Vorstengestag, n., *fore topmast stay*; - segel, n., *f. t.
staysail*; - - fall, n., *f. t. s.
halliard*; - - hals, m., *f. t. s.
tack*; - - leiter, f., *f. t. s. stay*;
- - Niederholer, m., *f. t. staysail downhaul*; - - schote, f.,
f. t. s. sheet; - - - schenkel,
m., *f. t. s. s. pendant.*
Vorstenge-want, n., *fore topmast shroud*; - wanten, f. t.
rigging.
Vorsteven, m., *stem*; - Aufklotzung, f., *s. deadwood*; -
knie, n., *stemson*; - - bolzen,
m., *s. bolt*; - niete, f., *stem
rivet*; - platte, f., *s. plate.*
Vortakel, n., *fore tackle.*
Vortank, m., *fore tank*; - Füll-
und Saugventilkasten, m.,
*f. t. filling and suction
valve.*
Vor-tau, n., *head fast*; - todholz, n., *fore deadwood.*
Vortoppsegel, n., *fore topsail*;
- brasse, f., *f. t. brace*; -
geitau, n., *f. t. clew line*; -
rahe, f., *f. t. yard.*
Vortreisegel, n., *fore trysail*;
- Ausholer, m., *f. t. outhaul*;
- baum, m., *f. t. boom*; -
Dempgording, f., *f. t. brails*;
- Einholer, m., *f. t. inhaul*;
- fall, m., *f. t. halliard*; -
gaffel, f., *f. t. gaff*; - - gerde,
f., *f. t. g. vang*; - - - schenkel,
m., *f. t. g. v. pendant*; - geitau, n., *f. t. brails*; - gerde,
f., *f. t. vang*; - hals, m., *f. t.
tack*; - Klaufall, m., *f. trysail
throat halliard*; - Piekfall,
m., *f. trysail peak h.*; - schote,
f. t. sheet.
vorüberfahren, *to pass*; in
Lee -, *t. p. to leeward.*

Vor- und Hinter-Schoner, m.,
fore and aft schooner; - - -
Segel, *f. a. a. sails.*
Vorunterbram-brasse, f., *lower
fore topgallant brace*; -
pferd, n., *l. f. t. foot rope*;
- rahe, f., *l. f. t. yard*; -
segel, n., *l. f. t. sail.*
Vorunterleesegel, n., *fore
lower studding sail*; -
Außenfall, n., *f. l. s. s. outer
halliard*; - Außenschote, f.,
f. l. s. s. tack; - Binnenfall,
n., *f. l. s. s. inner halliard*;
- Binnenschote, f., *f. l. s. s.
sheet*; - fall, n., *f. l. s. s.
halliard*; - hals, m., *f. l. s. s.
tack*; - rahe, f., *f. l. s. s.
yard*; - schote, f., *f. l. s. s.
sheet.*
Voruntermars-Bauchgording,
f., *lower fore topsail bunt
line*; - brasse, f., *l. f. t.
brace*; - - schenkel, m., *l. f.
t. b. pendant*; - pferd, n., *l.
f. t. foot rope*; - rahe, f., *l.
f. t. yard*; - segel, n., *l. f. t.*
Voruntertoppsegel, n., *lower
fore topsail*; - brasse, f., *l.
f. t. brace*; - rahe, f., *l. f. t.
yard.*
Vorwärmer, m., *steam heater.*
Vorwärtsexzenter, n., *go-ahead
eccentric*; - bügel, m., *g. a.
e. strap*; - scheibe, f., *g. a.
e. sheave*; - stange, f., *g. a.
e. rod.*
vorwärtsgehen, *to go ahead.*
vorwärtsgehende Bewegung,
f., *ahead motion.*
Vorwärts Geradführung or
- Gleitbahn, f., *ahead way
guides.*
vull und bi! *full and by!*

W.

waaken, *to wake.*
Wache, f., *watch*; - ablösen,
to relieve the w.; - auf Deck,

w. on deck; - haben, *to keep
the w.*; - halten, *to keep w.*;
- purren, *to turn out the w.*;

- setzen, *to set the w.*; - um
-, *w. and w.*; - zur Koje, *w.
below.*
wachen, *to watch.*
wachende Klippe, f., *lurking
rock*; - Riff, n., *l. reef.*
Wachrolle, f., *watch bill.*
wachsames Auge nach luv-
wärts, *to keep a weather
eye.*
Wachs-leinwand, f., or - tuch,
n., *oil cloth.*
wacht, die Boje -, *the buoy
is awake.*
Wacht-glas, n., *watch glass*;
- habender Offizier, m.,
*officer of the w. od. officer
on duty*; - schiff, n., *guard
ship*; - wimpel, m., *watch
pennant.*
Wagenkessel, m., *waggon
shaped boiler.*
Wägerung *see* Wegerung.
Wahl, nach -, *optional.*
wahre Breite, f., *true latitude*;
- Höhe, f,. *t. altitude*; - Kurs,
m., *t. course*; - Zeit, f., *t.
time.*
wahres Besteck, n., *ship's
place by observation.*
Wahr-tonne, f., *buoy*; -zeichen,
n., *mark.*
Waiger or Waigerung *see*
Wegerung.
waken, *to wake.*
Walboot, n., *whale boat.*
Walfisch, m., *whale*; - boot,
n., *w. boat*; - fahrer, m.,
whaler; - fang, m., *whale
fishery*; - fänger, m., *whaler.*
Wall-anker, m., *shore anchor*;
- gang, m., *1. wing passage*;
2. upper strake (of a boat);
- gänge, *gangways in the
hold*; - gangsschott, n.,
*watertight wing passage
bulkhead*; - nußholz, n., *walnut*; - schiene, f., *rubbing
strake.*
wallt, die Nadel -, *the needle
yaws.*
Walrückendampfer, m., *whaleback steamer.*

Walz-eisen, n., *rolled iron*; -
stahl, m., *r. steel.*
Walzenkessel mit innerer
Feuerung, m., *Cornish boiler.*
Wandelkragen, m., *mast hole
collar.*
Wanderbügel, m., *jib traveller
(of the jib).*
Wandering, *drifts.*
wandernde Sandbank, f.,
shifting sand.
Wandlampe, f., *bulkhead lamp.*
wanken, *to vacillate.*
Want, n., *shroud.*
Wanten, *shrouds*; - einbinden,
to turn in the rigging; -nach-
weben, *to square the ratlines*;
- schwichten, *to span in the
rigging*; - strecken, *to square
the dead eyes.*
Want - klampe, f., *shroud
cleat*; - klotje, n., *s. truck*;
- knopf or - knoten, m., *s.
knot*; einen - - einschlagen,
to k. a s. with a s. k.; -
kreuz, n., *rigging span*; -
matte, f., *hanging mat*; -
schlag, m., *shroud laid rope*;
- schraube, f., *rigging screw*;
- stopper, m., *shroud stopper*;
- takel, n., *shroud tackle*; -
tau, n., *shroud.*
Wanttau der Besahnbram-
stenge, n., *jigger topgallant
shroud*; - - Besahnmars-
stenge, *j. topmast s.*; - - Besahnstenge, *1. mizen t. s.*;
2. jigger t. s. (4 mast ship);
- - Bramstenge, *topgallant s.*;
- - Großbramstenge, *main
t. s.*; - - großen Stenge or
- - Großmarsstenge, *m. topmast s.*; - - Jiggerbram-
stenge, *jigger topgallant s.*;
- - Jiggermarsstenge, *j. topmast s.*; - - Kreuzbram-
stenge, *mizen topgallant s.*;
- - Kreuzmarsstenge, *m. topmast s.*; - - Marsstenge, *t. s.*;
- - Mittelbramstenge, *middle
topgallant s.*; - - Mittelmars-
stenge, *m. topmast s.*; - -
Stenge, *t. s.*; - - Vorbram-

stenge, *fore topgallant s.*; - - Vormarsstenge, *f. topmast s.*; - - Vorstenge, *f. t. s.*
Wanttau des Besahnmastes, *1. mizen shroud*; *2. jigger s.* (*4 mast ship*); - - Fockmastes, *fore lower s.*; - - Großmastes, *main s.*; - - Jiggermastes, *jigger s.*; - - Kreuzmastes, *mizen s.*; - - Mittelmastes, *middle mast s.*; - - Untermastes, *lower s.*

wantweise geschlagenes Tau, n., *shroud laid rope.*

Wärme-beschaffenheit, f., *temperature*; - durch Reibung, *heat by friction*; - einheit, f., *unit of heat*; - leiter, m., or - leitung, f., *1. transmission of h.*; *2. conductor of h.*; - messer, m., *calorimeter*; - messung, f., *calorimetry*; - schutzmasse, f., *non-conductor*; - stoff, m., *caloric*; - überführung or - übertragung, f., *transmission of heat*; - verlust, m., *loss of h.*

warmer Strom, m., *warm current.*

warmlaufen, *running hot.*

Warmwasser-pumpe, f., *hot water pump*; - rohr, n., *h. w. pipe.*

Warnungs-glocke, f., *signal bell*; - signale, *warning signals.*

Warp, n., *warp*; - anker, m., *kedge*; - boje, f., *warping buoy*; - pforte, f., *w. port*; - trosse, f., *w. line.*

warpen, *kedging.*

Warrel-block, m., *swivel block*; - bolzen, m., *s. bolt*; - haken, m., *s. hook.*

Warte, f., *observatory.*

Wasch-boot, n., *laundry boat*; - borde, f., *wash boards.*

waschen, *to buck (a sail).*

Wasch-hahn, m., *ash cock*; - jollen, *clothes lines*; - - tau, n., *c. l.*; - planken, *wash boards*; - platten, *w. plates.*

Waschwasser-hahn, m., *water service cock*; - rohr, n., *w. s. pipe*; - und Kühlwasser-Vorrichtung, f., *w. s. installations*; - Vorrichtungen für Reinigungszwecke, *w. s. for cleaning purposes.*

Wasser, das - beginnt zu laufen, *the tide is making*; - - fällt, *t. t. is falling*; - kentert, *t. t. is turning*; - - läßt nach, *t. t. slackens*; - - läuft ab, *t. t. is falling*; - - setzt um, *t. t. is turning*; - - steigt, *t. t. is rising*; - - steigt im Raum, *the water is making in the hold*; - - wird schwach, *the tide is getting slack*; - - wird schwächer, *t. t. i. g. weaker*; - - wird stärker, *t. t. is gaining.*

Wasser machen, *making water*; mehr - - als man auspumpen kann, *m. more w. than the pumps can throw up.*

Wasser übernehmen, *to ship water.*

Wasser-ablaßhahn, m., *water outlet cock*; - ballast, m., *w. ballast*; - Kompartiment, n., *w. b. compartment*; - - tank, m., *w. b. tank*; - bau, m., *hydraulics*; - - Ingenieur or - - Techniker, m., *hydraulic engineer*; - boot, n., *water boat*; - borde, f., *wash boards*; - brücke, f., *w. bridge (in boiler)*; - dampf, m., *steam.*

wasser-dicht, *water tight*; - dichte Gleitdichtung, f., *w. t. joint*; - - Kompartiment, n., *w. t. compartment*; - - Querschott, n., *w. t. bulkhead*; - - Schott, n., *w. t. b.*; - - Spant, n., *w. t. frame*; - - Tür, f., *w. t. door.*

Wasser-druck, m., *hydraulic pressure*; - - probe, f., *h. test*; - fänger über den Seitenfenstern, *wash rings over the side windows*; - faß, n., *water cask*; - - pumpe, f., *hand pump*; - galle, f., *wind gall*; - gang, m., *1. waterway (wooden)*; *2. deck stringer plate (iron)*; - - bolzen, m., *waterway bolt*; - hahn, m., *water cock*; - hose, f., *w. spout*; - kammer, f., *w. space (of condenser)*; - klerk, m., *w. clerk*; - klosett, n., *W. C. (i. e. water closet)*; - - rohr. n., *soil pipe*; - - tür, f., *W. C. door*; - lauf, m., *limbers*; - - loch, n., *limber hole*; - leitung, f., *water conduit*; - lieger, m., *leaguer*; - linie, f., *water line*; - machen, *to make w.*; - mangel, m., *short of w.*; - messer, m., *water gauge*; - paß, *horizontal*; - - Riß, m., *half breadth plan*; - pforte, f., *wash port*; - platz, m., *watering place*; - raum, m., *water space*; - recht, *horizontal*; - rinne auf Deck, f., *spurn water*; - riß, m., *floor plan*; - rohr-Hülfskessel, m., *water tube donkey boiler*; - rohrkessel, m., *w. t. boiler*; - sammler, m., *w. catcher*; - - garnitur, f., *w. c. fittings*; - schlange, f., *w. pipe*; - schlauch, m., *w. hose*; - schote, f., *lower studding sail sheet*; - schout, m., *Superintendent of a Mercantile Marine Office*; - schraube, f., *Dutch screw*; - segel, n., *water sail*; - spiegel, m., *level of the sea*; - stag, n., *bobstay*; - - band, n., *hoop for b.*; - - bolzen, m., *b. pin*; - - kette, f., *b. chain*; - - stange, f., *b. bar*; - stand, m., *water level (in boiler)*; - - anzeiger, m., *w. l. indicator*; - - apparat, m., *w. gauge column*; - - Dichtungsring, m., *w. g. glass ring*; - - glas, n., *w. g. g.*; - - hahn, m., *w. gauge cock*; - - lampe, f., *w. g. lamp*; - - rohr, n., *w. g. pipe*; - - zeiger, m., *w. g.*; - stiefel, m., *fishing boots*; - strahl,

m., *water jet*; - tiefe, f., *depth of w.*; gelotete - -, *soundings*; - tracht, f., *sea gauge*; - trichter, m., *water funnel*; - trompete, f., *w. spout*; - ventil, n., *w. valve*; - verbrauch, m., *consumption of w.*; - verdrängung, f., *displacement*; - - Tonnengehalt, m., *d. tonnage*; - vorrat, m., *supply of water*; - zuflußrohr, n., *w. s. pipe*.

Watt, n., *flat bank*.

Webeleine, f., *ratline*; - bändsel or - bindsel, n., *r. seizing*; - stich, m., *clove hitch*.

Wechsel-feuer, n., *alternating light*; - hahn, m., *distributing cock*; - ventilkasten, m., *communication box*; - weise Bewegung, f., *alternative motion*.

wechseln den Ankerplatz, *to shift the anchorage*.

Weg, m., *passage*.

weg-fieren, *to slack away, to veer out*; - geflogen, *carried away (sails)*; - geschlagen, *c. a.*; - lassen, *to leave out*; - laufen vor dem Winde, *to gale away*; - nahme, f., *1. capture, 2. seizure*; - sacken, *1. to sink (in water)*; *2. to vanish (on the horizon)*; - setzen, *to scuttle (a ship)*; - sinken, *to sink*; - stauen, *to stow away*; - weiser, m., *fairleader*; - - block, m., *leading block*; - - kauß, f., *wapp*; - - klotje, n., *fair lead truck*; - - latte mit Scheiben, *rack*; - - leine, f., *spurling line*.

Wege, weit aus dem - gehen, *to give a wide berth*.

Weger *see* Wegerung.

Wegerecht, n., *right of way*; - lampe, f., or - licht, n., *r. o. w. lamp* or *light*.

Wegering or Wegerung, f., *ceiling*; - latten, *cargo battens*; - legen, *to place the ceiling*; - luke, f., *c. hatch*; - planke, f., *c. plank*.

Wehr, n., *weir.*

Weiberknoten, m., *granny's bend.*

Weichenlampe, f., *right of way lamp.*

weicher Stahl, m., *mild steel.*

weiches Eisen, n., *soft iron;* - Holz, n., s. *wood.*

Weichlot, n., *soft solder.*

Weierpumpe, f., *weir pump.*

Weigering see Wegerung.

Weinzieher, m., *sampling tube.*

Weirpumpe, f., *weir pump.*

weisen, *to grow;* die Kette weist unter das Schiff, *t. g. underneath the vessel;* wie mit dem Stengstag -, *t. g. a short stay;* zum Springen steif -, *t. g. exceedingly.*

weiße Bö, f., *white squall;* - Licht, n., *white light;* - Tau, n., *w. rope.*

Weißeichenholz, n., *white oak.*

weißen, *to whitewash.*

Weiß-glut or - glühhitze, f., *white heat;* - metall, n., *w. metal;* - - garnitur, f., *w. m. lining;* mit - - ausfüllen, *to line with w. m.*

weitab, *aloof.*

weite Ringkette, f., *round linked chain.*

Weitenzirkel, m., *circle of amplitude.*

weiter dampfen, *to steam on;* - langen or - mannen, *to hand along;* - verfrachten, *to recharter;* - verfrachtung, f., r.

Well, f., *well;* - deckschiff, n., *w. d. ship.*

Welle, f., *1. wave (of the sea); 2. shaft (engine and propeller); 3. engine shaft (of steam winch); 4. main piece (of windlass); 5. barrel (of steering wheel); 6.* - mit 2 Kurbeln, *the two throw crank shaft.*

Welle entblößen, *to strip the shaft.*

Wellen-berg, m., *mountainous waves;* - beruhiger, m., *wave subduer;* - bock, m., *propeller shaft stay;* - brecher, m., *breakwater;* - bruch, m., 1. *broken shaft (of propeller);* 2. *breaker (of reefs);* - furche, f., *furrows between two waves;* - gebirge, n., *mountainous sea;* - gepeitscht, *wave beaten;* - geschwindigkeit, f., *speed of waves;* - kamm, m., *ridge of a vave;* - keilnute, f., *shaft key way;* - kupplung, f., s. *coupling;* - lager, n., s. *bearing;* - - deckel des Mittelbetings, m., *centre bitt keep;* - - - des Seitenbetings, *side b. k.;* - länge, f., *length of a wave;* - leitung, f., *shafting;* - periode, f., *period of waves;* - ringe, *thrust shaft collars;* - rohr, n., *stern tube;* - schlag, m., *shock of the waves;* - strang, m., *line of shafting;* - stück der Kurbelwelle, n., *crank shaft journal;* - tal, n., *trough of the sea;* - träger, m., *propeller shaft stay;* - tunnel, m., *shaft tunnel.*

Wellgrund, m., *shifting ground.*

Weltumsegelung, f., *circumnavigation of the world.*

Wende-hahn, m., *master cock;* - kreise, *tropics.*

Wendeisen, n., *tap wrench.*

wenden, *to go about (sailing by the wind);* auf derselben Stelle -, *to come round on the heel;* über den Achtersteven -, *to make a sternboard;* durch den Wind -, *to change the tack;* Klar zum -! *Ready about!*

Wendung, f., *to veer round;* in - liegen, *to be in stays;* - versagen, *to refuse staying.*

werfen, 1. *to cast (anchor);* 2. *to jettison (cargo).*

Werft, f., 1. *wharf (for mooring ships);* 2. *yard (for ship building);* - block, *launching block.*

Werft los! *Let go!*

Werftenblock, m., *careening block*.

Werg, n., *oakum*; - auskauen, *to expel the o. out of the seams*; - draht, m., *thread of o.*; - haken, m., *rave hook*; - zopf, m., *pledget*.

Werk, n., *works*; - führer or - meister, m., *foreman*; - statt, f., *1. loft (for sails and rigging)*; *2. workshop (machinery, &c.)*.

Werkzeug, n., *tool*; - halter, m., *t. holder*; - schärfen or - schleifen, *to grind tools*; - zum Rohreinsetzen, *tube fixing tools*.

Wertverminderung, f., *depreciation*.

West-indienfahrer, m., *West India trader*; - küstfahrer, *West Coast trader*.

westliche Länge, f., *west longitude*; - Mißweisung, f., *westerly variation*.

Westwind, m., *west wind*.

Wetter-deck, n., *weather deck*; - dicht or - fest, *w. tight*; - galle, f., *w. gall*; - küste, f., *w. shore*; - leuchten, n., *sheet lightning*; - loch, n., *cave of the wind*; - seite, f., *weather side*; - Stringerplatte, f., *gunwale plate*; - warte, f., *meteorological observatory*.

Wetter, vom - arg mitgenommen, *weather beaten*.

Wettfahrt, f., *race*; - zwischen Seglern, *sailing match*.

Wettrudern, n., *boat race*.

Wettsegeln, n., *regatta*.

Weymouthkieferholz, n., *white pine wood*.

Wider-halttau, n., *the running end of a rope*; - ruf, m., *countermand*; - see, f., *the back sweep of the waves*; - stand durch Reibung, m., *resistance by friction*; - kraft, f., *resisting power*; - stehen, *1. to resist*; *2. to weather out (a gale)*; - stehende Kraft, f., *resistance*.

widriger Wind, m., *head wind*.

Wiederaufnahme, f., *restoration (of classification)*.

wieder-ausbüchsen, *to rebush*; - ausfüllen, *to reline (the brasses)*; - durchscheren, *to rereeve*; - einhängen, *to reship (a rudder, &c.)*; - einnehmen, *to reship (cargo)*; - einschiffen, *to re-embark*; - einschiffung, f., *re-embarkation*; - einsetzen, *to reship (a mast)*; - holen, *to repeat (a signal)*; - holungsflagge, f., *substitute for the first flag*; - in Ordnung bringen, *to clear*; - verfrachten, *to recharter*; - verfrachtung, f., *r.*; - verlaschen, *to relash*; - verschalken, *to rebatten*; - verstauen, *to restow*.

Wiege, f., *cradle*; - amtsattest, n., *meter's certificate*; - attest, *weigh note*.

wiegen, *to rock (on the water)*.

Wiek, n., *cove*.

Wientakel, n., *double Spanish burton*.

wild, *wild (compass, ship)*.

Wimpel, m., *pendant*.

Wind, m., *1. wind, 2. gale (force 7-10)*; - abgeschnitten, *becalmed; an den - gehen, to lay a vessel close to the wind*; auf dem Winde liegen, *to lie head to wind*; - - - liegend, *wind rode*; - ist auf und nieder, *the w. is up and down*; - auffangende Segel, *drawing sails*; - aus einem Segel nehmen, *spilling*; beim Winde segeln, *to go near the wind*; dicht beim - halten, *hard alee*; - dreht mit der Sonne auf, *the wind keeps with the sun*; - läuft schulen, *the w. has becalmed*; - mit West, *w. with west*; dem Winde näher kommen, *to bring the loof round*; - recht von hinten, *wind right aft*; - - - vorn, *w. r. ahead*; in den -

schießen lassen, *to luff alee*; - schießt mit der Sonne auf, *the wind keeps with the sun*; - setzt wieder ein, *the w. is blowing back again*; - springt um, *the w. shifts*; vor dem Winde, *before the w.*; - wird achterlicher, *the w. draws aft*; - zwingt zum Kreuzen, *beating w.*
Wind *see also* Brise.
Wind-anker, m., *lower anchor*; - brett, n., *wind board*; - eisen, n., *tap wrench*; - fahne, f., *vane*; - fang habend, *to be wind taught*; - galle, f., *weather gall;* - hauch, m., *cat's paw*; - hose, f., *whirlwind*; - jammerer, m., *wind jammer*; - karte, f., *w. chart*; - kessel, m., *air vessel*; - messer, m., *anemometer*; - mühlenpumpe, f., *wind mill pump*; - reep, n., *mast rope*; - rose, f., *rhumb card of a compass*; nach allen Richtungen der - -, *to all quarters of the globe*; - segel, n., *wind sail*; - -bänder, *w. s. hoops*; - stärke, f., *force of the w.*; - - messer, m. *anemometer*; - stau, f., *high water by force of the wind*; - still, *calm*; - stille, f., *c.*; in - - *becalmed*; - stillengürtel, m., *calm belt*; - stoß, m., *gust*; - streifen, m., *wind band*; - strich, m., *1. compass point*; *2. weather line*; - tutsen, *ventilators*; - vierung, f., *quarter*; - - auf der Leeseite, *on the lee q.*; - - - - Luvseite, *on the weather q.*; - wärts, *windward*; - wolke, f., *wind cloud.*
Winde, f., *1. reel (for winding lines, &c. on)*; *2. winch (for loading, &c.)*; - kopf, m., *warping end*; - trommel, f., *chain drum.*
Winden-Dampfablaßrohr, n., *winch exhaust pipe*; - dreher, m., *w. handle*; - fischung, f., *w. partner*; - gestell, n.,

standards *of a w.*; - kappe, f., *w. cover*; - kessel, m., *w. boiler*; - Kupplungsklaue, f., *w. clutch*; - rohrständer, m., *w. pipe cradle*; - schwengel, m., *w. handle*; - Sicherungsvorrichtung, f., *w. guards*; - trommel, f., *barrel of a w.*; - Ueberzug, m., *w. cover.*
Windsch, f., *winch (see* Winde).
Wingfeeder, m., *wing feeder.*
Winkbake, f., *signal beacon.*
Winkel, m., *angle bar*; - anker, m., *palm stay (of boiler)*; - balken, m., *angle bar beam*; - bewegung, f., *angular motion*; - des Backsülls, *forecastle coaming angle bar*; - des Brückenhaussülls, *bridge house c. a. b.*; - des Deckhaussülls, *deck h. c. a. b.*; - des erhöhten Quarterdecksülls, *raised quarter deck c. a. b.*; - des Lukensülls, *hatchway c. a. b.*; - distanz, f., *angular distance*; - eisen, n., *angle iron*; - - stringer, m., *a. i. stringer*; - tasser, m., *protractor*; - förmig, *angular*; - holz, n., *angle staff*; - knie, n., *bent knee*; - maß, n., *square*; - schlinge, f., *angle bar carling*; - schmiede, f., *a. forge*; - schnitt, m., *angular cut*; - stahl, m., *angle steel*; - stringer, m., *bar stringer.*
Winsch, f., *winch*; - läufer, m., *cargo runner.*
Winsch *see also* Winde.
Winschen, an den - arbeiten, *to drive winches.*
Winter-fahrten, *winter navigation*; - lager, n., *w. quarters*; - seezeichen, n., *w. sea marks.*
Wippe, f., *whip for discharging cargo.*
wippen, *to whip.*
Wirbel, m., *eddy*; - block, m., *swivel block*; - bolzen, m., *s. bolt*; - haken, m., *s. hook*; - strom, m., *whirlpool*; -

sturm, m., *cyclone*; - wind, m., *whirlwind*.

wirken, *to act*.

wirkliche Pferdekraft, f., *effective horse power*.

Wirksamkeit des Dampfes, f., *efficiency of steam*.

Wirkung, f., *effect*.

Wischer mit Gummiplatte, m., *rubber mop*.

wöchentlicher Verkehr, m., *weekly service*.

wogende See, f., *surging sea*.

wohlbehaltene Ankunft, f., *safe arrival*.

wohlgestaltet, *shapely*.

Wolke, f., *cloud*.

Wolken-bruch, m., *rain spout*; - feger, m., *moonsail*; - raper, m., *skyscraper*; - schraper, m., *moon raker*.

Worp or Worpe, f., *transom*; - bolzen, m., *t. bolt*; - platte, f., *t. plate*.

Worpen, *bindings*.

Wrack, n., *wreck*; - boje, f, *w. buoy*; - güter, *derelicts*; - pumpe, f., *wrecking pump*; - trümmer, *wreckage*.

Wracker, m., *wrecker*.

Wreifholz, n., *1. wooden fender; 2. rubbing strake*.

wricken, *to scull*.

Wrickriemen, m., *sculling oar*.

wriggen *to scull*.

Wuhling or Wuling, f., *1. woolding; 2. glut (round the capstan)*; - gatt im Gallionsschegg, n., *gammoning hole*: - kette, f., *g. chain*.

Wulst, m., *collar*; - balken, m., *bulb beam*; - eisen, n., *bulb iron*; - platte, f., *b. plate*; - schiene, f., *b. p.*: - - balken, m., *b. beam*; - - schlinge, f., *bulb plate carling*; - stahl, m., *b. steel*; - T-balken, m., *T.-b. beam*; - winkel, m., *bulb angle bar*; - - balken, m., *bulb a. beam*; - - eisen, n., *bulb a. iron*.

Wurf, m., *cast*; - anker, m., *kedge anchor*; - - tau, n., *stream cable*; - leine, f., *heaving line*; - probe, f., *fall proof*.

Wurm-haut, f., *bottom sheathing*; - stichig, *worm eaten*.

Wurst in dem Want, f., *futtock staff*.

Würste or Wursten, *bow grace*.

Wurzel der Buhne, f., *the root end of a fascine work*.

W. z. N., *West by North*.

W. z. S., *West by South*.

Wyk, f., *creek*.

Z.

Zacken, *arms (of a knee)*; - rad, n., *tappet wheel*.

zackig, *indented*.

Zähfestigkeit, f., *tensil strength*.

Zähigkeit, f., *tenacity*; - probe, f., *tensile test*.

Zahlmeister, m., *purser*.

Zahn, m., *tooth*; - flanke, f., *flank of a t. of a wheel*; - hobel, m., *toothing plane*; - kupplung, f., *clutch*; - länge, f., *depth (of a cog)*; - loses Rad, n., *friction wheel*; -

rad, n., *cog w.*; - - kranz, m., *c. w. rim*.

Zange, f., *nippers*.

Zapfen, m., *pin, pivot, tenon*; - lager, n., *plummer block*; - - metall, n., *antifriction metal*; - loch, n., *mortise*; - - zum Vernageln, *m. to be bolted*.

zechengesiebte Kohlen, *colliery screened coals*.

Zedernholz, n., *cedar wood*.

Zeichen, n., *mark*.

Zeichner, m., *draughtsman*.

Zeichnung, f., *drawing*.

Zeigen der Flagge, n., *showing the flag*.

Zeiger, m., *gauge*; - am Manometer, *float stick*; - blatt a. M., n., *steam gauge dial*.

Z-eisen, n., *Z-iron*.

zeisen, *to seize*.

Zeisig or Zeising, m., *seizing* (*see also* Bändsel); einen - befestigen, *to nipper*; einen - an das Kabel (or die Kette) befestigen, *nipping the cable*.

Zeit-ball, m., *time ball*; - befrachtung or - charter, f., *t. charter*; - beobachtung, f., *t. sight*; - fracht, f., *t. freight*; - signalball, m., *t. ball*.

Zelt, n., *awning*; - baum, m., *a. boom*; - reepband, n., *a. hoop*; - ständer, m., *a. stanchion*; - strebe, f., *a. stretcher*.

Zement, n., *cement*; - stahl, m., *cemented steel*.

zementieren, *to cement*.

Zementierung, f., *cementing*.

Zenit, m., *zenith*; - distanz, f., *z. distance*.

Zente, f., *harpin*.

Zenterkielplatte, f., *middle line centre through plate keel*.

Zentral-Feuerbüchse, f., *centre furnace*; - kraft, f., *central force*; - lagerständer einer Pumpe, m., *centre bearing standard of a pump*.

Zentrifugal-kraft, f., *centrifugal power*; - pumpe, f., *c. pump*; - regulator, m., *Watt's regulator*; - ventilator, m., *screw fan*; - Zirkulationspumpe, f., *centrifugal circulating pump*.

Zentrum eines Zyklons, n., *centre of a cyclone*.

Zerbeizung or Zerfressung, f., *corrosion*.

zer-beulen, *full of dents*; - fetzen, *to tatter*; - fressen, *to corrode*; - reißen, *to tear, to part, to split*; die Segel

ganz in Stücke - -, *the wind blowing the sails all to smithers*; - reißprobe, f., *tearing test*; - schellen, *to be dashed to pieces*; - schlagen or - schmettern, *to smash*; - splittert, *broken in splinters*; - sprengung, f., *explosion*.

Zertifikat, n., *certificate*.

Zeug, n., *rigging*; - leine, f., *clothes line*.

Zeugnis, n., *discharge* (*of a sailor*).

Zickzack, n., *zig zag*; - kurs, m., *z. z. course*; - nietung, f., *z. z. riveting*; - schott, n., *z. z. bulkhead*.

ziehen, *to draw* (*ashes*).

Zifferblatt, n., *dial*.

Zille, f., *up-river barge*.

Zimmer, n., *room*; - arbeit, f., *carpenter's work*; - baas, m., *shipwright*; - mann, m., *carpenter*; - - hellegat, n., *carpenter's store room*; - - kammer, f., *c. r.*; - - knoten, m., *timber hitch*; - - maat, m., *carpenter's mate*; - - schnur, f., *c. chalk line*; - - stich, m., *timber hitch*.

Zimmerung, f., *repairs to a wooden hull*.

Zink-beschlag, m., *zinc sheathing*; - boot, n., *z. boat*; - haut, f., *z. sheathing*; - platte, f., *sheet of z.*; - weiß, n., *white z.*

Zirkel, m., *pair of compasses*.

Zirkulationspumpe, f., *circulating pump*; - Ausgußrohr, n., *c. p. discharge pipe*; - Ausgußventil, n., *c. p. d. valve*; - - deckel, m., *c. p. d. v. cover*; - - spindel, f., *c. p. d. v. spindle*; - Balancier, m., *c. p. lever*; - Dampfzuleitungsrohr, n., *c. p. steam pipe*; - deckel, m., *c. p. cover*; - Druckraum, m., *c. p. delivery space*; - Druckrohr, n., *c. p. discharge pipe*; - druckventil, n., *c. p. top valve*; - - Hubbegrenzer, m., *c. p. t.*

v. guard; - - Klappenfänger, m., *c. p. delivery valve guard*; - - sitz, m., *c. p. top valve seat*; - einsatz, m., *c. p. liner*; - exzenterbügel, m., *c. p. eccentric strap*; - - Paßstück, n., *c. p. e. s. liner*; - Fußventil, n., *c. p. foot valve*; - gelenk, n., *c. p. link*; - - Lagerschalen, *c. p. l. brasses*; - geschirr, n., *c. p. gear*; - Grundring, m., *c. p. neck bush*; - Halszapfen der Balancieraxe, m., *c. p. lever shaft journal*; - - - Traverse, *c. p. crosshead j.*; - Hauptausgußventilspindel, f., *c. p. main discharge valve spindle*; - kolben, m., *c. p. bucket*; - - ring, m., *c. p. b. ring*; - - stange, f., *c. p. piston rod*; - - und Kammer, *c. p. bucket and chamber*; - - ventil, n., *c. p. b. valve*; - - - Hubbegrenzer or - - - Klappenfänger, m., *c. p. b. v. guard*; - Kolbenventilsitz, m., *c. p. b. v. seat*; - körper, m., *c. p. chamber*; - - deckel, m., *c. p. c. door*; - Kreuzkopf, m., *c. p. crosshead*; - Luftauslaßventil or - Luftventil, n., *c. p. air valve*; - Plunger, m., *c. p. plunger*; - Probierhahn, m., *c. pump pet cock*; - Saugeraum, m., *c. pump suction space*; - Saugerohr, n., *c. p. suction pipe*; - Saugeventil, n., *c. p. s. valve*; - - Hubbegrenzer, m., *c. p. s. v. guard*; - - Klappenfänger, m., *c. p. foot v. g.*; - - sitz, m., *c. p. suction valve seat*; - Schnürhahn, m., *c. p. pet cock*; - stange, f., *c. pump rod*; - - Stopfbüchse, f., *c. p. r. stuffing box*; - Stopfbüchse, f., *c. p. s. b.*; - - deckel, m., *c. p. s. b. gland*; - Traverse, f., *c. p. crosshead*; - Ventil, n., *c. p. valve*; - - Hubbegrenzer or - - Klappenfänger, m., *c. p. v. guard*; - - sitz, m *c. p. v. seat*; -

Windkessel, m., *c. p. air vessel*; - Zylinder, m., *c. p. barrel.*

Zirkulationspumpenmaschine, f., *circulating pump engine*; - Absperrventil, n., *c. p. e. stop valve*; - Anlaßventil, n., *c. p. e. starting v.*; - Dampfabführungsrohr, n., *c. p. e. exhaust pipe*; - Exzenter, n., *c. p. e. eccentric*; - - bolzen, m., *c. p. e. e. bolt*; - - bügel, m., *c. p. e. e. strap*; - - Lagerschalen, *c. p. e. e. brasses*; - - scheibe, f., *c. p. e. e. sheave*; - - stange, f., *c. p. e. e. rod*; - Kolben, m., *c. p. e. bucket*; - - stange, f., *c. p. e. piston rod*; - - - Kreuzkopf, m., *c. p. e. p. r. crosshead*; - - Stopfbüchse, f., *c. p. e. p. r. stuffing box*; - - - - deckel, m., *c. p. e. p. r. s. b. gland*; - Kreuzkopflagerbolzen, m., *c. p. e. crosshead bolt*; - Kreuzkopflagerschalen, *c. p. e. brasses*; - - deckel, m., *c. p. e. connecting rod top end keep*; - Kurbelwelle, f., *c. p. e. crank shaft*; - - lager, n., *c. p. e. c. s. bearing*; - - - deckel, m., *c. p. e. c. s. b. keep*; - - - - bolzen, m., *c. p. e. c. s. b. k. bolt*; - Kurbelwellenlagerschalen, *c. p. e. c. s. bearing brasses*; - - Paßstück, n., *c. p. e. c. s. bearing liner*; - Kurbelzapfenlagerbolzen, m., *c. p. e. crank pin bolt*; - Kurbelzapfenlagerschalen, *c. p. e. c. p. brasses*; - - deckel, m., *c. p. e. connecting rod bottom end keep*; - Pleyelstange, f., *c. p. e. c. r.*; - - bolzen, m., *c. p. e. c. r. bolt*; - - fuß-Paßstück, n., *c. p. e. c. r. bottom end liner*; - Schieber, m., *c. p. e. slide valve*; - - kasten, m., *c. p. e. valve casing*; - - - deckel, m., *c. p. e. v. c. door*; - Schieberstange, f., *c. p. e. v. rod*; - - Stopfbüchse, f., *c. p.*

e. v. r. stuffing box; - - - deckel, m., c. p. e. v. r. s. b. gland; - Zylinderdeckel, m., c. p. e. cylinder cover; - - bolzen, m., c. p. e. c. c. bolt; - Zylinder-Entwässerungs- rohr, n., c. p. e. cylinder drain pipe.

Zisterne, f., hotwell.

zittern, panting.

Zoll, m., duty; - abfertigung, f., permit; - abgabe, f., duty; - amt, n., custom house; - aufseher, m., surveyor of customs; - beamter, m., custom house officer; - be- hörde, f., customs authorities; - fahrzeug, n., revenue vessel; - frei, duty free; - - schein, m., bill of sufferance; - ge- setze, custom house regu- lations; - kutter, m., revenue cutter; - laterne, f., custom light; - niederlage, f., bonded warehouse; - pflichtig, sub- ject to pay duty; - stander, m., revenue pendant; - ver- ordnungen, custom regu- lations.

Zone, f., zone.

zorren, to lash.

zu Anker gehen, to come to an anchor; - Lande, by land; - leicht bemastet, under- masted; - nahe dem Lande, too near the land; - niedri- ger Druck, m., insufficient pressure; - reichlich ver- sehen, over supply; - schwach bemannt, under- manned; - starker Druck, m., excessive pressure; - Wasser, by sea; - weit ab, too far off.

Zubehör, n., gear.

Zucker-Ahornholz, n., rock maple wood.

Zufluchtshafen, m., harbour of refuge; - reede, f., road of r.

Zufluß, m., flow.

Zug, m., 1. draught (of tunnel); 2. strain (on cables); 3. branch (of pumps); 4. airs (Wind).

zugänglich, approachable.

zugefroren, ice bound.

Zugerzeugungsmaschine, f., forced draught engine; - Ab- sperrventil, n., f. d. e. stop valve; - Anlaßventil, n., f. d. e. starting v.; - Dampfab- führungsrohr, n., f. d. e. exhaust pipe; - Dampfzu- leitungsrohr, n., f. d. e. steam pipe; - Exzenter, n., f. d. e. eccentric; - - bolzen, m., f. d. e. e. bolt; - - bügel, m., f. d. e. e. strap; - - bügel-Paß- stück, n., f. d. e. e. s. liner; - - Lagerschalen, f. d. e. e. brasses; - - scheibe, f., f. d. e. e. sheave; - - stange, f., f. d. e. e. rod; - Kolben, m., f. d. e. piston; - - stange, f., f. d. e. p. rod; - - - Kreuz- kopf, m., f. d. e. p. r. cross- head; - - - Stopfbüchse, f., f. d. e. p. r. stuffing box; - - - - deckel, m., f. d. e. p. r. s. b. gland; - Kreuzkopf- lagerbolzen, m., f. d. e. cross- head bolt; - Kreuzkopf- lagerschalen, f. d. e. c. brasses; - - deckel, m., f. d. e. connecting rod top end keep; - Kurbelwelle, f., f. d. e. crank shaft; - - lager, n., f. d. e. c. s. bearing; - - - bolzen, m., f. d. e. c. s. b. bolt; - - - deckel, m., f. d. e. c. s. bearing keep; - - - - bolzen, m., f. d. e. c. s. b. k. bolt; - Kurbelwellenlager- schalen, f. d. e. c. s. bearing brasses; - - deckel, m., f. d. e. c. s. bearing keep; - - Paßstück, n., f. d. e. c. s. brasses liner; - Kurbel- zapfenlagerbolzen, m., f. d. e. c. s. pin bolt; - Kurbel- zapfenlagerschalen, f. d. e. c. s. p. brasses; - - deckel, m., f. d. e. connecting rod bottom end keep; - Pleyel- stange, f., f. d. e. c. r.; - - bolzen, m., f. d. e. c. r. bolt; - - fuß-Paßstück, n., f. d. e. c. r. bottom end liner; -

Schieber, m., *f. d. e. slide valve*; - - kasten, m., *f. d. e. v. casing*; - - - deckel, m., *f. d. e. v. c. door*; - Schieberstange, f., *f. d. e. v. rod*; - - Stopfbüchse, f., *f. d. e. v. r. stuffing box*; - - - deckel, m., *f. d. e. v. r. s. b. gland*; - Zylinder, m., *f. d. e. cylinder*; - - deckel, m., *f. d. e. c. cover*; - - - bolzen, m., *f. d. e. c. c. bolt*; - Zylinder-Entwässerungsrohr, n., *f. d. e. cylinder drain pipe.*

zugesogen, *stopped accidentally (a leak).*

Zug-fähre, f., *horse ferry*; - feder, f., *spiral spring*; - festigkeit, f., *tensil strain*; - kessel, m., *flue boiler*; - leinen, *crowfoot lines*; - spannung, f., *strain*; - stange, f., *1. drag link (of eccentric gear)*; *2. purchase rod (of windlass)*; - werk, n., *block and tackle.*

zuhalten auf, *to steer for.*

Zunder, m., *touchwood.*

Zunge, f., *1. tongue piece (of machinery)*; *2. spindle (of a mast).*

zurichten, *to trim.*

zurren, *1. to lash, to seize*; *2. to gammon (the bowsprit).*

Zurring, f., *lashing*; - zweier Augen aneinander, *parrel l.*

Zurrings-brok, f., *boat's gripe*; - gat im Gallionsschegg, n., *gammoning hole*; - kette, f., *g. chain*; - tau, n., *lashing rope.*

zurück aus See wegen Wind und Wetter, *beaten back*; - backen, *to put aback*; - brassen, *to brace about again*; - dampfen, *to steam back*; - gehalten durch Unwetter, *weather bound*; - - durch Wind, *wind bound*; - - - - und Strömung, *backstrapped*; - gehen, *to go astern*; - gelegte Strecke, f., *distance run*; - geworfene See or Welle, f., *return sea*;

- kommen. *to put back*; - schlagen, *to back.*

Zusammen-drückung, f., *collapsion*; - fügen, *to connect*; - fügung, f., *connection*; - gesetzt, *compound*; - gesetzte Balkenkiel, m., *side bar keel*; - - Block, *made block*; - - Kurbel, f., *built-up crank*; - - - welle, f., *b. u. c. shaft*; - gesetzte Schraube, f., *b. u. propeller*; - legbares Boot, n., *folding boat*; - passen, *to adjust*; - pressen der Ladung, n., *steeving of cargo*; - schwichten, *to swift*; - stoß, m., *collision*; - stoßen, *1. to collide*; *2. to butt against (of timbers)*; - zeisen, *1. to frap*; *2. to seize*; - zwingen, *to heave in by means of a heaver.*

Zusatzerklärung, f., *additional declaration.*

zu-schärfen or - schrägen, *to snape*; - setzen, *1. to set more sails*; *2. to tally the sheets close a-board*; *3. to haul the tacks a.*; *4. to h. t. t. close a.* (soweit wie möglich); - stand, m., *state (of ship and cargo)*; - stellen, *to rig*; - steuern auf, *1. to bear in towards*; *2. to steer for.*

Zwei-deckschiff, n., *two deck vessel*; - drähtiges Segelgarn, n., *store twine*; - fache Expansionsmaschine, *double expansion engine*; - - Nietung, f., *d. riveting*; - felhafter Gesundheitspaß, m., *suspected bill of health*; - flügelige Schraube, f., *two bladed propeller*; - halbe Stiche, *two half hitches.*

Zweig-hahn, m., *service cock*; - kabel, n., *branch cable*; - rohr, n., *b. pipe.*

zwei-kurbelige Achse, f., *two throw crank shaft*; - mastig, *two masted*; - scheibiger Block, m., *double block*; - - Puppblock, m., *sister b.*; -

schrauben Dampfer, m., *twin screw steamer*; - wegehahn, m., *two way cock*; - wegschieber, m., *double ported slide valve*; - zylindrige Compoundmaschine, f., *d. cylinder compound engine*; - - Dampfmaschine, f., *d. cylinder steam e.*

zweite Buganker, m., *second bower*; - Kielschwein, n., *false keelson*; - Reff, n., *second reef*; - - band, n., *s. r. band.*

Zwillingsblock, m., *shoe block.*

Zwing-bolzen, m., *wring bolt*; - presse, f., *ferrule press.*

Zwinge, f., *ferrule.*

Zwinger, m., *wring staff.*

Zwischendeck, n., *1. between deck; 2. lower deck (of two deck vessel); 3. middle d. (of 3 or 4 d. v.); 4. steerage (for passengers)*; mit einem hohen or tiefen -, or tief verbunden im -, *high between deck.*

Zwischendeckbalken, m., *middle deck beam*; - Hängeknie, n., *m. d. b. hanging knee*; - Längsschiene, f., or - Lukenstringer, m., *m. d. b. tie plate*; - winkel, m., *m. d. b. angle bar.*

Zwischendeck-Balkweger, m., *middle deck beam shelf*; - band, n., *m. d. hook*; - Beplattung, f., *m. d. plating*; - Diagonalbänder, *m. d. tie plates*; - luke, f., *lower deck hatchway*; - - stringer, m., *l. d. beam tie plate*; - - süll, m., *l. d. hatchway coaming*; - Passagier, m., *steerage passenger*; - Schergang, m., *middle deck sheerstrake*; - Setzweger, m., *middle deck spirketting*; - stringer, m., *m. d. stringer*; - stütze, f., *m. d. stanchion*; - Unterbalkweger, m., *m. d. beam clamp*; - Wassergang, m., *m. d. waterway*; - weger, m., or - wegerung, f., *between decks ceiling.*

Zwischen - Gegenspant,   n.,

intermediate reversed frame; - hafen, m., *i. port*; - keil, m., *gib*; - platten, *intercostal plates*; - - Kimmstringerwinkel, m., *bilge i. stringer angle bar*; - - Seitenkielschwein, n., *side i. keelson*; - sente, f., *intermediate ribband*; - spant, n , *i. frame*; - träger, m., *intercostal girder*; - urteil, n., *interlocutary decree*; - Wind und Wasser, *between wind and water*; - - und Sturm liegen, *to ride b. wind a. tide.*

Zylinder, m., *cylinder*; - Abblashahn, m., *c. cock*; - Austrittskanal, m., *cylinder exhaust port*; - Bekleidung, f., *c. lagging*; - Boden, m., *c. bottom*; - Bohrmaschine, f., *c. boring machine*; - büchse, f., *c. liner*; - deckel, m., *c. cover*; - - bolzen, m., *c. c. bolt*; - - - mutter, f., *c. c. b. nut*; - deckel gesprungen, *c. c. gone*; - deckel-Stiftschraube, f., *c. c. stud*; - Drainagehahn, m., *cylinder drain cock*; - Drainagerohr, n., *cylinder d. pipe*; - einsatz, m., *c. liner*; - Entwässerungshahn, m., *c. drain cock*; - flansch, m., *cylinder flange*; - kessel, m., *cylindrical boiler*; - Mannloch, n., *cylinder manhole*; - mantel, m., *c. jacket*; - - rohr, n., *c. j. pipe*; - ohne Mantel, m., *unjacketed c.*; - öl, n., *c. oil*; - rand, m., *c. jaw*; - säule, f., *c. column*; - Sicherheitsventil, n., *cylinder escape valve*; - - Belastung, f., *c. e. v. load*; - - feder, f., *c. e. v. spring*; - - spindel, f., *c. e. v. spindle*; - Schmierbüchse, f., *c. lubricator*; - ständer, m., *c. column*; - Stopfbüchse, f., *cylinder stuffing box*; - - deckel, m., *c. s. b. gland*; - verkleidung, f., *c. liner*; - zapfen, m., *c. dowel.*

Berichtigungen und Zusätze.

auf Seite 53 ist hinzuzufügen: *crank bilge*, Kurbelbilge.

" " 71 lies *expel* anstatt *expell*.

" " 87 „ *furze* „ *furse*.

" " 103 „ *indented* „ *mortise*. versatztes anstatt versetztes Zapfenloch.

" " 303 ist hinzuzufügen: Grundlager, n., *main bearings*.

" " 330 gehört das nach Kreuzmarsstenge stehende u. nach Kreuzmarsstag.

" " 333 ist hinzuzufügen: Kurbelbilge, f., *crank bilge*.

" " 396 lies *launching* anstatt *lauching* in der letzten Zeile des Artikels „Stapel".

" " 410 lies *a v.* anstatt *a. v.* in der 3. Zeile des Artikels „übersegeln".

" " 107 ist hinzuzufügen: *jambing*, 1. einpressen, festlegen (*wood and casks*); 2. bekneifen (*ropes*).